THE ILLUMINATED BLAKE

THE ILLUMINATED BLAKE

ANNOTATED BY DAVID V. ERDMAN

ALL OF WILLIAM BLAKE'S ILLUMINATED WORKS
WITH A PLATE-BY-PLATE COMMENTARY

1974
ANCHOR BOOKS
ANCHOR PRESS / DOUBLEDAY
GARDEN CITY, NEW YORK

DAVID V. ERDMAN is Professor of English at the State University of New York at Stony Brook and Editor of Publications of The New York Public Library. He is the author of a number of works, including *The Poetry and Prose of William Blake*.

The Illuminated Blake is published
simultaneously in hard and paper covers
by Anchor Press.
Anchor Books Edition: 1974

Book design by M. F. Gazze

ISBN 0-385-06053-x

Printed in the United States of America

To
Enitharmon

While I was riding in an airplane at what seemed to be about the height of the eighth sphere, a voice speaking through the jet motors dictated the following words:

A line made by any idea moving a pen or burin on a surface (or a brush moving to make a surface) develops momentum. The delineating image itself grows, pulls the pen or brush, calls the idea forth. The poet hears the call gladly. The words come swiftly, dictated by spirits. But what the poet sees attracted him, the imaged idea moving of itself, *he* becomes. And he sees this to be happening. And when the becoming finishes, the flow of his milk and blood and glandous wine ceases. Is completed. It is a son or daughter, separate.

A line moving in crooked paths forward if accompanied by voice (music) and accompanied by picture (vision) has a second, and third, spatial life as well as the linear or temporal; the mortal worm becomes an immortal fly or bird singing Holy Holy.

A bird or butterfly sitting with wings closed—a human form sitting with arms and legs chained or with ears and eyes and mouth shut—is but a worm in a womb. To open these gates is to free the spiritual body, to greet the sunrise, the rainbow, the universe. To hesitate, to doubt, is to become the stone you dread.

"Hope and fear are—vision."

CONTENTS

KEY TO REFERENCES

1. The following abbreviations and short titles are employed for Blake's works:

A	*America*	*America a Prophecy*
Ah	*Ahania*	*The Book of Ahania*
E	*Europe*	*Europe a Prophecy*
FZ	*Four Zoas*	*The Four Zoas* (earlier title, *Vala*)
G	*Gates*	*The Gates of Paradise* (*For Children* and *For the Sexes*)
Gh	*Ghost of Abel*	*The Ghost of Abel*
J	*Jerusalem*	*Jerusalem the Emanation of the Giant Albion* (variant plate numbers for chapter II in copies D and E given in brackets)
Job	*Illustrations for the Book of Job*	
L	*Book of Los*	*The Book of Los*
LBD		*A Large Book of Designs*
M	*Milton*	*Milton a Poem*
MHH	*Marriage*	*The Marriage of Heaven and Hell*
N	*Notebook*	(The Rossetti Manuscript) See *The Notebook of William Blake, A Photographic and Typographic Facsimile,* Oxford, 1973
O		*On Homers Poetry and On Virgil*
R	*Religion*	*There is No Natural Religion* (series a and b)
Rs	*Religions*	*All Religions Are One*
S	*Songs*	*Songs of Innocence and of Experience* (copies of *Songs of Innocence* alone are cited as InA, InB, etc)
SBD		*A Small Book of Designs*
SL	*Song of Los*	*The Song of Los* (Africa; Asia)
T	*Thel*	*The Book of Thel*
U	*Urizen*	*The [First] Book of Urizen*
V	*Visions*	*Visions of the Daughters of Albion*
VLJ		*A Vision of the Last Judgment* (in *N*)

2. Plate numbers are given after short titles, using, despite some inconsistencies, the numbering established in the Keynes and Wolf *Census* (see below); except that a new numbering has been necessary for *Milton.* Line numbers are given by plate (as in *P&P*), but verse numbers are used for *Urizen.* Unnumbered prose, as in *Marriage,* is counted line for line, including title words.

The reference "Plate 2" is to Plate 2 of the work being described. References to plates in other works take the form: *Jerusalem* 2, *Thel* 6.

3. Letter abbreviations of titles (*J, T, Rs*) are used for brevity in the Index; elsewhere single letters, not in italics, refer to copies of works as designated in the *Census.*

4. Abbreviations for other frequently cited references:

Bible	Geoffrey Keynes, comp., *William Blake's Illustrations to the Bible: A Catalogue,* London and New York, 1957

Blunt Anthony Blunt, *The Art of William Blake,* New York, 1959

Census Geoffrey Keynes and Edwin Wolf 2nd, *William Blake's Illuminated Books: A Census,* New York, 1953

Dante Blake's drawings, by number, conveniently available in Albert S. Roe, *Blake's Illustrations to the Divine Comedy,* Princeton, 1953

Dict S. Foster Damon, *A Blake Dictionary: The Ideas and Symbols of William Blake,* Providence, 1965

Essays *William Blake: Essays for S. Foster Damon,* ed. Alvin H. Rosenfeld, Providence, 1969

Essick Robert N. Essick, "The Art of William Blake's Early Illuminated Books," diss., University of California, San Diego, 1969

Forms *Blake's Visionary Forms Dramatic,* ed. David V. Erdman and John E. Grant, Princeton, 1970

Frost Everett C. Frost, "The Prophet Armed: William Blake's *Marriage of Heaven and Hell,*" diss., University of Iowa, 1971

Gray Blake's drawings, by number for each poem, conveniently available in Irene Tayler, *Blake's Illustrations to the Poems of Gray,* Princeton, 1971

Hirsch E. D. Hirsch, Jr., *Innocence and Experience: An Introduction to Blake,* New Haven, 1964

Kauvar Elaine M. Kauvar, "Blake's Botanical Imagery," diss., Northwestern, 1970

Keynes Notes by Geoffrey Keynes in the Blake Trust facsimile edition of the work cited, e.g. *Songs* or *Jerusalem*

Mitchell W. J. T. Mitchell, "Poetic and Pictorial Imagination in Blake's *The Book of Urizen,*" *Eighteenth Century Studies,* III (1969) 83–107

Moore Donald K. Moore, "An Annotated Edition of William Blake's *Europe,*" diss., State University of New York, Stony Brook, 1972

Night Thoughts Blake's drawings (or engravings) for Edward Young's *The Complaint, and the Consolation; or, Night Thoughts,* soon to be available in a commentary edition by John E. Grant, Edward J. Rose, and Michael J. Tolley, Oxford

Prophet David V. Erdman, *Blake: Prophet Against Empire; A Poet's Interpretation of the History of His Own Times,* revised, Princeton and Garden City, 1969

P&P *The Poetry and Prose of William Blake,* ed. David V. Erdman, commentary by Harold Bloom, Garden City, 1966; fourth printing, revised, 1970

Raine Kathleen Raine, *Blake and Tradition,* Princeton, 1969, 2 vols.

Reading *MHH* David V. Erdman with Tom Dargan and Marlene Deverell-Van Meter, "Reading the Illuminations in *The Marriage of Heaven and Hell,*" pp. 162–207 in *William Blake: Studies in Honour of Sir Geoffrey Keynes,* Oxford, 1973

Sandler Florence Sandler, "The Iconoclastic Enterprise: Blake's Critique of 'Milton's Religion'," *Blake Studies,* v (1972) 13–57

W Joseph Wicksteed, *William Blake's Jerusalem,* 1953

INTRODUCTION

> If the Spectator could Enter into these Images in his Imagination approaching them on the Fiery Chariot of his Contemplative Thought if he could Enter into Noahs Rainbow or into his bosom or could make a Friend & Companion of one of these Images of wonder which always intreats him to leave mortal things as he must know then would he arise from his Grave then would he meet the Lord in the Air & then he would be happy . . . it is in Particulars that Wisdom consists & Happiness too.—*VLJ* (*P&P* 550)

THE FACT THAT William Blake wrote, printed, illustrated, and published his own poems by "a method of Printing which combines the Painter and the Poet" (670)—with no assistance but that of his wife Catherine—guaranteed the direct communication of the author's original and final "invention" and "illumination" to the fortunate reader and spectator of each original copy of his "Illuminated Books." No other English poet has had the power to invite his audience so fully into the particular shapes and colors of his images of wonder. Few original copies could be made, however, and although most of these seem to have survived, Blake's readers are rarely able to be spectators but have had to depend primarily on the reprinted words. Color facsimiles of most of the illuminated canon had been made by the end of the nineteenth century, some of them rather good but unreliable in details and often misleading in color. Much more faithful facsimiles have been made by the Trianon Press and distributed by the William Blake Trust during the past twenty years, and color slides have become familiar in many classrooms. But it still requires visits to several libraries in several cities to become directly acquainted with the variety of Blake's own illuminations as uniquely created in each copy he produced.

To the question often raised, whether Blake considered his poems or his designs the more important, the best answer is drawn from his comment to Dawson Turner (who wanted the pictures "without the Writing") that printing the pictures alone meant "the Loss of some of the best things," that the pictures "when Printed perfect accompany Poetical Personifications & Acts, without which Poems they never could have been Executed" (Blake to Turner, June 9 1818). And certainly the poems can stand alone, while many of the pictures cannot. Yet the poet's work is not perfectly "done" until that moment when the reader, travelling the line of text, becomes a spectator, seeing at one pulse beat the "single visualizable picture" (these words are Northrop Frye's) and then, between that and the next pulsation, leaving these mortal things, text and picture, to enter into Noah's rainbow, into "the eternal world that ever groweth" (these are the words of the Fairy who dictated *Europe*): "then he would be happy."

"Author and Printer" is the identification Blake gave himself in his first etched title page, and he refers back to it in the colophon of his last work in relief etching: "In 1822 W Blakes Original Stereotype was 1788" (*Ghost of Abel* 2), still calling attention to his particular method of reaching reader and spectator in one single or solid (stereo) impression (type). In his own advertisement of October 1793 (*P&P* 670), itself an example of his illuminated printing (the original now lost, a common fate of advertising fliers), he describes his invention of "a method of Printing both Letter-press and Engraving in a style more ornamental, uniform, and grand, than any before discovered," as "a phenomenon worthy of public attention." It is Blake's own attention to it that is worthy of ours. If we respect it, both author and spectator may be "sure of . . . reward." For we shall discover not only that becoming equally familiar with the bride and the groom of Blake's marriage of painting and poetry will enable us to share in the perfect happiness promised by Blake's art, but also that the substance of the work itself, the dialectal components of its design, the polar terms of its reference whether in thematic structure (at the center) or in ornament (at the circumference) will lead again and again to the struggle and symbiosis, the mutual embracing and mutual annihilation, of Poetry and Painting, of linear song and spatial image. All these symbolic levels only exist and act in human forms, as everyone knows but may sometimes forget.

For any writer there is some incorporation of his means into his ends, some awareness, reflected in the surface of his language, of the processes of putting pen to paper or fingers to keyboard. But for Blake there was a constant invention and revision of his own equipment, a concern about paper and ink but also about the copper surfaces of his plates, the varnish or ground that must hold its delineations firm and adhere to the copper rock, while his corrosive fires (aqua fortis) etched valleys around the exposed cliffs; then concern about the ink and its impression upon the "most beautiful wove paper that could be procured" (*P&P* 670): and then, a subject of experiment all his life, the painting of the printed paper, with translucent and opaque water colors, or with thick pigments by "colour printing." Even at the center of his early master work that undertakes for its vast subject *The Marriage of Heaven and Hell,* the text of one plate is devoted to an account of a "Printing house in Hell," with an illustration consisting of an emblem of the collaboration of the serpent of temporal delineation with the eagle of spatial illustration. Only when this collaboration, joined in by the spectator, is attended to and perfected as Illumination, can the poet's mental images arise from the grave or cave of copper into the universal air above "Time's troubled fountains" of acid and ink and such mortal things.

In short, Blake's text frequently incorporates images of delineation and coloring while his illustrations frequently incorporate images of thinking and writing. As a poet he keeps a constant eye on his own shadow or spectre—at first a harpist or piper whose musical notes materialize as clusters of flying birds (see Index)—or ripening grapes —promptly depicted by the painter, not dropping his quill but seizing an etching or engraving tool in his other hand (see *Urizen* 1 in mock of this). Later a blacksmith (Los) and architect (Urizen) whose furnaces and drawing board tend to throw each other out of focus: the "thought" of the architect with his geometer's circumscribing compasses turning the infinite options of "outline" into a serpent of stylized and countable coils that threaten to subside into a cypher. The resultant "wheel" may masquerade as useful, even as a means of obtaining bread, but is no more than a complicatedly redundant mill. To reach this extreme would be to reduce the poetic line to clichés and the illumination to journeymen's labor, at best meaningless except for an occasional witticism or spot of light. The opposite extreme, with Imagination taking the bit in its mouth and racing toward vision without the mercy of any timing, would send the sun plunging into the abyss, the nitric acid devouring every word and line on the surface until even Leviathan became formless and invisible.

To say that Blake was able, as author and printer, to keep all aspects of the production of his works under his own control is to reduce to an easy formula (the Urizenic triumph) the most difficult—and endless—struggle of his life, the effort to seize the symmetries that confronted him at every step, to create simultaneously and harmoniously in words, birds, lines, colors, a living city of Art that would resurrect us from our graves to meet the Savior in the air. Hands, tools, liquids, light, color were very real beings in Blake's furnace—and in Nebuchadnezzar's or Urizen's. As compared to the writer whose efforts shape thoughts and images into words to be set by journeyman printers, Blake felt the advantage and the responsibility of a process that allowed words to grow into vines and fruit and human forms, or into caves and forests and beasts of prey or comfort; into emblematic dramas or visions in human form, into sons and daughters shaking their bright fiery wings. In Plate 37 of *Jerusalem* we see the giant Albion bent over in melancholy, with a scroll across his lap which he is not reading, Blake's audience gone to sleep. But we see the Gulliver-sized William Blake sitting on the free coil of the scroll and busy with pen in hand inscribing a warning against melancholy for Albion when he does awake. It is written in mirror-writing because that is how Blake the printer must put the words on the plate to be legible when reversed by printing. Blake the artist has drawn a watery mirror in front of Albion up to the edge of the chalky cliff he sits on, where he will have to read the message. On the facing page, *Jerusalem* 36, which parenthetically refers to the poet's building "English, the rough basement," as the "stubborn structure of the Language" to act "against Albions melancholy, who must else have been a Dumb despair," Blake, having expelled his own despair, fills the illumination with a bouquet of color and life, prepared for Albion after his self baptism. A banquet, actually, an illumination of living vines by the unfurling of leaves and the lavishing of color. The eternal artist, Los, and his emanation, Enitharmon, residing for this occasion in their vehicular forms William and Catherine Blake, are joyously busy creating a gay tapestry of flourishing vines and ripening grapes for the Last Vintage and the annihilation of mortal melancholy. We are shown Blake's painting arm metamorphosed into three stems growing into grape vines and leaves, the longest dividing again into two stems, one spinning out a tendril of communication and another leaf, the other terminating in a scythe blade bravely flourished over the words "Eternal Death." His third "stem" arm branches downward as a paintbrush dripping with reds and blues. All the while his feet stride forward on the line (of text and delineation) which loops down the page, with several grape leaves and a large cluster of grapes, to divide into two ribbons terminating at the feet of Catherine Blake (serving as muse, inspiration, and colorist). Busy with both hands, she adjusts the color of the ripening grapes. Beside her is a double paintbrush hand wet with extra colors. The page exemplifies "our being fully employed" (see letter to Butts of July 6 1803).

Twelve pages further on—we are still only halfway through *Jerusalem*—after a page especially vibrant with birds of paradise and fertile leafage, there comes on Plate 49 a swift reversal. The voice uttering the poetry, the sad prophetic Erin, laments that now all the "Animals & vegetations . . . contained in the All Glorious Imagination are witherd & darkend." Albion, she says, has slid into such melancholy that his Emanation must be rescued and removed from "these terrible Surfaces." And we see that the text of this page is unadorned, stripped of all birds and leaves, of all interlinear ornament whatsoever, the poet-artist standing forlorn under a leafless tree looking up at its few shriveling colorless apples, his helpmate gone, his painting arm terminating in a scrawny twig with five skeletal fingers. (That he pictures it as the left arm does not mean literally that he painted with it.)

The most universal as well as the most personal themes of the poem are represented in these plates, and Blake is far from reducing his tale to the ups and downs of poetic and artistic endeavor. The very web and texture and color of his thinking derive and spin out and exfoliate from the daily acts of his labors on copper, from the minute particulars of the intimate, delicate, thread-thin and steel-strong interconnection of life and art. For the moment everything else is funneled through that vortex.

Much of the time, nevertheless, the printing house particulars are subordinated or transmuted nearly beyond recognition. The heroic bard exchanges harp and trump—not to mention graver and pencil—for the hammer and fire of the smithy. His adversary abstracts the tongs into compasses. The wheel of Hand becomes the enemy's printing house, though the wine-press remains Los's. When the successful work of turning night into day begins in earnest in *Jerusalem* 85 the picture of Los and Enitharmon extruding vines bearing grapes and blossoms refers primarily to the elemental extrusion and commingling of fibres of blood and milk and to the "Wine-presses of Love & Wrath" (the text is on Plate 88) and rather incidentally and in passing to the illumination of the book itself.

If the present annotations should appear at times reductively attentive to the embracing of ink and paper when the more obvious and more fully human referents are soul and body, female and male, father and child, I can only protest that one gets easily into the habit of seeing all marrying contraries as contained each in the other and fourfold or twenty-seven fold in one. I would wish in each instance to attend to the fold of meaning that seems uppermost, yet to take notice of Blake's workshop symbolism whenever it visibly links illustrations and text. In notes as brief as these there is often not time even to hint at the other meanings.

Putting this consideration aside, the direction of these remarks, when satisfactory, should be from illustration to Illumination. For I believe that the illumination has frequently been dimmer than it should be because of our tendency to neglect the simple level of direct illustration. It has become customary among students of Blake's pictures to suppose that very many of them do not directly concern the text, since we have never possessed an even rudimentary reading of them all—a lack which it is one purpose of this book to remedy. The larger pictures, it is true, have become increasingly familiar, at least on the simple story level of the postures and interaction of the Zoas. Yet the multitudinous but minute, even microscopic, animals and vegetations, or banners, scrolls, tendrils, even delete signs and snails and spiders, have been so overshadowed by the large pictures—or so difficult to associate with the text in any concreteness even when made out—that they have seemed even to our finest scholars little more at times than "irritating forms of punctuation" (an epithet coined by Northrop Frye, more in whimsy than in irritation, when seeking a term to contrast the hieroglyphs of *The Marriage of Heaven and Hell* and the full plate pictures of *The Book of Urizen*). We may be sure that Blake used an engraver's magnifying glass when drawing some of his minutiae—consider the tininess of the bird in its nest in *Jerusalem* 3. Spectators are well advised to use one for the marginal pictures in *Milton,* the interlinear population of *America,* and the marginal wraiths illuminating "The Keys to the Gates" (though we have photographically magnified the latter by 300 per cent: see *Gates* 17 and 18).

The present venture has been possible only because many of Blake's readers are becoming educated spectators also. When John Grant and I published *Blake's Visionary Forms Dramatic,* in 1970, a volume of essays on Blake's art by twenty educated contributors, including ourselves, I felt fairly confident that we twenty, at least, had learned how "to read Blake's pictorial language: to read its hieroglyphics, to see, to hear, to follow its choreography, its music, its mental drama" (p. vii), and was emboldened by that publication and the wide response it received to go on to the present task. When I came to writing picture notes on *America,* for example, a work upon which I had frequently lectured and now written, I would have simply to draw upon the reading I had already elaborated. What a shock it was to discover that there were numerous animal and human forms of punctuation that I had not noticed at all! Nor was their presence or absence unimportant in the drama of the work, not to mention the choreography. In Plate 15, for example, where I had dealt nicely with the sweep and succession of the large marginal pictures, the whole drama was changed when I discovered that the spaces between the lines and paragraphs of text were alive with scenes of returning soldiers, reunited families, and domestic rejoicing.

Just looking carefully, inch by inch, was half the work. The other half was in effect a borrowing of the eyes of enthusiastic collaborators, at every stage of the project. More Blakists than I can number, in classrooms and lecture audiences and by mail in animated criticism of Xerox copies of my draft notes, have pressed the hard questions and tightened the discussion, have corrected my misreadings and oversights. All have made valuable discoveries. Two products of seminar collaboration call for particular mention. In 1972 Donald K. Moore completed a doctoral dissertation in the form of an annotated edition of *Europe a Prophecy,* now being prepared for publication. And Tom Dargan and Marlene Deverell-Van Meter helped me prepare a well nigh exhaustive article on "Reading the Illuminations of *The Marriage of Heaven and Hell*" for the 1973 Festschrift for Sir Geoffrey Keynes. These studies considerably extend the interpretation of the Illuminations and supply more documentation for the present notes than I could have managed alone or would have time and space for in the other sections of them. Their air of confidence is partly a reflection of the sharing and assistance contributed by fellow scholars young and old.

The format originally chosen for this volume imposed a brevity on the notes which most of them retain. It was Enitharmon in the person of my wife Virginia who proposed the oblong design, simultaneously giving the pictures more freedom from reduction and opening up spaces for the notes that had begun to overflow. It has seemed wise, however, to keep most of the notes compact, so that they may function as a guide to the pictures, not a pontifical Covering Cherub or flaming sword fending off the unwary. The reader also must not risk "the Loss of some of the best things" by forgetting the poetry itself. Blake's pictures are never full translations of the text. And these notes attend to the text only as it relates to the pictures. It should be generally understood that an acquaintance with the poem or at least a fresh reading of it will be required to put these picture notes into meaningful perspective. Even when I seem to be telling "the story of the pictures," it should not be supposed that a story of the poem would be the same or even have the same plot. When I have introduced, as a way to present the meanings of the pictures, a synopsis of a whole illuminated poem, it should be tested against one's own full experience of the text and pictures, separately and together. (Slide projection, in color, on a large screen is an "Invention" which I am sure would have delighted Blake with the brilliance and size it can give to his "monuments" who dreamed of portable frescos "one hundred feet in height": *P&P* 518, 522.)

Color is for many reasons least adequately dealt with in these notes. Various effects of coloring, striking or contrastive or tonal, are reported, and some examples are given, in the first note on *Thel* and the first on the *Marriage,* of what the variations of coloring in different copies of the same plate amount to and signify, in verbal summary. But the colors cannot be pointed to here, and descriptions are unsatisfactory even in many words. I have tried as a rule to specify particular colors in particular copies (using superscript letters to identify copies, as with other variant details) in ways that are faithful to appearances though necessarily simplifying the reality. For one thing, the ink color of the basic printing of the plate is seldom mentioned (it would usually be some shade of brown, blue, green, or red, rarely black until *Jerusalem*). It is the added color (done with more or less thoroughness in most copies but seldom in all) that makes distinctions, and if I describe a flame or a bird as red or blue I am referring to added color—or at least isolated color. That is, all images in an unpainted page printed in red will be red but undifferentiated. If a bird on a page printed in blue or brown is painted red and the same bird on the same page printed in red is painted blue, I might say simply that the bird is prominently colored in both copies, or that the bird is red in most copies (if that were true) but blue in a copy printed in red. (I think that in Blake's color symbolism, to call it that, the distinction would hardly be a significant difference.) A copy printed in red, however, and then heavily painted, would have a prominently red bird if that image were isolated by the omission of added color. The note, "a red^{CFG} bird of paradise," should mean that the bird is prominently red in copies C, F, and G and *not some other color* than that of the printing ink in the other copies seen. In practice, if no critical point of interpretation seemed involved, I might simply call this bird red without citing copies; "red*" means in some copies.

Monotony Blake loathed, and when we consider how much variety he introduced into the printing and painting of his works, how distinctive each copy is in coloring and in the finishing of details, it is surprising how few truly variant details are to be found—if we set aside *Urizen,* where fluctuation so gets out of Urizenic control that even the plate representing the four elements cannot keep its full complement in all copies. The variants that do exist are often extremely interesting, but it is important, if sometimes very difficult, to distinguish true from more or less accidental ones. A clear-cut example of a truly intended variant is the large bunch of grapes in *Songs* 31 ("Earths Answer"), etched on the plate and strongly colored in some copies, removed without a trace from others, for example, copy Z. The alternatives require two different readings of the poem. *Songs* 4, in which the oval frames of the Tree of Jesse picture contain tiny figures or scenes, is more problematical. In all the copies I have seen (about seventeen), some of the scenes remain unchanged even when retouched: a seated woman and standing child, a woman sowing, a printer and printing press (attended, however, by a second man, and a parrot, in Z). Others change completely: a ruined castle, replaced by two towers (or persons) or by a mother and cradled infant; a figure seated, the position varied and once redrawn as standing. Though they can hardly affect one's reading of the poem, these changes are evidently intentional—yet perhaps caused chiefly by the fact that these details failed to print well and required retouching.

Even under-inking, however, can be intentional. The drooping lily in *Songs* 43 seems consistently under-inked to emphasize the lily's droop, for the electrotype made from Blake's original plate shows the image capable of printing clear and solid. A more certain example of an unclear image traceable to imperfection in the plate itself is that of a fish and fisherman in *Marriage* 22, where the fish always prints clearly, the fisherman seldom, the line or net connecting them, indicated by the tugging bend of the fisherman's arms and body, never all there. Evidently too thin a line had been etched. And yet Blake could easily have drawn it in; when he did retouch that section of the page, he sometimes made the fish into an ornament and obscured the fisherman. One supposes that Blake grew weary of his original intention, a visual pun on his scoffing remark that Swedenborg thought himself the only one who ever broke a net.

The fortunate opportunity to examine six of the nine copies of the *Marriage* in pairs side by side within the same few weeks made it possible to reach firm conclusions about some of the truly puzzling illustrations in that work. In Plate 11 Blake etched, and sometimes clearly painted, a mer-woman with one human leg and one dolphin leg, treated blithely as the skirt of a pink dress when he chose to keep the secret. And in the Argument page (Plate 2) the puzzling object, or non-object, being exchanged from hand to hand is manifestly meant to be beyond our ken, an enigma to tempt or test us at the gate. Is it a bunch of grapes, a package, a bird's nest? If he wished, Blake could have shown us; in nearly every copy this detail is retouched or repainted—to keep us from seeing. What we can almost see as green grapes, in one copy, is plainly just green leaves on a branch in another, and so on.

The evidence of Blake's intent is not always so unmistakable, but under the heading "enigmatic pictures" in the index below will be found a considerable number of more or less clearly intentional enigmas. See the notes on them for my understanding of what Blake is up to. As for the simply puzzling pictures, however, my interpretations will seem at times more confident than the blurred or indefinite details of the reproduced plate appear to warrant. I have tried to be careful in such matters, saying "perhaps" when the evidence is unclear. But what often happens is that a detail printing badly in every copy nevertheless reveals its sufficient outline when several copies are compared: for example, the fisherman cited above.

The punning hieroglyph of the fish breaking the net (that breaking could be the cause of its invisibility) is also in the category of the private joke (sometimes the private horror), a picture made explicit and shared with one or two customers, close friends who will not laugh or will laugh the right way. In effect Blake was issuing different editions for different audiences. The trustworthy Thomas Butts was sold a copy of the *Marriage,* copy F, that exhibits the mermaid in full amphibian visibility. The purchaser of copy G (unknown) was the only owner permitted to see, what had been etched on the plate but not brought out in other copies, the bloody trophy dropped by Ugolino in Plate 16. Only a few purchasers of *Visions of the Daughters of Albion* were trusted with the droll symbols of venery elaborated in Plate 1.

> That God is Colouring Newton does show
> And the devil is a Black outline all of us know

wrote Blake sarcastically (*N* 60). But it is the devil we are concerned with here, and the graphic lines which Blake declared were never drawn "without intention . . . most discriminate & particular (*VLJ: P&P* 550). Through dint of trial and error, and someone else's or my own later discovery, I have learned to respect the working assumption that every graphic image in Blake's illuminations has its seed or root in the poetry. A failure to find the textual referent is a failure to see something that is there—or that may have been there in an earlier version of the text.

Reference to the King's change from dragon form to "Angel form" pictured in the left margin of *America* 4 is missing from the text—but preserved in the canceled version of the same page, Plate b (see Appendix). Unfortunately no manuscripts (except of some of the Songs of Experience) and only a few canceled plates of any of the Illuminated Works survive. And there is evidence that before the completion, of *Jerusalem* for example, Blake moved the plates about a good deal. If the textual account of "fibres" illustrated in Plate 85 does not appear until Plate 88, it is easy to see why. The script of the latter plate is visibly not contemporary with the plates now adjacent to it; Plates 84 to 87, tightly linked together graphically and textually, cannot originally have followed Plate 83, there being no transition but an abrupt geological fault, as it were, between 83 and 84. Text and illustration must once have been closer together than they are now. Or, to consider a case where the graphic materials were rearranged, it takes considerable ingenuity—though not beyond what Blake often requires of his readers—to fit to the accompanying text the curiously abrupt shifts from bearded old man, to clean-shaven youth, to bearded old man in the appearance of Albion in *Jerusalem* 94–95–96. In origin we can see that this interpolating of the young Albion is a sophistication of the graphic text, in the bibliographical sense of the word, though done by Blake himself—who then obviously saw that it was a good thing to do. At the culmination of his story line all the male figures of his four chapters must be united in a single image. Instead of settling for an old man or a mature man in full vigor, he chose to alternate the two—continuing in the three final pictures with youth, age, and youth.

Again, the repeatedly confirmed assumption that Blake's imaginal particulars are in the first instance literal particulars lies behind the assurance with which, in my notes on *Songs* 34–36 and 51, I identify the lost girl on Plate 35 as Lyca, seven summers old, whose story is told on Plates 34 and 35, and the tall and much older loving couple on Plate 34 as Ona and her lover, whose story is told on Plate 51. Perhaps these two lost girls' songs were originally written and designed at the same time; there are eight copies of *Songs of Innocence* alone that lack the Lyca poems; conceivably they were invented for Innocence only when the Ona poem was invented for Experience. Perhaps, as seems more likely, the picture of lovers in Plate 34 was meant to "bring in" a tale not yet told but a tale subsequently spelled out as the story of Ona, for Experience. Perhaps an Ona poem was in Blake's original plans for *Songs of Innocence* but excluded from it. Firm evidence is lacking, but any of these possibilities seems more plausible than that Blake intended to illustrate the tale of a seven-year-old with the picture of adolescent lovers, except as analogue.

Sometimes, it may be, the textual base of an illumination may occur in another poet's text. The image of Urizen (in *Europe* i) resting his weight, compass-like, on a centered foot, is a graphic pun on a line of Milton not quoted in Blake's poem. But then there are reasons to believe that this textless picture was not designed for this poem but as an illustration for *Paradise Lost* presumably. The *Europe* title page (Plate ii) exists in several variants (see Appendix) one of which (ii a) seems to presuppose the absence of the present frontispiece, which perhaps fits in a miraculous way just because unrelated, except by invisible gravity, to the poem it now illumines. This perhaps overstates the matter, since lines 13–14 of *Europe* 2, asking "who shall bind the infinite . . . To compass it with swaddling bands?" constitute a wry and bathetic punning on the sublime of the golden compass-holder, and since the first of these lines is inscribed on a sketch for this picture, in *N* 96: a rather murky answer is that the *Notebook* Milton series in which it occurs considerably predates *Europe,* while the inscription can have been added later. A way to get "inside" such a curious posture as that of the Ancient in the *Europe* frontispiece, Donald Moore has shown me, is to attempt the position with one's body. Blake's drawings often begin with limbs and spine, and I suspect that he often used the living models of his own and his wife's bodies to try postures and gestures—not to copy them directly or in a mirror but to feel the spinal axes and the articulations of body and soul (see *Jerusalem* 45[31]:10). When their friend Butts came upon William and Catherine naked in their summer house, being "only Adam and Eve" (Gilchrist *Life* 97: Butts's often telling the tale is more convincing than his grandson's denying it years later) they were perhaps not merely "reciting passages from *Paradise Lost,* in character," but preparing Blake's imagination for his illustrations of that epic.

A quite different example from *Europe* involves a very small detail but a very precise linkage. My description of the four naked humans in the second Preludium page, three wrestling figures and a fourth racing away from them, remained only atmospherically related to the poem as long as I recognized them only generically, as, politically, analogous to the caricatures (by James Gillray) of a prime minister choking political opponents or rivals and, on the allegorical level marked by the glosses of Blake's friend Cumberland, human representations of "Horror, Amazement, and Despair." Yet an odd emphasis on the hair of the escaping man, with his eight fingers clutching it dramatically, histrionically, kept demanding an explanation. Each time I examined a different copy of the work, it struck me more that Blake was paying close attention to those fingers, and that I should too. Suddenly, when for the fiftieth time I was explaining to someone the pivotal historical peg of Pitt's dismissal of Lord Chancellor Thurlow from his cabinet in June 1792, pivotal only in Gillray's cartoons and in Blake's poem, where it is alluded to with unmistakable particularity in Plate 12 lines 14–20, I tumbled to the realization that those frantic fingers are Lord Thurlow's, clutching his judicial wig—which in reality or at least technically he had to relinquish to King George, but which the poet imagines, along with his judicial gown ("his furr'd robes & false locks"), adhering and growing "one with his flesh." This discovery of the particular point of illustration scarcely transforms the poem, but it does bring the whole Preludium into a clearer line of derivation—and into sharper focus. Again the working hypothesis was fruitful. A similar yet much more important signal that I was slow to respond to was the shorn hair of John Milton in *Milton* 18. Until the 1960s it was difficult to recognize a male figure in the other, very long-haired, Miltons in the book. Yet Blake might reasonably have counted on our seeing the shorn hair as an allusion to *Samson Agonistes;* the point made is central to his emphasis on *mental* war.

A different sort of attending to details corrected the emphasis in my note on "The Sick Rose" (*Songs* 39) as I revised it in response to the imperatives of the picture and text, "seen" together. Putting aside or into the background the analogue of Cupid and Psyche and the story-line of Gwendolen and Hyle, analogous characters who emerge years later in *Jerusalem,* I could see when I followed the images closely that the visible rose is sick in that it has a canker-worm at its core and has fallen to the ground, that its thorny stem has been no protection to it, that indeed the worm must have inched its way along the thorn path, evidently deflowering that sister rose earlier on the stem, as it passed her, and bypassing the other sister who is now in lamentation. These were details I had neglected when staying too much outside the picture.

BLAKE'S PRINTING HOUSE

Perhaps the most illustrative, and illuminating, product of the application of my literalist hypothesis is the reading which everyone can now "see" of the very literal illustrations of Plates 6 and 7 of *The Marriage of Heaven and Hell.* In these pages Blake describes and exemplifies his method of illuminated communication:

> When I came home, on the abyss of the five senses, where a flat steep frowns over the present world, I saw a mighty Devil folded in black clouds, hovering on the sides of the rock, with corroding fires he wrote the following sentence now percieved by the minds of men, & read by them on earth.
>
> How do you know but ev'ry Bird that cuts the airy way,
> Is an immense world of delight, clos'd by your senses five.

To reduce the infinite vision of his imaginative "walking among the fires of hell" (6:15) to illuminated printing, to words and pictures that can be read on earth, Blake must return home to his workshop from what the senses can only record as an abyss. (In Plates 17–20 an Angel and a Devil try each other's futures in the abyss, and in Plate 20 Blake pictures himself, as devil, hanging by the roots of a tree over a deep in which Leviathan is coiling, nay, sporting.) With corroding acid he must cut words and pictures in the sensory surface of this abyss (the mirror-like surface of the copper, looking *through* which we can see immense worlds of delight). From the perspective of "the present world" the copper plate looks like a flat steep, frowning or swagging overhead. The devil Blake sees in its clouds is himself at work on the printing surface or "sides of the rock"—which he pictures (at the bottom of Plate 6) as Dover cliff, the edge of dry land. There are some strokes that show us the cliff and some obscuring lines on the "H" (first letter of the "HOW" that begins his "sentence") that keep this Blake's secret until we look carefully. The "black clouds" in which his mirror image is folded and from which his phallic bolt of lightning strikes the rock are rounded like a woman's breasts. (Compare the poet as swan in *Jerusalem* 11.)

The bird that cuts the airy way opens up the spaces of the plate with color, sunbursts, Illumination. He is a living paintbrush in the artist's hand (compare *Milton* 25 and *Jerusalem* 36). In the "Proverbs of Hell" that follow, some of the pictograms continue the image of plowing the surface and opening immensity. Our thoughts return to the fire-threatened surface in the *Marriage* title page.

In Blake's description in *Marriage* 15 of "A Printing house in Hell" the immediate subject of text and pictures is Illuminated Printing, allegorically described. Each metal plate, cut and burnt into by tool and fiery acid, is a "cave," each process that the cave goes through is a "chamber" in the printing house. And the result of the process, the surface of paper printed and colored, which we also call a plate, is a "cave" too. The reader-spectator enters it to find the immense palaces which the poet-artist is building for his delight. (Perhaps one of the things Thel shrinks from, in *Thel* 6, is the making of a friend and companion of Blake's "images of wonder.") In the teamwork of eagle and viper, depicted at the bottom of Plate 15, the serpent's tongue performs the function of the lightning on Plate 6, but the eagle holds him so high *in the air* that his words are cut on clouds, not rocks. The "cave" that mediates between copper and cloud of vision represents "the minds of men," that is, the "cavern" through which man "sees all things" (see Plates 7 and 14).

BIRDS AND BANNERS

To the question whether there is a consistent symbolism in Blake's images I prefer to say, Read and look and see, and not to attempt general statements. Something should be said here, however, of my firm persuasion after reviewing all these works that one's instincts are right about *up* (see Index) as the right direction to look and fly, *onward* as the way to stride, rainbow colors and shapes as glorious, and so on. Birds of paradise are so frequently and so uniformly augurs of what their name tells that I have come to trust their presence as images of hope even in pages where no hope is otherwise offered by pictures or text: they remind us *how* to read the text, in these instances. On early pages these birds fly up beside such words as "percieve" and "perception," later beside "Salvation" in the refrain of the Bard's song in *Milton* and in the dialogue of Joseph and Mary in *Jerusalem* 61, where they have become half doves. In one version of the general title page of *Songs of Innocence and of Experience,* the bird of paradise that flies on an upward diagonal toward "Songs" carries in its mouth a golden apple, so that we may recognize bird as serpent metamorphosed.

Rainbows and ripe grapes can never be ambiguous in their affirmation, though, in the irony of mercy, clusters as large as humans can glut harlots (see *Jerusalem* 42) even at the climax of their bacchanalian devouring. Rising birds sometimes flock in a stormy scene, but as notes of contrast and hope. Even a bird swooping down or falling is an ironic negation of its own hopeful potential, not simply an evil force. Small images of flames or flowers or birds, closely applied to particular words, are I believe uncomplicated in their message as notes of approval or warning. Hence the rising bird above the name "Rousseau" in the Alps with Orc, in *Song of Los* 3 along with a waving banner on the name "Voltaire," seems a confirmation of my deduction years ago that Rousseau and Voltaire in this poem are positive figures, as they are not in the later lyric "Mock on Mock on Voltaire Rousseau."

My overview of the whole illuminated canon confirms also the impression that five birds with a sixth (often of paradise) signify the senses led by the imagination; that five giants sitting in a cell are five senses confined, that five stars, five blossoms, five daughters are ready, if the context at all allows, to invoke the same association—though never, of course, exclusively that. For Blake's focus and themes shift from work to work. Male and female figures can represent body and soul in the *Marriage,* illustrating a discussion of erroneous ideas about them, but we need not suppose that the body-soul problem is germane to the meaning of all such sexual dances in other works. Blake talks about "the Sea of Time & Space" in *Milton* (and once in *The Four Zoas* and once in a letter of 1802), but nowhere else, and I would hesitate to attach that label to all his pictures of ocean or abyss. Yet he may have had it in mind when, in the coloring of fairly late copies, he added water in the foreground of pictures previously resting on dry land.

Blake himself steps to the center of the stage in *Milton* and is present in the margins as well, wielding a knife as tool of his trade (engraving, sculpture in one sense) in contrast to Cain's wielding it in fratricide (compare *Milton* 15 and 21, 22, 24). But it is what happens in the poet, not in his work processes, that receives illumination in this poem. The garden, not the printing house, is the setting for Milton's and Blake's dance of death for life. And it is a pattern of dance, reinforced by a song about "the sweet Dance" of flowers and birds "all in order sweet & lovely" (34), that orders the plates, in which the major motifs are dancing, striding, and confronting. These posed actions display the separation and unity of contraries, of male and female, brother and brother, descent and ascent, wrath and pity, bread and wine. And the linking image is Milton's bright star that enters or is about to enter Blake's tarsus—a punning allusion to the light of heaven that transformed Saul of Tarsus into the apostle Paul, a conversion of negating wrath, by the creating wrath of Jesus, into pity. In dance form this is represented by the touching of foot to foot (*Milton* 2, 10, 33, 48) or by the binding on of sandals (8, 47, 50), the latter a symbol of preparation for the forward striding that unites the man and woman of the first and last plates in a spousal dance (after a coronal dance of woven flowers in 48). Inevitably the tight choreographical structure of this work has drawn most of my attention. Even the stone-and-skull altar (of 15 and 17) can be seen as stage property that is rearranged into descending and ascending stairs in 32 and 37. Yet I have left untraced many links that may be discovered between the large and the small marginal pictures.

THE INDEX

Thoroughgoing consistency will not be found, then, in these notes—nor in the Index. Nor have I room left even to summarize or recapitulate the discussions of particular and general points of interpretation that arise from time to time, sometimes only parenthetically, in the descriptive comment. The Index—to the pictures rather than to the notes—began as a brief guide to the most striking or interesting images. It has expanded into a fairly full itemizing of the distinctly definable particulars, including variants reported in the notes, but is still far from exhaustive. Dots of elision are inserted in entries known to be incomplete. A few entries will be found that attempt to deal with such imprecisely definable things as gestures and relationships, but these entries are to be taken as irregular and only suggestive. There are cross references in the commentary, but the Index does not include discussions of a given plate that occur in notes to other plates. The making of the Index (in which Jerry S. Blake, Tom Dargan, and Bob Waxler greatly assisted) exposed some glaring inconsistencies, for example in the naming of birds (whether lapwing or lark or swallow; eagle, falcon, or dove!), and some of these have resisted being cleared up by hasty arbitration. For one thing, functions, contexts, directions of movement enter into the identifications. A falcon as well as a lapwing can be a phoenix; a raven as well as an eagle. The flower identifications I believe are much clearer, perhaps because of the books consulted. Blake's catchfly may not look much like the living or photographed plant, but it resembles closely its graven image in eighteenth-century books. The Index will require some patience on the user's part, including that needed to locate the pictures by plate number and work (rather than page number). But it should prove more independently useful than the usual numbering would make it and more adaptable to one's own categorizing.

THE PLATES

The copies of the Illuminated Works chosen for reproduction in this book have been selected for clarity of detail. When individual pages in a clear copy have been found to be inadequate in this respect, usually from accidents of inking, substitutes have been introduced from other copies. In the *Songs of Innocence and of Experience* the best of the Gilchrist electrotypes have been introduced, for authenticity, despite the loss of consistency of tone and texture through the work. All the plates are reproduced in the exact size of the original, with some exceptions as noted, mainly the large pages of *America, Europe,* and *Jerusalem*. The different original copies, as designated in the *Census,* are indicated by superscript letters, thus: *Thel,* copy D, Plate 3: *Thel* 3^{D}. The Gilchrist electrotypes thus: *Songs* 18^{g}.

BLAKE'S WORKS IN ILLUMINATED PRINTING

Religions 1

Religions 2

Religions 3

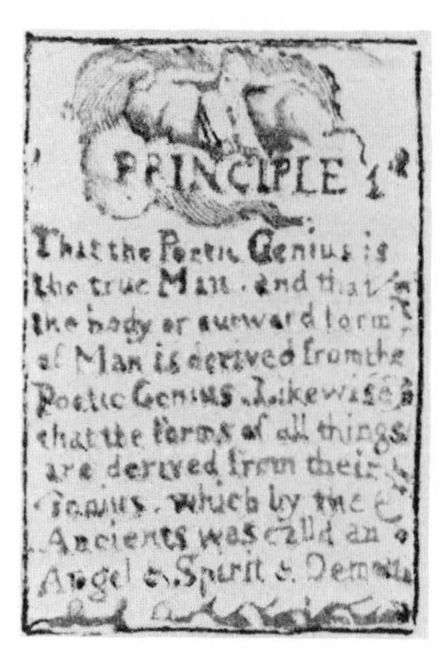

Religions 4

ALL RELIGIONS ARE ONE

FROM THE EVIDENCE presented by Geoffrey Keynes in his bibliographical note in the Blake Trust facsimile edition of *There is No Natural Religion,* 1971, the smaller tractate, *All Religions Are One* must now be recognized as technically earlier than the two series under the other title. It had traditionally been placed later.

Religions 1 (frontispiece). In a wilderness of close tree trunks and leaves, a youthful John the Baptist sits, Blake as prophet, naked except for his left knee, and points to the message of the following pages, etched by Blake as artist. On the rock beside him is a sheep or lion skin. The prophetic mantle on his knee will be appropriated by Urizen (compare *Europe* i) but will grow naturally as a cape from the poet's shoulders (compare *Milton* 22 and *Jerusalem* 36). His gesture will become that of the man in red in the Arlington Court picture. In 1822 Blake will remind us of this prophet "crying in the wilderness" when he inscribes the *Ghost of Abel.*

2 (title page). A winged angel, with arms around stone tablets of religious codes and a bearded priest or philosopher who looks up from an open book, conveys the message of the title, redirecting our attention from John's voice and hand: Wilderness (All): : Voice (One).

3 (Argument). A prone figure, head on hand, studies in the grass, which is beside him as in *Religion* a9, rather than above him as in b3.

4 (Principle 1st). A bearded man sits in clouds, his arms outstretched across rock-like clouds: the human form or spirit or demon of the cloud. (In *Marriage* 11 he is shown being abstracted; in *America* 8 he has become a tyrant god, Urizen.) A vine at the bottom shows living movement.

5 (Principle 2d). A half dozen sheep at bottom begin the theme that "all are alike." A vine leads us up a tree to the upper realm where the multiplication of human forms, growing up and looking up, implies "infinite variety." Blake will repeat this picture of the parturition of Eve from Adam in *Jerusalem* 31. The palm tree beside the sheep, "a traditional emblem of immortality and resiliency, may . . . symbolize the continual renewal of the same basic forms in nature" (Essick).

6 (Principle 3d). A scroll in viper form, with tongue darting forward, comes up from "think" to speak for two bearded philosophers seated beside Greek or Roman pillars (compare *Religion* a1), with books "adapted" from the Poetic Genius. The nearer man is writing with a pen, the other reading. (For a similar chair, see Plate 8 below and *Songs* 3.)

7 (Principle 4). A traveller with hat and staff strides forward (to the right); we see him again in *Gates* 14. Here his movement answers to the pointing of John the Baptist in the frontispiece and the direction of the viper's tongue in Plate 6.

Religions 5

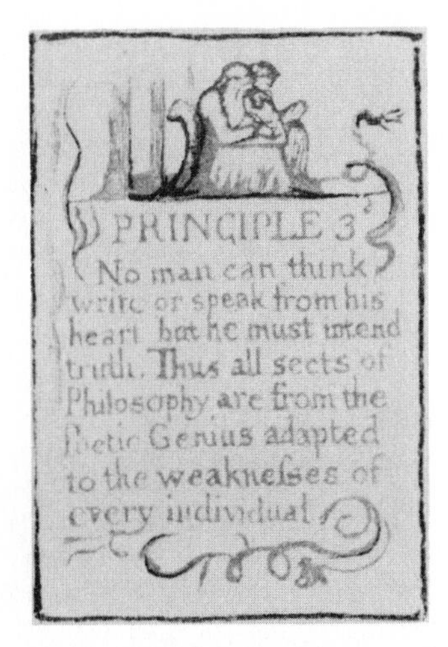

Religions 6

Religions 7

Religions 8

Religions 9

Religions 10

8 (Principle 5). Within a large tent or curtain (compare *Songs* 17) half a dozen children are receiving the Poetic Genius from a teacher seated in a philosopher's chair (see Plate 6). The thorny zigzag border under the title seems to be an early version of the binding briars of *Songs* 44. At bottom, under bracketing leaves, a "nude bearded man is plucking the strings of a harp while [looking up and] rushing with a long stride to the left" (Keynes), representing perhaps a unity of space and time: compare *Marriage* 3.

9 (Principle 6). At top are stone tablets of the "Jewish & Christian Testaments," in a cloud-shaped space; below a skirted figure gropes in darkness, illustrating "the confined nature of bodily sensation." We may contrast the running harpist of Plate 8, but their difference of direction should not be taken as absolutely symbolic. This groper is moving forward, in the direction pointed (see Plates 1, 6, 7). He seems to be among bulrushes, as the lost boy in *Songs* 13.

10 (Principle 7). At top the "true Man" (compare, below, *Religion* b9) appears with outstretched arms, above two figures on the ground, one sheltering his eyes with raised left arm, the other with head flung back (breasts suggesting a female). At bottom is a bird "hovering over dark waters" (Keynes).

The top scene, a Resurrection design, reappears in *Night Thoughts* 64 "to represent Christ before two pagans overcome by His light and glory" (Essick).

THERE IS NO NATURAL RELIGION
[Series a]

Religion a1[F] (frontispiece). Beneath two over-arching trees sit an elderly bearded man, clothed, and a sedate hooded woman, facing two naked youths who stand looking outward and down, respectively, the second with his left arm raised around the branching trunk. The two pairs are rather independent of each other (whereas in *Songs* 29 the young couple are absorbed in dependency upon the old). Similarly independent of each other are the two modes of thinking in the following tract—rational and prophetic. In the background are green hills; behind them a white[D] or pink[F] sky. The seat of the bearded man looks like a section of a fluted column (compare *Europe* 16).

At bottom, etched in reverse: "The Author & Printer W Blake."

Religion a1[F]

Religion a2^{C}

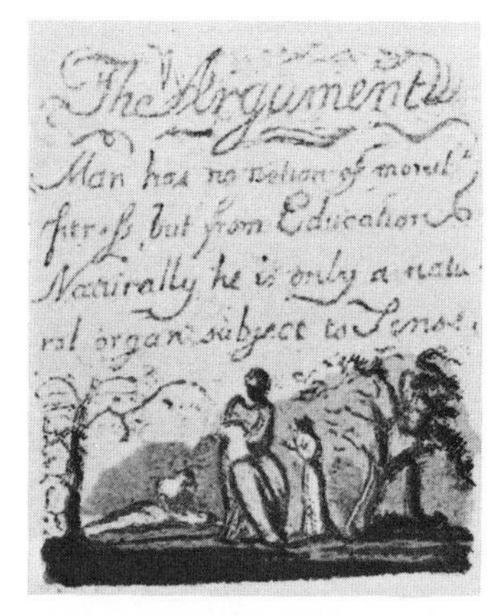

Religion a3^{F}

Religion a4^{C}

Religion a5^{G}

a2^{C} (title page). The title is on a door-like or window-like panel of Gothic tracery, with panels containing sketched figures, clothed but not winged, perhaps saints rather than angels. The larger central figure holds up his left hand; two flanking figures turn toward him in attitudes of prayer; the outer lower panels contain two pairs of standing figures. Between "is" and "NO" is a standing viper; beside "NO" a plumed bird. Four thin pilasters stand out from the panel, pointed at the top suggesting organ pipes or quill pens; two similar points stand up behind the panel. A door of perception, one surmises.

a3^{F} (The Argument). Among sketched trees, the one at left twined by a vine, perhaps flowering, a reclining figure may be writing, a sitting clothed woman holding a tablet, perhaps drawing, a gowned girl standing with open book; the word "Education" seems the relevant part of the text.

a4^{C} (I). A dog and an aged man with staff perceive each other with their "bodily organs." In contrast, a vine round the tree that encloses them spirals up into flowers and birds above the text, the birds launching into the infinite air. Four trunks are discernible in the green woods beyond.

a5^{G} (II). Under a bare vineless tree ("reasoning power . . . only") a mother is holding a child out toward a bird, which the child can see but is not permitted to touch. (The bird is at its finger tip in D, several inches away in G.) Flourishing trees are available in the background.

a6^{G} (III). Under a flourishing vine and tree (or double vine) a winged angel is instructing a man (beyond the senses). The man is not looking up, and his reaching hand (compare the child's in Plate 5) finds only his own leg.

a7^{G} (IV.). The three birds flying up at the top suggest the spiritual music rising from the pipe of the musician who sits with feathers or flowers in his hat, at the base of a tree. With music like this, vines aren't needed. The hat suggests to Damon "a 'natural' or Idiot"; to Essick, more properly, a primitive poet, one of those "naked civilized men" of the Ancient Britons; we meet him as the civilized Piper in *Songs* 3.

A bird rises^{G} above the woods in the background.

a8^{C} (VI). Without the restraining mother of Plate 5, a naked boy approaches a large bird, a swan in a pond who might be ridden. A hopeful vine grows up the lightly foliaged tree.

a9^{C} (VI). Reading or studying goes on in the arching grass (continuing the outdoor reading of Plate 3), beside a living tree with vine that holds a flower over the student's head. (All through these pictures, we see the vine of Education and the birds of song and flight outreaching the rational statements.) The grass at left almost suggests bulrushes: see *Songs* 13 and 22.

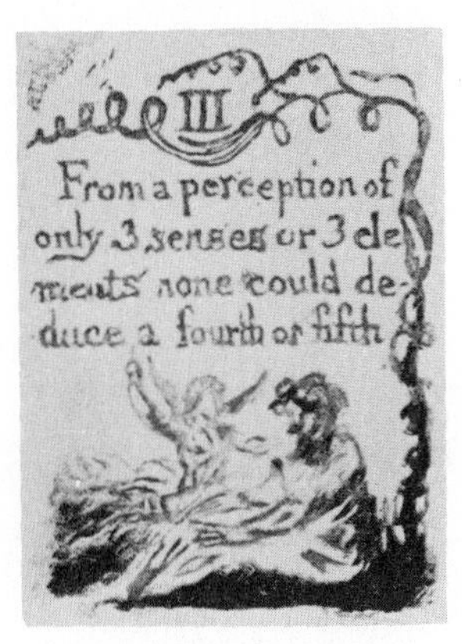

Religion a6^{G}

Religion a7^{G}

Religion a8^{C}

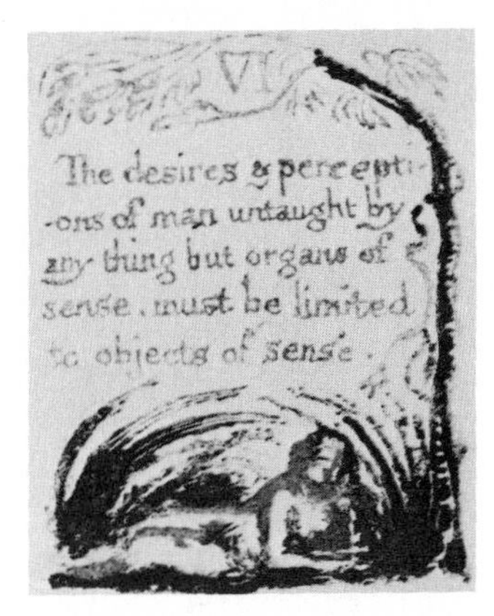

Religion a9^{C}

Religion b1[L]

Religion b2[L]

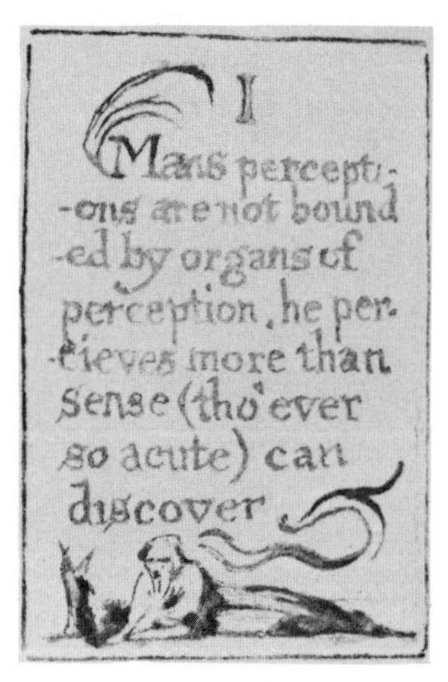

Religion b3[L]

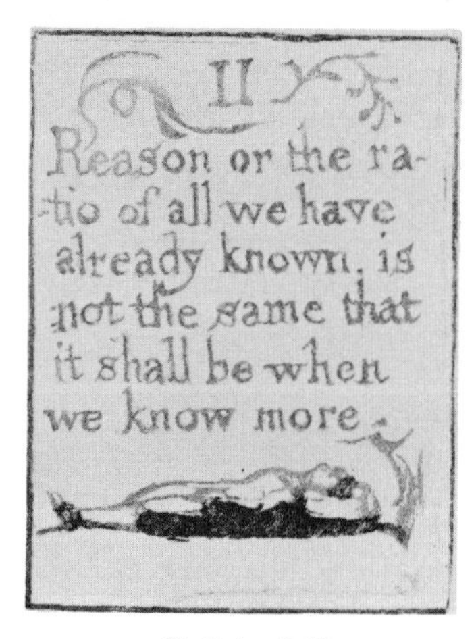

Religion b4[L]

THERE IS NO NATURAL RELIGION

[series b][L]

Religion b1 (frontispiece). A gowned figure stretches a left arm over a naked man, who responds by upward gesture and preparation to arise. (Christ raising Lazarus is the prototype.) Two Gothic panels behind them indicate the "Poetic or Prophetic character" at work. Compare *Songs* 18.

b2 (title page) (as for series a).

b3 (I). A bearded man lying on the ground (see a9, above) reads a book. A small stump beside him points like a human hand. A scroll ornament over the man's body calls attention to the text—and discoveries more acute than sensual perception. The grass curving high from "Mans" suggests a reach beyond.

b4 (II). A man lies supine and pillowed; we may take him to be asleep. At his head an ornamental figure leans over him with an arm or wand above his eyes, repeating the gesture of b1—a prophecy that "he will know more when he awakes" (Keynes). At top, the vegetative loops above "Reason" burst into a flower cluster at the right.

b6 (IV) [Plate 5 (III) is lacking]. The flowering foliage shows movements more complex than "complicated wheels."

b7 (V). In the foliage at each side of "Man" is a scroll-gowned figure soaring with hands raised, unsatisfied without "More!"

b8 (VI). At bottom a naked man chained and fettered by his ankles, "incapable of possessing," clutches his head in "despair." (Compare *Urizen* 4.)

b9 (VII). A naked man rising half out of a dark pit or cloud stretches out his arms (to possess—and share—infinitely). The vegetation on each side of the numeral echoes the gesture. His left hand shows a nail head, implying Christ crucified and now resurrected.

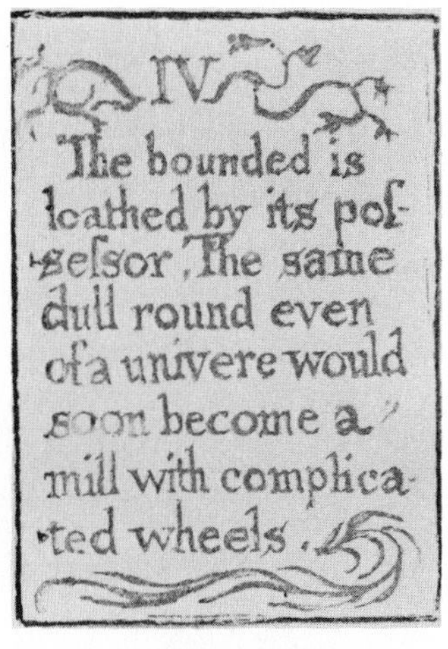

Religion b6[L]

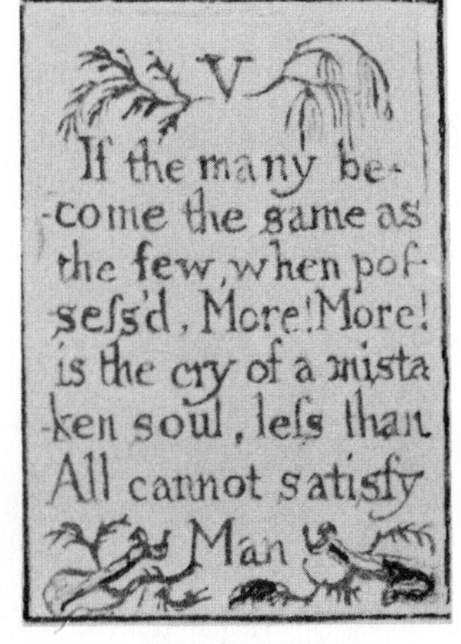

Religion b7[L]

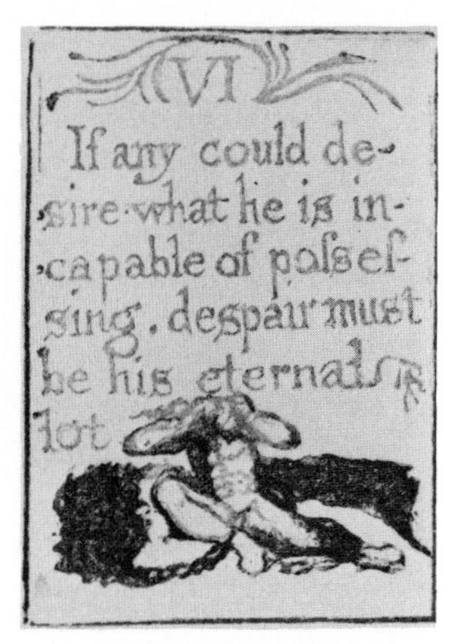

Religion b8[L]

Religion b9[L]

Religion b10L

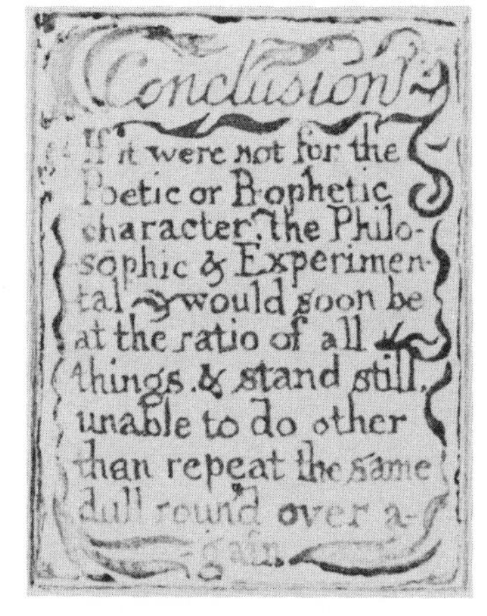

Religion b11L

Religion b12L

b10 (Application). A bearded man on hands and knees is drawing, on the ground, a triangle which mirrors the shape of his compasses. We see, in contrast, his human form and a tree bearing the flourishing text (i.e. we can see God as carpenter and the infinite flowering of life). Grant notes that the geometer is a combination of Newton and Nebuchadnezzar. Essick sees the design as a visual pun on the title, an "Application" of reason to earth.

b11 (Conclusion). A flowering conclusion.
(In preparing the Blake Trust facsimile, Keynes noted that in one set of the plates Blake's framing lines locate the "Conclusion" as a part of the "b" series; it had previously been placed by editors in the "a" group.)

b12 (Therefore). "A nude figure with radiations round his head is lying in an ecstatic trance on a rock" (Keynes); compare the sleeping traveller of *Gates* 19. The lettering is cursive and bursts into flourishes of vegetation, including the ivy we shall see in *Songs* 28 and 29. "The word (Blake's text) becomes the flesh (branches, leaves, etc); the flesh becomes the word" (Essick).

THE BOOK OF THEL

Thel is dated 1789 (though we evidently lack any copy completely produced that early), and pictorially and metaphorically it is a curious counterpart of Erasmus Darwin's "Loves of the Plants," published also in 1789 as part of *The Botanic Garden* (for which Blake engraved one plate in 1791). Darwin's book (cited in Nancy Bogen's edition of *Thel,* pp 69 and 71) is a poetic guide, in the idiom of "The Rape of the Lock," to the sexual behavior of the male and female parts of garden flowers, and some of Blake's flowers and their human forms seem to derive from Darwin's text, notes, and illustrations (though the latter are comparatively wooden diagrams). Darwin's emphasis on sexual encounter and aggressive masculinity seems particularly relevant. The long stamens at the top of Plate ii and in the fuchsia-like flowers of Plate 5 seem to derive from two flowers featured in the "Loves," the amaryllis formosissima and the Meadia (named after a Dr Mead, not Medea). Both are given engraved plates in Darwin and cross-referenced, both having very long stamens with many anthers: the amaryllis "six males, one female," the Media "five males and one female." Blake doesn't count anthers but depicts two large stamens hovering over Thel, in Plate 5. Blake's most recurrent flower in the poem, a spider or St Bernard's lily (anthericum liliago), is not found in Darwin, being perhaps too unpretentious in its blossoming; yet Darwin's account of fair Tulipa seems related to the text of *Thel*—and the picture in Plate 5. When Autumn blasts come, "Quick flies fair Tulipa the loud alarms, And folds the infant closer in her arms." And the "thousand fighting men" with "arrows ready drawn" of 6:13–14 may have been suggested by the armed guard of the Ilex, each of its four males grasping "a thousand arrows . . . A thousand steely points."

There are fifteen complete copies of *Thel* in color and another complete except for the Motto, produced over a period of twenty some years, with considerable variety in the coloring. One's general impression is that Blake was not or at least not consistently systematic in his use of color differences, and that even his use of them to emphasize dramatic contrasts, for example between the closed and the open flower on Plate 5, or in the leap from cloud to sunshine in copy N, was only occasional.

Nancy Bogen's report of the different colors of Thel's dress in Plates ii, 4, and 5 in the sixteen copies (pages 53–55 in her facsimile edition of copy M) affords a good opportunity to consider Blake's practice in this respect (though one may quarrel with her particular choices of color terms). If we ignore degrees of paleness or tone, Thel's dress in these four plates is unchanging from plate to plate in eleven copies. Blake slightly prefers pale shades of green or yellow (five copies) or pale pink or red (three), but uses vivid yellow in two, bright pink in one. In the other five copies, the change of color from Plate ii to Plate 5 is very slight in O (white with grey shading, noticeably darker in Plate 4) and a simple alternation between pale blue and pale purple in D. The only impressive changes occur in the late copy N (on 1815 paper) and the probably late copies I and J. In N the dress is "blue, gray, and greenish yellow shading" in the first three plates, bright yellow in Plate 5. The changes in copy I from greyish pink to light pink to pale purple, and in copy J from green to greyish yellow brown to yellowed green to greyish pink (or violet), are scarcely dramatic. And even the striking shift in N from a pale dress against a dark cloud in an otherwise yellow sky in Plate 4 to a bright yellow dress in Plate 5 is less impressive as an effect when we know that Thel begins the poem in a bright yellow dress, and keeps it unchanged, in copies A and F. The colors, in short, seldom suggest any change in Thel, either a growing up or a growing down. In copies D and L there is a warming from pale blue to pale purple or from pink to pale red; in I from light pink to pale purple; in J from yellowed green to greyish pink—but that is slight indeed.

Thel ii[I] (title page). Under a thin arching willow (tree of paradise or of sorrow) loosely entwined by a flowering vine dividing at its tip, the letters of the title stand like an inscription chiselled on a gravestone or a window (which the space shaped by the tree suggests) but sometimes made light as dawn air by color washes[J]. (For similar but varying combinations of thin tree and vine see *Songs* 8, 20, 27—and 34: two arching branches under which lovers embrace. See also *Songs* 10.)

The italic capitals of *"BOOK"* are alive with sinuous leaves that make buds of the three plump letters and form, against the "K," a calyx from which curved stamens rise in a pattern repeated in the soaring forms rising from blossoms of a similar shape at page bottom. In a preliminary flourish a youth sits reading (or writing).

Thel ii[I]

Inside the second "O" a shepherd, with hat, leans on a crook like Thel's below. The vine-trailing "of" is flanked by two birds, the first of paradise. (In V the first is blue, the second yellow. In N they are joined by three smaller birds.) Above the last letters of "THEL" soars a slightly gowned female pointing onward (holding a clump of three long curling silver leaves[O] shaped like the dividing vine growing on the "E"). But the name "THEL" stands rigid and upright though twined with coiling tendrils and scaled by acrobats—a boy (naked[DM] or clothed[O]) climbing the "T," arm-raising clothed girls below, and standing on, the bar of the "H." A small boy stands between "H" and "E" and a winged (angelic) reader sits in the "L." (The two words are colored contrastively in five copies; they are uncolored—or colored similarly—in eleven.)

In the foreground close to the tree, Thel as shepherdess ("a shining woman" but a "Virgin" 3:22, 25 etc) watches not sheep but the amorous embracing of a naked youth and gowned maiden in the blossoms of a pasqueflower, anemone pulsatilla, said to require the wind to open its petals "which are folded over the stamens in a singular and beautiful manner" (Darwin's note). (Colored appropriately shades of red or purple in most copies—yellow in C.) We might take Thel herself for Darwin's "sad Anemone" pining for the wind's "cherub-lips," since the two small figures beside her are performing Darwin's script: Zephyr, answering the Nymph's prayer, brings "blushing" color to her petals and, to her delight, "Tears with rude kiss her bosom's gauzy veil," flinging aside like a kerchief what Thel will think of as "a little curtain of flesh" (6:20). But in Blake's story these lovers are the human forms of the Dew and the Cloud (a cloud in motion being the zephyr's visible form), whose courtship, described in 3:13–16, "is reminiscent of the descriptions of pollination in Darwin" (Bogen 71). The unopened bud that bends close to Thel both suits her chaste demeanor—and is offered to her. When it opens, will she fling up her hands in joy—or horror—dropping her crook?

Thel 1N. In swash characters the name *"THEL"* comes to life, looping in tendrils with lily-like endings—except for a thicker initial stem with four finger-like roots, unearthed. Detached tendrils curve above and below the letters.

Leaping in the air at the name's beginning, a naked man with pointing right hand directs or points in the direction of an eagle flying horizontally. (Will it act the vulture and prey upon *"THEL"* as upon Oothoon in *Visions* 6 and *America* 13? Or illuminate her path and this poem?) Another naked youth soaring in the same direction points with lifted sword (with flame-shaped blade) and upheld shield, masculine counterpart of the bough-liftingO soarer of the title page. Both the eagle man and the armed man adumbrate the "fighting men in ambush" that haunt Thel in Plate 6.

Not apparently attending to these is the family group between title and text. A naked child is being welcomed in mid air (or tossed) by a scroll-gowned woman (compare *Urizen* 2) watched by a naked man half reclining on a head of ripe grain, canopied by a stem that arcs out of the first letter of text—though in N and O these leaves of barley (?) are incongruously attached to the trunk of a tree (or vineF) growing up the left margin from a field of nodding leaves (tops of ripe grain?) in the bottom margin. (In F another head of grain is painted in the right margin of the second strophe. In N there is water rather than sky below the figures.)

Thel 1N

Thel 2[N]. Under the only living branch of a white birch tree (traditional queen of the forest, fragile looking but strong), loosely entwined at its base by a leafing (and flowering[DV]) vine, Thel in a usually yellow*, sometimes pink* or purple* or white* dress with billowing skirt, held as if in formal curtsy, leans slightly (though still almost as statuesque as in Plate 1) toward the similarly dressed human Lilly (her dress white or uncolored)—who bows deeply, with arms folded, above a stem bearing six or seven white[LO] or blue[D] flowers of a St Bernard's lily and stands among its long slender leaves (which give it the name of spider lily) above the "verdant grass" (2:18). A second stem of lily flowers, with two curving leaves above it and two below, bows nearly to the ground in front of Thel. But behind the human Lilly a third stem of flowers (painted out in M) and several longer leaves bow almost as deeply in the other direction, marking their courtesy as habitual. In N and O there are a fourth and fifth stem of flowers fallen quite flat along the ground in front of the Lilly, losing their flower shapes and becoming rounder[O] as if turning from flower to fruit. On six of these —and on a fold of Thel's gown above her right foot—Blake puts tiny eyes[O] and mouths[O] (obscure in the facsimile) to suggest infant faces (as in the flowers of Gray *Spring* 3). When we reach Plate 4 we see the infant Worm "in the Lillys leaf" (4:3) and realize that these are the faces of tiny siblings here. A gentle hint to the virgin Thel? Also in O (and N) another birch trunk is crowded into the right margin: a wink, for the reader, about multiplying? In C the flowers Thel sees are uncolored, but the vine around the birch bears seven scarlet lily-like blossoms. In N Thel is backed by a heavy grey-blue cloud in a bright yellow sky, as though to suggest her isolation in a sunny world; in M by a green field or distant hill. But in J a purple cloud extends behind both figures and the tree trunk, with blue sky behind.

Thel 2[N]

Thel 3D. A curving branch of the seven-flowered lily stem which we have just seen opens the page; a small leafy flourish concludes it at lower right. In the top margin the Cloud is just beginning to materialize (in some copies) in patches of color wash or goldO. O has some brown edges of vegetation in the bottom and left margins.

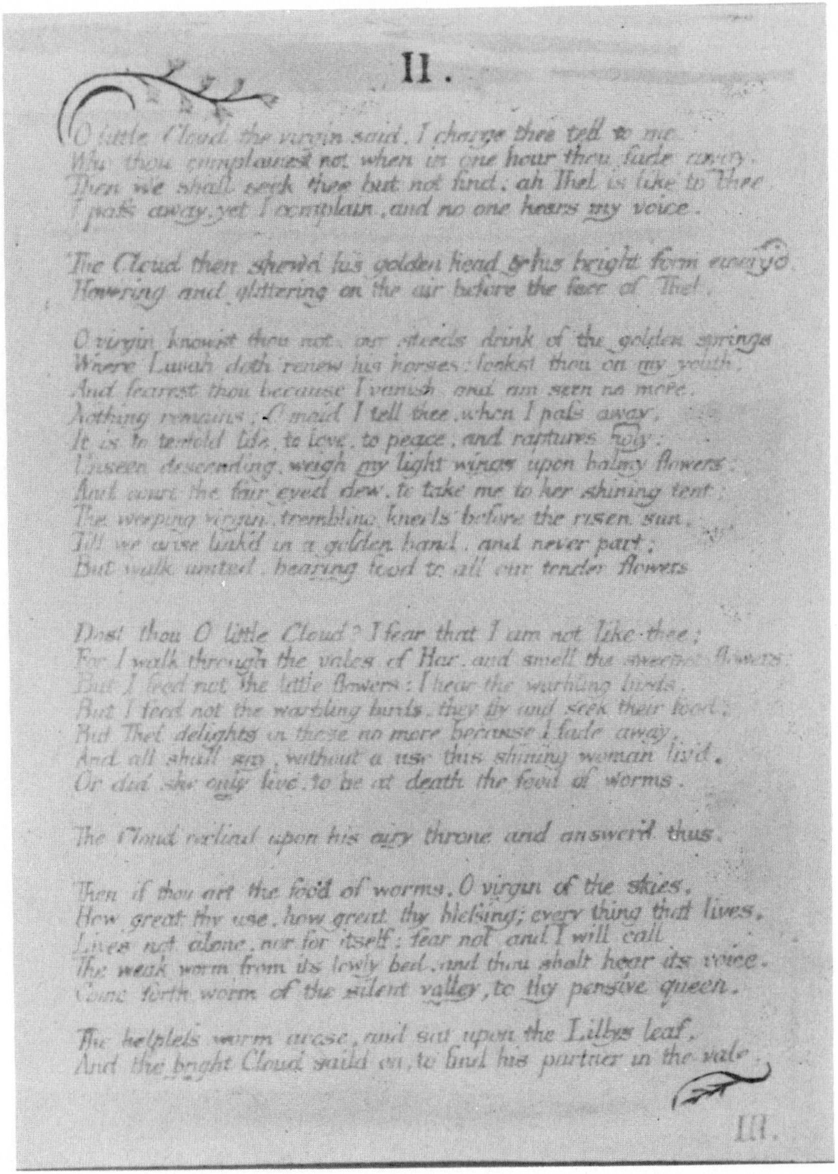

II.

O little Cloud the virgin said, I charge thee tell to me,
Why thou complainest not when in one hour thou fade away:
Then we shall seek thee but not find; ah Thel is like to thee.
I pafs away, yet I complain, and no one hears my voice.

The Cloud then shew'd his golden head & his bright form emerg'd,
Hovering and glittering on the air before the face of Thel.

O virgin know'st thou not, our steeds drink of the golden springs
Where Luvah doth renew his horses: look'st thou on my youth,
And fearest thou because I vanish and am seen no more,
Nothing remains; O maid I tell thee, when I pafs away,
It is to tenfold life, to love, to peace, and raptures holy:
Unseen descending, weigh my light wings upon balmy flowers;
And court the fair eyed dew, to take me to her shining tent;
The weeping virgin, trembling kneels before the risen sun,
Till we arise link'd in a golden band, and never part;
But walk united, bearing food to all our tender flowers

Dost thou O little Cloud? I fear that I am not like thee;
For I walk through the vales of Har. and smell the sweetest flowers;
But I feed not the little flowers: I hear the warbling birds,
But I feed not the warbling birds. they fly and seek their food;
But Thel delights in these no more because I fade away,
And all shall say, without a use this shining woman liv'd,
Or did she only live. to be at death the food of worms.

The Cloud reclind upon his airy throne and answer'd thus.

Then if thou art the food of worms. O virgin of the skies,
How great thy use, how great thy blefsing; every thing that lives,
Lives not alone, nor for itself: fear not and I will call
The weak worm from its lowly bed, and thou shalt hear its voice.
Come forth worm of the silent valley, to thy pensive queen.

The helplefs worm arose, and sat upon the Lillys leaf,
And the bright Cloud saild on, to find his partner in the vale.

III.

Thel 3D

III.

Then Thel astonish'd view'd the Worm upon its dewy bed.

Art thou a Worm? image of weakness. art thou but a Worm?
I see thee like an infant wrapped in the Lillys leaf:
Ah weep not little voice, thou canst not speak. but thou canst weep;
Is this a Worm? I see thee lay helpless & naked: weeping,
And none to answer, none to cherish thee with mothers smiles.

The Clod of Clay heard the Worms voice, & raisd her pitying head;
She bowd over the weeping infant, and her life exhal'd
In milky fondness, then on Thel she fix'd her humble eyes.

O beauty of the vales of Har. we live not for ourselves,
Thou seest me the meanest thing, and so I am indeed;
My bosom of itself is cold. and of itself is dark,

But

Thel 4[I]

Thel 4[I]. The human Cloud, a naked young man except for the white[O] or red[M] scroll-scarf (which indicates that the words he has just spoken are of prophetic import), stretches his arms as if both calling forth the worm (4:27–28) and gesturing goodbye to Thel. In some copies he is backed by a cloud[M], in others there is blue[JL] or purple[I] or pale[NO] sky behind him. Behind Thel and in the rest of the background there is more or less solid cloud, sometimes rose purple[F] or yellow[LIM]; sometimes a very bright yellow (green[M]) on the horizon and behind the infant[IN], dark[N] behind Thel. Her arms match the cloud's gesture but, with her downturned face, illustrate her astonishment at seeing, in human infant form, "the Worm upon its dewy bed" (1). Her skirts billow in the direction of the Cloud's flight, perhaps now feeling the spring zephyr (see Plate ii). The infant Worm "wrapped in the Lillys leaf" (3) lies on and among the long thin leaves of the St Bernard's lily, one flower cluster of which extends left of the infant. In copy O (in which baby faces were added in Plate 2) he shares his bed with five or more added shapes, of worm siblings no doubt; the lower two look like human legs bent at the knee. In this copy and N, Thel is given a full profile and the Cloud's face is repainted, so that he looks more directly at her than in other copies but she more undividedly down at the infant. The two faces as repainted look remarkably alike, but his sex is marked by a penis beneath the transparent scarf.

The birch tree at the right is incompletely sketched (but in O given a bare forked branch and carried to the top of the page; Blake will not, at this point, put a protective branch over Thel as he did in Plate 2). The vine around it is simplified to a five-looped tendril twining up (and, as etched, not touching the tree again) and one leaf pointing down. Roots are also extended down from the tree in O and water is indicated as filling the text area. In I there are distant trees.

Thel 5[N]. Sitting among tall flowers Thel, her face rarely visible[NO], bows her head and almost makes a cradle of her arms (compare the bowing Lilly in Plate 2) or simply folds them across her breast while watching the mother and child below her, who are identified in the text as "the matron Clay" and the infant Worm, still with the lily spray etched beside it—but obscured in most copies, since new flowers are now introduced. Beyond Thel's right elbow are two nodding stems of the colorless monotropa or corpse-plant, which lives without green tissue. Near her an opposite sort of plant, with long stems that cross each other, extends one blushing blossom above her head, still closed (compare the bud thrusting near in Plate ii) but beginning to put forth long stamens (a strongly phallic assertion in the Darwinian context), as is the opening blossom that bends the other way. This is Blake's version, with the bud at left usually paler in color than the flower at right, of Darwin's showy rose-colored or white Meadia or dodecatheon, with suggestions from his golden amaryllis, both over-supplied with what Thel would see as "fighting men in ambush" (6:14), laden with pollen. Blake gives this plant the long thin leaves of the St Bernard's or spider lily, thus, as it were, grafting lily to rose.

Usually he contrasts the bud at the left and the flower at the right, painting the flower a deep lavender[GI] or turquoise[D] or dark blue[L] and the bud pink[DGI] or green[L]. In two copies the sky blushes behind the flower (dark red[O] or deep blue[M]) but not behind the bud. Yet sometimes both bud and flower are the same rosy pink[MN] or blue and white (matching the lily)[O].

Emblematically ominous in a different way is the large plant at far left, gone all to leaves, spider-lily like, without flower or bud, often against dark sky.

In N the colors are all light, though the Meadia blossoms stand out in bright rose; a stream flows across the foreground and out of sight at the left; and in the bottom left corner, on the opposite shore, a lily-like vine with five blossoms is painted in. In some copies[INO] water is added around Thel's promontory, and beyond the barren plant, where the base of a tree trunk obtrudes from the left.

Kept innocent of all these growths, Thel, with her skirt wide like a great corolla, watches the naked matron and the naked infant with outflung arms and crossed legs who face each other with nothing to fear—to apply words which the matron uses to encourage Thel herself.

Thel 5[N]

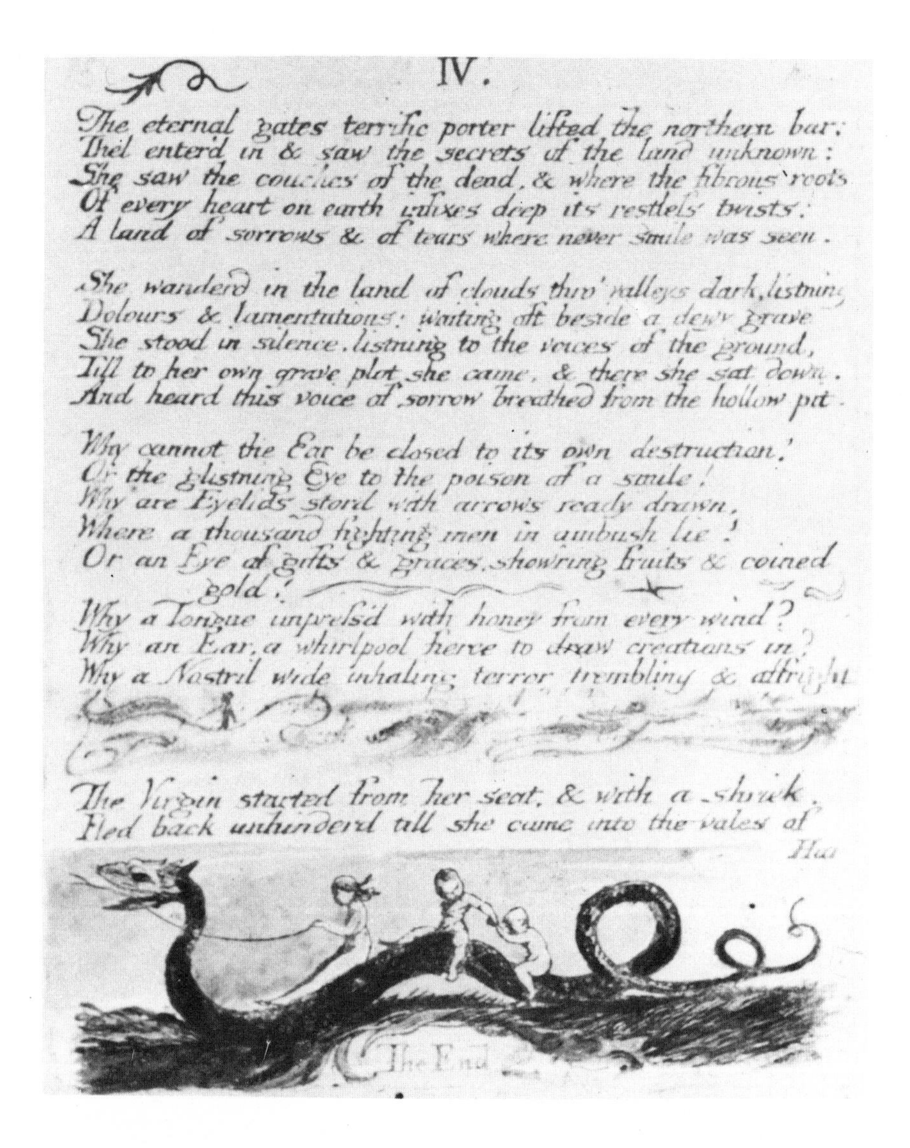

IV.

The eternal gates terrific porter lifted the northern bar:
Thel enterd in & saw the secrets of the land unknown:
She saw the couches of the dead, & where the fibrous roots
Of every heart on earth infixes deep its restless twists:
A land of sorrows & of tears where never smile was seen.

She wanderd in the land of clouds thro' valleys dark, listning
Dolours & lamentations: waiting oft beside a dewy grave
She stood in silence, listning to the voices of the ground,
Till to her own grave plot she came, & there she sat down.
And heard this voice of sorrow breathed from the hollow pit.

Why cannot the Ear be closed to its own destruction?
Or the glistning Eye to the poison of a smile!
Why are Eyelids stord with arrows ready drawn,
Where a thousand fighting men in ambush lie?
Or an Eye of gifts & graces, show'ring fruits & coined gold?
Why a Tongue impress'd with honey from every wind?
Why an Ear, a whirlpool fierce to draw creations in?
Why a Nostril wide inhaling terror trembling & affright

The Virgin started from her seat, & with a shriek.
Fled back unhinderd till she came into the vales of Har

The End

Thel 6I

Thel 6I. This concluding page and the Motto are later than other plates of *Thel* in style of lettering (for example in having leftward serifs on the *g*'s). Hence this plate may be a revised version of the poem's conclusion.

At the top a graceful sprig (akin to the concluding sprig on Plate 3) arches above "The eternal" (1). Between lines 15 and 16 an undulation, a flying bird, and two slight wisps of cloud (all given an upward pointing by the flight of the bird) emphasize the pleasant details of the "Eye . . . showring fruits" and the tongue's "honey from every wind."

In copies I and J lines 19–20 were deleted by erasure and covered by a pink wash^J or by figures^I of a man with a cane on a cloud-line and a gowned woman soaring: perhaps an ironic response to persons who asked Blake to erase references to the boy's "tender curb" and the girl's "curtain of flesh."

As a bridge over "The End" a green^DG or green-mottled^F or green-headed^MO serpent, making two curves and three loops, bears three children leftward, presumably "back . . . into the vales of Har" (22). (In *America* 11 a rather more cheerful serpent is carrying a more securely mounted but similar family inland from the fires of war.) Yet the girl holding the reins is not Thel but of the smaller fairy size of the human forms of dew and clay; her easy riding of the phallic serpent counterpoints Thel's fleeing "with a shriek" (21) at thoughts of genital curb and curtain. (She wears a dress in H.) Beside "The End" lies a broad leaf as big as the larger boy; it balances thin leaves like the lily's, under the girl. Perhaps it is meant for an oak leaf, the large kind that grow from new stems near the ground; there are similar leaves in *Songs* 33 and *Europe* 1 and 12.

The serpent and children may constitute a sort of lion and lamb emblem (compare *Songs* 36) of freedom in "a garden mild." Yet the serpent's head is sharper, flatter, and more sinister looking than in *America* and has three horn-like points of a crest. These, nevertheless, are more like the crests on the useful serpents of *Jerusalem* 9, 39, 72, and 98 than the horns of the beast in *Jerusalem* 75.

Thel i^{F} (Thels Motto). Usually unadorned, this postscript is encircled by a green vine with three grape leaves in copy F.

Thel i^{F}

SONGS OF INNOCENCE AND OF EXPERIENCE

TWENTY-ONE ORIGINAL copies of *Songs of Innocence* alone and twenty-seven of the combined grouping are known to exist, in nearly thirty public and private collections. Nearly a third of these have been examined, but the present notes are related most closely to the most available color facsimile, the Blake Trust version of *Songs* Z (Rosenwald collection, Library of Congress), and to the copies used for the present plates, namely copy I (Widener collection, Harvard) and the Gilchrist electrotypes (g) derived from Blake's original plates. Copy I is very simply colored and serves well for monochrome reproduction: copy U (Princeton) is adorned with silver and gold, making reproduction difficult, though details are often neatly outlined with a fine pen; copy Z is elaborately painted and has accustomed us to full, rounded trees (for example) on either side of the picture even when the etched plate gives only the inner outlines of such trees. One copy, Y (Metropolitan Museum of Art, New York), very delicated painted, adds semi-formal borders outside the plate area; these are briefly described here.

The plates are arranged in the order found in copy Z, partly for convenience, since it is the order followed in standard editions, and partly because it is the order which Blake settled down to in later years; yet even then he did not stop trying other arrangements. For a tabulation of all the different arrangements of plates in different copies, and some discussion of these, see the notes after Plate 27 and after Plate 54.

Songs 1[I]

Songs 1[I] (General title page). Variously colored flames, dark and light, sweep up and across the page (sulfur yellow[Z] flames downward between the two humans) and rise into a vine that loops into "SONGS" and foliates into an umbrella atop the first S—under which one thin figure stands, holding up a right hand for our attention, and another sits reading. At bottom, in the flames which their figleaves (his broad, hers dainty) show to be postlapsarian, are an Adam hiding his face from Eve (though not always from us: in U we see his profile) though bending over her (his arms in potential menace?) and an Eve bowed to the ground but looking back up at him, enigmatically* or seductively[I], or holding her eyes shut[Z], or looking up and out, mouth agape, at some terror offstage[UV], but sometimes[B] hiding her face toward the earth. (Compare their mutual self-enclosure to the postures of *Visions* 6; her seductiveness to Vala's in *Jerusalem* 24. When the plates were etched Vala had not been created, but she had been in Blake's mind quite a while by the time he painted copies I and Z.) For another view of Adam and Eve with the flame between them, see Plate 18. Compare also the postures of Cain and Abel in *Ghost of Abel* 1.

Usually there is grass* in the foreground, sometimes water[Y]. In Y, which has unique ornamental borders around all plates, green flames run up to *"INNOCENCE"* on each side, with loose tendrils above and pink flames further up and across the top. Grape leaves bracket both *"INNOCENCE"* and *"EXPERIENCE."*

Above *"INNOCENCE"* a large bird flies up and leftward, in the same direction as the flames, a direction that sometimes marks the return from flames to paradise (see *America* 11). In copy U the bird carries a yellow apple in its beak! Keynes aptly refers to this figure as a Bird of Innocence; I tend to distinguish this bird with long split tail as a bird of paradise, with *America* 7 as its identifying habitat, *Songs* 5 as a clear portrayal of its split tail and flight. In *Innocence* we shall see this bird in Plates 5, 15, and 27 with patches of lighter feathers (a lapwing effect noted in *Marriage* 2), and in Experience in Plates 34, 51, and 53 (one color but multiple tail in 34, two colors but tail with only two points in 51 and 53). Of these, Plates 34 and 53 were originally in Songs of Innocence, but 51 is a late addition to *Songs,* filled with birds perhaps to right the balance, for there are several Innocence pages with birds in them. Smaller birds with short but slightly divided tails often suggest swallows, not of the deeply cleft kind; such birds appear in

Plates 3, 4, 6, 15, 51. And there are a few, in Plates 15, 19, 26, and 43, that may be versions of the eagle Blake pictures so often in other works. Other kinds of birds occur in Plates 5, 15, 19, 43, and, in small marginal pictures, in a few others as noted. In some copies[BY] the flames beside the lower "Of" take the shape of a swan or raven. (For *Songs* 1[U] see Appendix.)

Songs 2[I] (Innocence frontispiece). On a cloud-blanket tucked among tight-foliaged trees a soaring naked child opens the world wide for the nakedly dressed bard or piper, striding forward with an instrument suitable for a chamber consort: no simple shepherd's pipe, it looks like an oboe. The trees, single and loosely twining together (anticipating Plate 4), set a stately rhythm for his dance. (The border[Y] repeats this twining with crossing briars, red and green, at the bottom, trellises at the sides, curving into the Tree of Jesse effect of Plate 4 above.) In some copies the piper's garment extends below his leg muscles; in BZY it stops below the knees, with a tie[BZ] at his left knee.

In various ways in different copies the cloud is strongly emphasized: the child is divine, celestial, a human form of the bird of innocence; the realm opened is that of imagination. The cloud is here, inside the protection of the branching trees; he rests on a fold of it—and the piper's head is up in it. A gentle breeze blows his hair forward over his left shoulder. (Compare the bard's hair in *Songs* 30.)

The living forest and grazing sheep as a visual chorus behind piper and child may be understood to announce for this work the theme of *Religions* 5: "all . . . are alike . . . & . . . have one source" and the Poetic Genius "is the source."

Songs 2[I]

Songs 3[g]

❧

Songs 3[g] (Innocence title page). In a wicker chair (painted* in various fashions) outdoors, a nurse (compare the cap in Plate 24) or mother holds open a book for boy and girl to read. Her head is sheltered by the word "Innocence," the first letter of which holds the piper (with wide brimmed, merrily curved hat) above her. The three upward flying birds (swallows?) may be seen as music rising from her head and his pipe. The children are sheltered by an apple tree twined loosely by a vine, and by the word "Innocence" which forces the tree to halt the growth of its central trunk or head and bend around its second branch to rise above the word and bear fruit—three[AA] or four[InP V] or six[YZ] apples, golden[YZ] or reddish[Y] or (three of the four) plum-colored[T] or blue and green[InP].

Allegorically (see Wynne's frontispiece emblem) the tree would represent the adult's teachings, the vine the children's learning. This vine does not yet bear flower or fruit, nor does it rise beyond the stunted head. The branches encircling the word emphasize the encroachment of Experience upon Innocence; the children's backs being turned away from the tree suggest their ignorance of its implications (Kauvar 82). A stream* with an island in it* separates this orchard from a distant hill and tree.

The word "SONGS" with its flourishes is the flaming (orange or red*) or fully leaving (green[Z] or blue[InF Y]) fanfare of the page (against dark blue sky*) and is inhabited by many human forms. Kneeling in the O is a miniature of the open-armed boy of the frontispiece, looking down toward the piper and nurse: the conductor of this orchestra. Leaning in the N is a winged scribe (haloed[Z AA]) writing with a pen (the author); above him is a tiny stick figure with arms akimbo toward past and future. A girl is holding up—or hanging the weight of her body from—the top of the G, with her arms together* or apart*, sometimes seeming to face us[Z] (compare *Songs* 23). Slight hints of human form may be intended in some of the bits of branches of the initial and terminal S's. (The border[Y] suggests edges of leaves or flames.)

Songs 4[I] Introduction (Innocence). Interweaving branches form eight panels, inhabited variously, as the Tree of Jesse in illuminated manuscripts and church windows (Blunt 45); here the heavily drawn oblong at bottom suggests a window frame or the bottom of a picture, with no roots below. From top left to bottom right the panels contain: (1) a seated woman and a standing child, repeating the motif of nurse and children in Plate 3—or perhaps a gowned man, seated, writing, and a standing young man or woman[U]; (2) a forward descending nude figure that combines the open hands of the child and the stride of the piper in Plate 2 (the left hand, drawn over the tree stem[UV], pointing to "Pipe") and is comparable to the figure in *Albion rose;* (3) a man standing (or sitting[V]) over a printing press, with a sheet of paper in it; in U this looks more like a plow; Z adds another figure beside him and a parrot above his head; Hirsch (174) sees an adult beside a bed; (4) a figure standing behind a hooded cradle, like the one in *Songs* 17 (headed the other way): this is clearly delineated in U and seems to fit the basic lines of the etching E—though these, unretouched, can look like a distant ruins including a castle tower; V replaces with a blue-gowned figure sitting on a pink toadstool; Z replaces the two blue-gowned figures; InP replaces with a woman leaning over an infant in an oval basket with no hood; (5) a bird (of innocence) flying upward, centered, with leaves or perhaps a cluster of fruit above it; (6) a huddled figure, legs crossed, head on hand; Jesse himself (suggests Essick) as in the Sistine fresco; or regarding or working at something in his lap[U], perhaps writing; (7) a woman sowing seed, with two birds flying near, a third rising above her head; (8) a seated figure, facing left, perhaps with an open book In[I] on knee; as retouched in U, a woman with a distaff at her right hand, a child's face and arm beside her knee, the arm reaching up for thread; the long pole of the distaff in front of her dress lets us mistake the divided dress as two knees; redrawn[Z] as a standing figure, or as figure with back toward us[Y]. (See Appendix in *Songs* 4[U].)

The small vines that flourish on both twining trees have leaves but no fruit (are they ivy?); they almost connect at the top, as the two flame scrolls of the title page, and, to varying degrees, between stanzas. In I the added oblong at bottom could be a stone sill; in most copies* it is running with water, narrowly contained. Since the tree was sometimes depicted as rising from Jesse's body, we may imagine a coffin here.

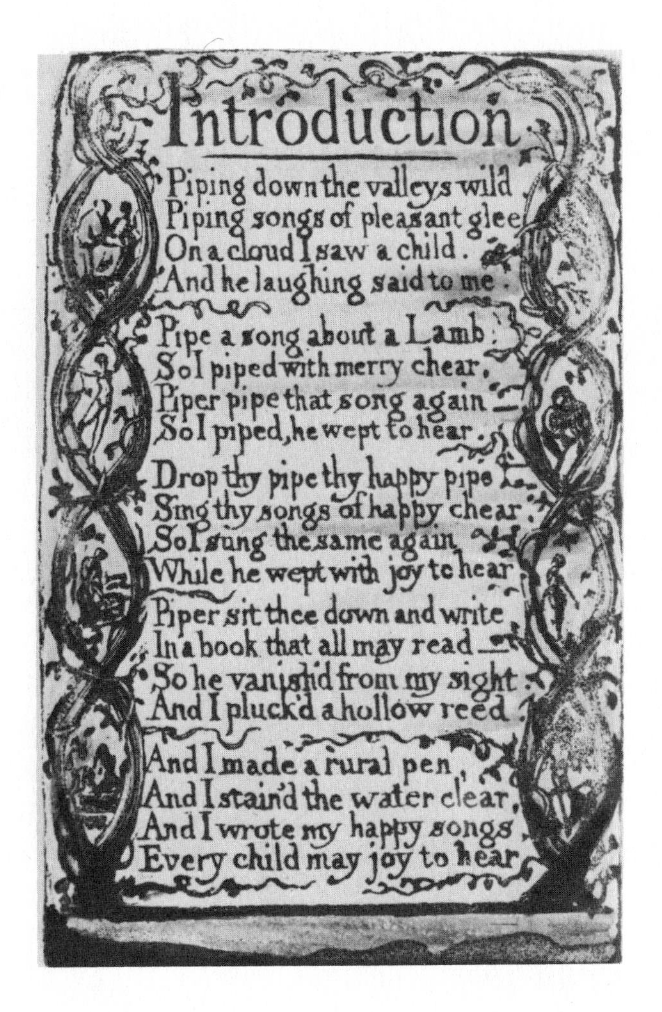
Introduction

Piping down the valleys wild
Piping songs of pleasant glee
On a cloud I saw a child.
And he laughing said to me.

Pipe a song about a Lamb;
So I piped with merry chear,
Piper pipe that song again—
So I piped, he wept to hear.

Drop thy pipe thy happy pipe
Sing thy songs of happy chear;
So I sung the same again
While he wept with joy to hear

Piper sit thee down and write
In a book that all may read—
So he vanish'd from my sight.
And I pluck'd a hollow reed.

And I made a rural pen,
And I staind the water clear,
And I wrote my happy songs
Every child may joy to hear

Songs 4[I]

Songs 5[I]

The Tree of Jesse as a symbol of God and his mercy makes a suitable emblem for Innocence; the motif recurs in Plates 7, 8, 20, 36, and especially 53, "The Schoolboy." Kauvar (83–84) finds in a Wither emblem an interpretation of the heavenly graft, in which Christ is the "wither'd branch . . . broken from the tree," which will spring back to life, a symbol of hope in the sign of a branch missing from the apple tree in Plate 2. (In the border[Y] faint red lines form an open book but are twined with green tendrils.)

Songs 5[I] The Shepherd (Innocence). A young shepherd watches his flock; one of the lambs, baaing, looks up at his face. His shepherd's scrip or wallet hangs at his right side; his crook is held upright beside an upright tree, while his curving body beside the crook is matched by a loosely twining vine around the tree. It bears four* or five* large blossoms like those of the lily in *Thel.*) He looks like but is not to be identified with the piper of the frontispiece: note his shorter hair, different neckline, tunic-like garment ending above the knees. The piper's role is prophetic, the shepherd's protective.

The luxuriant density of the flock, emblem of close content and comfort, is matched by the dense foliage of the trees above and behind them. A large bird of paradise (with light shoulder feathers* and divided tail*) rises above a radiant dawn (variously indicated*): we are looking east in summer. The hills are variously contoured.* Three smaller (or distant) birds are in the sky alongside, and two birds of lark size are on the branch just below them. These birds are sometimes obscured; sometimes [InB·B] a nest is suggested on the branch to the left of the small birds. (The border[Y] puts more grass at the bottom, red saplings with green vines up the sides.) In copy InP the ram's horns below the shepherd's wallet are delineated emphatically.

Songs 6^I The Ecchoing Green 1 (Innocence). The old folk sitting under a flourishing oak (in a park of trees) are two men with brimmed hats (the second man Old John, to whom a child looks up) and two mothers (as their caps indicate), the second fairly young, each tending a pair of weary or restless children. On the green two boys are batting a ball and three older children are standing or strolling. The oak in this context is parental and protective, a sort of axis mundi (notes Kauvar).

The title of the poem puts forth leaves and a vine all buds and blossoms, with very active sexual parts. Flanking the first stanza are a boy with a cricket bat and a boy rolling a hoop. Below each is a grapevine, the larger one bearing a ripe cluster of grapes toward which a swallow flies. The sky at right is red^V above the oak.

(The border^Y frames the top corners with acanthus leaf edges, suggesting green flame; at bottom it repeats very faintly the crossing briars of the Plate 2 border.)

Songs 6^I

Songs 7I

Songs 7I The Ecchoing Green 2 (Innocence). The children, a girl, a boy with kite, another with bat, are being directed home by "Old John with white hair," followed by one of the mothers holding an infant and accompanied by a small boy. (I adds long shadows.) Beside her walks a youth or small man with a hat that identifies him with the man sitting beside Old John on the preceding page; he holds out a bunch of grapes beside the small boy's face. Behind them a young woman with a wide-brimmed hat (making a halo effect) reaches up for a bunch of grapes being handed her by one of two boys for whom the two grapevines have become one living tree (needing no elm for support) which twines round itself and then supports the boys and brackets the text of the poem. The two unplucked bunches of grapes are larger than the two plucked, the very largest (more purple than the rest*) being perhaps just out of reach. But all these reachings can be managed in the world of innocent imagination in which vines are this sufficient and accommodating and the grapes of desire ripen in sunshine.

In UVZ the narrow stream of water that began under the Tree of Jesse continues here and in the next picture—the life's river or poetry of innocence, the "water clear" which the poet stains to make purple grapes—a condensation, Sevcik suggests, of the visionary cloud of Plate 2. (The border[Y] has simple lines at top and upper sides, then three formal panels on each side, alternating with leaves; at bottom curved lines of wing or cloud edges.)

There is a stream (or pond) in the background in Plate 3, with green hills beyond. In Plates 7, 10, and 23 the water in the foreground* may serve as a dividing boundary between the first and second of a pair of plates. Hirsch has noted (177, 181, 198, 199) that often the first and second plates of a pair refer to earthly life and Eternity. (In Experience there are no paired plates; the triptych 34–36, moved from Innocence, lacks water.) The reference may be doubtful in the case of "Night"; in "A Cradle Song" a rug must serve as river; and of course in the present plate the point is that Eternity is in an earthly village. Water in the foreground in single plates, e.g. 4, 8, 12, 24, makes the same point. The only foreground water in Experience is in Plate 47, where it serves an ironic purpose (Urizen in the bulrushes being equated to "The Little Boy lost").

Songs 8[I] The Lamb (Innocence). The dialogue of child and lamb (compare the shepherd and lamb exchanging looks in Plate 5) and the jubilation of embracing vines and sinuous trees need no detailed reckoning. The village oak stands beside the thatched cottage; the high-arching spirit of the foreground trees prevents any Urizenic oak grove domination.

The only birds in the picture are a pair of domestic doves, not in the air but standing together atop the thatched cottage with open door. A stream of water is painted into the foreground*. Blake liked to paint a background of strong blue* or purple* behind the cottage gable and the doves. The boy is usually naked*. (The border[Y] sketchily repeats the twined saplings, with roots at bottom turning up toward the water.)

Songs 8[I]

Songs 9[I]

Songs 9[I] The Little Black Boy 1 (Innocence). The southern trees are of wilder shape than the village oak or elm; the vine around the larger tree makes a more independent loop (often obscured*). Though vegetation is thicker, bodies are freer. The African mother, unlike the English, is clad only to the waist.

In Z and AA the foliage is stripped from the smaller tree at right, probably to make room for the large sunrise painted in (the sun, present in all copies but pale* or orange red[V] in a cloudless sky, rises south of east in African summer), perhaps also to associate that tree more particularly with the willow that bends in the same way over Christ and the children in the next plate. The marginal sapling and vine at the left echo motifs of the entwined saplings in The Lamb (Plate 8); the more active vines in the right margin suggest themes in Plate 6. But the flourish of sheltering foliage that grows over the title word "Boy" repeats again the willow's bending, emblematic of the suffering of Christ and all mankind as well as of his mercy. In the lines of the poem, the mother "pointing to the east" advises her child to look "on the rising sun," but as the black boy speaks these lines he points to the position of the noonday sun. We may understand him simply to be explaining what "black bodies" are like by pointing to "a shady grove" (15–16), but the gesture also suits the words "black as if bereav'd of light" (4). The bird rising up in the right margin near these words, however, reminds us that this life of sheltered innocence is but "a little space" which must be pierced to prevent its becoming a prison shutting us away from "joy in the noon day" (12). (I assume that the bird is well read in the text.) On the thematic warnings about "protective shade" in these two plates, see Kauvar 97–99. Yet the border[Y] shelters the scene at top and sides with four palm fronds like angel wings, from trees bearing clusters of coconuts (three at left, six at right beside the bird) with roots joining at bottom.

Songs 10[I] The Little Black Boy 2 (Innocence). The black boy has introduced the white boy to Christ, considering his education in love to be sufficient now, and is standing to "stroke his silver hair" (11) during the encounter. A willow of paradise hangs over them, and comparison with *America* 7 is suggestive. The willow is rooted in a green* bank, over a brown[VZ] rock, though in Z the roots grip the bank like fingers of a hand. The bank forms a seat for God as shepherd—with sun-like[XYZ AA] or pink[V] halo, or none [InDB]. The black boy is as light of skin as the English boy in some copies[BZ AA], quite black in others[InFIVY]—different ways of making the same points. (In U the black boy is blue black here, though brown in the preceding page; the white boy is pink and white; Christ is a compromise between them, the upper part of his face being almost as blue-black as the black boy.) The absence of distinct lambs in the background flock lets us see the boys as lambs. The upstanding St Bernard's lily (without leaves) at the left behind the boys was removed from the copper at some stage (it is present in U and V, not Z), but a variant form in the right margin persists in all copies. (In the border[Y] it is further stylized, as a wavy line with alternate attached pendulant flower shapes, up the left side, and with alternate centered spots up the right.)

A suggestion of water in the foreground, lacking in some copies[InF], is painted into a river in IUZ AA.

Songs 10[I]

Songs 11^{I}

Songs 11^{I} The Blossom (Innocence). All conventional images of vegetation and landscape are replaced by a branching flame-flower. (Though in Y, relenting, Blake fills the upper corners with green leaves and adds borders of grass at bottom, vines curving up the sides and top holding two shadowy blossoms in blue, two in green.) The flower's efflorescence consists of a central human madonna (winged and haloed^{Z}) with infant, and one wingless and five winged naked infants or joys: a wingless boy flying, with gestures combining those of the boy's arms and the piper's legs in Plate 2; one, winged but sitting sideways on the lower flame-branch and writing on a book or a sheet of paper or reading a broadside^{V}; two, above him, poised in flight and conversing with gestures toward the madonna and child (compare the conversation in Plate 21); two kissing each other in the higher flames. The mother, winged but clothed, usually stands out in color, of dress (blue^{InB} or green* or pink^{U}) or wing (rose^{I}, blue^{InF}); her back is toward the writer's back; the infant is scarcely discernible*, though sometimes redrawn to show its head at her right breast^{InP}.

We may think of the five winged joys as the aroused senses, capable of soaring, and the wingless but actually soaring boy as the imagination or genius. Compare "The Divine Image," Plate 18. The flames, which refer back to Plate 1 and ahead to Plates 18 and 25, are differently colored in different copies, ranging from red to green, often mixed reds and greens; in T pink, green, blue, and lavender, with an effect of iridescence; in U green, pink, yellow, and gold; in V rose and violet. The shape of the open flame-flower may suggest that of the swan for which the infant in *Religion* a8 is stretching his arms; the boy's gestures here signifying attainment. (See also the bird-shaped flame in Plate 1.)

Songs 12 The Chimney Sweeper (Innocence). At the bottom we see not the Angel of Tom's dream "who had a bright key" (13) but a realization of the Angel's promise of "God for his father" (20). The gowned figure (with halo*) who bends over and takes the left hand of a boy climbing out of a box coffin is Jesus himself (as in *The Woman Taken in Adultery* and several of Blake's New Testament illustrations); the key and the angel, who would have wings, melt off as a metaphor for the swiftness of salvation for chimney sweeps (see Swedenborg's *Earths in the Universe*). Compare the rescue of the lost boy in *Songs* 14.

Left of the coffin (not outlined in the plate and sometimes a simple hole in the ground*) the first freed boys raise their hands together, the next pair clutch each other, the next, still rejoicing with raised hands, run toward the river (indicated by lines at left, painted as water*). A further pair have begun wrestling; two beyond them seem running to dive. (Eleven boys in all.)

All the vegetation on the page is alive, with here and there a human form: in the C of the title a sweep carrying his sack of soot on his shoulders; astride the flourish above "eep" three vague figures, the second waving his sweep's brush in the air, the third leaning forward as if holding reins. At line 13, above "Angel," a small figure holds out the handle end of a key; in the right margin two figures reach toward each other (clear in InB and U). (The border[Y] has lily-like vines up the sides, vague lines of clouds or wings—or smoke—at top and bottom.) (The reproduction here is from a photographic conflation of several copies, made by John Wright, to recover badly inked details in the top and side margins.)

Songs 12

Songs 13[I]

Songs 13[I] The Little Boy lost (Innocence). Under a barren tree or two trees[Z AA] or none[B] (amid bulrushes[BIUY]) a gowned boy in a brimmed hat gropes after a triangular flare of swamp fire (surrounded by a burst of radiation[UYZ AA] like large petals[V]). In this and the following plate Blake uses a variety of methods to represent the boy's forlornness followed by comfort. The human figures are always central and prominent in their loose nightgown-like clothing; there is always a contrast between the shapeless light of the "vapour" here and the radiant countenances of humans adoring each other's lineaments in Plate 14. But sometimes the trees serve only as darkness, the vague shape of the enclosing night. Sometimes the arms of the tree or trees in Plate 13 mock the outstretched arms of the boy, while in Plate 14 they stand in protective arches, doubtless interlocking arms above the picture, offering both the enclosing shelter, and sorrow, of the mother and an infinite passageway.

The title lettering bears flowering and leafing vines; a man sitting in the loop edge of L with pipe at his mouth: not our friendly piper, in this position, but a wood sprite luring infants into swamps; a sleeper (a cocoon?) against the first stroke of B, an arm-waving figure in its bottom curve. Floating behind "Boy" is the swan of desire, fitter object for boy with outstretched arms to pursue (as seen in *Religion* a8). A long-necked water bird flies under a cattail (i.e. bulrush) above "lost," another below "Little," two gulls in spaces below the swan.

Four gowned angels (haloed[Z AA]) stand at the four corners of the text. At the bottom two gowned spirits wih scarves instead of angel wings and with tripling vines crossed by or attaching to their outstretched right and left arms, respectively, soar apart but upward, given respectively gold and yellow halos in Z (also haloed in AA); female and male in I (i.e. as etched): surrogates for mother and father anticipating the next page. In Z and AA blue sky with seven stars is added behind the lower figures, going partly up the margins with perhaps a star or two. Y emphasizes the bulrushes (identical to cattails, for Blake) and adds several in the side borders; compare his "Moses among the Bulrushes" and Plates 22, 23, 44.

Songs 14[I] The Little Boy Found (Innocence). Two tree trunks on the left, one on the right form a tunnel-corridor down which the boy is led (as in Plate 12) by the hand of "God ever nigh" (3), whose loose gown is lifted by a wind behind him—as somehow the boy's gown is also, though in Plate 13 it seemed to drag the ground. The savior father has a halo (variously pictured as a simple ring or wide band), which the boy's hat now seems to match (though removed in D and B). Beside the flourishing text another gowned spirit (from the bottom of Plate 13?), with halo[Z AA], extends a welcoming arm. The two spirits enact the roles of father and mother specified in the text.

The word "Found" extrudes banners of joy. "Boy," from its "y" which sported a simple leaf in Plate 13, now extends a rolling scroll of prophecy (if we compare *Marriage* 12 and 13) continuing down the left margin, which declares that this one of God's people has been *found* indeed. (The border[Y] puts fruit near the boy's head, perhaps coconuts such as the Black Boy dwells among in Plate 9.)

(The first letter of "Found" is usully transcribed as lower case, matching the "l" in "Little Boy lost"—but its descent below the line should not prevent our seeing that it has been raised into a swash capital.)

Songs 14[I]

Songs 15[I]

Songs 15[I] Laughing Song (Innocence). First off I should like to deduce that for Blake laughter, "the sweet chorus of Ha. Ha. He," means birds (potential words) in great variety of shape, movement, and color—the theme of the eleven or twelve variously great and minute winged spirits depicted here: for at least one of the three flying beside "the painted birds laugh in the shade" (9) is a humble house fly. The others, colored five different ways in I, for example, include (somewhat conjecturally): a swallow flying straight up left of the title, a crane or swan flying toward the S of "Song," a barn swallow farther right, another flying the same diagonal at bottom left, two birds of paradise, flying and perching, a third diving below the vine, a distant eagle, below it a lapwing, and a dove (a parrot in V) settling on the vine.

In this context, there is a feast for everyone at the table spread "with cherries and nuts" (10) under the village oak. Only the wine appears—on the cloth and held high by the youth who waves a fine hat (with plume* or fox-tail*, not always painted in) to lead us in toast and song. But there is much feasting on countenances (compare Plate 14) among these eight boys and girls (the third from the left not always visible; only two near us are clearly boys). The chairs are more reclining than the nurse's of Plate 3, rather Roman or Hellenistic. Long shadows indicate a declining sun. The hats on the girls at far left and far right are somewhat like haloes. (The border[Y] somewhat repeats the one for "The Lamb"—Plate 8—with saplings and vines.)

Songs 16[g] A Cradle Song 1 (Innocence). Suggestive, indeterminate vegetable and human forms of dreams, smiles, sweet moans, and sighs fill the verdure backed by night sky*. If we compare the solid flame flowers of Plates 11, 18, and 25 or the weltering green flames of *Urizen* 2, we see that the lullaby form of energy and desire thins into small strands or fibres, or flowers, that it flattens into "pleasant streams" and "happy silent moony beams" (3–4)—swarming, however, with people, not to mention the heads of ripe grain near the top left and bottom right corners and at the right of the fourth stanza.

The piper, hatless but piping, leans against A; a seated figure extends something from inside the C; a heavy man with brimless cap stands in the D. Four humans can be seen in the left margin: a woman stands with raised arm, invoking "Sweet sleep" (5); a winged joy points toward "Sweet smiles" (9); a mother with child in lap sits by "Sweet . . . Mothers smiles" (11); a tall figure with right arm raised and a long cape walks toward the bottom stanza (who the text suggests may be the savior of Plates 12 and 14). "Song" fills the top right margin with a dainty vine bearing nine or ten small flowers (or small blue berries[InB,U]). Just below these a person in left profile with bent head sits on a thin leaf sheet of "moony beams"—in the center of which one can just make out (but Blake often* clearly picks out) a gowned figure soaring (as it were) leftward. At the right of "happy child" a child holds two vine-stems as a swing; below him another extends both hands to one stem and stands with feet wide on another; down beside the fourth stanza a naked woman reclining on a vine looks down at a naked man walking away on the next curve.

The borders[Y] for this and the next plates consist of large enclosing curtains, quite theatrical in the first, with a patterned valance at the top, tasselled ties beside the ends of the first and second stanzas, and a rippling base; simpler in the second, fully closed at the bottom.

Songs 16[g]

Songs 17^{I}

Songs 17^{I} A Cradle Song 2 (Innocence). The dream verdure of the previous plate forms a beguiling canopy over this domestic scene, the only (partly) indoor picture in the *Songs*. In the left margin beside the first stanza an "infant small" is held by a gowned standing figure who can remind us of the figure beside the previous stanza and so represent here both the mother of Jesus comforting him "When he was an infant" and the savior with his "face that smiles on thee." Beside the final stanza a boy running down facing right and a girl down facing left represent his smiling "on all" (5).

Below this adorned text, a firm curtain and a hooded wicker cradle shelter the thickly wrapped, perhaps even threateningly swaddled, infant. The mother or nurse leans forward in a strong chair like that of Plate 3. It is "surely not by chance that the child's pillow forms a conspicuous halo" (Keynes). A flowing serpent motif develops in the carpet (often* replaced by other carpet designs). In V a shadow slants across the bottom left rug area.

Songs 18[g] The Divine Image (Innocence). At lower right the haloed* gowned savior as father (see Plates 12, 14, 16) stretches his left hand to raise up a naked man (Lazarus? Adam?). (In copy U, besides the halo of white and gold, there are long rays of white light streaming from the savior toward Adam.) And a naked woman (Eve? the Woman taken in adultery?) lifts up* her face awaiting her turn. The divine wrath and the divine mercy take the images, respectively, of a flower of naked fire (red and yellow and green[UYZ], variously yellow and green[InB,InD,BFIV]; compare Plates 11 and 25 and the relatively shapeless welter of Plate 1), and of a vine of tender filament that branches into leaves with lily shapes. One short petal of the flaming flower (sometimes omitted[BVYZ AA]) opens straight up to the height of Christ's right shoulder. Another opens at his left and roars between man and woman (like the flames behind Adam and Eve in Plate 1) to expand infinitely with infinite divisions and complex "motion and countermotion" into a gigantic reversed but not serpentine S (see Eben Bass *Forms* 302 ff, also for comparison of Plates 11 and 25). The tender thin vine also opens to the right and to the left of the savior (who is not only the true vine but the androgynous center of the flowering flame) and twines about the forms of flame as about a green elm or apple. It leaps swifter than the flame to make a Jacob's ladder ascent up the right side, and it surpasses the tips of flame, bending the longest back to shelter human forms. It explodes leafing hands against the hand of flame at the left which threatens to close its circle. This place of the meeting of contraries is thus held open for "The Divine Image," the name of this poem which speaks all to the vine's purpose, leaving the wrath to the illumination. A background of deep blue[Z] suggests that this flame is burning in the night.

(Elaine Kauvar suggests that the vine is an organic version of the polemonium caerulum or Jacob's ladder, but the differences seem greater than the similarities.)

On the top ground of flame thus drawn back, two children kneel with hands held up under the vine to "pray in their distress" (2), and toward them approach two gowned women, one moving swiftly to announce the children, the other walking toward them bearing a pitcher or cruet in her left hand and something round under her right arm, possibly a round loaf of bread (see esp V)—"a loaf of bread and a pitcher of wine" (Hirsch 194).

In Y the border adds stems turning into vines, with flowering at left center and a vigorous tendril looping inside the top left

Songs 18[g]

Songs 19[I]

corner. In InF the story is drastically simplified by the removal of Eve. In V both Eve and Adam are clothed in blue up to the waist, in InP only Eve. She is sometimes shown looking down*.

Songs 19[I] Holy Thursday (Innocence). At the top, nine pairs of charity school boys march two by two, led by two beadles with wands (sometimes only one wand*). The wands seem a parody of the true shepherd's staff (see Plates 5 and 10), and the boys are not only in uniform but grouped by their school colors (for example, three couples in gray coats, three in purple, three rather nondescript[Z]—or two in green, five in blue, two in red[I]—or three in green, four in pink, two in blue[V]). See Plate 7 for a free marching of intermingled ages and sexes, and garments. (Copy U approaches such variety, coloring the boy's garments in alternating pairs, green, blue, pink, grey, blue, pink, green, grey, with a final pair in which one boy wears pink coat and blue trousers, the other blue coat and pink trousers.) The charity school girls, trusted to one matron with wig and book but with no visible staff, march on grass rather than pavement, in more open pairs (seven to the boys' nine), and in an opposite direction. They sometimes[Z] have only one dress color under their white aprons; sometimes are grouped like the boys: two in yellow, two blue, one green, two pink[I]—or two in pink, three blue, two green[U]—or two in green, three pink, two blue[V]. But they are placed below the boys by the whole distance of the text. That this richly embroidered title and twelve lines are what Blake makes of the street between them is suggested by a whiff of smoky flame like that from the vagabonds' fires in the streets of Experience (*Songs* 45 and 46). It stands out (painted[Z] the purple of the coats above) between the title words "Holy" and "Thursday," rising from a small oval toward which a tiny boy runs from the left with an arm toward the fire.

With this clue, we can see that the two words are contraries potentially, such as the flame and vine on Plate 18, but now separated into negations: all dividing flame flaring up from the L of "Holy" (the left fork curling down toward the approaching boy); all leaf and contorting vine growing up from the Y and down from the S of "Thursday." The theme is repeated in the first line, where the flames go up and down from "a Holy" and the vines up from "Thursday," to support the vagabonds' fire. As the lines of verse advance, they are kept as open as "Thames waters" (4) by miniature flames and vines and other miniscule activity. After the first stanza a stork flies above "a multitude." After the second the busy vegetation opens for a dancing child who holds his hands wide under "innocent hands" and leaps up from "voice" between thin flames sent up by "the" and "song." At the bottom, feathery leafage dropping from "pity" waves over the matron and first girls, vines reach flower shapes down toward the other girls' heads—and if we look closely at the center of the line of vine we see an eagle with wings spread wide, standing on a vine and two-looped tendril in a fashion that anticipates Blake's emblem of the collaboration of line and illumination in *Marriage* 15. (The border[Y] has simple acanthus leaves at the bottom, loops up the sides, and somewhat scroll-like shapes at the top corners.)

Hirsch (196) notes that the two marching rows "suggest an immense line of children moving in a clockwise direction," i.e. "multitudes."

Songs 20[I] Night 1 (Innocence). The contemplator of the peaceful night as a heavenly garden ("I must seek for mine": 4) may be the robed figure at bottom left who steps toward* the text (John Grant's suggestion). (A later variant of this vision is Blake's *Il Penseroso* 1.) The objects in the left margin above him that are diagrammed rather than shown will be, from the top down, the "sun descending" (already down now), the "evening star" (four dots for stars below the sun, which is yellow in Z, then three farther down; sometimes a bright star[T] at right of line 12), and the full "moon like a flower" (5), a white disk[Z] beside the lower stars. Two of the birds that "are silent" sit on a branch, not "in their nest" (3), beside line 4, two doves facing each other like those on the thatched roof in Plate 8. Two of the seven "angels bright" who go their rounds with unseen blessing are just above the poet, one with head bent forward perhaps watching *him*. Another, with arms up, has a toe on the moon diagram. Another, just above, has wings and arms extended. (The two lower figures have wings also, the middle one apparently not.)

At lower right another winged angel with outstretched arms is about to alight on the green mound above the cave of a lion: "They visit caves of every beast" (19). The living tree beside the lion, loosely vine-entwined, branches just above the beginning of the text into a fork that holds a large-winged angel, resting, and above

Songs 20[I]

Songs 21[I]

that into another fork in which a winged angel stands with a vessel in his right hand (from which to "pour blessing": 13). A golden glow[Z] emanates from these angels in the tree (compare the comfort bearers near the children in Plate 18) and also forms an oval behind the title, "Night." There is water in the foreground in this plate and the next*, representing "life's river" (27:21). (The border[Y] is vaguely leafy.)

❧

Songs 21[I] Night 2 (Innocence). The text displaces the foliage of a tall oak (to guess from the leaves); there are three[TYZ], four[U], or six[AA] white stars in the night sky at right. In the left margin (i.e. up along the trunk) four angels (reduced to two[V]) are dimly seen tending nests. At bottom behind the tree is a tall St Bernard's lily, larger than those in *Thel,* unless the five girls walking in the garden and doing duty as angels are small. Usually they all* have "conspicuous halos" (K), sometimes a large glow for each group. Both groups are talking among themselves and seem about to share the news—which, if they are following the text of the poem in which a lion with ruddy eyes foretells his conversion to sleeping beside the "bleating lamb," whom he addresses, must have something to do with the lion's ruddier behavior in the present and the plight of the lamb he shall one day guard without the need of angels. If the girl at the left is holding a lamb in her arms, it is invisible. The lion swallowed it. The girl at the other side of the trio is holding something* at her left side, perhaps a lyre[InP] or harp[Z] (compare *Jerusalem* 70).

(The border[Y] consists of formal brackets at the top and bamboo poles at the sides, with three balls, then some green stems and leaves.)

Songs 22[I] and 23[I] Spring 1 and 2 (Innocence). In these two plates (which may be discussed as a unit) the large pictures focus on a single action, the embrace of "Little Boy Full of joy" (10–11), who is "here" with his "white neck" to be licked (20–22), and "Little Lamb," who is hailed, with "soft Wool" to be pulled and "soft face" to be kissed (19–26). The two little ones and the two mothers eye each other in the opening scene, a sunny meadow beside but not oppressively underneath an old oak, and are obviously in accord. The horizon is painted with various* indications of dawn, or colorful hills are shown beyond the plain.

The song is recited, however, not by the mother nor by the piper or flautist but by the poet, who has the piper at his disposal and in his purview a wider audience (and orchestra) that includes birds day and night, "Little Girl" as well as boy and lamb, and a barnyard rooster. For his illuminations, he simply lets the words and music exfoliate and animate. The capital S of "Spring" flows out into "a fanciful 'S' curve" (Eben Bass *Forms* 204) made out of budding grass stems pulled, perhaps, by the modest attendant sheep this side of the ewe and lamb. The piper's imagined response to the first line, "Sound the Flute!" is animated as a fairy angel piping on a symbolic flute (redrawn with trumpet effect in V) inside the grassy curve. The next line, "Now, it's mute," animates into a fairy angel being still, spreading his wings to call for illumination—and being accommodated by a fanciful form of the capital Y, from "Year." Beside the next stanza, a fanciful capital C, for the Cock who crows, supports, for the Girl as a vision of what her "Infant noise" can lead to, a fairy dressed in a flaring gown dancing (and singing) with arms extended "Merrily." (Years later, when he was coloring copy Z, and perhaps some others, Blake gave the Girl a capital G for her own by replacing the sad girl in the G of "SONGS" in Plate 3 with this merry dancer.)

In the final stanza we are taught quite firmly that the song of Spring is not so much for the Lamb as for the Boy, the fanciful capital letter here being a large B. It supports the fairy modestly hiding its head but raising angel-eagle wings in applause. Whereupon the ripening grass supplying the stems and flowering spikes for these fancies runs down the left margin and encloses the climactic vignette: ewe and ram watching Boy as he moves from pulling Lamb's wool to kissing Lamb's soft face. In B a purple cluster (of grapes?) is tucked beside the ewe at the left. In U the boy has a pink halo.

Songs 22[I]

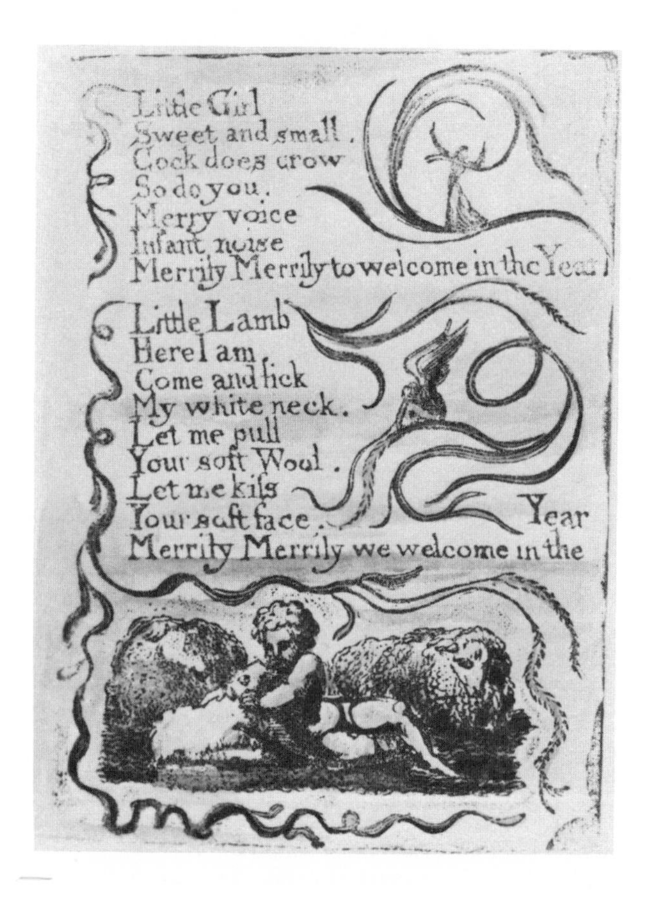

Songs 23[I]

In some copies[Z AA] water is added in the foreground beneath and behind the grasses, making the family stage into an island or promontory. In Y there is water in front but grass at the left, where a bulrush is added, matched by bulrushes in the border on each side—implying that we have here another hidden Moses, like the little boy lost in Plate 13.

Songs 24[g] Nurse's Song (Innocence). In the bottom scene a permissive nurse sits under an apple tree (the leaves and twigs few and scattered, as in Plate 3). On the other side of the playground a vine snakes its way up a young elm, vine and elm leaning toward the apple tree above the seven children. No apples or grapes are indicated; happiness is in the present play. The shadows indicate high noon. Nurse, reading a book to herself, sits on something low, not the fine chair of Plate 3. The children play their own game—not simply "dancing merrily in a circle" (Keynes) but making a chain with their hands, led by two boys (the others alternately girl and boy) to run under a kerchief held by a standing girl and boy—a version of "London Bridge" perhaps, or "Go in and out the windows." Mary Lynn Johnson notes that the chain's opening near the nurse includes her in the visual circle.

The title is in a jungle of proliferating foliage and human forms, with an impressive six-pointed green leaf, acanthus type, waving above the S. Beside it, walking on the stem of a small similar leaf growing to the right, a boy fairy holds up the stem of an unfurling tendril. The leafage spreading down the right margin recalls the "moony beams" in the same area in Plate 16. The leaflike extension from the end of "Song" makes a hammock for a reclining figure, while an active one climbs onto it. Above him in the S sits a large person, legs crossed, writing with a long-plumed pen. Above and to the left, over the apostrophe, a reader sits in a leaf that grows on the thin stroke of N (vine-twined, perhaps a miniature of the vine-twined flame-leaf of Plate 19). A naked figure climbs the first stroke of the N; another hangs down with one leg in the "u" to touch a small figure sitting on the hammock. The first words of the text encourage us to hear all this active and passive growth as "the voice of children . . . heard on the green"—and a mischievous boy points up from another green hammock to suggest a pun. Another, two lines farther down, sits reading[Z]. The text then absorbs our attention. If we now trace the gentle labyrinth of foliage which supplies resting places for these two, we see that it all grows from "within my breast" (3), the nurse's.

In the right margin, between the jungle of rest and laughter and the social playing below, a half-fallen willow hangs like rain over a pool—compare the willow over Christ and the children in Plate 10—in illustration of the paradisal spirit of the lines beside it: "we cannot go to sleep . . . birds fly . . . hills are all coverd with sheep" (10–12).

Songs 24[g]

Songs 25[I]

In coloring this page Blake often* picks out in green some of the acanthus leaves, the willow, and the "green" below, painting blue sky behind, sunlight on the horizon, the whole text as a cloud, rosy[Z] behind the title. Water is added in the foreground[U]. (The border[Y] is of simple lines.)

❧

Songs 25[I] Infant Joy (Innocence). A flower usually scarlet* (but blue in InA, InG, DEFIX), like the anemone of *Thel* ii but with different leaves, takes the vegetable form of the dividing flames of Plates 11 and 18 but in a sequence that seems to put twisting vine first, then flames, for a purer Joy. Then we see, from the flame-like tongues of the leaves, that in this plant the vine and the flame (line and surface, pity and wrath) begin as united contraries, with rhythmic moments when the flame asserts its force, mounting at the right to a phallic bud, at the top to a perfection such as anticipated by the lion's "tears of gold" (21:10). The nativity scene in the still but flaming center thus created is one of joy promising future joy. We saw (Plate 14) that the Little Boy lost when Found became a prophet. In "To Tirzah" (Plate 52) we shall see the adult in extremis finally "Raised a Spiritual Body." The Psyche-wings of the spirit at the staminal center of this flower, if Psyche stands for intellectual vision, promise the "Sweet joy" which the natural mother accepts as the boy's announced name: "two days" are enough time under these circumstances. (In Z the winged figure is given a halo, as mother and child are not, in InP her wings are a strong blue within the scarlet petals.)

Interesting comparisons could be made to the madonna and child of *Thel* 5, under the sign of a lily but the looming bud of desire, and of *Marriage* 11 in the maw of a water plant as animated by "ancient Poets." And we might wonder how Thel would regard the bud (which gets in her way in *Thel* ii) if she could see the present scene in the open blossom? (The border[Y] consists of three pairs of drooping leaves, the pair near the top resembling the drooping lily flower in Plate 43.)

Songs 26[I] A Dream (Innocence). The human form of the "watchman of the night" (16) stands in the lower right corner, with staff and lantern, in right and left hands. His glow-worm form may be seen on a blade of grass after "folorn" (5), or after "tear" (13) in Y (in gold) and in Z. It also appears, after "weep for me" (12), in composite form as the root to which a leafing plant is attached, like the forms in *Marriage* 5 and 19 that combine bird and serpent. (In Z and AA Blake adds a bright star just above the glow-worm part.)

In "A Dream" a reclining human sleeps in the curve of the A and another slumps over his reading inside the D. But the creative life and spirit within a dream are proclaimed by an eagle soaring above "dream" and an angel with wings and arms outspread above "weave" in line 1. The lost emmet (ant) is struggling in thick grass after line 3, and we see her again on a tangled spray below "her" (8). The beetle, whose hum she must follow (19), was not far from her (after line 4) when she first lost her way; we see him at the bottom, near line 17, in communication with the watchman. (A humming type, perhaps a click beetle of some sort—black in both positions in B; blue-black in the first only in Y; black only after 17 in T—he is the living form, of course, of the London watchman's rattle.) The watchman seems to be backed by a tree, but its branches seem very odd until we stop to think that a glow worm is very small and this is some garden plant.

Besides the star mentioned, two behind the title and an outlined star in the left margin of the third stanza are added in Z; four stars in T; three around the title in U; two in AA. (The border[Y] consists of drawn curtains.)

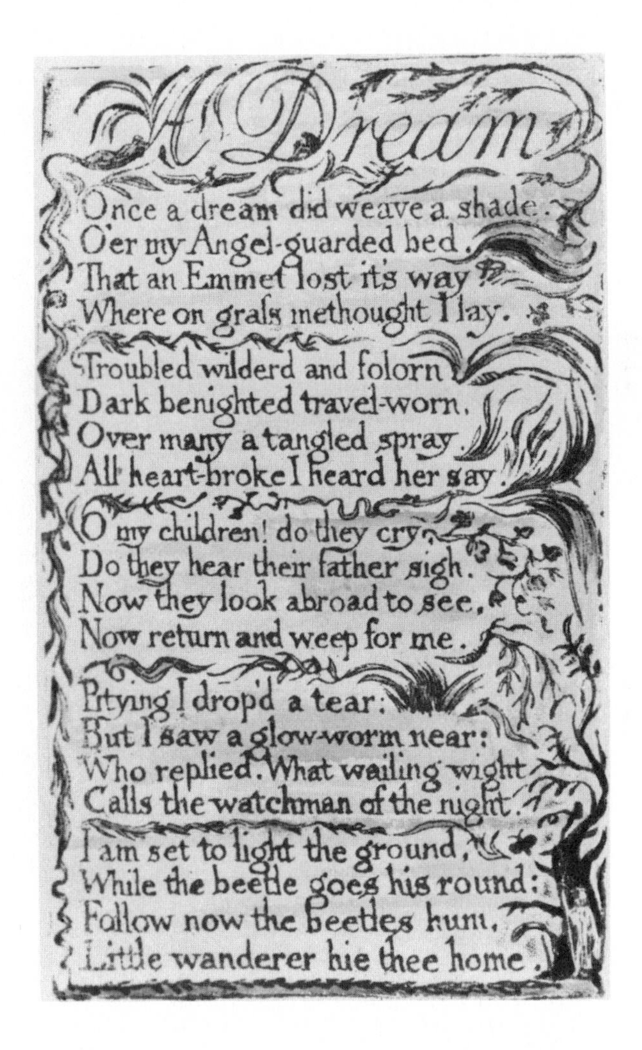

A Dream

Once a dream did weave a shade.
O'er my Angel-guarded bed,
That an Emmet lost it's way
Where on grass methought I lay.

Troubled wilderd and folorn
Dark benighted travel-worn,
Over many a tangled spray,
All heart-broke I heard her say.

O my children! do they cry,
Do they hear their father sigh.
Now they look abroad to see,
Now return and weep for me.

Pitying I dropd a tear:
But I saw a glow-worm near:
Who replied. What wailing wight
Calls the watchman of the night.

I am set to light the ground,
While the beetle goes his round:
Follow now the beetles hum,
Little wanderer hie thee home.

Songs 26[I]

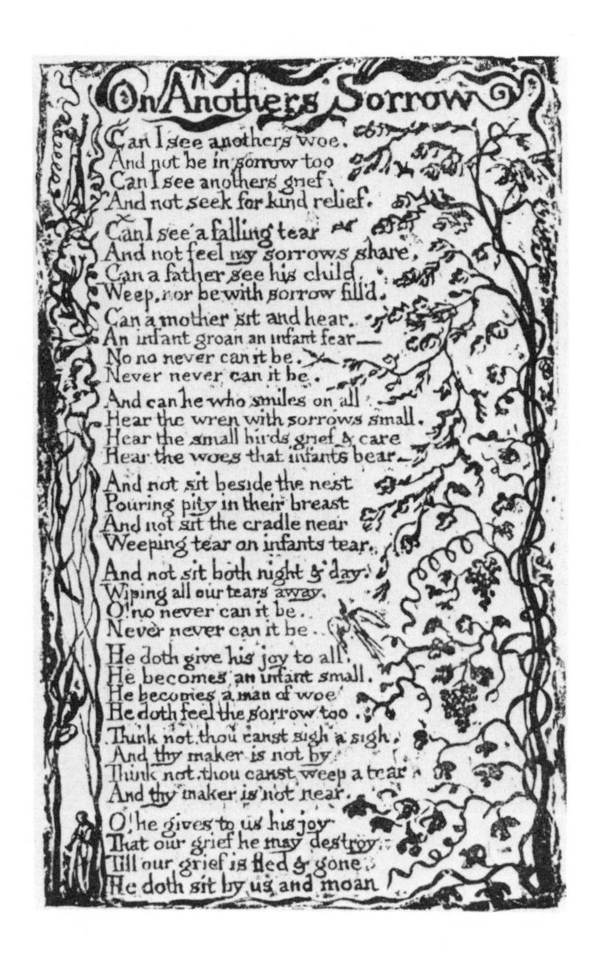
On Anothers Sorrow

Can I see anothers woe,
And not be in sorrow too.
Can I see anothers grief,
And not seek for kind relief.

Can I see a falling tear,
And not feel my sorrows share,
Can a father see his child,
Weep, nor be with sorrow fill'd.

Can a mother sit and hear,
An infant groan an infant fear—
No no never can it be.
Never never can it be.

And can he who smiles on all
Hear the wren with sorrows small,
Hear the small birds grief & care
Hear the woes that infants bear—

And not sit beside the nest
Pouring pity in their breast
And not sit the cradle near
Weeping tear on infants tear.

And not sit both night & day,
Wiping all our tears away.
O! no never can it be.
Never never can it be.

He doth give his joy to all.
He becomes an infant small.
He becomes a man of woe
He doth feel the sorrow too.

Think not, thou canst sigh a sigh,
And thy maker is not by.
Think not, thou canst weep a tear,
And thy maker is not near.

O! he gives to us his joy,
That our grief he may destroy
Till our grief is fled & gone
He doth sit by us and moan

Songs 27^{g}

Songs 27^{g} On Anothers Sorrow (Innocence). In this grand finale of the Songs of Innocence, night and day are brought together (in Z by the painting of blue sky in the left margin and top, green behind reddish branches and leaves and purple grapes in the right margin, and pale blue under the text, shading down to white below the bird of paradise, who marks the turn, the wiping away of tears, in the sixth stanza). (In V the bird is blue and bands of color underlie the foliage. In Y the base ink is red; the bird is one blue note in an indescribably festive yet delicate coloring of the page.) In the text the poet, speaking in the first person as poet, takes upon himself the burden of "a father," "a mother," of all (and of him "who smiles on all") to "seek for kind relief" (4) and to offer it, to smile on all. On the sunny right side of the page he festoons representative smiles and joys from all his Songs: the bird of paradise from "The Shepherd" (Plate 5), grapes from "The Ecchoing Green" (6–7), two doves (on a branch, after line 4) from "The Lamb" (Plate 8), the vine of mercy (from "The Divine Image" and elsewhere) multiplied, the woven shade promised in "Night" and "A Dream" spread like a laden table in noon day.

And the piper? Legs crossed, hat removed, (given a halo^{V}), smiling (surely) down at a listening dog*, he plays his pipe beside the line, "That our grief he may destroy" (42). And the margin above him shows how it is done. Growing up from beside his feet, bare thin leafless branches struggle to form spaces as in the tree of Jesse (Plate 4), and human forms struggle to people them: a climber reaching the first loop; at the top (beside the first stanza) a man raising a compassionate hand; below him (beside lines 6–8) a dark figure, perhaps a slave trapped in the vines, raising both hands in supplication. And then the image which the poet insists we *must* believe, of "thy maker" who "doth feel the sorrow" and is by, is near. A face of sorrow, eyes, nose, mouth, looking a bit downward to the left, can be made out beside lines 10–14, the empty branches below not quite forming a body. (In InB and InP the eyes, nose, and mouth are slightly emphasized. In V a larger face is indicated, facing the text. In Y the original face is brought out prominently. In Z, using a smaller head shape, facing the text, Blake outlines a distinct head and body beside lines 11–21.) Below these fanciful true images the piper must keep up his conjuring music though he may weep and others weep to hear. Like his later avatar, Los the prophet, he cannot cease building, to change lost into found, Plate 13 into Plate 14, to *discover* the deity which is the poetic imagination in every breast, who becomes a little child that we may "feel the sorrow too" (28) and "bear the beams of love" (9:17).

The arrangement of plates followed here leads easily to the frontispiece for Experience which follows, in which the piper having dropped his happy pipe (see 4:9) to cross the ford, like a St Christopher, with a firm hold on the spiritual body of the child, is preparing to walk through the graveyard (see Plate 29) and use his voice as bard without other instrument.

OTHER ARRANGEMENTS bring other juxtapositions and other emphases, and Blake tried a new arrangement every time he assembled a copy of *Songs of Innocence* or* of the combined *Songs*. For example, "On Anothers Sorrow" concludes only two of the twenty copies of the separately issued *Songs of Innocence* for which Blake's order is known; three copies[AHN] end with "The Divine Image," three[EJP] with "A Cradle Song," two[MO] with "The Little Boy Found." All these convey, in different ways, some image of God appearing as father. Taking all copies with reliable report of order of plates, including the combined *Songs of Innocence and of Experience,* a total of forty-two copies, twelve conclude the Innocence group with "On Anothers Sorrow," seven with "The Little Boy Found," one with "The Chimney Sweeper" (another containing the savior image). A quite different conclusion emphasizes the lion as friend of lambs and children; eight copies end with "Night," where the lion is quoted, two with "The Little Girl Found" (Plate 36), where lions lie down with children. Two copies end with "The Voice of the Ancient Bard" (Plate 54), one each with "The Shepherd," "The School Boy," "Infant Joy," "A Dream."

For each fresh reading of Blake one might try the *Songs* in a fresh arrangement. Here are the twenty different orders Blake proposed in the separately issued *Songs of Innocence.* For the fourteen other orders, in combined issues of *Songs of Innocence and of Experience,* see below, after Plate 54.

(Copy A of *Innocence* only is abbreviated InA, and so on.)

InA: 2–5, 25, 16–17, 15, 9–10, 54, 6–7, 24, 19, 27, 22–23, 53, 26, 34–36, 11, 8, 13–14, 20–21, 12, 18.

InB: 2–5, 25, 27, 53, 19, 24, 15, 9–10, 54, 6–7, 12, 18, 26, 34–36, 13, 14, 16–17, 22–23, 11, 8, 20–21.

InC: 2–4, 16–17, 13–14, 18, 12, 27, 22–23, 53, 8, 11, 26, 34–36, 15, 9–10, 54, 19, 24, 6–7, 20–21, 25, 5.

InD: 2–4, 6–7, 15, 9–10, 54, 11, 8, 26, 34–36, 24, 19, 25, 5, 20–21, 13–14, 18, 12, 16–17, 27, 22–23, 53.

InE: 2–4, 18, 12, 6–7, 11, 8, 15, 9–10, 54, 5, 25, 27, 22–23, 53, 24, 19, 14, 13, 26, 34–36, 20–21, 16–17.

InF: 2–5, 25, 8, 11, 15, 9–10, 54, 13–14, 18, 12, 16–17, 20–21, 27, 22–23, 53, 26, 34–36. (Lacks 6–7, 19, 24.)

InG: 2–4, 26, 34–36, 8, 11, 6–7, 18, 12, 25, 5, 20–21, 16–17, 13–14, 24, 19, 27, 22–23, 53, 15, 9–10, 54.

InH: 2–5, 25, 15, 9–10, 54, 6–7, 16–17, 20–21, 24, 19, 11, 8, 27, 22–23, 53, 13–14, 26, 34–36, 12, 18.

InI: 2–4, 5, 9–10, 54, 16–17, 11, 34–36, 8, 24–25, 27, 13–14, 12, 22–23, 53, 15, 26, 19, 18, 6–7, 20–21.

InJ: 2–5, 9–10, 54, 18, 26, 6–7, 27, 25, 8, 22–23, 11, 24, 12, 16–17. (Lacks 13–15, 19–21, 34–36, 53.)

InK: 2–4, 6–7, 15, 9–10, 54, 11, 8, 26, 22–23, 53, 25, 5, 16–17, 24, 19, 12, 18, 13–14, 20–21, 27. (Lacks 34–36.)

InL: 2–5, 25, 24, 19, 27, 22–23, 53, 15, 9–10, 54, 6–7, 16–17, 13–14, 8, 11, 18, 12, 20–21. (Lacks 26, 34–36.)

InM: 2–4, 25, 5, 15, 9–10, 54, 27, 22–23, 53, 16–17, 19, 24, 6–8, 11, 18, 12, 21–20(?), 13–14. (Lacks 26, 34–36.)

InN: 2, 4, 3, 5–8, 19, 24, 16–17, 15, 9–10, 26, 12–14, 27, 11, 20–21, 53, 22–23, 25, 18. (Lacks 34–36, 54.)

InO: 2–5, 25, 9–10, 27, 22–23, 15, 53–54, 12, 8, 19, 18, 20–21, 26, 16–17, 11, 24, 13–14. (Lacks 6–7, 34–36.)

InP: 2–4, 25, 6–7, 22–23, 18–19, 53, 13–14, 27, 26, 15, 11, 20–21, 8, 5, 54, 12, 24, 9, 16. (Lacks 10, 17, 34–36.)

InQ: 2–4, 6–7, 11, 22–23, 25, 54, 5, 9–10, 27, 16–19, 8, 12, 26, 53, 15, 24, 13–14, 20–21. (Lacks 34–36.)

InS: 2–21, 53, 22–25, 54, 26–27. (Lacks 34–36.)

InT: 3, 2, 4–5, 25, 27, 19, 24, 9–10, 54, 6–7, 12, 18, 26, 34–36, 13–14, 16–17, 22–23, 11, 8, 20–21. (Lacks 15, 53.)

InU: 3, 2, 25, 6–7, 9–12, 15, 8, 53, 24, 13–14, 20–21, 19, 26, 16–17, 25, 54, 22–23, 5, 27, 18, 34–36.

(It is important to realize that the alphabetical arrangement of copies of *Songs of Innocence* does not represent an established chronological sequence.)

In early copies (or in copies early in the *Census* ordering) certain songs appear grouped together frequently. Donald Ross, who is making a computer-aided study of the arrangements of the songs, calls attention to the following clusters in copies of Innocence alone,

Songs 28I

more or less broken up in late copies and combined copies of Innocence and Experience:

"Introduction," "The Shepherd," and "Infant Joy" appear consistently as the first three songs in InABFLT and in *Songs* E; in two other copies (InE and *Songs* V) the second and third songs remain paired though moved away from the "Introduction"; in six the pair begins with "Infant Joy": InCDGKM; *Songs* C.

"Laughing Song," "The Little Black Boy," and "The Voice of the Ancient Bard" are grouped together, in varying positions in the series, in thirteen copies: InABCDEFGLM; *Songs* CDEV. A fascinating enclosure of the children and savior between a feast and a bardic prophecy.

"On Anothers Sorrow," "Spring," and "The School-Boy" are grouped in that order, in various positions, in eleven copies: InACDEFGLM and *Songs* CDE. The group concludes the Innocence series in InD.

"A Dream," "The Little Girl Lost," and "The Little Girl Found" (the two latter bound together in the etching) are grouped in that order in InABCDEFGT.

Paired poems include the obvious "The Little Boy lost" and "The Little Boy Found" (once inadvertently reversed: InE) and "The Lamb" and "The Blossom," eight times in that order (InCFGKLM; *Songs* CD) and six times reversed (InABDET; *Songs* E), "The Chimney Sweeper" followed by "The Divine Image" in four copies (InABCT), reversed in nine (InDEFGLM; *Songs* CDE), "Holy Thursday" followed by "Nurse's Song" in four (InBCM; *Songs* D), reversed in eight (InADEGKL; *Songs* CE).

It will be seen that these groupings and pairings occur generally in the same copies, constituting, within the variables of shifting positions of the groups and of other songs, what Ross properly refers to as the Old Order, from which about half of the Innocence copies (of known order) depart and nearly all the combined copies.

Songs 28I (Frontispiece: Experience). The shepherd-piper with neither crook nor pipe (see *Songs* 27 note) strides forward with his right foot advanced (it was his left in Plate 2), both hands holding the hands of a naked boy who is not now on a cloud but is winged for potential flight; he is also given a halo* (as not in Plate 2: see copy Z). The infant and poet were looking at each other; now both look directly at us, to fix the message of "On Anothers Sorrow." The flock graze, as in Plate 2, not looking up as in 5, but in other respects the setting is like the shepherd's, as is the bard's dress. We are even further out of the sheltering woods—both a good thing and a dangerous thing. The child and his St Christopher hold tight and look us directly in the eye as they step directly forward.

The lines of the blue* hill in the distance (with a slighter indication[YZ] of sun behind: but sometimes a sunrise[ABT]) and of the tree at the right are severe, but both trees are verdant. At left there are sometimes[BIZ] two trees with crossed trunks. A small ivy vine with triangular leaves ascends the large and lightning-scarred trunk at the right, a contrast to the younger tree entwined by flowering vine in Plate 5. (In late copies and, as shown by posthumous copies, on the copper, the branch at top extends in an arch to the left edge of the picture. An earlier state of the plate, in which the branch reaches only part way, the foot is farther back, and the leaves and shadows are darker, may be represented in B and I.) The border[Y] contains tendrils and criss-crossed briars, repeated less emphatically in the next page, which is draped by pink curtains at top and sides.

Songs 29[I] (Title page, Experience). Beside a solid wall, of a cemetery or garden (suggesting also a paneled church interior), a young man and woman, clothed and more upright than the Adam and Eve of Plate 1, bend over the stiff bodies of an old man and woman, ambiguously dying in bed or become effigies on a marble pillow. The girl with the father, the boy with the mother, are in stylized mourning. Compare *Gates* 13 to see that this is a vision of fear; the top, bright half of the page is a vision of hope. Whether the "of" and the ivy connecting these halves lift Experience into Songs or pull Songs down is conditional upon our reading. Ivy can grow over the scars of experience (see Plate 28) but by itself it yields no flowers or fruit. The word "EXPERIENCE" like an iron fence seems to shut off hope, and most of the leaf tips point down. But the foliage is alive, and on "SONGS" it opens into elaborate leaves and flowers and a tendril spinning toward infinity (eight loops plus). A small figure on the first S calls attention to the upward flourishing. And the larger pointing girl and boy, dancing on tip-

Songs 29[I]

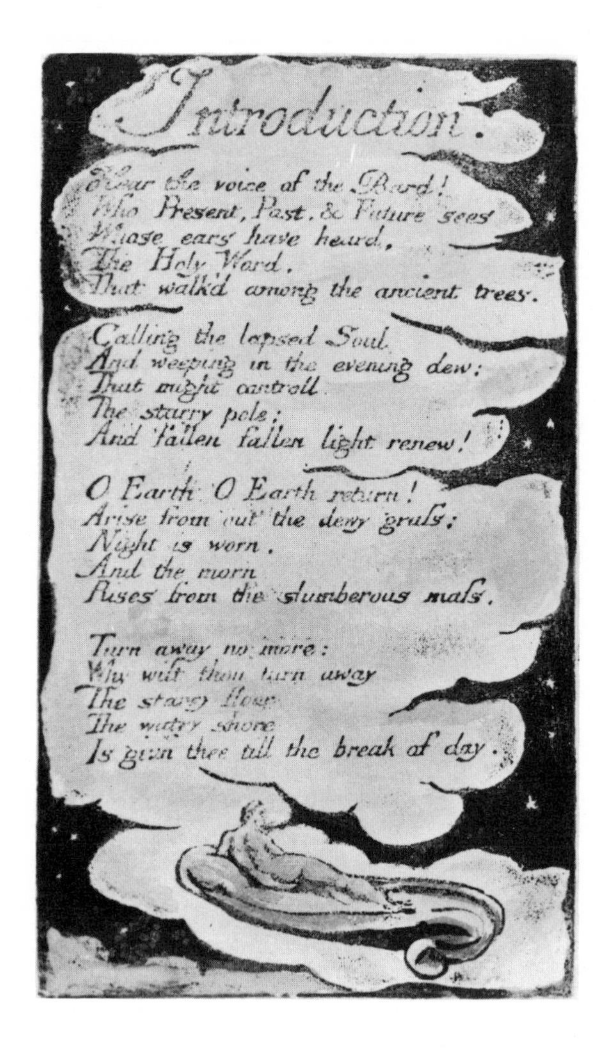

Songs 30[I]

toe, may be recognized as the true human forms of the mourners below—often* dressed in the same colors to confirm the identifications.

(The belief that there are two versions of this plate seems mistaken; the Gilchrist electrotype seems not to have been made from Blake's copper plate but from a redrawing of the page made for Gilchrist's need, the original copper being presumably missing. Several of the lines exemplify what is known as a forger's tremble.)

Songs 30[I] Introduction (Experience). The text, in which "The Holy Word," heard by the Bard whose voice is now to be heard by us, calls "the lapsed Soul" or "Earth," to rise "from out the dewy grass," is written on a multiple cloud in a starry indigo* sky. (There are variously nine[AA] or twelve[A], fourteen[I], fifteen[Y], twenty-one[B], or twenty-five[O] stars; twenty in Z including, in the right margin from top to bottom, Orion's belt, the Pleiades, and Aries.) On a scroll-couch on a lower or nearer cloud a naked figure reclines, with hair streaming under the chin (sometimes changed[I] to a break in the clouds), sometimes given a halo[YZ AA], who looks into the western sky, as the constellations[Z] indicate. It must be early winter, if it is anywhere near "the break of day" (16) as we are told by the voice and shown by a faint glow[YZ AA] on couch and clouds, coming up from behind or shed by the halo or both.

I incline to interpret this figure as the bard, aloft in clouds on a prophetic scroll from which he can see "Present, Past, & Future" (2)—or the human form of The Holy Word, which would account for the halo. He calls to Earth, benighted in the dark past and present, to turn eastward (as she apparently has lapsed from doing) to renew "fallen fallen light" (8). In her "Answer" (Plate 31) she protests that Jealousy keeps her heavily chained in her "den." Both Keynes and Grant hold that this reclining figure must be Earth herself, who is shown in somewhat this posture arising at the lark's call in *L'Allegro* 2 and at the nativity of Jesus in the watercolor for Milton's Nativity *Hymn* (figures 162 and 175 in Raine). But Earth in these scenes lies very much on the earth or on the grass, with some sort of vegetable pillow. This cloud-borne "lounging divan" (Bass *Forms* 208) seems quite out of character, whereas it is very much like scroll desk and divan in *Night Thoughts* 5 (*Forms* plate 73) on which a reclining poet faces us so that we can see the pen in his hand. According to the text of this poem Earth is neither arisen from her den, though it be but grass, nor ready for a halo. (Figures in the sky with scrolls seem usually to have prophetic or spiritual missions; see *Europe* 3 and the spirits of mercy in *Job* 19.) Compare the more gently wind-blown hair of the bard's alter ego, the piper, in *Songs* 2.

For border[Y] the corners are bracketed by thin green vines bearing a few tiny leaves.

Songs 31[I] Earth's Answer (Experience). Stems (enlarged into trunks[Z]) on the left send thin lines into the text, branching downward, but with some upward movement beside the title and the first stanza, and with an independent grapevine that springs out of "father of" (10) with tendrils, leaves, and a bunch of grapes in the right margin. (The grapes are usually purple* but green in Y and quite painted out and replaced by a separate tendril in Z.) On the ground an almost worm-like serpent glides and hisses; it has one small coil, and its tail turns up, directing attention to the stems in the left margin that eventuate in the life in the right. In InB and B the grapes and the serpent are purple; in T only the grapes; in AA the grapes are rosy, the serpent pink, blue, and white. In Y the serpent's head is in a white sunrise with lavender rays; in Z he has horns. (For a similar serpent, without the coil but on a contrarious mission, see *Jerusalem* 72.) (There is a formal leaf border in Y.)

The relationship of the serpent to the grapes, far above his head, may be seen as a curious counterpoint to the relationship, in the text, of Earth to the light of which she is deprived by a jealous father. From the manuscript (*Notebook* 111) we can discover a symbiotic relationship between this poem and the lines eventually drawn upon for "Infant Sorrow" (*Songs* 48). In this poem a woman, in the other a man, has grown grey haired with deprivation and "free Love . . . bound" by a jealous "father," and what the lamenting male is chained from enjoying (just as the lamenting female Earth is chained from enjoying the light of day) is "the fruit or blossoms" or "Clusters of the wandring vine" (*P&P* 719). It seems apparent that the grapes and serpent brought in to illuminate "Earth's Answer" represent the parallel lament of the bound male, turned to a serpent by deprivation.

EARTH'S Answer.

Earth rais'd up her head,
From the darkness dread & drear.
Her light fled:
Stony dread!
And her locks cover'd with grey despair.

Prison'd on watry shore
Starry Jealousy does keep my den
Cold and hoar
Weeping o'er
I hear the father of the ancient men

Selfish father of men
Cruel jealous selfish fear
Can delight
Chain'd in night
The virgins of youth and morning bear.

Does spring hide its joy
When buds and blossoms grow?
Does the sower?
Sow by night?
Or the plowman in darkness plow?

Break this heavy chain.
That does freeze my bones around
Selfish! vain!
Eternal bane!
That free Love with bandage bound.

Songs 31[I]

Songs 32I

Songs 32I The Clod & the Pebble (Experience). Under branches of a tree, with sparse foliageOZ or noneB or almost noneIM, and drinking from a "brook" which floats the text, stand four sheep who have somehow lost their charm since we saw them in *Innocence*. The lamb has grown, the ram shows horns, the two ewes aren't involved in motherhood; beside them tower two horned oxen. HereI we see their faces; sometimes the mouths of the ram and the ewe near him are down in the waterOZ. Eating and drinking is their whole business, and if the "little Clod of Clay" feels he is building a heaven for himself by letting them trample him, they couldn't care less. They also illustrate ironically the clay's words below their mouths: the eyes of one BI AA or both* of the oxen look up uncordially as if fending off the awareness that they too will give themselves, as food.

On the other side of the water, and beside the pebble's part of the argument, we see a floating duck, two frogs, a worm between them, a small vine over the sitting frog and another beside the leaping frog that sends up large green leaves into the text. The text is retraced in red inkZ. There may be a food cycle among these lower creatures also, but at least they express a certain amount of individual "delight" (10); they are not *shown* "each in turn preying on the other" (Keynes). The sitting frog and worm we shall see again in *Jerusalem* 98. (The borderY is of stems with two or three bellflowers near each upper corner, a cheerful effect.) The design stresses "richness and variety" (Hirsch 218).

Songs 33[I] Holy Thursday (Experience). A child lies dead on the ground, a gowned mother stands appalled under a barren oak. There is usually* a body of water behind her; beyond it the hills at left and right represent one smooth grassy* breast and one craggy and barren, or snowy[Y], exposing the assumption of benevolent nature. In the margin gigantic oak leaves displaced from the barren tree grow green* above and below a weeping woman and two children, a boy hiding his eyes, a girl clinging to her. Below, a half upside down cruciform figure lies fallen among oak leaves and spear grass. (Compare fallen Albion in *Jerusalem* 9.) A lily-like row of leaves grows under the title, emphasizing the word "Holy," from stems reaching up the left margin; the stems between stanzas are thin and leafless. The star-shaped leaf beside "HOLY" is sometimes green* sometimes gold[Y].

This picture of what adults have made of Ascension Day, of the rising of man as God, contrasts with the Innocence picture (Plate 19) of what children manage to make of it anyway. The border[Y] is filled with briars all around, criss-crossing at bottom.

Songs 33[I]

Songs 34g

Songs 34g The Little Girl Lost 1 (Experience). (Electrotype with marginal surplus removed.) At the top a bird of paradise (blue[Z] or blue and white[B] or red and yellow[I]) flies upward linking the words "In futurity I prophetic see" to "Girl" in the title. At bottom right we see, not Lyca "Seven summers old" (13) but an older girl and boy, embracing under paradisal arches of willow and airily free vine, with an anemone leaf at their feet which reminds us of the love-making fairies in the anemone blossoms of *Thel* ii. More directly these lovers represent the "youthful pair" of Plate 51 (A Little Girl Lost), the maiden Ona and youth who meet "in garden bright" in the holy light of dawn. At the left a slightly sturdier vine grows without supporting tree, even without roots, but with much flowering, including four large bells (to celebrate a free marrying?); indeed it supports an undulant, prophetic serpent with single coil (see Plate 31) in a fork that singles out the "prophetic" introductory stanzas. This serpent's tongue is busy writing (reading) the announcement of "a garden mild" (8); his head is turned modestly away from the mild couple. (The sinister crested serpent in *Satan Watching Adam and Eve in Paradise* also looks the other way, but his tongue threatens to destroy the flowering vines that form their marriage arch.)

The maiden's left hand points up to (and as) the bird of paradise, as though to lead her lover to "futurity" (the garden where love is not thought a crime: see Plate 51), as Lyca in the text, by getting lost, leads her parents. (We may read the picture shift as saying that Ona and her lover, frozen out of Plate 51 by an outraged parent, find their garden in the fear-free dell attained by the family of Lyca.)

The young man is naked in early copies*, more frequently clothed in copies printed after these plates were moved from Innocence to Experience. On the first loop of the vine at left sits a bird of paradise, with another diving downward toward it. (The border[Y] contains some tendrils and leaf shapes like the leaf at Ona's feet modified as acanthus.)

Songs 35[I] The Little Girl Lost 2 (Experience). The Little Girl Found 1 (Experience). A girl's lostness (how Ona will feel if she wakes up in a land of Experience) is illustrated by Lyca feeling "Lost in desart wild" (34:21) underneath a leafless birch tree, seeing no humans but a living oak and three companionable birches in the background. In the poem, sweet sleep does come to her, and she is found by God as a "kingly lion" (34:37). Compare the sheltering tree trunks within which God as his father appears to the little boy lost, in Plate 14. (In some copies[InF ABY] the dresses of Ona on Plate 34 and Lyca on Plate 35 are colored differently, to keep us from confusing them.)

The "Found" picture introduces the lioness, who entered in the final stanza of the "Lost" poem to act as nurse and mother. She stands under a barren tree; we are still in the desert; yet the branch reaching to the left margin bursts into blossom when it meets a version of the free spiralling wedding vine of Plate 34, here putting forth two matching lilies and running up to write the title, ending in a serpentine tendril that unites the first two words.

Both the girl and the lioness look on toward the next page, with good reason. (There are sometimes[Z AA] dawn colors behind the lioness; the border[Y] is of vines, barren but thornless.) There are some tiger-like stripes on the lioness, as if to include the other beasts, "Leopards, tygers," around Lyca.

Songs 35[I]

Songs 36g

Songs 36g The Little Girl Found 2 (Experience). In the fairy tale of the text Lyca's parents are led to his palace by the royal lion, a "vision" (46), find their daughter sleeping among "tygers wild" (48), and remain in this "lonely dell" to live fearless ever after. The tale of the picture is that there is nothing lonely about living in a sunny dell where children of all ages and sexes can sleep without fear beside a lioness mother (who doesn't look so much like a tiger here) and a redeemed lion father; where (on the left) very young sapling and vine can grow upward, without bowing, together but free, and (on the right) tightly embracing elms can grow old together, their trunks kept leafy by vines, even ivy: in Z and AA a line of ivy is added up the surface of the lower bark like the ivy covering lightning scars in Plate 30; for this pair when more youthful, see Plate 2. The boy astride the lioness may remind us of the children riding a serpent in *Thel* 6 and *America* 11; we may also be reminded of the two boys sleeping on and beside a ram in *America* 7. The boy talking to the lion presumably has his left hand in the mane, for this is another vision of the boy in the family of sheep in Plate 23. The sleeping girl has no dress to identify her as Lyca or Ona. Our not seeing Lyca's lost mother and father anywhere impells us to recognize that the story of their finding their daughter is seen here as the daughter's finding *them,* transformed from beasts of prey to royal protectors. Poems and pictures together present the liberating, rescuing, and family reuniting savior of the Songs of Innocence as also (hinted there too, of course) a relibidinizing "spirit arm'd in gold" (36). One effect of Blake's moving these poems from Innocence to Experience is the planting of a strong image of paradise and prophecy of love not thought crime right in the midst of songs of woe.

In copy Z, in which the texts are retraced in various colors in all plates, it is noteworthy that reddish ink is employed for poems encouraging sexual love—"The Blossom," "Laughing Song," "A Divine Image," and "Garden of Love"—with a still clearer red for "The Clod & the Pebble" (I am not quite sure what to make of that) and the present plate. (The border[Y] is of tendriled vines at top, acanthus leaves at bottom.)

❧

Songs 37[I] The Chimney Sweeper (Experience). A London sweep, with his wire brush in his right hand, holds a sackful of soot over his shoulder with his left. He looks up anxiously into driving snow in an unshovelled street and walks past closed window and door. He is usually* bareheaded but shod; in Z AA he wears a hat but has bare feet. In T his face is as black as the houses.

Foliage from his title runs down to underline his prophetic role: "to sing the notes of woe." (The border[Y] suggests snowy clouds.)

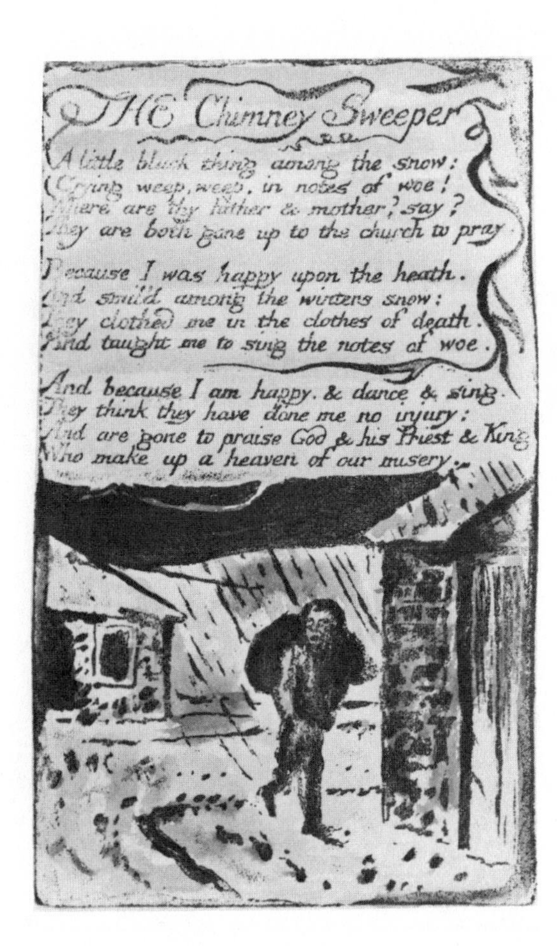

Songs 37[I]

Songs 38[I]

Songs 38[I] Nurses Song (Experience). Upright lintels of a simple doorway, paralleling the lines of the nurse's dress and as stiff as her poised comb, enclose the vignette of her restrictive tutelage of the boy, defined in the poem. But the girl reads even in the angular doorway. And vines burgeoning with purple* or blue[I] clusters (two on the right, three[I], two*, or one[BYZ AA] on the left) busily grow across these bounding lines and mock the stilted propriety of the standing figures as well as the wintry language of the text. The word "Song" is demoted from its prominence in Plate 24; yet it can explode one looped trumpet of purple[BZ AA] or green[I] blossom. A sort of thwarted blossom rises in a curve on the N of "NURSES," with a personage, chrysalis-like, sleeping in it.

The picture is a parodistic variant of the plate Blake designed and engraved for the frontispiece of Mary Wollstonecraft's *Original Stories* (1791), "Look what a fine morning it is."

The border[Y] is a formal one of squared loops, though acanthus leaves retain some hold on the top corners.

Songs 39[I] The Sick Rose (Experience). "O Rose thou art sick," we agree, seeing her crimson globe fallen to the ground, her two rosy* buds forlorn—the lower a woman huddled on a thorny stem as if weeping, with yellow hair hanging down; the upper a woman lying on thorns, her head buried in her arms, her left leg pulled up but dangling, her long scroll-skirt tangled almost worm-like down the main stem. At top left a brown* or green[V] (sometimes rose*) cankerworm has inched his way to a green leaf to eat it. Sometimes[YZ] another worm shape is added between the next two leaves on that branch. At bottom another worm, who must have inched his way along the main stem, encountering and ravishing the prostrate sister on his way to the open blossom, extends a curved phallic body out from the flower center and about the waist of the human form of Rose, also yellow-haired*, who stretches out her arms possibly in joy, probably in terror: her face usually* an enigma. (In V, redrawing puts the worm behind the woman and shows her emerging fully clothed.) On first thought it is her life that the poet or gardener sees being destroyed by the worm—who came "invisible . . . in the night" and "storm," like the worm and storm that Jehovah sent to wither up Jonah's gourd and remind him of the frailty of mortals (Jonah 4). These caterpillars on leaf and petal remind us of the grief derived from the assumption that life is mortal (see *Gates* i), against which thorns are no protection. (In V the huddled woman is yellow green, the others rose colored.)

In Y there is no enigma. The flower and girl are white, though her sisters above are pink and blue. Her face registers desperation, and we see the sharp proboscis of the worm turning out from below her dress as about to attack her.

What clues may clarify the riddle of woman and worm? The sister flowers may imply the Cupid-Psyche script (or that of Gwendolen and Hyle in *Jerusalem* 82), the "invisible worm" being what jealous sisters think Love is really like. The similarity of the picture to *Thel* ii, where blossom-borne lovers are obviously enjoying themselves whatever Thel may think, suggests that it might be only the secrecy or the jealousy that caused the flower to fall to the ground. The scroll-dress of the clutching sister may imply the Cassandra pessimism of the female in *Europe* 3. We are all victims of pessimism to the extent that we are compelled to see the "dark secret love" as vermiform. (In copies where he remains invisible[AB] it is only our acceptance of the speaker's view that compels this. In B only the rose, not the woman, is blushing.) Yet the living color of

Songs 39[I]

Songs 40[I]

the full blossom and her human form with arms flung free have a message of life. Caterpillars are also emblems of eternity, reminding us that a worm hidden in secret may be reborn as a boy or girl found. Rose is another lost girl, in a clime where sweet love is thought a crime, but her winging arms indicate her potential as "a newly hatched butterfly rising on its first flight" (Chayes *Forms* 227).

The letter of title and text is unadorned. This is a song of Experience; yet only the pessimist need read its ironies fatalistically. (The border[Y] is of vines, spiky at bottom but interweaving at top.)

❧

Songs 40[I] The Fly (Experience). Two barren trees make a squarish arch over the poem and scene, with a stiff tendril separating the two columns of stanzas. The title begins with a single whip, as does "The Sick Rose"; "brush'd away" concludes with a double whiplash. At the last words a bird or bat or moth (a "happy fly" perhaps) rises, countered across the page by a lifeless shuttlecock dropping toward the girl's battledore. If (we may see) "want Of thought is death" (15–16), then the girl (given yellow shoes in A, red in T) may be learning to be thoughtless about winged things, and the efficient nurse (identified by cap and uniform; see Plates 3 and 24) leading the gowned boy to walk, may be guiding him into a thoughtless (since lifeless) universe, under that barren arch, on grassless ground, turned away from the only living things in it. (The tree at left is almost off the page; the one at right seems intended for a birch, inviting readers of "The Little Vagabond"—Plate 45—to identify "modest dame Lurch" here.) This could develop into the kind of education we see in *America* 14.

All the relations pictured are of entrapment and blind domination: the trees' roots (added on top of the ground[Z]) complete the trap closed above by their branches; the nurse holds the child in an iron grip and obscures his vision with her body; the girl relates to a winged thing with blind force (Sevcik). Contrast the girl in Plate 36 being taught by her little brother to ride the lioness—or, with his mother's assistance, "The Infant Jesus Riding on a Lamb" (suggested by Grant). (The simple border[Y] runs to coils at the top.) It is possible, at the same time, to sense "the *élan vital* surging" through both children (Hirsch 241).

Songs 41[I] The Angel (Experience). An auburn-haired maiden[Z AA] (grey-haired[B] ultimately, according to the text) tells the story of her life as "a Dream" that she does not understand. (This is signified in AA by a dark blue wash over the text, by very tangled border vines in Y.) The picture arrests the critical moment when she armed herself, in fear, against the mild angel who was her secret "hearts delight" (8). The armor consists of her hands' insisting (against his cheek and against her own) on a vision of life as but a mortal span (compare *America* 14 and *Jerusalem* 4). The angel-boy, naked and large-winged but grounded, makes blandishing pitiful attempts—not to push past that armed assertion but to reach around it or implore her not to turn away. Blake gives her a spiked crown[VZ AA b] befitting her dream that she "was a maiden Queen" (2) but removes it in some copies[B]. The boy has a halo* (but in AA his white wings look like tombstones). Sometimes the tightness of the girl's waist is emphasized, sometimes the bulging of her breasts.

The vegetational entrapment is more oppressive than in Plate 40. The barren tree that closes overhead like a mausoleum vault droops to the ground (in mock of the paradise willow) and nourishes coiled vines, viper-like if tongueless. The sprig of ivy beside the title has leaves that point both ways. The weeping "both night and day" (5) engenders a grapevine that has upward as well as downward possibilities. But below it a vaguely serpentine flourish that extends leftward below the text swings round to point a sharp arrow at "grey" (16). And the title seems strapped in by a tight belt down the left margin. Yet, with various emphases*, there is passionate coloring in the sky, his wings, and her dress—as though the fires of *Marriage* 1 were not impossibly distant.

Songs 41[I]

Songs 42[I]

Songs 42[I] The Tyger (Experience). This tiger is not in the "garden mild" anticipated in Plate 34—nor clearly headed for it like the somewhat tiger-striped lioness of Plate 35—but in the "desart" of Experience, represented by a barren tree (probably a birch, with some of his stripes on the bole) and a colorless clump of vegetation (spear grass?) at the end of a whip that drops straight from a strap looping from the first T of "The Tyger." In the last line of text another whip points to the tiger from "thy"; tendril and whip compete for the two y's of "symmetry." Yet the tree, often light and colorful and usually* given above its third branch-arm a bogy face of some kind more absurd than frightening, seems helplessly collapsed at base (when we try it as a human form) and feckless in its skinny arms. This effect, and the light of pink[Z] sky behind the tiger, as well as the tiger's own aplomb, tend to dismiss either forest or night as perdurable. The tree, indeed, has been scared leafless.

The tiger, on all fours but in no such agony as Nebuchadnezzar (in *Marriage* 24), is painted or drawn differently in different copies, with expressions varying from smiling (in B and perhaps Y) to worried[T] to supercilious[Y AA] to patient[V] or gentle[Z] and with total effects said (by Keynes) to range from "a ferocious carnivore painted in lurid colours" (this I have not seen) to "a tame cat." His eye is often marked comically, with an X[A] or dot and circle[BVYZ AA] or heavy lid[T]. His body is orange and dark[Z AA] or banded with red, blue, and yellow[T] or red, lavender, and dark blue running into a sort of rainbow effect in the sky[I].

In short, this picture, like the poem it illuminates, remains one of Blake's contrived enigmas—a contrivance forced upon him by the truth, one feels. But the eagle(?) flying above the tiger's name in the first line should remind us to lift up our heads in the presence of "a portion of Genius" (*Marriage* 9). The border[Y] has grasses in the lower half, crossing in rather formal pattern beneath the tiger, and splendidly wing-like acanthus leaves embracing the upper corners.

Songs 43[g] My Pretty Rose Tree; Ah! Sun-Flower; The Lilly (Experience). The only thorn in the top picture is on the S of "ROSE." A leafing grapevine, fruitless, springs around the barren tree that leans away from and rises above the frustrated, jealous couple. The man hides his head, huddling, with spear grass at his back; the woman is half turned away, somewhat like the "maiden Queen" of Plate 41, an Earth refusing to rise from the grass. One large and nine small birds are flying up diagonally leftward as are a bird of innocence and two smaller birds under the title. Very lively tendrils flourish around the letters. In Z a sunshine effect is introduced behind the woman, and the sky gets wonderfully blue toward the top. (AA is similar, with less blue and more sunshine, reaching the Lilly title also.) But the leafless and crooked tree (compare those of Plates 42 and 47), possibly an apple or a birch, certainly not a "Rose-tree," seems to hold the humans' attention away from the promissory winged life in the background.

The Sun-flower, seen in human form, is imagined as living atop a tendril-spiral, with root feet uprooted and petal arms held up and hair streaming—ready to leap toward a sun etched among clouds after the word "Sun" in line 2. (But often* no sun is shown there; in Z a great golden puff of sunshine surrounds the girl herself. In V there is no sun or sunlight; the girl is running and has no root connections.) In *Night Thoughts* engraving 49 (used for *Four Zoas* 47) the sunflower has a stalk as well as a looping tendril; the girl yearns with outstretched arms toward an Apollo in human form, and a large disk of sun is indicated behind both the sunflower and Apollo.

The line marking off the next poem is straddled by a worm with serpentine loops and tail, its head presumably buried in the line.

The lily flower is shown in the right margin, a day lily (the leaves and flower shape indicate) which fades and closes at the day's end, bent downward as though, despite the text's promise of immunity to threat, being crucified with the head downward. Blake often leaves it without color[BE] or paints it white[PY AA] or dull blue[AV], but sometimes green[GTYZ]. (For an extensive discussion of this plate see John E. Grant "Two Flowers in the Garden of Experience," *Essays* 341 ff.)

In a bit of ironic byplay, a heavy ribbon attached to "The modest" (Rose) reaches down around the poem to confront, with a deletion loop, a short wide ribbon from the Lilly's "beauty." The

Songs 43[g]

Songs 44[I]

border[Y] offers two tear-shaped fruits, figs perhaps, at each side of "Ah! Sun-flower," acanthus leaves at the upper sides.

❧

Songs 44[I] The Garden of Love (Experience). Kneeling beside an open grave in the green, a boy and girl with hands in prayer (and behaving like the standing figures in Plate 29) join a bald monk's ritual reading from the black book, his gesture earthward, toward the grave. Darkness, with a more or less vague suggestion of trees, presses at their backs; a leaning gravestone at right imitates the human form in rock, beneath a church window (the diamond leading* of which repeats the crossed diagonals of briars below). Under the last line, "binding with briars my joys . . . ," a grave mound is indicated by the traditional criss-crossed briars bound around the turf-covered coffin: what will go into the black hole being worshipped above. (In some copies only the briars show.)

In a macabre variation of his usual adornment of the text with vines and verdure, Blake treats the text area as underground and introduces four or five red* worms as stanza dividers. The leaves and tendrils—or are they roots?—that grow on the title all strive downward. (The border[Y] repeats the crossed briars and the window diamonds.)

Songs 45[I] The Little Vagabond (Experience). At the top, a naked* vagabond is comforted by a rejoicing "God like a father" (13), haloed with rosy[I] or yellow[Y] or white[BZ] flowers, in a cathedral of forest trunks. The scene repeats, at a more desperate level, the father-like savior's rescue of boy in forest in Plate 14. Below, in an open green* field, a homeless family surround a blazing fire. The exhausted father with head on left hand sits on a mound or a pile of goods, right knee bent, right hand behind back (or at side[YZ]), the suggestion of a sheep beside him[B], a small boy standing ignored at his side. The mother on the other side of the fire crouches and hides her face (though Blake can give her a face looking up*), with one child kneeling before her, reaching its arms around her knee and neck, another ignored at her left knee. Only the two ignored children see or accept the light of the fire.

The title generates some banners that bend up toward the scene of comfort, and a grapevine down the right margin that manages one leaf and some tendrils and greets two birds flying beside "drink & sing" (9). The happy final stanza is illuminated by another small bird—and a very long-tailed bird of paradise, in leftward flight. (The border[Y] is of thin vines, with some criss-crossing; see Plate 44.)

Songs 45[I]

Songs 46[g]

Songs 46[g] London (Experience). Another vagabond boy at a smokier street-fire than the family's fire in the previous page is, however, actively warming his hands. His flame we have seen in miniature under the title of "Holy Thursday" (Innocence) Plate 19. At the top a similar lad is guiding a long-bearded barefoot man with crutches along a cobblestone pavement, past a closed door. (In *Jerusalem* 84 we see the same aged man, named London, being similarly led toward an open door.) A beam of strong light (narrowed in some copies[Z]), matching the boy's deed, saves man and child from any "cry of fear" (6). (In AA both are given faint haloes.)

Hirsch (265) sees the "crippled old man" as a "replica of Urizen. The weakness and woe he symbolizes is also the weakness and woe he has caused." The "marks," however, point to salvation.

Banners at left of the title and along the page are treated as leaves, not serpents or straps. The one at bottom, attached to "And," has a sort of foot and appears, sometimes clearly[I], as a worm, keeping the bottom of the page aerated. Once, at least, he is given a plume at right[AA]. The border in Y is particularly impressive: a Gothic window frame surrounds the page, with four miniature windows in a vertical row on each side.

Songs 47[I] The Human Abstract (Experience). "Cruelty" knitting "a snare" (7) and kneeling down "with holy fears" (9) seems to be entangling himself in a net of his own knitting. Etched as a rope on the left, held by both hands across his head and joining a parallel rope on the right with two or three cross strands[AB], the snare is sometimes chain-like in its blackness[B] and sometimes painted without cross strands[VZ]. The cross bars on the tree at the right, etched there but sometimes[Z] obscured, seem to identify this Tree of Mystery with the birch tree of Plate 42; the base relates it also to the tree of Plate 43. The raven shape[I] at its top branch is usually indistinct. The bulrushes at the left are repeated in the border[Y] in the unusual form of two crossed pairs. Black[B] or white* water is usually added in the foreground.

The chain effect in B relates this Urizen web to the "mind-forg'd manacles" of Plate 46; yet we must remember as well the spider kings of Asia in *Song of Los* 6:1–8.

Songs 47[I]

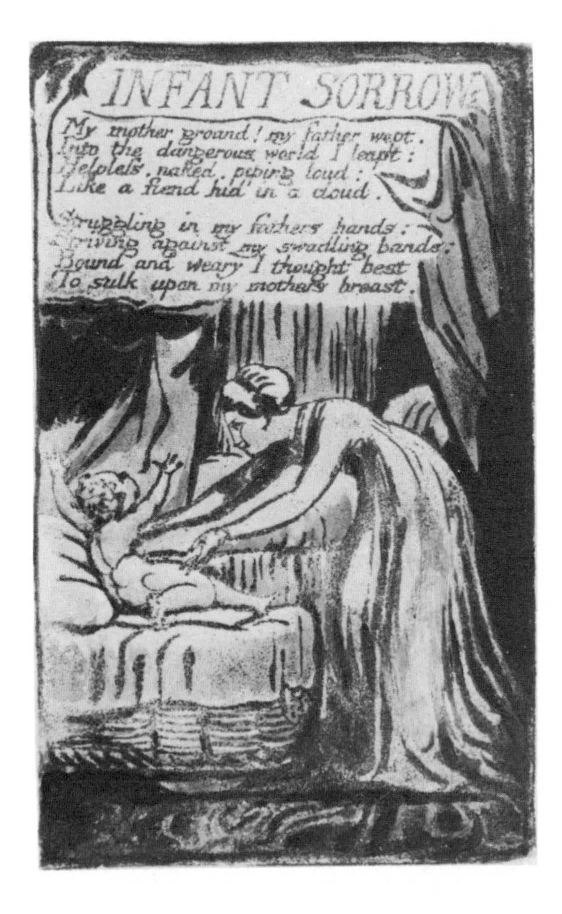

Songs 48[I]

Songs 48[I] Infant Sorrow (Experience). The boy's nakedness in anger contrasts with all the heavy cloth hanging around the larger bed and on the mother's body. His own wicker bed is unenclosed, a further contrast to the swaddled infant of "A Cradle Song" (Plate 17). His arms, reaching up and out—the gesture is not like that of the girl half out of the rose in Plate 39, for his elbows are bent (as the drawing in Z confirms, the etched arms being rather simplified)—suggest his "unwilling surrender to his mother's arms" (Keynes), the bent elbows conveying the unwillingness.

The mirror-like surface of the floor, established in the etching, disappears in Z and AA with new carpets. (The border[Y] adds a further, slight curtain.)

Songs 49[I] A Poison Tree (Experience). The naked "foe outstretchd" (16) lies in a barren land like that of "Holy Thursday" (Experience), Plate 33, and in a head-down cruciform position like that of the appalled child at the bottom of that plate, though with body out flat, legs behind the tree. Wrath without pity (see note on Plate 18) can grow into a tree of death—like but not identical to the Tree of Mystery grown by the human brain (Plate 47). The tree pictured is something like the birch of Plate 47, more like the tree of Plate 41 in its extending like a vault over the dead body beneath it, but we must accept it as a poison apple tree. That it grew from the suppressed wrath of the speaker, and not really out of the ground, is shown by a coup de theatre managed by Blake as designer. From the ironic word "My" in the last line—ironic in that "My foe," my ultimate triumphant possession, is now nothing and no longer mine—a small twig grows, up the page, enclosing the title, and expanding down the right margin, to become a tree of seventy years' growth, rooted in the earth and dying.

In some copies[Ib] an odd effect of reversal is achieved by letting the trunk above the fourth stanza look like a hand that seems to grasp the trunk above it as by the leg of an elongated human torso. This makes the rooted body of the tree seize the upper structure as the handle of a whip that lassoes the title and ultimately should exert a crack-the-whip effect on "My." This may sound absurd in the telling, but the point is one that Blake was concerned to make. He explains it in *Marriage* 11, where he shows man abstracting an external deity from his own breast and then submitting to the abstraction in slavish worship.

Sometimes there are indications of dawn[A] or at least light on the horizon[Z]—more distant than in Plate 33. The border[Y] brackets the top corners with sharp-pointed large leaves and fences the bottom with angular thorny briars criss-crossed by strands of leaves like green holly.

Songs 49[I]

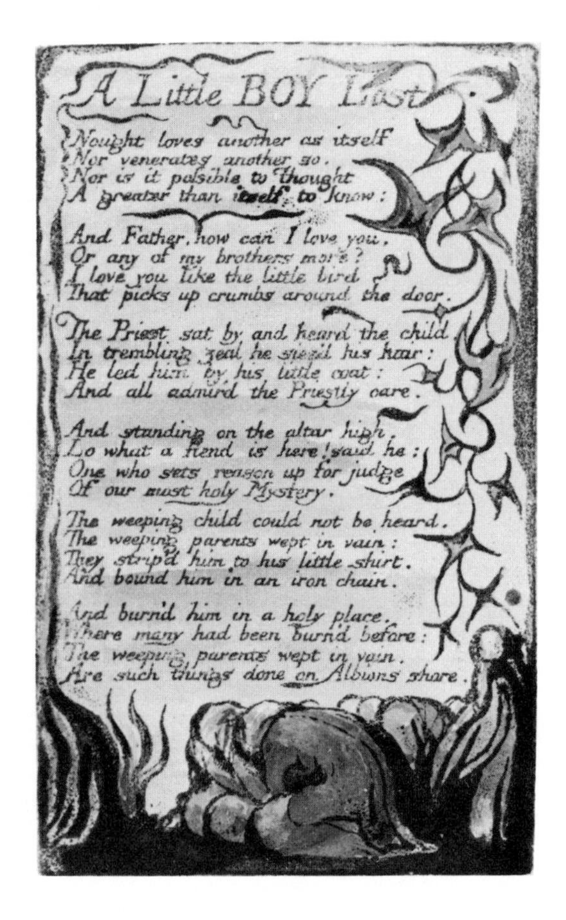

Songs 50[I]

Songs 50[I] A Little Boy Lost (Experience). The boy who is "burn'd . . . in a holy place" (21) for uttering a sentiment like the Pebble's in Plate 32 is not shown. We see neither holy place nor priest but the edge of the sacrificial fire, at the left. The unenclosed flames are parodistically like the fires of the vagabonds in field and street (Plates 45 and 46). The kneeling people recall the family of Plate 45 but are all faceless and vague in shape, something like the Daughters of Albion who hide from Oothoon's voice in *Visions* 7. The self-clutching ones kneeling in front must be the "weeping parents" (18); heads of three or four* indicate the congregation behind them, all trapped in the net of cruelty and the doctrine of humility. The one standing at the right has turned away, with hand at neck. (Sometimes mistaken for the priest, who would hardly officiate from this position.) In copy Z this person is allowed to look up (as one of the daughters in *Visions* 7), and we see a woman in a green dress, in left profile, looking toward the invisible altar, her left hand at her throat, her right sheltering her face. In the same copy Blake paints a red, yellow, green, blue rainbow through the text.

The outraged foliage may or may not be menacing "vengeance" (Keynes); it shows that the green values of life are being seared, the edges of leaves yellowed[BZ AA] by the flames. It is not in the poem or the pictures that the sacrificed life calls for revenge. The most striking interlinear ornament is a judicious bracket attached to "how" (5) presumably asking how love can be weighed in a balance. (The border[Y] has curving vines with drooping tendrils.)

Songs 51I A Little Girl Lost (Experience). In this self-styled "indignant page" (2) there is immense libidinal energy and, in the text, devastating frustration: tenderest love between bright youth and maiden under "the holy light" of dawn that makes the present the "Age of Gold" (5), then one book-dimmed look from Ona's father that strikes her dumb and him hoary! Yet emblems of joy and energy fill the page. A grapevine twines in huge leaps up a barren tree in the right margin, evidently a birch. First the vine extends a bracket and a thirteen-loop tendril to dismiss "hoary hair"; at its next turn, a stem puts out three leaves and a small tendril; at its next, after dodging around a squirrel who stands in the first crotch, it extends what ought to be a small bunch of grapes (left reddish brown in Z and AA) and a backward-looping tendril; then it puts forth two looping tendrils and three leaves, one of them, oddly, a plume. It ends twining a branch beside the "Age of Gold" stanza. Also the page teems with birds: eight in the lowest break, including a bird of paradise above "Ona!" (30), two above the grape leaves, four near the squirrel, including another bird of paradise, one opposite "fear" (19), three above "rising day" (15). And the title and first prophetic stanza are flanked by five birds, two of them of paradise, one perhaps a swallow (these three blue and purpleB). The "GIRL" of the title is linked by a plume and coil vine to "Children of the future Age" (1). (The borderY has slightly interweaving vines and rounded acanthus leaves at the top corners.)

Only from the text would we realize that all this life and promise can be negated (though not forever) by the barrenness of the parent tree! For more of Ona's story see note on Plates 34 and 35. But first notice the small figure in the top curve of the vine: is it Ona grasping vine and tree, like the girl inside the G of "SONGS" in Plate 3 and like the girl of Plate 23, though more collapsed than they and forlorn?

Songs 51I

Songs 52[I]

Songs 52[I] To Tirzah (Experience). Near a green* hill, under a vine-like branch that bears seven red[V] or yellow[Z] or pale green[AA] apples (five in Y, where the border adds three more on each side), a body is decaying into "the Earth" (2) with legs already gone or buried (though painted in again in YZ and AA, fingers too). (In V the fingers are enrooting.) Compare the apples of Plate 3. Compare the bodies consumed in *Gates* 16 and *Jerusalem* 92 and 93. We may suppose that the body is "supported by . . . Mother-love and Sex-love, who failed to save him" (Keynes) or see in the look between dying man and mother the mesmerism of Rahab upon Albion in *Jerusalem* 25 (see Chayes *Forms* 240). But if we turn from fearful to hopeful vision (compare *Jerusalem* 33) may we not see the two women and the pitcher-offering old man (the pitcher is golden in V) as spiritual comforters like the two angels bringing pitcher and other relief to the children in Plate 18? As the "Mortal part" is consumed, the "Spiritual Body" is welcomed into the Garden, and love does give support.

In early copies of *Songs of Innocence and of Experience* (BCD) Blake concluded with a spiritual body borne aloft by winged cherubs (Plate a: see Appendix). Later (copies EIOS) he put in its place "To Tirzah" with the same concluding message: "It is Raised a Spiritual Body." Looking at either of these plates—or at *Gates* 16—we can understand that the Eternal Man "has risen," out of the realm of "Contrary States."

Probably still later (TUWXYZ AA) he moved "The School Boy" and "The Voice of the Ancient Bard" from *Songs of Innocence* to come after "To Tirzah," showing the spiritual bodies of children up in the tree and letting the Bard sound the concluding note. In any of these arrangements the concluding plates imply an apocalyptic metamorphosis at the end of a series of emblems, beyond Innocence and Experience.

(Copies FGH lack Plate 52, ending with 40, 51, and 47 respectively; copies LNPQRV have Plate 52 further inside the Experience group and conclude with various Songs other than "The Voice," without the strong terminal effect of rising; copies J and M are not certainly in arrangements made by Blake. When locked inside the series, the apocalyptic prophecy may seem only promissory, even ironic.)

Songs 53^{g} The School Boy (in Innocence originally, remaining there in *Songs* A–K and OQRS; in Experience in LNPT–Z AA). Three children are playing marbles at the bottom of the page; the one at right, backed by stems curving the shape of the body, seems to be a girl; the five visible marbles are in front of her. At the left rises a thin, dividing sapling entwined by a barren vine that ends in a loop beside "By sorrow" (25). Above that, in a fork, leans a clothed figure with right arm down, left holding what may be a pipe (or a viol). The tree ends beside line 6; above it coil tendrils from "The" in the title; on them sits, with wings out to fly, a bird of paradise (standing for the "sky-lark" in line 4). The title with its bouncing tendrils seems to be running away. But at the top right a boy reading a book is sitting in an outdoor school, true "learnings bower" (14). Below him, in the irregular intertwinings (compare the regular ones of the Tree of Jesse in Plate 4) of two trees whose leaves are plumes (a sensitive plant: mimosa) and a grapevine with a purple* cluster at line 19, are two climbing boys (at stanzas 2 and 4).

Below them (as it took John Grant to point out) the naked* figure who seems at first glance to be one of the climbing boys (and has a disguising leotard in InB, YZ) is a figure out of Ovid, Daphne dendrifying—though Blake could have intended a dendrifying boy. Her left arm extends up as a vine—and seems to be producing that cluster of grapes. (The effect, quite clear in V and in g, is often removed*.) Her right leg is growing downward. The classics brought to life. It may well be her arms that produce the plumes of mimosa leaves on up the cycle. For the boys this is all a part of "their joy in the springing day" (24). (The border^{Y} is of thin stems and roots.)

Songs 53^{g}

Songs 54[I]

❧

Songs 54[I] The Voice of the Ancient Bard (in Innocence originally, remaining there in *Songs* A–S; in Experience in O, T–AA [in both sections in O]). This plate, occurring more often in Songs of Innocence and made to serve there, often early in the book, may help us recognize that the bard and the piper are two voices of one poet. At the end of the double work it serves as a quiet finale, a gathering of actors and audience for an epilogue by the author. A gentle invitation to join the group, all easy human beings, a working harp, materials for decoration: a simple vine, three anemone leaves, a palm frond. No heavy trees or flames or livestock or flying things. When the recitation is over we may want to ask the bard why there are bands or cuffs on his right wrist and ankle. Ingenuity will conjecture which of the roles these eight "Youth of delight" may have been playing in the illuminations: Lyca, Ona, sweep and vagabond, angel and virgin queen, Mary and Susan and Emily? The bard, of course, in the parts of Human Abstract, and London.

The border[Y] crowns the upper corners with acanthus leaves, adds tendrils below.

❧

In the twenty-four copies of Songs of Experience for which we know Blake's order of arrangement of the plates, he tried eighteen different arrangements. All but two of these (KN) being extant as a combined sequence of Innocence and Experience, these copies present the Innocence songs in fourteen new orders—two copies (RS) repeating the order of InS—making a total of thirty-four different orders for the Songs of Innocence. (See note at *Songs* 31).

Copies TUWXYZ AA follow the order used in the present volume. The other seventeen arrangements are:

A: 3, 2, 4, 22–23, 6–7, 9–10, 13, 20–21, 11, 24, 27, 54, 15, 18, 12, 19, 53, 14, 8, 5, 16–17, 26, 25; Experience: 29, 28, 30–31, 40, 32, 41, 37, 42, 48, 45, 38, 47, 34–36, 44, 49, 46, 39, 33, 43. (Lacks 1, 50–52.)

C: 2, 1, 3–4, 25, 5, 16–17, 8, 11, 24, 19, 6–7, 27, 22–23, 53, 18, 12, 15, 9–10, 54, 20–21, 13–14; Experience: 28–31, 48, 51, 38, 41,

39, 44–45, 47, 26, 34–36, 50, 37, 40, 49, 46, 42–43, 33, 32, a. (Lacks 52 but has a, as do B, unpaginated, and D.)

D: 2, 1, 3–4, 15, 9–10, 54, 27, 22–23, 53, 6–7, 16–17, 20–21, 5, 25, 24, 19, 8, 11, 18, 12–14; Experience: 28–31, 40, 49, 46, 42, 39, 44, 26, 34–36, 48, 51, 47, 45, 50, 37, 41, 38, 33, 43, 32, a. (Lacks 52 but has a.)

E: 1–5, 25, 11, 8, 15, 9–10, 54, 18, 12, 16–17, 6–7, 27, 22–23, 53, 24, 19, 13–14, 20–21, 26; Experience: 28–31, 15, 34–36, 50, 37, 42, 46, 44, 39, 38, 41, 45, 47, 40, 49, 48, 51, 33, 43, 52. (Lacks 32, duplicates 15.)

F: 2–5, 9–10, 27, 6–7, 12, 22–23, 53, 15, 26, 13–14, 8, 24, 34–36, 54, 18–19, 16–17, 25, 11, 20–21; Experience: 28–32, 38, 33, 46, 41, 49, 42, 50–51, 37, 47, 43, 40. (Lacks 1, 39, 44–45, 48 and 52.)

I: 2, 1, 3–5, 11, 9–10, 22–23, 19, 6–7, 25, 8, 24, 15, 12, 18, 26–27, 53–54, 16–17, 20–21, 13–14; Experience: 28–33, 48, 41, 39, 40, 50–51, 43, 37, 45, 49, 44, 46–47, 38, 42, 34–36, 52.

J: 1–5, 22–23, 19, 15, 24, 18, 8–10, 25, 6–7, 16–17, 53, 20–21, 27, 26, 13–14, 11–12, 54; Experience: 29–31, 48, 32, 44, 40, 42, 50, 33, 43, 41, 38, 34–36, 47, 37, 52, 49, 51, 46, 39, 45. (Lacks 28.)

K (and e): Experience only (but Blake's foliation—28 is numbered "30"—implies a lost Innocence Series): 28–32, 38, 48, 42, 33, 41, 46, 40, 47, 45, 50–51, 44, 34–37, 49, 43, 52. (Lacks 39.) (37 and 52 misnumbered in *Census*.)

L: 1–4, 6–7, 12, 9–10, 19, 22–24, 5, 26, 16–17, 20–21, 11, 13–14, 25, 8, 54, 15, 18, 27; Experience: 28–31, 34–36, 42, 40, 33, 48, 32, 37, 52, 45, 47, 44, 50, 41, 39, 38, 49, 46, 51, 43, 53.

M: 3, 1–2, 4, 8, 6–7, 15, 20–21, 19, 18, 13–14, 27, 9–10, 26, 11, 54, 5, 22–25, 16–17, 12; Experience: 28–32, 49, 42, 41, 39, 52, 44, 50, 51, 37, 47, 34–36, 38, 48, 45, 40, 46, 53, 43, 33.

N: Experience only: (but Blake's foliation—29 is numbered "30"— implies a lost Innocence series): 29–32, 37, 49, 48, 42, 40, 39, 47, 51, 34–36, 44, 41, 43, 50, 52, 46, 45, 33, 38, 53. (Lacks 28 and 54.)

O: 1–5, 12, 19, 6–7, 11, 15–17, 25, 27, 24, 54, 22–23, 18, 53, 8, 26, 13–14, 9–10, 20–21; Experience: 1, 28–32, 38, 34–36, 42, 48, 37, 44, 39, 46, 43, 49–50, 40, 47, 45, 51, 41, 33, 54, 52. (Has 1 and 54 twice.)

P: 2, 1, 3–7, 25, 9–10, 27, 22–23, 15, 53–54, 12, 8, 19, 18, 20–21, 26, 16–17, 11, 24, 13–14; Experience: 28–31, 48, 42, 40, 32, 34–36, 49, 39, 33, 47, 38, 51, 50, 52, 43, 46, 45, 37, 41, 44.

Q: 2–4, 6–7, 5, 11, 22–23, 12, 54, 53, 25, 15, 26, 8–10, 16–17, 19, 24, 27, 18, 13–14, 20–21; Experience: 28, 1, 29–31, 48, 42, 37, 34–36, 38, 32, 40, 50, 47, 52, 39, 44, 46, 51, 41, 49, 45, 33, 43.

R: 1, then as in InS; Experience: 28–49, 52, 51, 50.

S: 1, then as in InS; Experience: 28–32, 38, 42, 37, 49, 45, 33, 43, 47, 50, 41, 48, 34–36, 46, 44, 39–40, 51–52.

V: 1–4, 6–8, 5, 25, 9–10, 15, 22–23, 16–17, 24, 19, 11–12, 18, 20–21, 26–27, 13–14; Experience: 28–31, 38, 40, 42, 34–36, 32, 45, 33, 49, 41, 39, 52, 54, 43–44, 50, 48, 53, 46, 51, 37, 47.

THE MARRIAGE OF HEAVEN AND HELL

Nine complete copies are known, and two incomplete. Salient differences are indicated here; the variations in the title page are given rather fully; but for a detailed account of all the designs of this work, and most of their variations, see "Reading *MHH*."

Marriage 1[C] (title page). Two couples, the first strolling, the second kneeling and reclining on green* grass, are framed and separated by arching trees stripped of most of their branches. Above the strollers two birds fly under an enclosing branch held out by four (or two[EF]) paired but leafless trees. At right a half-fallen tree leaning against a larger upright tree backed by a broken trunk extends the only living bough, green with leaves[EG], over a kneeling musician serenading (with lyre, not pipe for the shape is oval) a woman who lies on her left side with legs drawn up, pillowing her head against the living trunk. Above this musical couple rise an improbably long-necked eagle (see Plate 15) perhaps, or raven (see Plate 27) and five smaller birds—a configuration often suggesting the five senses escorted by the imagination (see also Plates 17 and 27). "*MARRIAGE*" in looped swash capitals lies across broken branches to end between leaves and birds, and a circled scroll with thickened tip as of an ear of grain.

Marriage 1[C]

Below the apparent surface is an abyss or another sky, teeming with naked children and couples, who dance, embrace, soar, in the warmth of flames that leap toward "and" (which makes a scroll round itself and tapers off as if drawn by the bird just beyond) to join "HEAVEN" and "HELL"—deadly block letters in themselves. Opposite the flaming side of the abyss are tiers, that seem earth or rock from an earthly perspective, emerging as a triangle of clouds in the heaven of Hell, from which a reclining angel (we assume) turns to embrace a devil, each looking the other squarely in the eye—though to call them angel and devil (when there is a halo—blue[A] or gold[I]—they share it) or to inquire into their sexes, neither manifestly male, may be to fall into an error like those corrected by the Devil on Plate 4.

An impression of the variety of effects achieved in different copies may be conveyed by a brief report of some salient variations upon the etched base of this plate. In copies A through E the shapes of flames and trees are fairly identical, representing what was etched in the copper; in H and I the flames on one side and the tier of cloud-rocks on the other are extended into the page center, by painting. In I the three stumps at top right have been painted into three fat trunks rising beside and partly replacing the original single tall tree backed by a stump. In E the trees are black and charred as well as blasted. In D two figures are added, huddled together among the roots at left.

The sky behind the trees is more or less clear in all copies, with some bands of blue or other light colors except in E. The lower sky area is uncolored[BE] or grey[FC], or pale blue and pink[DG]. In I it has patches almost as blue as the upper sky. But the coloring of this lower area in A and H hardly suggests sky at all. In A deep purples and blue make the whole underground space a dark foil (of night sky) for the triangle of strawberry-red and pink flames and the triangular shelf of clouds which are the golden-brown of the printing. The pale brown world above ground seems ignored rather than threatened by the flames or the embracing light-haired angel and devil. The painting of H conveys an opposite impression: the angel has a mere shelf of yellow cloud to rest on, the upper tiers are burnt into golden smoke; the flames lick at the roots and seem already to have consumed the stumps of the upper world; at the left a surge of gold from the flames runs up alongside the trees.

Elaine Kauvar notes that in alchemical tradition (see Paracelsus) truncated trees may signify death as an instrument of transformation, preparing the way for new life, Energy.

Marriage 2[C] (Argument). On the green surface of the earth, now at page bottom, recline a single girl or boy, chin in hand, backed by a large leaf, and a naked couple making neither music nor love. The "deep" with its fires and clouds appears only in the text that hangs heavy over these humans. (The refrain is in red, the inner stanzas in blue[H].) Yet above them five birds fly, sparks of life and hope. The bird above "serpent" (17) is perhaps a swallow. The largest is distinctly a lapwing (with crest, and two-color effect[F]); it appears to spring from the five-looped tendril of a tough but thwarted grapevine that is kept apart from its natural support, a parental elm. Clasping the tree instead is a tall maiden (with hair spiralling on both sides of the trunk), usually naked down to her midriff[ABC] or in a topless gown[DF] (full in later copies). She is handing or receiving something to or from a woman in the tree, but we are not allowed to see it, and her legs are crossed as Gwendolen's (in *Jerusalem* 81) when clutching an invisible "falshood." The gift or theft looks almost like green grapes or birds' heads poking from a nest, in C; in D and G like leaves on the branch behind; in EHI like nothing at all. The hander-down, with bare breast[ABC] and a garment of gravity-defying scrolls (a poetic or prophetic—or Satanic—character), is sometimes mistaken for an Adam (because of the text on the next page). Yet both figures are feminine in build; the picture seems intentionally cryptic, like the poem alongside.

The twisting garment of the figure in the tree suggests Satan in serpent form tempting Eve. Anne Mellor observes that Michelangelo at least once (in the Sistine Chapel ceiling) painted Satan as a woman-serpent when handing mysterious fruit to Eve. In the context of correction of errors (Plate 4) we may take the illustrated Argument as a corrective enigma. The fires shaken by tyrannous Rintrah supply regenerative warmth for the just man; the illusion of "the religious" that a serpent's gift turned woman's love to sin is confronted by the Devil's account that trouble comes when joys are stolen in secret. By this reading the two humans here are not up to any good, but the title page has shown how they might be. In copy D the red flames there are repeated as red sky behind the cross-legged girl. The lapwing flying back toward the flame asks us to start over.

At top (except in DE) the leaves seem to have been displaced from the living tree to a detached sprig near "Rintrah."

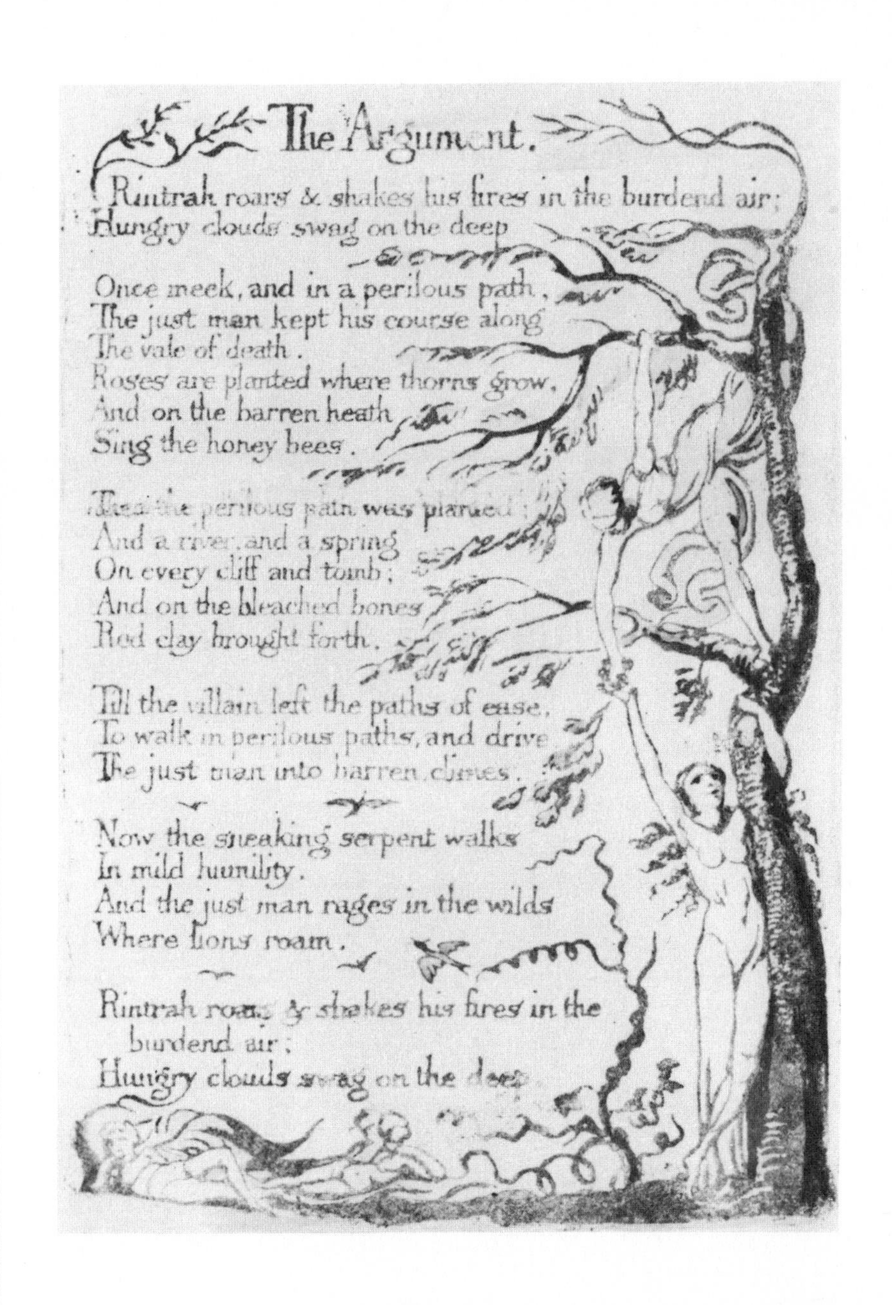

Marriage 2[C]

Marriage 3^{E}

Marriage 3^{E}. As the "new heaven" (1) palls, "Eternal Hell" (2) is reviving and is being welcomed by five naked humans with outstretched arms: at top a female comfortable in strong flames (compare the title-page devil); at bottom, a woman swept by energy's flames to give birth, the infant awake at first breath and both mother and child looking up with open arms; then male and female contraries embracing—a girl, still in space, but kissing a boy as he flies: except for crossed legs (see Plate 2), the girl is like the woman in flames, above; the running boy, except for the direction of his running, is like the young man with outstretched arms running in flames in *Urizen* 3. Note the optical illusion of married perspectives of time and space: the legs insist that she is still, he is running, but the heads, arms, torsos that they are embracing. Again, a paradoxical emblem illuminates the paradoxical text, of marriage without restraint.

In the small interlinear figures, a gowned readers' welcomer above "a new" (1)—fresh from the title page of *Thel*—mimics the flame-girt welcomer above. There follow a plume or leaf, swirling banners, a rising bird (2), and more banners. Marking the "return of Adam" (5–6) a soaring man points forward. And the declaration in behalf of Contraries (9) is followed by a picture of companionability or neighborliness, a man and woman clasping hands on an ogee curve of beauty (see Hogarth): a greeting of Heaven and Hell.

The flames of the left side of the title page are now at the top; the beds of cloud that were on its right side now support the whole lower scene. We are in the abyss and find it no desert.

In copy H all the text is retraced in strong colors: red for "As a new," then blue-grey to "Now . . . necessary to," which is all in red, then "Human existence" grey on red; then grey until the last line, except for "contraries" in black; the last line golden red. In F "1790" is added above the soaring figure of line 1.

Marriage 4^{E}. Flanking "The voice of the Devil" are three cloaked angelic trumpeters (formerly emblems of biblical prophecy and the poetic muse) who announce the Devil's corrigenda list. Under the trumpets are living notations of the voice: banner-unfurling tendrils and leaves and a rising bird or insect; after "Errors" (2) a soaring mother and child, free (not quite touching hands).

After error No 1 (that Body and Soul are two) a flying figure leaves a figure seated on a leaf—presumably Soul leaving Body, which then becomes vegetable. Correction No 1 (down the page, lines 13–16) ends in a thrusting branch and then a vignet of Soul, above clouds, turning back toward Body, who leaves his vegetable wrapping to spring toward Soul. (Other figures in the line belong to correction No 2.) After error No 2 (treating Energy as evil and bodily, Reason as good and "alone from the Soul") five active, varied figures (the senses of course) sporting are followed by three huddled stone-like reasoners (perhaps monkeys) on a flat greensward. After error 3 (that God will torment us for following our energies) a heel-flinging animal is watched by two unattended children, while another child is directed by an adult to consider the patient (grazing) ox. Surrounding correct answers 2 and 3 (hailing Energy as life and Delight and Reason as its outward circumference) a man is led by a small animal on a leash (under "inlets of" 13)—i.e. is following his energies—and a child is groped toward by a bearded, blind or blindfolded adult followed by what may be a shadow or ghost (or perhaps the whole scene is set off by bracket-like trees). At the left of the next lines, an adult walks with a cane. Between answers 2 and 3 we see a procession of six figures moving forward, on their own but exhorted by Reason following them; then a bracket-like leaf (or a man[I]); then two horses drawing a man, who holds invisible reins, in a chariot or cart: Energy drawing Reason?

Keynes writes that the exhorting figure and his audience suggest Blake's relief-etching thought to be of Joseph of Arimathea (founder of the Christian church in England) preaching to the Britons. The bracket-like object would be his staff, a thorn which enrooted and sprang into a Christmas-blossoming tree. Application: the errors having been corrected, true preaching is accompanied by eternal delight. (The contrast of false preaching is shown in Plate 11.) The horses "of instruction" (Plate 9) are ready to spring up as the "eternal horses" (Plate 27) "of intellect."

At bottom, perhaps showing the jealous separation of soul and

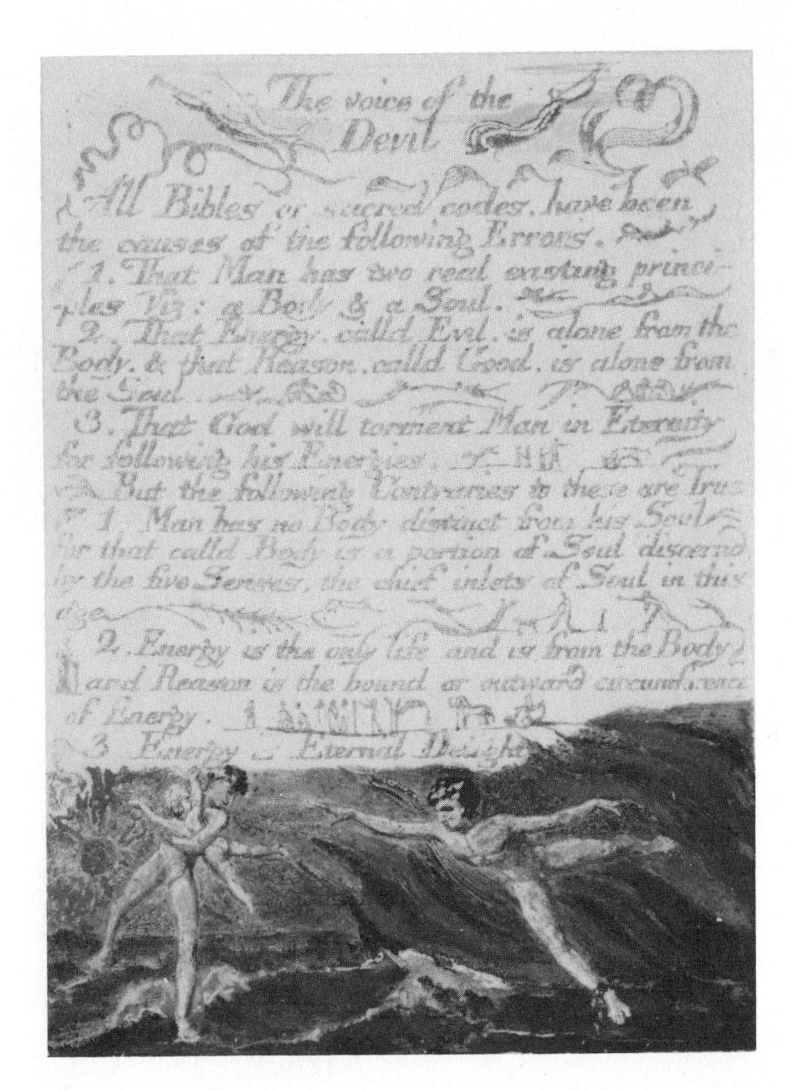

Marriage 4^{E}

Marriage 5E

body, a naked couple, with a small boy, seem to be lunging toward each other—but scarcely heading for the embrace of Plate 1. He is backed by flames, she by a rayed sun; both seem to be running on the deep, but they are kept apart by her clutching of the infant and by a chain* on the man's right ankle. The infant's outstretched limbs suggest not the joy of birth (Plate 3) but fear. In unretouched copies the woman and man have facing profiles, eyes open, and the child with its face turned toward its right arm appears to be regarding the man. In copy H child and mother look solemnly at him; his eyes are open. In copy I the child is drawn with shut eyes and his mouth an open O for crying; the woman looks at the man, but he has eyes shut or looking downward.

There is no chain or manacle on his ankle in copies ABC, but a manacle perhaps in D. The chain is visible in copies E through I; there are both manacle and chain in the color-printed drawing, in reverse, called *The Good and Evil Angels:* these both stand in air, and not over water but over surf and shore; they are not clearly male and female, either.

Blake would have known that an eagle thus rising but chained to a log is an emblem of Ambition. When he added the chain, was he making a thematic link to the eagle in Plate 15? That is, might the serpent there become the eagle's chain?

Marriage 5E. Phaëton-like, down hurtle a naked man and sword and a horse with saddle cloth and broken chariot wheel (spokes visible*) into flames. Falling with them, or lighting them, is an orb, pinkish or bright red, or (in I) painted yellow and black with a larger orb added at the far left, red and flaming. The red orb may be the sun, or Mars (see *America* 5:1–5); the added burning orb, as sun, would leave the smaller orb, yellow with black crescent, to serve as moon. Yet the crescent, in the original etching, can suggest an occulted sun. Presumably the picture is adaptable to both parties' histories of the fall (see text). The man's spread hands are braced to hit solid ground, but it is already in flames. Reason must have forgotten to let the horses do the pulling; a sword is not a bridle. But Energy must have accepted restraint (see text pp 4 and 5). Between them they've let the sun fall, connoting (Plate 26) universal ruin.

A human reclining, in line 3, is "weak enough" (2); lying flat in a desert he becomes a "shadow" (5) (green* like the grass beside him). Under "Paradise Lost" (6) a reclining figure is instructed by a man with compasses, his back to a serpent headed away from them. Someone in front of the next line escapes, groping. Under "Satan" (9) is a flying red* serpent with bat wings—a conflation of eagle and viper, in present terms soul and body, i.e. a tiny emblem of the marriage we must not forget when we see (in line 12) the red and black serpent alone, wingless but spiralling rapidly along on a strip of green* with red* tongue active. (We saw the same energy in isolation in the corkscrew tendrils of the vine on Plate 2.) (The passive figures in lines 3, 5, 7 repeat the languor we noticed on Plates 2 and 3.) The twig and leaf in lower left margin are green* as is the grass at bottom in G and I. In H the paragraphs of text are, respectively, red, golden, blue, blue on red, blue, pale golden, bluish.

Marriage 6[E]. Under the Devil's charge that Reason "formed a heaven of what he stole from the Abyss" (1–2) a fleeing figure hands something—we remember the obscure transaction of Plate 2—to someone who reaches both hands for it. The thief runs like Cain in *Milton* 15 (q.v.). The green vegetation around them puts forth two squarish leaves behind the first figure and a bumpy serpentine flourish behind the second.

The deletiŏn of the word "Devil" in line 6 is covered by a flame[D] or a red and gold blot[I]. Illustrating ". . . after Christs death, he became Jehovah" (7) a figure of Christ risen subtly combines the trailing gown of the benevolent Jesus (as in "The Little Boy Found": *Songs* 14) with a suggestion of a serpent tail. Around "A Memorable Fancy" appear joyous flames—like those of the title page, not with threatening points as in Plate 5—and three merry figures (compare the three trumpeters of the previous subtitle, Plate 4) giving themselves to "the enjoyments of Genius" (16): one walking on fire (as on water: see Plate 4), one giving his head to the flames (his hands not defensively downward as Phaëton's on Plate 5); one dancing above the word "walking," all three defying Nebuchadnezzar, so to speak.

At page bottom Blake describes and diagrams the etching process he must come "home" to (22) if he is to communicate such enjoyments. Preparing to etch a copper surface, Blake sees

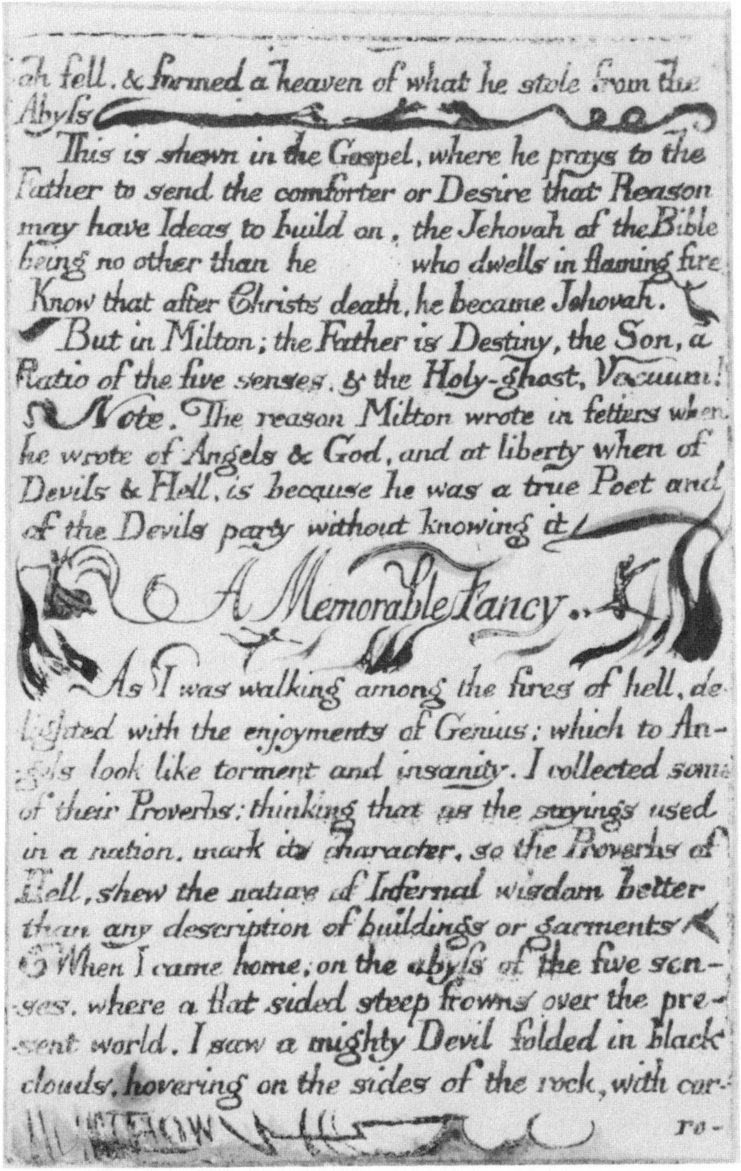

ch fell. & formed a heaven of what he stole from the
Abyss
This is shewn in the Gospel, where he prays to the
Father to send the comforter or Desire that Reason
may have Ideas to build on, the Jehovah of the Bible
being no other than he who dwells in flaming fire.
Know that after Christs death, he became Jehovah.
But in Milton; the Father is Destiny, the Son, a
Ratio of the five senses. & the Holy-ghost, Vacuum!
Note. The reason Milton wrote in fetters when
he wrote of Angels & God, and at liberty when of
Devils & Hell, is because he was a true Poet and
of the Devils party without knowing it

A Memorable Fancy.

As I was walking among the fires of hell, delighted with the enjoyments of Genius; which to Angels look like torment and insanity. I collected some
of their Proverbs: thinking that as the sayings used
in a nation, mark its character, so the Proverbs of
Hell, shew the nature of Infernal wisdom better
than any description of buildings or garments.
When I came home; on the abyss of the five senses, where a flat sided steep frowns over the present world. I saw a mighty Devil folded in black
clouds, hovering on the sides of the rock, with cor-
ro-

Marriage 6[E]

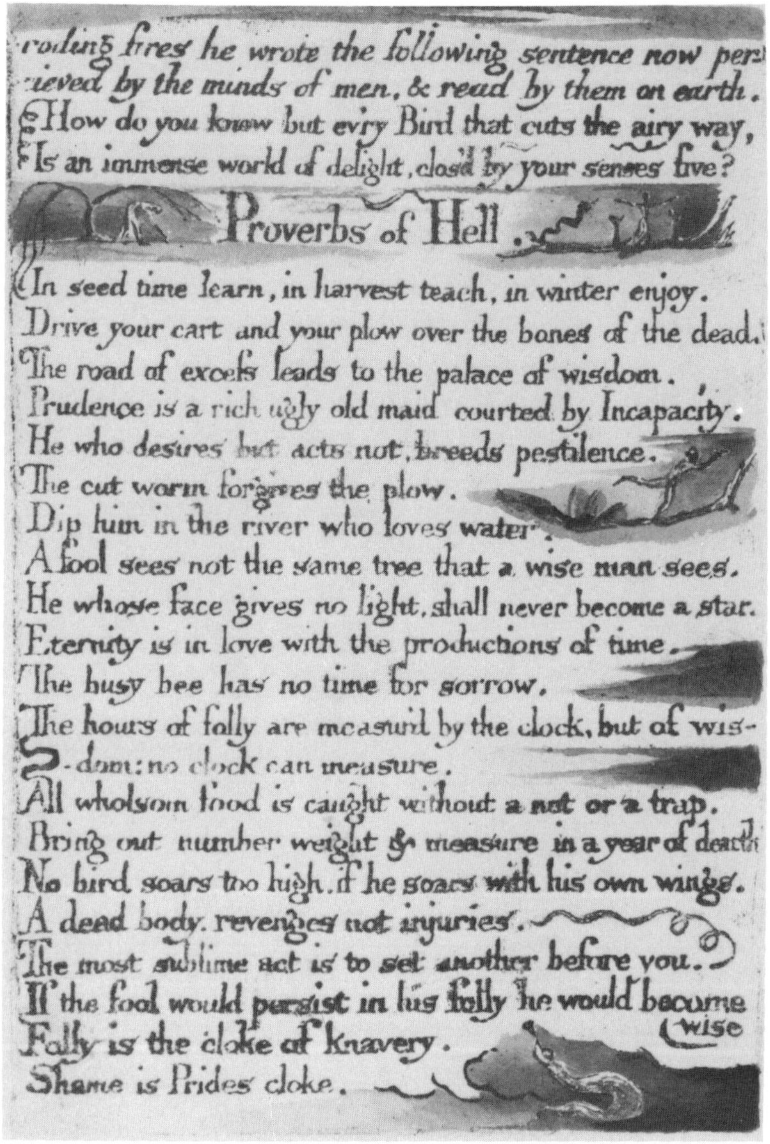

roding fires he wrote the following sentence now per-
ceived by the minds of men, & read by them on earth.
How do you know but ev'ry Bird that cuts the airy way,
Is an immense world of delight, clos'd by your senses five?

Proverbs of Hell

In seed time learn, in harvest teach, in winter enjoy.
Drive your cart and your plow over the bones of the dead.
The road of excess leads to the palace of wisdom.
Prudence is a rich ugly old maid courted by Incapacity.
He who desires but acts not, breeds pestilence.
The cut worm forgives the plow.
Dip him in the river who loves water.
A fool sees not the same tree that a wise man sees.
He whose face gives no light, shall never become a star.
Eternity is in love with the productions of time.
The busy bee has no time for sorrow.
The hours of folly are measur'd by the clock, but of wis-
dom: no clock can measure.
All wholsom food is caught without a net or a trap.
Bring out number weight & measure in a year of dearth.
No bird soars too high, if he soars with his own wings.
A dead body, revenges not injuries.
The most sublime act is to set another before you.
If the fool would persist in his folly he would become
wise
Folly is the cloke of knavery.
Shame is Prides cloke.

Marriage 7^{E}

himself as a "Devil folded in black clouds" at work on "the sides of the rock," which he pictures as Dover cliff, the edge of dry land. We see, darting from black^{D} clouds, a streak of lightning cutting the letters "HOW"—the first word of the verse presented on the next plate beginning "How do you know" and identifying birds as "airy" engravers; compare the eagle in Plate 15. That word "HOW" is Blake's own secret stolen "from the Abyss" to build a heaven; we must look again at the figure in the tree of Plate 2 and her scroll/garment hinting at a devil/poet.

(For a fuller account, see Introduction.)

Marriage 7^{E}. The preliminary loops before "How" (3) suggest that it is the serpent who draws the line or does the lettering, his tongue the lightning of Plate 6. The bird that "cuts the airy way" (represented by a free curve below "cuts": 3) opens the mental space rising infinitely above the line, "an immense world of delight." We are to read the "Proverbs of Hell" with our whole minds/bodies. Before the "Proverbs" title a stooping figure, tree enclosed, pokes the ground with a small stick or dibble ("In seed time learn": 6), presumably learning while seeding the surface. After the title (with a happy banner on "Hell") in a green valley beside a rising cliff (we are *inside* the copper rock) we see a gowned upright figure with joyous hands outstretched over two hand-raising children: parent and children, teacher and pupils all sharing the serpent's messages of delight. The serpent, now rising at an angle that marries horizontal and vertical, symbolizes the liberated line of text.

After "The cut worm forgives the plow," we are shown a runner (like the second dancer in flames in Plate 6) cutting the air with his right hand, in a green valley: the poet plowing a furrow in the copper plate; ourselves running as we read a line of text. The ground and cliff edge repeat the frame of the scene just above. We are *in* the etched "rock." The runner in the narrative line is matched at page bottom by a robe-trailing trumpeter in clouds, apocalyptic spacial illumination that transcends linear time. (Compare the Body and Soul figures of Plate 4.) The line that loops and curves about "you" after proverb 18 diagrams the "sublime act" of that proverb.

In copy I the line below "wise" loops into a serpent head facing the trumpeter, in D a flying wingless snake; in I there is a suggestion of a recumbent figure below the trumpeter, being awakened —as all the recumbent figures we have seen must be.

Marriage 8C. Acorns among oak leaves and a serpentine grape tendril adorn the title, and the margin hints at immense joys: ripe grapes (red or purple), tendril and leaf, and four birds identifiable as (from left to right) lapwing, gull or dove, bird of paradise (the color of the grapes above), and swallow. A fifth bird, an eagle looking up (also grape color) with open beak, is busy in the next line illustrating figures in the text: lion, man, woman, sheep. The man and woman are at work, presumably making clothes of skins. Above "watch the roots" (19) a foolish man is watching an empty-handed tree with neither roots nor fruits—or, as Everett Frost suggests (p 220), the adjacent proverb, "What is now proved was once, only imagin'd," may be intended: the watching figure, a boy, imagines while the dead tree proves. Wiser watchers (lion, tiger, horse, elephant: 20) are marked by a cluster of acorns, at left, and a branch of hazelnuts.

A landscape-seascape illustrates the cistern-fountain idea and the proverb "One thought, fills immensity" (23–24). Down a rocky cliff a tall force of water falls into the ocean (drops filling immensity) which carries a boat and ships, near and distant (one going over the horizon). Ocean and cliff repeat the shape of valley and rock in Plate 7. The stream of thought fills the valley (prepared copper surface), carries the vessels, nourishes a green palm tree (with coconutC) on the cliff edge, and innumerable birds (eagle or paradise bird grape-colored at left), which flow out to fill the air—and overflows into text and illumination conveying (to read on) "an image of truth."

In the next images—a snake coiled to strike and a stag lunging toward it, after "speak your mind, and a base man will avoid you," Blake draws on the tradition that stags and serpents are natural enemies. Grape leaves at the bottom, with the eagle's submitting "to learn of the crow," may hint at the fable of fox and crow.

(The copy H version of this page is reproduced in color in Keynes *Bibliography* 1921.)

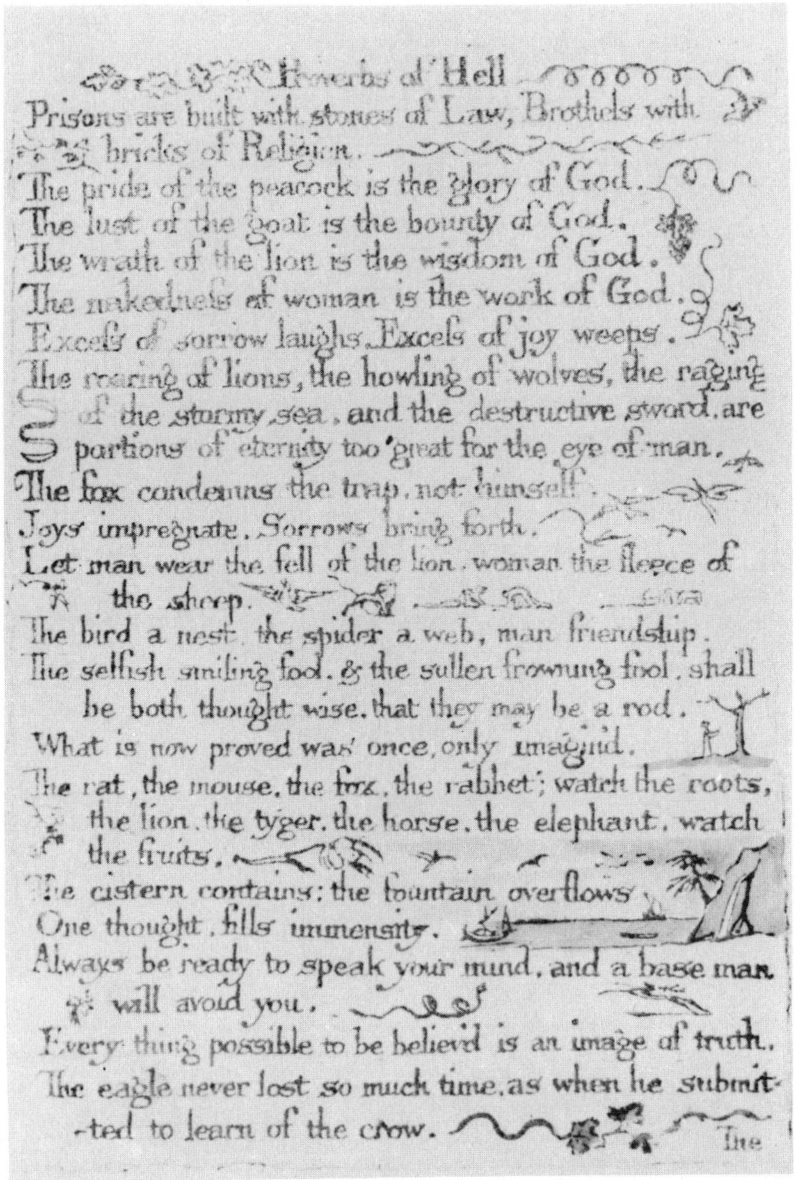

Proverbs of Hell
Prisons are built with stones of Law, Brothels with bricks of Religion.
The pride of the peacock is the glory of God.
The lust of the goat is the bounty of God.
The wrath of the lion is the wisdom of God.
The nakedness of woman is the work of God.
Excess of sorrow laughs. Excess of joy weeps.
The roaring of lions, the howling of wolves, the raging of the stormy sea, and the destructive sword, are portions of eternity too great for the eye of man.
The fox condemns the trap, not himself.
Joys impregnate. Sorrows bring forth.
Let man wear the fell of the lion. woman the fleece of the sheep.
The bird a nest, the spider a web, man friendship.
The selfish smiling fool. & the sullen frowning fool. shall be both thought wise. that they may be a rod.
What is now proved was once, only imagin'd.
The rat, the mouse, the fox, the rabbet; watch the roots, the lion, the tyger, the horse, the elephant, watch the fruits.
The cistern contains: the fountain overflows
One thought. fills immensity.
Always be ready to speak your mind, and a base man will avoid you.
Every thing possible to be believ'd is an image of truth.
The eagle never lost so much time, as when he submitted to learn of the crow. The

Marriage 8C

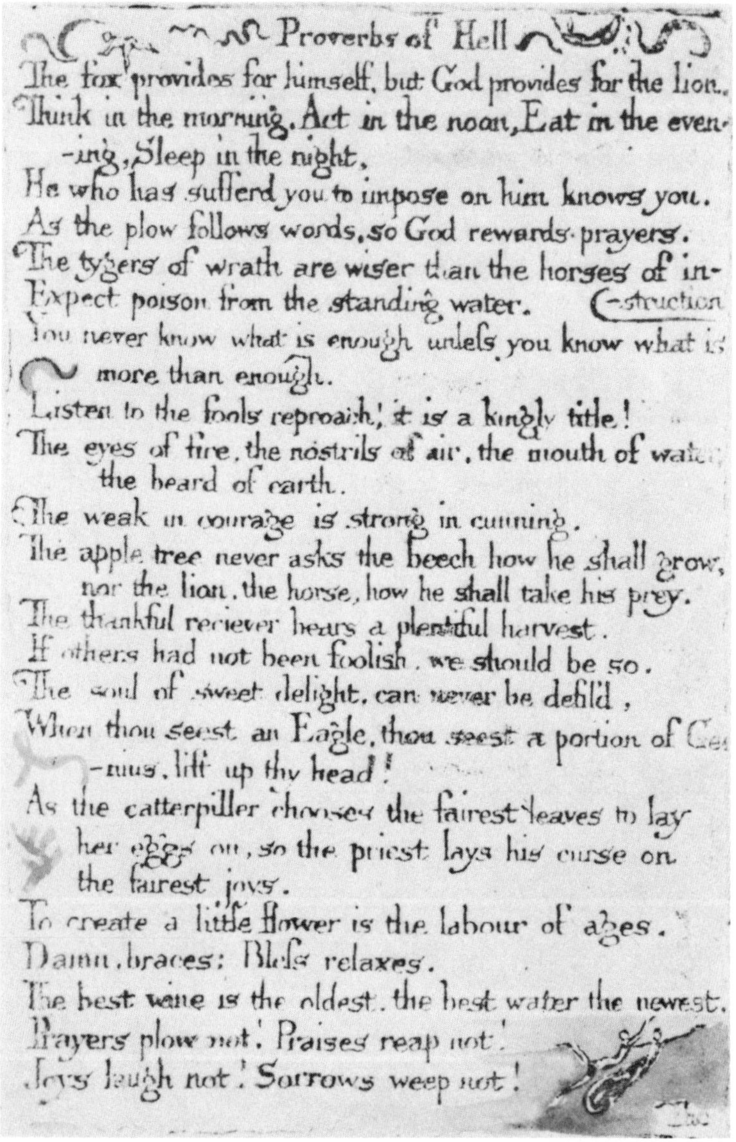

Proverbs of Hell

The fox provides for himself. but God provides for the lion.
Think in the morning. Act in the noon, Eat in the even-
-ing, Sleep in the night.
He who has sufferd you to impose on him knows you.
As the plow follows words, so God rewards prayers.
The tygers of wrath are wiser than the horses of in-
Expect poison from the standing water. (-struction
You never know what is enough unless you know what is
more than enough.
Listen to the fools reproach! it is a kingly title!
The eyes of fire, the nostrils of air, the mouth of water,
the beard of earth.
The weak in courage is strong in cunning.
The apple tree never asks the beech how he shall grow,
nor the lion, the horse, how he shall take his prey.
The thankful reciever bears a plentiful harvest.
If others had not been foolish, we should be so.
The soul of sweet delight, can never be defil'd,
When thou seest an Eagle, thou seest a portion of Ge-
-nius, lift up thy head!
As the catterpiller chooses the fairest leaves to lay
her eggs on, so the priest lays his curse on
the fairest joys.
To create a little flower is the labour of ages.
Damn, braces: Bless relaxes.
The best wine is the oldest. the best water the newest.
Prayers plow not! Praises reap not!
Joys laugh not! Sorrows weep not!
The

Marriage 9E

Marriage 9E. The repeated title is flanked by sinuous scrolls and two figures, a boy at left who directs us to read, "The fox provides for himself," and someone above "God provides for the lion" who may be a lazy reader in a hammock. The proverbs otherwise are allowed to proceed without aid. We may read them with active cunning, like foxes, or receptively, like lions. Blake's confidence that we are reading properly is indicated at the bottom of the page, where a dancing and pointing couple assist the catchword in directing us onward. These figures, having represented body and soul separately on Plates 3, 4, and 7, here fly forward together, dressed somewhat like the strolling couple on the title page.

Marriage 10^{E}. After the wish of the crow that "every thing was black" and of the owl "that every thing was white," the body and soul figures pose together (body darker, over soul in a moment of embrace) and apart. Below "murder an infant" (12) a vegetable infant is approached by a man holding out a rope for strangling; behind him a human infant soars upward. And dancing beside "barren," to show how life is "Where man is," are body and soul together again, with, perhaps, a lapwing and gull.

Vegetation at top contrasts elm leaves (compare Plate 2) and leaves of grape and chestnut. The infant-holding leaf below contrasts with the seaweed under "sea . . . contempt" (4). Contrasting ivy and grape leaves flank "Enough! or Too much" (17), the first angular, the second broad on a looping vine—evaluated by a grape leaf on "Truth." Below, a trap-like jaw of vegetation (a catchfly or dionoea muscipula) beside the slow learner on the Devil's right is in contrast to a large wing-like leaf with a viper tendril rising from it, on his left. This and the coiling vine and leaf above prepare us for the eagle and serpent emblem of Plate 15. (Geoffrey Keynes suggests that the wing-like plant derives from an adjacent plate to that of the catchfly in Darwin, the gloriosa superba, whose six petals are grouped in a roughly wing-like cluster. Yes, but the tendril flower that rises from the wing derives from yet another Darwin plate, that of the vallisneria spiralis, a water plant that uses spiral stems to keep its blossoms above water. Blake thus grafts land and water plants together—another marriage of contraries. See his next plate.)

The instructing Devil, reaching the end of his (snake-like) scroll of proverbs (though in D Blake forgets and puts a balancing roll on that end), points one bat-like wing (almost occulted by his head) to "Enough!" and the other to "Too much." The apprentice at his left may be Blake himself (cross-legged) who has just finished writing down these Proverbs, and whose profile matches the Devil's, sharing concern for the Theotormon-like angel's progress. In some copies the ground beyond the grass on which the Devil kneels suggests a brink or cliff edge; in some^{HI} a stream fills this area, inky, or with white foam; in G flames.

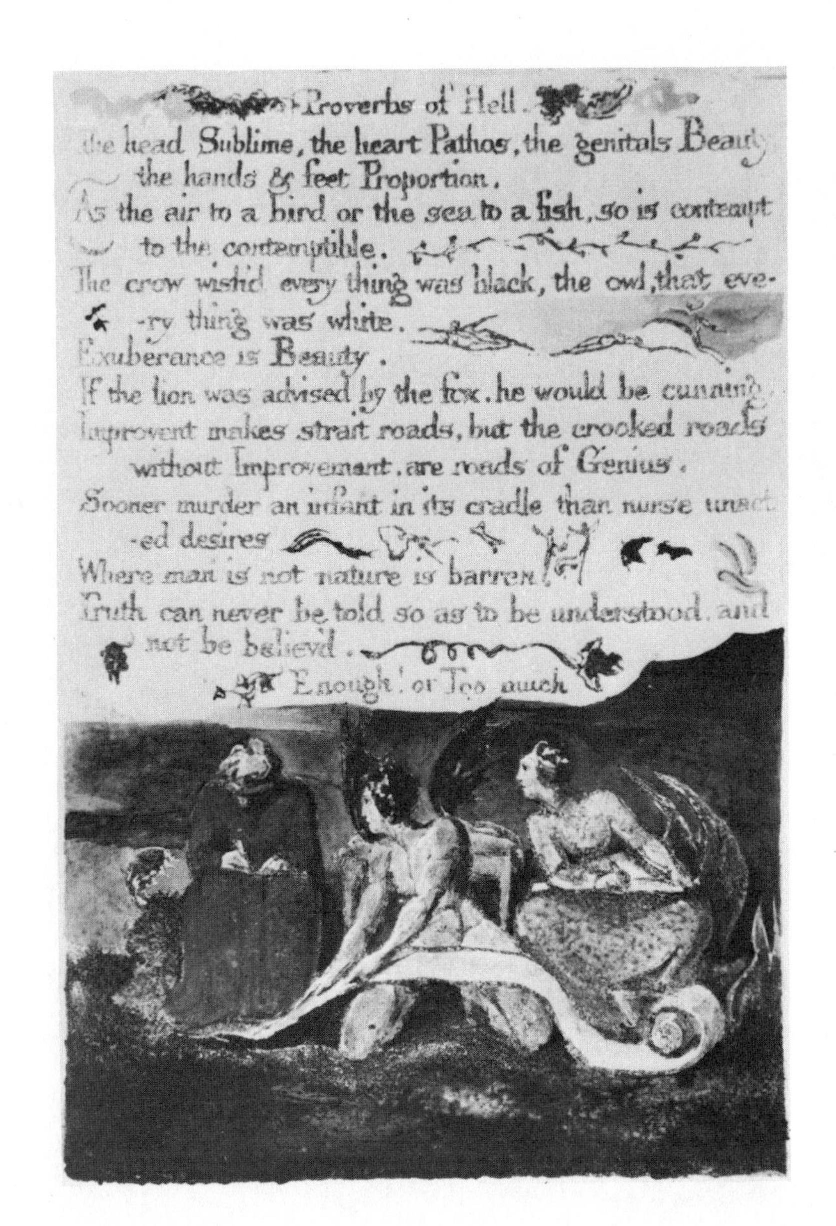

Marriage 10^{E}

Marriage 11^I

Marriage 11^I. The top picture illustrates poets' animating of "sensible objects with Gods or Geniuses" (1–2). On the left we see the divine human form of the sun or (also) of a daisy or sunflower rising over the horizon, or from the earth; next an old stump with bearded face (compare Urizen's face in *Milton* 19); extended in some copies and more like a water spout. Beside it are two groping hands on slender arms (stems) reaching up (from ground or water). A large open plant or flower, the top "wing" of which bears the viper tendrils we saw in Plate 10, extends a lower wing, undulating like flames or waves, to form a bracket of shelter in which a mother and infant face each other with gestures of embrace—geniuses of earth and flower (or worm: see *Thel* 5). The woman, like the plant, is of both sea and land. For her right leg, crossed under her left, is that of a mermaid: it changes, just below the hip, to a formless fabric like artists' depictions of dolphins' tails (and there are engravings of two-tailed mermen that could have suggested this). In copy F the finny fabric is visible on this side of the human leg as far down as below the knee, as if forming a sort of skirt for the human leg to rest on, the rest flaring out at the far side of the human leg. In some copies^GI this effect is half hidden. In some Blake hides it altogether; the woman is given a dress and her fins become a skirt. (In G her hair is like a sunflower crown and there is a bright red flower near her fingertip and the infant's navel.) In copies G and I we view this scene from within a cavern.

An ancient poet or blue-robed Druid stands beside "The ancient Poets" as we enter the text. Between the lines, words are animated as birds: ten, including a large red^EH or blue^FGI one after "percieve," lapwing or eagle. Banners on letters, often serpentine, keep up the animation until "thus began Priesthood" (11) leads to a cut-serpent abortion masked as vegetation. The second paragraph begins with a human standing in a curve of engraving (6).

After priests have "pronounced that the Gods had ordered such things" (13–14) a black stick figure (priest or animated stump?) directs four devotees, two kneeling and two huddling, in the worship of a headless warrior with sword (ocean waves behind him). In copy D the kneeling figures are in the orange color of the sun and sun-god at the top of the page, implying that the poets' animation has turned to sword worship. The waves, abstracted thus, suggest British worship of Neptune. If (on Plate 4) the Everlasting Gospel was brought by Joseph of Arimathea, it has been changed now to Druid blood sacrifice.

At page bottom we see the illusion that deity is a bearded man in a cloud whose outstretched finger creates man. Our thin modern Adam, "weak" (see Plates 2 and 5), drifts away from the cloudy God he has abstracted, forgetting where "All deities reside" (15).

There is a curious analogue for this plate, as emblem, in Thomas Rowlandson's sarcastic print of *The Historian Animating the Mind of a Young Painter* (1784). The painter neglects his proper subject, the beauty of a mother and child, to focus his attention on a bewigged old historian. The similarity implies not so much an influence as a residual theme: the proper study of art.

Marriage 12E. The serpent line runs right into the title, and two naked humans and two birds come running and flying to see and hear. These and the few other animal and human figures on this page and the next may seem little more than elegant printer's indicators. Yet the grape leaf at the first paragraph and the open-mouthed serpent beginning the next are introducing prophets; in contrast the figures surrounding the words "cause of imposition" are a bird flying upside down (perverted inspiration) and a headless contrary to the serpent, a mazy worm. Above "perception" in the eighth line a small bird flying upward reminds us of the large bird flying so beside "percieve" in Plate 11. Flying upward, birds open the airy way to infinite delight; downward they may act as beasts of prey, like Theotormon's eagle (in *Visions* 5 and *America* 11) or descend as doves of peace. The important statement, "All poets believe . . . thing" is set off by soul and body figures flying respectively left and right, flanked by serpentine scrolls. Firmly categorizing the import of these scrolls is the elaboration of rising and descending strokes in the word "prophecying" in the bottom line; for its human extension see Plate 13. (In E the bottom scroll is doubled in length.)

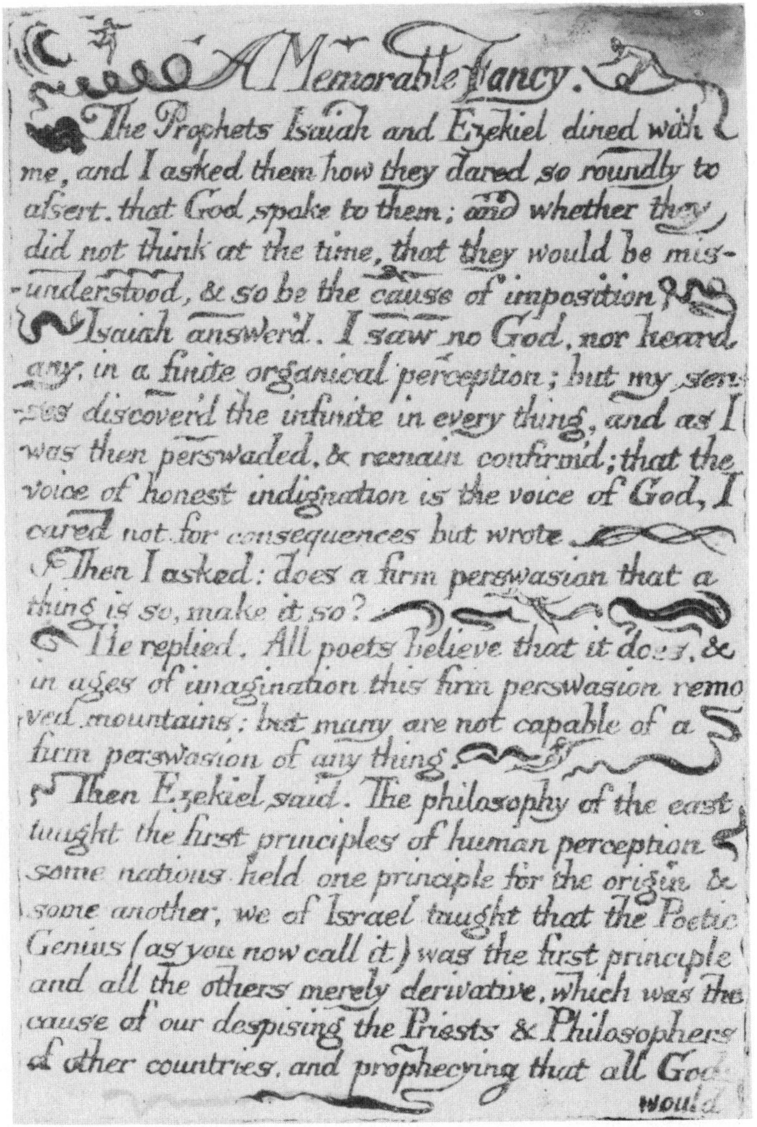

A Memorable Fancy.

The Prophets Isaiah and Ezekiel dined with me, and I asked them how they dared so roundly to assert. that God spake to them; and whether they did not think at the time, that they would be mis-understood, & so be the cause of imposition.

Isaiah answer'd. I saw no God. nor heard any, in a finite organical perception; but my senses discover'd the infinite in every thing, and as I was then perswaded. & remain confirm'd; that the voice of honest indignation is the voice of God, I cared not for consequences but wrote.

Then I asked: does a firm perswasion that a thing is so, make it so?

He replied. All poets believe that it does, & in ages of imagination this firm perswasion removed mountains; but many are not capable of a firm perswasion of any thing.

Then Ezekiel said. The philosophy of the east taught the first principles of human perception some nations held one principle for the origin & some another; we of Israel taught that the Poetic Genius (as you now call it) was the first principle and all the others merely derivative, which was the cause of our despising the Priests & Philosophers of other countries, and prophecying that all Gods would

Marriage 12E

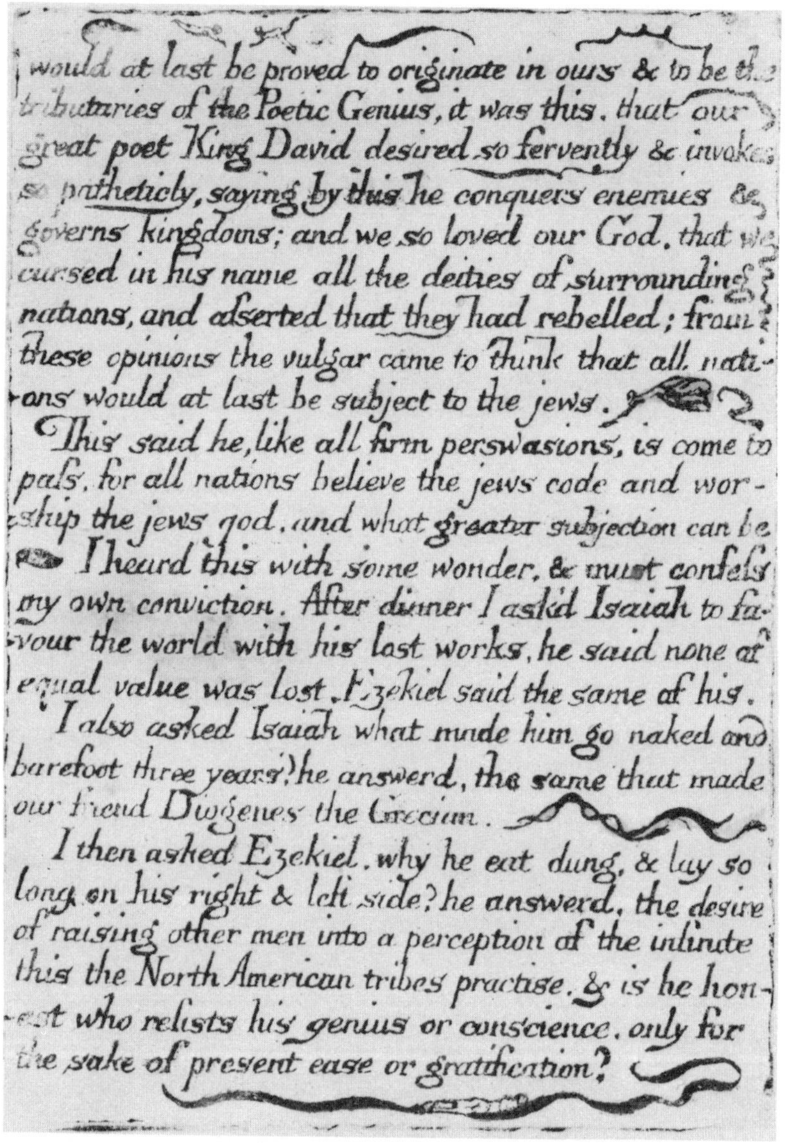

would at last be proved to originate in ours & to be the
tributaries of the Poetic Genius, it was this. that our
great poet King David desired so fervently & invokes
so patheticly, saying by this he conquers enemies &
governs kingdoms; and we so loved our God. that we
cursed in his name all the deities of surrounding
nations, and asserted that they had rebelled; from
these opinions the vulgar came to think that all nati-
-ons would at last be subject to the jews.

This said he, like all firm perswasions, is come to
pass, for all nations believe the jews code and wor-
-ship the jews god, and what greater subjection can be

I heard this with some wonder, & must confess
my own conviction. After dinner I ask'd Isaiah to fa-
-vour the world with his lost works, he said none of
equal value was lost. Ezekiel said the same of his.

I also asked Isaiah what made him go naked and
barefoot three years? he answerd, the same that made
our friend Diogenes the Grecian.

I then asked Ezekiel. why he eat dung, & lay so
long on his right & left side? he answerd, the desire
of raising other men into a perception of the infinite
this the North American tribes practise. & is he hon-
-est who resists his genius or conscience. only for
the sake of present ease or gratification?

Marriage 13E

Marriage 13E. In line 1 two infants signal the word "be," and when the word recurs its rising stroke is given a looping banner. Emphatic underlining is given to "fervently" and "patheticly," but a very wormy downward squiggle drops from "we" alongside "cursed in his name. . . ." At the end of the paragraph the cloaked soul figure directs our attention onward. After "Diogenes the Grecian" (19) two horizontally twining grasses with spikes at their right ends support a caterpillar on their first curve. At page bottom, in the curve of a long banner, Ezekiel lies on his right side (see 20–21), the banner perhaps taking the pun in "lay so *long.*" The prophet's evident comfort seems to belie his spoken denial of "present ease." But his hammock is painted dark against sulfur sky in copy G.

Marriage 14[E]. In variously colored flames which, like those of Plate 4, burn in reverse direction to the flames of the title page and Plate 3, a woman with streaming hair and a black or purple blindfold (except in G and I) hovers above a naked greyish male body on green grass[GI]. In G and I her face is made visible, shouting[I]—implying, in the iconography of *Jerusalem,* a vision of the soul as that portion of man that wakes him from sleeping as body. (Grant suggests that in the blindfold version the hovering figure serves as Covering Cherub, while the effect with eyes and mouth open is that of *Visions* 8.)

In the center, chestnut leaves and burs follow "sensual enjoyment," and another leaf hangs from "body" (compare the hanging lily in "The Lily" *Songs* 43). Near the bottom a naked prancing chestnut[D] horse against pink sky[F] suggests the "infinite" prospect when "the doors of perception" are open. We saw an energetic but falling horse on Plate 5; this one is on his feet and going fast. The whips that unfurl from the first and last letters of "has closed" (just beneath) seem flung apart by the horse's free movement, the first whip negating itself by a knot-like deletion sign (noted by Grant). We shall see still more energetic displays on Plate 27.

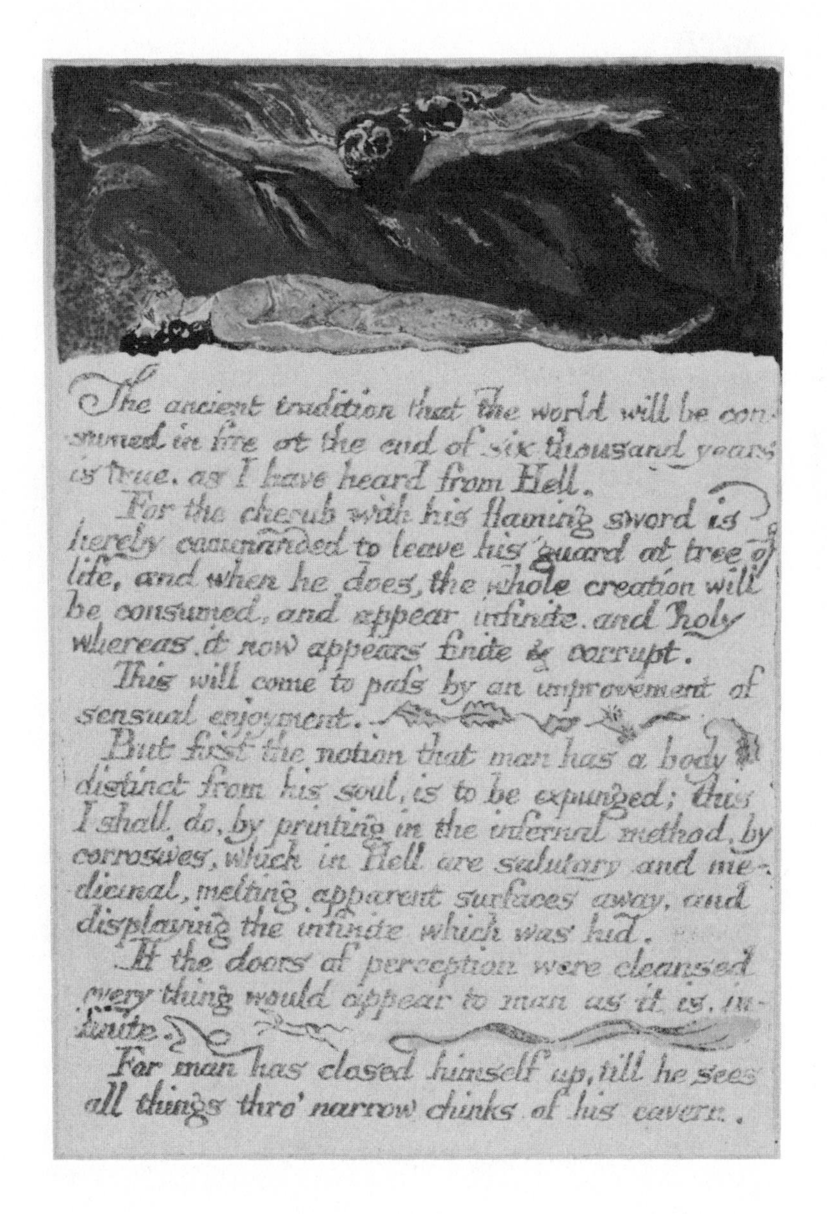

The ancient tradition that the world will be consumed in fire at the end of six thousand years is true. as I have heard from Hell.

For the cherub with his flaming sword is hereby commanded to leave his guard at tree of life, and when he does, the whole creation will be consumed, and appear infinite. and holy whereas it now appears finite & corrupt.

This will come to pass by an improvement of sensual enjoyment.

But first the notion that man has a body distinct from his soul, is to be expunged; this I shall do, by printing in the infernal method, by corrosives, which in Hell are salutary and medicinal, melting apparent surfaces away, and displaying the infinite which was hid.

If the doors of perception were cleansed every thing would appear to man as it is, infinite.

For man has closed himself up, till he sees all things thro' narrow chinks of his cavern.

Marriage 14[E]

A Memorable Fancy
I was in a Printing house in Hell & saw the
method in which knowledge is transmitted from generation to generation.
In the first chamber was a Dragon-Man, clearing away the rubbish from a caves mouth; within, a
number of Dragons were hollowing the cave,
In the second chamber was a Viper folding round
the rock & the cave, and others adorning it with gold
silver and precious stones.
In the third chamber was an Eagle with wings
and feathers of air, he caused the inside of the cave
to be infinite, around were numbers of Eagle like
men, who built palaces in the immense cliffs.
In the fourth chamber were Lions of flaming fire
raging around & melting the metals into living fluids.
In the fifth chamber were Unnam'd forms, which
cast the metals into the expanse.
There they were reciev'd by Men who occupied
the sixth chamber, and took the forms of books &
were arranged in libraries.

Marriage 15[I]

Marriage 15[I]. Body on the left of the title and soul on the right are threaded together by the line that writes "Fancy," and after the words about transmitting knowledge (3–4) a continuous worm-tendril ends ironically in a delete sign. In the first chamber of the "Printing house" (1) the "Dragon-Man clearing away the rubbish" from the surface of the copper ("caves mouth") is depicted as a burin or graver given head, arm, and legs (at left of line 4). The sprig of leaves in line 6 hints at the preparation of printed leaves. The "adorning" process (8) is represented by a standing and a reclining human figure with something lying between them, presumably a plate or book, preceded by a viper-shaped scroll; the second figure may be melting into the ground. Leaf-topped curves after "immense cliffs" (13) mark the cliff edge, i.e. the edge of the cavity in the copper plate, of which we saw two examples in Plate 7. Studding the curves are dots or leaves of diamond shape, representing the application of "precious stones" (9). Following "expanse" (17) is a feathery scroll. Following the words about books in libraries (19–20) a viper line and an oak leaf combine to suggest ink and paper, the leaf of a tree being an easy hieroglyph for the leaf of a book.

Under "libraries" (20) a distant bird flies leftward above the large emblem of serpent and eagle—who are not fighting each other, as in the Homeric omen, but collaborating to produce linear text and infinite illumination. In several copies[EFGI] their being inside the cave (of the copper) is indicated by cloud-rock sides and floor, into which the snake's tongue cuts as the lightning on Plate 6. The space shown is the abyss, as in the title page and Plates 4, 10, and 20. But the eagle, like the bird on the title page, looks upward, drunk with vision. According to the text the eagle, with "feathers of air" (11), causes "the inside of the cave to be infinite" and builds "palaces," i.e. these Illuminated Writings, "in the immense cliffs." Technically I take this to imply the application of picture to copper and then color to paper. Actual feathers were used in the etcher's work, for example to "get an even surface" on the wax applied to the plate (to "receive any impression minutely") (Blake to Cumberland 6 Dec 1795) or to keep the acid circulating evenly during the biting.

The snake and bird together constitute a plumed serpent (notes John Grant); the small cognate emblem of snaky twig and oak leaf is repeated in Plate 20, where William Blake takes the place of the leaf. There the poet is to the root as the eagle here is to the snake. Consider too that the Devil of Plate 10 with a serpentine scroll in his grasp has wings spread. Note that the tendrils of the isolated vine on Plate 2 turn down, but the similarly looping tail of the collaborating serpent here turns upward (as the bird's head), then forward and up (like the viper's body in Plate 7 at right of the part title). Vine and leafing tree, divided, could bear no blossom or fruit; serpent and bird, married, like body and soul, poet and artist, craftsman and genius, can together transmit "knowledge . . . from generation to generation" and cause the inside of our cave to be infinite.

❧

Marriage 16[I]. In the large top picture we see what happens if the collaborators of Plate 15 separate, if cunning priests impose their errors of abstraction (Plate 11): our senses sit in prison not palaces. In *Gates of Paradise* 12, where the motto referring to priestly vengeance indentifies these five, differently grouped, as Ugolino and his kindred, they are shown as lean, exhausted, presumably on the verge of their legendary self-devouring. Here, in copies A to C at least, the jailing of gigantic potential is the point. The "Giants" who form the world of "sensible objects" (Plate 11) *seem* "to live in it in chains" (2–3) but would be freed by altered vision. The five in prison are stout bodies grouped in one rank and clutched together like the fingers of a closed hand; their garments are colored variously as symbolic of variety. Only the father's face is not hidden, his eyes at first blank[ABC], later staring directly forth[EF] or to the right[DGHI]. (In F a large eye is visible in the face farthest left. In G when we follow Ugolino's incredibly long arms to the right we see below his open left hand a bloody red lump gleaming on the floor, flesh he has tried eating! Copy I remits this horror, but guilty eyes still peer sideways; the youth at his right now shows his face; the youth at left opens an eye; the background is lightened.)

At the end of the paragraph the small light figure sitting on a long line illustrates the proper soul-body relationship: arms outstretched as wings, body balanced in a trough of line. At the next break a little flower shows how to fill the immense. At the next, the light soul and dark body, separated and backed by vegetation but reaching toward each other, diagram the reference to "existing beings"—and to what follows, "two classes of men."

The Giants who formed this world into its
sensual existence and now seem to live in it
in chains; are in truth. the causes of its life
& the sources of all activity, but the chains
are, the cunning of weak and tame minds. which
have power to resist energy. according to the proverb, the weak in courage is strong in cunning.
Thus one portion of being, is the Prolific. the
other, the Devouring: to the devourer it seems as
if the producer was in his chains, but it is not so,
he only takes portions of existence and fancies
that the whole.
But the Prolific would cease to be Prolific
unlefs the Devourer as a sea recieved the excefs
of his delights.
Some will say, Is not God alone the Prolific?
I answer, God only Acts & Is, in existing beings
or Men.
These two clafses of men are always upon
earth, & they should be enemies; whoever tries

Marriage 16[I]

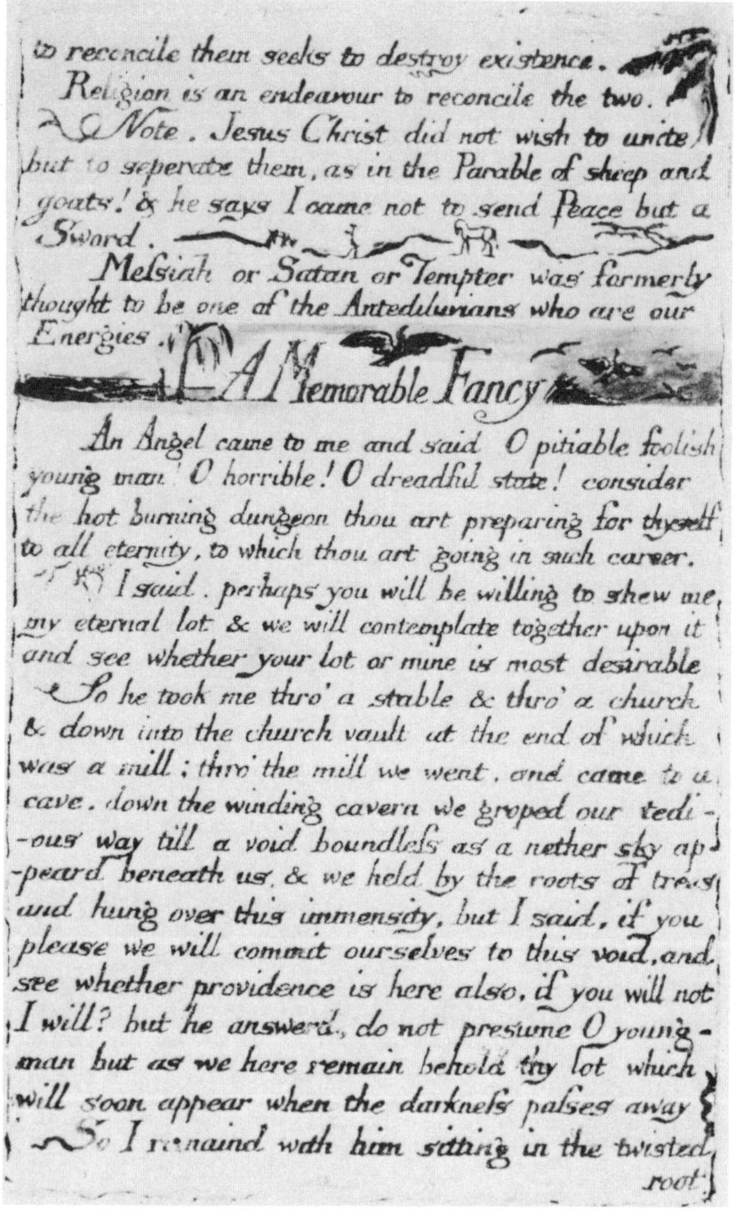

to reconcile them seeks to destroy existence.
Religion is an endeavour to reconcile the two.
Note. Jesus Christ did not wish to unite
but to seperate them, as in the Parable of sheep and
goats! & he says I came not to send Peace but a
Sword.
Messiah or Satan or Tempter was formerly
thought to be one of the Antediluvians who are our
Energies.

A Memorable Fancy

An Angel came to me and said O pitiable foolish
young man! O horrible! O dreadful state! consider
the hot burning dungeon thou art preparing for thyself
to all eternity, to which thou art going in such career.
I said. perhaps you will be willing to shew me
my eternal lot & we will contemplate together upon it
and see whether your lot or mine is most desirable
So he took me thro' a stable & thro' a church
& down into the church vault at the end of which
was a mill: thro' the mill we went, and came to a
cave. down the winding cavern we groped our tedi-
-ous way till a void boundless as a nether sky ap-
-peard beneath us, & we held by the roots of trees
and hung over this immensity, but I said, if you
please we will commit ourselves to this void, and
see whether providence is here also, if you will not
I will? but he answerd, do not presume O young-
man but as we here remain behold thy lot which
will soon appear when the darkness passes away
So I remaind with him sitting in the twisted
root

Marriage 17[E]

Marriage 17[E]. A pine tree with three branches holds the top right margin. In illustration of Christ's opposites, sheep and goats, Peace and Sword (4–6), we see a horizontal sheep and an upright goat, a walking and a leaping horse. The pictorial translation of "Sword" into active goat and horse reminds us that Christ's force is for intellectual not corporeal war, for loosing the horses (compare the giants) from dens imposed by "weak and tame minds" (16:5). These horses of prophetic instruction are visions released from the caves of copper and paper. Again, see the liberated horses on Plate 27.

Above "A Memorable Fancy" a red* phoenix (our eagle of Plate 15) flies from the drooping willow at left (the phoenix's mythical resting place after burning) toward a watery area, or perhaps a heath, indicated by reeds, or trees, beyond "Fancy," probably the abyss of the vision that follows, over which our familiar five birds are circling, the lapwing (or the reborn phoenix?) in the center. Looking quite the other way stands a traveller with staff[AEC], his back to the tree: there is just nothing in sight, though in I there is a pool beside the tree, perhaps implying an oasis. Considering the parable of the text, is this the angel Reason, looking out upon nothing, contrasted to the red diabolic "young man" who sees with imagination and senses?

During the frightened Angel's speech and vision that begin the Memorable Fancy, no living emblems can fly; there are only some crevices (or roots) in front of the second paragraph, and suggestions of rebellious viper shapes in "So" and upward from "twisted" (28–29).

Marriage 18ᴱ. The vision of the angel imposes barenness on the lettering, except for an occasional floral flourish on "deep," "vast," "deep," and "sea," all wilting downward. But the approach of the spiritual Leviathan is marked in some copies, by a touch of green or a marginal check-mark, or, in copy H, by the picking out in blue-black ink of the word "Leviathan."

root of an oak. he was s• pended in a fungus
which hung with the head downward into the deep:
By degrees we beheld the infinite Abyss, fiery
as the smoke of a burning city; beneath us at an
immense distance was the sun, black but shining
round it were fiery tracks on which revolvd vast
spiders, crawling after their prey; which flew or
rather swum in the infinite deep, in the most terrific shapes of animals sprung from corruption.
& the air was full of them, & seemd composed
of them; these are Devils. and are called Powers
of the air, I now asked my companion which was my
eternal lot? he said, between the black & white spiders
But now, from between the black & white spiders
a cloud and fire burst and rolled thro the deep
blackning all beneath, so that the nether deep grew
black as a sea & rolled with a terrible noise: beneath us was nothing now to be seen but a black
tempest, till looking east between the clouds & the
waves, we saw a cataract of blood mixed with fire
and not many stones throw from us appeard and
sunk again the scaly fold of a monstrous serpent.
at last to the east, distant about three degrees appeard a fiery crest above the waves slowly it rear
ed like a ridge of golden rocks till we discoverd
two globes of crimson fire. from which the sea
fled away in clouds of smoke, and now we saw, it
was the head of Leviathan, his forehead was divided into streaks of green & purple like those on
a tygers forehead: soon we saw his mouth & red
gills hang just above the raging foam tinging the
black deep with beams of blood, advancing toward
us

Marriage 18ᴱ

us with all the fury of a spiritual existence.
My friend the Angel climb'd up from his station into the mill; I remain'd alone, & then this
appearance was no more, but I found mys[illegible] sitting on a pleasant bank beside a river by moon
light hearing a harper who sung to the harp. &
his theme was, The man who never alters his
opinion is like standing water, & breeds reptiles
of the mind.
But I arose, and sought for the mill &
there I found my Angel, who surprised asked
me, how I escaped?
I answerd. All that we saw was owing to your
metaphysics: for when you ran away, I found myself
on a bank by moonlight hearing a harper, But &
now we have seen my eternal lot, shall I shew you
yours? he laughd at my proposal; but I by force
suddenly caught him in my arms, & flew westerly
thro' the night, till we were elevated above the
earths shadow: then I flung myself with him direct
ly into the body of the sun, here I clothed myself in
white, & taking in my hand Swedenborgs volumes
sunk from the glorious clime, and passed all the
planets till we came to saturn, here I staid to rest
& then leap'd into the void, between saturn & the
fixed stars.
Here said I! is your lot, in this space, if space
it may be calld, Soon we saw the stable and the
church, & I took him to the altar and open'd the
Bible, and lo! it was a deep pit, into which I de
scended driving the Angel before me, soon we saw
seven houses of brick, one we enterd; in it were a
num

Marriage 19E

Marriage 19E. The angel and his dark vision having departed, the soul and body figures (at line 9), flying parallel, escape horizontally through clouds toward, or as, two rising birds. After the angel's asking "how I escaped?" (12) a curlicue of communication points, again, to two birds; then a human form comes running with "I answered" (13).

Finally, when "I . . . leap'd into the void" (25), soul and body hold hands in free space, beside a gull and a marvelous eagle-winged viper or a serpent-tailed bird, red and black or yellow and green (or in a red band of sky), compacting into a small hieroglyph the eagle-snake emblem of Plate 15 (and see Plate 5).

In copy I, liberally adorned with patches of gold leaf in Plates 1 to 14 and 16 to 19, Blake's supply of gold seems to have given out at this point. There is a slight glint on the serpent in Plate 20; faint smudges of gold in Plates 23 and 27 seem to have been transferred by thumb from remaining dust or from earlier pages. It would be unwise to infer a symbolic intent in this sudden reduction of illumination.

To single out only the effects that can be easily defined: in Plate 1 the gold supplies a halo for the embracing devil and angel, in Plate 2 a patch of light on the grass, in Plate 3 a center of fire and bright bands outlining the woman in the flames, half shaping a halo over her forehead. Gold encircles the sun in Plate 4, adds tips to the flames in Plate 5, emphasis to fires and lightning in Plate 6, bands of light beside the contrasting plants in Plate 10. In Plate 11 it gives a halo to mother and infant, lies in patches above her thigh and at her feet, and makes a heap (of rainbow gold?) on the blue plant behind the infant. In Plate 14 it glows around the legs of the naked man and forms a large mound at his feet. In Plate 18 gold is used between lines, in Plate 19 in a streak of blue at the top. After the glint in Plate 20, the faint smudges in Plates 23 and 27 give golden emphasis to the sleeping horse, to the name of the Raven, and to the final "Holy." The intent, but for this technical failure, might surely have been greater climactic splendor.

Marriage 20[I]. The phantasy that Blake imposes on the angel is barren of adornment, only concluding with three figures (14) for "monkeys, baboons, & all of that species" (1)—or monkeys with their tails eaten off (see text). At bottom, hanging over the deep, is Blake sitting as described at the Fancy's beginning, "in the twisted root of an oak tree" (17:29–81:1). Since both the Angel and Blake sit there, the picture can be of either, but since it is a prophetic position like Ezekiel's in Plates 13 and 23, from the reader's point of view the sitting figure is Blake. Actually, at the right margin, sketched in a bend of the oak root as it grows down from Aristotle's "works," is what appears in some copies to be another figure, the Angel.

In the large picture, the Leviathan, showing three bodily loops above the tide, is churning the deep with "all the fury of a spiritual existence" (19:1). As a biblical, apocalyptic version of our prophetic viper working in the cave with corrosive fires, Leviathan directs his bright red tongue straight upward, in a position deliberately reminiscent of the eagle's beak in Plate 15. He is variously multicolored as described (18:26–32). White foam indicates the fury of his movement (compare the acid bath of Plate 10). A dawning of rose and gold (variously shaded, more like a dull red cloud in D) spreads from the left horizon. In G and I clouds have been added to the sides, as in Plate 15. (In I the artist has carelessly colored the angular wave seen through the first loop as though it were a part of the serpent's body.)

Detail from Copy E

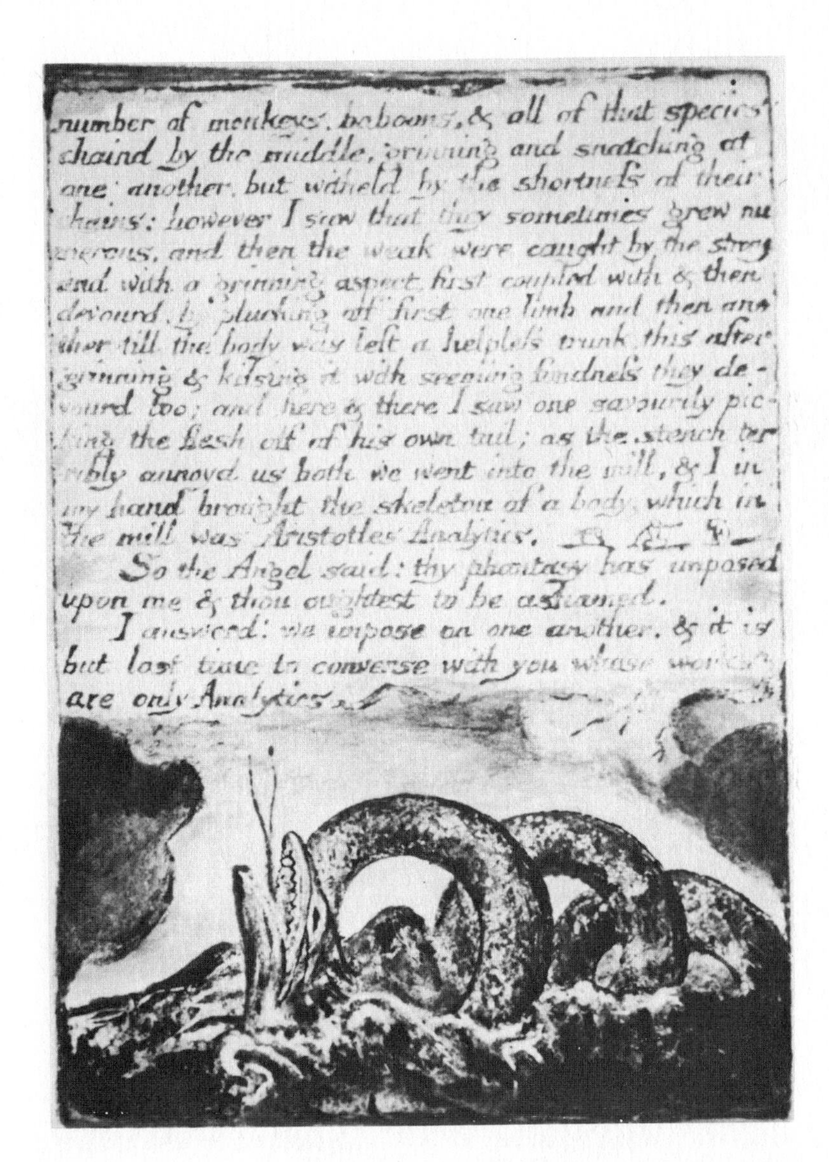
number of monkeys, baboons, & all of that species
chaind by the middle, grinning and snatching at
one another, but witheld by the shortness of their
chains: however I saw that they sometimes grew nu
merous, and then the weak were caught by the strong
and with a grinning aspect, first coupled with & then
devourd, by plucking off first one limb and then ano
ther till the body was left a helpless trunk. this after
grinning & kissing it with seeming fondness they devourd too; and here & there I saw one savourily pic
king the flesh off of his own tail; as the stench ter
ribly annoyd us both we went into the mill, & I in
my hand brought the skeleton of a body, which in
the mill was Aristotles Analytics.

So the Angel said: thy phantasy has imposed
upon me & thou oughtest to be ashamed.

I answerd: we impose on one another, & it is
but lost time to converse with you whose works
are only Analytics.

Marriage 20[I]

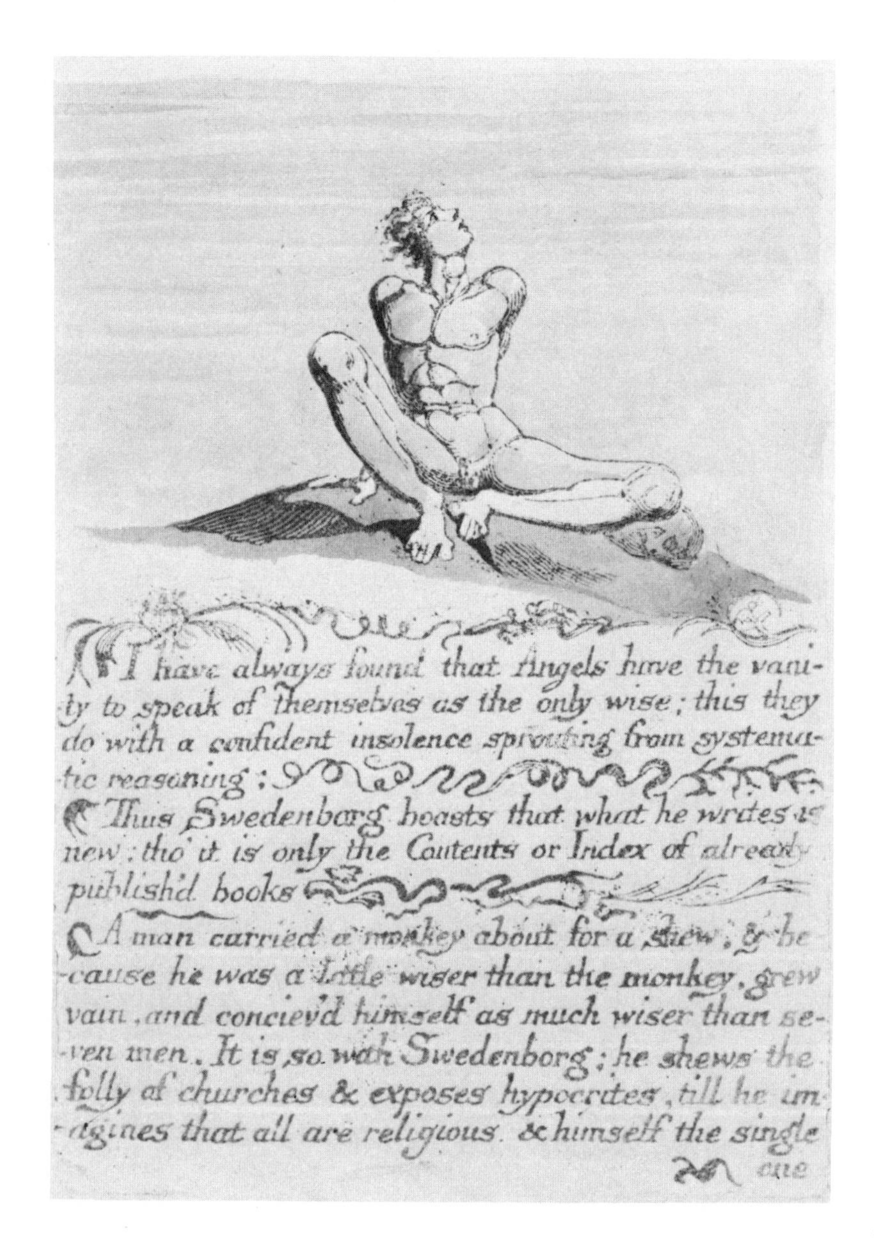

I have always found that Angels have the vanity to speak of themselves as the only wise; this they do with a confident insolence sprouting from systematic reasoning:

Thus Swedenborg boasts that what he writes is new; tho' it is only the Contents or Index of already publish'd books

A man carried a monkey about for a shew, & because he was a little wiser than the monkey, grew vain, and concievd himself as much wiser than seven men. It is so with Swedenborg; he shews the folly of churches & exposes hypocrites, till he imagines that all are religious. & himself the single one

Marriage 21[C]

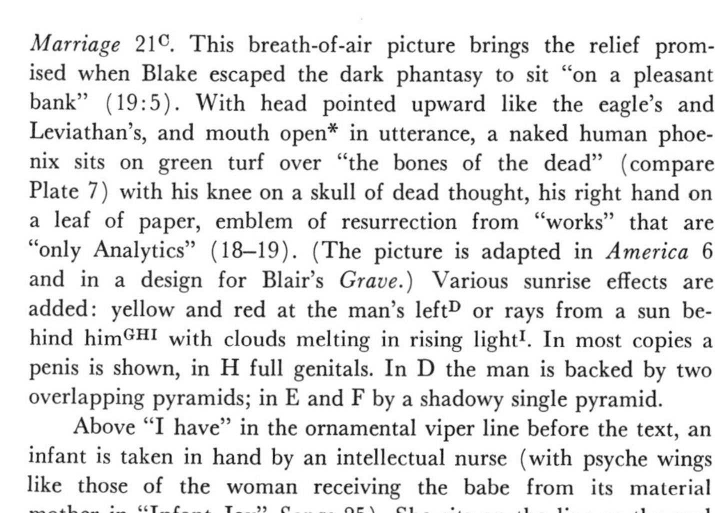

Marriage 21[C]. This breath-of-air picture brings the relief promised when Blake escaped the dark phantasy to sit "on a pleasant bank" (19:5). With head pointed upward like the eagle's and Leviathan's, and mouth open* in utterance, a naked human phoenix sits on green turf over "the bones of the dead" (compare Plate 7) with his knee on a skull of dead thought, his right hand on a leaf of paper, emblem of resurrection from "works" that are "only Analytics" (18–19). (The picture is adapted in *America* 6 and in a design for Blair's *Grave.*) Various sunrise effects are added: yellow and red at the man's left[D] or rays from a sun behind him[GHI] with clouds melting in rising light[I]. In most copies a penis is shown, in H full genitals. In D the man is backed by two overlapping pyramids; in E and F by a shadowy single pyramid.

Above "I have" in the ornamental viper line before the text, an infant is taken in hand by an intellectual nurse (with psyche wings like those of the woman receiving the babe from its material mother in "Infant Joy" *Songs* 25). She sits on the line as the soul in Plate 16 and across a ripe ear of grain.

The title given this picture in the Cumberland copy, "Satan's Address to the Sun," alludes to *Paradise Lost* IV 32 ff, where Satan recalls how fallen, once glorious, he is. In Milton his address is uttered "with no friendly voice"; from Blake's Devil's point of view, the address has been misreported. Some years on (count the curves and loops) a child and a nurse (with red[E] skirt) study together. Then, free of this vine, the independent schoolboy reads in a leafy cave (like the treetop reader in "The School-Boy" *Songs* 53). The educational progress shown leads to the naked humanity of the large picture. The laughing characterization of "Swedenborg" receives graphic comment only in squiggles, not wholly unsympathetic: rollicking brush-work following the colon after "systematic reasoning" (3–4), fat and thin leaves (the former shaped[I] into legless chicken and duck) after "publish'd books."

Detail from 1868 facsimile

Marriage 22[E]. After "ever broke a net" (1) a large fish twists in a long net, its broken end held by a fisherman (often unclear*) sitting on a slope of shore at right. (Compare Los with a net full of fish in *Four Zoas* 64.) After "falshoods" (4) someone in a scroll garment on a leafing branch directs us to "hear the reason" (5). Swedenborg's inability to converse with devils (6–8) gives us a discontinuous diagram of the transmission of knowledge (contrast 15:4). His "superficial" writings are marked by flat green leaves (10–11) the; "infinite number" of delights obtainable from Dante or Shakespeare is suggested by a motley company: a fish, a long-tailed bird of paradise, a distant falcon perhaps, a green slug, a swan perhaps with feet showing, and an ampersand. His candle-holding futility is represented by a man vainly trying to reach the tail of the viper of true delineation (below "master": 18).

The title "A Memorable Fancy" is vibrant with diabolic lines —for this section contains the central conversion of Angel to Devil in Plate 24—above and below "Fancy"; jestingly vertical at the left, where the audience (that schoolboy of Plate 21 now lying on his right side) is ready to read *this* book (i.e. to watch the action directly: "Once I saw"); and coiling up the cliff edge at right. The conversion will occur when the Angel reaches out to embrace the fire (24:3). Here in dumb show a figure stretching out his arms receives an arrow (invisible: of intellectual affection) from a leaping archer, naked. (Compare Milton's star shooting into Blake's tarsus in *Milton* 32 or the cupid-winged archer shooting a woman in the genitals in *Four Zoas* 19.)

Between the announcement of the Devil's words and the words themselves are a thorny wild rose and a flying worm, diabolic contraries. At page bottom a thick flourish that can be made to look like a salamander[D] swims leftward.

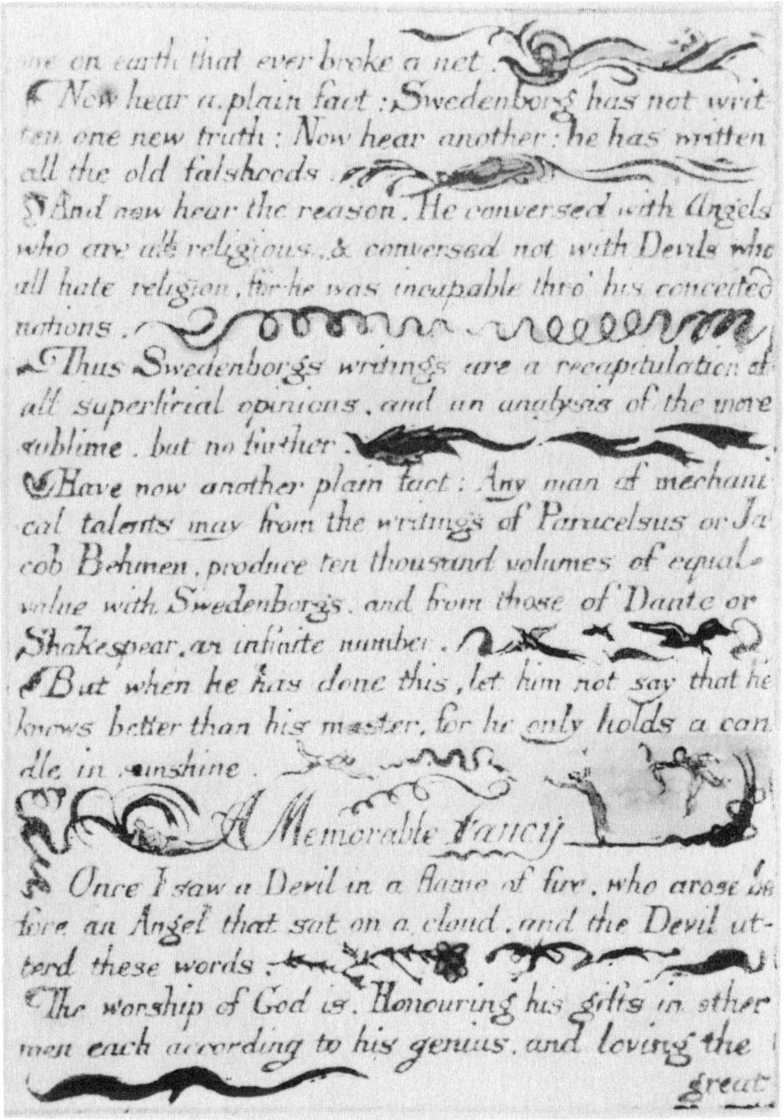

ne on earth that ever broke a net.
Now hear a plain fact: Swedenborg has not written one new truth: Now hear another: he has written
all the old falshoods.
And now hear the reason. He conversed with Angels
who are all religious, & conversed not with Devils who
all hate religion, for he was incapable thro' his conceited
notions.
Thus Swedenborgs writings are a recapitulation of
all superficial opinions, and an analysis of the more
sublime, but no further.
Have now another plain fact: Any man of mechani-
cal talents may from the writings of Paracelsus or Jacob Behmen, produce ten thousand volumes of equal
value with Swedenborgs. and from those of Dante or
Shakespear, an infinite number.
But when he has done this, let him not say that he
knows better than his master, for he only holds a candle in sunshine.

A Memorable Fancy

Once I saw a Devil in a flame of fire, who arose before an Angel that sat on a cloud. and the Devil utterd these words.
The worship of God is. Honouring his gifts in other
men each according to his genius. and loving the
great

Marriage 22[E]

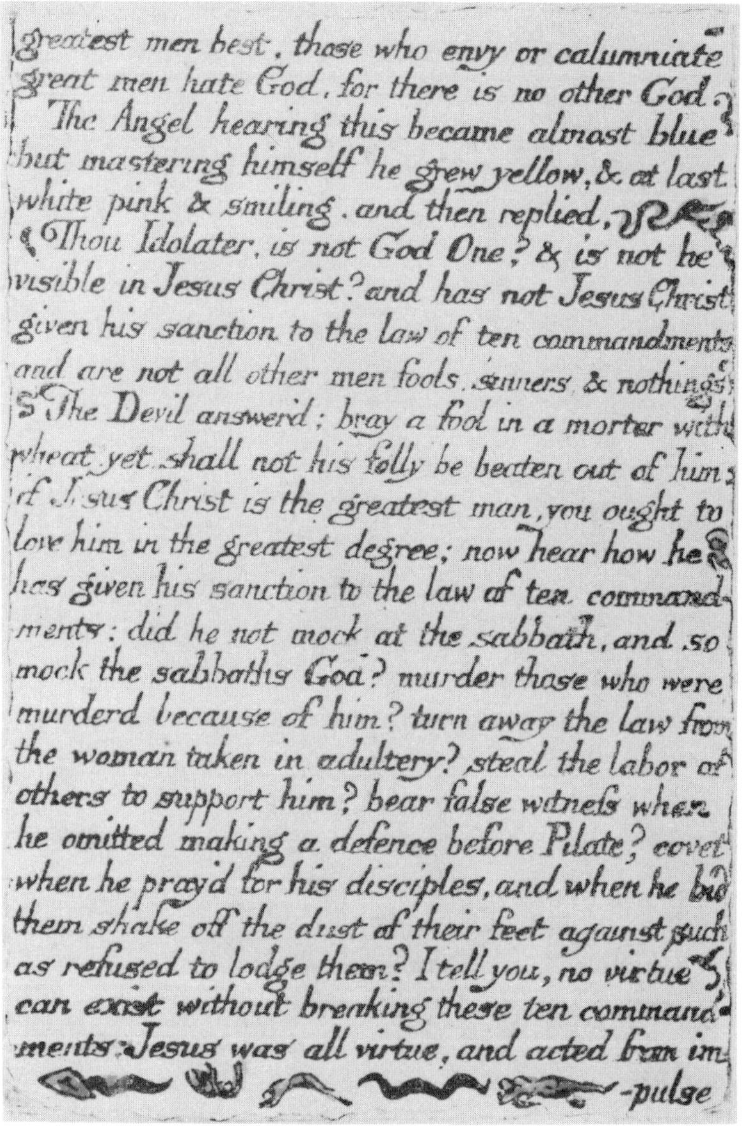

greatest men best. those who envy or calumniate
great men hate God, for there is no other God.
The Angel hearing this became almost blue
but mastering himself he grew yellow, & at last
white pink & smiling. and then replied,
Thou Idolater, is not God One? & is not he
visible in Jesus Christ? and has not Jesus Christ
given his sanction to the law of ten commandments
and are not all other men fools, sinners, & nothings?
The Devil answer'd; bray a fool in a morter with
wheat. yet shall not his folly be beaten out of him:
if Jesus Christ is the greatest man, you ought to
love him in the greatest degree; now hear how he
has given his sanction to the law of ten commandments: did he not mock at the sabbath, and so
mock the sabbaths God? murder those who were
murderd because of him? turn away the law from
the woman taken in adultery? steal the labor of
others to support him? bear false witness when
he omitted making a defence before Pilate? covet
when he pray'd for his disciples, and when he bid
them shake off the dust of their feet against such
as refused to lodge them? I tell you, no virtue
can exist without breaking these ten commandments: Jesus was all virtue, and acted from im-
-pulse

Marriage 23[E]

Marriage 23[E]. The characterization of angelic rhetoric (5) seems consistent with 21:4. When the Devil speaks of Jesus Christ (13) a very plain pictogram of man with halo accompanies the pronoun "he." (Huddled, perhaps to fit the cramped space.)

At page bottom, under "Jesus was all virtue, and acted from impulse," float two curious squiggles and three dead or resting bodies. The first squiggle has a triangular shield for a head, with perhaps a Greek or a Hebrew letter approximated in its center—an emblem of a triune God? The third human, at right, lying on his left side, may be Ezekiel again (see Plate 13). The second squiggle is a human (or dog[D]) upside down; the third a human diver.

Marriage 24E. At the end of the devil's persuasive argument, we see the angel before and after conversion: first a figure huddled in doubt on a vegetable curve, then a light figure walking on waves, wind filling his scarf. Told of the angel's conversion to arise as Elijah, we see a faintly sketched soaring figure after his name (4). Then a line is filled with a seminar of five prophets with a horse (facing away from them at the left) who "often read the Bible together" (6–7), bracketed by four books at right and some larger fascicles (prints, perhaps, or fodder?) piled at left. A shadowy figure (clearly meant to be so) at the left, seen from behind, has angel wings and dangling legs but no head; he seems to be holding out a dripping head toward the seminar: this may well be the angel before mental decollation (i.e. consuming). The viper-tendrilled foliage at the right is unique in its variety of shapes and directions, and the rest of the paragraph burgeons with foliage and loops and banners, culminating in a Shandean doodle after "whether they will or no" (10). After "if they behave well" (8) a runner (compare 7:11) is behaving well, i.e. going rapidly forward, toward a two-volume Bible in scroll shape. The supra-serpentine coilings on this page depart widely from the viper lines of simple transmission; life is richer when "One Law" (11) is no more.

In the finis picture, of the oppressor (King Nebuchadnezzar) with spiked crown, retreating in terror on all fours, we see the face of the bearded god on Plate 11, now returning to the tree stump. The two great trunks behind him, in elephantine embrace (with the suggestion of another pair behind) may remind us of the less gigantic paired trunks in the title page—or the amiable pair in *Songs* 36.

Marriage 24E

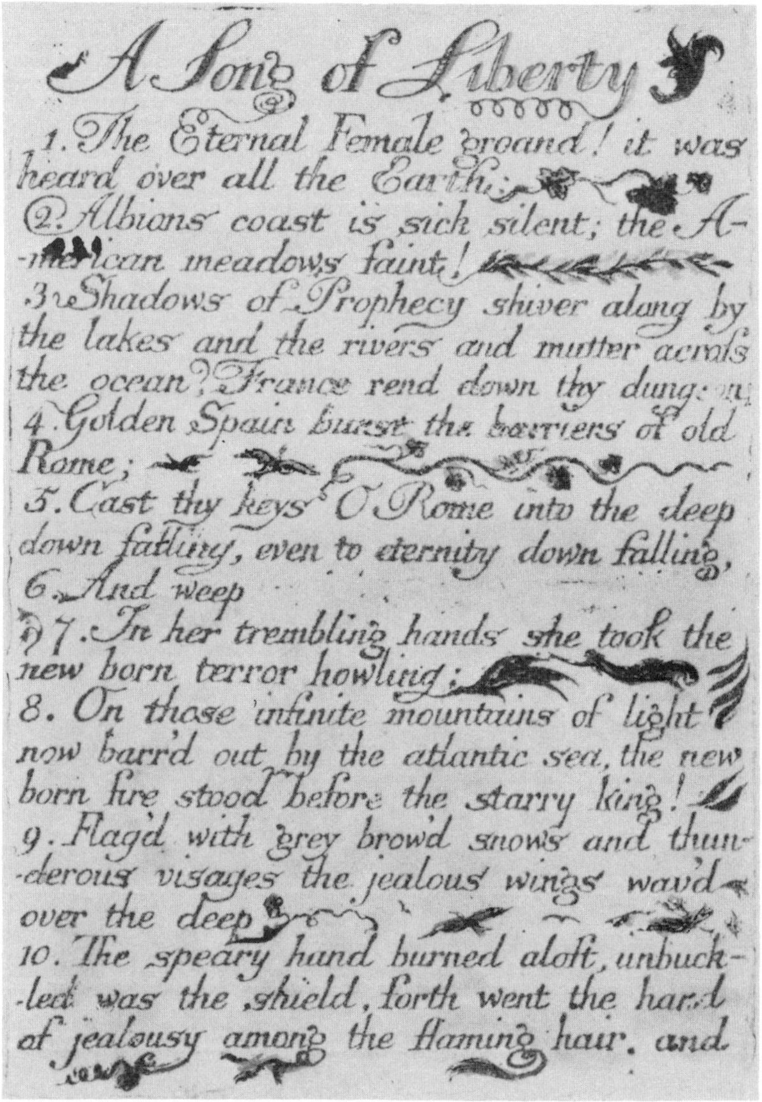

A Song of Liberty
1. The Eternal Female groand! it was
heard over all the Earth:
2. Albions coast is sick silent; the A-
-merican meadows faint!
3. Shadows of Prophecy shiver along by
the lakes and the rivers and mutter across
the ocean? France rend down thy dungeon;
4. Golden Spain burst the barriers of old
Rome;
5. Cast thy keys O Rome into the deep
down falling, even to eternity down falling,
6. And weep
7. In her trembling hands she took the
new born terror howling;
8. On those infinite mountains of light
now barr'd out by the atlantic sea, the new
born fire stood before the starry king!
9. Flag'd with grey brow'd snows and thun-
-derous visages the jealous wings wav'd
over the deep.
10. The speary hand burned aloft, unbuck-
-led was the shield, forth went the hand
of jealousy among the flaming hair, and

Marriage 25[E]

Marriage 25[E] (A Song of Liberty). That a "Marriage" which culminates in a gathering of prophets to "read the Bible" should end with a "Song" in biblically numbered verses should not be surprising, nor should the primacy now given the word. There are no more large, separate pictures; instead, the lettering is given more space and fills it more liberally. But the small pictures are also ampler and free to dilate with the lettering (see Plate 27) with the effect of a sort of levelling *up*. The familiar emblems of tendril and leaf establish their importance at once in the adornment of "Liberty" in the title with a looping tendril such as grew from "Fancy"—and the connecting of "Song" and "Eternal" with loops like those in the title page after *"MARRIAGE"* and around "and." Grape leaves, lacking since the Proverbs of Hell, propitiously return, qualifying the groan "heard over all the Earth" (1) and putting small banners on the vine lifting "keys" beside rising red birds. The red-gowned "Female" (15) taking the green flames in "her trembling hands" looks like a variant of our earlier soul figure; her accepting the new infant before it is visible in human form seems an act like the angel's embracing the flame.

Three birds, bringing the total to five, and some drifting vegetation mock the "jealous wings" of verse 9; the large red bird near the wild red rose on a vine running up from "deep" suggests the rose vine as a variant of the eagle-serpent emblem. In the last line (24) a knot is tied (overgrown with a leaf[EI]) in the graphic line below "jealousy"; the line is divided in three under "among" and spread wide under "flaming."

Marriage 26^E^. The threatening stag (in line 2), who represented "a base man" in Plate 8 when threatening a serpent, may represent the jealous king; his antagonist, the "new born wonder" or falling "fire" (1, 3), appears as a red^D^ human form. Between them is a bush or bent tree with branches that repeat the menace of the stag's raised hooves. Metamorphosed into a bush or tree (painted as tawny^D^ as the stag) he can threaten the human wonder only statically. (Compare the similarly horizontal human tree in *Milton* 20 that menaces the approaching new-born bard.) The "starry night" (1–2) is drawn in a shape perhaps related to the cloudy cliffs of the title page.

After Blake's advice to the Londoner as Jew and African, two sitting figures like those in the street bonfires of *Songs* 45 and 46, one preparing something, the other blanketed, beside a tree stump (beyond which a long whip attaches to "shot") may be studying to become prophets, i.e. to "look up"; compare the seminar of Plate 24. After verse 14 a strip of bare earth is all that remains when the ocean has "roaring fled away" (12). The falling of king and warriors in verse 15 is shown as blades of seeding grass bent horizontal; the consequence in verse 16 is pictured as a flying back of soul toward green^D^ body, their hands outstretched to touch (reversing the abstracting process of Plate 11). The scene of verse 17 is enacted by four counsellors or warriors, in two pairs, hailed by their "gloomy king," the man at the right with a long train and an outstretched arm.

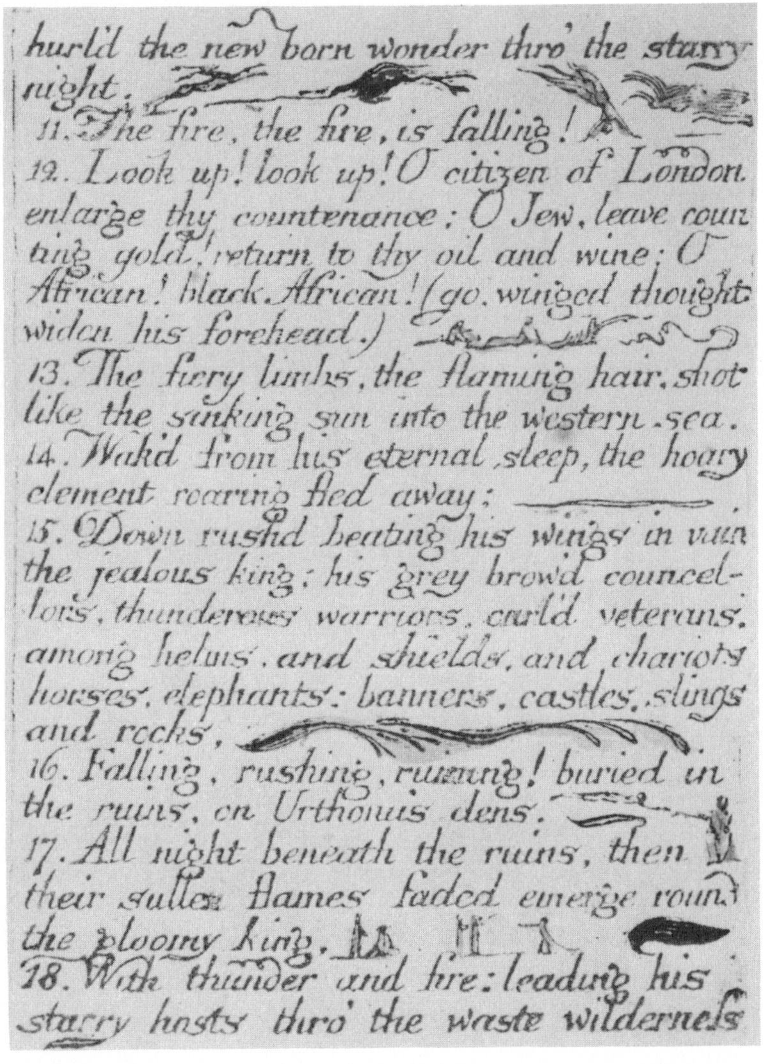

hurl'd the new born wonder thro' the starry
night.
11. The fire, the fire, is falling!
12. Look up! look up! O citizen of London.
enlarge thy countenance: O Jew, leave coun
ting gold! return to thy oil and wine: O
African! black African! (go. winged thought
widen his forehead.)
13. The fiery limbs, the flaming hair, shot
like the sinking sun into the western sea.
14. Wak'd from his eternal sleep, the hoary
element roaring fled away:
15. Down rush'd beating his wings in vain
the jealous king: his grey brow'd councellors, thunderous warriors, curl'd veterans,
among helms, and shields, and chariots
horses, elephants: banners, castles, slings
and rocks,
16. Falling, rushing, ruining! buried in
the ruins, on Urthona's dens.
17. All night beneath the ruins, then
their sullen flames faded emerge round
the gloomy king.
18. With thunder and fire: leading his
starry hosts thro' the waste wilderness

Marriage 26^E^

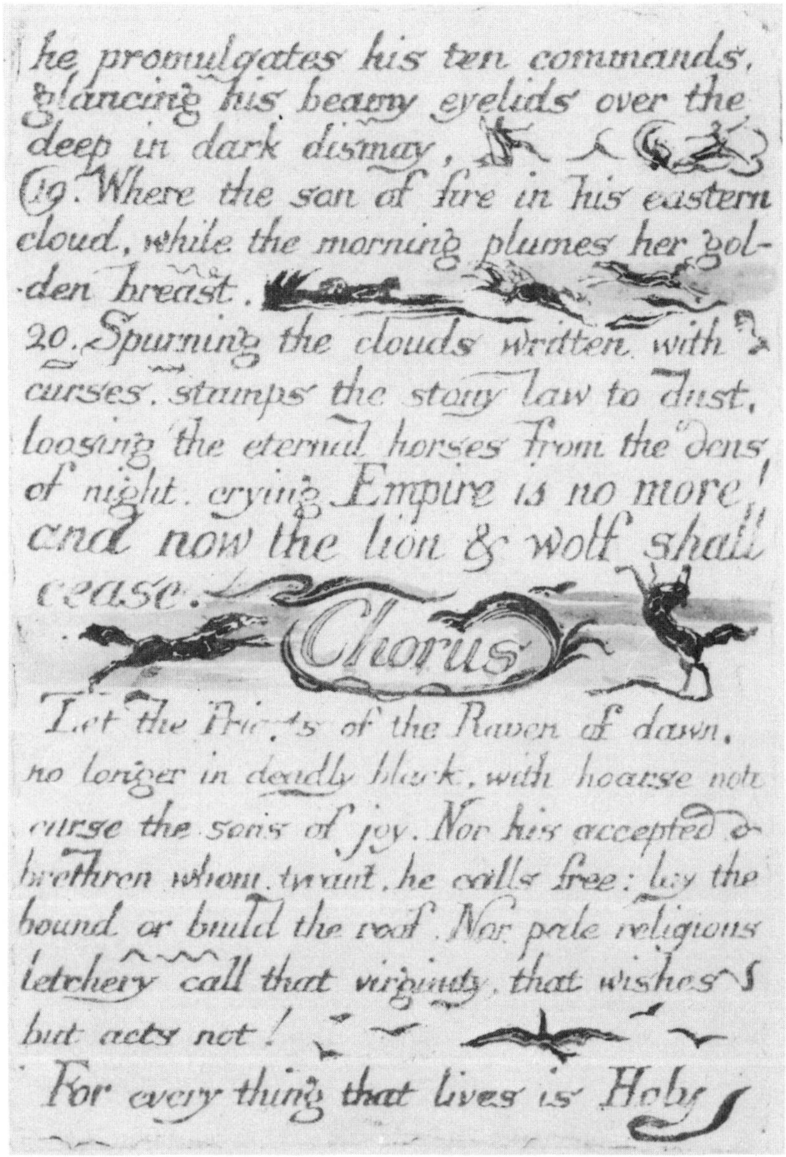

he promulgates his ten commands,
glancing his beamy eyelids over the
deep in dark dismay,
19. Where the son of fire in his eastern
cloud, while the morning plumes her gol-
-den breast.
20. Spurning the clouds written with
curses, stamps the stony law to dust,
loosing the eternal horses from the dens
of night, crying Empire is no more!
and now the lion & wolf shall
cease.

Chorus

Let the Priests of the Raven of dawn,
no longer in deadly black, with hoarse note
curse the sons of joy. Nor his accepted
brethren whom, tyrant, he calls free; lay the
bound or build the roof. Nor pale religious
letchery call that virginity, that wishes
but acts not!
For every thing that lives is Holy

Marriage 27^{E}

Marriage 27^{E}. At the end of line 3 we see "the son of fire in his eastern cloud" (4–5), image of the boy running in Plate 3, now with left foot forward but no girl on the cloud behind him. The figure with arm and right leg stretched toward him is either the king giving chase with spear in hand, falling backward as he runs, or, more likely, a shepherd-priest with crozier or crook, fallen on one knee "in dark dismay." Spurning the curses, the son of fire is "loosing the eternal horses" (8), and we see two resting in a golden meadow (the first facing us, with its head against the tail of the second) and two others approaching at a gallop, one carrying a man, the other riderless. All may be enjoying liberty in different ways; compare the horse with rider to the swan carrying Paul Revere in *America* 11.

At the "Chorus" we see two horses rearing and riderless, the second learning to stand on two feet with head up like the eagle's in Plate 15, the leviathan's in Plate 20, and the resurrected man's in Plate 21. Bird feather and serpent-tendril intertwine around the word, with a flying bird above, something like the loop and bird around the marrying word "and" in Plate 1. A warning banner is attached to the last false note, "call" (19). In the final picture the bright phoenix, our eagle, with five attendant birds, springs up from the fiery meaning of "every thing that lives is Holy." In copy H the final line is picked out in red, the word "Raven" in the first line of the Chorus in blue. Raven and eagle have attained similar prophetic roles now that "Empire is no more!"

With its final upward look the bird directs our understanding to the human form "in his eastern cloud," the bright sun which our imagination must steal from the abyss whither the dying sun plunged in Plate 5.

VISIONS OF THE DAUGHTERS OF ALBION

TWELVE OF THE POSSIBLY seventeen extant copies (plus proofs designated "a" and extra pages with copy F) have been examined at various times, but not all these have been checked for the variant details cited here. The *Census* defines two states of Plates i, ii, and 8, and reports the earlier state for copies A to H, the later state for IJK and M, but fails to report for copies LNOPQ. I find that L is of the later state, in respect to these plates, but P (the Fitzwilliam copy, on paper watermarked 1815, as are N and O) is of the earlier state, and O is early in Plate ii but late in Plate 8. Furthermore, a unique variant in Plate 1 in copy C, the angel with outstretched wings and arms, requires us to recognize C as the earliest copy. (I have not seen copies INQ, but I and N are reportedly on relatively late paper.) A revised chronology of copies would be: CABDEFGH, P, O, LMN with Q unknown.

Visions i[K] (frontispiece; tailpiece in copy A). In the mouth of a cave on the water's edge, with darker, "black jealous waters" (2:4) inside the cave, naked Bromion, Oothoon, and Theotormon seem locked or paralyzed in the postures revealed by their speeches in the poem. They do not see the sun that shines from an eye-like opening in the clouds, pale orange sun and clouds with blue sky[A] or the same sun in pink sky with orange-edged purple clouds[L] or red and white sun in red and black sky[F] or rose and gold sun[O] in yellow sky[BO] or brown[C] or orange[HP] sun in pale brown sky, among blue-black[F] or purple[CHPO] clouds. (Pale yellow sun in yellow sky in pink-edged purple clouds in the duplicate page in F.) Oothoon herself is aware of the cloudy sun, but being in a cave sees only its shadow: "Instead of morn arises a bright shadow, like an eye In the eastern cloud" (2:35–36).

We are strongly compelled to see, in many copies, a human face in the sky, with the straggling clusters of leaves that hang from the roof of the cave as locks of hair. In some copies[AEGPO] there is a second, blank, eye in the clouds above Theotormon (in O the dark grey eyeball shading into purple clouds); in some[CBFHK] it is

Visions i[K]

closed but leaves a seam. In G (red iris in yellow eye at left, blue eye with no center at right, in a grey face) we feel directly stared at. In one-eyed versions the sky face seems in left profile. Yet from the viewers' perspective, the cave edge and brow of foliage seem the skull socket and brow of our own eyes, seen through as a single opening. A still different perspective is suggested by a marked division* of the arch of the cave into three rough-hewn stones separated by mortar, implying a builded doorway or gateway. In P the unbroken arch looks like the main branch of a tree whose trunk grows from the rock beside Theotormon.

What Bromion the rapist and slaver sees, the only one of the three using his eyes, is some terrifying prospect offstage left. His reaction is like that of the drinker at Belshazzar's feast pictured in *Night Thoughts* 33, who sees his fate in the handwriting on the wall. In copy A this plate follows Plate 8, so that what Bromion sees is the storm cloud with a wrathful Oothoon at his head: he has chained her body, but her spirit soars aloft—to draw on the language of the *America* Preludium. When Blake placed this plate at the front of the book, I believe he expected us, when we reach "The End" in Plate 8, to recognize the dialectic of first and last plates and to recreate this confrontation—as we are invited to do with the first and last plates of *Milton,* where the confrontation of Milton and Ololon must become an embrace. Implicitly there could be a happy ending here too, of course, if Bromion-Theotormon (dragon and angel forms like those of the Prince of Albion in *America*) would reassume the human. In short, a precarious and threatened stasis is what we see in this tableau. Bromion's ankles are manacled to a chain from which a large manacle hangs over Oothoon's leg. She, "the soft soul of America" (1:3), is not visibly manacled, though she and Bromion are in Theotormon's opinion "bound back to back" (2:5). He, the jealous lover, keeping apart, cannot let himself look or listen; he covers his ears and face and squats "weeping upon the threshold" (2:21). Yet it is his lack of vision that produces the impasse. The cave is Bromion's, but Theotormon summoned the black waters which threaten this precarious threshold—on which he takes the highest ground in "secret tears" that are as invisible as Oothoon's bonds. The sea is still, but some tidal foam rises inside the cave. The dark green* or brown* (or gold[O]) leaves hang motionless.

Visions ii[J] (title page). In vivid contrast to Plate i, the title page offers visions of storm, high seas, fiery action, and sunshine opened wide into a double* rainbow. In copy A the static Plate i is at the work's end, but in other copies Blake insists upon this sequence of despair and hope. Oothoon with arms outstretched, hair streaming, and backward glance, runs toward us on the trough of an ocean wave between foaming crests. Apparently bearing down upon her is a jealous god, soaring with horizontal wings but perhaps stopped on his cloud; his mouth is open above a cloven beard (he is Urizen as the ghost of Theotormon's curses), but he is on fire, and his face has an inward look of woe if also anger. Like Theotormon, he hugs himself, not Oothoon, his right hand scratching his left shoulder, his left hand fending off the flames.

The brightly colored rainbow spanning three tiers of cloud (or four[A-H,OP]) hides part of Urizen's right wing and illuminates a scarf dance of three fairy "creatures of the element" (see *Notebook* 30), whose open arms and running legs echo the running of Oothoon. (We fail to understand fairies if we think his wing is scattering them: that's up to us.) A fourth dancer arches her body alongside the "A" of "Albion"; a small huddled figure sits on the cloud above "bi." On the cloud above, lie two disheveled figures (like Oothoon and Bromion in Plate 1), one leaning down and pointing to a naked woman on the lower cloud whose arms behind her suggest Oothoon's position in Plate i. At the top of the rainbow, partly in its light, sits a cross-legged conjuror (called "The Evil Demon" in a separate pencil drawing) seeming to direct the storm that rains from the dark side of the clouds (and incidentally directing us into this book); but what he directs its force against are two very grim rock cliffs below Urizen's left wing. In some copies[ELOP] the two rock masses are picked out as two human forms with bowed heads and long hair down which the rain pours. The lower figure, near the margin, has long pink[O] arms that hang lifeless. The figure nearer Urizen is a variant of Theotormon in Plates i and 4; his head is lower than his knees; his pink[O] legs form a V, his feet presumably meeting beneath his hair. (A group of similar figures, with dangling arms and heads and cascading hair, may be seen at upper right in Blake's frontispiece for Bürger's *Lenore.*)

The rainbow coloring establishes a bright red* or pink* which will reappear on the final page. Oothoon's running under it continues a journey that began in joy ("Over the waves she went in wing'd exulting swift delight": 1:14); we are invited to help her sustain the faith whereby she still walks on the waves, despite the menaces of Bromion and Theotormon under the aegis of the selfish jealous father-god Urizen.

Visions ii[J]

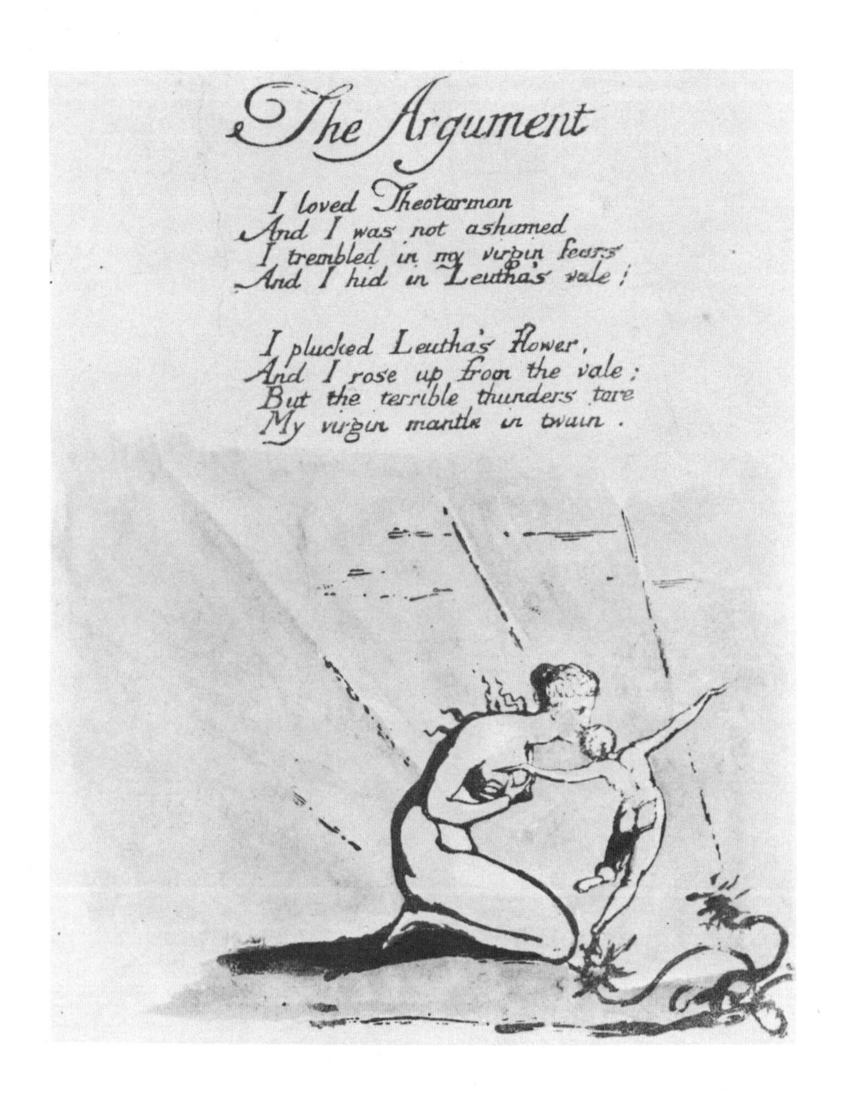

Visions iii[J]

Visions iii[J] (Argument). From a sunrise source (a two-flowered Marygold at bottom right) radiate five bands of colored light (marked by four dividing lines in the etching)—a sort of transposition of the five color ribbons of the rainbow on the title page (though often* painted simply pink and orange). (In copy F the rainbow colors are adjusted to include the green of the grass in its correct position in the prismatic sequence: from left to right the bands are yellow, orange, red, violet, blue. In O a double rainbow arches behind the curve of Oothoon's back.) Sharing the light, a naked Oothoon, kneeling, holds her crossed hands against her very full breasts and kisses the joyous human form of the Marygold: "I see thee now a flower: Now a nymph!" (1:6–7). According to the text Oothoon is plucking the flower and putting it "between my breasts" (1:11–12); it can "glow" there because, as the picture makes us see, she does not "bind" the joy to herself (contrast Plate i) but kisses it "as it flies . . . in eternity's sun rise" (*Notebook* 105, a passage universally found appropriate).

Elaine Kauvar notes that this Marygold, the *caltha palustris* of Darwin commonly called May-flower, was used to protect fertility in May Day festivals. It opens only to rays of sun, innocent love in daylight. It is a miniature, here, of the emblem of Experience in *Thel* 1.

Visions 1[J]. At page bottom, collapsing on separate rock pillows on green ground, "prostrate and exhausted after their sin" (Keynes)—to take their accuser Theotormon's view of their copulation—lie naked Oothoon, head downward like the woman of Fuseli's *Nightmare,* and naked Bromion, their faces not visible. His right hand is held out in an empty grasp. Hers is empty too, but her left hand touches what might seem a heap of her shed clothing (hidden by paint in P). That it is, more precisely, the deflated cloud of her vision of the act of plucking the flower of love we learn from the five or six[G] fairy mimes around the title word "Visions" enacting a grotesque pageant of the joys and terrors of "the moment of desire" (7:3), in a sky that continues the rainbow* or dawn* coloring of Plate iii.

On the forward curve of the "V" sits a female trumpeter holding a phallic serpent horn to her mouth (compare Gray *Spring* 5), her stockings half off[A], more or less naked*. Next, replacing the dot of the first "i" and holding in her right hand a loose rein attached to the top of the "V" (compare the reins held by girls riding serpents in *Thel* 6 and *America* 11) a naked female rides with her legs astride a horse-like cloud (often tan[CG]) beyond which trails a long horse tail. (The tail *could* be an extension of her own hair; yet see Plate 5.) Her hold is looser than the serpent-riders', and the reins hang down to her left ankle. She leans back almost meditatively, with cheek on hand and elbow on cloud. In what must be the earliest copy (C), because removed from the plate in others, a small naked male angel stands in her lap, with outstretched arms (one just behind her head) and outstretched eagle-like wings that trail pink and yellow vapor. (Contrast the flaming Urizenic figure in Plate ii.) Where the cloud-horse might have a neck we see instead a pair of testicles, serving as a sort of pommel for the riding woman, and a short round penis. (The dangling bridle strap falls across the division between penis and testicles.) The woman's right foot extends just beyond and below the penis, but the design is ingeniously ambiguous, so that we may, if we wish, ignore that right foot and see the nearer fold of testicle as the woman's right knee (the leg folded somehow out of sight). This side-saddle effect seems emphasized in some copies[AO]. In copy G the rider is white in an otherwise dark page, and a brown bill (duck's or swan's?) is added to the penis, which is painted green like a bird's head (though the bird is given no eye). If we compare the position of the naked man riding a swan in *America* 11, we may recognize the posture of the

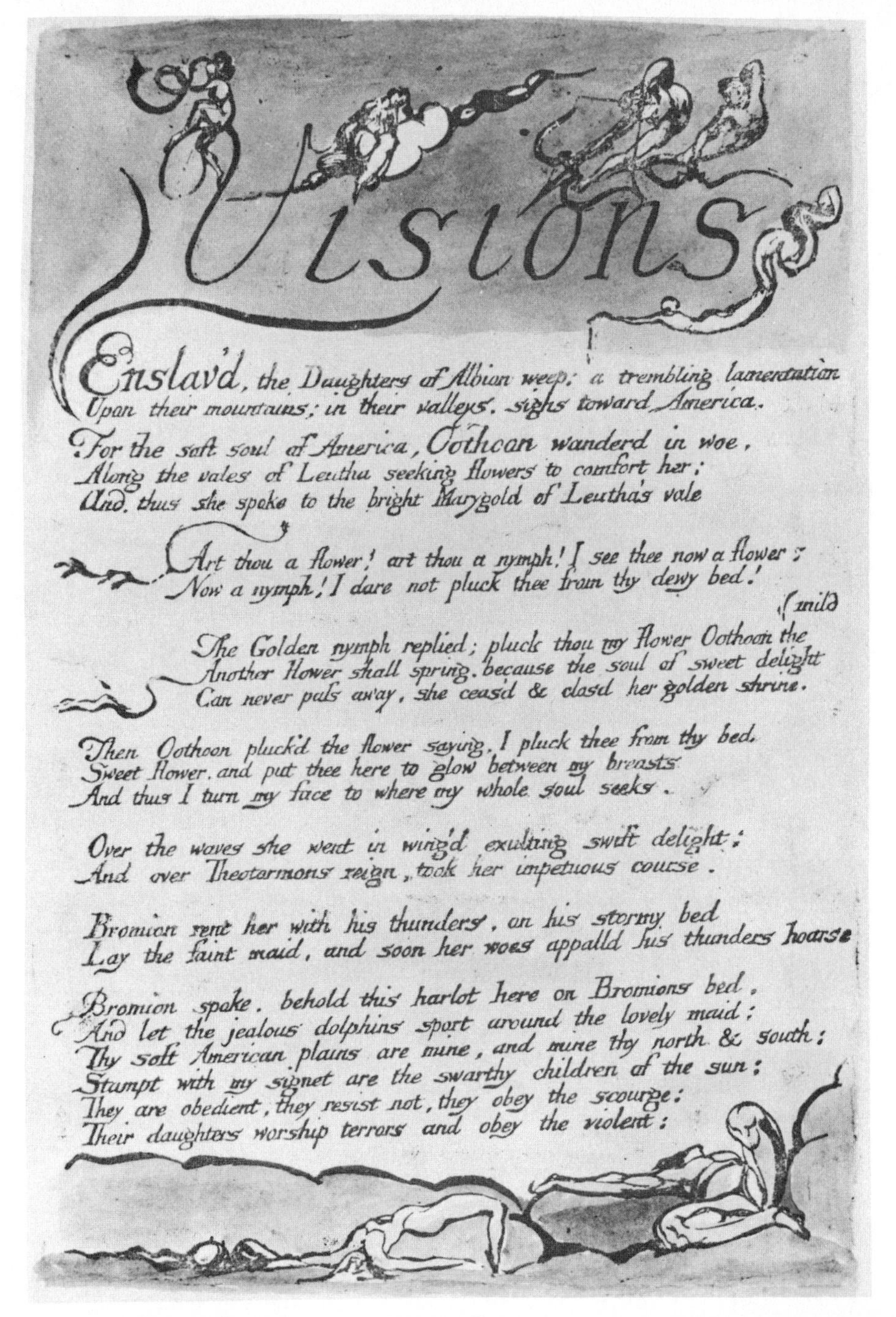

Visions 1[J]

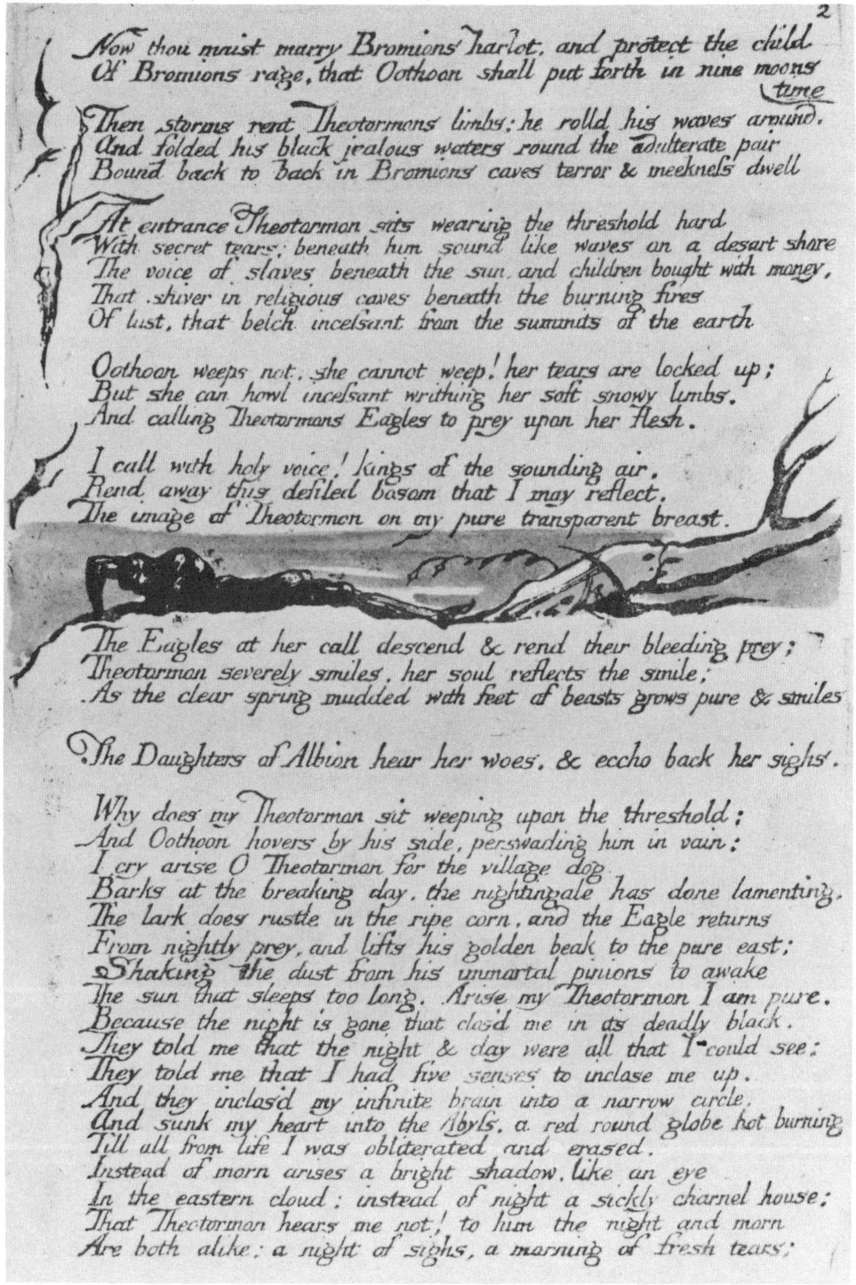

2

Now thou must marry Bromions harlot, and protect the child
Of Bromions rage, that Oothoon shall put forth in nine moons time

Then storms rent Theotormons limbs; he rolld his waves around.
And folded his black jealous waters round the adulterate pair
Bound back to back in Bromions caves terror & meekness dwell

At entrance Theotormon sits wearing the threshold hard
With secret tears; beneath him sound like waves on a desart shore
The voice of slaves beneath the sun, and children bought with money,
That shiver in religious caves beneath the burning fires
Of lust, that belch incessant from the summits of the earth

Oothoon weeps not: she cannot weep! her tears are locked up;
But she can howl incessant writhing her soft snowy limbs.
And calling Theotormons Eagles to prey upon her flesh.

I call with holy voice! kings of the sounding air,
Rend away this defiled bosom that I may reflect.
The image of Theotormon on my pure transparent breast.

The Eagles at her call descend & rend their bleeding prey;
Theotormon severely smiles. her soul reflects the smile;
As the clear spring mudded with feet of beasts grows pure & smiles.

The Daughters of Albion hear her woes, & eccho back her sighs.

Why does my Theotormon sit weeping upon the threshold;
And Oothoon hovers by his side, perswading him in vain:
I cry arise O Theotormon for the village dog
Barks at the breaking day. the nightingale has done lamenting.
The lark does rustle in the ripe corn, and the Eagle returns
From nightly prey, and lifts his golden beak to the pure east;
Shaking the dust from his immortal pinions to awake
The sun that sleeps too long. Arise my Theotormon I am pure.
Because the night is gone that clos'd me in its deadly black.
They told me that the night & day were all that I could see;
They told me that I had five senses to inclose me up.
And they inclos'd my infinite brain into a narrow circle,
And sunk my heart into the Abyss, a red round globe hot burning
Till all from life I was obliterated and erased.
Instead of morn arises a bright shadow, like an eye
In the eastern cloud; instead of night a sickly charnel house;
That Theotormon hears me not! to him the night and morn
Are both alike: a night of sighs, a morning of fresh tears;

Visions 2^J

cloud-rider as a relaxed version, in reverse, of that of the swan-rider.

At the bottom of the page, the objects beside Oothoon include a horse tail (except in copy O) and must constitute the deflated remnant of the horse-cloud above "Visions." (For a reappearance of the horse-tailed cloud as a pillow, see Plate 5. And for an eagle with a swan-like bill, see Plate 3.)

Next, at top, soar two naked* male archers with cupid bows, the first ready to shoot; the second, having done so, reaches toward an invisible quiver for another arrow. (Compare the fighting men who threaten in *Thel* 1 and 6.) For the climax of this enactment, a scroll-gowned female like an apocalyptic angel pours liquid from a thin phial to drip beside "weep" (1).

The two indented stanzas of Oothoon's speech are marked by a stem of leaves with a *tiny* Marygold (see Plate ii) on its curve of beauty (see *Marriage* 3) and a couch, bracketed to "Another flower shall spring," on which lies a tiny imitation of Oothoon exhausted (but her head at a more comfortable angle).

Visions 2^J. In the upper left margin a distorted vision of the "soft snowy limbs" of Oothoon shows them hanging downward (not dancing or diving like the rainbow fairy in a similar position beside "A" in Plate ii), presumably "writhing" while she howls "incessant" (12). The figure is without developed feet or hands or head, almost all "body"—though in copy F Blake somewhat relents and sketches in the details of a thin profile. Sometimes^C the cloud edges above are backed by blue sky.

Across the center of the page a black African "beneath the sun" strains to hold his head out of the dust; his human form is symmetrically balanced by a less fallen tree, against which a pick-axe rests. The tree, similar in position to the tree in *America* 4, manages some leaves, only near its base.

Visions 3[J]. Oothoon on a white (or purple[H] or orange[P]) cloud, still fallen back as in Plate 1 (or rather as the more comfortably lying marginal imitator) and writhing as in Plate 2, receives the beak of Theotormon's preying eagle, a genius turned vulture. Yet this image is a product of Oothoon's rhetorical imagination and is shown as cloud-borne, though in at least one copy[A] the cloud seems to rest on earth, painted green at lower left. The image reappears in *America* 13, where it is a true vision of the horrors of war and where the beak of the eagle, whose wings are outspread like Urizen's in the *Visions* title page, is sharply ravenous. Here the beak of "Theotormon's" eagle (2:13) is rather like the bill of a swan (as in *Night Thoughts* 157) or a duck (see note on Plate 1).

And none but Bromion can hear my lamentations.

With what sense is it that the chicken shuns the ravenous hawk?
With what sense does the tame pigeon measure out the expanse?
With what sense does the bee form cells? have not the mouse & frog
Eyes and ears and sense of touch? yet are their habitations.
And their pursuits, as different as their forms and as their joys:
Ask the wild ass why he refuses burdens: and the meek camel
Why he loves man: is it because of eye ear mouth or skin
Or breathing nostrils? No. for these the wolf and tyger have.
Ask the blind worm the secrets of the grave, and why her spires
Love to curl round the bones of death; and ask the ravnous snake
Where she gets poison: & the wingd eagle why he loves the sun
And then tell me the thoughts of man, that have been hid of old.

Silent I hover all the night, and all day could be silent.
If Theotormon once would turn his loved eyes upon me;
How can I be defild when I reflect thy image pure? (woe
Sweetest the fruit that the worm feeds on. & the soul preyd on by
The new washd lamb tingd with the village smoke & the bright swan
By the red earth of our immortal river: I bathe my wings.
And I am white and pure to hover round Theotormons breast.

Then Theotormon broke his silence. and he answered.

Tell me what is the night or day to one oerflowd with woe?
Tell me what is a thought? & of what substance is it made?
Tell me what is a joy? & in what gardens do joys grow?
And in what rivers swim the sorrows? and upon what mountains

Visions 3[J]

Wave shadows of discontent! and in what houses dwell the wretched
Drunken with woe forgotten. and shut up from cold despair.

Tell me where dwell the thoughts forgotten till thou call them forth
Tell me where dwell the joys of old! & where the ancient loves?
And when will they renew again & the night of oblivion past?
That I might traverse times & spaces far remote and bring
Comforts into a present sorrow and a night of pain
Where goest thou O thought! to what remote land is thy flight?
If thou returnest to the present moment of affliction
Wilt thou bring comforts on thy wings. and dews and honey and balm;
Or poison from the desart wilds, from the eyes of the envier.

Then Bromion said: and shook the cavern with his lamentation

Thou knowest that the ancient trees seen by thine eyes have fruit;
But knowest thou that trees and fruits flourish upon the earth
To gratify senses unknown? trees beasts and birds unknown:
Unknown, not unpercievd, spread in the infinite microscope,
In places yet unvisited by the voyager. and in worlds
Over another kind of seas, and in atmospheres unknown:
Ah! are there other wars, beside the wars of sword and fire!
And are there other sorrows, beside the sorrows of poverty?
And are there other joys, beside the joys of riches and ease?
And is there not one law for both the lion and the ox?
And is there not eternal fire, and eternal chains?
To bind the phantoms of existence from eternal life?

Then Oothoon waited silent all the day, and all the night,

Visions 4J

Visions 4J. Oothoon, chained by her ankle in the wave-flame of enslaved desire or condoned slavery, clasps her hands (not on her breasts as in Plate iii) and laments over Theotormon, who sits like a stone mourner, thinking without seeing or hearing, between rock and ocean. His advanced right toes may remind us of *Urizen* 1, but Urizen there is at least busy trying to communicate.

In most copies* a bright sun is rising over the water—her lamentation renewed "when the morn arose" (5:1), but Theotormon does not sense the difference: "Tell me what is the night or day . . . ?" (3:22). The wave-flame is colored as the water; geographically it represents the element in which the slave trade is conducted. Oothoon as the soul of America is in chains above the American shore; as a slave she is shipwrecked in mid-passage. Yet there are large cracks in the rock behind her. (In copy C the sun is lacking here but added in Plate 6.)

(In copy F "a thin, leafless brown tree has been added in ink at the bottom right margin, and the sun is only a quarter circle rather than a semicircle": Bentley. There is the trunk of a tree, with a quarter sun, in O.)

Visions 5[J]. Oothoon's outcry to Urizen, epitomizing her philosophy yet accepting his Demonic authority as "Creator of men!" even though "mistaken," is marked out by a vigorous grape stem bearing five leaves and one threefold and one fourteenfold tendril, but no fruit. Near the bottom of the page a woman lies with her face in a "night pillow," her left hand at her head, bare to the waist (or covered except for one hand[F]), below which she is entangled in a green* (or blue[FL] or gold[H] or rose[P]) sheet or garment—illustrating Oothoon's call for liberation: "and must she drag the chain Of life, in weary lust?" (22–23). In copy A her black hair distinguishes her from Oothoon and identifies her as one of the still benighted daughters in Plate 8, also in green. (In other copies[BP] too her dress color identifies her as one of the daughters in 7 or 8.) When she turns from this position and looks about she will be like Nature in *On the Morning of Christ's Nativity* or Earth in "Night Startled by the Lark," *L'Allegro* 2, where the soaring figure of Dawn will help us understand what Oothoon is doing in Plate 8. (Yet the horse tail on her pillow equates it with the fairy's mount in Plate 1 and the deflated cloud beside Oothoon at the bottom of that plate.)

5

But when the morn arose, her lamentation renewd,
The Daughters of Albion hear her woes, & eccho back her sighs.

O Urizen! Creator of men! mistaken Demon of heaven;
Thy joys are tears! thy labour vain, to form men to thine image.
How can one joy absorb another? are not different joys
Holy, eternal, infinite! and each joy is a Love.

Does not the great mouth laugh at a gift? & the narrow eyelids mock
At the labour that is above payment, and wilt thou take the ape
For thy councellor? or the dog, for a schoolmaster to thy children?
Does he who contemns poverty, and he who turns with abhorrence
From usury: feel the same passion or are they moved alike?
How can the giver of gifts experience the delights of the merchant?
How the industrious citizen the pains of the husbandman.
How different far the fat fed hireling with hollow drum;
Who buys whole corn fields into wastes, and sings upon the heath:
How different their eye and ear! how different the world to them!
With what sense does the parson claim the labour of the farmer?
What are his nets & gins & traps. & how does he surround him
With cold floods of abstraction, and with forests of solitude,
To build him castles and high spires. where kings & priests may dwell.
Till she who burns with youth. and knows no fixed lot; is bound
In spells of law to one she loaths: and must she drag the chain
Of life, in weary lust! must chilling murderous thoughts. obscure
The clear heaven of her eternal spring? to bear the wintry rage
Of a harsh terror driv'n to madness, bound to hold a rod
Over her shrinking shoulders all the day; & all the night
To turn the wheel of false desire: and longings that wake her womb
To the abhorred birth of cherubs in the human form
That live a pestilence & die a meteor & are no more.
Till the child dwell with one he hates. and do the deed he loaths
And the impure scourge force his seed into its unripe birth
E'er yet his eyelids can behold the arrows of the day.

Does the whale worship at thy footsteps as the hungry dog?
Or does he scent the mountain prey, because his nostrils wide
Draw in the ocean? does his eye discern the flying cloud
As the ravens eye? or does he measure the expanse like the vulture?
Does the still spider view the cliffs where eagles hide their young?
Or does the fly rejoice. because the harvest is brought in?
Does not the eagle scorn the earth & despise the treasures beneath?
But the mole knoweth what is there, & the worm shall tell it thee.
Does not the worm erect a pillar in the mouldering church yard?

Visions 5[J]

6

And a palace of eternity in the jaws of the hungry grave
Over his porch these words are written. Take thy bliss O Man!
And sweet shall be thy taste & sweet thy infant joys renew!

Infancy, fearless, lustful, happy! nestling for delight
In laps of pleasure; Innocence! honest, open, seeking
The vigorous joys of morning light; open to virgin bliss.
Who taught thee modesty, subtil modesty! child of night & sleep
When thou awakest, wilt thou dissemble all thy secret joys
Or wert thou not awake when all this mystery was disclos'd!
Then camst thou forth a modest virgin knowing to dissemble
With nets found under thy night pillow, to catch virgin joy,
And brand it with the name of whore; & sell it in the night,
In silence, ev'n without a whisper, and in seeming sleep:
Religious dreams and holy vespers, light thy smoky fires:
Once were thy fires lighted by the eyes of honest morn
And does my Theotormon seek this hypocrite modesty!
This knowing, artful, secret, fearful, cautious, trembling hypocrite.
Then is Oothoon a whore indeed! and all the virgin joys
Of life are harlots: and Theotormon is a sick mans dream
And Oothoon is the crafty slave of selfish holiness.

But Oothoon is not so, a virgin fill'd with virgin fancies
Open to joy and to delight where ever beauty appears
If in the morning sun I find it: there my eyes are fix'd

Visions 6[J]

Visions 6[J]. Theotormon, pressing his forehead with his right hand, looks unhappily at his raised left arm which wields a three-thonged "cat" over himself. This is his "sick mans dream" to match Oothoon's trying the torture of his ideas, in Plate 3. The knots on the whip look uncannily like the heads of the Marygold flowers in Plates iii and 1 (especially in the miniature there). He ignores Oothoon, who is also self-absorbed, striding by with her face buried in her hair and hands, in a sort of desperate variant of her stance in Plate ii. He rests back on a cloud or hill (his vortex, which her stride should carry her over); sunlight is pushing from behind clouds at her back[HJ] or from a golden sun on the horizon[C]. (His cloud, though it gets orange tinted near her, extends on up the right margin, like Vala's veil—see *Jerusalem* 85—in P and O. It rests on a vortex in the bottom right corner in O.)

Visions 7[J]. Five of the Daughters of Albion (not three, pace Keynes) "are crouching in attitudes of despair." The two smaller ones are huddled at the left, one with hand dangling down, the other with curly head (and clenched right fist[O]) showing above the hip of the first. Only the top central figure is looking and listening; only her hair (and perhaps a strand of the black-haired daughter in front) is blown by the invisible wind. (Compare the five huddling members of the "Ugolino" family in *Marriage* 16, five "Giants" if they will look up.)

A separate print of this design (*SBD* 17) is inscribed: "Wait Sisters Tho' all is Lost." In G the right margin is filled with pale maple leaves and a grey trunk.

Visions 8[J] (The End). Of the three Daughters shown here, two with young faces are now looking up—at Oothoon, who soars in a stormcloud rolling up from the horizon and above the ocean. (She is up free from the cave, like Orc in *America* 3.) Wrapped now in flames like Urizen-Bromion in the title page yet bearing a contrary prophetic message, she soars with her arms for wings, is not self-clutching. The flames are not consuming her—this reverses her cloud vision of Plate 3—but flowering out in the shape of her breasts (as in Plate iii). Her hair blows outward from her head as center. The Daughters, attentive, are at the water's edge, but their rock is the highest visible land. Their garments and the painted clouds compose a rainbow scene that grows brightest in the bright red* or orange* or purple[P] flame—which burns largest near her heart (an idea symbolized differently, but also with rainbow colors, in *Jerusalem* 85). In copy G there is some black in the red and yellow flames; the cloud is very dark as it funnels up from the horizon over black water (a vortex) and then yellows under Oothoon, who seems to rise on its crest like the living figure-head of an approaching storm, an image that would suit Shelley's of a fierce Maenad with streaming locks. (In late copies the cloud behind Oothoon has been removed from the plate, except for a few traces, yet is usually[JKLO] restored in the coloring process.)

In copy A this picture of the stormcloud bearing and now

In happy copulation; if in evening mild. wearied with work;
Sit on a bank and draw the pleasures of this free born joy.

The moment of desire! the moment of desire! The virgin
That pines for man; shall awaken her womb to enormous joys
In the secret shadows of her chamber; the youth shut up from
The lustful joy. shall forget to generate. & create an amorous image
In the shadows of his curtains and in the folds of his silent pillow.
Are not these the places of religion, the rewards of continence!
The self enjoyings of self denial? Why dost thou seek religion?
Is it because acts are not lovely, that thou seekest solitude,
Where the horrible darkness is impressed with reflections of desire.

Father of Jealousy, be thou accursed from the earth!
Why hast thou taught my Theotormon this accursed thing?
Till beauty fades from off my shoulders darken'd and cast out,
A solitary shadow wailing on the margin of non-entity.

I cry, Love! Love! Love! happy happy Love! free as the mountain wind!
Can that be Love, that drinks another as a sponge drinks water?
That clouds with jealousy his nights, with weepings all the day:
To spin a web of age around him. grey and hoary! dark!
Till his eyes sicken at the fruit that hangs before his sight.
Such is self-love that envies all! a creeping skeleton
With lamplike eyes watching around the frozen marriage bed.

But silken nets and traps of adamant will Oothoon spread,
And catch for thee girls of mild silver, or of furious gold:
I'll lie beside thee on a bank & view their wanton play
In lovely copulation bliss on bliss with Theotormon:
Red as the rosy morning, lustful as the first born beam,
Oothoon shall view his dear delight, nor e'er with jealous cloud
Come in the heaven of generous love; nor selfish blightings bring.

Does the sun walk in glorious raiment, on the secret floor

Visions 7[J]

Visions 8J

ironically defining the "soft soul of America," on a verso page, is immediately followed, on the facing recto page, by the usual frontispiece of the seaside cavern from which Bromion looks Westward open-mouthed. The effect is a confrontation of Oothoon and Bromion that accounts for the intense looks on their respective faces—and that compels us to see that here are two "visions" of Oothoon, enslaved and free, available to the Daughters of Albion. (Compare Orc in the earth and in the air, in *America* 2 and 3.) When the seashore and cave picture is in its more usual position preceding the title page (except in G, where it follows it), we may discover this effect more slowly than we do the links and contrasts between Plate 8 and the title page, but both discoveries will tighten our grasp of the work. We may also find the effect of a cycle renewed in experience that began in innocence, when we compare Oothoon's expression and situation here with the spirit of "exulting swift delight" in which she originally "wing'd" over the waves (1:14). (It has become customary to apply to the ocean depicted in these plates Blake's later term, "the Sea of Time & Space"—found in *Milton* 15[17]:39, 46; 34[38]:25; in *Four Zoas* iv 265; and in a letter of January 10, 1802—but the "Atlantic sea" of *America* is a more appropriate primary designation. It is the deep between Oothoon and the realm of Theotormon which she is determined, and inspired, to bridge as promised by the rainbow of the title page.)

AMERICA A PROPHECY

(Reduced from about 9 by 6½ inches)

America i[N] (Frontispiece). Under a cloudy sky (its apparent eye empty: compare *Visions* i), after a battle that has left a cannon barrel and a sword hilt (obscured[KM]) on the ground inside a city wall, a naked giant with eagle or angel wings sits in the broken wall with his face buried in acceptance of defeat. Tyranny's stony law has been breached, but the rebel champion who calls himself Orc (8:1) has been manacled by his wrists and chained into the breach like a human rock. A naked woman sheltering two children sits with her legs crossed, on a carved stone fallen from the wall, and contemplates the fallen cannon. By 1793, the date on the title page, the American Revolution as a chapter in the revolt of people against monarchs and of minds against mental chains has been stopped dead as far as the people of Albion are concerned. (Albion is here a name for England, not yet the "Ancient Man" of later prophecies.) The Atlantic ocean as a dividing gulf has replaced the "Atlantean hills" which once united the nations and afforded access "to the Golden world" (10:6–7). As an emblem of the divided shores of America and Albion, the stage area of the action of the poem, this broken wall shows us also the remedy. The spirit of independence in living form can fill and mend the breach. Also, when the rock becomes Orc again, no chains will hold.

This and the simpler battlefield scene in Plate ii derive from Blake's *A Breach in a City the Morning after the Battle* (*Forms* Plate 23) exhibited in 1784 after the American war. That breach was heaped with bodies, a descending vulture screamed near (compare Plate 12), and four women and an old man searched the slain for signs of life. Blake now puts before us this vision of death as one we must search as he helps us replace it with a vision of life. When Orc looks up he will see the breach—the stone under his feet was the threshold of a gateway and could be so again—and that the "soul of America" is still alive (see *Visions* 1:3), Oothoon, with whom we may identify the naked female in this symbolic context. The climax of the prophecy will come in Plate 16 with the melting of Orc's chains, the "five gates" of the "law-built heaven" of throned tyrants (16:14–23), a melting that begins with the unlocking of human eyes and ears and voice.

(See *Forms* 92–114 for a more thorough analysis of *America,* though these notes contain new information and perspectives.)

America i[N]

America ii^{N}

America ii^{N} (Title page). On ground level the battlefield scene continues, with sleet or rain falling but sometimes* beams of light. This serializing of the picture leads us from stasis (Plate i) to active embracing, by a less symbolic man and woman: he still clutching his sword hilt on a heap of bodies, she clothed and confident that her kiss will wake him—to words which enter in an active cloud: the letters of "AMERICA" stiff, of *"a PROPHECY"* leaning forward. In the mental realm of the prophetic cloud a female and male philosopher are assisted by a page-turning child and three naked youths toward the reading of this prophecy. The alert female is already doing so, for the girl at her back is directing us, not her, to the subtitle and the battlefield. The male's reading requires redirection. The bodies rise to a crescendo in the leaping female who turns the page.

America 1K (Preludium 1). The poem beginning on Plate 3 presents a potentially cyclic revolution of rise and fall, rebellion and enslavement, threatening a perpetual dull round. The Preludium, added after the first etched state of the work, previews the revolution from a perspective that sees the cycle as capable of being melted—or breached like the stony wall of death.

The illumination of this page, which leaves one side open, can be read in either direction (see *Forms* 100). If we hurry from the headless worm of sixty winters (six coils) to the human form underground, sitting up but self-clutching, and move on, we see human bodies or torsos twining and rising but becoming less animal than vegetable, to emerge from the ground as a willow tree that must remain rooted to exist. Yet on the grassy surface lies a lusty young man who can look and speak up—but is chained in crucifixion to the rock, like the black rebel in Blake's engraving of *The Execution of "Breaking on the Rack."* That humans can stand up we see next in the Eve and Adam under the tree (of paradise, or of sorrow), who, however, cannot enjoy their freedom but hearing the youth's cry must turn and look back, as the women toward fallen warriors in Plates i and ii. This ironic sequence may seem to trap hope, risen from the worm, and send it back to the worm.

Right at Orc's foot this point is made by a three-coil miniature of the larger worm, and as we look down the page we may find its motif in the bottom line, "In vain!" Although interlinear ornament pervades the text, the effect is of a carpet rather than a garden. Loops, banners, zigzags attach to nearly every letter that stands above the line; a wind seems to be blowing leftward, but to be caught in stillness. Leafing and flowering vines hang quietly in the left margin (where root effects are prominent) and put forth leaves in the right. Unattached shapes are few, a bird above "awful" (8), a headless vine-serpent above "anon a serpent" (15)—a most feeble response—and two mere suggestions of birds near the banner on "eagle" (13). A tiny bird above "limbs" (16) is tied by a string.

(See *Four Zoas* 62 for a redrawing of this scene in illustration of the vain attempt of Los and Enitharmon to free Orc from the chain of Jealousy in which Los had bound him.)

America 1K

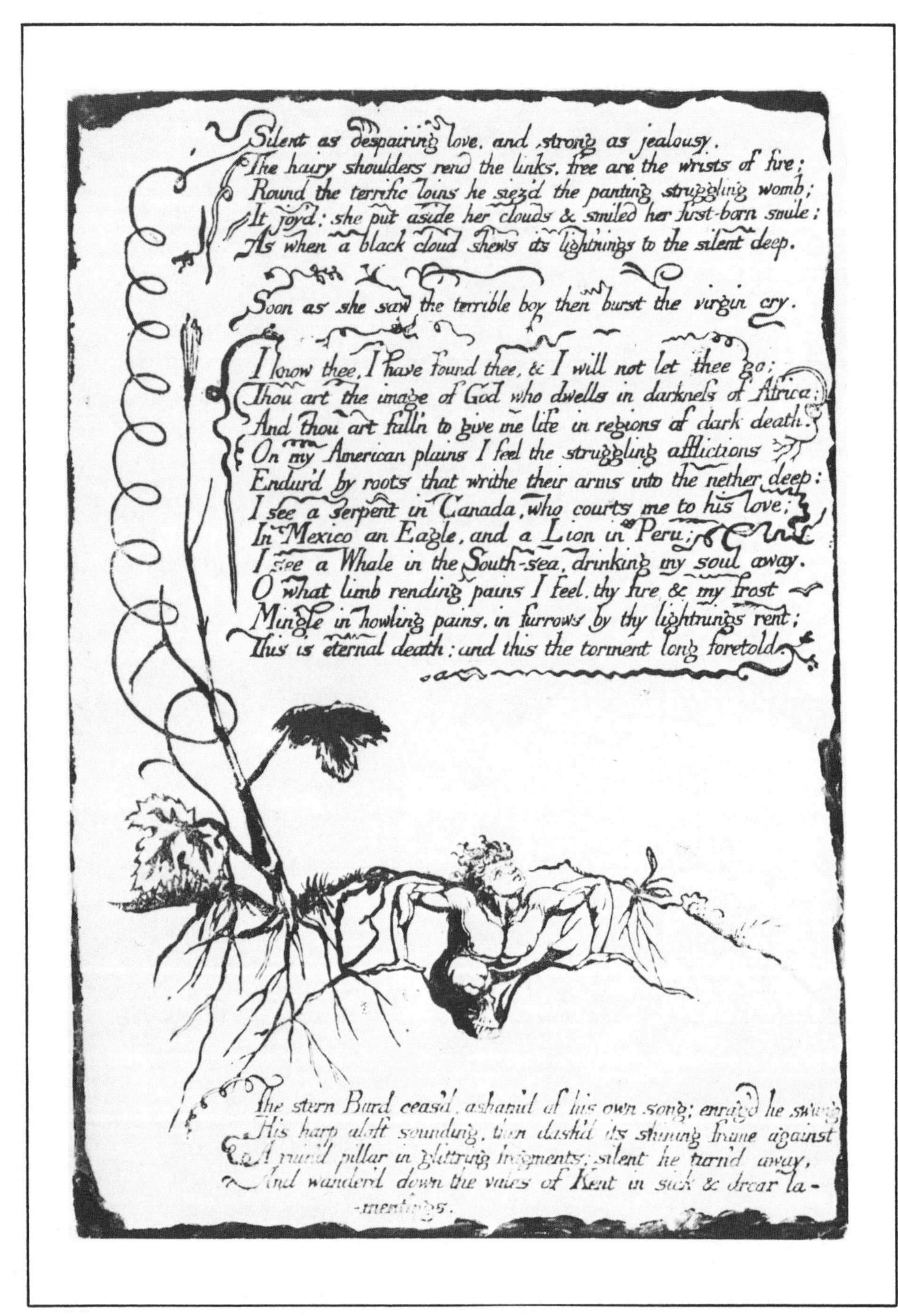

America 2[N]

America 2[N] (Preludium 2). Now, in text and pictures, action springs: life reaching from earth though rooted in it—a grape shooting up taller than Adam, a sprout of wheat, and Orc, free of chains, crouching in a furrow. That he can rise above the earth like a sun is hinted by a grace note of yellow light behind his head[M] or by sunlight on the open horizon[AK].

The grape stem bears an opening umbrella of future grapes; a heaven-scaling tendril of ten loops guides us to the text. In it the banners are fewer and blow both ways. Note "despairing love" (1) with a pattern of opposing impulses eloquently repeated in line 6—florally on "Soon . . . saw," like whips on the opposition of boy and virgin—more gently in 7, and so on. At the end, "foretold" sprouts clover leaves and a scroll of prophecy (compare *Marriage* 12). A complex of rooty scrolls grows down from "nether deep" (11); a bird flies below "away" (14); an acrobat leaps from one viper line to another above "I have found" (7) toward a scroll-seated figure above "I know." An almost-horse plunges beside a looped strap attached to "The hairy shoulders" (2).

The four lines of bardic denial, below the picture, were covered during the printing of most copies.

America 3N. At the top of the page Orc, flexing his left arm and rising swiftly as from the furrow of Plate 2, trails broken chains—sobering evidence that he did not bypass the slavery or crucifixion of Plate 1. At the bottom citizens running from flames reach up, needing to get there too. The title words ornamented with loving care seem Blake's most confidently enthusiastic; how swiftly he has brought us from the battlefield to this bright life: the five (or six) birds gaily colored*, the spikes of wheat green and golden*. "A" begins in a lily, mocks Orc's chains with a dangling bellflower, and ends in ripe wheat for an approaching lapwing (nearby a butterfly is added in brown ink[B]). *"PROPHECY"* is alive with prophetic tendrils (how mild the scrolls of *Marriage* 12 and 13 by comparison) with initial and medial lilies and three great deviant spirals, one springing *out from the page* from the central "O." Five birds (of course) fly in the word's spaces, including two birds of paradise, one singing.

The text begins with a sobered lily form (on "T") and a tendril on "Guardian" flattened from vine to viper, and then eschews ornament to make room for a naked soaring trumpeter blowing flames (a flag-bearer stood in these flames in cancelled plate a: see Appendix) and a lower crackling row of flame tops as of a burning coastal village (behind the text) from which three Americans escape, stand-ins for Orc and his parents of Plate 1.

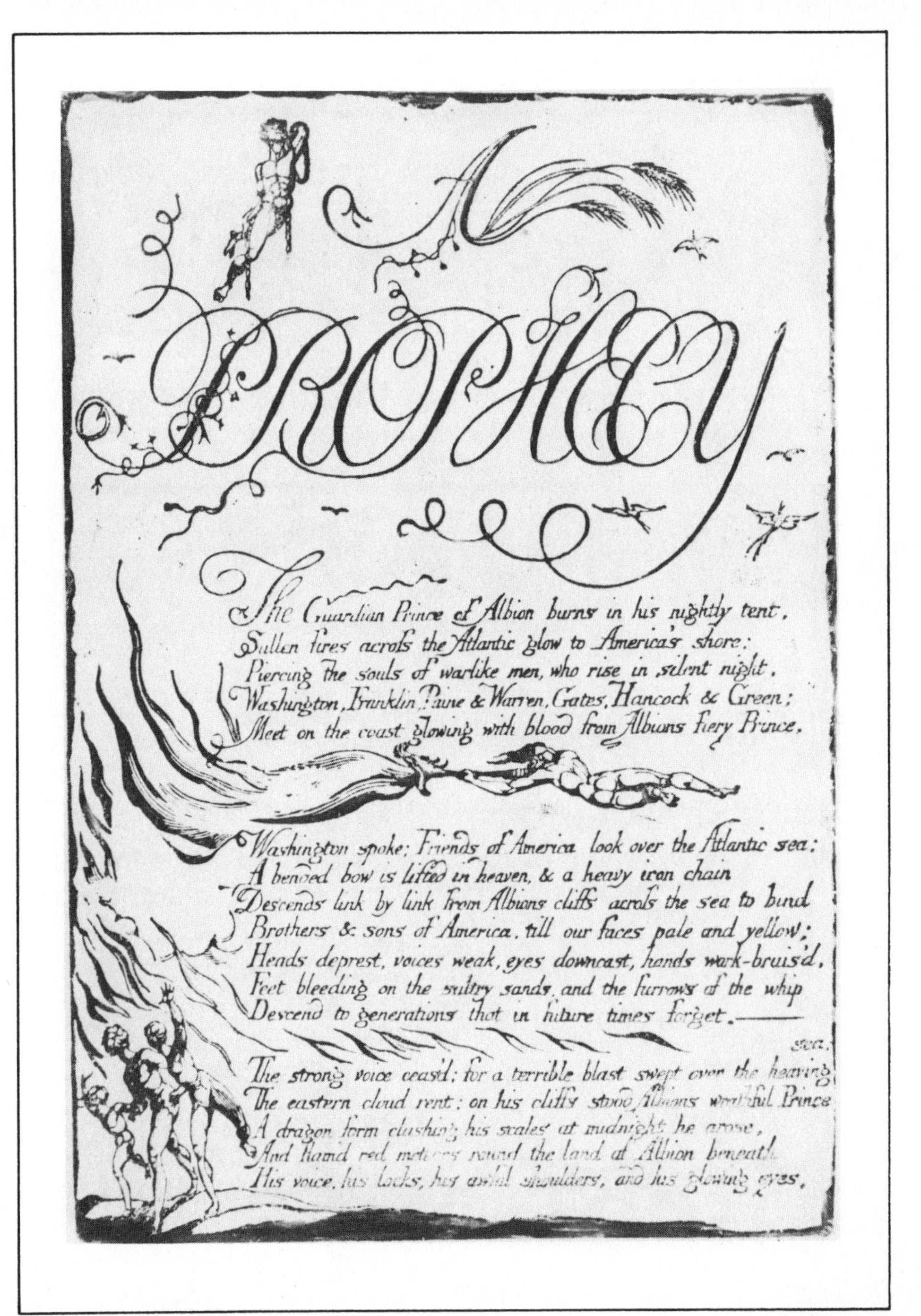

America 3N

America 4N

America 4N. The illustrations belong to (hence retain in the poem) lines not repeated from cancelled plate b (see Appendix). In the final text Albion's Prince (George III) arises "A dragon form" flaming round "the land of Albion" (3:15–16), and his voice, locks, shoulders, eyes "Appear to the Americans" (4:1). These features "Reveal the dragon thro' the human" in b:1, and before flying to America the king renews "his Angel form" to appear before an English Parliament. At the top we see his dragon form, revealed as human by its feeble human hands (compare the hands and feet of the Satanic bat in *Gates* 19). His angel form dives down the left margin, law book clutched behind his back, scepter held in his left hand like a magic wand. He is preceded and followed by lightning like a trademark of wrath. In his naked human form, below the clouds, he clutches his head and contemplates a beached sea monster (an orc or revolutionary whale: see 2:14). "The King of England looking westward trembles . . ." (12). His bearded counselor beside him seems to be looking up at the dragon and angel forms in the clouds—or perhaps only seeing the lightning (since "Shut out from mortal sight the Angel came" b:10). He shelters a young child (possibly twoM): compare the woman in Plate i; there are children on both sides in a war.

Behind the humans a huge oak bends down like the lodged wheat in Plate 9 or the forest crushed by a revolutionary tempest in *Song of Los* 6. With their lightning the dragon and angel forms sow the wind; the human forms (and the tree, of life) reap the whirlwind.

Kathleen Raine (I 117, fig 52) sees the dragon form as a basilisk (king-killer): "Has the falling aged figure of Urizen been killed by the glance of the basilisk (Orc?) . . . ?" The text and the aged hands of the man inside the dragon rule out the dragon-Orc identification. But Blake may be making ironic use of the legend: what kills the King will be his assumption of the dragon form of tyranny.

America 5N. Here is another contrast in perception. As the King enters the flames, still clutching his head in fear as in Plate 4, he sees the adversary as a coiled serpent awaiting him amid hellfire. (Compare the more literal violence of cancelled plate c: Appendix.) What we see (not mentioned in the text) is a revolutionary tribunal of three naked youths up in the heavens, like Orc risen in chains in Plate 3, with fiery sword and scales of justice. This progressive cartoon, unlike Plate 1, can be read in only one direction. At the top the King, bound, is tried and found wanting (compare Dante 37, *The Devil about to hurl a Magistrate into the Boiling Pitch Pool of Corrupt Officials*), then sent hurtling to the bottom, where his possibly decapitated body is encircled by a blood-red serpent with human face but forked tongue. Does the cloud on which the rebel holds the King signify that this is only a dream, a possibility? The King and Queen of France had recently (January 1793) been guillotined. Compared to *Song of Los* 6 or *Ahania* 6 (and see *Forms* 108) this picture is enigmatic; kings if they correct their vision in time, i.e. if they keep their heads, can—keep their heads.

It would help kings to study the two visions of prophetic coils, here and in Plate 2, visions respectively of fear and of hope. Fear moves geometrically downward in a vortex that tapers to nothing, to no return. Hope grows vitally upward in endless communication that expands into words and poetry; even though the first word the living vine produces may be "Silent," it ineluctably transvalues itself.

In line 4 "planet red" is preceded by a leafing banner and followed by a twisting vine ending in an angular leafless bush, a design as elusive as the whole epic simile it adorns.

America 5N

America 6N

America 6N. In this design, redrawn from *Marriage* 21, an older and sturdier young man emblematizes the text (below) of burst grave, redemption from slave labor: life, liberty, and the pursuit of happiness "in the bright air" (7). The sky above indicates "a fresher morning" (13), while the clouds backing man and text indicate that true independence when "Empire is no more" (15) is not yet more than a vision, a prophecy. The skull, moved to the man's right side and also looking up, more clearly suggests the dead self as of the same person; the open page under his right hand is gone, but a living book is indicated by two grape leaves below it and a six-leaved grapevine growing from the grave mound on the left, accompanied by a coiling tendril that starts off the pen or eye writing the words, and branches of delicate bellflowers (beside two more grape leaves) at the right: the whole group—leaves, flowers, mound, skull, and naked man—forming a half wreath about the text appropriate to its function as a monumental engraving of Blake's poetic version of the Revolutionary Declaration of Independence of 1776.

At the bottom a single thistle in flower bends down (like the tree in Plate 4) as if conceding that its "indignant . . . bitterness" (see the Blake *Concordance* and *French Revolution* 145 for the thistle as a symbol of oppression) "shall cease." Its companions—a redM salamander or eft darting his tongue at a fly and a brown toad confronting a wirey rearing viper—move about freely among flowers and grass, liberated from their traditional habitat as emblems of tyranny, the "dungeon" of "the inchained soul shut up in darkness and in sighing" (11, 9).

Has the thistle lost his prickles and become a harmless knapweed? The broad leaves and smooth stem say yes. (Compare Plate 9.)

America 7^{N}. Two naked children sleep on and beside a resting sheep (its eyes sometimes open^{K}) on a grassy flat ground beside still water, under a weeping birch with its drooping catkins in flower (used as a tree of paradise in *Night Thoughts* designs such as 244; more impressionistically rendered than the birches in *Thel*). In context this is an emblem of times of peace before the war and prophesied to follow the revolution; not in present times a suitable model for adults, whose sleeping may mean death: see Plates i and ii.

Three birds of paradise (with split tails) sit in the branches (two painted red^{K} or red and yellow^{M}), another (purple^{M}) flies upward among them, as does a large moth or butterfly. Two distant birds approach. Between tree and sheep a large grape leaf springs on a coiled stem from the grass; another lies at the water's edge at lower right. (Contrast the large leaf in *Thel* 6 below the serpent bearing children.) Rays of sunlight—certainly sunrise—are indicated by five radial lines, the spaces between them painted in rainbow colors in M, replaced by horizontal color in K.

(Compare the lioness and lion with naked children sleeping and awake in *Songs* 36.)

America 7^{N}

America 8N

America 8N. If this is Urizen above all heavens (16:3), the divine form of George III, why is he looking upM or up left? After all, he has just addressed Orc as a rebel in the deep and is now listening to "the terror's" answer (see text). The reason must be that he fears that the adversary may be above him, that he sees Orc rising in fire and feels himself sinking to the ocean, whose waves are only the distance of seventeen lines of text below him, and turbulent. His looking offstage left is like Bromion's in *Visions* i. In other words—and this may be a hopeful sign—he does not really believe his own phantasy of human rebellion as a Leviathan in the deep (see *Marriage* 20). Orc in Plate 10, in a stance that seems the mirror opposite of this, also looks to the left, but somewhat downward (confirming the impression that he is rising higher than the tyrant). In fact the mirror effect is momentary; Orc's right leg (hidden in some copiesKM) is lower and he is springing up, not sitting (or sinking) like Urizen. Hence Urizen's extended arms are, like the clutching king's, holding tight as well as marking possession and power. Compare also the arms resting on his stony law in *Urizen* 28. Compare also *Milton* 18.

America 9N. The ripe wheat lodged by a heavy storm marks the efforts of British soldiers ("my punishing Demons") to "smite the wheat" and "quench the fatness of the earth" (3–5). But it arches leftward, making shelter for a "new born child" (as the French Revolution is called in the Fayette poem: *P&P* 491), dead white in some copiesM, living pink in othersK. This is a symbolic variant of the battlefield pictures of Plates i and ii adapted to the immediate text.

Bright green* wild flowers continue to grow among the wheat as though no storm had blown. Fresh stems to bear new flowers are shooting up on each side of the child. The base leaves look somewhat like those of the knapweed or thistle on Plate 6, but it is poppies that grow (legendarily a sign of good farming) among the wheat; the flower that looks like this in old herbals is the daucus criticus that "groweth in wheat," with a purple flower and leaves like a wild poppy but whiter. Blake adapts the stems to his prophetic tendrils.

The marginal ornaments along the right side consist largely of flowering plants or vines growing or falling downward, a motif of contradictory effects which begins with the first two words, where the whips on the first "Sound!" (of the king's war cry) are challenged by a reverse whip on the second "sound!" (1).

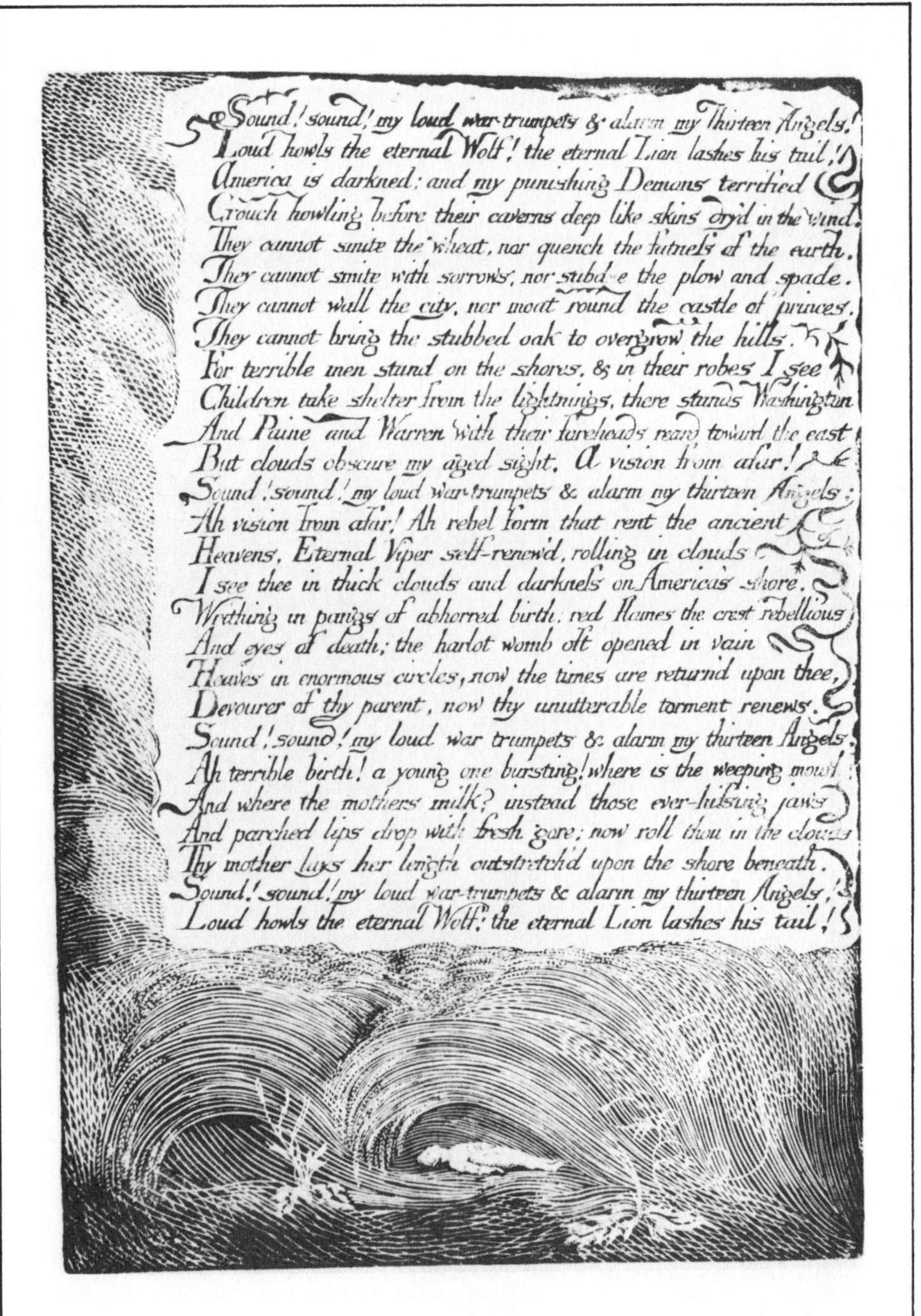

Sound! sound! my loud war-trumpets & alarm my Thirteen Angels!
Loud howls the eternal Wolf! the eternal Lion lashes his tail!
America is darkned; and my punishing Demons terrified
Crouch howling before their caverns deep like skins dry'd in the wind.
They cannot smite the wheat, nor quench the fatness of the earth.
They cannot smite with sorrows, nor subdue the plow and spade.
They cannot wall the city, nor moat round the castle of princes.
They cannot bring the stubbed oak to overgrow the hills.
For terrible men stand on the shores, & in their robes I see
Children take shelter from the lightnings, there stands Washington
And Paine and Warren with their foreheads reard toward the east
But clouds obscure my aged sight. A vision from afar!
Sound! sound! my loud war-trumpets & alarm my thirteen Angels:
Ah vision from afar! Ah rebel form that rent the ancient
Heavens; Eternal Viper self-renew'd, rolling in clouds
I see thee in thick clouds and darkness on America's shore.
Writhing in pangs of abhorred birth; red flames the crest rebellious
And eyes of death; the harlot womb oft opened in vain
Heaves in enormous circles, now the times are return'd upon thee,
Devourer of thy parent, now thy unutterable torment renews.
Sound! sound! my loud war trumpets & alarm my thirteen Angels!
Ah terrible birth! a young one bursting! where is the weeping mouth!
And where the mothers milk? instead those ever-hissing jaws
And parched lips drop with fresh gore; now roll thou in the clouds
Thy mother lays her length outstretch'd upon the shore beneath.
Sound! sound! my loud war-trumpets & alarm my thirteen Angels!
Loud howls the eternal Wolf! the eternal Lion lashes his tail!

America 9N

America 10ᴺ

❧

America 10ᴺ. Orc answering Urizen (of Plate 8: see note) looks rather downward though shown (as Urizen imagines him) in flames of hell. In Blake's account of the war it is "Albions Angel" who in fear of the flames of rebellion launches war (Plate 9) and spreads "the red flames of Orc" among the citizens of New York, Boston, Pennsylvania, Virginia (14:11–16). The flames beating up against the four lines of text at the top threaten to ignite "the Colonies," but they "refuse the loud alarm."

Orc's left leg imitates (or is imitated by) Urizen's right, in Plate 8, but Orc is not squatting on his right leg (as Urizen must be on his left); he extends it for climbing. Both figures stretch out their arms, Urizen to hold on to his clouds, Orc to encourage his flames (if also to climb: for a more passive invitation to flames, see *Marriage* 3). Their contrasting nakedness and heavy clothing, snaky red* hair and smooth white hair and beard, enforce the life and death contrasts of fire and cloud, freedom and Empire, that structure the whole prophecy. Orc is also present to Urizen on Plate 8 in that the text below Urizen is Orc's reply to his challenge. "The visibly stony womb of plate 8 encloses Orc's apocalypse, with Urizen sitting over it like a hen on an egg, until two plates later it 'gives birth' to fiery Orc, as though verbal seeds had burst into visionary flames" (George Quasha in *Forms* 280–81; see also Janet Warner in *Forms* 180–82). Orc's hair and facial expression suit the description and function of Los in *Europe* 15:9–11: "Then Los arose his head he reard in snaky thunders clad: And with a cry that shook all nature . . . Call'd all his sons to the strife of blood." For in *America* it is Orc who exercises the prophet's concern (Los not yet being invented, though we find his picture in the Adam of Prelude 1) to cry out upon "Empire" and "the Lion & Wolf" (6:15) and arouse the inhabitants and all resources.

America 11N. Text and pictures grow specific. In the speech by Boston's Angel (Samuel Adams in Congress in 1774 calling for "Independence": see *Prophet* 24[26]) the speaker stands above his word "commanded" (7) which shoots up a goatish squiggle behind him, and a horse comes running to his (or Paul Revere's) aid (from *Marriage* 27). Behind him the words "what," "God," and "Angel" extrude mere empty banners. In the larger scene the swan and serpent, already bridled and mounted, hasten from Albion's fires, the British bombardment of coastal towns, to safer homes inland (compare the family running from flames in Plate 3). The adult rider of the swan—continuing the naked Orc-Los image of Plate 10 (the poet himself in disguise, too, like Horace: see *Jerusalem* 11)—may be taken as Adams (the label "Bostons Angel" standing just above his head), or as Tom Paine whose "pen" is mentioned (14:15), for this must be a pen swan, or as Revere riding to spread the alarm.

Both swan and snake are of course serpentine images of Orc (see 1:13–15, 2:12–14), as the five small birds above and below "the energies" (10) remind us. And the two large birds of paradise accompanied by four smaller birds, seen against clouds near the swan and above the serpent, show that the flight inland can be reversed toward paradise (the Atlantic Mountains), a message reinforced by hopeful signs in the "dark night" (3), the pleiades at the left (seven stars and an eighth) and a new moon and star (Venus?) near the serpent's mouth. In contrast to the child-carrying serpent in *Thel* 6, who is horned, green-faced*, and glaring and points his tongue forward (to the left), this serpent smiles, points upward, is attentive to us and his riders (with the middle child more securely mounted and sunnier toward his brother). John Howard has called my attention to the traditional interpretation of the serpentine Dolphin carrying a naked child on its coiling, scaly back as representing "Safety" or freedom from danger. (For some reason the serpent in this plate was originally etched with three tails, remnants of which are still visible.)

America 11N

America 12N

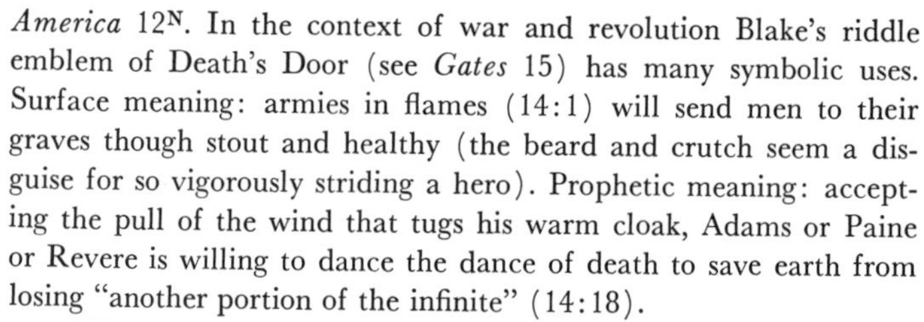

America 12N. In the context of war and revolution Blake's riddle emblem of Death's Door (see *Gates* 15) has many symbolic uses. Surface meaning: armies in flames (14:1) will send men to their graves though stout and healthy (the beard and crutch seem a disguise for so vigorously striding a hero). Prophetic meaning: accepting the pull of the wind that tugs his warm cloak, Adams or Paine or Revere is willing to dance the dance of death to save earth from losing "another portion of the infinite" (14:18).

What happens inside the tomb? Thick foliage flourishes on the birch that rises above its hewn stones and oaken door. And the angle of the strong trunk (looking, at its rooty base, like the beached orc of Plate 4) exactly parallels the angle of the man's backbone—and the angle of flight of the birds of paradise in Plate 11. But what of the scarred and evidently topless second tree? A mate of the living birch, its bark stripped; not bending so far, did it break instead? Emblem of a king's fate? The clouds in the lower background suggest storm.

America 13N. Here Blake depicts the Atlantic center of his prophetic stage, with the once bright "Atlantean hills" (10:6) sunk to a tidal rock. On it and at sea bottom he displays the physical and mental horrors of war as felt by female and male bodies (see a later depiction in *Jerusalem* 58). In the text the end is in sight as "British soldiers thro' the thirteen states" begin to surrender (6), but the pictures show the darkest hour of human anguish. We may think we have seen the "soft soul of America" before, preyed upon by an eagle, but that was only a soft concept (*Visions* 3) of the reality: there is no cloud "frame" here. Oothoon's vulture was just an idea, without talons and only swooping toward her, assisting a rhetorical gesture toward a jealous lover. Here the eagle is upon her with blood on its wingsN (and isn't that a strip of flesh under its beak?); and the surf is at her thigh. Her head flung back and arm dangling lifeless, she is in a swoon which Blake will remember for the sleep of Jerusalem in the title page (see *Jerusalem* 2); both are serious versions of Fuseli's melodramatic *Nightmare*. Prophetically, if the inchained soul will wake and laugh at the eagle, that genius will do wonders of illumination to outstrip the swan. (For a simpler version see Plate c: Appendix.)

From the same perspective the war victim at sea bottom is letting himself be immobilized by the helpless feeling one gets under water; he hasn't been eating (notice those ribs), and his fingers are turning into claws or taking root in the sea floor! If the boa constrictor around his legs (kin of the serpent on Plate 11, from its face) and the three open-mouthed fish and a water snake can sufficiently frighten him into his senses (symbolized by five close-mouthed fish swimming in the other direction below the text) he will be in time to join the rushing together of inhabitants in the next page. (Two blueK whelks and two or three twisty eels or water snakes assist.)

In the left margin beside roots or vines connecting upper and lower scenes, an upright viper "speaks" to Oothoon's palm and guides us to a row of hieroglyphs about the English Governors' "Shaking their mental chains" (3–4): one governor sitting on the edge of a leafy divan (this is how a governor would surrender) reaches his left hand toward a half-scroll (his recall or his resignation) brought by a fairy secretary. The "rush" that follows sprouts helter-skelter foliage, then two leaves being measured by an inchworm.

America 13N

America 14N

America 14N. The good news—that the Americans' standing firm causes the plagues to disobey the voice of Albion's Angel and to recoil—is accompanied by many small loops and banners. A scroll-gowned figure soaring above "flames" points to a bowknot of grain and blossom on "stood," followed by a sort of centaur on "view'd," blossoming in each direction, then a pinkM swallow, a multiple leaf, a dancing half-human flame, a greenM banner, and a bright redM double banner—matched in color by a large redM flame in the bottom left corner which is uttered like laughter by an abbreviated serpent. A redM bird of paradise flies up leftward between scrolls attached to "been lost" and "fire" (17, 19).

But the page is dominated by a hideous tree monster, leafless, leaning over the scene with left arm up, right arm cut off—or is that the arm of a birch trunk behind the monster? Its roots run down to resist "fire" with an angry knee and claw toward the laughing serpent. Behind it the clouds swag heavier and uglier. Under its barren branches a young scholar, kept ignorant of the bright flames, not opening the testaments under his elbow (the upper volume showing a gleaming* leather spine, the lower its front edge), worshipfully accepts instruction from a death-preaching sibyl. Her thumb and fingers demonstrate that life is but a span. From her womb speaks a lean but eloquent serpent, one of the monsters of error that breed in the womb of Moral Virtue (see *Prophet* 204–6, 240[221–23, 260]). Compare Orc's early instruction by the "shadowy daughter" (1:1) before he broke his chains. The cowled sibyl we shall see, reduced to more enigmatic communication, in *Gates* 16; we shall come to recognize her in *Jerusalem* as Vala, spanning again in Plate 4 and generally committed to mortality and morality, turning prophetic clouds to intestines of greed.

America 15[K]. At this point the poem gets so excited that it makes almost as much use of pictures as of words. While the text details the effects of the fire and plague of disobedience in England, the interlinear pictures show us what happens in Bristol and London when the spirit of Empire sickens and the soldiers "cast their swords & spears to earth" (5). Their wives and children greet them, and their brothers embrace them. A large bird with curving wings flies up over "Albions Angels" (1). In line 3 a liberated horse bears the news that "Albions Guardian" is collapsing, and under that phrase a boy and man greet each other on a bracket built of the "d" of "Londons"—a minuscule version of the man and urchin of the "London" illustration (*Songs* 46). Someone sits waiting on a looping, trumpet-like vine growing from "Spirit," and a welcoming committee of eight pigeons fly up, barked at by a dog held on invisible leash by a woman half sitting on a hill-line drawn down from "plague" (2). Another pigeon is near the first banner from "bands" (i.e. troops), above which a reformed eagle flies upward—waved at or pointed toward by a tall, skirted (or tree-like?) figure followed by a man tossing a child. In the space following "threw off their hammerd mail" a blasted stump shelters a cat and dog beside two men rushing together with open arms, counterpointing the phrase above them ("howl of anguish"). For comparable rejoicing see the freed chimney sweepers in *Songs* 12. A strong line under this whole scene attaches securely to "earth" (5) and proceeds to put forth a grape leaf. Figures bracketed by strokes above the next words are (a) leaping forward mightily and (b) reclining in peace: both serving as human forms of the gaily flapping banners on the words "naked multitude." Below the latter word is a soaring trumpeter, to arouse us all.

An inverted "V" like the mitre on a chimney joins the words "ancient" and "miter'd" (9) (preceding which a bent-winged vulture appears, suggesting the bird we thought an eagle in line 1). The paragraph ends with a diagonal viper above "sky" paralleled by a spike of yellow barely from the "y." In the break two humans wide apart reach toward each other across a gulph occupied by scroll and whip-like banners on "snowy" and "plagues." There are also a flowering and an eagle-winged banner and two birds in the break; yet for the rest of the text area the motif of "burning winds . . . flames of Orc" departs from human illustration. The flowering banner, attached to "winds," suggests flames; the eagle wing is on "driven"; other banners suggest reptiles and zigzag lightning. A

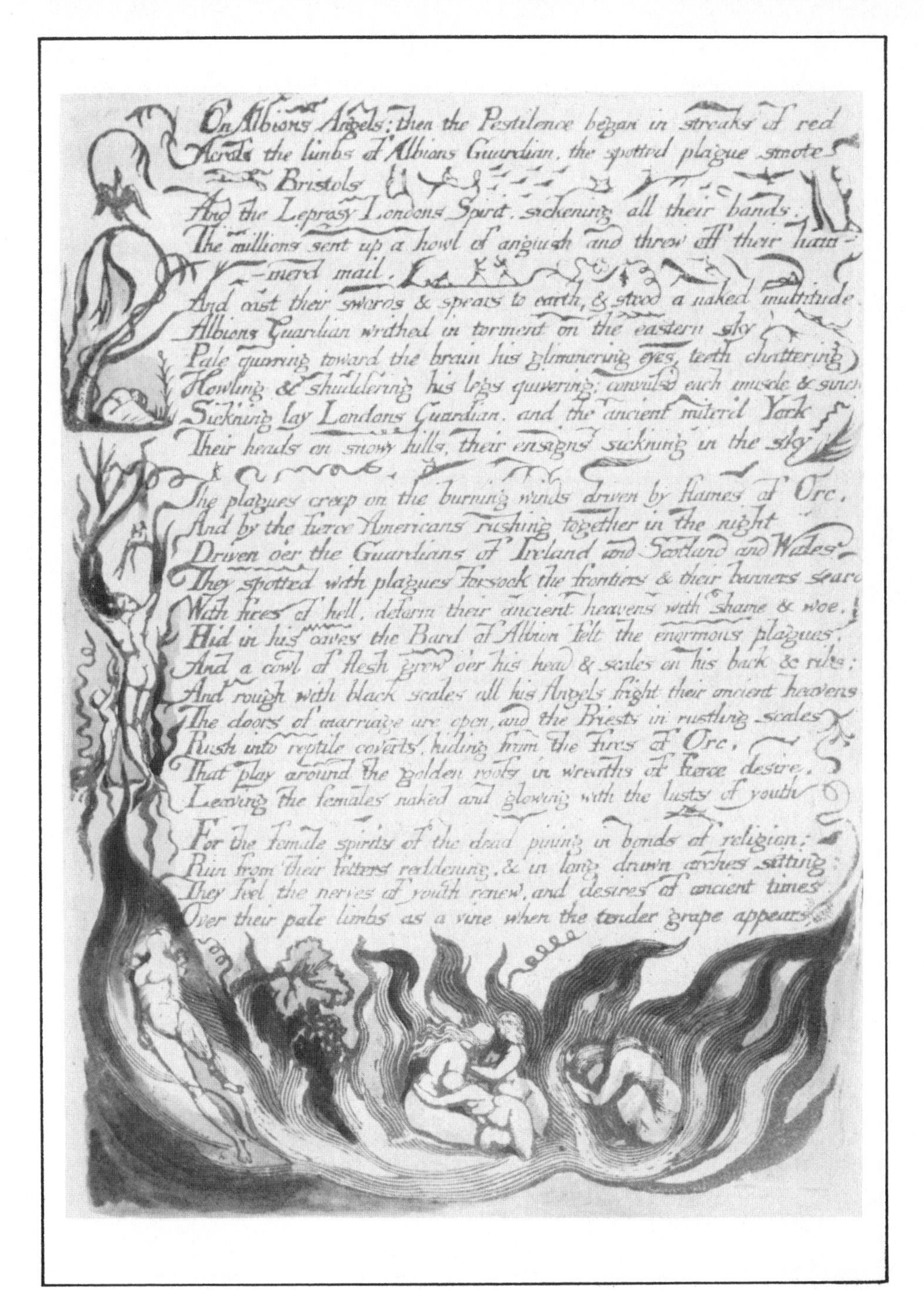

America 15[K]

America 16N

free soaring viper darts against the wind above "enormous" (16); another wind flower, with three red buds, hangs down from "scales" (19). Birds continue—three tiny ones in lines 12 and 15, two larger ones in the next break, the central bird an eagle hovering, or flying right at us, under "glowing." Coming toward it, as if also flying, is a leaping stag that makes a line from "religion" (beside which a moth flutters) to "lusts."

One civil effect of the end of combat—that the "doors of marriage are open" (19)—is illustrated in the larger pictures, in the bottom and left margins. Read as a cartoon progressing from bottom right to upper left (see *Forms* 104), the thawing combination of flames, ripening grapes, and "females naked and glowing" (22) begins with a self-enclosed single girl, then a cluster of three, self-involved (if they have a secret child they are not showing it, though in copy M the woman reaching in is given a face looking out), then an open woman (yet with left hand behind her back) rising in a rising flame, then a Daphne dendrifying beside an enrooting child; finally, on the earth's surface, a small, clothed female still "pining in bonds of religion" (23). Read, however, as a cross section (like *Marriage* 1) of quiet on the green surface and "desires of ancient times" erupting from below, the woman rising in flames is an Oothoon rising to melt away the "bolts and hinges" (16:22) from the wooden gates of Daphne and family (note the mother and child on her wooden right arm, a link with the returning soldier theme) and to dispell the "mildews of despair" (16:20) inhibiting the bowed woman on the surface. Beside Daphne the naked boy enrooting is nevertheless holding up a large flame (paralleled by a viper tendril behind him), such as the vagabond's flame in *Songs* 19 and 46. And beside the bowed woman there is already a sunflower ready to bloom when she looks up (miniature of the sunflower in *Night Thoughts* 87, engraving 26). The tree and vine at her back are ready to open out for Paradise (compare the tree and beginning vine on Plate 7), and the eagle in the treetop is auspiciously looking straight up and prepared to fly, reversed from his vulture role in Plate 13. (The eagle on the curving vegetation is also a mutation of the eagle collaborating with the serpent in *Marriage* 15.)

America 16[N]. Approached through this reading of Plates 14 and 15, the mysterious figure here, whose hair provides the Niagara Falls for the tale of Urizen's "icy magazines" that halted the spread of the Revolution, can be seen as a conflation of the worshipful male of 14 and the bowed female of 15 (compare the conflation of persons toward the end of *Jerusalem*), now enlarged for us to see that all the apparently "blasting fancies and . . . mildews" (20) are metaphors of hope. The four blasted human trees, one headless yet with a branch-arm pointing prophetically onward, are renewing their "nerves of youth." The world which the bowed praying human will inhabit when the gates limiting perception are consumed is etched for *us* to see on the frozen body itself: lovers embracing against the bare toes, a savior stag rearing (above the word "rage") on the calf, a flock of sheep with resting shepherd on the line between calf and thigh, four sheep and a dog on the next level, where a spreading tree, like the one on Plate 15 opened out, grows from the sexual center and accommodates the leaning body of the piping poet of innocence (his hat brim a bit shorter than in *Songs* 3). At the top a seminar is gathering (compare *Marriage* 24). A robed young woman with a book watches a young man who seems to be flying a kite—or pointing to the invisible eagle. The man sitting on the head, whom we saw in the title page, must now be reading *America,* too absorbed to notice the waterfall or the "FINIS" sign below.

That sign, written on the body of a serpent (and sometimes cancelled[M]), lets him put paid to the shuddering thrones and the cold mists. Coiling among thorny but blossoming red* roses, his head another rosebud, he directs his tongue in the proper prophetic position (see *Marriage* 15, where he points his tail). And as our eyes adjust to their tiny fairy size, we see other human forms very much alive: a woman walking the thorny branch toward the rose at the serpent's mouth, a man shaking or waving a small rose or leaf[M] under "flames," and someone diving toward the flamy scroll in the left corner. (See also *Forms* 104–5.)

(See Appendix for Plates a, b, c.)

For the stag symbolism, see the stag above the right hand of Raphael in the Boston version of *The Archangel Raphael with Adam and Eve.*

EUROPE A PROPHECY

(Reduced from about 9 by 7 inches)

Ten of the twelve extant copies (plus proofs designated a and b) have been examined. Plate iii occurs in only two copies. Retouched versions of Plate ii are reproduced in the Appendix, pages 396–98, below.

Different copies are illuminated in quite different color schemes, but there are few significant variants in the details of coloring.

Europe i[I] (frontispiece). When the Almighty "took the golden Compasses" in his hand to circumscribe universe and creatures, "One foot he centred, and the other turn'd" (*Paradise Lost* VII 224–28). How his outreaching hand may find whereon to fix one of his compasses' feet in that "vast profundity obscure" we may wonder. But his human form has been given, by his creator Blake, one centered foot (the right, bearing his body) and one free to do some turning: though knee and foot already mark the bound of his disk world—a sun (possibly a shield covering a sun) which rays out from it (or from behind it). A strong lateral wind in his beard and hair shows this opening in the clouds to be a moment in the storm of eternity. Yet we can see that art transcending time has fixed this vision, that beneath the shifting color masses of the clouds an engraver with tools as pointed as the compasses has fixed their shapes with infinite labor of cross-hatching.

As a portrait of Urizen this shows him in his finest hour, in solitude. (Contrast his self-reflectivity in *Urizen* 1, his worship of his own abstract obscurities in *Song of Los* 1, his slanging match with Orc in *America* 8.) Blake once thought to put him into the title page with his contrary the serpent (see *Europe* ii a, Appendix), trying to write his laws while riding the coiled monster. But a greater confrontation of reason and energy or desire is this Newton-like assumption that the black abyss is a tabula rasa, this brave pretence that seeking to "bind the infinite" (2:13—see *Notebook* 96) does not presuppose a leviathan who needs binding (or bounding) "even at the cost of every thing that breathes" (as Urizen will come to feel: *Four Zoas* VIII).

The potential heart shape in the clouds behind his beard is emphasized in strawberry red in copy C—a phenomenon outside Uri-

Europe i[I]

zen's realm, yet taking the sun's strongest light. His own regal assumption of prophetic power is quietly indicated by the royal purple[G] (or white: Whitworth Institute print) edge of his garment visible beside his left foot (compare the garment on John the Baptist's knee in *All Religions Are One* i).

(In the British Museum there is a drawing of this picture, obviously a forgery, which brings the right hand forward out of balance.)

The power of this emblem is beyond satire because the artist is not outside the picture but in its core, simultaneously demonstrating the control required to "frame" living forms and, like Canute, slyly exposing the absurdity of imposing a "just Circumference" (*Paradise Lost* VII 31).

Europe ii[I] (title page). A living form from the abyss, partly resting on flame-like leaves, his tail too long to fit the printed page, the adversary rears his coiling force into the heavens, borrowing rainbow colors from the sun and clouds of Plate i. Embodying energy, desire, phallic power, the fiery tongue, he turns his back on the geometer, looks us directly in the eye, and points on up into the Prophecy we must study.

The lettering of "*EUROPE*" can be read in either direction, as the forward-springing coils on *E* and the backward-pulling trumpet tugging on *R* (colored like vegetation) imply. Will the serpentine prophetic movement which has enlivened the first three letters sweep on through the second three, or will the stiffness in those spread back to freeze all "*EUROPE*" solid? "PROPHECY" remains cold stone—unless we read on. Hills, lighter in the distance, and dawning light in some copies (simple grey hills in C and H) suggest more going on ahead than behind; and the letter E formed by the upright coils of the serpent's body stands out against clear sky, to imply an identification of his open mouth as a prophetic trumpet. (In B a trumpet mouth is added to the coils on "E" to parallel the serpent's mouth.)

The title plunges us into geography and prophetic history and the year 1794. We shall find that the text focusses on events in London in 1792 (see *Prophet* chapters 9 and 12), leading to war with the Republic of France in January 1793, colored by the English antijacobinism of 1794. The theme is of ideological war turned into a "strife of blood" (16:11), of war, launched to circumscribe Albion from the outer darkness of France and its dark but red revolution, accompanied by suppressions and jailings in England that may, nonetheless, mature an English jacobinism.

Europe ii[I]

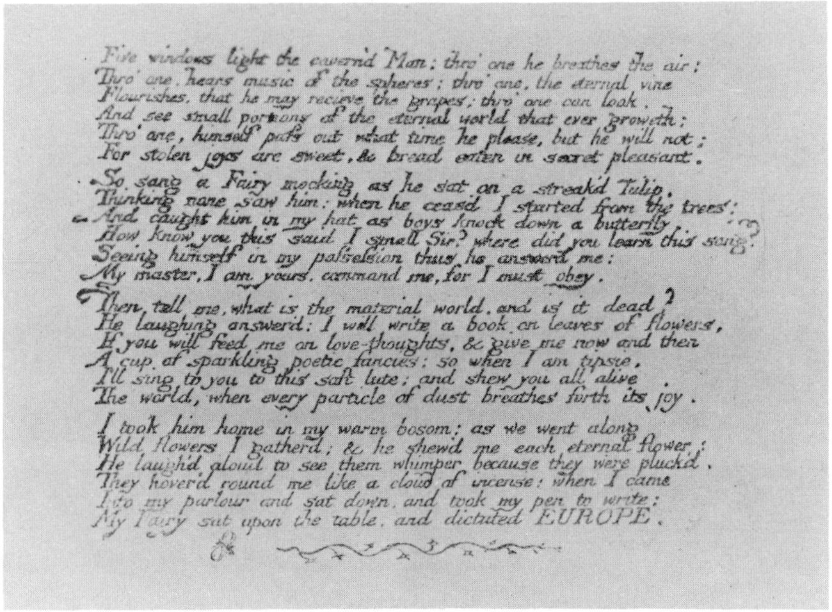

Five windows light the cavern'd Man; thro' one he breathes the air;
Thro' one, hears music of the spheres; thro' one, the eternal vine
Flourishes, that he may recieve the grapes; thro' one can look.
And see small portions of the eternal world that ever groweth;
Thro' one, himself pass out what time he please, but he will not;
For stolen joys are sweet, & bread eaten in secret pleasant.

So sang a Fairy mocking as he sat on a streak'd Tulip,
Thinking none saw him: when he ceas'd I started from the trees;
And caught him in my hat as boys knock down a butterfly.
How know you this said I small Sir? where did you learn this song?
Seeing himself in my possession thus he answerd me:
My master, I am yours. command me, for I must obey.

Then tell me, what is the material world, and is it dead?
He laughing answer'd: I will write a book on leaves of flowers,
If you will feed me on love-thoughts, & give me now and then
A cup of sparkling poetic fancies; so when I am tipsie,
I'll sing to you to this soft lute; and shew you all alive
The world, when every particle of dust breathes forth its joy.

I took him home in my warm bosom: as we went along
Wild flowers I gatherd; & he shew'd me each eternal flower:
He laugh'd aloud to see them whimper because they were pluck'd.
They hover'd round me like a cloud of incense: when I came
Into my parlour and sat down, and took my pen to write:
My Fairy sat upon the table, and dictated EUROPE.

Europe iii^H (reduced proportionally)

Europe iii^H (preface). The question "where did you learn this song?" (10) brings the first flourish, of viper loops on the question mark. The tails on y's tend to quaver, also, especially on "I am *y*ours" (12) and "M*y* Fair*y*" (24). The closing ornament, a small "butterfly" (9) as easy to knock down as a Fairy, and a sustained undulation of sharp-leaved ivy, only very slyly prepares us for the gigantic effects that follow, more solemnly adumbrated by the man-in-the-sun in the frontispiece who is trying to catch the universe or create it, and the tongue-darting serpent in the title page who saves half his coils for the struggling times. This Fairy found sitting "on a streak'd Tulip" (7) seems as detached from the *Europe* he dictates (24) as do the fairies sitting in the center of the *Song of Los* (see below) seem from the *Africa* and *Asia* that enclose them.

Copy K has a sort of muted sunburst effect (or explosion) at bottom right, with rays in sepia brush strokes, and some sprinkled gold. This prefatory plate is found only in copies H and K, the latter on paper watermarked 1818–20, the former perhaps dating around 1800. The etching of the plate, with idiosyncratic serifs on the g's, can have been done as late as 1803. Thus the poem may be a late addition, though it may have been made early and held back and only selectively published, like the bardic quatrain on *America* 2. Copy L, lacking it, on paper dated 181[3?], may precede copy K. That it did not show up when the posthumous copy (M) was printed gives some support to the *Census* hypothesis (p 79) that the plate was mislaid.

❧

Europe 1^I (Preludium 1). The youthful traveller, equipped like Bunyan's Christian (in his opening dream) but dressed in the buff and blue of George Washington adopted by the Foxite Whigs of the 1790s—for we are plunged at once into political prophetic caricature with idiom borrowed from the prints of James Gillray (see *Prophet* Plates Va, b)—had better take note of "The Assassin" (George Cumberland's caption for this page) lurking in the windy cave, i.e. Parliament, where Edmund Burke (whose profile this is) flourished a dagger in a Jacobin-baiting speech in December 1792. Unless the watchful pilgrim, now looking offstage, discovers the villainy of this unshaven[DEG], slope-browed, cross-legged trickster, he will fall into as gloomy a depression as the self-clutching figure below, wrapped in backward flung if somewhat forward looping prophetic scrolls. Clued by Gillray's caricature of Charles Fox in the Slough of Despond, we can see this gloomy figure as Fox (the likeness fairly strong in K). Batwings, like the devil's in *Marriage* 10, show his potential for flying—and note the ten birds in the abyss beside him, the only sky on the page.

The pilgrim's left hand behind his back suggests reserves to draw upon. The assassin points upward as if threatening to despatch him to heaven (an irony: the right direction properly understood) but expects him to plummet in manacles like a slave—as shown in the abyss beside Fox. (Even this manacled figure, painted black in two copies, blue with black iron in a third[D], is struggling with his legs.) We see the traveller (perhaps) twice more: first jailed, stripped, and shackled but evidently not defeated (in Plate 13)—one of the stout citizens jailed for the trials of '94—and then in Plate 15 busy saving women and children.

Of the contrasting foliage at the top, the boughs over the cave are probably oak; they suggest hair on the cave-skull, with Burke sitting in the eye cavity (compare *Visions* 1). All vines in the text area hang or turn downward but twist like vipers. One vine supports an infant viper (or two) (or a black caterpillar[D]) at the intersection above the slave's right foot. The small flies (two in the air), a cabbage moth on the fruiting vine at right and a spider directly left of it, a dragon fly at line 12, and the black birds (two more at right: all perhaps ravens: compare *Marriage* 27) are emblems of corruption; more will follow. The "day of dismal thunder" (7) has clouds, lightning, and up-thrusting two-forked vegetation. The large leaves, sometimes blue* (green[D]), at the traveller's heel are like the leaf below the serpent in *Thel* 6.

Europe 1^I

Europe 2ᴵ

Europe 2ᴵ (Preludium 2). The traveller reader who gets this far will take some encouragement from the text, where the balance between "shady woe, and visionary joy" (12) is tipped toward joy by five birds flying (with two more above "vig'rous progeny" 8). After "milk and honey?" three birds fly, but then a wavy vine is choked or crossed out by something, and a corkscrew pointing toward "ceast" gives finality to "my voice is past" (16). In the cloud-borne scene we are shown what Cumberland's gloss interprets as convulsions occurring in Parliament ("Where . . . imprison'd tempests rave") which produce "Horror, Amazement, and Despair" in "hideous forms": three statesmen, naked and minus their wigs, in a power struggle in which the cool one (pink skin*) holds vised in his right arm an opponent turned green*, while he strangles another turned blue* and howling. (In C the coloring is more natural, but the first victim is yellowing, the second turning green.) We may think of the color changes of the angel in *Marriage* 23 who, scandalized by radical blasphemies, becomes "almost blue." It is of course the three victims of the strangling tyrant who translate as Horror, Amazement, and Despair.

The scene recalls young Hercules strangling serpents in his cradle; in a cartoon of 1784 Gillray had identified "The Infant Hercules" as the young William Pitt, boy wonder become prime minister, strangling two political opponents. In the text we will find Pitt's expulsion of the Lord High Chancellor Thurlow from the cabinet, and the effect on his wig. (See *Prophet* 197–200[214–17].) Yet the strangler looks more like Dundas, Pitt's right-hand man, while a close graphic analogy is Gillray's "The Impeachment, or, 'The Father of the Gang, turnd King's Evidence'" (May 1791), in which Burke stands between Sheridan and Fox and seizes them by their wigs.

The fourth naked man, escaping up the cloud bank, is clutching his black hair with tightly flexed fingers—like Burke's on those wigs. Yet he has the skin color (red orange[G] or rose red[F]) of the "flush of health in flesh exposed to the open air" (*P&P* 536), i.e. of an uncorrupted descendant of Blake's ideal Ancient Britons—or free American Indians. Thurlow, expelled from Pitt's cabinet, lost his judicial gown and wig; in Blake's vision these "furr'd robes & false locks" turned, by an irony of the vital force of freedom, into his own living flesh: the exposure to open air working instantly, they "Adhered and grew one with his flesh, and nerves & veins shot thro them" (12:16–17). Even while still "with dismal torment sick," and still clutching his locks, the judged judge is transformed into his own man, with his own hair and living flesh. (Just as the king who clutches his head in *America* 5 will live if he doesn't lose his head by acting the tyrant, so the "Guardian of the secret codes" is free once he escapes from the secrecy and falsehood of codes of justice. This infant Hercules emblem, then, anticipates Blake's ironic history painting of Pitt's "Apotheosis" (after his death in 1806) as a God of War. Milton's Nativity Ode, echoed with sympathetic irony in the verses that follow, celebrates the infant God who "in his swaddling bands" could control all the serpent gods like "Typhon huge ending in snaky twine." Rintrah-Pitt attempts just such tyranny to end tyranny. (On the theological ironies inferable, see Sandler 33–36.) The escape and metamorphosis of false judge into true human, pictured here, should influence the spectator's escape from any temptation to worship the strangler (shown as an infant only in his baldness) or to mistake the ever newly born "infinite" (13) for a "secret" hypocrite. The effectual power of Typhon gods is to bring on their own destruction: see Rintrah's attempt to "blow the iron tube!" (13:2). The smile (see line 16 and compare "The Tyger") is on the face of the creating-resurrecting savior.

The falling action of the group wrestling in the sky may be contrasted with the embracing in the nether sky in *Marriage* 1.

Europe 3^{I} (A Prophecy). What joys the "secret child" (2) will bring are mimed by human and flower forms in the title cloud. At the fixed compass feet of "A" grow a human willow and a fruiting date palm. Dancing fairies at left (note their spiral hair as in Plate 9) and angels at right (winged) mock stolen and familiar embraces. Vines on "PROPHECY," flowering first with Thel's lilies and then tendrils, spurred on by flames under the center P and the final Y, join two pointing soarers with loops like the E and serpent of Plate ii. Eight or nine humans sport in the letters: a climber with one leg hanging down, a parent tossing an infant, a reader, a shepherd with flock (in the O), a climber on "CY" with a walking figure (or woman and child[G]) above, and a reader between flames and tendril. The letters remain stiff, and grief is expressed in the

Europe 3^{I}

Europe 4[I]

bent body of the figure on a cloud above the flaming P; yet signs point east, even the lily and the reluctant fairy (top left), whose scarf repeats the E, cannot go back.

Halted but potentially swift flight eastward is indicated also in the scroll-garmented, huge-winged Cassandra (a contrary of Oothoon in *Milton* 49) who should be soaring fast yet rains her black locks straight down toward the flaming orb of the new born. (Her gown is pink[CF] or blue[D] or violet[E] but the scroll-tail is black[C], her wings mottled[CEF] or purple[D] with the serpent's colors of Plate ii.) Below her waist two fairy angels of annunciation with a serpent trumpet fly up from "secret child"; on the looping flourish lifting from the first line of text a leaf, or a butterfly on a bud, poises and a gowned female gestures diagonally. A black* raven is the large bird among the five beside her, but the bird of paradise rising from below the stanza is red[F], with perhaps an eagle alongside.

The scroll of the next stanza is more worm-like; there is one bird near it, but two small figures mime Enitharmon reclining on a couch and a son or daughter rising "around" (6). Two birds mark Los's "num'rous sons," but the humans crawling toward, and leaning on, a bare rock suggest a hard night rather than a night to enjoy. Altogether the illumination of the page impresses us more with the importance than with the momentum of the prophecy. (Donald Moore remarks of the soaring woman, identified by Cumberland as "A Comet" "importing change," that her face is like Occasion's, which one cannot see until too late, and that the figure in the burning orb below resembles Occasion's offspring Furor in *Faerie Queene* 2.4.1–15.)

Europe 4[I]. To paraphrase: scorn not the moths and butterflies, four marking the threat to "warbling joys" (4), another above the next "joy" (9), and three near the grain which a grasshopper approaches; for a Last Judgment draweth nigh. Such perhaps always is the import of Blake's swarming humblest creatures: compare *Song of Los* 3, *Jerusalem* 98. The old order passeth.

Six naked or nearly naked children, Enitharmon's presumably, unaware of the approaching end of eighteen hundred years of idle pleasure for royalty, are "at sport beneath the solemn moon" (14:32; compare 13:10–12). One bathes in the sun on the upper cloud as on a horizontal surface; two kick their heels in a waltz;

three lie exhausted (one still on her elbows) from some orgy (compare Oothoon and Bromion after the rape: *Visions* 1).

Enitharmon herself, flirting with danger (counting on "lucky hours": 9), lifts the bedclothes (unless her gesture contradicts her call, "Arise O Orc") from that "horrent Demon," for she believes him safely bound (13–15) by Urizen—or by Burke: she is a Marie Antoinette type, we shall see. His flaming head and the absence of visible manacles or chains indicate that she is mistaken. The secret child has reached manhood; when Orc goes into action in "the vineyards of red France" (15:2) there will be no mock crowning of his "head with garlands of the ruddy vine" while his hands are "bound" (12–13), but chariot wheels "dropping with blood" (15:5). (On the Cupid-Psyche analogue see *Forms* 115, 128, 218–19.)

Yet we must also notice that the stem of grain bearing the grasshopper grows up from "Arise O Orc" and that a grapevine illustrates "garlands of the ruddy vine": Orc when truly awake will get us to the harvest feast and The End.

Europe 5[I]. If hair color and curl are a guide, the angel queen behind Rintrah's sword arm is Enitharmon, though both queens' mouths are open, perhaps pleading in unison "That Woman, lovely Woman! may have dominion" (3). In the picture sequence she is now piously avenging Orc's lack of interest in her ruddy vine by demanding a court order "that Womans love is Sin" (5). She is not looking down, but the flame-like leaves (blue on green[D]) which they all stand on were recently the bed of the serpent (see Plate ii).

In the political allegory these are the queens of France and England (both daughters of Enitharmon, in effect). What they are up to, we see from Plates 6, 7, and 15, may be defined by the title of Blake's watercolor of 1784, *War unchained by an Angel—Fire, Pestilence, and Famine following.* Their wish for a ban on "all Joy" (8) rationalizes the domestic repression. Their young champion in kingly crown and chain mail, or rather scales that even cover his face and have become a part of his nature (without hiding his nakedness), is Rintrah the Zoa of wrath enlisted under the code of Urizen. The sword he carries lies broken on the ground in *America* i. In the present Prophecy he is Pitt, the prime minister and knight

Europe 5[I]

Europe 6[I]

errant of modern times, who pleased the memory of the Queen of France (invoked by Burke, whom we see in Plate 1, probably Enitharmon's son Palamabron mentioned here) and the alleged dominion of the Queen of England when he blew the trumpet of war against the Republic. The Cumberland gloss titles this page "War" and capitalizes "Minister" in the defining comment, "O War! thou Son of Hell, whom angry heavens do make their Minister!" (See *Prophet* 205[222].)

There is little ornament in the text but a small fleck of a bird over "race" and two flies under "life awaits." The wings of the angels are mottled in the serpent's color, blue on brown[C].

Europe 6[I]. Blake's comment on the consequences of war is silent but eloquent. Not content simply with indicating that the camp followers of war are famine, pestilence, and fire (Plates 6, 7, 15), he indicates that it is the rich and powerful who devour the children, the young who die of plague, women and children who perish in flames.

Here the infant victim of war whom we saw in a storm-lodged wheat field in *America* 9 lies dead (of starvation) by a blazing hearth and is presumably destined for the pot coming to a boil. The Cumberland gloss, with the title "Famine," hints at the fatal consequences of cannibalism with a text from Dryden—". . . to prolong our breath We greedily devour our certain Death"—and at the meaning of the scene: "Preparing to dress the Child." In his Notebook emblems (73, 83) Blake had drawn contrasting women with dead infants: a humbly dressed mother holding the child and regarding it mournfully; an elegant woman in a throne-like chair with the child in her lap but using her hands to dramatize the situation. Here the rich woman in an elegant chair, with a red (coral) necklace and fine coiffeur and yellow[CD] or pink[G] stocking, hugs herself and watches the pot. The humbler woman, with bare feet and no necklace and squatting on the floor with her skirt folded (perhaps against the cold), is bent in helpless grief. The infant's shroud (very white[C]) protects his body from the floor; it is not folded over him, for he is past help from warmth.

The flames somewhat match those from Orc's head in Plate 4. They leap out into the room; their smoke makes a shadow across the top of the room[DH].

Europe 7^{I}. A closed oak door in a brick wall is marked with the legend "Lord Have Mercy On Us" and a crude cross, sealing the family within from contaminating the rest of the population with the pestilence. Three citizens on the street side of the sealed door have been stricken anyhow, two women turning green^{C} (pale^{G}), one frantic, the other despairing, and a tawny youth whose face is beginning to turn grey green^{CG}—as is the bellman's^{CG}. The latter's dark clothes and shielding hat make the gloom official; he will have been responsible for the inscription on the door; he looks away from the dying but rings his bell for the death cart.

In Blake's Notebook list of subjects for his engraved *History of England* (not extant) he included "The Plague" (i.e. of 1665 in London) and "The fire of London" (i.e. of 1666), and his paintings of Pestilence, Plague (and Famine) are extant. In historical perspective the great plague was emblematic of a collapsing order. The royal family, for example, fled the city though inhabitants were compelled to remain because infected. The irony of the "Lord Have Mercy" inscription, with darkness* slanting across it as in *Urizen* 26, includes the signification that edicts can wall citizens apart from each other but infection respects no bounds. (An emblem in *Notebook* 25 shows a similar dying group, at a more elegant door. See also *Song of Los* 6, where the context is a storm that flattens the forests of tyranny.)

Apt words in the Cumberland inscription are the title, "Plague," and "hark! the Bell Of Death beats Slow!"

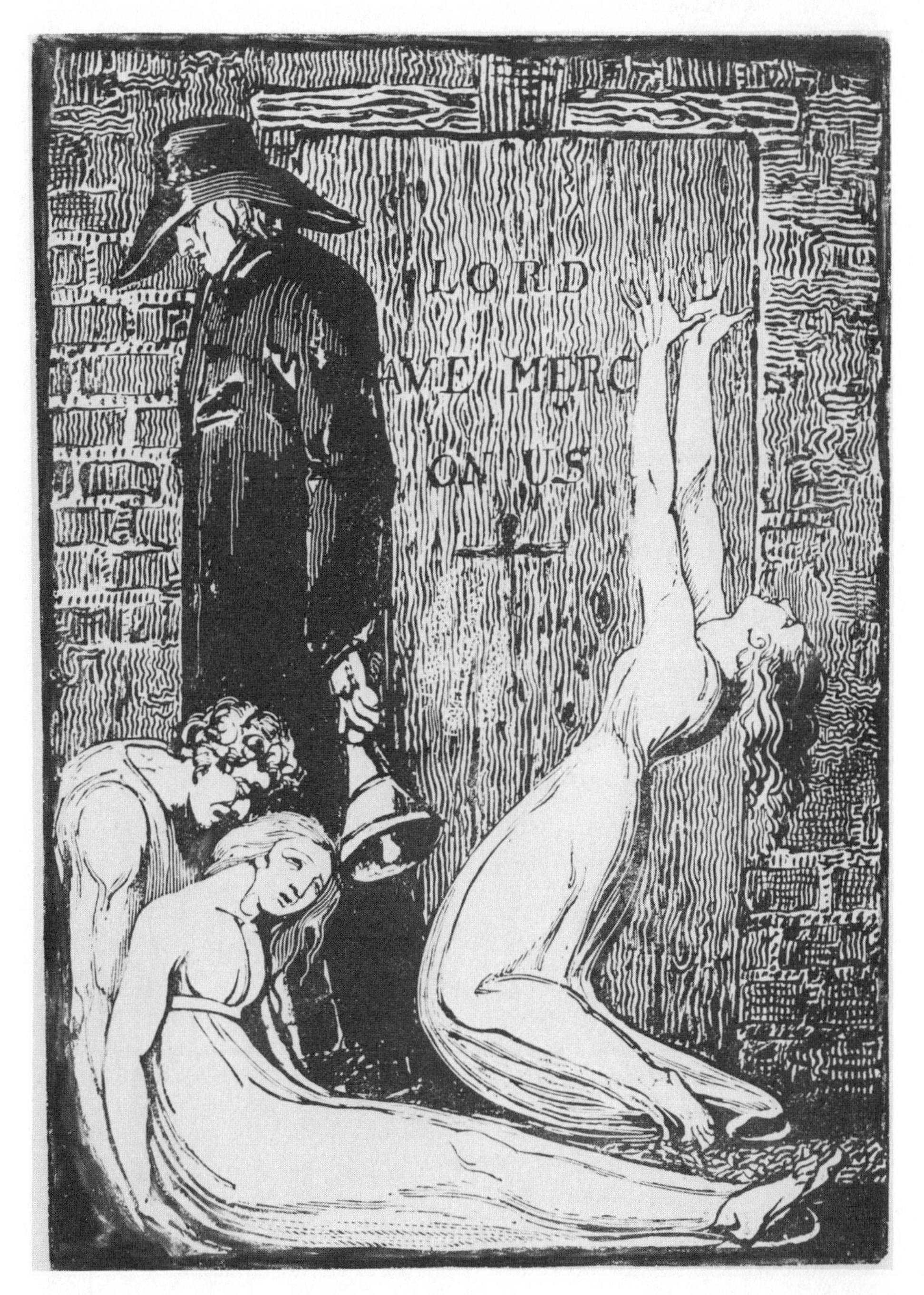

Europe 7^{I}

Europe 8I

Europe 8I. The text lacks ornament except for emphatic y-tails in the paragraph break—that on "lovely" is made ironic by the next word, "jealous" (7)—and a triple horse-tail on "A" immediately following "each ramping his golden mane shakes" (11), as though to imply that what Enitharmon sees as the "innumerable race" of Rintrah's chivalry are literally cavalry.

Is the white-bearded, gowned ancient denouncing—or warding off—persons or terrors he sees in the west? King Tiriel as an avatar of King George denounces his rebellious sons in *Tiriel* 8 in identical stance, though with his palms held forward (and shorter beard). Is the gowned woman, with hair hanging down like the angel's in Plate 3, pleading, as five daughters do around Tiriel, or clinging for protection? Michael Tolley (*Forms* 33) sees the old man as "Albion's guardian angel, simultaneously denouncing the Americans and warding off the clouds of pestilence he himself has provoked with his curses." His eye is sometimes severe[DG] but expresses less authority than fear, though less terror than Bromion's in *Visions* i. His hands are feeble like those of the King's dragon form in *America* 4. The simplest level of explanation must be that something fiery is threatening from the west, which casts a glow on the edges of the clouds: specifically war, which leaves women and old men exposed to destruction.

The Cumberland gloss, modified from Dryden's *Aeneis,* describes Troy in flames: "Thus Deluges descending on the plains Sweep o'er the yellow year &c." Troy is again the half-buried locus of the fire in Plate 15. If Cumberland got Blake's symbolism right, the aged king here represents the yellow year threatened by the revolutionary deluge. In Plate 13 his hosts fall, "Yellow as leaves of Autumn," when the trumpet is blown. The picture concurs with those of famine and plague in signifying the decay of the old order and the imminence of a Last Judgment. Compare *Song of Los* 4.

❧

Europe 9[I]. Two fairies that look like giants, until we adjust to the scale, for they are in an S-curve of ripe grain, blow serpent trumpets from which pour flecks of "Mildews blighting ears of Corn" (to quote Cumberland). These fairies or human forms of plague winds, female and male, are quite impersonal about their work; or rather, they know (compare the king of fairies watching from a flower in the center of *Song of Los*) that they are trumpeting the apocalypse. And the fairy who dictated *Europe* knows. The political symbolism is repeated from *America* in the text: war divided the rulers of Europe ("fleeting bands . . . Divide the heavens of Europe": 6–7) until "Albions Angel smitten with his own plagues fled with his bands" (the British attempt to sow division by warfare in America ended in the surrender and flight of troops or "bands" and division against the war in Bristol and London). (See *Prophet* chapter 4.)

In Blake's historical sources there is no clear distinction between one kind of pestilence and another; plague winds filled with insects bring fire that burns, mildew that blights, locusts that devour grain and, directly and indirectly, citizens. The myriads of blights that fall within the text area may turn as we look into birds, their prophetic opposite; at least three seem to do so in line 11.

The flower growing entwined around the grain seems more like lily than poppy (see *America* 9), but it promises to keep the corn healthy, by ancient belief. Tolley (*Forms* 131) identifies the grain as barley, from its long whiskers; it was the grain ripe enough to be smitten in Exodus 9:31.

Europe 9[I]

following

In thoughts perturb'd they rose from the bright ruins silent
The fiery King, who sought his ancient temple serpent-form'd
That stretches out its shady length along the Island white.
Round him roll'd his clouds of war; silent the Angel went,
Along the infinite shores of Thames to golden Verulam.
There stand the venerable porches that high-towering rear
Their oak-surrounded pillars, form'd of massy stones, uncut
With tool; stones precious; such eternal in the heavens,
Of colours twelve, few known on earth, give light in the opake,
Plac'd in the order of the stars, when the five senses whelm'd
In deluge o'er the earth-born man; then turn'd the fluxile eyes
Into two stationary orbs, concentrating all things.
The ever-varying spiral ascents to the heavens of heavens
Were bended downward; and the nostrils golden gates shut
Turn'd outward, barr'd and petrify'd against the infinite.

Thought chang'd the infinite to a serpent; that which pitieth:
To a devouring flame; and man fled from its face and hid
In forests of night; then all the eternal forests were divided
Into earths rolling in circles of space, that like an ocean rush'd
And overwhelmed all except this finite wall of flesh.
Then was the serpent temple form'd, image of infinite
Shut up in finite revolutions, and man became an Angel;
Heaven a mighty circle turning; God a tyrant crown'd.

Now arriv'd the ancient Guardian at the southern porch,
That planted thick with trees of blackest leaf, & in a vale
Obscure, enclos'd the Stone of Night; oblique it stood, o'erhung
With purple flowers and berries red; image of that sweet south,
Once open to the heavens and elevated on the human neck,
Now overgrown with hair and coverd with a stony roof,
Downward 'tis sunk beneath th'attractive north, that round the feet
A raging whirlpool draws the dizzy enquirer to his grave.

Europe 10I

Europe 10I. Here the lively serpent of the title page is turned to bronze—head, crest, tongue, and flames are bronze colored in D—"petrify'd against the infinite" (15), with seven monotonous coils, infinity divided by time into seven days, the order of encompassing creation, instead of the "ever-varying spiral ascents to the heavens of heavens" (13) that his improvement into divinely human form would mean. Flames revolve every way from his fiery tongue, and his horns, scarcely developed in Plate ii, have grown into five crown-like spikes. Urizen, in short, has triumphed: "Thought [has] chang'd the infinite to a serpent" (16), even flattening his top and bottom turns into right angles.

Some free spiralling occurs in the lettering, though: twists defying the completeness of "petrify'd"; a strong banner under "tyrant crown'd" (24) that mimics, with a difference, the bends of the serpent; a loop that ties a knot in time, on "Now" (25) and an appropriately backward trumpet mouth; a dizzy drop from "dizzy." After "an ocean rush'd" (19–20) grow some sea vines and a very long-winged water bird (between banners). Yet at the center a potential tendril is thinned and flattened to a worm, above "chang'd."

Europe 11[I]. Here, heavily disguised (and revealed in his dragon form as a spectre bat) is King George himself. Or, perhaps we should say, if the Assassin of Plate 1 is Burke, the strangler and warrior of Plates 2 and 5 Pitt, and the angel queens the queens of France and England, then this pope of the established church, on his Gothic throne which (if we don't notice its side posts) looms almost like a cathedral occulted by his gross majesty, is as close as Blake dared come to representing George the Third. The facial resemblance is no more imprecise in one direction than Gillray's in another. The text identifies him as "Albions Angel" who has been acting the King's part in *America;* it also indicates that the book on his knees is a (paper) copy (made by "Kings & Priests . . . on Earth": he is dressed as both) of the "brazen" edition issued by Urizen and now selling widely "from North to South." The design of saints on his robe makes it a substitute for the cathedral door, notes Donald Moore.

The angel queens, from Plate 5 where they were urging Rintrah-Pitt to proclaim the rationale for counterrevolution, now dip scepters in hypocritical (crossed) obeisance, with French fleurs de lys—and serpents dart from their robes, complete with scales[K]. Said Blake in *Notebook* 99 (*P&P* 491): "The Queen of France just touchd this Globe And the Pestilence darted from her robe." Their wing tips touch the tips of his bat wings; in some copies[BC] triangles of tracery in the chair have been exaggerated into bat ears for the King. In C he wears a silver necklace like a choking manacle. The small cross-topped orb at the top of his crown, a feature shared by the papal tiara and the royal crowns of kings of England, is sometimes modified to a simple orb[B], sometimes to a simple cross[K].

Cumberland's gloss is "Pagan [corrected to Papal] Superstition," the mistake perhaps evidence that he was taking down the words from Blake's fairy's dictation and misheard at first.

Europe 11[I]

And the clouds & fires pale rolld round in the night of Enitharmon
Round Albions cliffs & Londons walls; still Enitharmon slept:
Rolling volumes of grey mist involve Churches, Palaces, Towers:
For Urizen unclaspd his Book: feeding his soul with pity
The youth of England hid in gloom curse the paind heavens; compelld
Into the deadly night to see the form of Albions Angel
Their parents brought them forth & aged ignorance preaches canting,
On a vast rock, percievd by those senses that are closd from thought:
Bleak, dark, abrupt, it stands & overshadows London city
They saw his boney feet on the rock, the flesh consumd in flames:
They saw the Serpent temple lifted above, shadowing the Island white:
They heard the voice of Albions Angel howling in flames of Orc.
Seeking the trump of the last doom

Above the rest the howl was heard from Westminster louder & louder:
The Guardian of the secret codes forsook his ancient mansion,
Driven out by the flames of Orc; his furrd robes & false locks
Adhered and grew one with his flesh, and nerves & veins shot thro' them
With dismal torment sick hanging upon the wind: he fled
Groveling along Great George Street thro' the Park gate; all the soldiers
Fled from his sight: he dragd his torments to the wilderness.

Thus was the howl thro Europe!
For Orc rejoicd to hear the howling shadows
But Palamabron shot his lightnings trenching down his wide back
And Rintrah hung with all his legions in the nether deep

Enitharmon laughd in her sleep to see (O womans triumph)
Every house a den, every man bound; the shadows are filld
With spectres, and the windows wove over with curses of iron:
Over the doors Thou shalt not; & over the chimneys Fear is written:
With bands of iron round their necks fastend into the walls
The citizens: in leaden gyves the inhabitants of suburbs
Walk heavy: soft and bent are the bones of villagers

Between the clouds of Urizen the flames of Orc roll heavy
Around the limbs of Albions Guardian, his flesh consuming.
Howlings & hissings, shrieks & groans, & voices of despair
Arise around him in the cloudy
Heavens of Albion. Furious

Europe 12I

Europe 12I. The motif of insect life as symbolic of the decay of the old order is again (as in Plate 4) counterpoised to Enitharmon's ignorance of what time it is. Present desperation of the rulers is detailed in the first three stanzas, with interlinear banners noting the howling "from Westminster" (14) at the scorching flames of Orc. But Enitharmon laughs "in her sleep" (25) seeing repression complete, "Every house a den, every man bound" (26), and sources of light "wove over with curses of iron" (27).

We see the weaving, but it is of spiderwebs not iron; even a spider-sized fly can break it (see fly at center right, beneath the highest spiders—a thin-legged one beside "soldiers" and a vaguer large one diagonally above it). A caterpillar can travel on it (near that fly). And myriads of insects can escape these webs, dancing merrily in the spaces between stanzas: three double-winged flies, seven or more single winged, one with spotted wings, and scores too tiny to describe, blending into blotches like the mildews of Plate 9. Enitharmon dreams that the bones of villagers are "soft and bent" (31); we see one human, at bottom right, not only soft-boned but shrunk to the size of three grape leaves—and impossibly twisted on his hips, apparently praying dutifully to the spider-gods above and also apparently bound tight in a woven web: perhaps painted on his body by his imagination, like the chain scales on Rintrah. (See also *Jerusalem* 45.) We recall the angel in *Marriage* 18 who imagined the poet's eternal lot to be "between the black & white spiders." The larger of Blake's six spiders have beautiful bodies of many colored velvet, though only six legs until someone corrected him (another pair of legs is given the lower spider in B and K and the large central spider as well in E). Behind the webbed human are two vaguely pyramidal hills*, sometimes[CG] painted yellow-brown. The large oak leaves at lower right, some turning brown*, are like the leaves in the path in Plate 1.

The Cumberland gloss quotes Dryden's *King Arthur* on a dungeon "stow'd with snakes and adders" and rats and toads ("paddocks").

Europe 13[I]. The momentous announcement that a mighty spirit named Newton has blown "the enormous blast" which sends the "myriads of Angelic hosts" falling like autumn leaves is quietly marked by a single fly, a spider in flattened interwoven grass, and a sort of broken root or green* stem bent around below "Judgment" (sometimes[G] bearing two or three thin caterpillars). This is to say that the philosophy that builds prisons and eventuates in the utter futility of imprisonment was proclaimed initially by Newton and only given a finishing shove by Pitt's war upon the Republic. Below the spider's nest Enitharmon continues her anachronistic song ("tho' the earth-worm call: Let him call in vain"—i.e. ignore these insects and caterpillars) to pass the time until "human solitude is past!" If the tyrant hosts are falling, it already is past. Then what is this naked giant doing in chains and consternation? Who is his green jailor with two black keys (sometimes obscured*) and a thin coating of imaginary webbing or scaly armor on his body? We are in Newgate or the Tower in London in 1794; the flames of Orc are just a little slow reaching this cell from Westminster. But this is the present event, not a scene in Enitharmon's dream; the shackled leg-crossing prisoner doesn't seem willing to settle down quietly. (Moore suggests that the jailor seems to be clad in some sort of garment that covers the front and sides of his body and that what horrifies the prisoner is this sudden view of his scaly back side.)

The Cumberland title is "Imprisonment," with a quotation that anticipates long waiting in this "world," however. Apropos the spider, Moore notes that a spider was the only friend of a prisoner in the Bastille in one of Mary Wollstonecraft's *Original Stories.*

Do the jailor's stride and oddly knobbed hair—though we see enough of both arms to know that his fingers can't be in it—mean to remind us of the top figure in Plate 2?

Europe 14[I]. Every crawling or flying kind of life—including the earth-worm, under "thy" (8)—is calling on this penultimate page, or being called by Enitharmon—who is now wide awake but quite unaware that it is no longer the year one. What we see as birds and butterflies cutting the airy way (her "crystal house" 13:14) she sees as her children. Those who "flock around" Ethinthus "Like the gay

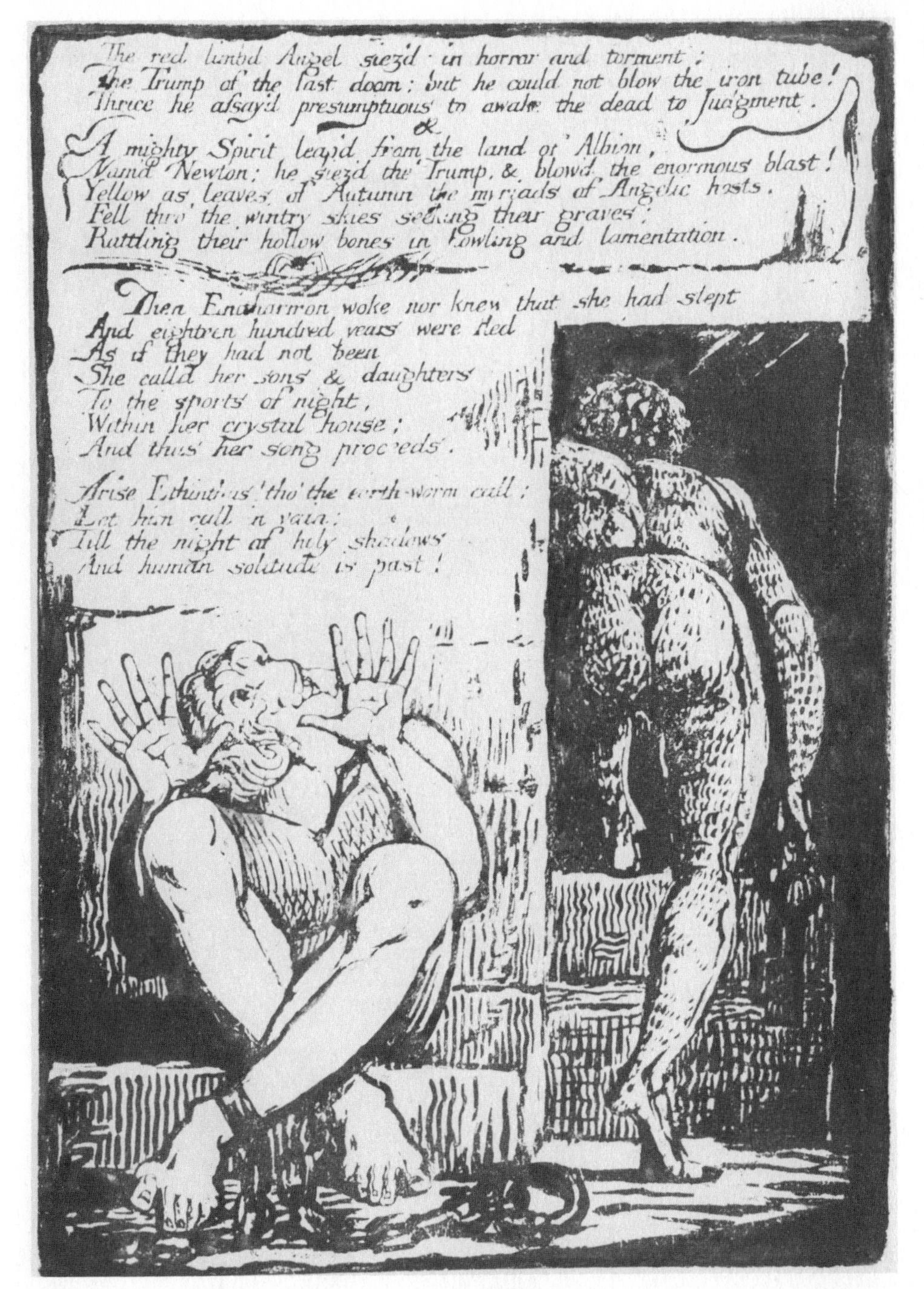

Europe 13[I]

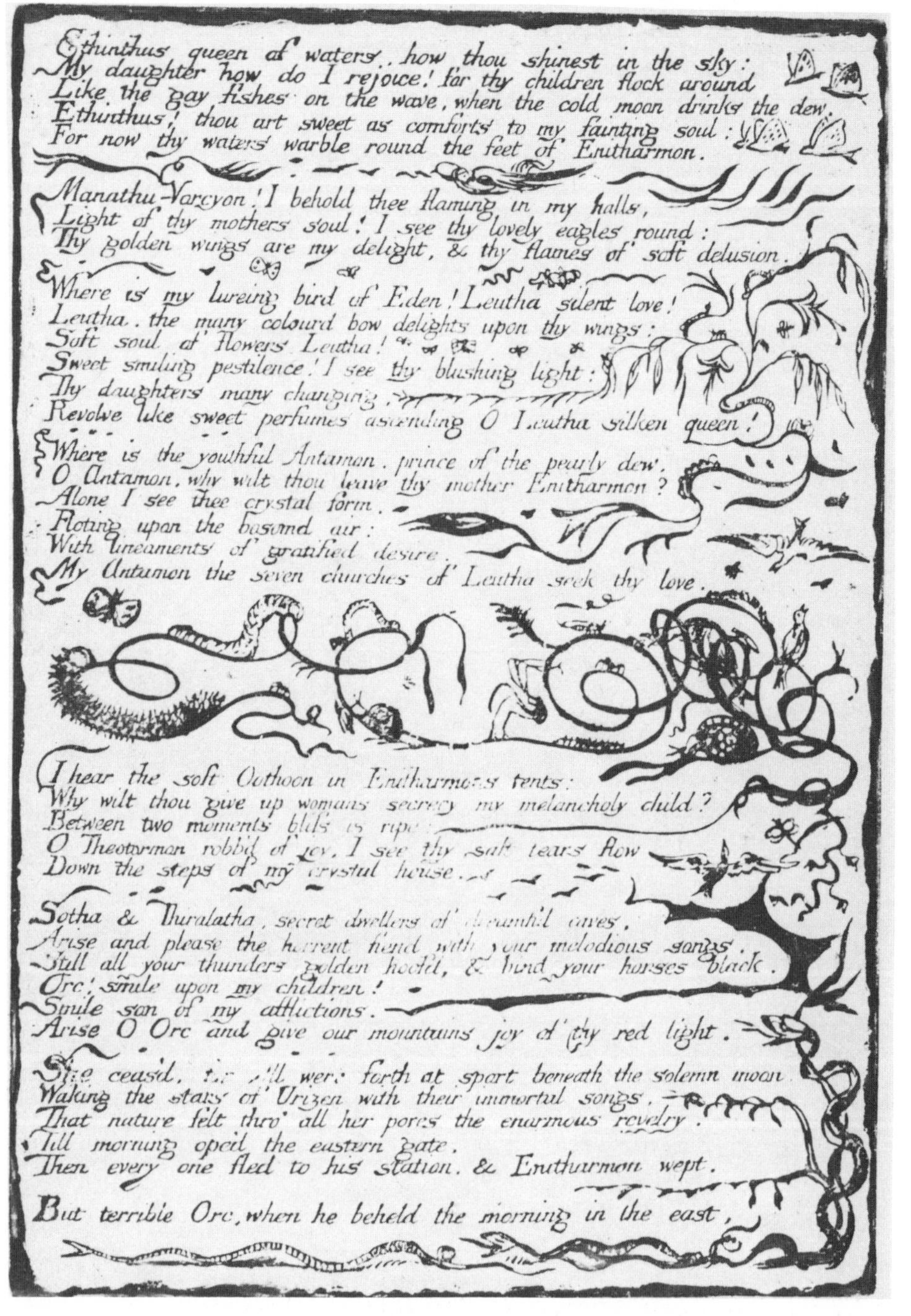

Europe 14[I]

fishes on the wave" (2–3) are five fish-like butterflies in the top right corner, colored like flames[BC]. Above "flaming in my halls" (6) an eagle-winged, horse-tailed creature (compare *Visions* 1 perhaps?) soars among birds and flames. Possibly it is one of Manathu-Vorcyon's "lovely eagles" (7), but farther down two unmistakable eagles fly toward each other above and below the central tangle. Meanwhile below "Thy golden wings are my delight" (8) we see two distant birds, two butterflies, and then the worm (perhaps only a banner on "Leutha") and a pair of moths (or one with two heads) and a cloud. On the other hand Leutha, the "lureing bird of Eden" with rainbow "delights" upon her wings (10–11), is manifest not as a bird but as five tiny butterflies or moths, suiting (as birds would not) the further description, "smiling pestilence." As for "Antamon, prince of the pearly dew," a "crystal form Floting upon the bosomd air: With lineaments of gratified desire" (15–19), we have our choice of nine caterpillars and two snails, crawling on stems beside and below the stanza, one moth under "Antamon" (20), three small spiders on each of the two stem clusters—one about to be eaten by a goose-like bird reduced to the large spider's size (as is a lark singing nearby)—or those two eagles. They, however, might go better with Theotormon weeping (24), his "salt tears" underpinned by five distant birds flying. Enitharmon awake, we realize, can see the human forms of the myriads of flying creatures, each "an immense world of delight, clos'd by [our] senses five" (*Marriage* 7). Three serpent forms are all *we* see, at bottom, of her son Orc; though he, even to her, is a "horrent fiend" (27), and even to the poet "terrible Orc" (37): but compare "terrible Blake" (*P&P* 491).

In some copies[BCD] most of the creatures on the page are given the serpents' colors. And so are the flowers, which we must not overlook. In the top cluster of vegetation there are two open blossoms of the Meadia, the long-stamened flower we saw just opening in *Thel* 5; lower down a lily-like bud and flower. Of the caterpillars, four are wooly, four or five are canker- or inch-worms, busy measuring. The general color and bustle on the page convey a sense of the "enormous revelry" (34) that the text calls for. At the same time the swarming creatures "are curiously reminiscent," notes Donald Moore, "of the newts and blind-worms, weaving spiders, beetles black, worms, snails, and the like, which were not supposed to come near the fairy queen in Act II, scene ii, of *A Midsummer Night's Dream*. Perhaps Enitharmon's association with these creatures is a measure of her difference from Titania—or, considering the latter's delusion and mistaken love—her resemblance" (Moore 167).

Europe 15[I]. Following Orc down "from the heights" (1) we end in the flaming "vineyards of red France" (2), pictorially like the flaming ruins of Troy. We know that Newton has trumpeted the Last Judgment; so this is Armageddon. The artist's test is not to lose sight of the flying worlds of delight (there are three or four small caterpillars among the leaves growing out from "red"—after the grapevine growing from "vineyards"—and a small bird taking wing, perhaps a miniature eagle, and four flies or moths) while he calls all his talents ("all his sons") to the bloody field and flaming city. Striding from flaming ruins to marble steps (like those behind "William" and "Robert" when Milton's star descends with bardic afflatus in *Milton* 32 and 37) and a ruined fluted column, who but Los (known later as bard and blacksmith) can rescue his children (the daughters here; the sons who "shook their bright fiery wings" in Plate 3 are busy etching these pages) as Aeneas did father and child (see *Forms* 133n, 134n, 214)? (Compare the rescue effort to *Job* 3, where it is not brought off, and to *America* 3.)

The cloth trailing from the woman who has fainted on Los's shoulder (extending below her dress[B]) suggests bedclothes snatched up in haste. The younger daughter is not so much looking back as waving at the bold eagle just above the flames who is flying the proper diagonal (ever-varying spiral) to Eternity—at the same angle as Los's body, and the flames. (In K the girl is given a face looking toward the rescuer.) Los's determination to frame into prophetic symmetry the "furious terrors" of armies of lions and preying tigers (4–7) is marked by the vine of furious sharp-leaved ivy that springs from his name in line 9 and translates into a bardic garland the "snaky thunders" binding his head. The ivy leaves act as small but pointed critics of "wheels dropping with blood," of "groans . . . cries . . . anguish," and indeed of "snaky thunders."

The concluding flourish is a branch of five oak leaves with a naked acorn, matched by the penis below (sometimes covered by a wide[F] or narrow[DG] scroll of cloth). The emblem seems a quotation, freed of viper shapes, of the leafing branch beside the printing-house eagle in *Marriage* 15.

Cumberland's gloss—"Fire," with a description of flames as "flaky Plague"—continues the apocalyptic motif.

Europe 15[I]

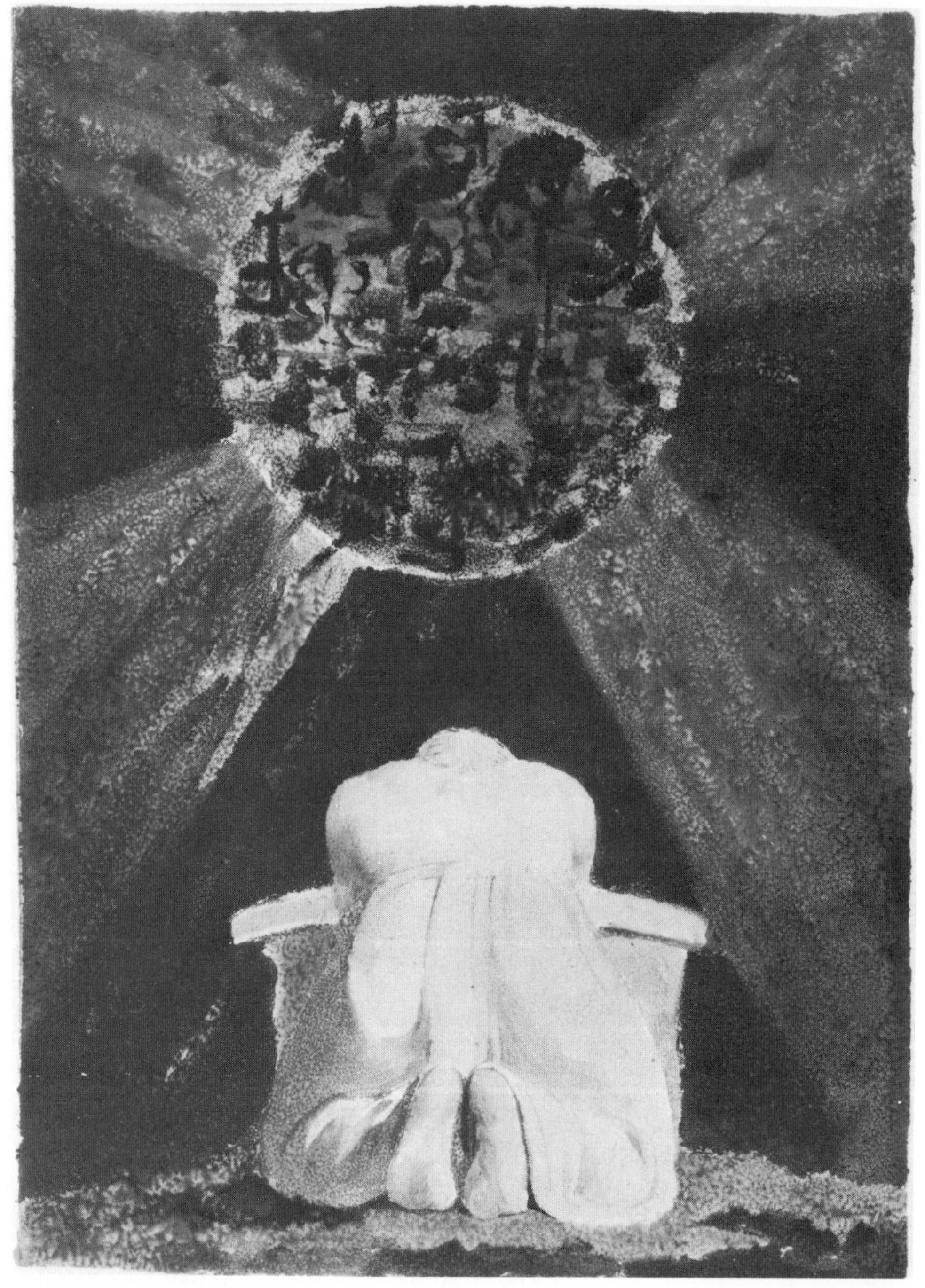

Song of Los 1A

THE SONG OF LOS
(Reduced from about 9 by 7 inches)

Song of Los 1A (frontispiece). A bowed, kneeling figure who can be seen as Urizen (note the reference to "his woven darkness above" 7:25) worships a dying or occulted sun (written over with mysterious hieroglyphs in copy D, more chaotic in A, irregularly spotted in B, drab blurs in E: see Mitchell 1969 on this mysterious "order" as obvious chaos). A bright contrast to this woven darkness is afforded by the white or whitish body and garment of Urizen himself, his bare feet the most living thing in the picture. In this praying position (compare Noah and Job before altars) he cannot read the open book—which may, to him, seem to be "his Laws to the Nations" (3:8) but sung by Los will make him weep (7:41). If we compare his open book in *Urizen* 1 and 5, we may conclude that his laws and curses have been projected or abstracted onto the sun. (In the Butts copy of Blake's *Job* 1, the first part of the Lord's Prayer is written across the sun.) The curved earth beneath him is green. See the sun reforged to visibility by Los in Plate 8.

(Compare the Devil in *Marriage* 10, reading from a scroll with the stool-throne behind him; a poet sleeping in a book in *NT* 7; "The Sacrifice of Jephthah's Daughters" *Bible* 50.)

In A and D the dark cone over Urizen is tent-like; in B a dark hill rises between the altar and the two lower bands of light; in E these pour in front of the hill and there is a general diffusion of light between the four lopsided bands.

When we look back, having finished the Song, we see that the writing on the sun is the text of "Africa," the first part, the history of mankind under philosophies of tyranny.

Song of Los 2[E] (title page). The lettering is pale and unadorned but lean and strong; it fills the heavens; the name "LOS," in scroll forms, in the "middle air" where the devils of *Paradise Regained* now dwell, covers Urizen's world; and the three* birds by flying up leftward (like the birds in *America* 11) indicate that the Song may return us to paradise. The mouth of the large bird of paradise (red[A] or dark blue[E]) is open for singing. Urizen does not see the birds but, perhaps[AD], the serpentine "S"—or perhaps only the inside of his own eyelids. His face is pink and his eyes blue; he may think he is acting the part of the heavenward-looking man in *Marriage* 21 (see *America* 6), but his hand is on the skull not the book, and his body is decaying into the earth as in *Jerusalem* 92. (The *Census* editors—p 91—see him as Adam, reasonably enough; he may soon play Noah too: see 3:10–16.) The implications of his look of pious selfhood (compare *Job* 1) are made explicit in the opening lines of Night II of the *Four Zoas* illustrated by a variant of this design (p 23; see also p 130): the Ancient Man, rising upon his Couch of Death but weary unto death, "Turning his Eyes outward [sic] to Self, losing the Divine Vision."

The disorder—or machine-like regularity—of Urizen's world is indicated by the intermixture of ocean waves and hills and valleys; his immediate hill is grass green, with brown earth under him and for his pillow, but the distant hills are colored and shaped like waves. This weltering effect is symbolic of things to come.

Song of Los 2[E]

Song of Los 3E

Song of Los 3E (Africa). The titles "Africa" and (Plate 6) "Asia" suggest histories of continents to match *America* and *Europe* but prove only allusive. "Africa" surveys the past history of mankind under Urizen's code of hypocrisy and war, from Adam's shuddering and Noah's fading, down to King George's burning at the beginning of revolution, in America (4:21). "Asia" depicts the present tempest of revolution: kings losing their heads as they lose their grip, and the earth turning from tomb to womb, swelling "with wild desire" (7:36).

The profuse foliation around the stiff title letters of "Africa" evolves only one animal form, a lizard climbing the *A,* and no human forms. Their civil stiffness is overpowered by a boa constrictor from the jungle (compare *America* 16). Insects abound, not birds, marking the decay and corruption of the old order (compare *Europe* 14). The only human we see is asleep, a shepherd with face buried and legs drawn up, beside his huddling sheep (see the comment of Night to Cloud, 13–16). The bottom of the page may be flooded; beside line 17 we see "the waters" (that seem like animals) but not Noah. The black and red and gold serpentAC, however, forms a kind of heart (for "heart-formed Africa" line 3) with his middle coils; his down-darting tongue is as red as the paradise bird on Plate 2; also red and black are some of the insects near the tongue, the bat-winged insect below "Eternity" (9), and the caterpillar on the vine beside the sheep. Also touched with Orc's fire are the lilies on the vine below line 9 (but they are blue in D) and the three birds flying above it. And very much alive are the tendrils curling near "sunny African." But slavery quickly turns leaves square (12) and brings the flood. When the serpent darts his tongue *upward,* we will have the situation of *Marriage* 20.

Song of Los 4D. As Eternity, not accepted as vision, is obliterated "like a dream" (4), the tendrils grow downward, chiefly a twelve-loop coil below the name "Urizen!" (17). The wings of the person flying with arms *and* wings to escape the fate of "doleful forms" (8) are oblong and seem artificial (perhaps Daedalian); they are painted sky-blueD (illusory?) almost blackA or brown and blackE (deathly), and there is a patch of raven-blackAE foliage beside the flier's left wing. Below, Har and Heva fleeing from the "War & Lust" of their brothers and sisters (5–6)—before they became the senile idiots of *Tiriel* and before Thel fled to *them?*—are followed by two birds, painted so black they must be ravens, near Heva's hand. As they simultaneously run and embrace, her arm around Har's head makes a halo. Her flesh is pink, his darker*, the earth green against red and yellow hills and dark blue sky, in A; in D the hills are mottled blue and the sky dark red. (In D the faces are fairly calm, in other copies more distressed.)

The bird flying above "Rousseau" and the matching banner on "Voltaire" confirm the deduction that these Alpine figures are pillars of fire if not light, in the "European darkness" (7:26); see *Prophet* 258.

Song of Los 4D

Song of Los 5D

Song of Los 5D. *Europe a Prophecy* was "dictated" to Blake by a fairy (see the Preface poem). Here a crowned fairy king, beside his sleeping queen (they are identified as "Oberon and Titania" in a separate painting), watches humanity from a world of stars and lilies quite outside this poem—or rather from an Eternity far *within* it, thus affording an opening for Imagination between the pulsations of Africa and Asia. In A and D he watches us, as we read; in C he looks up; in E he looks apprehensively ahead, his hand drawn holding his scepter tighter, anticipating the bitterness of the "Kings of Asia" expressed in the next plate.

At bottom we see mottled green earth, then a stream of water, then a darker band of earth, then dark blue sky sprinkled with white stars—about forty in A, ten in C, twenty-two in D, only seven in E.

The leaves and shape of their flower throne indicate a day lily, the flowers of which flourish and die quickly but successively. Is the history surveyed in "Africa" a dream in Titania's memory (as it is in Enitharmon's in *Europe*)? Is Oberon a mental prince who like Los watches the present revolution, "Asia"? If so, the lily bud bending forward among the stars must hold the spirit of the time to come, not a king but a joy. These perfect lilies foretell a paradisal regeneration.

Compare the Bard among stars in *Songs* 30 "Who Present, Past, & Future sees."

Songs of Los 6[E] (Asia). The text is a lament of kings; the pictures show that the tempest of revolution has struck. Cross bars on the lettering of "A" and "IA" give the effect of rigging on a ship (suggested by the cloud background). Human figures in the lettering fall or seem drawn toward the welter below—of waves, or (as we look down the page) treetops of a forest. In *America* 9 tyranny lodged the ripening grain over a newborn child; here forests of oppression are flattened over a youth and maiden (a detail from Blake's painting of "Pestilence"), perhaps the last victim of the kings' "Pestilence" (line 11). Strap-like branches or roots are thrown below the Councellor's "curb" (16); beside them a crouching kneeling body has a great hole where its head should be (edged by blood; unmistakable in copy A); compare Blake's more enigmatic hint to kings in *America* 5. And note the head-clutching figure at top center of the "ASIA" title/ship.

At top left, outside the "ship" but sitting with left leg drawn up on the first stroke of the letter "A," a naked youth reminds us of the liberated man of *Marriage* 21 and *America* 6—looking up whence the wind bloweth. In the lower curve of "S" a gowned woman huddles under a looped leaf or wave, which in E seems to have a head. Between "S" and "I" a man holds a woman with scarf flying up, knees bent to jump overboard. ("ASIA" is a sinking ship.) Under the final "A" a naked man reclines on a heap of bodies and holds up a severed head[A] for inspection (a battlefield vignette?) or just his hand[D]. Some of these effects (and the one next described) are subdued or lacking in copies C and A.

On or above the welter above the two youths are two shadowy headless forms (lacking in AD) that look like winter underwear being blown; are these cast off garments the selfhoods of the man and woman, (Har and Heva?), the "sexual garments" (see Gates 18)? Compare the shadows of the errors of Job and his wife in *Job* 2 and 16. In the political context we may take them for the flayed bodies of beheaded monarchs (see *Urizen* 6). In E the garments are green (vegetable?), the forest under them brown and yellow, the "ship" pale lavender.

Song of Los 6[E]

Song of Los 7D

Song of Los 7D. In sequence, Plate 7 seems to continue the forest of Plate 6; the boughs that crowd the left margin—an unusual effect—can be the ends of those bent down in the right margin of 6. Yet there is a difference as of stillness after storm. Seen as a separate picture, the brown branches and green leaves are not in motion but form a nest around the text. The naked figure at the top right is the only inhabitant; falling as if an embodiment of all the bloody action of the preceding pictures, faceless but with a head that can be recovered if we imagine it tilted sharply back (compare *America* 5). Except for the tendrils following the spider kings' cry (after 8) there are no other distinctive forms on the page. The text is given priority, within this green nest. What hatches in it is a rebirth: the final stanza is of tomb turned womb, for a cosmic orgasm, apocalypse, regeneration.

Then the last words, "Urizen Wept," an echo of John 11.35, "Jesus wept," implying humane compassion not hypocritical selfhood, direct us to recall our reading of the frontispiece (Plate 1) and to view that picture, of Urizen in a posture of contrition as a prophetic contrary of Plate 8.

❧

Song of Los 8D (tailpiece). The poet/blacksmith Los, naked (in contrast to skirted Urizen in Plate 1) with his steel hammer in a firm cushion of cloud, rests "wearied" from his intellectual labors (see *Jerusalem* 99:2), and regards the completed song/sun with anxious compassion (his brows knit and forehead creased)E. In his open "Furnaces of affliction" (*Jerusalem* 73, q.v.) he has purged the sun of the runes of Urizenic mystery (see frontispiece)—an action which is a variant of stamping the stony law to dust (*America* 8:5), i.e. a revolutionary destruction of the old order. It is now blood red (see the globe of life blood in *Urizen* 17, a biological variant of this cosmological emblem) but still obscured by clouds. In A the clouds are dark and the disk itself is blackened and the rays spurt like blood; in copies B and D the clouds are few and small; in E the sun appears to float in a sea of shallow stratus.

(The next stage will be to shape a human face in the sun: see Los attempting to do so, in *Songs* b: Appendix, below.)

From the clouds behind him on each side spires of light radiate upward, brighter than the sun's and suggesting a divided or threefold source. These beams are not at an angle to represent rays from the visible orb, which may represent the material sun, or history, the corporeal war which Los is forging into vision. To the more bright light behind him compare the dawning light behind Jerusalem in *Jerusalem* 92, where she is contemplating the effect of mortal warfare in front of her with a comparable facial expression. (Los lifts the sun in *Jerusalem* 97, after the hammering shown in 32 and 73, and it is borne head-high in 100.)

Song of Los 8D

THE [*FIRST*] BOOK OF URIZEN

Note: The plates of *Urizen* are differently arranged in each of the seven known copies, thus presenting seven different picture "narratives." Using the Keynes model numbering, based on copy D, and italicizing the numbers of plates containing text, these arrangements are given here, listing copies in their most probable order of production. (Present locations are noted.)

Copy C—*1–4* 12 *5 6* 9 *10 11 13* 22 *15* 14 *18* 17 *19* 21 *20 23* 27 24 *25* 27 28. Binding order. (Lacks *7, 8,* 16.) (Paul Mellon)

Copy F—*1 2 3 5* 12 *6 7* 14 *10 8* 9 *11* 13 22 *15 18* 17 *19 20* 21 *23* 24 *25* 26 27 *28*. Binding order. (Lacks *4,* 16.) (Harvard)

Copy D—*1–3 5–8* 9 *10 11* 12 *13* 14 *15* 17 *18–20* 21 22 *23* 24 *25* 26 27 *28*. Numbered by Blake. (Lacks *4,* 16.) (British Museum)

Copy E—*1 3 5* 12 *2 6* 14 *7 10 8 11* 22 *13 15 18* 17 *19* 12 *20* 21 23 26 27 *28*. Census collation (not verified), but this gives 12 twice; "lacks 4, 9, 16, 24"—but what of *25?* (Private collection)

Copy B—*1–4* 14 *5–7 10* 12 *8 11* 22 *13* 9 *15* 16 *18* 17 *19* 24 *20* 21 *23 25* 26 27 *28*. Blake's numbering. (*Census* "15–19" is mistaken.) Morgan Library (Mrs Thorne)

Copy A—*1 2* 22 24 *3 4* 12 *5 6 7* 17 *8 10 11* 14 *13 18* 21 *19 15* 16 *20* 9 *23* 26 *25 28* 27. This is simply the order as bound; it is certainly mistaken in placing 15 after 19 despite the running heads; these pages were not so numbered by Blake, whose own partly erased numbering, however, fails to include numbers for Plates *1, 7, 8, 9, 15, 23* (perhaps because their positions were obvious, except for 9) and wavers between using Plate 12 as eighth and moving it to follow the title page ("7" deleted, "1" added); has 24 and 25 both numbered "23" (deleted); and gives position "24" first to Plate 28, then to 27. Putting text pages in their necessary order, Blake's numbers would produce the sequence: *1* 12 *2 3 4 5 6* (*7*) [12] (*8*) *10 11?* 17 14 *13* (*15*) *18 20* 16 ( ) *19* (but 19 after 20 won't do) 26? 22? 24/*25* 27 *28?* (Perhaps 9, unnumbered, belongs after 16.) (Paul Mellon)

Copy G—*1 2 3* 9 *5* 12 *6* 14 *7 8* 22 *10 11* 16 *13 15 17 18 19 20* 21 *23* 27 24 *25* 26 *28*. Numbered by Blake. (Lacks *4*.) (Rosenwald collection)

Copy G is on paper watermarked 1818; the other six copies may all have been done in the 1790s. "It is almost impossible to arrange these in any definite order of sequence . . ." (*Census* 70). In *P&P* 725–26 I suggested, on the hypothesis that the earlier copies would have the emblem plates closer to their textual referents and the later farther away, the order of copies CB F D E A G, with A the climactic exemplar of the original series and G following at a distance. On the evidence of etching style, Plates 7 and 8 were made later than the other text plates; their absence puts copy C earliest. Their insertion permitted the removal of Plate 4, thus avoiding two chapters IV, but did not require it; copy B dealt with that problem by changing numbers. Plate 16, present only in copies ABG, is evidence pointing to the revision of my hypothetical sequence to the order given above: C FDE BA G. Neither should be considered firmly established.

Urizen 1[B] (title page). Urizen is writing his own book with his left hand[BA] or his right[DG] (holding a quill) and illustrating it with the other (holding an etching needle or a "pencil," a brush for fine work). (Simmons notes that the left-right symbolism of early copies is markedly reduced in the late G.) With eyes shut he copies what he can read with his toes, from nature's book (his own invention). Efforts at drawing a leaf are visible[BG] on the page under his right foot; on the other page, efforts at writing the letter "W," a revealing choice: see "Will Blake" in the imprint line that supports the whole self-portrait. (Copies are cited in the sequence suggested in the note below.)

He is writing secrets and commandments, but the copy-book is enrooting; the closed books on which he is transcribing may be seen as a single coffin-lid[D]; the Mosaic tablets at his back (where the proverb-communicating Devil of *Marriage* 10 has living wings) suggest a double tombstone: are both Testaments stony to Urizen? (Compare *Religions* 9.) A barren trunk and a branch from the Tree of Mystery form a barrel arch (cave-like[DA]) above the solitary solipsist, duplicated farther back by two similar trunks. ("FIRST" is replaced, in G only, by another branch.)

As a combination frontispiece and title page (Urizen must do and be everything at once), this plate is anything but an invitation into the poem. We might well say, with the Eternals of chapter 3, "What is this? Death" (6:9). Yet there are patches of blue sky[G] between the stones and the first and second arcades which invite us to explore its absurdity (no law can be written this mechanically) and to test its pretense of seamless power (there must be cracks everywhere: a one-man tyrant must be a desperate fraud—or a grim jest). The serpentine adversary (see *Europe* ii) is at work in the lettering of "URIZEN," though his loops on the first letter turn to whips on the last. Blake's caption for this plate in *A Small Book of Designs* (*SBD* 1)—where Urizen's eyes are open—is "Which is the Way The Right or the Left."

Urizen 1[B]

Urizen 2[B]

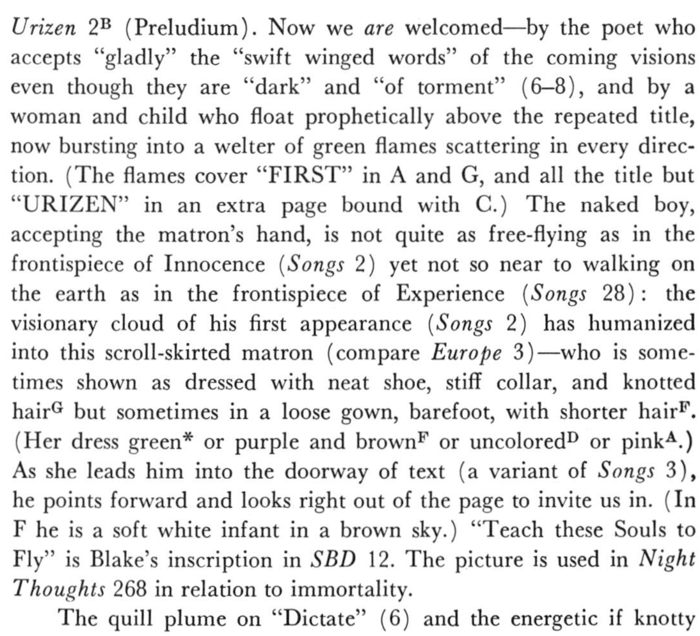

Urizen 2[B] (Preludium). Now we *are* welcomed—by the poet who accepts "gladly" the "swift winged words" of the coming visions even though they are "dark" and "of torment" (6–8), and by a woman and child who float prophetically above the repeated title, now bursting into a welter of green flames scattering in every direction. (The flames cover "FIRST" in A and G, and all the title but "URIZEN" in an extra page bound with C.) The naked boy, accepting the matron's hand, is not quite as free-flying as in the frontispiece of Innocence (*Songs* 2) yet not so near to walking on the earth as in the frontispiece of Experience (*Songs* 28): the visionary cloud of his first appearance (*Songs* 2) has humanized into this scroll-skirted matron (compare *Europe* 3)—who is sometimes shown as dressed with neat shoe, stiff collar, and knotted hair[G] but sometimes in a loose gown, barefoot, with shorter hair[F]. (Her dress green* or purple and brown[F] or uncolored[D] or pink[A].) As she leads him into the doorway of text (a variant of *Songs* 3), he points forward and looks right out of the page to invite us in. (In F he is a soft white infant in a brown sky.) "Teach these Souls to Fly" is Blake's inscription in *SBD* 12. The picture is used in *Night Thoughts* 268 in relation to immortality.

The quill plume on "Dictate" (6) and the energetic if knotty lettering of "URIZEN" suggest that Blake himself is taking up the pen of his blind hero. But that the text will arrive only uncertainly at the human birth and instruction symbolized above, and only in recoil from Urizen, is hinted at in the looping line running forth from "solitary" (4) and knotting and then coiling backward into "Eternals" (5)—also by the knot in the coil under "unfold" (7), and the scarcity of living things within this green fire: a winged fly under "R" and a butterfly with spotted[F] wings poised together for the moment in the circle after "N".

Urizen 3B. We now see the bloody and golden side (flames red* or goldenG or red and goldenF) of the green welter of flame in Plate 2. From the perspective supplied by the text of chapters 1 and 2 we may identify the naked youth running leftward as one of the Eternals looking outward from bright eternity—a solar center in which life is too full of "unquenchable burnings" (4:13) and "fluctuation" (4:11) for the self-exhiling Eternal, Urizen, to tolerate it—into the "soul–shudd'ring vacuum" (5) where Urizen or Death hides in darkness (indicated by black patches between flames). The running is a human dance form of the "sound of a trumpet" (40) which awakes the heavens in alarm; this Eternal will emerge in chapter 3 (misnumbered "II" in copy B, Plate 4) as Los keeping watch. The Plate 3 picture will adapt to verses 8, 9, and 14 of chapter 3 if we see Los as rousing his fires and circling round "the dark globe of Urizen" or "around the dark Demon" Urizen himself (5:38; 6:2)—the solar center being also a fiery circumference *within* which Urizen's world is "A void . . . dark & deep" (4:16). We may also—although Urizen was never that youthful, being "Born Poor, Aged Sixty three" (*P&P* 631)—see this Plate 3 picture as *his* vision of his heroic fighting "with the fire" (4:14). The cruciform position of the arms is not coincidental; for a much later, walking version, see Hand in *Jerusalem* 26. (See *Jerusalem* 62 for a variant in which the identification with Los/Blake is foremost.)

The ten birds after "cloud" (17) and the vines and three flying insects nearby in the right-hand column can illustrate both the genesis of "shapes . . . Of beast, bird" etc (14–16) in Urizen's world and the condition in which "eternal life sprung" (39). In the right-hand column four lines lower Blake adds a bird of paradise, under "Immensity" (43), with two tiny trumpeters, one winged, flying left and right for the "trumpet" reference in the next line (44). (A long-stemmed bud and an open St Bernard's lily flourish just left of the center line.) For Urizen, seeking a universe he can divide and measure, all this springing darkens Eternity; in his own book of Genesis it shows up as "conflictions" (14)—disturbing as the birth of a child. (The same naked runner serves at the top of the Genesis title page [*Dict* plate 2] to keep watch and to ward off the void theatening Eden.) The page ends with leaves like footsteps.

Chap: I

1. Lo, a shadow of horror is risen
In Eternity! Unknown, unprolific?
Self-closd, all-repelling: what Demon
Hath form'd this abominable void
This soul-shudd'ring vacuum?—Some said
"It is Urizen". But unknown, abstracted
Brooding secret, the dark power hid.

2. Times on times he divided, & measur'd
Space by space in his ninefold darkness
Unseen, unknown: changes appeard
Like desolate mountains rifted furious
By the black winds of perturbation

3. For he strove in battles dire
In unseen conflictions with shapes
Bred from his forsaken wilderness,
Of beast, bird, fish, serpent & element
Combustion, blast, vapour and cloud.

4. Dark revolving in silent activity:
Unseen in tormenting passions;
An activity unknown and horrible;
A self-contemplating shadow,
In enormous labours occupied

5. But Eternals beheld his vast forests
Age on ages he lay, clos'd, unknown,
Brooding shut in the deep; all avoid
The petrific abominable chaos

6. His cold horrors silent, dark Urizen
Prepard; his ten thousands of thunders
Rang'd in gloom'd array stretch out across
The dread world, & the rolling of wheels
As of swelling seas, sound in his clouds
In his hills of stor'd snows, in his mountains
Of hail & ice; voices of terror,
Are heard, like thunders of autumn,
When the cloud blazes over the harvests

-tion

1. Earth was not: nor globes of attrac-
The will of the Immortal expanded
Or contracted his all flexible senses.
Death was not, but eternal life sprung

2. The sound of a trumpet the heavens
Awoke & vast clouds of blood roll'd
Round the dim rocks of Urizen, so nam'd
That solitary one in Immensity

3. Shrill the trumpet: & myriads of Eter
-nity,

Urizen 3B

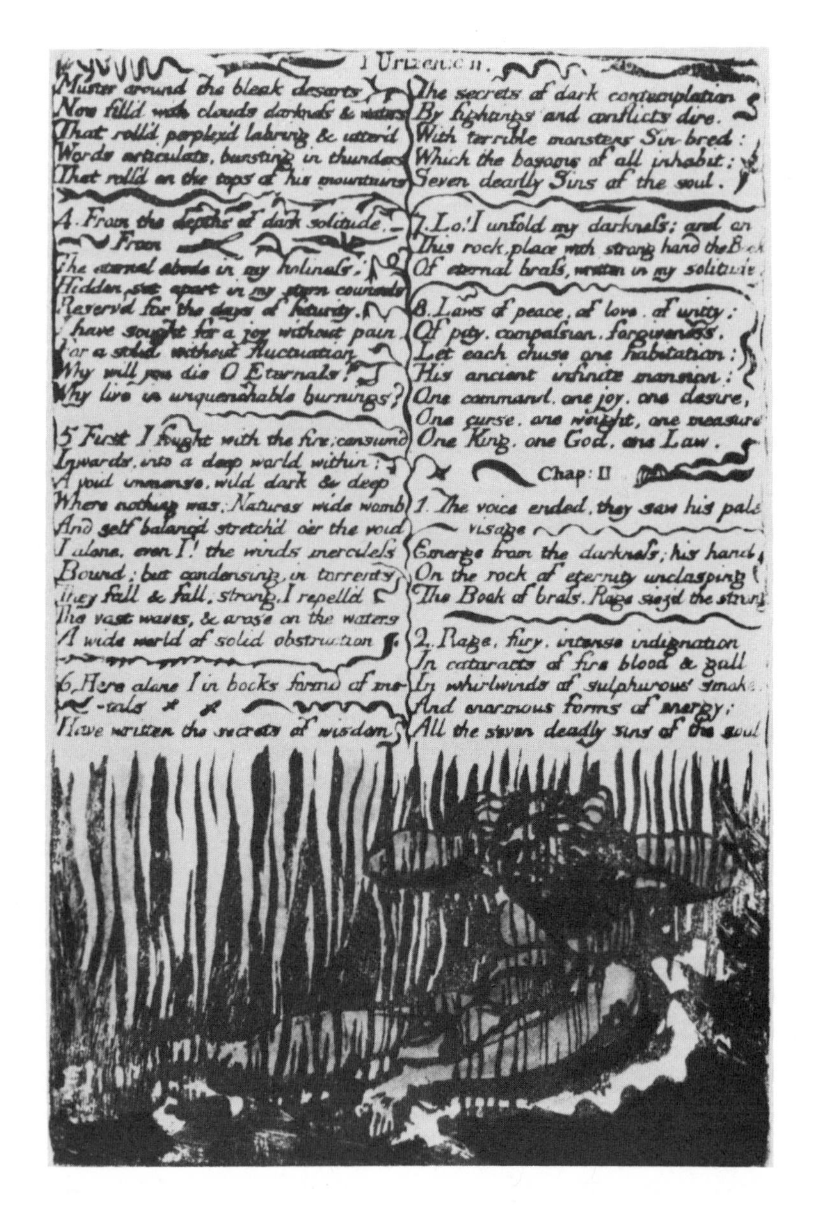

Muster around the bleak desarts
Now fill'd with clouds darkness & waters
That roll'd perplex'd labring & utter'd
Words articulate, bursting in thunders
That roll'd on the tops of his mountains

4. From the depths of dark solitude. From
The eternal abode in my holiness,
Hidden set apart in my stern counsels
Reserv'd for the days of futurity,
I have sought for a joy without pain,
For a solid without fluctuation
Why will you die O Eternals?
Why live in unquenchable burnings?

5 First I fought with the fire; consum'd
Inwards, into a deep world within:
A void immense, wild dark & deep,
Where nothing was; Natures wide womb
And self balanc'd stretch'd o'er the void
I alone, even I! the winds merciless
Bound; but condensing, in torrents
They fall & fall; strong I repell'd
The vast waves, & arose on the waters
A wide world of solid obstruction

6. Here alone I in books form'd of me-
-tals
Have written the secrets of wisdom
The secrets of dark contemplation
By fightings and conflicts dire,
With terrible monsters Sin-bred:
Which the bosoms of all inhabit;
Seven deadly Sins of the soul.

7. Lo! I unfold my darkness: and on
This rock, place with strong hand the Book
Of eternal brass, written in my solitude.

8. Laws of peace, of love, of unity:
Of pity, compassion, forgiveness.
Let each chuse one habitation:
His ancient infinite mansion:
One command, one joy, one desire,
One curse, one weight, one measure
One King, one God, one Law.

Chap: II

1. The voice ended, they saw his pale
visage
Emerge from the darkness; his hand
On the rock of eternity unclasping
The Book of brass. Rage siez'd the strong

2. Rage, fury, intense indignation
In cataracts of fire blood & gall
In whirlwinds of sulphurous smoke:
And enormous forms of energy;
All the seven deadly sins of the soul

Urizen 4B

Urizen 4B (lacking in FDEG). The question "Why live in unquenchable burnings?" (13) is now seen from Urizen's perspective: a naked Eternal inside the curtain of raining fire clutches his head and sits on fluctuating ground more liquid than solid. In A the fire seems to rise like blades of black grass.

The central flowering stem continues, with extensions between verses. Frequent banners leaf leftward from the tall letters, as does a long serpent, free flying, after line 5. In the next space a dragonfly and an ascending redA bird (equal in size!) flank a triune leaf (three sprigsA) growing from "holiness" (7) (Urizen's holiness being Trinitarian?). Two birds fly in the second line of verse 6, perhaps a bird of paradise at the verse's end. After "Chap: II" (i.e. III) a spider stands at the beginning of a dividing banner.

⁂

Urizen 5B. Urizen with crown-like (spikyBFD) halo—or a radiant sun *behind* his head—stretches out his arms, not to create but to reveal his "book of brass," fixing us with his eyes. ("The Book of My Remembrance": *SBD.*) Is its "secret" that memory cannot decipher nature's hieroglyphs (shown sometimes as a riot of colorsD or muddy shapesF—as, in effect, chaos)? Above "departing" (8) flies a bird of paradise (blue greenFDA); above and beside "the flames of Eternal fury" (18) dance four or five human forms (the horizontal one may be a viper: see those enjoying Hellfire in *Marriage* 6 and 7). The words trail a tremulous westward underline, no good devil's spiral, but the viper in the opposite column at "Los . . . Urizen" (38) is redA or red and blackD.

At the end of verse 6 (line 27) a locust confronts a running man (compare *Marriage* 7): "To the desarts . . . he ran . . . To hide, but he could not" (20–21). In verse 7 the verbal image of Urizen's world as a black heart from which pour rivers of blood is translated pictorially as a plant drooping from a bulb on "globe" (33); the vein running up from "veins" (30) is redA. Fires that "pour thro' the void" (15) encode as nine flying birds in the left column, two closer up (and blueF) in the right. There is a blueF fly above "dark'ning" (3).

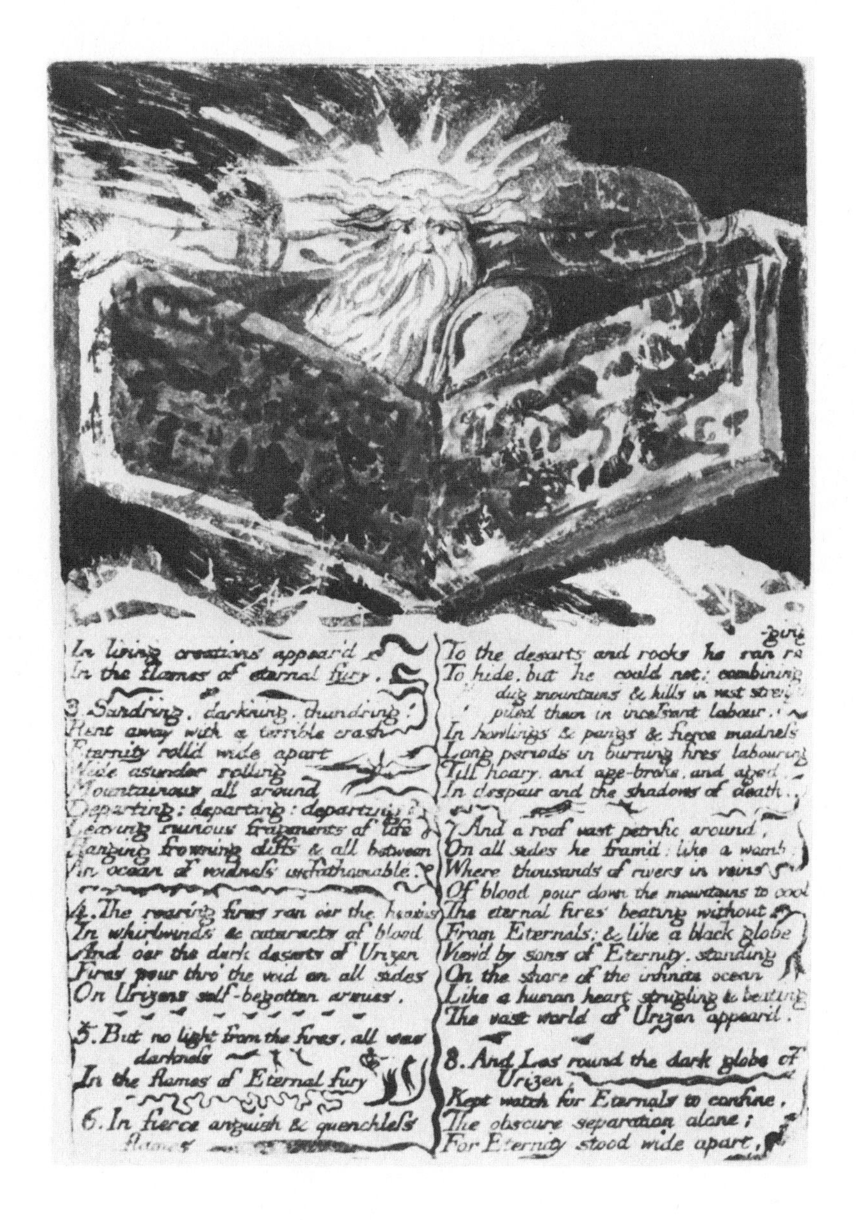

Urizen 5B

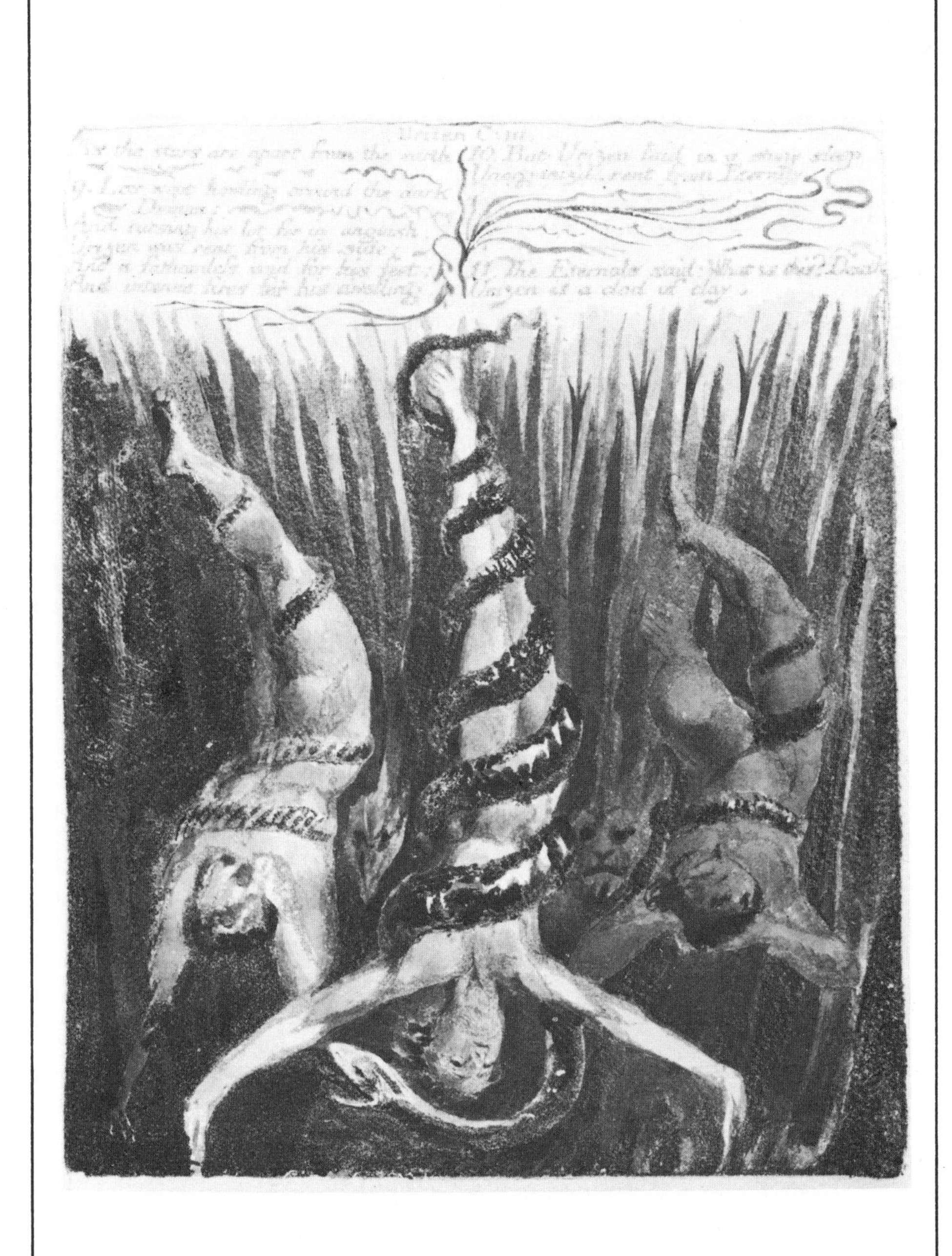

Urizen 6[A]

Urizen 6[A]. The text tells of Los "cursing his lot" as Urizen is "rent from his side" leaving him in "intense fires" with "a void for his feet"—Urizen's departure heats up heaven (turning light to heat, pity to wrath) as well as opening an abyss—and leaving Urizen in "stony sleep Unorganiz'd." The illumination depicts a Satanic host defeated by a war in heaven (four arrows from the Almighty's bow at upper right[BA] only partly visible[D]. As with the fall shown in *Marriage* 5, both parties can interpret this as the lot of their adversaries: a Satan "falling headlong wound round by the tail of the serpent" (*VLJ* 76: *P&P* 546) or a Messiah crucified "with the Head Downwards" (*VLJ* 87), prophetic of resurrection. The youthfulness of the central figure encourages us to see not Urizen with his "self-begotten armies" (4:16) but Los or Orc constricted by the serpent which Urizen's thought engenders in Eternity (see *Europe* 10:16). The two youths falling beside him, also serpent-bound, clutch their heads in despair—the note of Los's "anguish" (3) at his apparent lot—but the gesture of the central figure already calls "Arise!" (to interpret from *Paradise Lost*). The effect is to reverse the anguish of the Laocoön.

The two other falling figures, shadowy in the flames between the falling youths, prove to be the flayed heads and skins of aged, bearded kings (crown spikes discernible on both heads[AG]), the head on the left thin, with walrus mustache[FG] or goatee[BA] (an almost bird-like effect), the head on the right human-lion like. (The complete flayed body of the walrus-mustached old man may be seen in *Let Loose the Dogs of War,* a presumably contemporary drawing by Blake related to *Night Thoughts* 117; his head is attached as a trophy to the side of a crowned Nimrod hunting with hounds, and the skin of his legs trails out behind.) Here the flayed bodies trailing behind the heads end not in legs but in twisting serpent skins—a help toward identifying the living serpents, and toward realizing that *both* parties are falling, men and serpents: but these ghosts of bodies, with humanoid heads and serpent skins, are perhaps of no party, mere relics of the battle. (In D the falling figures are all painted out except for the central crucifixion.)

If we compare the eagle holding the serpent in *Marriage* 15, we see the serpent dominant here, his tail at the top pointing forward but only slightly upward, the eagle now in human form with arm-wings outstretched. They are both falling, but there is an eagle also among the five upward flying birds at top left who underline the comparison of Eternals to "stars . . . apart from the earth" (1).

Stars must fall to earth for saviors to be born; compare *Milton* 2. The squiggles from "anguish" (3) steady into undulations and a vine that grows with leaves downward toward the serpent's undulations. (The hatching or ornament in the right column covers deleted lines.)

Urizen 7^{B} (lacking in C). Los becomes stupified, howling dismally with round mouth (teeth and red tongue added in G), covering his ears, and shortly reduced to "gnashing"—because (as we can tell from his face) he sees Urizen's vision of the separation (of Plate 6) as valid, himself crucified, his arms as the serpent body. Yet the very fright of it rouzes his fires: see the ascending vines contorting under "the wrenching" but taking shapes approaching the Urizenic alphabet above "Los rouz'd his fires."

Urizen 7^{B}

Urizen 8B

Urizen 8B (lacking in C). Though Los is "smitten" (1) it is only "with astonishment"; there are now six birds (dark blue[AD] or blue and brown[F]) flying, one his eagle (all very simply drawn): the senses and the imagination. And Los begins to form nets and to fix with rivets of art the changes (verses 4–6) in the foetal skeleton of the old man (for, like Stothard, Urizen begins life "extreme old": *P&P* 499). We see a cowl of flesh begin to form over the spine and behind the head of his aged greenish[DG] bones, and a blue spinal nerve[DF].

In Plates 7 and 8 Los and Urizen, like orbs in space potentially sun and earth, are in "whirlwinds" of the abyss—a furnace for Los to work in, a womb for Urizen to grow human in.

Urizen 9B (lacking in E). Urizen, choosing to be "Hidden set apart in my stern counsels," sought "For a solid without fluctuation" (4:8, 11). What he experiences is a rocky solid as fluctuating as fire, and an isolation that threatens to be crushing instead of life-giving. Cloud (there are patches of blue skyG toward the top), earth, and human form appear moving toward uniformity or chaos—with elimination of the human form in either event. But Urizen is not about to give up. A print of this plate (*SBD* a) is captioned "Eternally I labour on." His labors are like a bulb's within the earth.

Urizen 9B

Urizen 10B

Urizen 10B. At first glance this may seem a view from behind of Urizen laboring on Plate 9, but this more youthful Atlas is not pondering but pushing, not the dormant bulb of Urizen in "stony sleep" while "ages roll'd over him" (1) but Los—described in the text as engaged in the "restless" work of a blacksmith "Incessant" (16–17)—going at the rock with his hands, causing gaps to open between the rocks. In verse 3, when the corrosive foam settles into a lake (like an etched plate coming clean out of the acid bath in Blake's alchemical printing), three flying birds appear. The ground under Los's feet has the form (not in F) of the whale (or Orc) in *America* 4. Plates 9 and 10 both recall Orc crouching in the earth in *America* 2—with the great difference that Orc could look and therefore rise up without obstruction. Los here must either remove the stone or push his head through it (as he half seems to be attempting). In some copies the features of his adversary Urizen appear on the adjacent rock: in a patch of light by Los's left handB, or as ghost's eyes above his right handA, or as a face near his left kneeG.

Compare "Earth" stuggling into life in *Gates* 3—more by thought (as Urizen) than by energy (as Los or Orc). The *SBD* inscription: "Does the Soul labour thus In Caverns of The Grave."

Urizen 11B. (Copies DBA are similar, F darker. In G the structures behind Los are almost completely hidden by the flames, which have spread to his side of the page; Urizen's skull as well as his body has been given more flesh, also teeth and nostrils, and the chains are gone from his legs.)

The vine and tendrils in the text are growing upward now; the loops at left are pulled "down into the Abyss" but they shelter a greenAD grape leaf, and the tendril above "The pangs of hope" moves forward from loops into vine. Urizen is now really in the smithy, his greenish bronze flesh still lacking skin, and he too is looking up. In the early copies the blacksmith's credentials as builder of cities are present in a Roman dome (earth shaped with a grid of longitudes and latitudes) and a leaning tower like Pisa's that is surely falling. Los is clutching his hammer very close to the steel, to do better this time, but his face expresses "dismal woe"DBA if not anguishG.

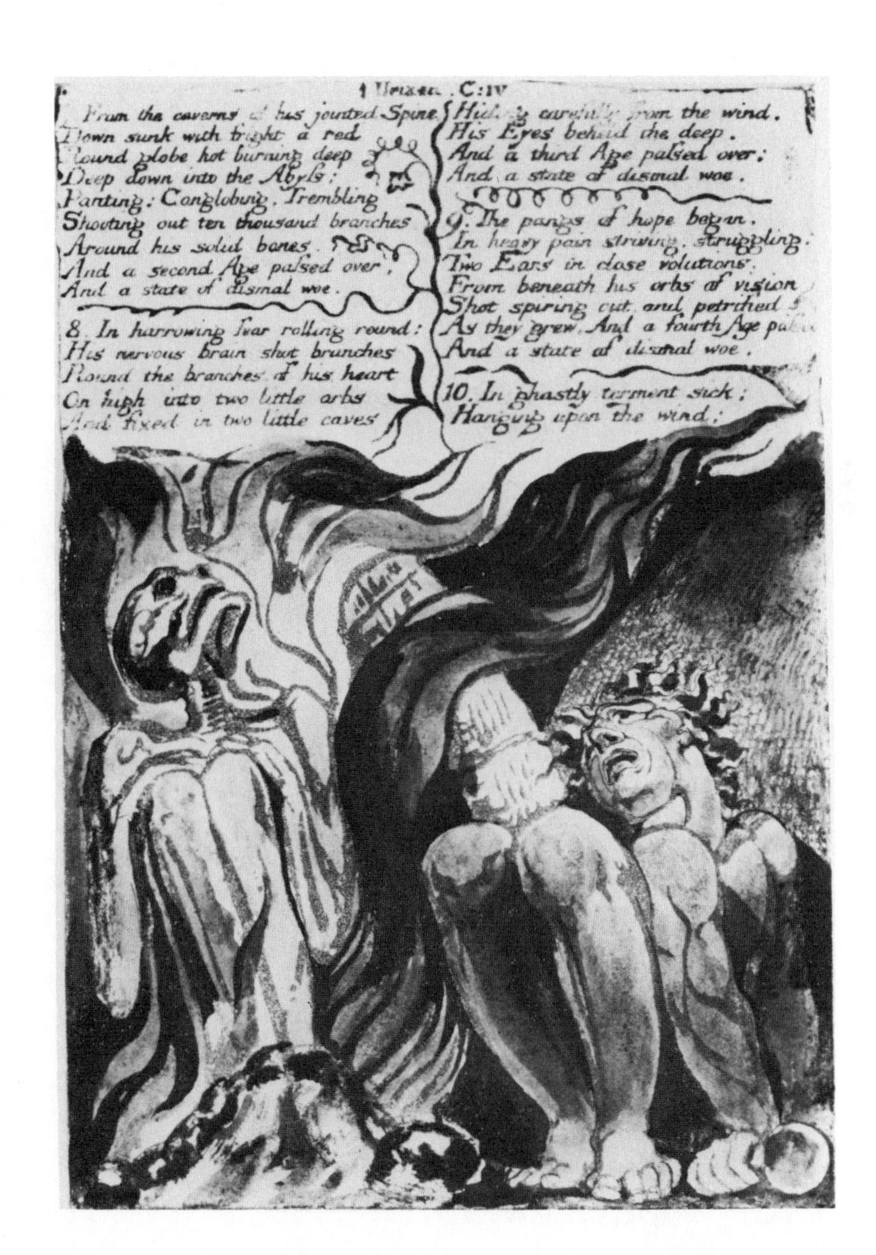

Urizen 11B

Urizen 12^B

Urizen 12^B. The baptism of the thinker as athlete swiftly reduces his dignity (is he still sitting?) and sends his beard streaming in opposite directions. The elemental liquid is water (blue green^B or blue and green^D and black^F) or darkness (dark, with no color in front of his body^A, or grey and black^G with lines of orange brown); the text has him "hiding in surgeing Sulphureous fluid his phantasies" (10:13–14) or, earlier, strongly repelling the "vast waves" (4:21–22, his own account). This is Urizen's contribution to the etching process and to regeneration. It is hard to tell whether, as a swimmer, he is trying to rise or sink. But his hands imitate the resurrection posture of Los in Plate 6 (an adjacent picture in FG, nearby in CDEB). His feet are splashed with silver in G; they have black stigmata in D (compare Hand in *Jerusalem* 26). A print of this plate is inscribed "I labour upwards into futurity" (*SBD* b).

Urizen 13^B^. With her back to us a naked woman with hair streaming in two directions as if in a storm center (compare Urizen's in Plate 12) (streaming only leftward in FBA) divides the cloudy heavens, opening the sky to the constellations[G] of the seven Pleiades and the belt of Orion—setting the sun and moon apart or in their places: this combines Urizen's work of separating and Los's of fixing, and it sets his clock. (The effects vary; in D there do not seem to be clouds with the crescent moon at right; in most copies the object of her pushing at the left seems to be a globe, not clear of clouds and scarcely lit; in most copies a possible interpretation is simply the parting of dark clouds—with bright edges—in dark sky. Compare Christ parting clouds in *Night Thoughts* 1 and Apollo doing so in *Job* 14.

The picture recurs in *Ahania* 1; here she is "Pity" who "divides the soul" (51–53), subsequently named Enitharmon. The small pictures dividing the "dismal" images of the text seem to illustrate the "wisdom & joy of life" which "Roll like a sea" around Los: two butterflies (one dark blue[A], one spotted white[A] or red and yellow[F]) and two distant birds; seven birds winging beside "eternal life" and one above the "anguish" where pity begins; very exuberant vines that put twenty-four loops at "Los wept," a flower hand against "dismal woe," and other flower shapes near the top. (On this plate as the dividing center of the work, see Simmons in *Forms* 149.)

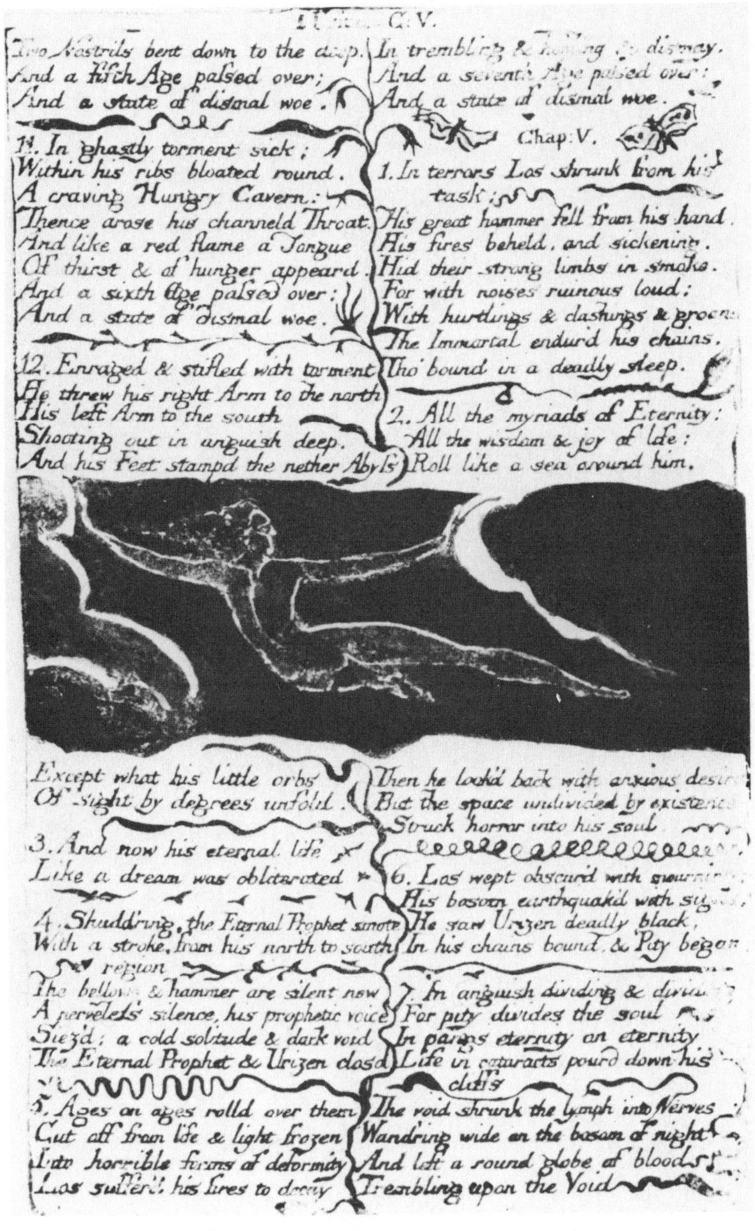

Urizen 13[B]

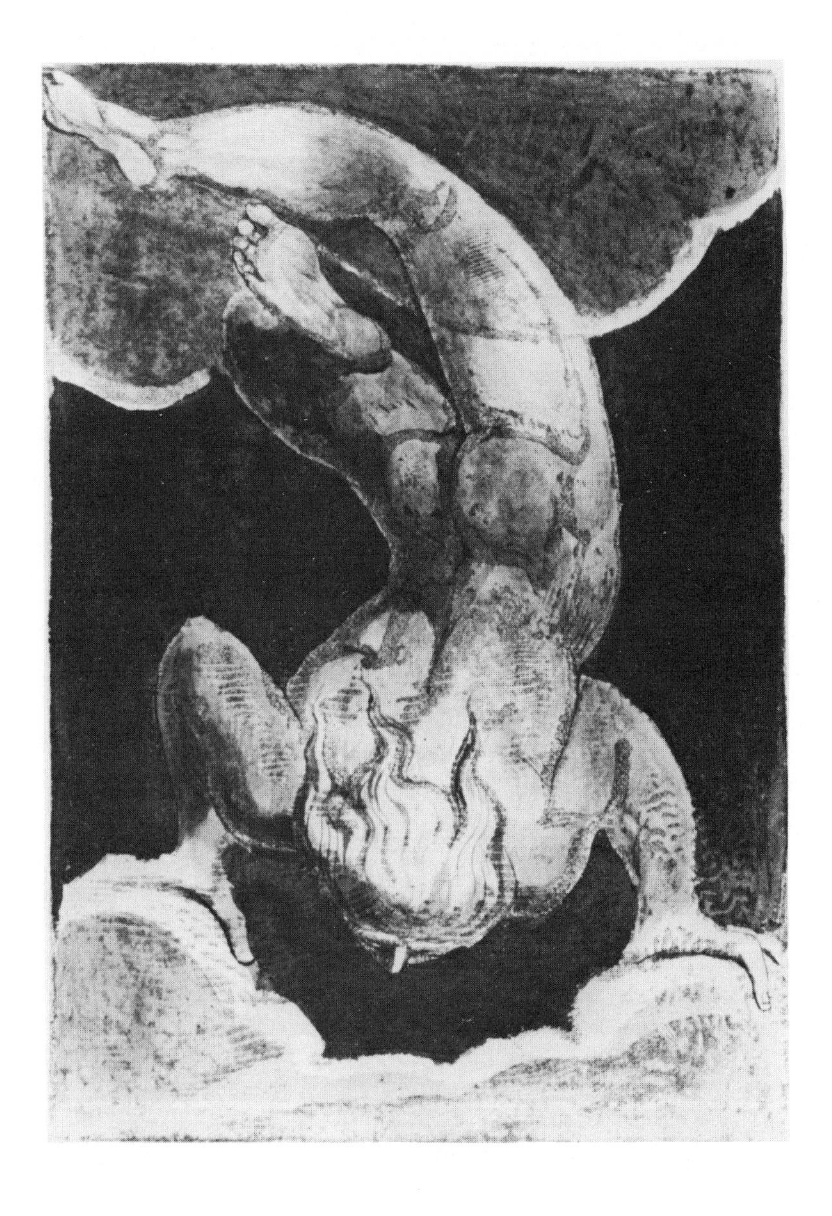

Urizen 14B

Urizen 14B. In the group of full-page pictures of the four elements, this is Air (Earth being Plate 9, Water Plate 12, Fire Plate 16). Is this Urizen seeking solid and perhaps finding it another cloud? Has he become a Tantalus, as engraved by Goltzius in this sort of position, seeking in vain to drink? The ambiguity of drawing is prophetic; that is, Blake did not simply intend to draw rocks (or clouds) but fail to make his intent clear; he drew, as in *Marriage* 1, masses that must be seen as rocks but also as clouds or, as in the embracing couple in *Marriage* 3, a figure that combines motion and stasis, diving and a hand stand. See Mitchell (p. 103) on this design as embodying "the paradoxical fusion of expansion and contraction, movement and stasis which characterizes Urizen's world." (But it is in G, not A, that the "continuity of the human form with its spatial container is emphasized by coloring" and in G, not B, that Urizen's beard is, slightly, visible.) In D a black void yawns between upper clouds and lower cloud-rocks.

Urizen 15B. "As glasses discover Worlds In the endless Abyss of space" (to quote the text here), three[D] or four[G] Eternals and an eagle[BG] (top left) are beholding "the dark visions of Los"—only the curved surface of a globe or skull before Los's left hand delineates the surface by applying his illumination. In *Marriage* 6–7 a Devil (Blake) is described as hovering over the rock surface while etching; here Los as Blake reaches down to add light, colored lines to the blank dark surface of a globe or skull, and an Eternal at his left (a stand-in for Urizen if this is Urizen's skull) trails his beard like a paintbrush. In terms of the forming of Urizen, this is a step after the nerves and sinews of Plate 11, an addition of flesh and skin. The text relates it (also) to the "globe of life blood" which we see in Plate 17 (preceding this in A only). (Blake's relief etching required applying the lines of text and picture in varnish or "ground" to the plate before etching.) The collaboration of these two is emphasized by their seeming to share a cloak[BG] of blue[G] (sky?) which however divides them from the other Eternals, one with a beard that curves under Los's cloud, another just above[G], a young beardless face with white cloak, and an eagle whose neck and head, in blue[G], fill the top left corner with perhaps a long wing stretched out beside the cloak. The presiding eagle of the printing house, perhaps. The light on the horizon is red[DA] or red and yellow[G] or rose and purple[F].

A flower form (dark green[DFA]) that hangs down from "appear'd" repeats the bending down of Los and divides into finger-like petals trailing color as his fingers do.

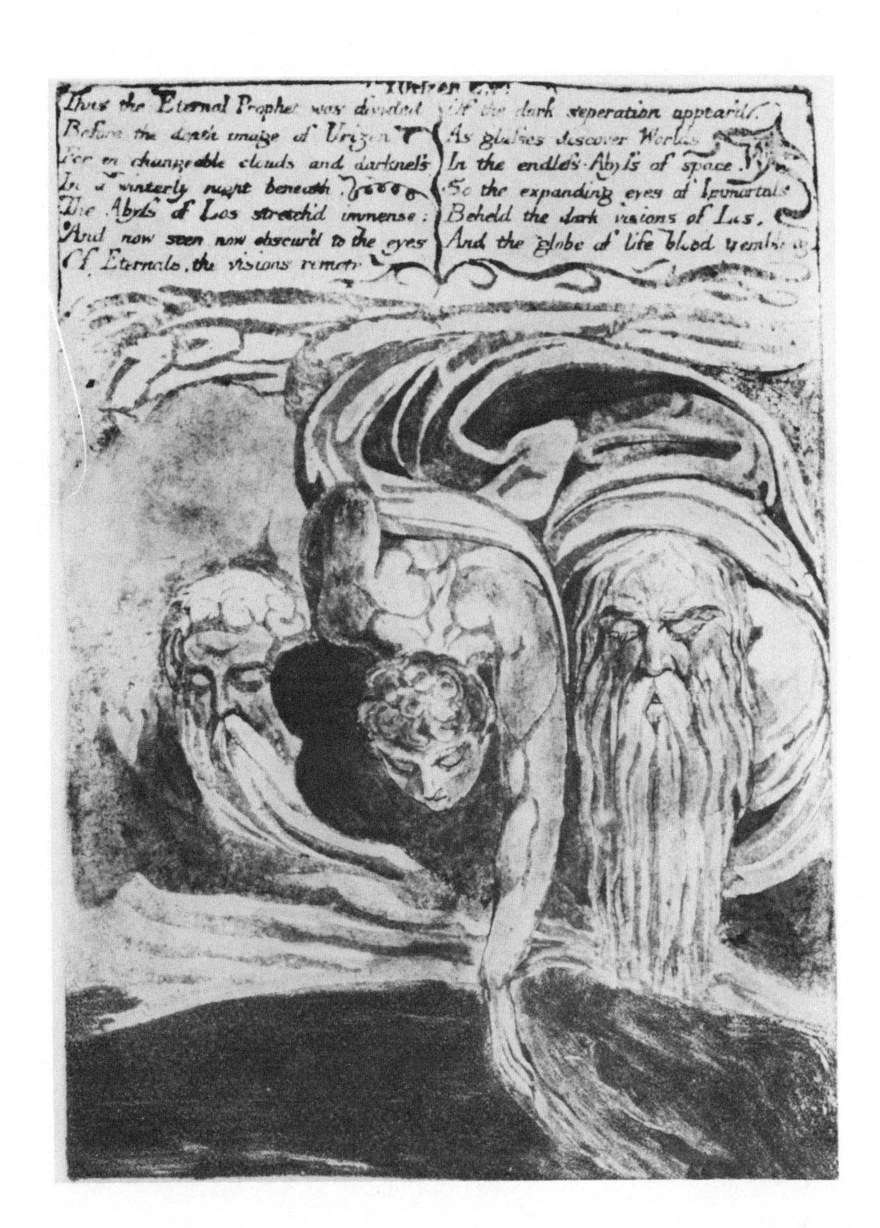

Urizen 15B

Urizen 16B

Urizen 16B (lacking in CFDE). Probably an afterthought to supply a full-page Fire picture to go with Earth (9), Water (12), and Air (14). Los sits with hands behind his head in a boss of yellow and red flames, his body dark and redG (from the smithy?), his hair and the flames blowing in contrary directions (like Urizen's hair in Plate 12 and Enitharmon's in Plate 13). Is he being torn but resisting division? Is he moving or at the center of motion? His facial expression varies from the narrow mouth and tearful cheeks of B to the closed mouth and bearded sadness of A—where the flames seem at the top only and he is in a "giving-up fall through liquid dying flames" (Simmons)—to the open howling mouth and upturned anguished eyes of G.

The symmetrically matching portrait is Urizen's in Plate 22. But note that when Los is weeping (in copy B) Urizen is not; when Urizen is weeping (in G) Los is not.

Urizen 17[B]. The "anguish dividing & dividing" Los's soul mounts to pulsations of labor eventuating in the birth of Enitharmon, the Pity engendered by his response to Urizen's plight or need. The process takes "eternity on eternity" and he holds his hands against his ears, as if to shut out noise, or to keep his head from melting away, or to extrude the placental globe of blood. "Life in cataracts pourd down his cliffs" (see the veins of blood[G] down his spine and back), "The void shrunk the lymph into Nerves Wand'ring wide on the bosom of night And left a round globe of blood Trembling upon the Void" (V 7). (For some of Blake's ideas about fibres of life see note on *Jerusalem* 85.) In B the veins are few but make a network on the globe; in CDA there are more veins on the body but the globe is red and fairly smooth; in G the body is veined, the globe not distinctly so, but veins surround it, like a nest. (In F the clothing gathers at the waist in thick red and silver folds that carry blood down the sides, not down the back; the globe is red and smooth.)

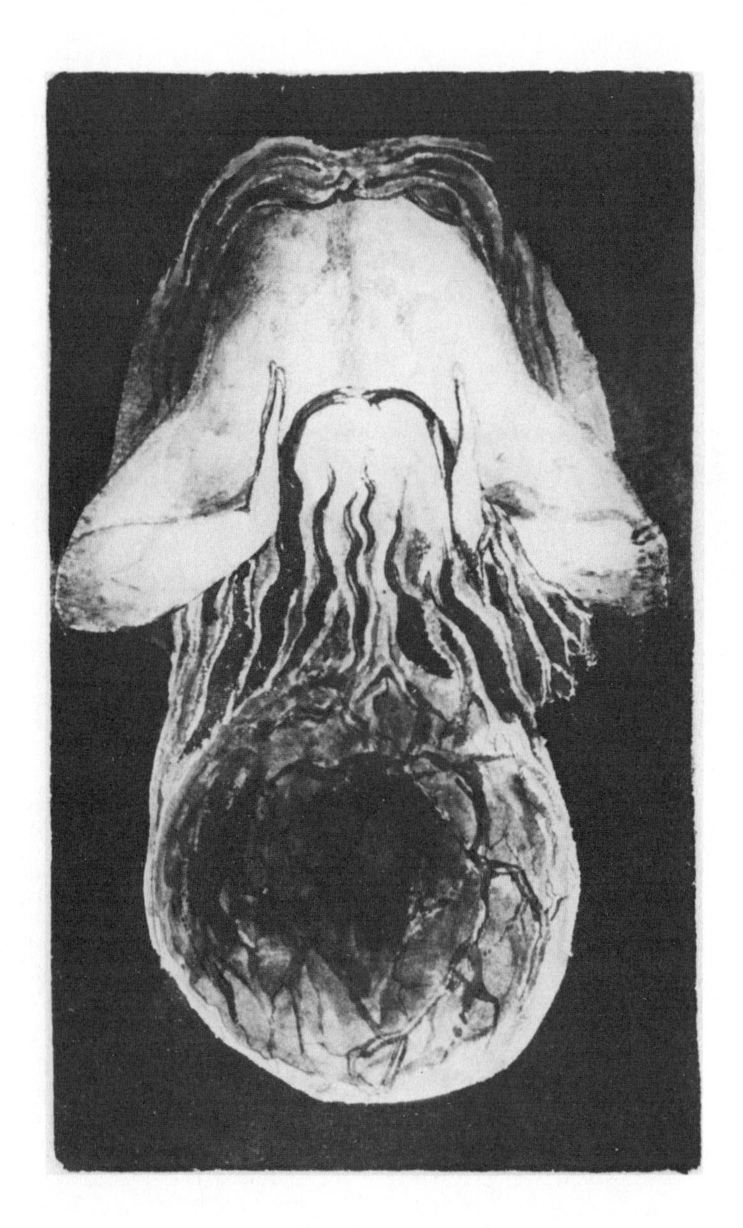

Urizen 17[B]

Urizen 18^{B}

Urizen 18^{B}. From the fiery heart's center where the hammer pounds the anvil (here held resting on it) Los looks with selfless pity—hands in crucifix position without letting go the hammer—toward the trembling globe. (In page sequence, Plate 17 immediately precedes 18 only in D and G, but immediately follows it in CFEB.) It has become "the first female now separate" (10).

Los's right arm rests on a rounded stone, and a similar stone is behind his left arm (thinner than the right, distinctly withered in A); it is as though he were occupying the same position Urizen does in Plate 28! (Stones and anvil are green^{F}.)

In A and F flames engulf Los's right foot; in G he does not lack genitals. The words "trembled" and "Wonder" produce most of the interlinear foliage, all naked as flames.

Urizen* 19[G]. Scarcely out of the fire (but after his embrace of pity: note how she rises from the word "Pity"), she "wept, she refus'd In perverse and cruel delight" (11–12). (The chapter title in the first column is flanked by figures soaring toward it, if not each other, a gowned female and a naked male. Los, having covered his ears during labor, now covers his eyes—translating the text, "She fled from his arms, yet he followd," to signify "he followed suit": they cooperate in the perversity of separation by turning their faces away or inward. Compare, for his role and a reverse of hers, *Visions* 6; for hers, *Visions* 8.

In some copies there are simply "curtains of darkness" behind them (B, dark red background, she greenish, he reddish; A, odd scratch lines behind her); in others she stands in pink[D] or grey[F] smoke (pink, white, and gold[G]) like a magician's puff. In G there is a rock behind Los and the gold flames near him seem solidifying as part of it; there is a green carpet under him; a patchwork of green and brown leaves[F].

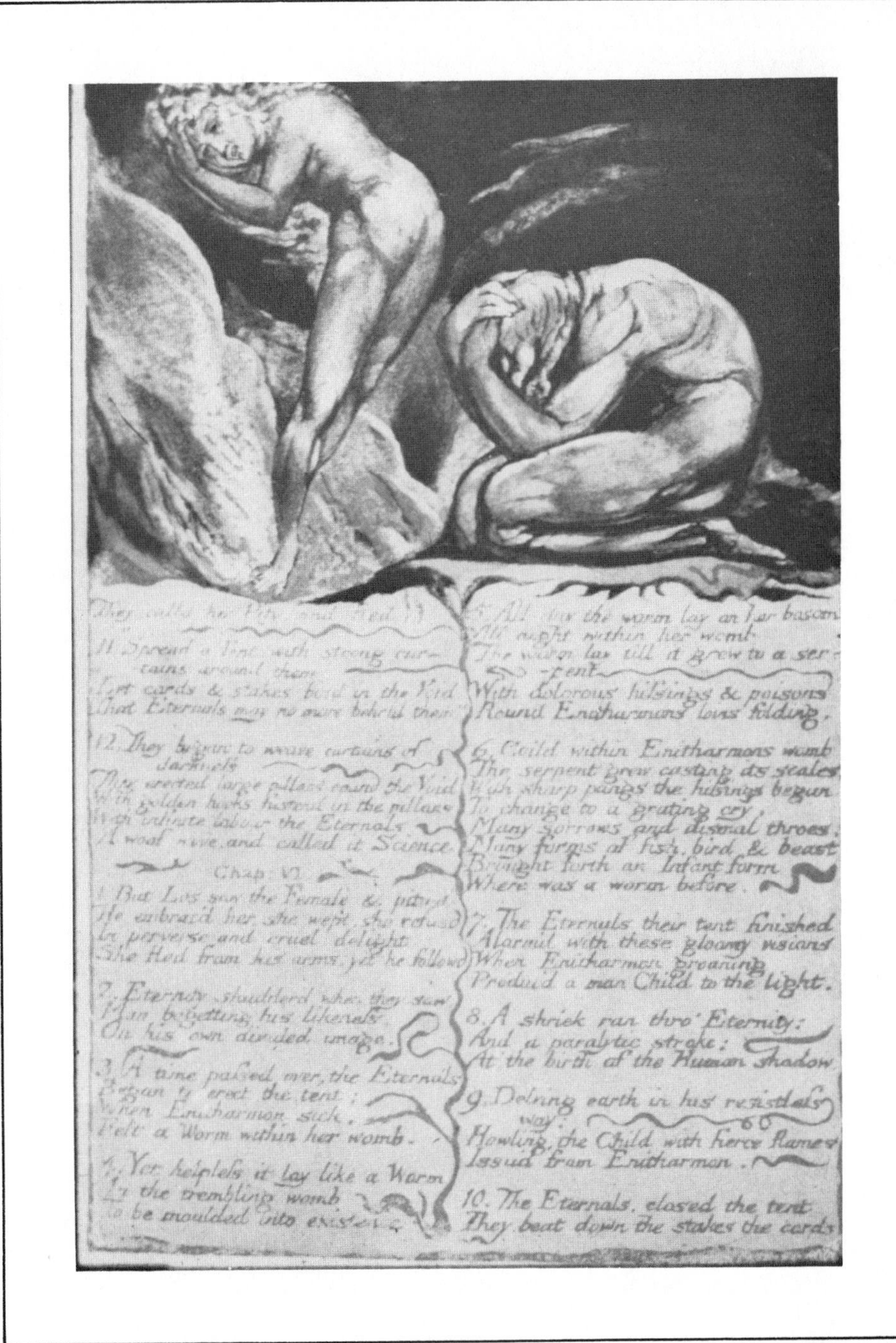

Urizen 19[G]

Urizen C. VII

Stretch'd for a work of eternity:
No more Los beheld Eternity.

11. In his hands he seiz'd the infant
He bathed him in springs of sorrow
He gave him to Enitharmon.

Chap. VII.

1. They named the child Orc, he grew
Fed with milk of Enitharmon

2. Los awoke her; O sorrow & pain!
A tight'ning girdle grew,
Around his bosom. In sobbings
He burst the girdle in twain,
But still another girdle
Oppress'd his bosom. In sobbings
Again he burst it. Again
Another girdle succeeds
The girdle was form'd by day;
By night was burst in twain.

3. These falling down on the rock
Into an iron Chain
In each other link by link lock'd

4. They took Orc to the top of a mountain.
O how Enitharmon wept!
They chain'd his young limbs to the rock
With the Chain of Jealousy
Beneath Urizens deathful shadow

5. The dead heard the voice of the child
And began to awake from sleep
All things. heard the voice of the child
And began to awake to life.

6. And Urizen craving with hunger
Stung with the odours of Nature
Explor'd his dens around

7. He form'd a line & a plummet
To divide the Abyss beneath.
He form'd a dividing rule:

8. He formed scales to weigh;
He formed massy weights;
He formed a brazen quadrant;
He formed golden compasses
And began to explore the Abyss
And he planted a garden of fruits

9. But Los encircled Enitharmon
With fires of Prophecy
From the sight of Urizen & Orc.

10. And she bare an enormous race

Chap. VIII.

1. Urizen explor'd his dens
Mountain, moor, & wilderness,
With a globe of fire lighting his journey
A fearful journey, annoy'd
By cruel enormities: forms

Urizen 20^{B}

Urizen 20^{B}. The child Orc is born in a welter of variegated red flames yellow or white at the center (compare the green ones in Plate 2, the red in Plate 3—but the human form now outward indicating joy not terror), arms out (like the child in birth in *Marriage* 3) but, as newborn infants are traditionally said to do, "Delving earth in his resistless way" (19:44), the earth brown^{FG} with blue or black (flames-water) pouring onto it. The boy's genitals are outlined^{BF}. Very strong vinework grows up through the page center, heated by the flames. It manages to diagram the text, e.g. at VII 2:5, showing the formation of girdle after girdle.

❧

Urizen 21B. Orc has grown rapidly "Fed with milk of Enitharmon" (VII 1) but so has the chain formed of Los's daily girdles of jealousy now hanging from the current one. Los's beard shows how Urizenic or mortal he has become, choosing to take Orc up the mountain to chain his limbs to the rock. He has brought hammer and anvil to the mountain (in one copy the anvil is improvised from three rock slabs; in F it is an old greenish rock). The actions of Abraham toward Isaac and Jupiter toward Prometheus are precedents without so much maternal cooperation. For the next scene, see *America* 1. And compare *Four Zoas* 60.

A red sun (omitted in A) sinking (presumably) behind the green hill puts blood on Los's chain. (In F there is an incredibly plum-colored sun; the girdle and chain are strawberry red.) In FDB there are folds of drapery behind the embracing mother and child: to what purpose? The stance of Los here and in *Jerusalem* 100 hints at the lameness of Hephaestos, the god of blacksmiths. In F and in a color-printed proof of this plate the drapery is also present; Enitharmon's right hand is at her side instead of on Orc's back.

Urizen 21B

Urizen 22[B]

Urizen 22[B]. This statue of Urizen manacled and chained is placed, ironically, near Plate 21 (Los with chain) only in copy D. In CFEB it is near the text-bearing Plate 13. Plate 16 (Los sitting in flames, lacking in CFDE) was first placed fairly near (in B) as its mate near the same text. "Both plates, with matching poses, refer to V 1–6, the moment (ages) of stasis when Los finishes Urizen and is . . . struck with despair; the moment ends with the creation of Enitharmon (pity) which leads eventually, through Orc, to Urizen's rebirth" (Simmons). There are tears on his cheeks, almost invisible[FBA] or prominent[G]. His halo (or the radiation behind his head) is dull white and purple[F] or red[D] or bright yellow[B], or red, white, and black (with some gold)[G], the hill behind him green[G].

Blake's caption for this plate in his *Large Book of Designs* stresses contrary aspects of Urizen's chains: forged by his own mind to mock the world, they lock him into his own torments: "Frozen doors to mock The World: while they within torments uplock."

Urizen 23^{B}. The lion at the right is either extremely shaggy—or is wearing sheep's clothing: a bit of clowning that suggests that the artist himself is inside the lion, watching (compare the human swan in *Jerusalem* 11). Urizen doesn't recognize him, and there will be no collision, we can see from the position of his left foot. With that heavy lamp of his, issuing bloody-smoky rays, ironically described as "a globe of fire lighting his journey" (20:48), he can hardly see where he is going and has to grope with his left hand—an ironic version of Diogenes. All he makes out is one of the "cruel enormities" (i.e. forms "Of life") on his godforsaken mountains. *Four Zoas* 74 shows Urizen in the same position, without the lion, having, in 71, tried seizing "a lion . . . By the fierce mane . . . in vain." For a lion accepted as guide, see the one near the head of the procession in Blake's *Faerie Queene* painting (*Dict* plate 8). For lions confronting tyrants see Stothard's Bunyan illustration of Feb 1 1791, "The Affright," in which two lions confront Greatheart armed; the positions are similar. Blake's Bunyan 8 is similar symbolically but not pictorially. For a lion in a cave (as in G) see *Songs* 20.

The interlinear foliage runs to whip-like roots that drop below the text and mock the shape of Urizen's head and shoulders. Beside the word "enormities" (2) Blake shows what unblinded people can see, three normal flying birds, one perhaps the eagle. (This and another are reddened in F.)

(Mitchell observes that if Urizen were St Jerome, who holds his red cardinal's hat the way Urizen does his globe when retiring to the wilderness to prepare his secret book, the New Testament, he would make the lion his friend by pulling a thorn from his paw.) In context the design is a sort of anticipatory parody of *Jerusalem* 1.

Urizen 23^{B}

Urizen 24B

Urizen 24B (lacking in E). Urizen's four sons, who disgust him by breeding forms of life (22:46–50) are crudely elemental: flaming Fuzon at the top; Thiriel, hair curly blueD or brownG, his head in a bubble of air; Utha emerging "From the waters" and lamenting at once; and Grodna, climbing right up out of the parched earth, the cracks in which seem to him Heavens. (Grodna's clamp-like hands anticipate the motif of Albion's possessiveness in *Jerusalem* 4.) In some copiesBA the chaos of their environment is but vaguely differentiated; in othersDG there is sunlight on the horizon. In F a red scarf flying from Thiriel's waist makes a sort of sun. In D, the copy in which the falling figures on Plate 6 are reduced to one and the Eternals on Plate 15 to three, only two Elements are present: Utha in black water and Thiriel in a sky of clouds that replace Fuzon—as does a red sun half risen in the exact center. Grodna and his earth are replaced by sea and sun.

The absence of this plate from copy E seems related to the absence of the Earth and Fire plates (9 and 16) as well. I suspect that these omissions and the changes in D were made to remove the four-element theme from these copies, for some reason.

The red scarf, a sun of sorts, appears also in C and A. Thiriel has outstretched arms, with palms open, in CAG. There is a separate plate in which only Utha appears. (Reported by W. J. T. Mitchell.)

Urizen 25[B]. Urizen's daughters are also disobedient to his "iron laws" and seem, from his "darkness," the brood of monsters and worms. The variations in copies of this plate only complicate the difficulty of sorting out the limbs and serpent coils in this can-of-worms picture. In early copies[DBA] a winged creature at the top has a human head close to a face with human hand which clutches a horn-like worm (or two hands that clutch the head[D]) and may belong to some of the large scaly coils that loop toward and around the daughter reclining at lower left; her body extends like an almost human thigh across the page, not scaly but ringed (compare *Jerusalem* 75). In F there are two pink female faces at top; the central monster, bronze, crocodile-like, has the wings, and a woman's head with black hair; in G another human face is added near the winged knee, and the winged monster's face is gone; perhaps the wings, with a serpentine extension around and down the right edge of the picture, are now assigned to the new face. The wings are turning green, and the leafy platform below the coiling group is greenish blue.

There is probably a caterpillar (or blue[A] chrysalis) just below this platform. And some of the interlinear foliage is worm-like. There is an unusual intermixture of flying insects and humans after line 4, perhaps two insects followed by two running or dancing children and a soaring gowned figure. A human flees from "fire" after verse 7, a gowned human descends beside "human brain," and a bird rises (in the lower right column) after "eternal life" (replaced by a flower in A). Two human forms barely emerge from lines after IX 1.

Urizen 25[B]

Urizen 26B

Urizen 26B. Is this begging child with his "Dog at the wintry door" (25:2) in the same England as the mother and child of the Preludium (Plate 2)? There is a long graphic tradition, rather sentimental, of begging children with their dogs, probably alluded to by Blake when he spoke of taking a dog for one's schoolmaster (*Visions* 5). For Blake at least one home picture is desirable in every prophecy, a reminder that he is writing to and of existing beings and men. (For cognates see *Songs* 37 and 46, *Europe* 6 and 7.)

But the city over which Urizen drops his tears of selfish Pity (25:14) is contorted by the Urizenic carpentry: the human form is squared to the cruel shape of the door and its panels, the dog flattened to a doormat with right-angled head. The pity is in the lifeless poster. Even the shadows are triangles (reversed from right to left in F and A, the whole area dark in D). The boy nevertheless illuminates this darkness, if more like a candle than a happy infant.

Urizen 27[B]. A multi-purpose emblem. When this plate follows Plate 5 (as in copy B) it does for Urizen's launching his new world (see 5:37) without supplying the vaguest notion of its shape. When it follows Plate 23 (as in G) it suggests his taking both hands to push the sun he has been carrying. But in G the color of the globe in Plate 23 is pale white ranging through yellow to pink, with red and brown rays; the color of what he is pushing here is grey green with an aura of dark red, two touches of yellow, a blue background, more probably world than sun. (The evidence of *Four Zoas* 74 helps to suggest a vortex.) In FDA he seems rather to be fleeing through circular spaces (his head yellow in black and red clouds[D]) so that his hands seem flung up beside his head as fending off shadows upon his solipsistic existence. In the context of Plates 25 and 28 (which are near in most copies) our attention is drawn more to his robe, the folds of which, flesh pink as though part of his body[G] (paper white as his neck and hair[F]), suggest the embrio-web drawn out from his sorrowing soul which follows Urizen wherever his footsteps take him over the cities (VIII 6).

Urizen 27[B]

Urizen 28ᴮ

Urizen 28ᴮ. The finis line, "The End of the [*First*] Book of Urizen," is almost a double entendre, or the picture makes it one. Urizen sits about where he was in Plate 1—a mirror image is suggested by his left foot's replacing his right—yet hands and feet are no longer occupied with making or copying his book but with the web become a Net of Religion that none can break, twisted "like to the human brain" (25:21); compare *Songs* 47. The tombstones (of Natural law) are his arm rests. (The stony law which Los is in a position to stamp to dust in Plate 18.) The pedant of Plate 1 has become the tyrant God of his own Religion, eyes open, face harder, posture upright, still a halo of thin points of light from his head (or from a sun behind it)—more completely in command of his own universe: and completely trapped in it. Note the inverted pyramid formed by his arms, net, and foot. His index fingers point *down*.

A tiny drawing under the finis line makes the point: a faceless corpse, the human form in extremis. "Urizen's green footstool is doubtless the Earth, our neck, alas" (Grant); in F it is a stone as grey as his foot; the ropes are very black.

Yet a defiant counter energy expresses itself in the column-dividing central vine: growing up from the earth above Urizen's head, it lets us see him as a bulb planted in the ground (see Plates 9 and 10); from it one great green leaf (touched with yellowᶠ) springs just where the grape leaf and tendril grew on Plate 11; a perfected form of the large leaf of Los on Plate 15. And flame-tendrils strongly bracket and separate out verse 8, of the departure of "the remaining children" altogether. All that living things can do is leave. (Nothing more can happen in *this* book: Simmons.)

THE BOOK OF AHANIA

(Reduced from about 5¼ by 4 inches)

Ahania i (frontispiece). This work is printed by intaglio etching in black ink; the three illustrations are colored with care. In the frontispiece Urizen, with his back against "his mountains of Jealousy" (2:33), squats behind the diminutive Ahania ("so name his parted soul": 32), "Kissing her and weeping over her." He has called her Sin and is ready to hide her in darkness (as he has already hidden his own face).

Ahania 1 (title page). This is the "lamenting voice of Ahania" (4:45: Ahania herself having "no form" 49) "Distant in solitary night" (48). The form we see suggests Ahania's "circling dark Urizen, As the moon anguished circles the earth" (2:39–40). Above a curved horizon, her body touched with blue against a blue sky (darkening at left) so that her white face is moon-like, in a transparent gown that forms a round scroll under her left foot, she soars away yet turns her head, owl-like, over her shoulder. Her hair indicates swift flight, her hands a halting effort(?). Whorls in a streak of white cloud above her right arm suggest "her tears from clouds" falling (4:50).

Compare the use of this image in *Urizen* 13, and see *Night Thoughts* 1.

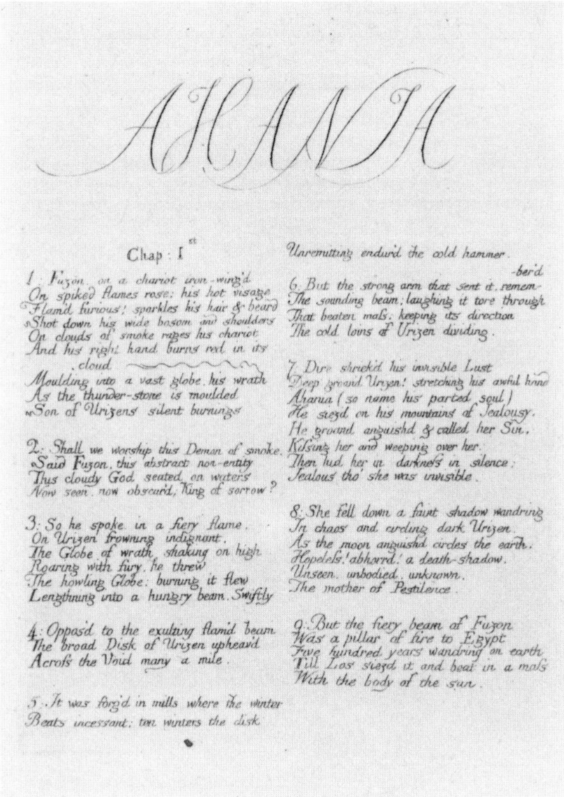

AHANIA

Chap: I[st]

1: Fuzon, on a chariot iron-wing'd
On spiked flames rose; his hot visage
Flam'd furious! sparkles his hair & beard
Shot down his wide bosom and shoulders
On clouds of smoke rages his chariot
And his right hand burns red in its
cloud
Moulding into a vast globe, his wrath
As the thunder-stone is moulded
Son of Urizens silent burnings

2: Shall we worship this Demon of smoke,
Said Fuzon, this abstract non-entity
This cloudy God seated on waters
Now seen, now obscur'd, King of sorrow?

3: So he spoke in a fiery flame,
On Urizen frowning indignant,
The Globe of wrath shaking on high
Roaring with fury, he threw
The howling Globe: burning it flew
Lengthning into a hungry beam. Swiftly

4: Oppos'd to the exulting flam'd beam
The broad Disk of Urizen upheav'd
Across the Void many a mile.

5: It was forg'd in mills where the winter
Beats incessant; ten winters the disk
Unremitting endur'd the cold hammer.

6. But the strong arm that sent it, remem-
-ber'd
The sounding beam; laughing it tore through
That beaten mass: keeping its direction
The cold loins of Urizen dividing.

7. Dire shriek'd his invisible Lust
Deep groan'd Urizen! stretching his awful hand
Ahania (so name his parted soul)
He siez'd on his mountains of Jealousy.
He groand anguish'd & called her Sin,
Kissing her and weeping over her;
Then hid her in darkness in silence;
Jealous tho' she was invisible.

8: She fell down a faint shadow wandring
In chaos and circling dark Urizen,
As the moon anguish'd circles the earth;
Hopeless! abhorr'd! a death-shadow,
Unseen, unbodied, unknown,
The mother of Pestilence.

9: But the fiery beam of Fuzon
Was a pillar of fire to Egypt
Five hundred years wandring on earth
Till Los siez'd it and beat in a mass
With the body of the sun.

Ahania 2

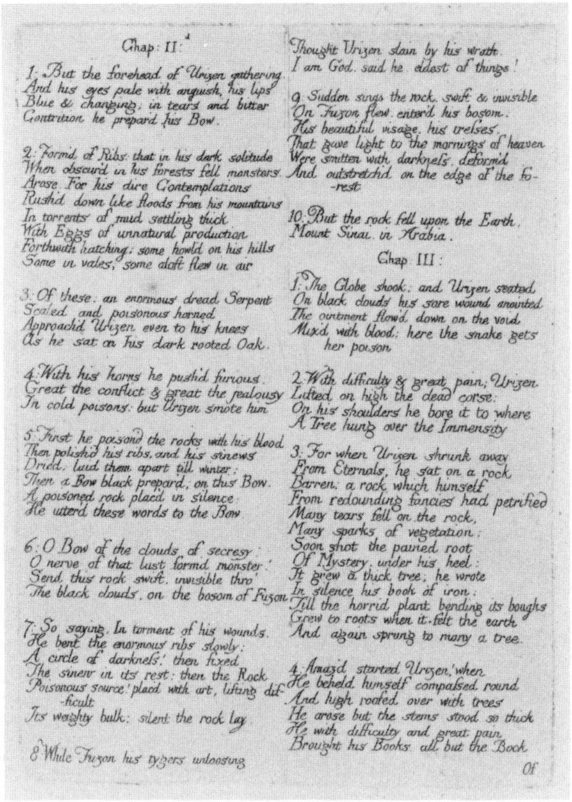

Chap: II:

1: But the forehead of Urizen gathering,
And his eyes pale with anguish, his lips
Blue & changing; in tears and bitter
Contrition he prepar'd his Bow.

2: Form'd of Ribs: that in his dark solitude
When obscur'd in his forests fell monsters,
Arose. For his dire Contemplations
Rush'd down like floods from his mountains
In torrents of mud settling thick
With Eggs of unnatural production
Forthwith hatching; some howl'd on his hills
Some in vales; some aloft flew in air

3: Of these: an enormous dread Serpent
Scaled and poisonous horned
Approach'd Urizen even to his knees
As he sat on his dark rooted Oak.

4: With his horns he push'd furious.
Great the conflict & great the jealousy
In cold poisons: but Urizen smote him

5: First he poison'd the rocks with his blood
Then polish'd his ribs, and his sinews
Dried; laid them apart till winter;
Then a Bow black prepar'd; on this Bow,
A poisoned rock plac'd in silence:
He utter'd these words to the Bow.

6: O Bow of the clouds of secresy!
O nerve of that lust form'd monster!
Send this rock swift, invisible thro'
The black clouds, on the bosom of Fuzon

7: So saying, In torment of his wounds,
He bent the enormous ribs slowly;
A circle of darkness! then fixed
The sinew in its rest: then the Rock
Poisonous source! plac'd with art, lifting dif-
-ficult
Its weighty bulk: silent the rock lay.

8: While Fuzon his tygers unloosing
Thought Urizen slain by his wrath.
I am God. said he, eldest of things!

9: Sudden sings the rock, swift & invisible
On Fuzon flew, enter'd his bosom;
His beautiful visage, his tresses,
That gave light to the mornings of heaven
Were smitten with darkness, deform'd
And outstretch'd on the edge of the fo-
-rest

10: But the rock fell upon the Earth,
Mount Sinai, in Arabia.

Chap: III:

1: The Globe shook; and Urizen seated
On black clouds his sore wound anointed
The ointment flow'd down on the void
Mix'd with blood; here the snake gets
her poison

2: With difficulty & great pain; Urizen
Lifted on high the dead corse:
On his shoulders he bore it to where
A Tree hung over the Immensity

3: For when Urizen shrunk away
From Eternals, he sat on a rock
Barren; a rock which himself
From redounding fancies had petrified
Many tears fell on the rock,
Many sparks of vegetation;
Soon shot the pained root
Of Mystery, under his heel:
It grew a thick tree; he wrote
In silence his book of iron:
Till the horrid plant bending its boughs
Grew to roots when it felt the earth
And again sprung to many a tree.

4: Amaz'd started Urizen! when
He beheld himself compassed round
And high roofed over with trees
He arose but the stems stood so thick
He with difficulty and great pain
Brought his Books, all but the Book
Of

Ahania 3

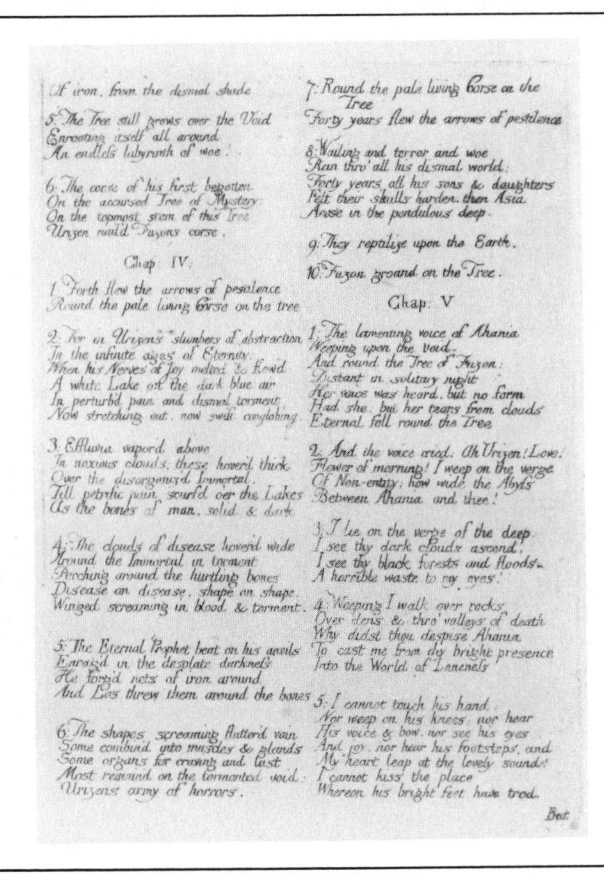

Of iron, from the dismal shade

5. The Tree still grows over the Void
Enrooting itself all around
An endless labyrinth of woe!

6. The corse of his first begotten
On the accursed Tree of Mystery:
On the topmost stem of this Tree
Urizen naild Fuzons corse.

Chap: IV:

1. Forth flew the arrows of pestilence
Round the pale living Corse on the tree

2. For in Urizens slumbers of abstraction
In the infinite ages of Eternity:
When his Nerves of Joy melted & flowd
A white Lake on the dark blue air
In perturbd pain and dismal torment
Now stretching out, now swift conglobing.

3. Effluvia vapord above
In noxious clouds; these hoverd thick
Over the disorganizd Immortal,
Till petrific pain scurfd oer the Lakes
As the bones of man, solid & dark

4. The clouds of disease hoverd wide
Around the Immortal in torment
Perching around the hurtling bones
Disease on disease, shape on shape,
Winged screaming in blood & torment.

5. The Eternal Prophet beat on his anvils
Enragd in the desolate darkness
He forgd nets of iron around
And Los threw them around the bones

6. The shapes screaming flutterd vain
Some combind into muscles & glands
Some organs for craving and lust
Most remaind on the tormented void:
Urizens army of horrors.

7. Round the pale living Corse on the Tree
Forty years flew the arrows of pestilence

8. Wailing and terror and woe
Ran thro' all his dismal world:
Forty years all his sons & daughters
Felt their skulls harden; then Asia
Arose in the pendulous deep.

9. They reptilize upon the Earth.

10. Fuzon groand on the Tree.

Chap: V

1. The lamenting voice of Ahania
Weeping upon the void.
And round the Tree of Fuzon:
Distant in solitary night
Her voice was heard, but no form
Had she: but her tears from clouds
Eternal fell round the Tree

2. And the voice cried: Ah Urizen! Love!
Flower of morning! I weep on the verge
Of Non-entity; how wide the Abyss
Between Ahania and thee!

3. I lie on the verge of the deep.
I see thy dark clouds ascend,
I see thy black forests and floods,
A horrible waste to my eyes!

4. Weeping I walk over rocks
Over dens & thro' valleys of death
Why didst thou despise Ahania
To cast me from thy bright presence
Into the World of Loneness

5. I cannot touch his hand:
Nor weep on his knees, nor hear
His voice & bow, nor see his eyes
And joy, nor hear his footsteps, and
My heart leap at the lovely sound!
I cannot kiss the place
Whereon his bright feet have trod.

But

Ahania 4

But I wander on the rocks
With hard necessity

6. Where is my golden palace
Where my ivory bed
Where the joy of my morning hour
Where the sons of eternity, singing

7. To awake bright Urizen my king;
To arise to the mountain sport,
To the bliss of eternal valleys;

8. To awake my king in the morn:
To embrace Ahanias joy
On the breath of his open bosom:
From my soft cloud of dew to fall
In showers of life on his harvests

9. When he gave my happy soul
To the sons of eternal joy:
When he took the daughters of life
Into my chambers of love:

10. When I found babes of bliss on my beds.
And bosoms of milk in my chambers
Filld with eternal seed
O! eternal births sung round Ahania
In interchange sweet of their joys.

11. Swelld with ripeness & fat with fatness
Bursting on winds my odors,
My ripe figs and rich pomegranates
In infant joy at thy feet
O Urizen sported and sang;

12. Then thou with thy lap full of seed
With thy hand full of generous fire
Walked forth from the clouds of morning
On the virgins of springing joy,
On the human soul to cast
The seed of eternal science.

13. The sweat poured down thy temples
To Ahania returnd in evening
The moisture awoke to birth
My mothers-joys, sleeping in bliss.

14. But now alone over rocks, mountains
Cast out from thy lovely bosom:
Cruel jealousy! selfish fear!
Self-destroying: how can delight
Renew in these chains of darkness
Where bones of beasts are strown
On the bleak and snowy mountains
Where bones from the birth are buried
Before they see the light

FINIS

Ahania 5. Fruit of the guillotine: illustrating the historical analogy of the use of the guillotine in the French Revolution, implied by the symbolism of the text. Fuzon flings a Globe of wrath "Lengthning into a hungry beam" at Urizen, who makes a bow of a serpent's ribs and sinews to shoot back with a poisoned rock and then nails Fuzon's corse to the Tree of Mystery (3:13–40, 4:5–8; see *Prophet* 314–315). Blake depicts with close realism a heap of severed and unsevered heads: in the center a headless male chest and belly; left of it a bodiless head of black hair; below a shoulder and head with pink cheek and brown hair; at bottom right a black head of hair below a torso severed and bleeding just below the shoulders; resting on it the severed and bleeding head of a brown-bearded man, presumably Fuzon/Moses/Robespierre.

THE BOOK OF LOS
(Reduced from about 5½ by 4 inches)

Book of Los 1 (frontispiece). This must be "Eno aged Mother . . . Sitting beneath the eternal Oak" (lines 1–4). We have seen her, perhaps, more self-confident as the sibyl in *Gates* 16. This and the title-page design illustrate the dark enclosure and the prophetic struggle within the womb/egg of the title diagram on Plate 3.

Book of Los 2 (title page). A naked giant sits wedged among rocks —metaphorically related to the "Human Illusion In darkness and deep clouds involvd" which Los finally achieves in this book (5:56–57, the concluding lines) and to the situation of the blacksmith Los in chapter 1 (though there he is standing, but see 3:42–44) especially 4:4–7, where "the fierce raging Immortal" is bound in "a Solid . . . Black as marble of Egypt."

Book of Los 3. Opening a Center. Although the spider inside the central egg/letter of "LOS" is Urizen, bearded, triple-crowned, holding open his book, his squatting (with his left shoulder and kneecap side by side) blends suggestions of hunched despair and foetal pre-birth. His apparent crown (compare *Europe* 11) is but a swatch of his web, and the Adam and Eve lying in the web's furthest extension—a naked man at left turning away but looking back, a naked woman at right hiding her breasts with both arms and also looking toward the law-book, are free of the web and trapped only by their eyes. That Los has "expanding clear senses" (4:10) we are shown, diagram fashion, by the thread which begins at the "S" of his name, provides the woof for Urizen's fabric, and curves around not to form merely a larger egg but to spiral infinitely forward (again, pointing a prophetic direction to readers). This is opening a center (see *Four Zoas* and *Jerusalem,* via the *Concordance*).

1

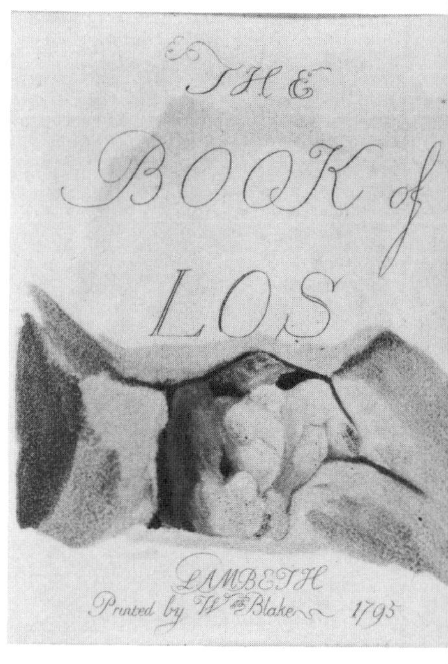

2

On the "Chap. I" heading the necessary reader is shown how he will have to move his whole body: if Adam, just above, turns away from Urizen he will find himself on the line toward the spiralling; so too the reader, if he or she will turn about and follow the loop and small spiral toward the text.

3

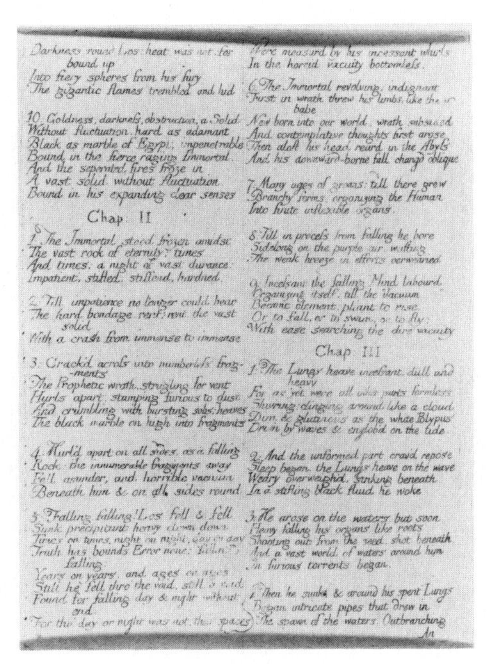

4

5

Book of Los 4. The line from "spaces" (bottom of first column) seems meant to be attached to "Then" in the second column.

Book of Los 5. At the finis, Los with outstretched arms joyously enacts the form of Human Illusion existing within the "darkness and deep clouds" of the last line. But we are given, as in the first text page, a leading string, from the "S" into the infinite abyss—where the sun is more than half risen (reason for and reward of Los's joy) though only faintly visible ("self-balancd" 7:5) behind clouds. (Compare the end of the *Song of Los.*)

Coloring. In the only known copy of this book in intaglio etching, there is a brown wash on the title page and subdued coloring throughout—except for blue sky at the sides of the frontispiece and blue, green, and yellow clouds above and earth beneath the sibyl and the *dark* hill that frames her grey robes and hair somewhat like the dark earth around the grave doorway of "Death's Door." Los has light brown hair and light colored flesh in the title page, where the rocks are brown. In Plate 3 the net is grey blue and the human figures are brown. In Plate 5 the sun is brown with brown rays; the skin of Los is also brown; so are the lower clouds, though the upper are greenish. Can these browns have darkened from some lighter pink or orange coloring?

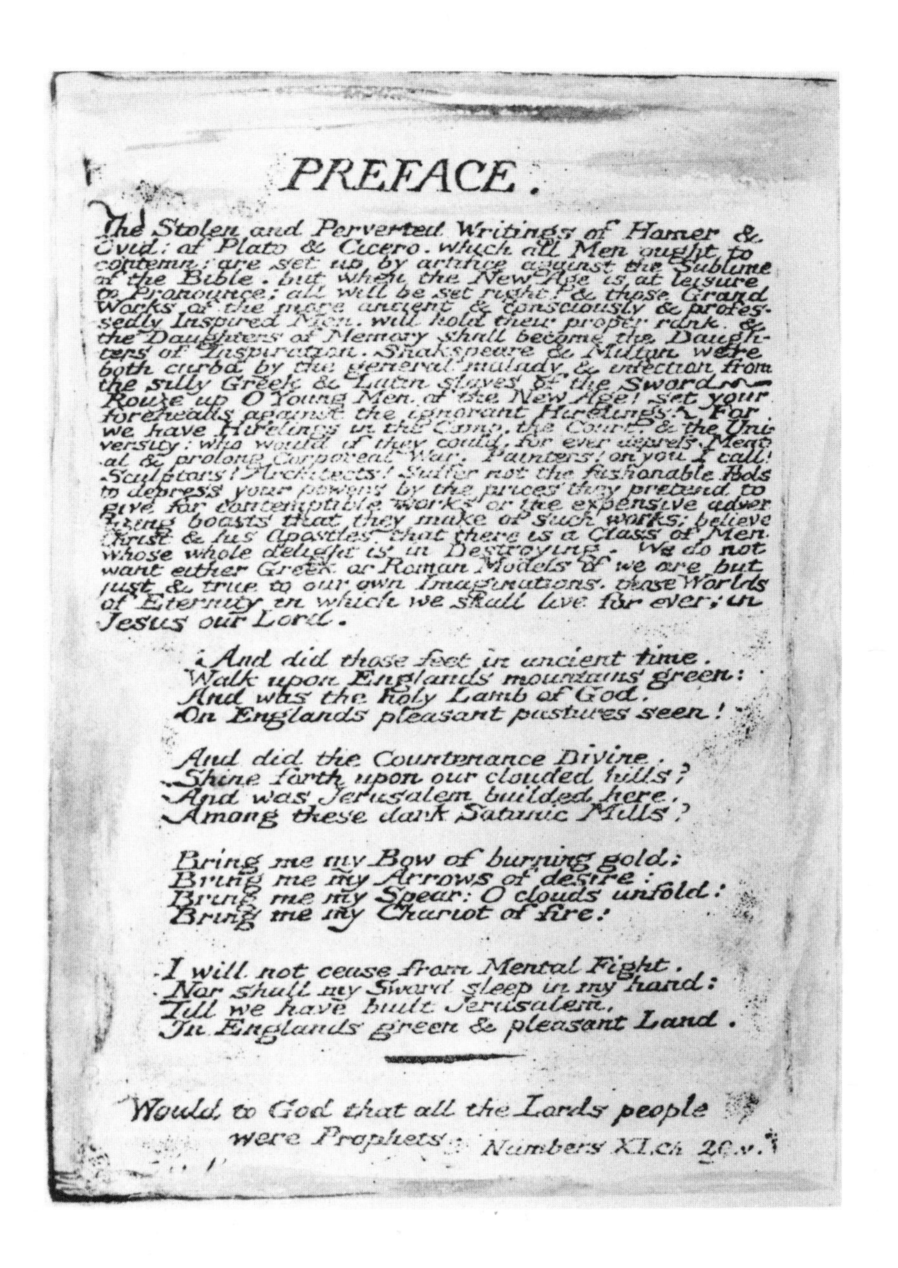

PREFACE.

The Stolen and Perverted Writings of Homer & Ovid: of Plato & Cicero. which all Men ought to contemn: are set up by artifice against the Sublime of the Bible. but when the New Age is at leisure to Pronounce; all will be set right: & those Grand Works of the more ancient & consciously & professedly Inspired Men, will hold their proper rank, & the Daughters of Memory shall become the Daughters of Inspiration. Shakspeare & Milton were both curbd by the general malady & infection from the silly Greek & Latin slaves of the Sword.

Rouze up O Young Men of the New Age! set your foreheads against the ignorant Hirelings! For we have Hirelings in the Camp, the Court, & the University: who would if they could, for ever depress Mental & prolong Corporeal War. Painters! on you I call! Sculptors! Architects! Suffer not the fashionable Fools to depress your powers by the prices they pretend to give for contemptible works or the expensive advertizing boasts that they make of such works; believe Christ & his Apostles that there is a Class of Men whose whole delight is in Destroying. We do not want either Greek or Roman Models if we are but just & true to our own Imaginations, those Worlds of Eternity in which we shall live for ever; in Jesus our Lord.

And did those feet in ancient time.
Walk upon Englands mountains green:
And was the holy Lamb of God,
On Englands pleasant pastures seen!

And did the Countenance Divine,
Shine forth upon our clouded hills?
And was Jerusalem builded here,
Among these dark Satanic Mills?

Bring me my Bow of burning gold:
Bring me my Arrows of desire:
Bring me my Spear: O clouds unfold!
Bring me my Chariot of fire!

I will not cease from Mental Fight,
Nor shall my Sword sleep in my hand:
Till we have built Jerusalem,
In Englands green & pleasant Land.

Would to God that all the Lords people were Prophets. Numbers XI. ch 29 v.

Milton iA

MILTON A POEM IN 2 BOOKS

THE DATE of the side panel ("The Author & Printer W Blake 1804") is that of the *Jerusalem* title page (*Jerusalem* 2), though neither work was completed in its extant form until many years later. The date does suggest that they were planned together, and some indication of their relationship is supplied by size and shape. The plates of *Milton* are exact halves of the plates of *Jerusalem,* probably made from similar sheets of copper cut in half. And the work is fifty pages long, half the hundred pages of *Jerusalem.* Hence *Milton* cannot afford (so to speak) both frontispiece and title page —though it did acquire a Preface, unadorned and not graphically counting as a page. It also divides into two books, as against the four chapters of *Jerusalem*—but these symmetries were some time in forming; the title pages, when first etched, were inscribed to announce, respectively, twelve books and twenty-eight chapters. Cutting *Milton* down from twelve books, however brief, must have involved drastic reduction. What it made possible was the conflation of many lines of action to a single "moment" of descent and (incomplete) ascent, rehearsed and repeated in Milton's descent and uniting with Blake, Blake's uniting with Los, Ololon's descent and sixfold separation uniting as One Woman to embrace Milton, Albion's sleep and imperfect rising (the complete story saved for *Jerusalem*). Thematically the moment reveals the separation and union of the contraries of wrath and pity; visually it shows male and female, brother and brother, wives and daughters, with choreography which represents a right relation by a dance position of

---

Milton iA (Preface) [K1] (AB2; not in CD). This plate was presumably withdrawn by Blake; it is here assigned a number outside the fifty-plate sequence; the graphic movement in any case leaps from 1 to 2. Printed in black ink, with pale ink and blue washes in A, pale yellow in B.

(In the notes that follow, quotations of Geoffrey Keynes are from his notes in the Blake Trust facsimile of copy D.)

tarsus to tarsus (reminding us of the conversion of the avenging Saul into the apostle Paul), or by two persons receiving one star or binding on one sandal. Plates 32 and 37, which analyze a scene already pictured in Plate 17, may have been designed to emphasize, in the two-book plan, the symmetry of descent and ascent. Each book also starts with a tarsally touching pair, like two blossoms on one plant, suggesting the unity of wrath and pity shown in *Songs* 18 where Christ stands in the center. Like the light from heaven that brought the voice of Jesus to Saul of Tarsus, the star implies a similar center in these pictures; and the rows of flaming human grain in Plate 50, with Ololon stepping into the center and toward us, in consummation and illumination (which we are invited to join) imply a convergence at the moment when Milton joins Ololon to become One in Jesus.

Milton as the warrior Samson also steps into the drama, metamorphosing into Milton-Blake as sculptor in Plate 18.

There are four copies of *Milton:* A (British Museum), B (Huntington Library), C (New York Public Library), D (Rosenwald Collection, Library of Congress). Copy A is used except where otherwise indicated, but the pagination of copy D (complete except Preface, here designated Plate i) is employed in which Blake establishes a series of fifty plates. References to the text are made in the same numbering; to find passages in the Keynes or Erdman editions, the "K" numbers given for each plate must be employed.

Milton 1A (title page [Ki] (AB1, Ci, D1). We plunge, or are drawn, into "MIL / TON a Poem" without frontispiece, following the striding poet of the title, naked amid flames (of prophetic wrath), as he pushes and announces his way through the center of his name and through a vortex of billowing smoke. (In B all the flames are colored as smoke.) When we follow Milton's hand through by turning the page, we see him as a flaming star (on Plate 2) from the perspective of This World. (On Plate 18 his striding foot breaks through the center of the word "Self-hood"—an equivalent act. In both pictures Milton's nakedness represents this act as a shedding of all garments.)

The clothed traveller of the *Jerusalem* frontispiece, who is Blake/Los stepping into the door of a walled city or garden, is in symmetrical contrast to this heroic nude traveller stepping into the

Milton 1A

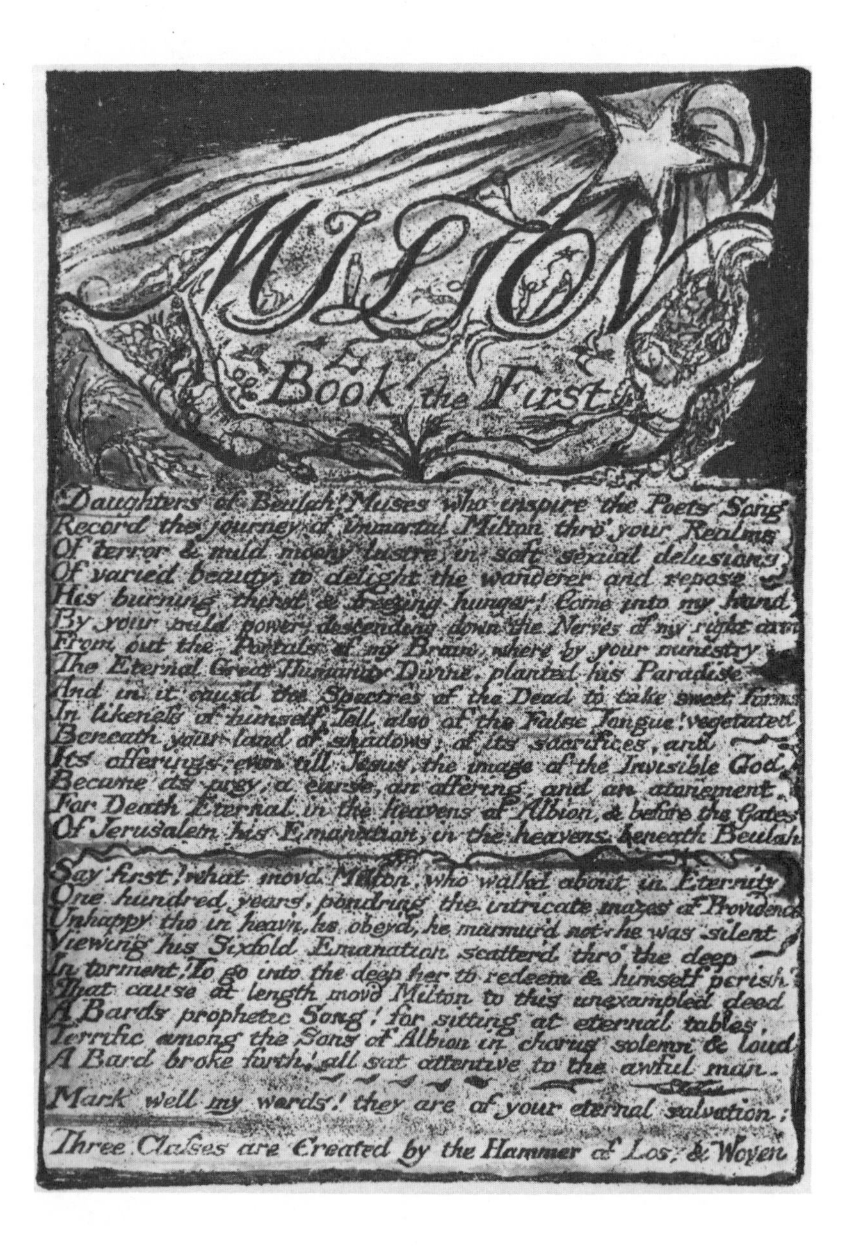

Milton 2A

flames of annihilation, this "Christian Agonist, undertaking the Hero Journey into the black cloud of Time and Space" (Sandler 16). The gesture of Milton's raised right hand balances that of Los's left but is unambiguous in its thrust. The fingers of Los's lowered right hand enter the disk of his lantern/sphere; the fingers of Milton's left hand similarly enter the cloud and flame[D] that billow and flare unenclosed. But Los's act in *Jerusalem* is domestic, mundane, the step of an observer-participant; Milton's is sublime (haloed[C]), universal, self-committing and self(name)-transforming. Yet the cloud at his left hand bears, prophetically, the name of the new "Author & Printer W Blake," who joins in repeating the vow (under Milton's feet) "To Justify the Ways of God to Man" (this time).

Milton 2[A] (Book the First) [K2] (AB3, C1, D2). "Woven into the heading . . . is a representation of Milton as a star irradiating the bread and wine of life" (Keynes)—for, as Los knows (26:42), Milton's return is "the Signal that the Last Vintage now approaches." The star is yellow with bloody streamers[A] or orange[B] or red[D] with yellowish rays (sprinkled with gold[D]), for the irradiation brings also the terror of consuming fire—to falsehood. We have moved back a split second *before* the act that will split open the name "MILTON," liberate the six garmented humans loitering among its letters (see below), and not only ripen but consume the grain and grapes, the bread and the wine here seen as male and female blossoms attached by their right feet to a living plant—his at its base, hers a little higher, implying perhaps Adam's seniority to Eve. Bread is the male at the left, above ripe (or green[B]) heads of grain, wine the female at the right against a tangle of vines bearing ripe grapes, blue[A] or red[B], each grape the size of an apple in proportion to her body (compare the fairies in the grain in *Europe* 9). Each seems to bear a token of the other; a tendril springs from his head (which also seems to be fruit-heaped); a small head of wheat grows at her thigh. A bird (of paradise?) flies leftward near her face, another near his tendril, and a smaller bird over the "B" of "BOOK." She wears a girdle, obscured in copy D. There is a cliff or tree behind her. The star will free their human forms to dance, not vegetate as they do now, "Mortal & Vegetable in Sexuality" (39:24). (On the touching of feet, see note on Plate 10.)

The adult inhabitants of the unmoved "MILTON" may represent the sixfold persons of Ololon sharing Milton's unhappiness in a "heav'n" (18) reminiscent of the vale of Har in *Tiriel* 3. Their garments and postures hide their hands and feet. One lies against the slope of the "M" (in a parody of the posture of the alert youth on the "A" of "ASIA" in *Song of Los* 6); one sits in its last curve. Another stands stock still on the front loop of "L." Another sits on the top of "T" (down the stem of which a vine extends, with middle and terminal leaves, the latter repeating the shape of the star, as though to enter and open up "BOOK"). Another, accommodating his body to the tilt of the egg-shaped "O," watches a child playing with a bird on a string (contrast the lark's soaring later on). Again, more like the cage of Har than Heaven. The sixth clothed figure leans against the "F" of "FIRST." The annihilation and resurrection of Milton, the opening of this Book, will awake this sleeping multitude, "the Lords people" (Plate i), to "live for ever." On Plate 10 we see the fire of this star burning up Satan; all Beulah will be surprised at "fury & fire" as a form (or true contrary) of pity (see 38:3–7).

In the text area, above the word "words!" and above "they are of your eternal salvation," fly five birds, then a larger one, toward a tiny woman in flames (compare Oothoon in *Visions* 8).

Milton 3^{D} [K3] (C2, D3, not in AB). In the right margin we see three stages of the separation of the female form (29–34). Suggestions of green grass in the background indicate arrival on earth (gilded in D). The first stage is hairless with legs not separate and only a hint of breasts; the second shows a long shapeless left arm working free, a right leg with foot unformed; the third a right arm beginning to frame the face and emphasize the breasts, a leg line forming. These are pink, an outflowing from the "red round globe" (heart) (11). Below are the blue vessels, the "blue fluid exuded in Sinews" (35) which will become separated "into a Male Form" (36)—the priority now suggested being of female to male.

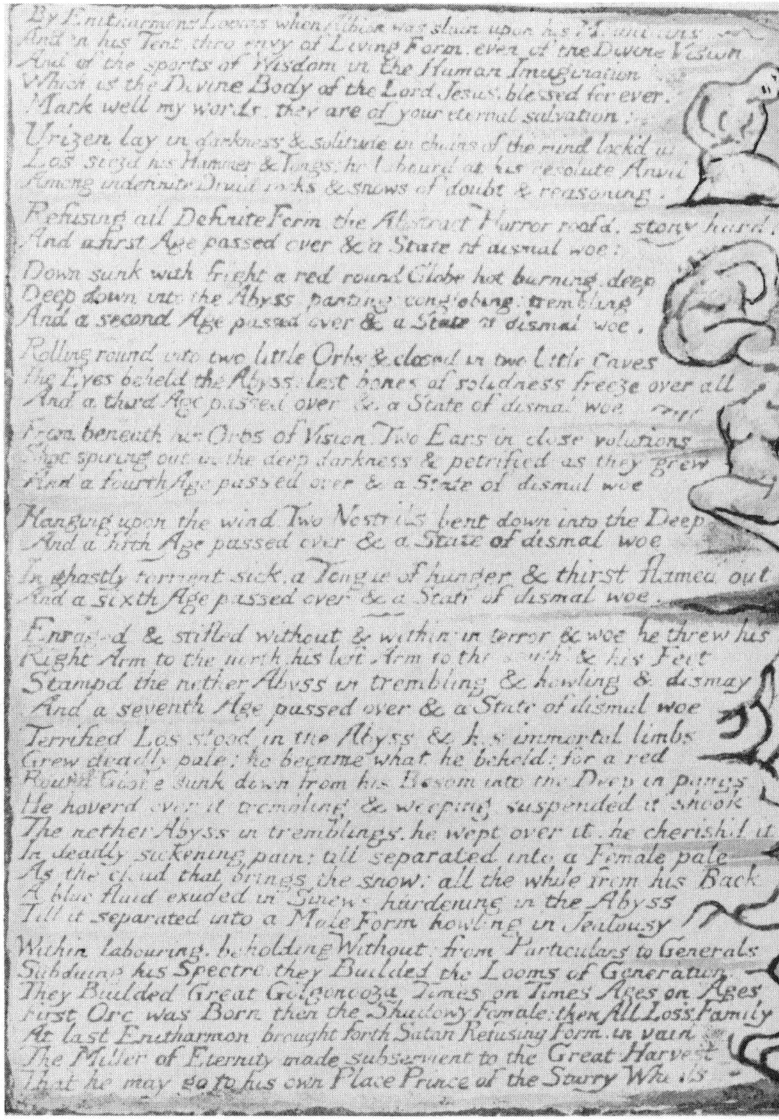

Milton 3^{D} [K3]

Milton 4D [K4]

Milton 4D [K4] (C3, D4, not in AB). Fibres alluded to in lines 4–5 extend from the word "Satan" (2). Textual reference to Satan's "Mills" (12, 14) is followed by a trilithon, a sketched group of three standing and three sitting figures, a large unsquared stone, and an irregular row of squared stones, the first and last trilithons seen sideways (note top segments)—scattered components potentially of a stone altar, if we look ahead to Plates 15 and 17. Los at his forge prevents Satan from replying by rolling "his loud thunders" (15), and a line down from the last word seems to start or continue flames which roll up from under the refrain "Mark well my words . . ." (note the varying emphasis given the refrain in Plates 2, 3, 4, 7, 9, and 12).

At bottom, below Los's prophecy of a mocking of Druidical stonework and sacrifice by a display of "Naked Beauty with Flute & Harp & Song" (22: an anticipation of the top picture in Plate 18), we see (under three trilithons that loom on the hill, potentially the three crosses on Calvary—place of the skull—mentioned in line 21) the uncut boulder again, the world-rock of Plate 6, here shaped as potential mundane egg—or skull. On it sits a bowed, pink-clothed female, now fully formed, with hair, but like a "Sick Rose" (see *Songs* 39, on lower branch, reversed) unopened—midpoint between the two visions—yet flanked by standing women holding distaffs and spindles (and both belted like the "wine" woman of Plate 2). Theirs is a graceful dance—though sad, for beside the left spinner a huddled human mourns and behind the right one a threefold trilithon (Druid form of Tyburn gallows) seems ready to trap the red spindle-tear of human thread (compare *Jerusalem* 100). Yet in blue sky above the upheld distaff (and on the other side of the hill) three birds fly amid rosy clouds.

Florence Sandler suggests that Blake is recapitulating the tradition that treats as one and the same place in mystic geography the world-stone or foundation-stone, Adam's burial place, the temple/palace of Melchizedek (who built an altar of twelve stones and offered bread and wine over the earth that closed over Adam's body), the altar within Solomon's temple (a thunderbolt or firestone left upon the threshing floor when the Lord sent fire from heaven), the place where Satan's skull was crushed (i.e. the Crucifixion), and the Sepulchre purporting to hold the Lord of Life in death, from which he comes forth having discarded his grave-clothes. The women recognize that they are confounded in—and released from—the task of spinning and weaving the grave-clothes which are our mortal bodies when Mary of Magdalene meets Jesus in the garden: compare Ololon's meeting with Milton in Blake's garden and trembling before him. The place of Resurrection is also the rock in the desert from which water flowed when Moses struck it. Blake reverses the application to death and sacerdotalism of all these signs of heavenly descent. In 39:46–60 the renovating Moment of Ololon's descent—without which Milton's descent would not avail—is described as "a Fountain in a rock Of crystal" or "on the Rock of Odours," in a garden of regained Paradise that mocks the enrooted oak groves and Tyburn's brook, the oak groves being Canaanitish as well as Druidical. (For details see George Every's chapter "The Place of the Skull" in his *Christian Mythology,* London 1970.) The links are forged by Los "at his resolute Anvil" (3:7) on "Tyburn's brook" (6:11), implying the traditional interconnection of meteorites, sacred rocks, anvil and forge, foundation-stone, temple, and altar of sacrifice. (See Mircea Eliade, *The Forge and the Crucible: The Origin and Structures of Alchemy, 1962.*)

Milton 5ᴰ [K5] (D5, not in ABC). The tale is (lines 40–44) that when King James called for fires (compare *Song of Los* 6) and Satan fainted (compare "Urizen wept": *Song of Los* 7), the Druidic "Mathematical Proportion was subdued by Living Proportion." And the tiny interlinear and marginal sketches show grass developing tendril loops (4), rising birds (at 15 and 35—above "a faint delight"—and perhaps at 11 and 20). A very meaningful serpentine spiral grows out of "Created" (42), which after ten loops bends down (the king himself "Created" the fires by a Druidic command for destruction of Golgonooza, the City of Art) but then rises triumphantly in four larger loops spiraling into the sky. (Compare the rising tail of the printing-house serpent in *Marriage* 15.) Note that this imitates, *in reverse,* the movement of the lettering of "MIL / TON a Poem" in the title page.

At bottom left, in a bed of gold-painted, blue or black tipped flames that lick toward the word "Created," bathes a pink female form, further developing from the series of three on Plate 4: see her fully alive in *Marriage* 3.

Milton 5ᴰ [K5]

Milton 6ᴬ [K6]

Milton 6ᴬ [K6] (ABC4, D6). Near the top the "lulling cadences" of the loom are echoed in thread-like tendrils. Below is a Druid scene to match *Jerusalem* 70. In a deep blue patch in a blue evening sky shines a waning crescent moon (but the whole sky is redrawn in D: see below). Eight large stars were etched, one seen through the trilithon, but only five left bright in A; one of these[BC] was above the moon, one[BC] below it in a curious gulf of sky that appears as an abyss into which a large Rocking, or Logan, Stone (precarious image of our world—and our skull—loosed from the spinning women of Plate 4) seems capable of being toppled: it is painted to resemble a ship under sail, with grey hull. (In D all the large stars are removed, the moon, still a waning crescent, has the full moon in its arms, the clouds are whiter, and the blue gulf is filled with five gilded stars forming an impossible dipper.)

A traveller on a prancing horse approaches the stone ship along a road cut into the hill beneath the trilithon. Since Satan in the poem is, on the simplest human level, the tyrannously good-natured selfhood of William Hayley, Blake's patron at Felpham, about whose riding Blake was solicitous and satiric—"Felpham Billy rode out every morn . . . over the fields of corn" (*P&P* 495)—we may see him here on one of "Palamabrons horses" which he will shortly madden (7:43–44) and may imagine his riding toward the abyss beyond the skull-ship as illustrating Palamabron's prophecy of his "future course thro' darkness and despair to eternal death" (7:24). Palamabron's own emotional state, "reddening like the Moon in an eclipse" (7:20), may be alluded to in the redrawing of the moon in D, where the edges are reddish.

The hill is grass green, with two (or one[D]) greenish oak trees against the stone, and a forest of the same color behind. Beside four nearer trees (two[D]) is a pastoral scene with sheep and a man with some staff or tool in his hand (a rake in D).

Florence Sandler suggests that this stone gate to the stars, following a reference to "Babel" as frowning "over the Nations in glory & war" (23–24), should be thought of as the negation of the "Crystal Gate" (39:61), the entrance of the First Heaven, where the larks meet. Ancient Babylon (Babel), from Bab-ilu, gate of the gods, had anticipated Newtonian England in making a religion out of calculations of the movements of the stars. Also, if Blake is thinking of the *gate* of Babylon (Ishtar's Gate, through which the Jews went into exile) or more precisely of the hardened Urizenic form of the Ishtar's gate/womb-entrance, then perhaps the moon and the ark-rock should be seen as the shrunken form of the female in a landscape and skyscape where the male rides to "glory & war" —the distant moon implying a potential Ololon with moony ark, or Oothoon weeping ark-like over the harvest (Plate 49).

Milton 7A [K7] (ABC5, D7). LoopsD at top cover a deletion. Under "plow" (3) a bird flies, and beyond it is a sketch that may be plow or bird. Above and below the refrain "Mark well . . . salvation" are three birds (a fourth in C) beginning under "words," a zigzag of lightning curving into a headless serpent, and at the end a tongue-darting viper with two or three unformed companions. Compare *Marriage* 15; here the collaboration of eagle and viper, illumination and words, is only approaching.

Below the word "Harrow" (18) sits a large woman confronted by a child. After "prophetic I behold" (23) are a star and a moon in potential ark position. After "pretence of pity and love to me" (26) a figure kneels in a furrow, and at the next break a figure with no face but a hair-line that shows he is facing right stands or walks off, on green grass. In the space behind him a bird flies above "wind of" and a four-looped root, attached to "hills," assists the reading of "unroots the rocks & hills." Beside "Palamabrons horses" (43) a horse trots off to the right, free of any rider.

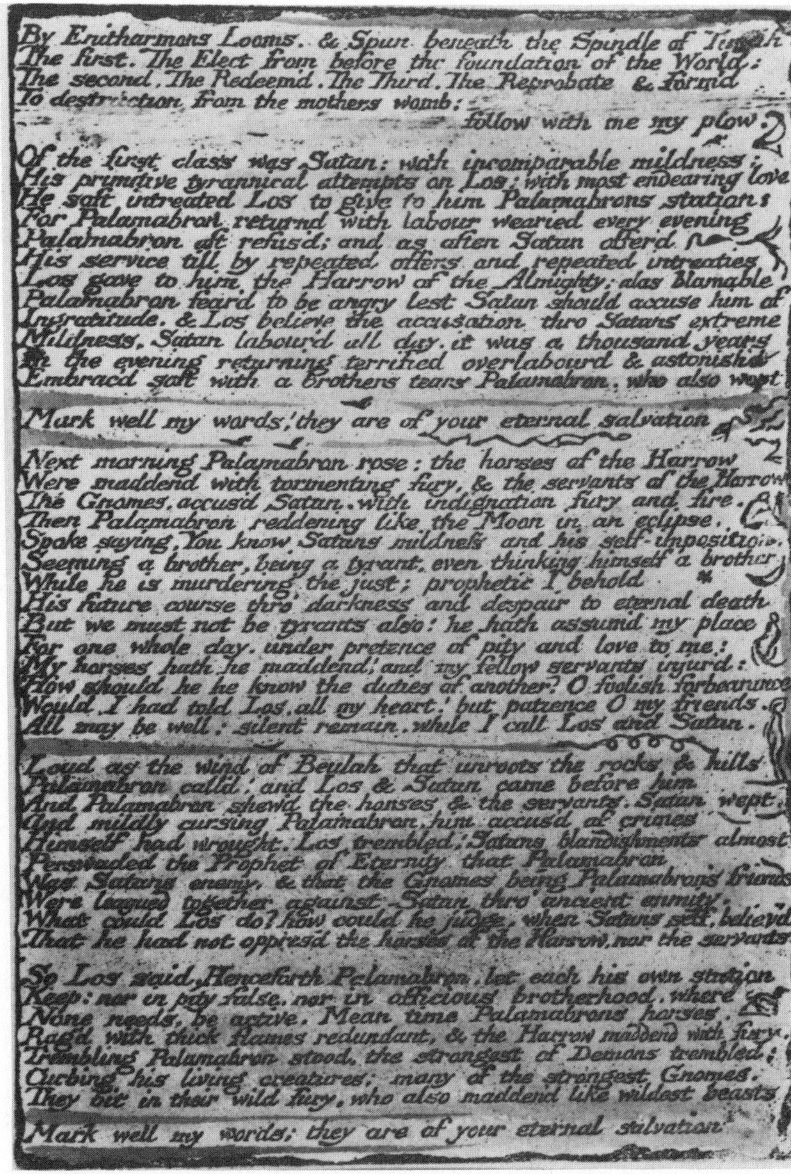

By Enitharmons Looms. & Spun beneath the Spindle of Tirzah
The first. The Elect from before the foundation of the World:
The second. The Redeemd. The Third. The Reprobate & formd
To destruction from the mothers womb: —
follow with me my plow.

Of the first class was Satan: with incomparable mildness;
His primitive tyrannical attempts on Los: with most endearing love
He soft intreated Los to give to him Palamabrons station;
For Palamabron returnd with labour wearied every evening
Palamabron oft refusd; and as often Satan offerd
His service till by repeated offers and repeated intreaties
Los gave to him the Harrow of the Almighty; alas blamable
Palamabron feard to be angry lest Satan should accuse him of
Ingratitude. & Los believe the accusation thro Satans extreme
Mildness. Satan labourd all day. it was a thousand years
In the evening returning terrified overlabourd & astonishd
Embracd soft with a brothers tears Palamabron, who also wept

Mark well my words; they are of your eternal salvation

Next morning Palamabron rose: the horses of the Harrow
Were maddend with tormenting fury, & the servants of the Harrow
The Gnomes, accusd Satan, with indignation fury and fire.
Then Palamabron reddening like the Moon in an eclipse,
Spake saying, You know Satans mildness and his self-imposition,
Seeming a brother, being a tyrant, even thinking himself a brother
While he is murdering the just; prophetic I behold
His future course thro darkness and despair to eternal death
But we must not be tyrants also: he hath assumd my place
For one whole day, under pretence of pity and love to me:
My horses hath he maddend! and my fellow servants injurd:
How should he he know the duties of another? O foolish forbearance
Would I had told Los, all my heart! but patience O my friends.
All may be well: silent remain, while I call Los and Satan.

Loud as the wind of Beulah that unroots the rocks & hills
Palamabron calld! and Los & Satan came before him
And Palamabron shewd the horses & the servants. Satan wept,
And mildly cursing Palamabron, him accusd of crimes
Himself had wrought. Los trembled; Satans blandishments almost
Perswaded the Prophet of Eternity that Palamabron
Was Satans enemy, & that the Gnomes being Palamabrons friends
Were leagued together against Satan thro' ancient enmity.
What could Los do? how could he judge, when Satans self, believd
That he had not oppresd the horses of the Harrow, nor the servants.

So Los said, Henceforth Palamabron, let each his own station
Keep: nor in pity false, nor in officious brotherhood, where
None needs, be active. Mean time Palamabrons horses.
Ragd with thick flames redundant, & the Harrow maddend with fury.
Trembling Palamabron stood, the strongest of Demons trembled:
Curbing his living creatures; many of the strongest Gnomes,
They bit in their wild fury, who also maddend like wildest beasts

Mark well my words; they are of your eternal salvation

Milton 7A [K7]

Mean while wept Satan before Los. accusing Palamabron;
Himself exculpating with mildest speech. for himself believ'd
That he had not opress'd nor injur'd the refractory servants.

But Satan returning to his Mills (for Palamabron had serv'd
The Mills of Satan as the easier task) found all confusion
And back return'd to Los. not fill'd with vengeance but with tears.
Himself convinc'd of Palamabrons turpitude. Los beheld
The servants of the Mills drunken with wine and dancing wild
With shouts and Palamabrons songs, rending the forests green
With ecchoing confusion, tho' the Sun was risen on high.

Then Los took off his left sandal placing it on his head,
Signal of solemn mourning: when the servants of the Mills
Beheld the signal they in silence stood, tho' drunk with wine.
Los wept! But Rintrah also came, and Enitharmon on
His arm lean'd tremblingly observing all these things

And Los said. Ye Genii of the Mills: the Sun is on high
Your labours call you! Palamabron is also in sad dilemma;
His horses are mad! his Harrow confounded! his companions enrag'd.
Mine is the fault! I should have remember'd that pity divides the soul
And man, unmans: follow with me my Plow. this mournful day
Must be a blank in Nature: follow with me, and tomorrow again
Resume your labours, & this day shall be a mournful day

Wildly they follow'd Los and Rintrah, & the Mills were silent
They mourn'd all day this mournful day of Satan & Palamabron:
And all the Elect & all the Redeem'd mourn'd one toward another
Upon the mountains of Albion among the cliffs of the Dead.

They Plow'd in tears! incessant pour'd Jehovahs rain, & Molechs
Thick fires contending with the rain, thunder'd above rolling
Terrible over their heads; Satan wept over Palamabron
Theotormon & Bromion contended on the side of Satan
Pitying his youth and beauty; trembling at eternal death:
Michael contended against Satan in the rolling thunder
Thulloh the friend of Satan also reprov'd him; faint their reproof.

But Rintrah who is of the reprobate: of those form'd to destruction
In indignation. for Satans soft dissimulation of friendship!
Flam'd above all the plowed furrows, angry red and furious.
Till Michael sat down in the furrow weary dissolv'd in tears
Satan who drave the team beside him, stood angry & red
He smote Thulloh & slew him, & he stood terrible over Michael
Urging him to arise: he wept! Enitharmon saw his tears
But Los hid Thulloh from her sight, lest she should die of grief
She wept: she trembled! she kissed Satan; she wept over Michael
She form'd a Space for Satan & Michael & for the poor infected
Trembling she wept over the Space, & clos'd it with a tender Moon

Los secret buried Thulloh, weeping disconsolate over the moony Space

But Palamabron called down a Great Solemn Assembly,
That he who will not defend Truth, may be compelled to
Defend a Lie, that he may be snared & caught & taken

Milton 8A [K8]

Milton 8A [K8] (ABC6, D8). Above Satan's "tears" (6) rise four loops ending in perhaps a naked human figure in full-length profile (or a mere patch of border[AC]). Single birds appear in the next two breaks, but in the right margin are three human figures vaguely delineated. The first may represent Los placing "his left sandal . . . on his head" (11), a squatting figure leaning over perhaps with sandal in hand. The next figure kneels, perhaps with burden on back. Next a clothed figure bends upward, aspiring to escape this "mournful day" (22). Jags of lightning shoot down from "Molechs" to "reproof."

At bottom a reclining figure (a man meditating, i.e. calling a "Great Solemn Assembly" [46] in his thoughts) is flanked by a stem of leafing foliage and a tendril that reaches to, or grows from, the cliff on the right.

Milton 9ᴬ [K9] (ABC7, D9). The text is filled with expressions of the wrath of Rintrah: it flames high in Satan (11); in Los it causes him to curse and rend up nations and displace continents (13–16); and, on his own, Rintrah rears up walls of rocks with moats of fire (43–44). All this is said to occur "hidden beneath . . . mildness" (19), and presumably the illustrations represent repressed (vegetated) wrath. The top figure, beside "rage" (10), is a dancer with swirling skirt (tango effect) whose arms flare out into green flower flags: the larger one, held up high, serves as the only ornamentation of the refrain "Mark well . . . salvation." Midway down, under "Jehovah" (22), is a potentially human figure with hands raised in rage—completely turned into a green leaf-flag. A floating (or seated?) figure lower down, with raised arm, is superficially angelic. Below, alongside the "solemn universal groan" (37), a naked man facing away from us and reaching high seems turning into a tree trunk at the bottom and extruding from the end of his raised hand (or hands) a rock from which extends a green branch with an umbrella-like leaf. Is the bump by his left hip the head of a kneeling man?

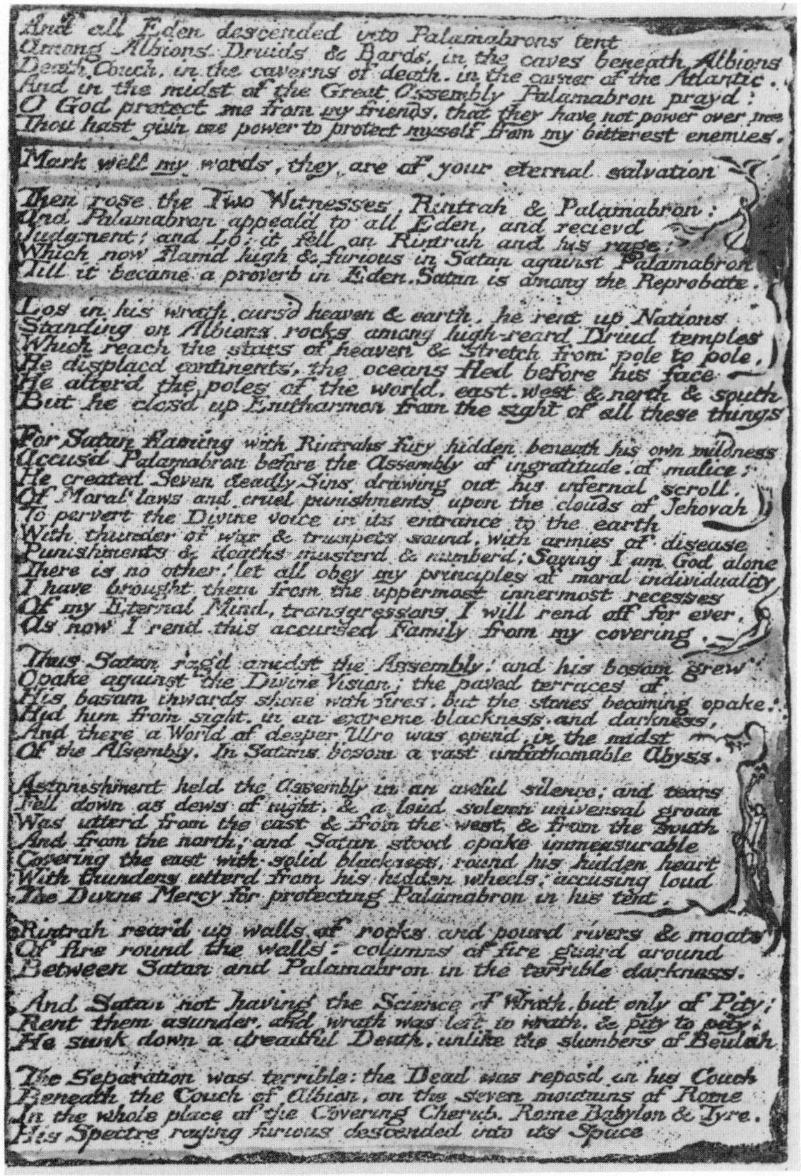

And all Eden descended into Palamabrons tent
Among Albions Druids & Bards, in the caves beneath Albions
Death Couch, in the caverns of death, in the corner of the Atlantic.
And in the midst of the Great Assembly Palamabron prayd:
O God protect me from my friends, that they have not power over me
Thou hast givn me power to protect myself from my bitterest enemies.

Mark well my words, they are of your eternal salvation

Then rose the Two Witnesses, Rintrah & Palamabron:
And Palamabron appeald to all Eden, and recievd
Judgment: and Lo! it fell on Rintrah and his rage:
Which now flamd high & furious in Satan against Palamabron
Till it became a proverb in Eden. Satan is among the Reprobate.

Los in his wrath cursd heaven & earth, he rent up Nations
Standing on Albions rocks among high-reard Druid temples
Which reach the stars of heaven & stretch from pole to pole.
He displacd continents, the oceans fled before his face
He alterd the poles of the world, east, west & north & south
But he clos'd up Enitharmon from the sight of all these things

For Satan flaming with Rintrahs fury hidden beneath his own mildness
Accus'd Palamabron before the Assembly of ingratitude! of malice:
He created Seven deadly Sins drawing out his infernal scroll,
Of Moral laws and cruel punishments upon the clouds of Jehovah
To pervert the Divine voice in its entrance to the earth
With thunder of war & trumpets sound, with armies of disease
Punishments & deaths musterd & number'd; Saying I am God alone
There is no other! let all obey my principles of moral individuality
I have brought them from the uppermost innermost recesses
Of my Eternal Mind, transgressors I will rend off for ever,
As now I rend this accursed Family from my covering.

Thus Satan rag'd amidst the Assembly! and his bosom grew
Opake against the Divine Vision: the paved terraces of
His bosom inwards shone with fires, but the stones becoming opake!
Hid him from sight, in an extreme blackness and darkness,
And there a World of deeper Ulro was open'd, in the midst
Of the Assembly. In Satans bosom a vast unfathomable Abyss.

Astonishment held the Assembly in an awful silence: and tears
Fell down as dews of night, & a loud solemn universal groan
Was utterd from the east & from the west & from the south
And from the north; and Satan stood opake immeasurable
Covering the east with solid blackness, round his hidden heart
With thunders utterd from his hidden wheels: accusing loud
The Divine Mercy, for protecting Palamabron in his tent.

Rintrah reard up walls of rocks and pourd rivers & moats
Of fire round the walls: columns of fire guard around
Between Satan and Palamabron in the terrible darkness.

And Satan not having the Science of Wrath, but only of Pity:
Rent them asunder, and wrath was left to wrath, & pity to pity.
He sunk down a dreadful Death, unlike the slumbers of Beulah

The Separation was terrible: the Dead was reposd on his Couch
Beneath the Couch of Albion, on the seven mountains of Rome
In the whole place of the Covering Cherub, Rome Babylon & Tyre.
His Spectre raging furious descended into its Space

Milton 9ᴬ [K9]

Milton 10A

Milton 10A (ABC8, D10). This tableau of three naked men who look like brothers (two are sons of Los) translates the message of the Bard's song (9:31–49) into the choreography of human gestures. Satan, standing on one of the "paved terraces of His bosom" with his head flung sideways (like Nelson's in the drawing, not the painting, of *The Spiritual Form of Nelson Guiding Leviathan,* where lightning strikes Nelson's neck as the flames here scorch Satan) is the Selfhood revealed by the light of the flaming star of Milton's descent (Plate 2) and being consumed by its fire, the light and the fire representing a life-giving unity of mercy and wrath. The flames are sulfur yellow at center, then red, turning to "solid blackness" immeasurable. Beside Satan, wringing his hands in mistaken sympathy, stands the brown-bearded Rintrah. Behind Rintrah is mild, blond-bearded Palamabron, touching toes with Satan in mistaken sympathy, too, but turning away with his body and hands, inside a blue space resistant to the opacity. (In ABC the beards are not colored in, but the lines on the jaws indicate them.) In D the flames around Satan are gilded, and golden ashes (small flamesC) fall just behind Palamabron's extended foot.

The touching of feet (one left and one right) is a sort of parody of the relationship of bread and wine in Plate 2; it should represent a marriage of true Contraries (as it does in Plate 48), and the brothers Rintrah and Palamabron should be touching each other, joining fraternal pity and wrath. They cannot truly pity nor hate the selfhood Satan, a mere negation that will go up in smoke (see Plate 32). He has momentarily rent pity and wrath "asunder"—"The Separation was terrible"—but to look for Satan's "hidden heart" is to look into "a vast unfathomable abyss" (9:35–49).

The key to the foot-touching in these illuminations is Blake's pun on Saul of Tarsus who, when irradiated by the light of heaven, became Paul hearing the voice of Christ. The burning up of Satan (i.e. Milton's recognition and annihilation of his Selfhood) will put wrath and mercy into right relation as components of one psyche, just as the fiery star's entering the tarsus (the articulation of the foot that energizes walking forward) of William Blake and of Robert Blake (in Plates 32 and 37) unites them in the light of the imagination. Brothers who are divided and not receiving the light nor the voice will act as Cain and Abel (see Plate 15).

The blue space that Rintrah and Palamabron stand in, separating them from Satan's consummation, suggests the blue gulf into which the stone ship of Plate 6 may launch. But see the text of the next plate.

In the 12-book *Milton,* which Blake intended (see title page) and at least partly wrote, there was evidently a prophetic vision of the English Civil War (see references in Plate 5 to artillery and to James and Cromwell; and see *Prophet* 424). I suspect that the historical dimension of the problem of uniting pity and wrath involved the right relations of Parliament (Palamabron, who calls "a Great Solemn Assembly") and the Army (Rintrah).

Milton 11D [K10] (C8*, D11, not in AB). Enitharmon appears in the space of generation as "An aged Woman raving along the Streets" (4). In one perspective this is a London street scene, matching that of *Songs* 46 and *Jerusalem* 84 and showing us where the "Cry of the Poor Man" of Plate 49 comes from. But a door in a cellar or mine is suggested by the squat shape and overhanging arch and supporting beam: in other perspective we are with Enitharmon *inside* the cave house of generation and death. Her arms and flowing hair suggest swift flight, but her right ankle seems manacledD and perhaps tethered and her left hand is bent against wood and stone; she is "measuring" the span of mortal space, trying to open it up. But the fragmentation of existence into fixed, separate, opake globes, atomic particles like dark spots caused by the shooting of "the arrows . . . of Jealousy" (17–18), is suggested by a chaos of dots and splotches on the door and post and arch, running up into the text area and asserting themselves above the words "Female Space" (6) and in the space above and after "over Satan who triumphant" (21). The dots are held at bay by the flowing prophetic banner waving below "Humanity" (11), though only at the cost of their triumph under "against the Divine." The dots' identification with "Satan" is indicated in the ensuing line.

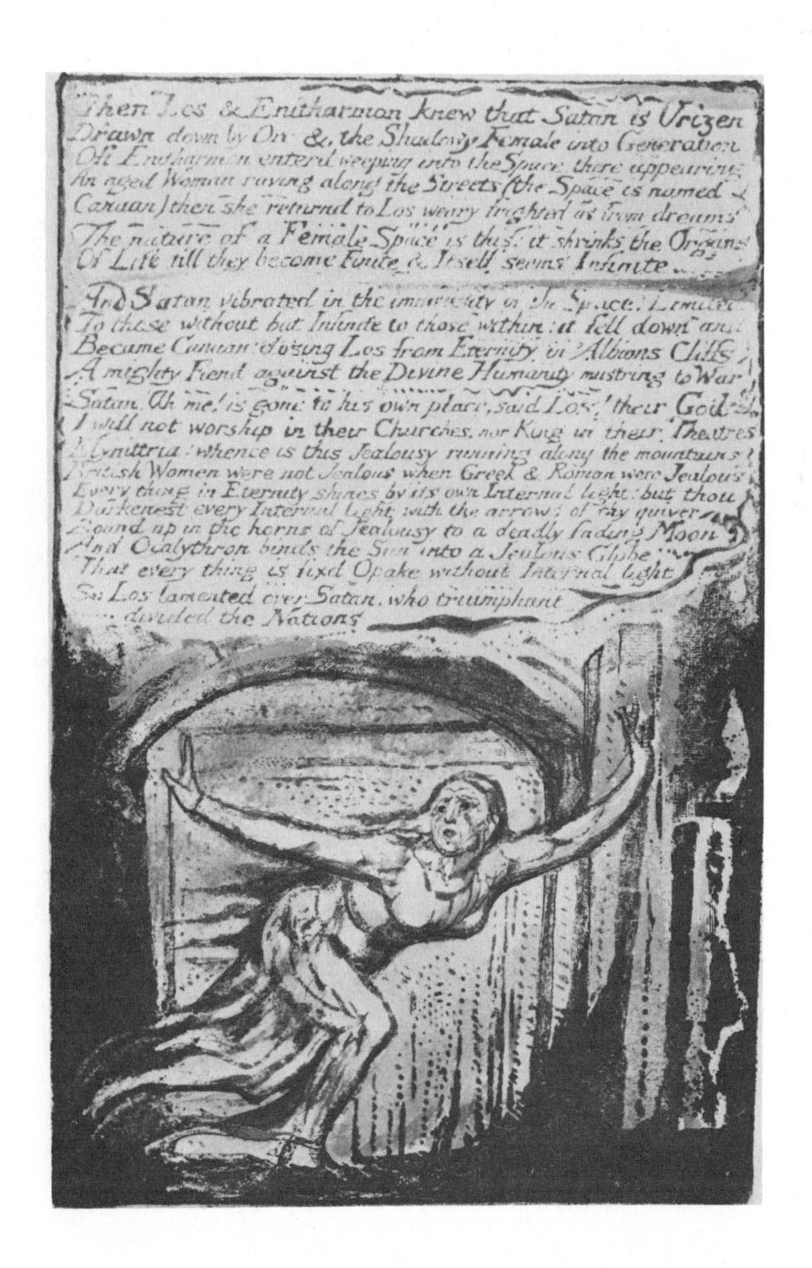

Milton 11D [K10]

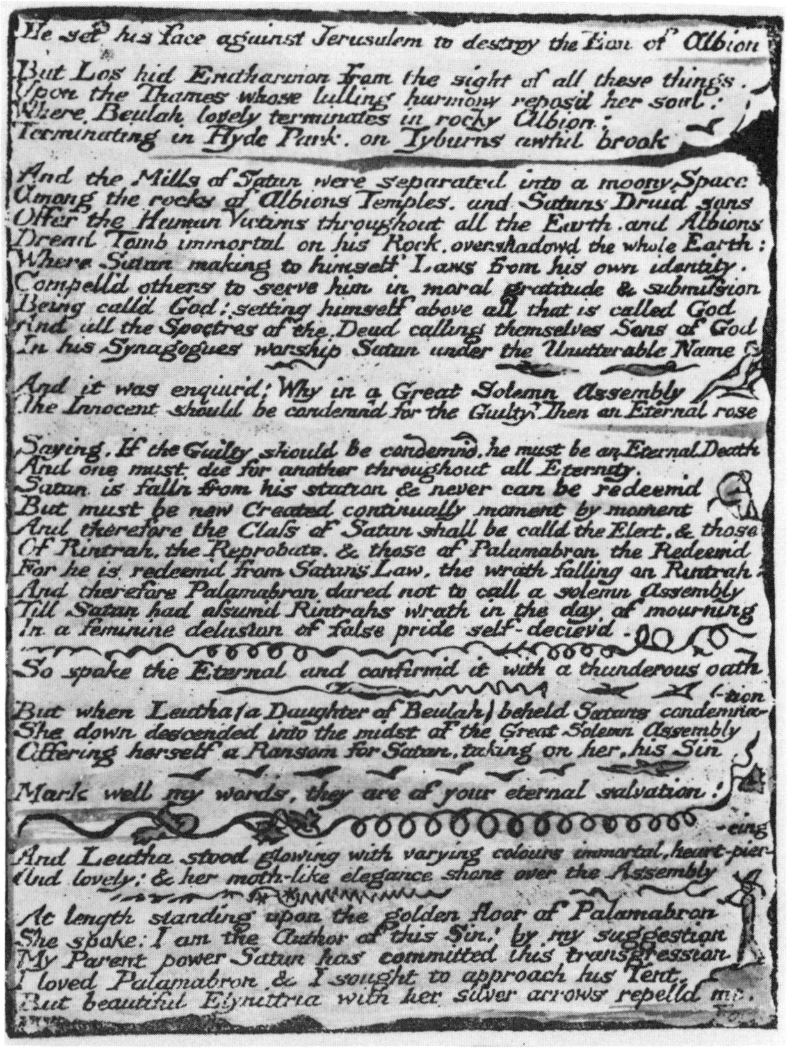

He set his face against Jerusalem to destroy the Eon of Albion

But Los hid Enitharmon from the sight of all these things.
Upon the Thames whose lulling harmony reposd her soul:
Where Beulah lovely terminates in rocky Albion:
Terminating in Hyde Park. on Tyburns awful brook

And the Mills of Satan were separated into a moony Space
Among the rocks of Albions Temples. and Satans Druid sons
Offer the Human Victims throughout all the Earth. and Albions
Dread Tomb immortal on his Rock. overshadowd the whole Earth:
Where Satan making to himself Laws from his own identity.
Compelld others to serve him in moral gratitude & submission
Being calld God: setting himself above all that is called God
And all the Spectres of the Dead calling themselves Sons of God
In his Synagogues worship Satan under the Unutterable Name

And it was enquird: Why in a Great Solemn Assembly
The Innocent should be condemnd for the Guilty? Then an Eternal rose

Saying. If the Guilty should be condemnd, he must be an Eternal Death
And one must die for another throughout all Eternity.
Satan is falln from his station & never can be redeemd
But must be new Created continually moment by moment
And therefore the Class of Satan shall be calld the Elect. & those
Of Rintrah. the Reprobate. & those of Palamabron the Redeemd
For he is redeemd from Satans Law. the wrath falling on Rintrah.
And therefore Palamabron dared not to call a solemn Assembly
Till Satan had assumd Rintrahs wrath in the day of mourning
In a feminine delusion of false pride self-decievd.

So spake the Eternal and confirmd it with a thunderous oath

But when Leutha (a Daughter of Beulah) beheld Satans condemnation
She down descended into the midst of the Great Solemn Assembly
Offering herself a Ransom for Satan. taking on her. his Sin

Mark well my words. they are of your eternal salvation:

And Leutha stood glowing with varying colours immortal, heart-piercing
And lovely: & her moth-like elegance shone over the Assembly

At length standing upon the golden floor of Palamabron
She spake: I am the Author of this Sin; by my suggestion
My Parent power Satan has committed this transgression
I loved Palamabron & I sought to approach his Tent.
But beautiful Elynittria with her silver arrows repelld me.

Milton 12ᴬ [K11]

Milton 12ᴬ [K11] (ABC9, D12). In this page the seventh and final occurrence of the Bard's refrain "Mark well my words . . . of your eternal salvation!" (31) is illuminated by a flight of seven birds plus a large eighth (perhaps swan or eagle; compare the "Eighth Image Divine" 17:5–6) and by a strong vine with four green leaves and a tendril of fifteen coils which rise to hold the fourth leaf high: a triumph of completed communication, the coils putting right-side-up the "transmission" image of *Marriage* 15, and the wing-leaf not simply clutching the serpent, as there, but growing from him. In copy C a rainbow spans the page from top left to center right, and a five-pointed star is added above "Enitharmon" (2)—though Los hides her from "All these things" (see Matthew 1:19–20) the star tells that a savior will be born. The stanza ends with a rising bird.

Under the next, about those who "worship Satan" (14), only one figure is soaring toward the penant under "worship"; one is flying, another climbing, away from it. Lower down a hunched figure sitting on a rock may be doing compass exercises. But the words of true gospel spoken by "an Eternal" (16–26) are endorsed by a full row of freely looping vine, and his "thunderous oath" (27) by a more angular vine, on which a human reclines (like Ezekiel in *Marriage* 13) and toward which a bird and moth are flying.

Leutha's "moth-like elegance" (33) as she rehearses for Milton the annihilation of selfhood is underlined by a leafy and a zigzag vine, with two Marygold star blossoms centered in a curve of beauty. This opens the blue air for a striding piper with a similarly curved hat whose music puts flourishes on nearby words. (Compare the piper in *Songs* 3.)

❧

Milton 13A [K12] (ABC10, D13). The text is now so crowded that a very small picture story exists marginally. A swaddled child illustrates the seized "new born son" (3). Two women, one feathered(?) the other a mermaid(?), symbolize the exclusively "feminine" perceptions (5–7). Leutha's being seen by colorists ("servants of the Harrow" 14) as a mere rainbow on the hills (15)—in copy B a large wash rainbow begins to the left of this passage and sweeps down to the lower right corner (moved to the preceding page in C)—is represented by a vaguely luscious blond woman with barely visible head but lots of hair; beside her a cupid flies, touching her thigh with his wing tips. Below line 23 she enacts how her own Hell's "flames still gird me round" (her feminine body leaping above fires). She sits on a hummock with an idle girdle or strap in her right hand when telling how she was "armd to say The most irritating things" (32). At line 42 she is apparently inside a skull or "Brain" with arms and hair sticking out, explaining her hiding herself in the "inmost Palace of his nervous fine wrought Brain."

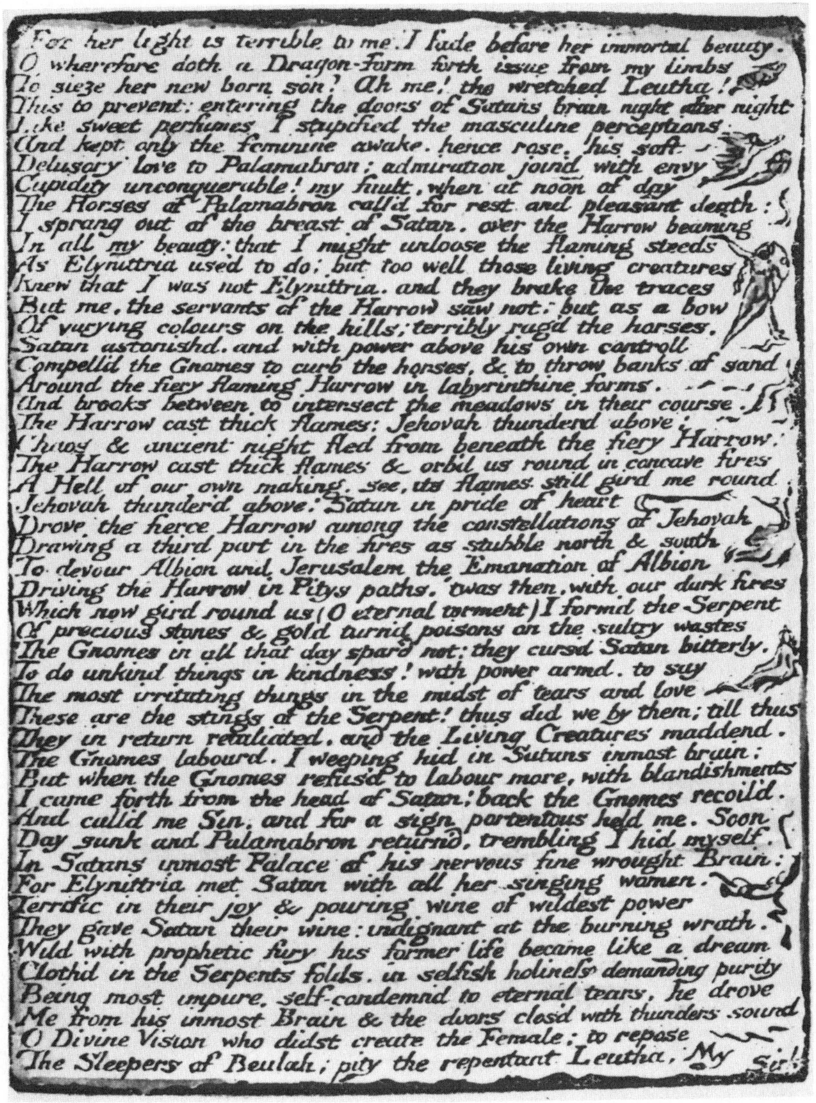

For her light is terrible to me. I fade before her immortal beauty.
O wherefore doth a Dragon-form forth issue from my limbs
To sieze her new born son? Ah me! the wretched Leutha!
This to prevent: entering the doors of Satans brain night after night
Like sweet perfumes I stupified the masculine perceptions
And kept only the feminine awake. hence rose his soft
Delusory love to Palamabron: admiration join'd with envy
Cupidity unconquerable! my fault, when at noon of day
The Horses of Palamabron call'd for rest and pleasant death:
I sprang out of the breast of Satan, over the Harrow beaming
In all my beauty: that I might unloose the flaming steeds
As Elynittria use'd to do; but too well those living creatures
Knew that I was not Elynittria, and they brake the traces
But me, the servants of the Harrow saw not: but as a bow
Of varying colours on the hills; terribly rag'd the horses.
Satan astonishd, and with power above his own controll
Compell'd the Gnomes to curb the horses, & to throw banks of sand
Around the fiery flaming Harrow in labyrinthine forms.
And brooks between to intersect the meadows in their course.
The Harrow cast thick flames: Jehovah thunderd above:
Chaos & ancient night fled from beneath the fiery Harrow:
The Harrow cast thick flames & orb'd us round in concave fires
A Hell of our own making. see, its flames still gird me round.
Jehovah thunder'd above: Satan in pride of heart
Drove the fierce Harrow among the constellations of Jehovah
Drawing a third part in the fires as stubble north & south
To devour Albion and Jerusalem the Emanation of Albion
Driving the Harrow in Pitys paths. 'twas then, with our dark fires
Which now gird round us (O eternal torment) I formd the Serpent
Of precious stones & gold turn'd poisons on the sultry wastes
The Gnomes in all that day spar'd not; they cursd Satan bitterly.
To do unkind things in kindness! with power armd, to say
The most irritating things in the midst of tears and love
These are the stings of the Serpent! thus did we by them; till thus
They in return retaliated, and the Living Creatures maddend.
The Gnomes labourd. I weeping hid in Satans inmost brain;
But when the Gnomes refus'd to labour more, with blandishments
I came forth from the head of Satan; back the Gnomes recoil'd.
And call'd me Sin, and for a sign portentous held me. Soon
Day sunk and Palamabron return'd, trembling I hid myself
In Satans inmost Palace of his nervous fine wrought Brain:
For Elynittria met Satan with all her singing women.
Terrific in their joy & pouring wine of wildest power
They gave Satan their wine: indignant at the burning wrath.
Wild with prophetic fury his former life became like a dream
Cloth'd in the Serpents folds, in selfish holiness demanding purity
Being most impure, self-condemn'd to eternal tears, he drove
Me from his inmost Brain & the doors clos'd with thunders sound
O Divine Vision who didst create the Female: to repose
The Sleepers of Beulah: pity the repentant Leutha. My
Sin!

Milton 13A [K12]

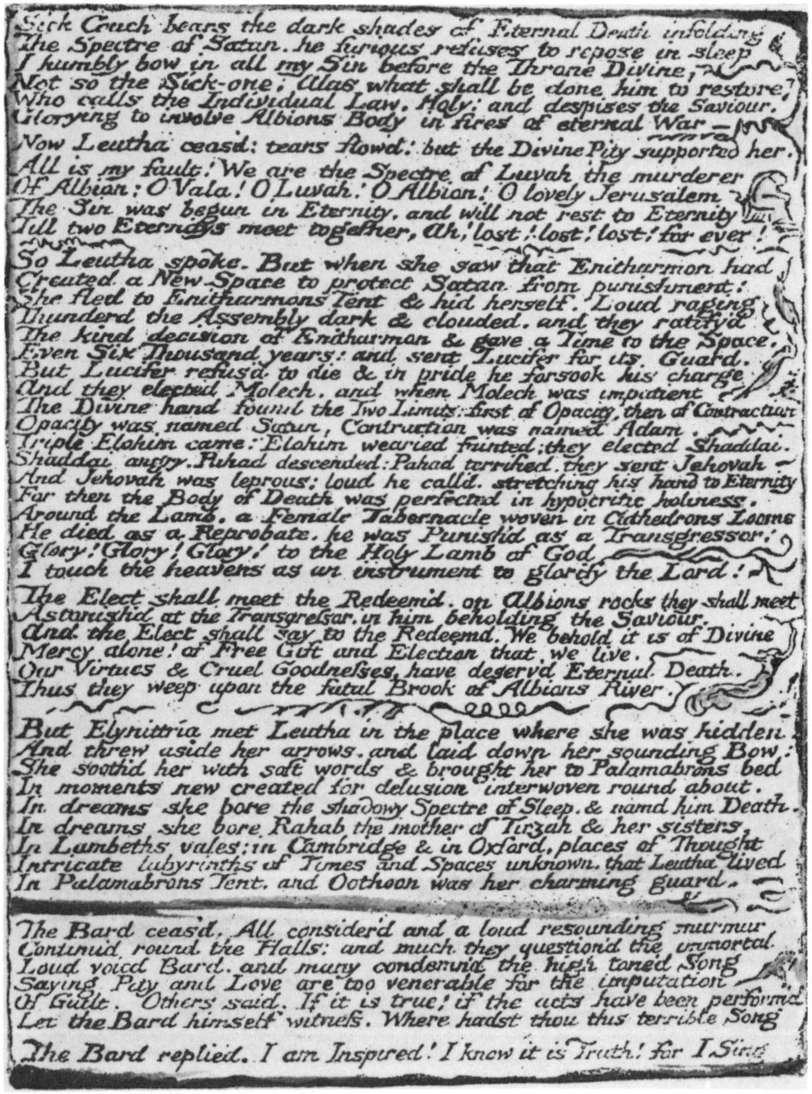

Sick Couch bears the dark shades of Eternal Death infolding
The Spectre of Satan. he furious refuses to repose in sleep
I humbly bow in all my Sin before the Throne Divine,
Not so the Sick-one; Alas what shall be done him to restore?
Who calls the Individual Law, Holy: and despises the Saviour.
Glorying to involve Albions Body in fires of eternal War—

Now Leutha ceas'd: tears flow'd: but the Divine Pity supported her.
All is my fault! We are the Spectre of Luvah the murderer
Of Albion: O Vala! O Luvah! O Albion! O lovely Jerusalem
The Sin was begun in Eternity, and will not rest to Eternity
Till two Eternitys meet together, Ah! lost! lost! lost! for ever!

So Leutha spoke. But when she saw that Enitharmon had
Created a New Space to protect Satan from punishment;
She fled to Enitharmons Tent & hid herself. Loud raging
Thunderd the Assembly dark & clouded. and they ratify'd
The kind decision of Enitharmon & gave a Time to the Space,
Even Six Thousand years; and sent Lucifer for its Guard.
But Lucifer refus'd to die & in pride he forsook his charge
And they elected Molech. and when Molech was impatient
The Divine hand found the Two Limits: first of Opacity, then of Contraction
Opacity was named Satan, Contraction was named Adam.
Triple Elohim came: Elohim wearied fainted: they elected Shaddai.
Shaddai angry. Pahad descended: Pahad terrified. they sent Jehovah
And Jehovah was leprous; loud he call'd. stretching his hand to Eternity
For then the Body of Death was perfected in hypocritic holiness.
Around the Lamb. a Female Tabernacle woven in Cathedrons Looms
He died as a Reprobate. he was Punish'd as a Transgressor!
Glory! Glory! Glory! to the Holy Lamb of God
I touch the heavens as an instrument to glorify the Lord!

The Elect shall meet the Redeem'd. on Albions rocks they shall meet
Astonish'd at the Transgressor. in him beholding the Saviour.
And the Elect shall say to the Redeemd. We behold it is of Divine
Mercy alone! of Free Gift and Election that we live.
Our Virtues & Cruel Goodnesses, have deserv'd Eternal Death.
Thus they weep upon the fatal Brook of Albions River.

But Elynittria met Leutha in the place where she was hidden.
And threw aside her arrows. and laid down her sounding Bow;
She sooth'd her with soft words & brought her to Palamabrons bed
In moments new created for delusion interwoven round about.
In dreams she bore the shadowy Spectre of Sleep. & namd him Death.
In dreams she bore Rahab the mother of Tirzah & her sisters,
In Lambeths vales; in Cambridge & in Oxford, places of Thought
Intricate labyrinths of Times and Spaces unknown, that Leutha lived
In Palamabrons Tent. and Oothoon was her charming guard.

The Bard ceas'd. All consider'd and a loud resounding murmur
Continu'd round the Halls; and much they question'd the immortal.
Loud voic'd Bard. and many condemn'd the high toned Song
Saying Pity and Love are too venerable for the imputation
Of Guilt. Others said. If it is true! if the acts have been perform'd
Let the Bard himself witness. Where hadst thou this terrible Song

The Bard replied. I am Inspired! I know it is Truth! for I Sing

Milton 14A [K13]

Milton 14A [K13] (ABC11, D14). Leutha's lament ending "lost! for ever!" (11) is accompanied by a pink and clothed figure sitting on a bench of slats and bowed over (probably Blake the artist; we see him again in this spot in Plate 21). The slatted effect is seen also in a fragmented line under "War" (6), after which a firm vine, flowering at the top, connects "supported" (7) to the "Throne Divine" (3) (though slightly broken in D). Lucifer's and Molech's being sent down but proving impatient (17–19) is probably the point of the light and dark figures coming or going in the margin. At line 21, "Contraction was named Adam," a lightning serpent is drawn. And then, at 29, a flowering vine springs from the "f" of "glorify the Lord!" At the paragraph's end Leutha soars up carrying a torch after a line of verdure with a four-looped tendril, above the deep blue of "Albions River."

Reference to Oothoon in line 44 inspires a sketch of her floating figure (see *Visions* 8). Below, beside the passage describing the "resounding murmur" and sharp questioning when "the Bard ceas'd," a stout man is shown running off stage—Blake the poet in his modest vegetable body (no features drawn) evading responsibility for the "Loud voicd Bard" who can answer back: "I am Inspired! I know it is Truth!" Blake's suit is brownA, or pinkBC, or blueD. We see him again, naked, in Plate 24; wearing his suit, beside his cottage, in Plate 40.

Milton 15^A [K14] (ABC12, D15). Here we see what could have happened to Palamabron and Rintrah if Milton's star had not descended (see Plate 10). (In C there is a row of small gold stars after the line ending with "refuge in Miltons bosom" 9.) Cain, at right, has slain Abel, at left (to use the familiar names; Blake repeats the same particulars in *Ghost of Abel* 1). Cain is simultaneously running fast and too extended to move. There is a knife in his outstretched hand; in copy C he is given a halo of gold and black spikes: compare Hand in *Jerusalem* 26. It is this continuing fratricide that compells Milton to descend: "The Nations still follow after the Gods of Priam" (14–15) (as in the days of Achilles and Hector).

The altar of blood sacrifice behind the two brothers is a wall of human skulls (touched with gold^C) and stones—the latter perhaps also skulls that have lost human form on "becoming opake," the condition to which Satan's once luminous "paved terraces" are said to contract (9:31–32). Three stones in the three sections of the altar are faceless pink^A heads (an effect somewhat obscured by a grey wash in D). Vegetation reaching out from the stones extends budding branches over Abel, barren ones over Cain; shoots spring up before him: the beginning of a forest? Fratricide separates human form into a collapsed body and a fleeing spectre. No star has entered Cain's tarsus and hence Abel's; both worshipped at a stone altar: we see the danger of Palamabron's foot on the Satanic terrace in Plate 10.

See Blake in Abel's position at the altar in Plate 17, struck by Milton's star not a fraternal knife. See Milton's concern for the collapsing body of Urizen in Plates 18 and 45. Yet consider that the sculptor also uses a knife as well as his shaping hands: wrath and pity again as contraries?

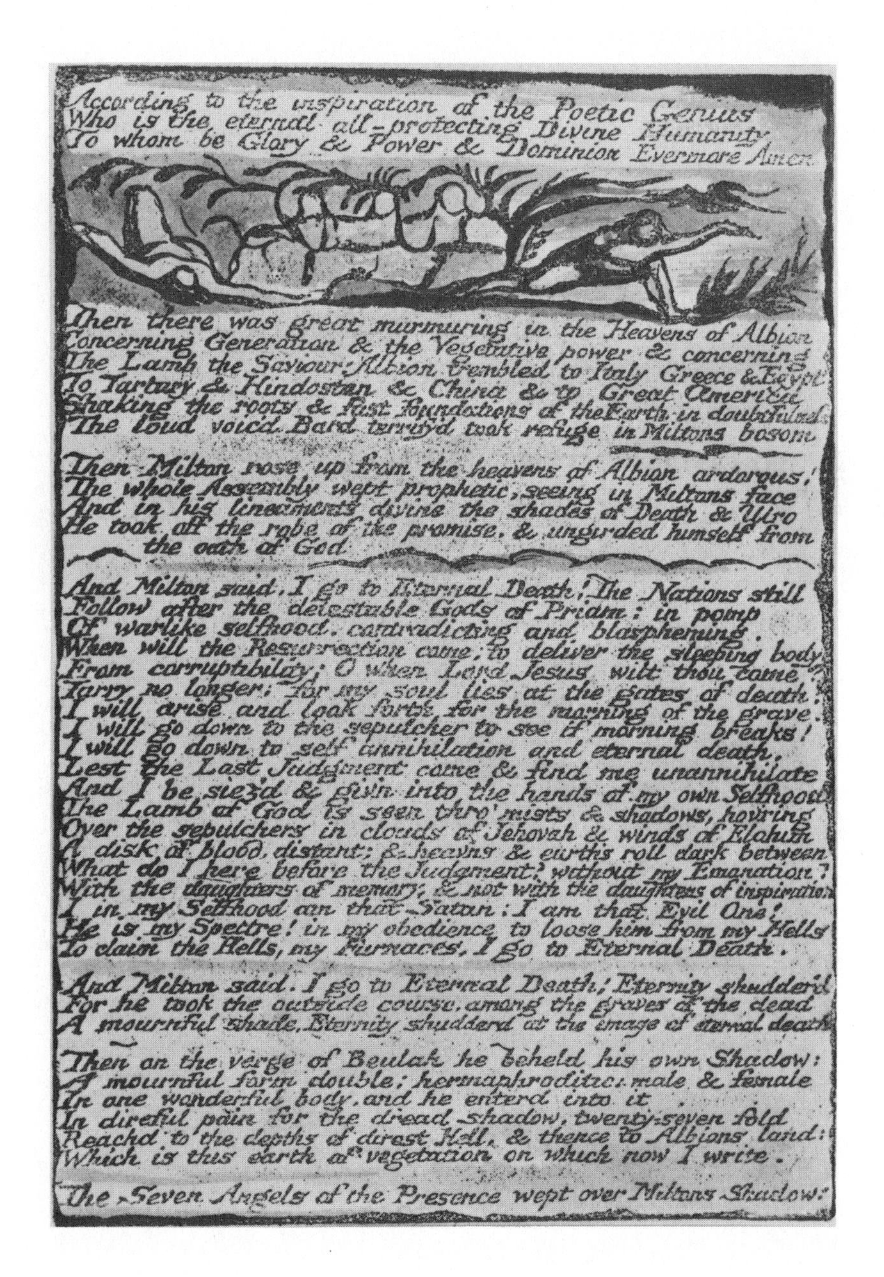

According to the inspiration of the Poetic Genius
Who is the eternal all-protecting Divine Humanity
To whom be Glory & Power & Dominion Evermore Amen

Then there was great murmuring in the Heavens of Albion
Concerning Generation & the Vegetative power & concerning
The Lamb the Saviour: Albion trembled to Italy Greece & Egypt
To Tartary & Hindostan & China & to Great America
Shaking the roots & fast foundations of the Earth in doubtfulness:
The loud voic'd Bard terrify'd took refuge in Miltons bosom

Then Milton rose up from the heavens of Albion ardorous!
The whole Assembly wept prophetic, seeing in Miltons face
And in his lineaments divine the shades of Death & Ulro
He took off the robe of the promise, & ungirded himself from
the oath of God

And Milton said, I go to Eternal Death! The Nations still
Follow after the detestable Gods of Priam; in pomp
Of warlike selfhood, contradicting and blaspheming.
When will the Resurrection come; to deliver the sleeping body
From corruptibility: O when Lord Jesus wilt thou come?
Tarry no longer; for my soul lies at the gates of death.
I will arise and look forth for the morning of the grave.
I will go down to the sepulcher to see if morning breaks!
I will go down to self annihilation and eternal death,
Lest the Last Judgment come & find me unannihilate
And I be siez'd & giv'n into the hands of my own Selfhood
The Lamb of God is seen thro' mists & shadows, hov'ring
Over the sepulchers in clouds of Jehovah & winds of Elohim
A disk of blood, distant; & heav'ns & earths roll dark between
What do I here before the Judgment? without my Emanation?
With the daughters of memory, & not with the daughters of inspiration
I in my Selfhood am that Satan: I am that Evil One!
He is my Spectre! in my obedience to loose him from my Hells
To claim the Hells, my Furnaces, I go to Eternal Death.

And Milton said. I go to Eternal Death! Eternity shudder'd
For he took the outside course, among the graves of the dead
A mournful shade. Eternity shudderd at the image of eternal death

Then on the verge of Beulah he beheld his own Shadow;
A mournful form double; hermaphroditic: male & female
In one wonderful body. and he enterd into it
In direful pain for the dread shadow, twenty-seven fold
Reachd to the depths of direst Hell, & thence to Albions land:
Which is this earth of vegetation on which now I write.

The Seven Angels of the Presence wept over Miltons Shadow;

Milton 15^A [K14]

Milton 16A

Milton 16A (ABC13, D16). (White-line engraving, with color, as in title page.) Milton, inspired, is shown as he "took off the robe of the promise, & ungirded himself from the oath of God" (15:13). "In contrast with that commanding gesture of so many Renaissance depictions of Apollo bringing the world under the rule of his ordering harmony, Blake has been at pains to show the poet as one who is casting away everything he posesses" (Raine II 250). But he is also readying himself for the combat with Urizen (Plate 18) in which he will combine wrath with mercy. Rays of the fiery nimbus round his head "mingle with the rays rising from the globe of a setting sun" (Keynes). (In A and B the sun is yellow, the nimbus in A reddish then bluish, in B blue, white, and pink; in C the sun is golden with rays of green, red, and gold, the nimbus a plain greyish halo with rays in white line; in D the color of nimbus and sun's rays is blood red, and the sun's disk though touched with gold is dark.)

The face and body of Milton subtly differ from copy to copy and are completely redesigned in D. John Grant sees A as the sublimest Milton, B as the most mysterious, C as the strongest, and D as the most companionable. In D his locks are much more prominent, he has a distinct penis (touched with red) and testicles, the white clothes and belt stand out sharply—and his robe has been extended along the ground so that he can step on it, as dirt beneath his left foot. Milton's striding forward is as in the title page but from a different perspective—and, to judge from his still having a garment to put off, a bit earlier in time; in the next plate we again see his star descending, as in Plate 2, but a bit later in time, now reaching its destination. If we look ahead for a matching picture, we shall find Ololon in Plate 50.

Milton 17A [K15] (ABC14, D17). At the lower left Milton's comet or "falling star" (47) is about to enter the tarsus of William Blake's left foot (49), having descended "perpendicular" through Beulah (44, 48). The "Three Heavens of Beulah" which Milton knew in his earthly "pilgrimage" (51–52) are pantomimed in the perpendicular vignettes of three women in pink dresses in the right margin, as Mary Lynn Johnson has helped me see. At top, on a spectre-edged cloud (topped with greenA grass), a mother holds an infant upright. The next woman twists sideways in alarm after word that Milton goes "guarded within" (20). The third, another Leutha perhaps, kneels beside a spiral viper, her arms raised in alarm or to conjure the serpent to collaborate. A fourth woman, in a somewhat paler dress, stands beside the altar, turning away as the star falls; she must be the poet's "sweet Shadow of Delight" who will "tremble" until he is by her side (49:28).

But what are William and Catherine Blake doing at opposite ends of the stony altar of sacrifice—enacting the story of Cain and Abel? In what spirit had Blake been approaching? Perhaps like Saul of Tarsus before his illumination, "breathing out threatenings and slaughter" (Acts 9.1). (In Blake's watercolor drawing [*Bible* 154], Saul, in a variant of this posture, though on horseback [recall Plate 6], has been leading armed men; Christ, extending his arms within a star-like radiance, countermands the pointing of their spears.) Catherine, halted in a forward stride toward William, with knees thrown together, head turned, right arm hiding her face, may be shielding herself from Blake's wrath before the intercession of the star—or from the terror of its approach. The analogy of Saul's transformation into Paul suggests that William Blake has been saved, by Milton's illuminating descent, from some act of connubial persecution comparable to the fraternal persecution that culminated in the slaying of Abel. By employing the stage property of the altar of sacrifice of Plate 15 as background and center of this male-female confrontation, Blake transfers the theme of false and true relation from brotherly to marital contraries, and even permits a pun about the altar.

The star will not only transform Blake by relaying Milton's decisive forward stride of self-annihilation to the articulation of Blake's forward foot; it will also transform the stones of the altar, by dividing them into two useful stairways (see Plates 32 and 37) and putting them behind the uniting brothers. (No "black cloud redounding" [60] spreads from Blake's foot, though in D there is a

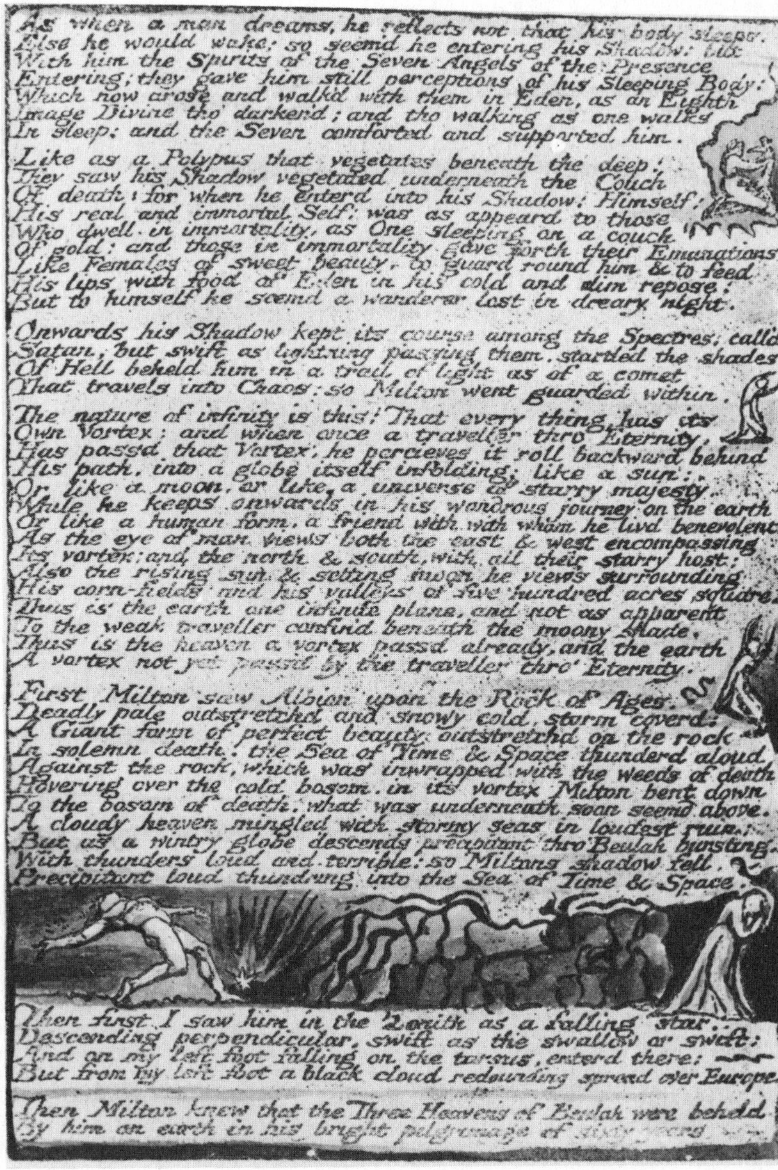

As when a man dreams, he reflects not that his body sleeps.
Else he would wake; so seemd he entering his Shadow: but
With him the Spirits of the Seven Angels of the Presence
Entering; they gave him still perceptions of his Sleeping Body;
Which now arose and walkd with them in Eden, as an Eighth
Image Divine tho' darkend; and tho walking as one walks
In sleep; and the Seven comforted and supported him.

Like as a Polypus that vegetates beneath the deep;
They saw his Shadow vegetated underneath the Couch
Of death: for when he enterd into his Shadow: Himself:
His real and immortal Self: was as appeard to those
Who dwell in immortality, as One sleeping on a couch
Of gold; and those in immortality gave forth their Emanations
Like Females of sweet beauty, to guard round him & to feed
His lips with food of Eden in his cold and dim repose:
But to himself he seemd a wanderer lost in dreary night.

Onwards his Shadow kept its course among the Spectres; calld
Satan, but swift as lightning passing them, startled the shades
Of Hell beheld him in a trail of light as of a comet
That travels into Chaos: so Milton went guarded within.

The nature of infinity is this: That every thing has its
Own Vortex; and when once a traveller thro Eternity,
Has passd that Vortex, he percieves it roll backward behind
His path, into a globe itself infolding; like a sun:
Or like a moon, or like a universe of starry majesty,
While he keeps onwards in his wondrous journey on the earth
Or like a human form, a friend with whom he livd benevolent.
As the eye of man views both the east & west encompassing
Its vortex; and the north & south, with all their starry host;
Also the rising sun & setting moon he views surrounding
His corn-fields and his valleys of five hundred acres square.
Thus is the earth one infinite plane, and not as apparent
To the weak traveller confind beneath the moony shade.
Thus is the heaven a vortex passd already, and the earth
A vortex not yet passd by the traveller thro' Eternity.

First Milton saw Albion upon the Rock of Ages,
Deadly pale outstretchd and snowy cold, storm coverd;
A Giant form of perfect beauty outstretchd on the rock
In solemn death: the Sea of Time & Space thunderd aloud
Against the rock, which was inwrapped with the weeds of death
Hovering over the cold bosom, in its vortex Milton bent down
To the bosom of death, what was underneath soon seemd above.
A cloudy heaven mingled with stormy seas in loudest ruin;
But as a wintry globe descends precipitant thro Beulah bursting,
With thunders loud and terrible: so Miltons shadow fell,
Precipitant loud thundring into the Sea of Time & Space.

Then first I saw him in the Zenith as a falling star,
Descending perpendicular, swift as the swallow or swift;
And on my left foot falling on the tarsus, enterd there;
But from my left foot a black cloud redounding spread over Europe.

Then Milton knew that the Three Heavens of Beulah were beheld
By him on earth in his bright pilgrimage of sixty years

Milton 17A [K15]

dark shadow at each end of the altar, which itself is cast into greyness. There are now not three but four or five faceless stone heads—four, given some features, in D.)

Milton 18ᴬ [K16]

Milton 18ᴬ [K16] (ABC15, D18). As Milton, more youthful after having "ungirded himself" (15:13) and with shorn hair (compare Plate 16 but also 45), strides across the river (Jordan) to grapple with his "Self-hood," the tarsus of his right foot cuts apart the two syllables of that word just as his hand, in Plate 1, pushes apart the syllables of "MIL / TON." Milton meets his negative John the Baptist (see the text of Plate 21) in the form of Urizen knee-deep in the flood, who grasps the stone tablets of the Law as they fall apart, like the divided syllables, at Milton's approach. Urizen's body, collapsing like Abel's, appears to sink into the water; his grey arms and head and tablets threaten to subside into the condition of the stone wall of commanded sacrifice, the altar of Plate 17. Not having the science of wrath, Urizen is terrified at the stern bard's approach. Milton does not, like Cain, wield a knife and turn away, but uses his feet to express his wrath and his hands to save the human form of his adversary. "When with cold hand Urizen" pours the river water "on To Miltons brain" (to turn his skull into another altar stone), Milton takes "of the red clay . . . and filling up the furrows" (an image that makes sculpture a metaphor for etching —an artist's pun on "sculpsit") creates "new flesh on the Demon cold" (21:7–14). (For a schematic diagram of this uniting of the fourfold Adam through earth, see Plate 36.)

If we note that the difference between the hand's cutting with a knife and the hands' shaping by building up is like one of the differences between the processes of intaglio engraving or etching and relief etching, we must also note that Milton's method, like Blake's relief etching, combines both the cutting of furrows and their filling up. Wrath and pity again?

In Exodus 20.25 the God of Law commanded that the stone of his altars must not be shaped by tool wielded by human hand. In Blake's view only the creativity of the hand can release the shape of the altar from death.

Milton's shorn hair makes this picture a comment on his persona Samson agonistes, another Saul of Tarsus, who felt powerless shorn (of selfhood) because power meant pulling down the temple of Dagon (Urizen) to destroy enemies (and self). In *Night*

Thoughts 537 Blake had painted the biblical Samson, with his hair growing back, grasping the tottering pillars (mocked here by the collapsing tablets). (Stuart Curran points out that Milton himself had distinguished his own mental warfare from the physical combat of the biblical Samson.) Thematic implication: timing, an anxiety that fury be not premature, is the concern of physical warriors; Milton-Samson need not wait for his proud hair to grow back. The transformation that gives life can be instantaneous.

The yellow sunlight behind the steep hill (the dark earth-rock that almost occults the sun) illuminates a young Bard with halo[D] and harp (held like a wing: he is an eagle of genius), accompanied by four dancing musicians, one blowing a trumpet, two shaking tamborines, one blowing a serpent horn—and a fifth, not clearly etched but given a face in D and a triangle to play. These may have been sent forth as seducers by Rahab in aid of Urizen (see 21:27–31). But from Milton's perspective they are the promised display of naked beauty, with "Harp & Song" if not "Flute" (4:28). The sunrise behind them relates them to the life-giving act of Milton; they must represent the five liberated senses or daughters, not the "self-dividing," "the Double-sexed" that Rahab and Tirzah thought they were sending. Indeed this row of living artists announces the potential of the rows of stone in the altar plates, a potential achieved partially in Plate 19, fully in Plate 48. Compare also Blake's *Job* 21.

Milton 19[A] [K17] (ABC16, D19). At the top Ololon appears as a human wall consisting of Milton's three wives and three daughters. The daughters—green, blue, pink[AC]; rose, white, pink[B]; all grey[D]—dance sinuously, while the wives, sharing a sofa, turn away from these Salomes. The wives (and sofa) are blue in ABC and they look into darkness; in D they are red and they see three dancing red flames—symbolically the three daughters—in the right corner. Or possibly they have a distant view (see line 3) of Milton's consuming selfhood, threefold. Similar flames appear in the same corner, lower down, in Plate 33. The three daughters are neither singing nor making music, and if the rigidity of the wives spreads, a stone wall could be the result. Yet the wives are still practically touching the daughters (garments hide their feet); if they decide to join the dance, the result will be the harmony of Plate 48. In B there is a knife (of Cain) in the raised right hand of the first daughter.

Milton 19[A] [K17]

And Tharmas Demon of the Waters, & Orc, who is Luvah
The Shadowy Female seeing Milton, howld in her lamentation
Over the Deeps, outstretching her Twenty-seven Heavens over Albion
And thus the Shadowy Female howls in articulate howlings
I will lament over Milton in the lamentations of the afflicted
My Garments shall be woven of sighs & heart broken lamentations
The misery of unhappy Families shall be drawn out into its border
Wrought with the needle with dire sufferings poverty pain & woe
Along the rocky Island & thence throughout the whole Earth
There shall be the sick Father & his starving Family! there
The Prisoner in the stone Dungeon & the Slave at the Mill
I will have Writings written all over it in Human Words
That every Infant that is born upon the Earth shall read
And get by rote as a hard task of a life of sixty years
I will have Kings inwoven upon it, & Councellors & Mighty Men
The Famine shall clasp it together with buckles & Clasps
And the Pestilence shall be its fringe & the War its girdle
To divide into Rahab & Tirzah that Milton may come to our tents
For I will put on the Human Form & take the Image of God
Even Pity & Humanity but my Clothing shall be Cruelty
And I will put on Holiness as a breastplate & as a helmet
And all my ornaments shall be of the gold of broken hearts
And the precious stones of anxiety & care & desperation & death
And repentance for sin & sorrow & punishment & fear
To defend me from thy terrors O Orc! my only beloved!

Orc answerd. Take not the Human Form O loveliest. Take not
Terror upon thee! Behold how I am & tremble lest thou also
Consume in my Consummation; but thou maist take a Form
Female & lovely, that cannot consume in Mans consummation
Wherefore dost thou Create & Weave this Satan for a Covering
When thou attemptest to put on the Human Form, my wrath
Burns to the top of heaven against thee in Jealousy & fear.
Then I rend thee asunder, then I howl over thy clay & ashes
When wilt thou put on the Female Form as in times of old
With a Garment of Pity & Compassion like the Garment of God
His garments are long sufferings for the Children of Men
Jerusalem is his Garment & not thy Covering Cherub O lovely
Shadow of my delight who wanderest seeking for the prey.

So spoke Orc when Oothoon & Leutha hoverd over his Couch
Of fire in interchange of Beauty & Perfection in the darkness
Opening interiorly into Jerusalem & Babylon shining glorious
In the Shadowy Females bosom. Jealous her darkness grew:
Howlings filld all the desolate places in accusations of Sin
In Female beauty shining in the unformd void & Orc in vain
Stretch'd out his hands of fire, & wooed: they triumph in his pain

Thus darkend the Shadowy Female tenfold & Orc tenfold
Glowd on his rocky Couch against the darkness: loud thunders
Told of the enormous conflict Earthquake beneath: around
Rent the Immortal Females, limb from limb & joint from joint
And moved the fast foundations of the Earth to wake the Dead
Urizen emerged from his Rocky Form & from his Snows

Milton 20D [K18]

In the margin of the first break is a curl of green drapery or flame. At the bottom, on the green turf of England, Milton is confronted by Los as a "Vehicular terror" (i.e. mistaking him for Satan). Los shoots his limbs forth "like the roots of trees"—and we see that he is almost headless. He stands on his left foot (or his right[B]). Urizen, nothing but head, peers from the ground and beholds "the immortal Man" (36). The picture is an analytic variant of the wrestling of Plate 18: it is the *division* of Los and Urizen from being fraternal contraries that makes Los act like a body whose hands are all fingers and whose feet are going backward and Urizen seem an Abel collapsing back into the ground; Milton's task is to annihilate their separation. Looking again at Plate 18 we can see that Milton is replacing Urizen's head. Historically the separation of England's head and body is what happened in the "fury premature" of 1649; it was justified by the republican Milton, but the ensuing Civil War did not achieve a resurrected England. In the Bard's song (5:39) King Charles "calls on Milton for atonement." Compare the Voice of Abel's blood in *The Ghost of Abel.*) But the naked Milton now confronts the problem of making whole what is already asunder, of resurrecting the Spiritual Body. In the twelve-book, historical *Milton* (perhaps lost, perhaps only planned) Blake may have posed the problem of combining wrath and mercy in a true brotherhood as that of joining Parliament (Palamabron) and Army (Rintrah), with Cromwell interfering as the Satanic illusion. See Plate 5.

Milton 20D [K18] (C17, D20, not in AB). The sad nude woman kneeling in the upper right margin is probably Orc's "Shadowy Female" (who utters the lament alongside). Below her (at line 20) is a covered figure, perhaps, lying with his head raised. The dark shadows edging the lower half of the text suggest the edge of a stone tablet.

Milton 21^A [K19] (AB17, C18, D21). For several pages a marginal narrative having few direct textual referents seems to pursue an almost independent course, dealing with the artist at work as central figure. On the present page Milton's efforts to build "with new clay a Human form" (14) suggest that form-building may be involved in the pictures of a large pink rose or anemone bud taking human form: second figure from top and sixth and seventh figures. And a despairing creator may be the male figure huddled at bottom (in a blue-green suit in D like the Blake figure in Plate 14). From his spine green stems rise toward (while not actually connecting with) the humanizing buds above him. Similar despair may afflict the slightly less bowed figure third from the top sitting on a green mound from which the stem of the pink human bud above him arises. (In D this figure is pink, unlike the lower one, but in A both are pink, like the rose in full bloom, and in B they are both blue, in C brown.)

The man on the mound has a sort of cape, perhaps a modification of the pilgrim's pack which bows a smaller figure at the top. The two standing figures in the central area, a naked athlete preparing to throw or put something and, above him, a blond-haired figure with overlong purple gown possibly wielding a knife in the left hand, may be analogues of the wrestling of Milton with Urizen, the labors of Milton/Blake as sculptor.

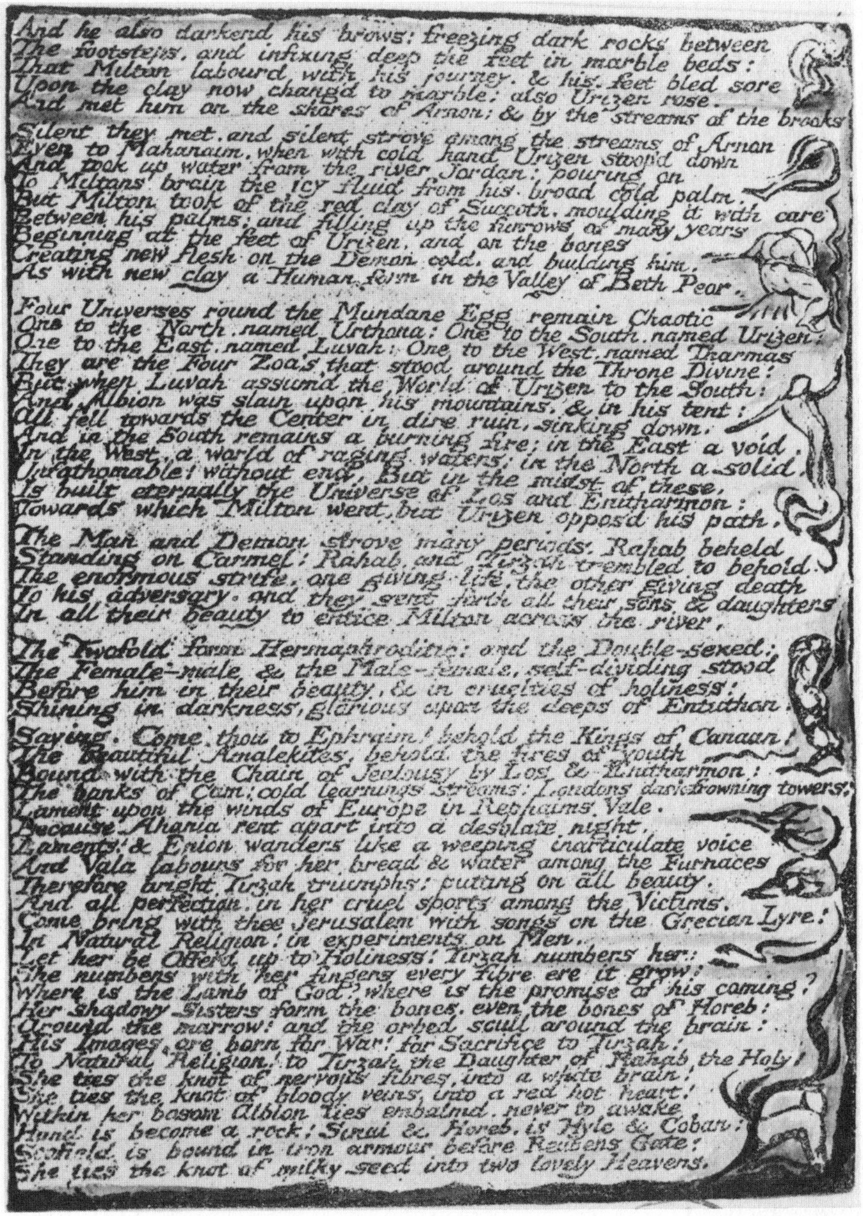

And he also darkend his brows: freezing dark rocks between
The footsteps, and infixing deep the feet in marble beds:
That Milton labourd with his journey, & his feet bled sore
Upon the clay now changd to marble; also Urizen rose,
And met him on the shores of Arnon; & by the streams of the brooks

Silent they met, and silent strove among the streams of Arnon
Even to Mahanaim, when with cold hand Urizen stoop'd down
And took up water from the river Jordan: pouring on
To Miltons brain the icy fluid from his broad cold palm.
But Milton took of the red clay of Succoth, moulding it with care
Between his palms; and filling up the furrows of many years
Beginning at the feet of Urizen, and on the bones
Creating new flesh on the Demon cold, and building him,
As with new clay a Human form in the Valley of Beth Peor.

Four Universes round the Mundane Egg remain Chaotic
One to the North, named Urthona: One to the South, named Urizen:
One to the East, named Luvah: One to the West, named Tharmas
They are the Four Zoa's that stood around the Throne Divine:
But when Luvah assumd the World of Urizen to the South:
And Albion was slain upon his mountains, & in his tent;
All fell towards the Center in dire ruin, sinking down.
And in the South remains a burning fire; in the East a void.
In the West, a world of raging waters; in the North a solid
Unfathomable! without end. But in the midst of these,
Is built eternally the Universe of Los and Enitharmon:
Towards which Milton went, but Urizen opposd his path.

The Man and Demon strove many periods. Rahab beheld
Standing on Carmel; Rahab and Tirzah trembled to behold
The enormous strife, one giving life, the other giving death
To his adversary. and they sent forth all their sons & daughters
In all their beauty to entice Milton across the river,

The Twofold form Hermaphroditic: and the Double-sexed;
The Female-male & the Male-female, self-dividing stood
Before him in their beauty, & in cruelties of holiness:
Shining in darkness, glorious upon the deeps of Entuthon.

Saying. Come thou to Ephraim! behold the Kings of Canaan!
The beautiful Amalekites, behold the fires of youth
Bound with the Chain of Jealousy by Los & Enitharmon;
The banks of Cam: cold learnings streams: Londons dark-frowning towers;
Lament upon the winds of Europe in Rephaims Vale.
Because Ahania rent apart into a desolate night,
Laments! & Enion wanders like a weeping inarticulate voice
And Vala labours for her bread & water among the Furnaces
Therefore bright Tirzah triumphs: putting on all beauty.
And all perfection, in her cruel sports among the Victims.
Come bring with thee Jerusalem with songs on the Grecian Lyre:
In Natural Religion: in experiments on Men,
Let her be Offerd up to Holiness! Tirzah numbers her;
She numbers with her fingers every fibre ere it grow;
Where is the Lamb of God? where is the promise of his coming?
Her shadowy Sisters form the bones, even the bones of Horeb:
Around the marrow! and the orbed scull around the brain:
His Images are born for War! for Sacrifice to Tirzah!
To Natural Religion! to Tirzah the Daughter of Rahab the Holy!
She ties the knot of nervous fibres, into a white brain!
She ties the knot of bloody veins, into a red hot heart!
Within her bosom Albion lies embalmd, never to awake
Hand is become a rock! Sinai & Horeb, is Hyle & Coban:
Scofield is bound in iron armour before Reubens Gate:
She ties the knot of milky seed into two lovely Heavens,

Milton 21^A [K19]

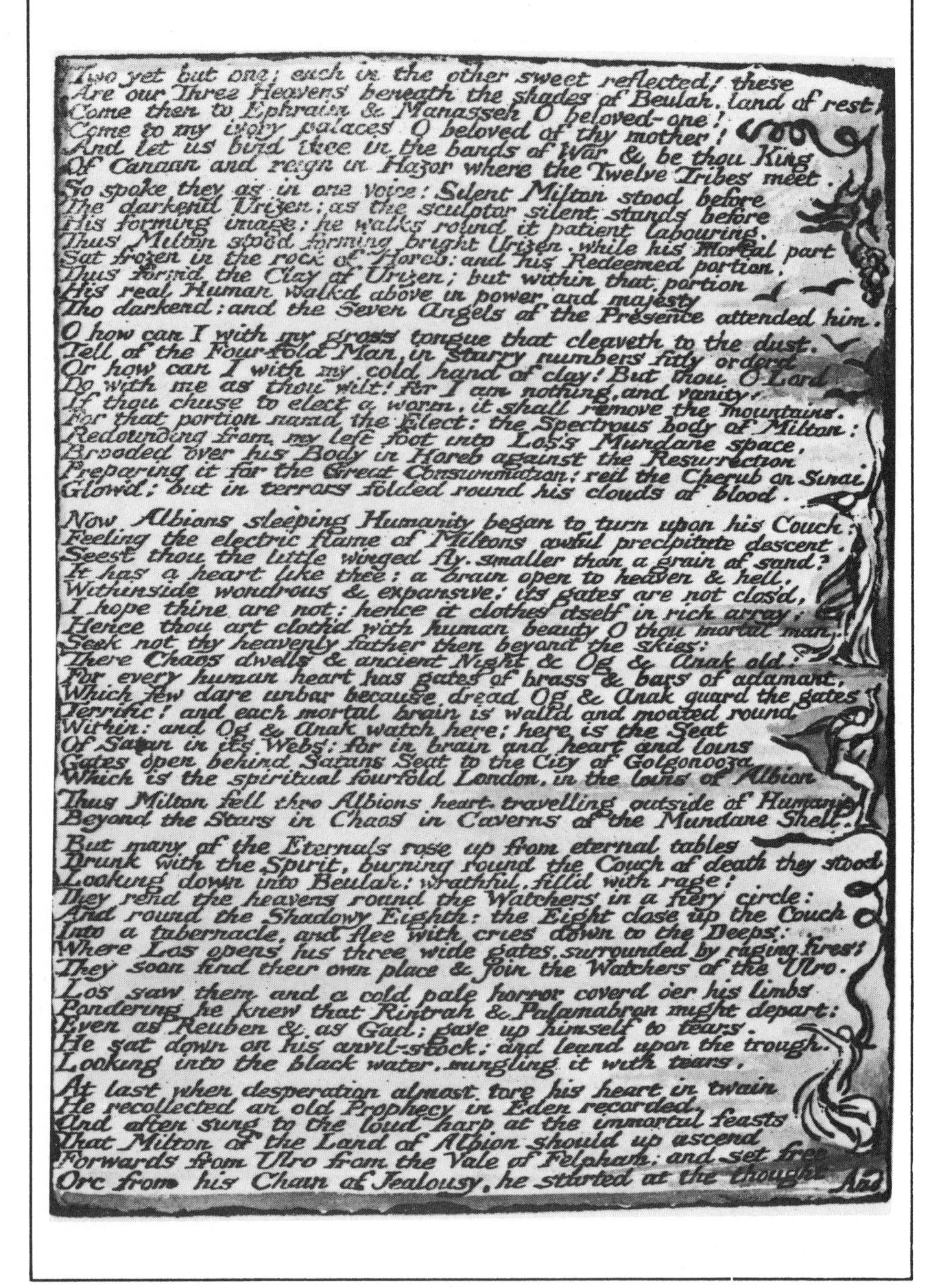

Two yet but one: each in the other sweet reflected; these
Are our Three Heavens beneath the shades of Beulah, land of rest!
Come then to Ephraim & Manasseh O beloved-one!
Come to my ivory palaces O beloved of thy mother!
And let us bind thee in the bands of War & be thou King
Of Canaan and reign in Hazor where the Twelve Tribes meet.
So spoke they as in one voice: Silent Milton stood before
The darkend Urizen; as the sculptor silent stands before
His forming image; he walks round it patient labouring.
Thus Milton stood forming bright Urizen, while his Mortal part
Sat frozen in the rock of Horeb: and his Redeemed portion,
Thus formd the Clay of Urizen; but within that portion
His real Human walkd above in power and majesty
Tho darkend; and the Seven Angels of the Presence attended him.
O how can I with my gross tongue that cleaveth to the dust,
Tell of the Four-fold Man, in starry numbers fitly orderd
Or how can I with my cold hand of clay! But thou O Lord
Do with me as thou wilt! for I am nothing, and vanity.
If thou chuse to elect a worm, it shall remove the mountains.
For that portion namd the Elect: the Spectrous body of Milton:
Redounding from my left foot into Los's Mundane space,
Brooded over his Body in Horeb against the Resurrection
Preparing it for the Great Consummation; red the Cherub on Sinai
Glowd; but in terrors folded round his clouds of blood.
Now Albions sleeping Humanity began to turn upon his Couch;
Feeling the electric flame of Miltons awful precipitate descent.
Seest thou the little winged fly, smaller than a grain of sand?
It has a heart like thee; a brain open to heaven & hell,
Withinside wondrous & expansive; its gates are not clos'd,
I hope thine are not: hence it clothes itself in rich array;
Hence thou art clothd with human beauty O thou mortal man.
Seek not thy heavenly father then beyond the skies:
There Chaos dwells & ancient Night & Og & Anak old:
For every human heart has gates of brass & bars of adamant,
Which few dare unbar because dread Og & Anak guard the gates
Terrific! and each mortal brain is walld and moated round
Within: and Og & Anak watch here; here is the Seat
Of Satan in its Webs; for in brain and heart and loins
Gates open behind Satans Seat to the City of Golgonooza
Which is the spiritual fourfold London, in the loins of Albion
Thus Milton fell thro Albions heart, travelling outside of Humanity
Beyond the Stars in Chaos in Caverns of the Mundane Shell.
But many of the Eternals rose up from eternal tables
Drunk with the Spirit, burning round the Couch of death they stood
Looking down into Beulah: wrathful, filld with rage;
They rend the heavens round the Watchers in a fiery circle:
And round the Shadowy Eighth: the Eight close up the Couch
Into a tabernacle, and flee with cries down to the Deeps:
Where Los opens his three wide gates, surrounded by raging fires!
They soon find their own place & join the Watchers of the Ulro.
Los saw them and a cold pale horror coverd oer his limbs
Pondering he knew that Rintrah & Palamabron might depart:
Even as Reuben & as Gad; gave up himself to tears.
He sat down on his anvil-stock; and leand upon the trough.
Looking into the black water, mingling it with tears.
At last when desperation almost tore his heart in twain
He recollected an old Prophecy in Eden recorded,
And often sung to the loud harp at the immortal feasts
That Milton of the Land of Albion should up ascend
Forwards from Ulro from the Vale of Felpham; and set free
Orc from his Chain of Jealousy, he started at the thought
And

Milton 22ᴬ [K20]

Milton 22ᴬ [K20] (AB18, C19, D22). In the center of the right margin we see the naked and clothed athletes again, perhaps, the naked one dancing with (sculptor's) knife, to work in clay—or with graver in one hand and pen in the other: see him emerge as the Blake figure in Plate 24. The garmented figure could be the sculptor's "forming image" (9), with the garment falling aside (as Milton's in Plate 16) to reveal the "real Human" (12). In this way, perhaps, Los "opens his three wide gates" of art (49). Their opening is celebrated or signified by the five birds that fly up together from the figure's lifted left arm, toward the cluster of purple grapes with leaf and tendril at the top. At the bottom a dancer in swirling skirt, possibly celebrating Los's starting at a hopeful "thought" (last line), wields a great whip of a line that forms a path for the sculptor's foot (compare the star entering Blake's in Plates 17 and 32). The cheering thought is that Milton, whose *descent* to Felpham's vale is rehearsed from many angles in this poem, will then *ascend*, "up" and "Forwards" (59–60). (The personal parallel is Blake's retreat from Lambeth to Felpham—a journey for which he borrows the sandals of Los in Lambeth [24:9–11]—seen as preparation for his return to mental war in London. The two moves are the pulsations between which the whole poem lives.)

The knife wielding figure dancing on the line and the skirted figure wielding it (or coloring it?) can be seen in similar collaboration in *Jerusalem* 36.

Milton 23A [K21] (AB19, C20, D23). In the top right margin, with face turned up and arm reaching toward Heaven (see line 6), walking a leafing line is William Blake—though he leaves out his features, as in Plate 24—walking "forward thro' Eternity," knowing now "that it was Milton" (8). And we, looking back, are permitted to surmise that one of the free spirits laboring was Milton, the other Blake. Just below him flames of grass flourish after "living banks" (18). The next marginal group (beside 22–32 but unclear except in D) seems to represent the descent of Milton's star and spirit (seen as a cloudy form with human head, a version of Ololon perhaps) toward Blake, who now understands, stepping through tall grass. The next group may be "all the Family Divine" weeping "as One Man . . . over Ololon" (41–42). Leaning on a four-looped grapevine ("the Family Divine collected as Four Suns": 37), a gowned Christ turns toward a gowned kneeling Ololon. Below that we see Ololon standing with arms flung high exclaiming "How is this wondrous thing? . . . let us enter . . ." (47–50). (The object beside her could be an opening wooden gate.) The bottom figure, gathering to spring with wing-like arms, is perhaps William Blake, rather than Ololon, responding to the divine command to "Watch over this World . . . with your brooding wings" (55). In coloring (a heavy pink in D) and stoutness this naked muscular figure is identified with the Blake figure on the next plate.

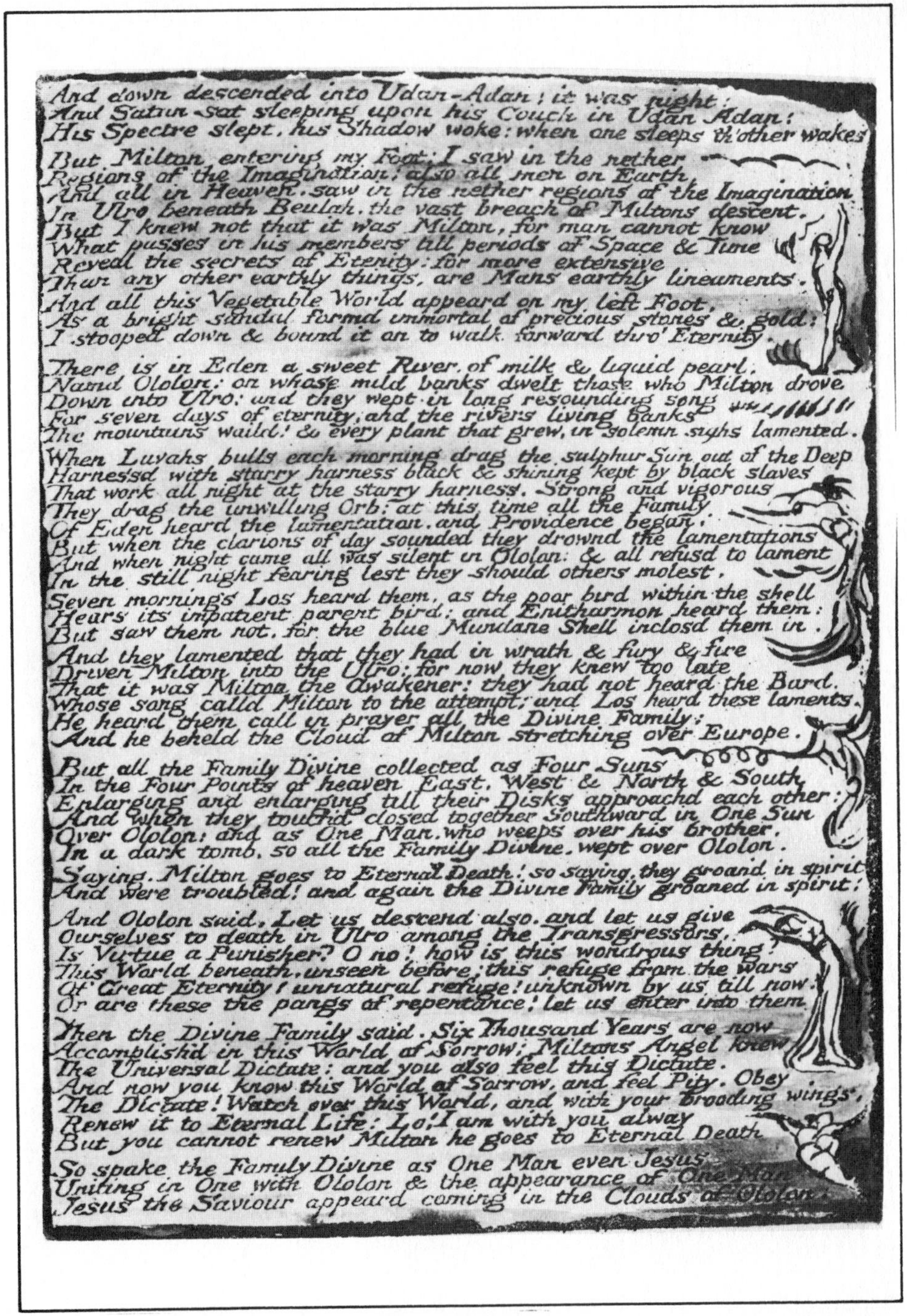

And down descended into Udan-Adan; it was night:
And Satan sat sleeping upon his Couch in Udan-Adan:
His Spectre slept, his Shadow woke: when one sleeps th'other wakes

But Milton entering my Foot; I saw in the nether
Regions of the Imagination; also all men on Earth
And all in Heaven, saw in the nether regions of the Imagination
In Ulro beneath Beulah, the vast breach of Miltons descent.
But I knew not that it was Milton, for man cannot know
What passes in his members till periods of Space & Time
Reveal the secrets of Eternity: for more extensive
Than any other earthly things, are Mans earthly lineaments.
And all this Vegetable World appeard on my left Foot,
As a bright sandal formd immortal of precious stones & gold:
I stooped down & bound it on to walk forward thro' Eternity.

There is in Eden a sweet River, of milk & liquid pearl,
Namd Ololon; on whose mild banks dwelt those who Milton drove
Down into Ulro: and they wept in long resounding song
For seven days of eternity, and the rivers living banks
The mountains waild! & every plant that grew, in solemn sighs lamented.

When Luvahs bulls each morning drag the sulphur Sun out of the Deep
Harnessd with starry harness black & shining kept by black slaves
That work all night at the starry harness, Strong and vigorous
They drag the unwilling Orb: at this time all the Family
Of Eden heard the lamentation, and Providence began;
But when the clarions of day sounded they drownd the lamentations
And when night came all was silent in Ololon: & all refusd to lament
In the still night fearing lest they should others molest.

Seven mornings Los heard them, as the poor bird within the shell
Hears its impatient parent bird; and Enitharmon heard them:
But saw them not, for the blue Mundane Shell inclosd them in.

And they lamented that they had in wrath & fury & fire
Driven Milton into the Ulro; for now they knew too late
That it was Milton the Awakener: they had not heard the Bard,
Whose song calld Milton to the attempt; and Los heard these laments.
He heard them call in prayer all the Divine Family;
And he beheld the Cloud of Milton stretching over Europe.

But all the Family Divine collected as Four Suns
In the Four Points of heaven East, West & North & South
Enlarging and enlarging till their Disks approachd each other;
And when they touchd closed together Southward in One Sun
Over Ololon: and as One Man, who weeps over his brother,
In a dark tomb, so all the Family Divine, wept over Ololon.

Saying, Milton goes to Eternal Death! so saying, they groand in spirit
And were troubled! and again the Divine Family groaned in spirit!

And Ololon said, Let us descend also, and let us give
Ourselves to death in Ulro among the Transgressors.
Is Virtue a Punisher? O no! how is this wondrous thing?
This World beneath, unseen before: this refuge from the wars
Of Great Eternity! unnatural refuge! unknown by us till now!
Or are these the pangs of repentance? let us enter into them

Then the Divine Family said. Six Thousand Years are now
Accomplishd in this World of Sorrow; Miltons Angel knew
The Universal Dictate; and you also feel this Dictate.
And now you know this World of Sorrow, and feel Pity. Obey
The Dictate! Watch over this World, and with your brooding wings,
Renew it to Eternal Life: Lo! I am with you alway
But you cannot renew Milton he goes to Eternal Death

So spake the Family Divine as One Man even Jesus
Uniting in One with Ololon & the appearance of One Man
Jesus the Saviour appeard coming in the Clouds of Ololon!

Milton 23A [K21]

Tho driven away with the Seven Starry Ones into the Ulro
Yet the Divine Vision remains Every-where For-ever. Amen.
And Ololon lamented for Milton with a great lamentation.

While Los heard indistinct in fear, what time I bound my sandals
On; to walk forward thro' Eternity, Los descended to me:
And Los behind me stood; a terrible flaming Sun: just close
Behind my back; I turned round in terror, and behold.
Los stood in that fierce glowing fire; & he also stoop'd down
And bound my sandals on in Udan-Adan; trembling I stood
Exceedingly with fear & terror, standing in the Vale
Of Lambeth: but he kissed me and wishd me health.
And I became One Man with him arising in my strength:
Twas too late now to recede. Los had enterd into my soul:
His terrors now possess'd me whole! I arose in fury & strength.

I am that Shadowy Prophet who Six Thousand Years ago
Fell from my station in the Eternal bosom. Six Thousand Years
Are finishd. I return! both Time & Space obey my will.
I in Six Thousand Years walk up and down: for not one Moment
Of Time is lost, nor one Event of Space unpermanent
But all remain: every fabric of Six Thousand Years
Remains permanent: tho' on the Earth where Satan
Fell, and was cut off all things vanish & are seen no more
They vanish not from me & mine, we guard them first & last
The generations of men run on in the tide of Time
But leave their destind lineaments permanent for ever & ever.
So spoke Los as we went along to his supreme abode.

Rintrah and Palamabron met us at the Gate of Golgonooza
Clouded with discontent. & brooding in their minds terrible things

They said. O Father most beloved: O merciful Parent!
Pitying and permitting evil, tho strong & mighty to destroy.
Whence is this Shadow terrible? wherefore dost thou refuse
To throw him into the Furnaces; knowest thou not that he
Will unchain Orc; & let loose Satan, Og, Sihon & Anak,
Upon the Body of Albion? for this he is come; behold it written
Upon his fibrous left Foot black; most dismal to our eyes
The Shadowy Female shudders thro' heaven in torment inexpressible:
And all the Daughters of Los prophetic wail: yet in deceit,
They weave a new Religion from new Jealousy of Theotormon:
Miltons Religion is the cause: there is no end to destruction!
Seeing the Churches at their Period in terror & despair:
Rahab created Voltaire; Tirzah created Rousseau;
Asserting the Self-righteousness against the Universal Saviour,
Mocking the Confessors & Martyrs, claiming Self-righteousness;
With cruel Virtue: making War upon the Lambs Redeemed;
To perpetuate War & Glory, to perpetuate the Laws of Sin:
They perverted Swedenborgs Visions in Beulah & in Ulro:
To destroy Jerusalem as a Harlot & her Sons as Reprobates;
To raise up Mystery the Virgin Harlot Mother of War,
Babylon the Great, the Abomination of Desolation!
O Swedenborg! strongest of men, the Samson shorn by the Churches!
Shewing the Transgressors in Hell, the proud Warriors in Heaven:
Heaven as a Punisher & Hell as One under Punishment:
With Laws from Plato & his Greeks to renew the Trojan Gods,
In Albion; & to deny the value of the Saviours blood.
But then I rais'd up Whitefield, Palamabron raisd up Westley,
And these are the cries of the Churches before the two Witnesses:
Faith in God the dear Saviour who took on the likeness of men:
Becoming obedient to death, even the death of the Cross
The Witnesses lie dead in the Street of the Great City
No Faith is in all the Earth: the Book of God is trodden under Foot:
He sent his two Servants Whitefield & Westley; were they Prophets
Or were they Idiots or Madmen? shew us Miracles!
Can

Milton 24A [K22]

Milton 24A [K22] (AB20, C21, D24). Los, descending and becoming "a terrible flaming Sun" (6), is shown as a falling naked figure closely followed by a gowned one (Ololon perhaps) against yellow bursts of light. A viper shape is beside his outstretched right hand, and his left reaches down toward a triumphant trumpet-like flower growing out from line 26. Below dances stout William Blake, a paintbrush in one raised hand, a knife turning into a bird (N.B.) flying from the other. (These looked like wings in the hands of the bottom figure on Plate 23.) His face, with modest economy, is left to what our imagination can make of a nose and eyes from the "gs" of "things" (28); no other lines are drawn for the head. This figure represents not simply Blake but "us"—Los and Blake as one—defiant (see the text alongside) of the pitiful accusations of Rintrah and Palamabron, who fear the revolutionary unchaining of Orc.

What follows? Is that twining double form, golden[B] or blue[D] (with yellow head[CD]) coiling about pink, an image of what Rintrah and Palamabron fear, the Daughters' weaving a "new Religion from new Jealousy of Theotormon" (38)? Possibly, since the lowest figure on the page (bluer than the others) is Theotormon brooding (as in *Visions* i). The two birds soaring and the boy playing on the shore above him may indicate the folly of such fears.

The artist at work seems to be the central marginal figure in Plates 21–24.

Milton 25^{A} [K23] (ABC22, D25). Imposed upon by the dark vision of Rintrah and Palamabron, Blake-Los sits, in center right margin, more bowed than before, his garment almost growing into his green earthen stool. Above him we may be seeing the "secret Obscurities" which Los says are necessary awhile (39–40): a blond, naked woman running^{A} or soaring^{BCD} (her left leg on the ground in A, replaced by foliage in B, by a suggestion of a detached pair of legs in CD) has vague fibres for arms and seems to be flying a kite—or, in D, pursuing a vision of infants, still unformed cocoons. The sitting and kneeling women below Los are almost human but without faces or definite hands and feet. They too are hiding or turning away from what might be potential birds (just below Los). Below them is a sketchy forest, of vaguely human shape. At the very bottom a twig figure is lifting the edge of the sheet of paper on which the text is inscribed, to turn the page (and get us out of this as fast as possible).

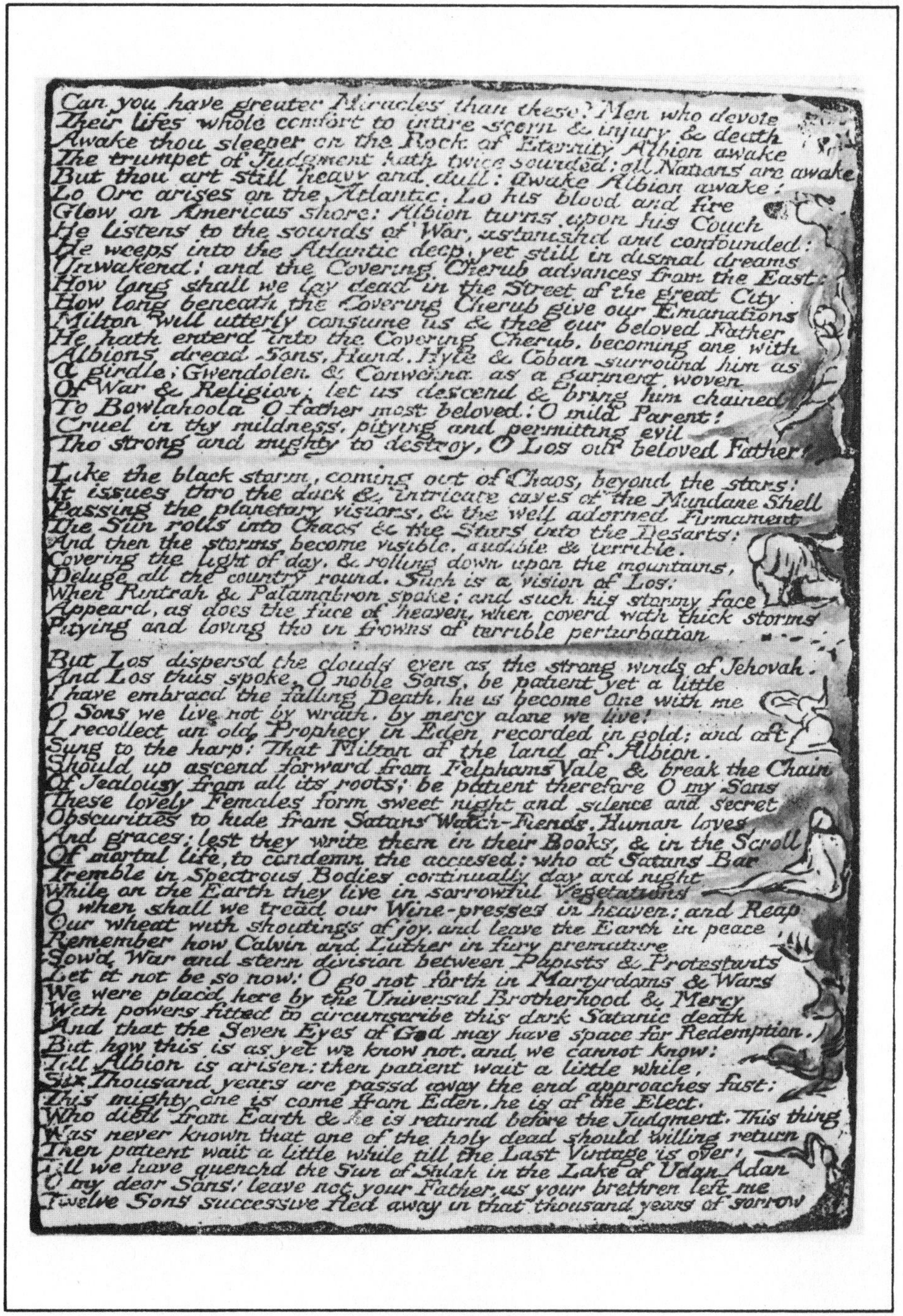

Can you have greater Miracles than these? Men who devote
Their lifes whole comfort to intire scorn & injury & death
Awake thou sleeper on the Rock of Eternity Albion awake
The trumpet of Judgment hath twice sounded: all Nations are awake
But thou art still heavy and dull: Awake Albion awake!
Lo Orc arises on the Atlantic. Lo his blood and fire
Glow on Americas shore: Albion turns upon his Couch
He listens to the sounds of War, astonishd and confounded:
He weeps into the Atlantic deep, yet still in dismal dreams
Unwakend! and the Covering Cherub advances from the East:
How long shall we lay dead in the Street of the great City
How long beneath the Covering Cherub give our Emanations
Milton will utterly consume us & thee our beloved Father
He hath enterd into the Covering Cherub, becoming one with
Albions dread Sons, Hand, Hyle & Coban surround him as
A girdle; Gwendolen & Conwenna as a garment woven
Of War & Religion; let us descend & bring him chained
To Bowlahoola O father most beloved! O mild Parent!
Cruel in thy mildness, pitying and permitting evil
Tho strong and mighty to destroy, O Los our beloved Father!

Like the black storm, coming out of Chaos, beyond the stars:
It issues thro the dark & intricate caves of the Mundane Shell
Passing the planetary visions, & the well adorned Firmament
The Sun rolls into Chaos & the Stars into the Desarts;
And then the storms become visible, audible & terrible,
Covering the light of day, & rolling down upon the mountains,
Deluge all the country round. Such is a vision of Los;
When Rintrah & Palamabron spoke; and such his stormy face
Appeard, as does the face of heaven, when coverd with thick storms
Pitying and loving tho in frowns of terrible perturbation

But Los dispersd the clouds even as the strong winds of Jehovah.
And Los thus spoke. O noble Sons, be patient yet a little
I have embraced the falling Death, he is become One with me
O Sons we live not by wrath. by mercy alone we live!
I recollect an old Prophecy in Eden recorded in gold; and oft
Sung to the harp: That Milton of the land of Albion.
Should up ascend forward from Felphams Vale & break the Chain
Of Jealousy from all its roots; be patient therefore O my Sons
These lovely Females form sweet night and silence and secret
Obscurities to hide from Satans Watch-Fiends. Human loves
And graces; lest they write them in their Books, & in the Scroll
Of mortal life, to condemn the accused: who at Satans Bar
Tremble in Spectrous Bodies continually day and night
While on the Earth they live in sorrowful Vegetations
O when shall we tread our Wine-presses in heaven; and Reap
Our wheat with shoutings of joy, and leave the Earth in peace
Remember how Calvin and Luther in fury premature
Sowd War and stern division between Papists & Protestants
Let it not be so now: O go not forth in Martyrdoms & Wars
We were placd here by the Universal Brotherhood & Mercy
With powers fitted to circumscribe this dark Satanic death
And that the Seven Eyes of God may have space for Redemption.
But how this is as yet we know not, and we cannot know;
Till Albion is arisen; then patient wait a little while,
Six Thousand years are passd away the end approaches fast;
This mighty one is come from Eden, he is of the Elect,
Who died from Earth & he is returnd before the Judgment. This thing
Was never known that one of the holy dead should willing return
Then patient wait a little while till the Last Vintage is over:
Till we have quenchd the Sun of Salah in the Lake of Udan Adan
O my dear Sons! leave not your Father, as your brethren left me
Twelve Sons successive fled away in that thousand years of sorrow

Milton 25^{A} [K23]

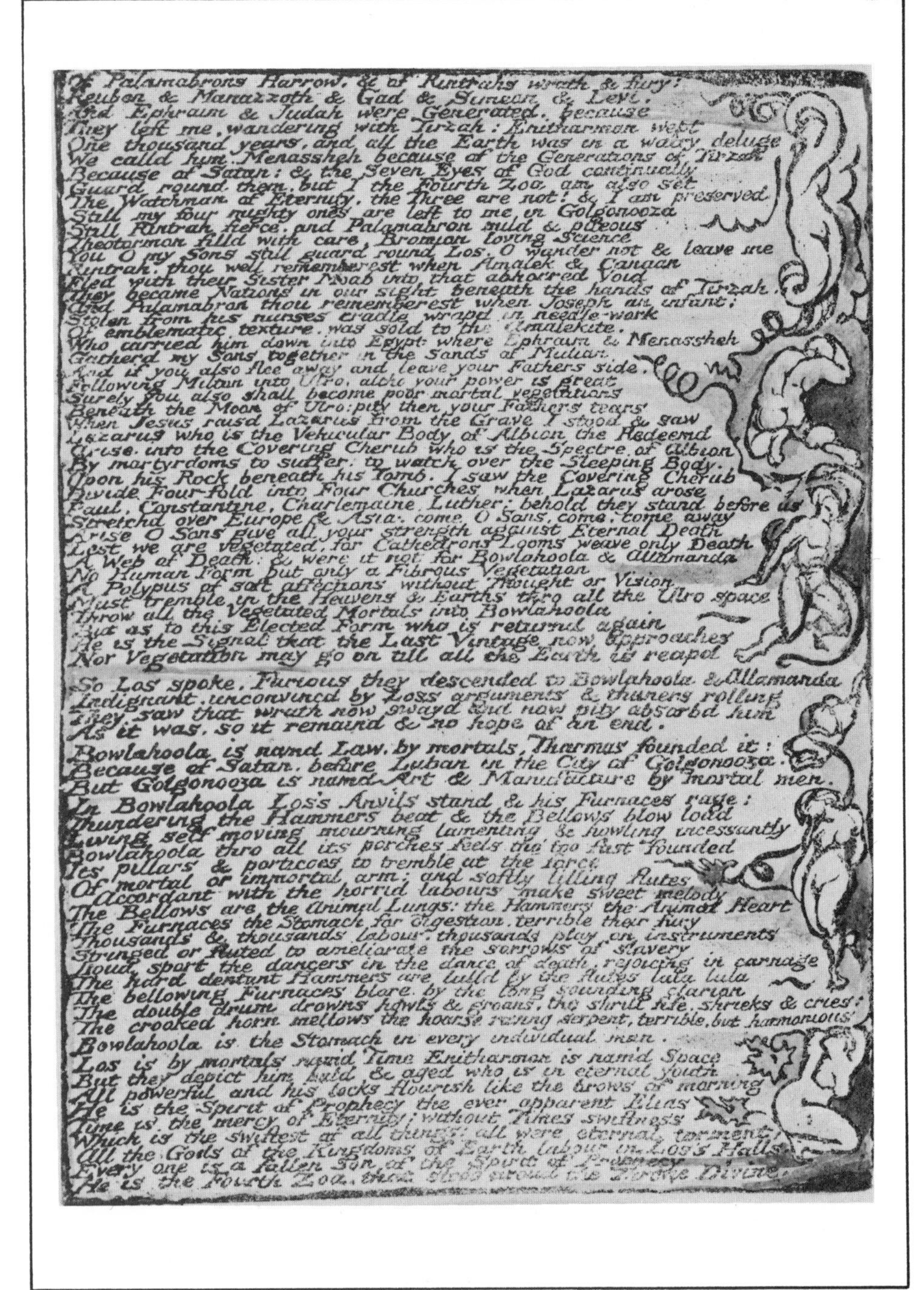
Of Palamabrons Harrow, & of Rintrahs wrath & fury:
Reuben & Manazzoth & Gad & Simeon & Levi,
And Ephraim & Judah were Generated, because
They left me, wandering with Tirzah: Enitharmon wept
One thousand years, and all the Earth was in a watry deluge
We calld him Menassheh because of the Generations of Tirzah
Because of Satan: & the Seven Eyes of God continually
Guard round them, but I the Fourth Zoa am also set
The Watchman of Eternity, the Three are not! & I am preserved
Still my four mighty ones are left to me in Golgonooza
Still Rintrah fierce, and Palamabron mild & piteous
Theotormon filld with care, Bromion loving Science
You O my Sons still guard round Los. O wander not & leave me
Rintrah, thou well rememberest when Amalek & Canaan
Fled with their Sister Moab into that abhorred Void
They became Nations in our sight beneath the hands of Tirzah.
And Palamabron thou rememberest when Joseph an infant;
Stolen from his nurses cradle wrapd in needle-work
Of emblematic texture, was sold to the Amalekite,
Who carried him down into Egypt where Ephraim & Menassheh
Gatherd my Sons together in the Sands of Midian.
And if you also flee away and leave your Fathers side,
Following Milton into Ulro, altho your power is great
Surely you also shall become poor mortal vegetations
Beneath the Moon of Ulro: pity then your Fathers tears
When Jesus raisd Lazarus from the Grave I stood & saw
Lazarus who is the Vehicular Body of Albion the Redeemd
Arise into the Covering Cherub who is the Spectre of Albion
By martyrdoms to suffer: to watch over the Sleeping Body.
Upon his Rock beneath his Tomb. I saw the Covering Cherub
Divide Four-fold into Four Churches when Lazarus arose
Paul, Constantine, Charlemaine, Luther; behold they stand before us
Stretchd over Europe & Asia. come O Sons, come, come away
Arise O Sons give all your strength against Eternal Death
Lest we are vegetated, for Cathedrons Looms weave only Death
A Web of Death: & were it not for Bowlahoola & Allamanda
No Human Form but only a Fibrous Vegetation
A Polypus of soft affections without Thought or Vision
Must tremble in the Heavens & Earths thro all the Ulro space
Throw all the Vegetated Mortals into Bowlahoola
But as to this Elected Form who is returnd again
He is the Signal that the Last Vintage now approaches
Nor Vegetation may go on till all the Earth is reaped

So Los spoke. Furious they descended to Bowlahoola & Allamanda
Indignant. unconvincd by Loss arguments & thuners rolling
They saw that wrath now swayd and now pity absorbd him
As it was, so it remaind & no hope of an end.

Bowlahoola is namd Law, by mortals, Tharmas founded it:
Because of Satan, before Luban in the City of Golgonooza.
But Golgonooza is namd Art & Manufacture by mortal men.

In Bowlahoola Los's Anvils stand & his Furnaces rage;
Thundering the Hammers beat & the Bellows blow loud
Living self moving mourning lamenting & howling incessantly
Bowlahoola thro all its porches feels tho' too fast founded
Its pillars & porticoes to tremble at the force
Of mortal or immortal arm: and softly lilling flutes
Accordant with the horrid labours make sweet melody
The Bellows are the Animal Lungs: the Hammers the Animal Heart
The Furnaces the Stomach for digestion. terrible their fury
Thousands & thousands labour. thousands play on instruments
Stringed or fluted to ameliorate the sorrows of slavery
Loud sport the dancers in the dance of death, rejoicing in carnage
The hard dentant Hammers are lulld by the flutes lula lula
The bellowing Furnaces blare by the long sounding clarion
The double drum drowns howls & groans, the shrill fife, shrieks & cries:
The crooked horn mellows the hoarse raving serpent, terrible, but harmonious
Bowlahoola is the Stomach in every individual man.
Los is by mortals namd Time Enitharmon is namd Space
But they depict him bald & aged who is in eternal youth
All powerful and his locks flourish like the brows of morning
He is the Spirit of Prophecy the ever apparent Elias
Time is the mercy of Eternity; without Times swiftness
Which is the swiftest of all things: all were eternal torment:
All the Gods of the Kingdoms of Earth labour in Los's Halls.
Every one is a fallen Son of the Spirit of Prophecy
He is the Fourth Zoa, that stood around the Throne Divine.

Milton 26A [K24]

Milton 26A [K24] (ABC23, D26). In an interpretation of Los's words (twelve sons "left me, wandering with Tirzah: Enitharmon wept": 4) two naked sons are shown among tendrils or vines that seem trying to trap them, their heads and bodies turned away from sad Enitharmon caught in a fruitless vine below them and toward the beast-harlot Tirzah above, represented as a female torso formed between serpent coils in the visceral veil of Vala (compare *Jerusalem* 24). She has no face (except in D) and her left arm becomes a coil around her head; in D the coil seems like a fine hat brim: we can recognize her in *Jerusalem* 12.

The seductive woman between grape leaves at page bottom is Rahab or Vala herself supervising the process, as in *Jerusalem* 24. At the same time she symbolizes the ripe grapes—as Los recognizes in hailing Milton's return as "the Signal that the Last Vintage now approaches" (42). Compare the wine woman of Plate 2.

Milton 27A [K25] (AB25, C24, D27). This and the next three plates depart from the style of Plate 26 with its series of human forms in the right margin, resumed in Plate 30.

Twelve birds flying, one above "Seed" (8), two toward "Golgonooza" (12), one in mid-page risking capture by Blake-Los (or is he speeding it on its flight?), four around the vital words "energy," "tears," "moment," "eternity," and four after "she weeps & looks abroad" (54), mark the singing "at the Vintage" (8). Actually Los may be saluting "the Labourers of the Vintage in . . . awe" (16). And a thirteenth, larger bird may be intended by the strokes above "Strife," but perhaps only a cloud shape.

Lower down, beside Los's warning not to break forth in "wrath lest you also are vegetated by Tirzah" (57–58) runs a figure human up to the waist, vegetable (cactus?) or caterpillar above. (Mary Lynn Johnson notes that his legs are in the same position as Milton's in his fully human, successful striving against the polyp on Plate 46.) Below, "spiritual Vegetation" exemplified by "the Constellations" (61–62, 66) may be illustrated by the living but rather barren trellis after "Night" (compare the stellar vines in *Jerusalem* 57). (But see also the vegetation on the altar in Plate 15.)

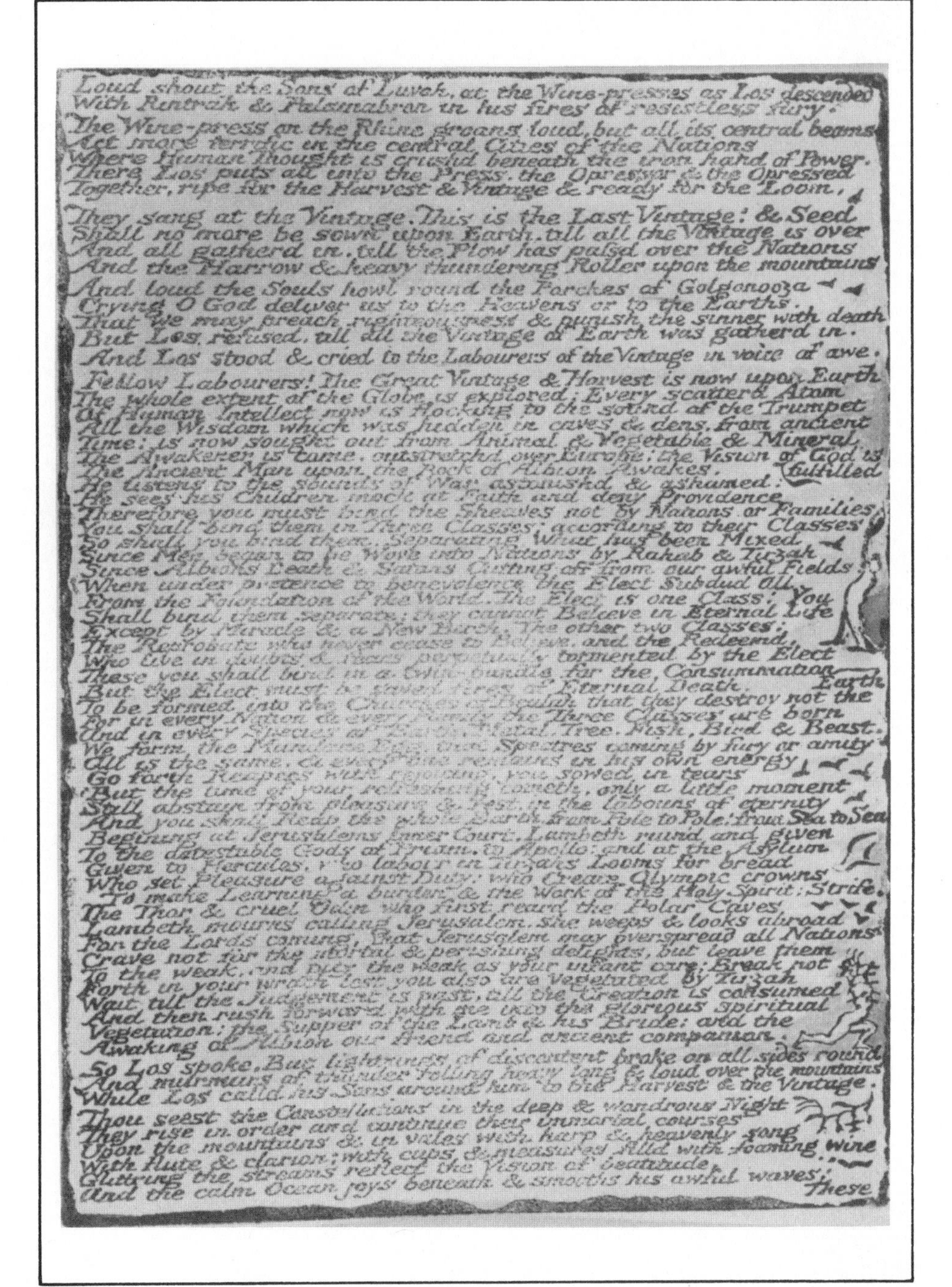

Loud shout the Sons of Luvah, at the Wine-presses as Los descended
With Rintrah & Palamabron in his fires of resistless fury.
The Wine-press on the Rhine groans loud, but all its central beams
Act more terrific in the central Cities of the Nations
Where Human Thought is crushd beneath the iron hand of Power.
There Los puts all into the Press, the Opressor & the Opressed
Together, ripe for the Harvest & Vintage & ready for the Loom.

They sang at the Vintage. This is the Last Vintage! & Seed
Shall no more be sown upon Earth, till all the Vintage is over
And all gatherd in, till the Plow has passd over the Nations
And the Harrow & heavy thundering Roller upon the mountains

And loud the Souls howl round the Porches of Golgonooza
Crying O God deliver us to the Heavens or to the Earths,
That we may preach righteousness & punish the sinner with death
But Los refused, till all the Vintage of Earth was gatherd in.

And Los stood & cried to the Labourers of the Vintage in voice of awe.

Fellow Labourers! The Great Vintage & Harvest is now upon Earth
The whole extent of the Globe is explored: Every scatterd Atom
Of Human Intellect now is flocking to the sound of the Trumpet
All the Wisdom which was hidden in caves & dens, from ancient
Time; is now sought out from Animal & Vegetable & Mineral
The Awakener is come. outstretchd over Europe! the Vision of God is fulfilled
The Ancient Man upon the Rock of Albion Awakes,
He listens to the sounds of War astonishd & ashamed;
He sees his Children mock at Faith and deny Providence
Therefore you must bind the Sheaves not by Nations or Families
You shall bind them in Three Classes; according to their Classes
So shall you bind them. Separating What has been Mixed
Since Men began to be Wove into Nations by Rahab & Tirzah
Since Albions Death & Satans Cutting off from our awful Fields;
When under pretence to benevolence the Elect Subdud All
From the Foundation of the World. The Elect is one Class: You
Shall bind them separate: they cannot Believe in Eternal Life
Except by Miracle & a New Birth. The other two Classes;
The Reprobate who never cease to Believe, and the Redeemd,
Who live in doubts & fears perpetually tormented by the Elect
These you shall bind in a twin-bundle for the Consummation—
But the Elect must be saved fires of Eternal Death, Earth
To be formed into the Churches of Beulah that they destroy not the
For in every Nation & every Family the Three Classes are born
And in every Species of Earth, Metal, Tree, Fish, Bird & Beast.
We form the Mundane Egg, that Spectres coming by fury or amity
All is the same, & every one remains in his own energy
Go forth Reapers with rejoicing. you sowed in tears
But the time of your refreshing cometh, only a little moment
Still abstain from pleasure & rest, in the labours of eternity
And you shall Reap the whole Earth, from Pole to Pole! from Sea to Sea
Begining at Jerusalems Inner Court, Lambeth ruind and given
To the detestable Gods of Priam, to Apollo: and at the Asylum
Given to Hercules, who labour in Tirzahs Looms for bread
Who set Pleasure against Duty: who Create Olympic crowns
To make Learning a burden & the Work of the Holy Spirit: Strife.
The Thor & cruel Odin who first reard the Polar Caves
Lambeth mourns calling Jerusalem. she weeps & looks abroad
For the Lords coming, that Jerusalem may overspread all Nations
Crave not for the mortal & perishing delights, but leave them
To the weak, and pity the weak as your infant care; Break not
Forth in your wrath lest you also are vegetated by Tirzah
Wait till the Judgement is past, till the Creation is consumed
And then rush forward with me into the glorious spiritual
Vegetation; the Supper of the Lamb & his Bride; and the
Awaking of Albion our friend and ancient companion.

So Los spoke. But lightnings of discontent broke on all sides round
And murmurs of thunder rolling heavy long & loud over the mountains
While Los calld his Sons around him to the Harvest & the Vintage.

Thou seest the Constellations in the deep & wondrous Night
They rise in order and continue their immortal courses
Upon the mountains & in vales with harp & heavenly song
With flute & clarion; with cups & measures filld with foaming wine.
Glittring the streams reflect the Vision of beatitude,
And the calm Ocean joys beneath & smooths his awful waves!
These

Milton 27A [K25]

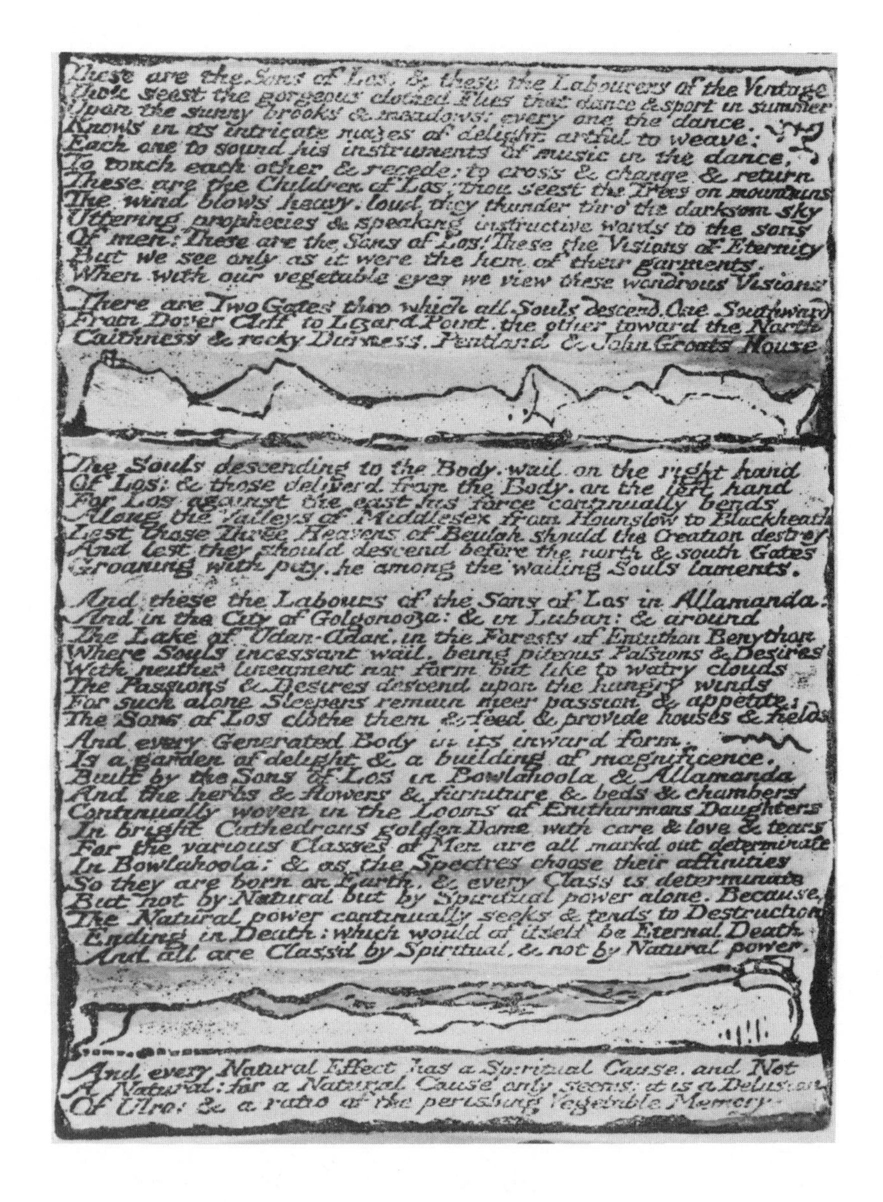

These are the Sons of Los, & these the Labourers of the Vintage
Thou seest the gorgeous clothed Flies that dance & sport in summer
Upon the sunny brooks & meadows: every one the dance
Knows in its intricate mazes of delight artful to weave:
Each one to sound his instruments of music in the dance,
To touch each other & recede; to cross & change & return
These are the Children of Los; thou seest the Trees on mountains
The wind blows heavy, loud they thunder thro' the darksom sky
Uttering prophecies & speaking instructive words to the sons
Of men: These are the Sons of Los! These the Visions of Eternity
But we see only as it were the hem of their garments
When with our vegetable eyes we view these wondrous Visions

There are Two Gates thro which all Souls descend. One Southward
From Dover Cliff to Lizard Point. the other toward the North
Caithness & rocky Durness, Pentland & John Groats House.

The Souls descending to the Body, wail on the right hand
Of Los; & those deliverd from the Body, on the left hand
For Los against the east his force continually bends
Along the Valleys of Middlesex from Hounslow to Blackheath
Lest those Three Heavens of Beulah should the Creation destroy
And lest they should descend before the north & south Gates
Groaning with pity, he among the wailing Souls laments.

And these the Labours of the Sons of Los in Allamanda:
And in the City of Golgonooza: & in Luban: & around
The Lake of Udan-Adan, in the Forests of Entuthon Benython
Where Souls incessant wail, being piteous Passions & Desires
With neither lineament nor form but like to watry clouds
The Passions & Desires descend upon the hungry winds
For such alone Sleepers remain meer passion & appetite;
The Sons of Los clothe them & feed & provide houses & fields

And every Generated Body in its inward form,
Is a garden of delight & a building of magnificence,
Built by the Sons of Los in Bowlahoola & Allamanda
And the herbs & flowers & furniture & beds & chambers
Continually woven in the Looms of Enitharmons Daughters
In bright Cathedrons golden Dome with care & love & tears
For the various Classes of Men are all markd out determinate
In Bowlahoola; & as the Spectres choose their affinities
So they are born on Earth, & every Class is determinate
But not by Natural but by Spiritual power alone. Because
The Natural power continually seeks & tends to Destruction
Ending in Death: which would of itself be Eternal Death
And all are Classd by Spiritual, & not by Natural power.

And every Natural Effect has a Spiritual Cause, and Not
A Natural: for a Natural Cause only seems: it is a Delusion
Of Ulro: & a ratio of the perishing Vegetable Memory.

Milton 28ᴬ [K26]

Milton 28ᴬ [K26] (AB26, C25, D28). Profiles are shown of the two gates for "Souls descending to the Body" (16): first the northern coast of Scotland from John o' Groats House (indicated on the eastern point: we are looking from the north) to "rocky Durness" in the west; below, the southern coast of England, viewed from the south, from Lizard Point in Cornwall to Dover Cliff in the east, shown topped by the ancient Roman fortress. The northern view of Britain's island is wet and rocky; the southern shows no strip of ocean and affords a glimpse of green downs and valleys.

Are these stone "gates" in effect the stone altars of Druid Britain, turning into single slabs preparatory to becoming preciously luminous pavements for Milton's and Los's ascent? Does the insertion of twenty-eight lines of poetry between them open them for that purpose? See note on Plate 37.

After mention of the "inward form" of the "Generated Body" (31), a thin worm is shown.

Milton 29A [K27] (AB24, C26, D29). Except for two rows of five flying birds (at 18 and after 48) and two indistinct figures at the top, the second possibly a bird, the margins are given to the creatures who "Dance round the Wine-presses of Luvah" (13)—reading down from line 12: a bird-like flier that must be an insect; a scorpion fly; two flies; then, in procession, centipede (or, more likely, caterpillar), spider, gold beetle, earth-worm, grasshopper, and an improbable toad darting its tongue at a tongue-darting "Serpent clothd in gems & gold" (22) (legless and not, pace Keynes, a "venomous Newt," unless Blake is making a metaphoric jest).

These creatures are touched with pink in A, with gold and silver (particularly the scorpion fly) in C. The page is given a rainbow effect in D by colors in the margin. It is a significant omen that the birds are flying in united families of five.

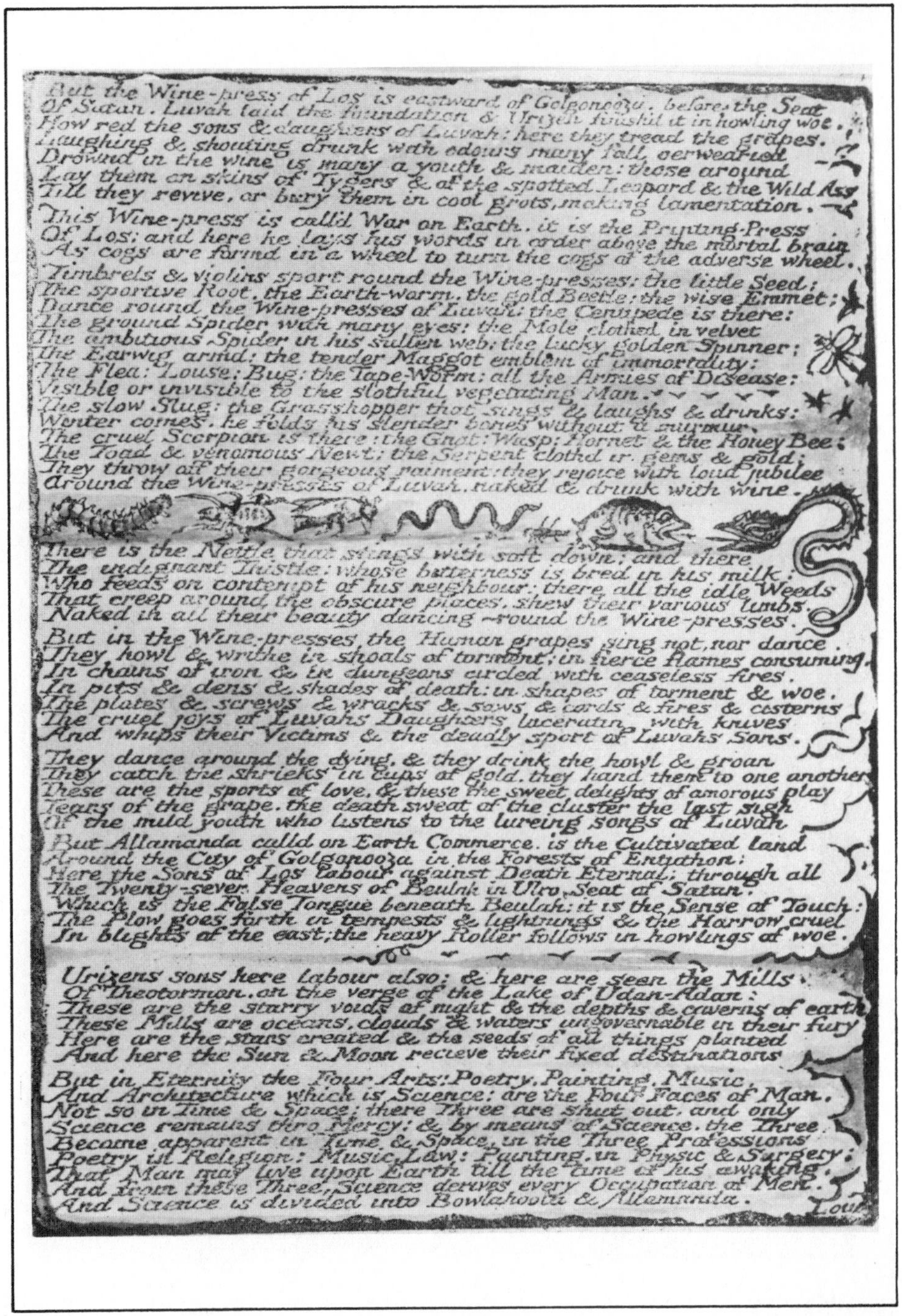

But the Wine-press of Los is eastward of Golgonooza, before the Seat
Of Satan. Luvah laid the foundation & Urizen finish'd it in howling woe.
How red the sons & daughters of Luvah! here they tread the grapes.
Laughing & shouting drunk with odours many fall, oerwearied
Drownd in the wine is many a youth & maiden: those around
Lay them on skins of Tygers & of the spotted Leopard & the Wild Ass
Till they revive, or bury them in cool grots, making lamentation.

This Wine-press is call'd War on Earth, it is the Printing-Press
Of Los; and here he lays his words in order above the mortal brain
As cogs are formd in a wheel to turn the cogs of the adverse wheel.

Timbrels & violins sport round the Wine-presses; the little Seed;
The sportive Root, the Earth-worm, the gold Beetle; the wise Emmet;
Dance round the Wine-presses of Luvah: the Centipede is there:
The ground Spider with many eyes: the Mole clothed in velvet
The ambitious Spider in his sullen web; the lucky golden Spinner;
The Earwig armd: the tender Maggot emblem of immortality:
The Flea: Louse: Bug: the Tape-Worm: all the Armies of Disease:
Visible or invisible to the slothful vegetating Man.
The slow Slug: the Grasshopper that sings & laughs & drinks:
Winter comes, he folds his slender bones without a murmur.
The cruel Scorpion is there: the Gnat: Wasp: Hornet & the Honey Bee:
The Toad & venomous Newt; the Serpent clothd in gems & gold:
They throw off their gorgeous raiment: they rejoice with loud jubilee
Around the Wine-presses of Luvah, naked & drunk with wine.

There is the Nettle that stings with soft down; and there
The indignant Thistle: whose bitterness is bred in his milk:
Who feeds on contempt of his neighbour: there all the idle Weeds
That creep around the obscure places, shew their various limbs.
Naked in all their beauty dancing round the Wine-presses.

But in the Wine-presses the Human grapes sing not, nor dance
They howl & writhe in shoals of torment; in fierce flames consuming,
In chains of iron & in dungeons circled with ceaseless fires.
In pits & dens & shades of death: in shapes of torment & woe.
The plates & screws & wracks & saws & cords & fires & cisterns
The cruel joys of Luvahs Daughters lacerating with knives
And whips their Victims & the deadly sport of Luvahs Sons.

They dance around the dying, & they drink the howl & groan
They catch the shrieks in cups of gold, they hand them to one another:
These are the sports of love, & these the sweet delights of amorous play
Tears of the grape, the death sweat of the cluster the last sigh
Of the mild youth who listens to the lureing songs of Luvah

But Allamanda calld on Earth Commerce, is the Cultivated land
Around the City of Golgonooza in the Forests of Entuthon:
Here the Sons of Los labour against Death Eternal; through all
The Twenty-seven Heavens of Beulah in Ulro, Seat of Satan,
Which is the False Tongue beneath Beulah: it is the Sense of Touch:
The Plow goes forth in tempests & lightnings & the Harrow cruel
In blights of the east; the heavy Roller follows in howlings of woe.

Urizens sons here labour also; & here are seen the Mills
Of Theotormon, on the verge of the Lake of Udan-Adan:
These are the starry voids of night & the depths & caverns of earth
These Mills are oceans, clouds & waters ungovernable in their fury
Here are the stars created & the seeds of all things planted
And here the Sun & Moon recieve their fixed destinations

But in Eternity the Four Arts: Poetry, Painting, Music,
And Architecture which is Science: are the Four Faces of Man.
Not so in Time & Space: there Three are shut out, and only
Science remains thro Mercy: & by means of Science, the Three
Became apparent in Time & Space, in the Three Professions
Poetry in Religion: Music, Law: Painting, in Physic & Surgery:
That Man may live upon Earth till the time of his awaking,
And from these Three, Science derives every Occupation of Men.
And Science is divided into Bowlahoola & Allamanda.

Lou

Milton 29A [K27]

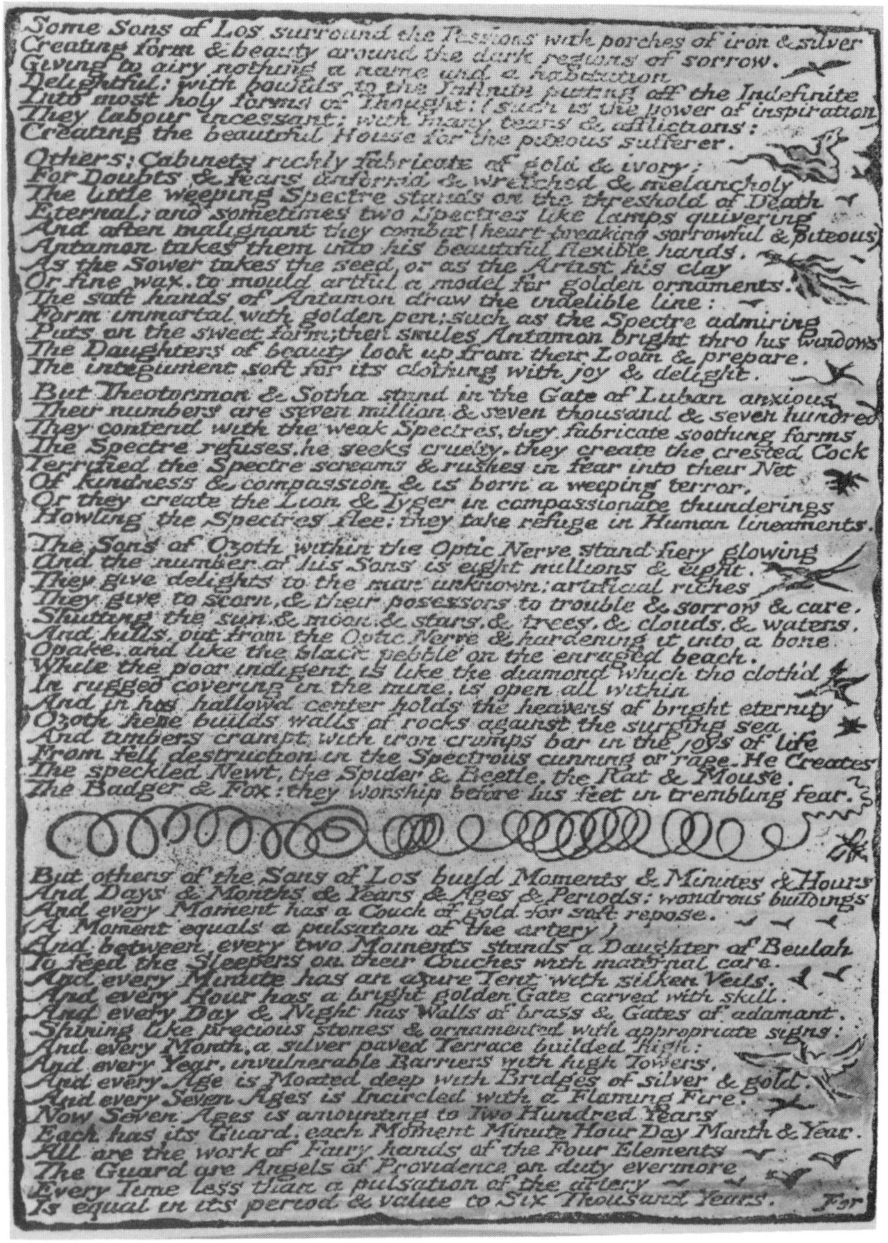

Some Sons of Los surround the Passions with porches of iron & silver
Creating form & beauty around the dark regions of sorrow.
Giving to airy nothing a name and a habitation
Delightful: with bounds to the Infinite putting off the Indefinite
Into most holy forms of Thought: (such is the power of inspiration)
They labour incessant; with many tears & afflictions:
Creating the beautiful House for the piteous sufferer.

Others; Cabinets richly fabricate of gold & ivory;
For Doubts & fears unform'd & wretched & melancholy
The little weeping Spectre stands on the threshold of Death
Eternal; and sometimes two Spectres like lamps quivering
And often malignant they combat (heart-breaking sorrowful & piteous)
Antamon takes them into his beautiful flexible hands.
As the Sower takes the seed, or as the Artist his clay
Or fine wax, to mould artful a model for golden ornaments.
The soft hands of Antamon draw the indelible line:
Form immortal with golden pen; such as the Spectre admiring
Puts on the sweet form; then smiles Antamon bright thro his windows
The Daughters of beauty look up from their Loom & prepare.
The integument soft for its clothing with joy & delight.

But Theotormon & Sotha stand in the Gate of Luban anxious
Their numbers are seven million & seven thousand & seven hundred
They contend with the weak Spectres, they fabricate soothing forms
The Spectre refuses, he seeks cruelty, they create the crested Cock
Terrified the Spectre screams & rushes in fear into their Net
Of kindness & compassion & is born a weeping terror.
Or they create the Lion & Tyger in compassionate thunderings
Howling the Spectres flee: they take refuge in Human lineaments.

The Sons of Ozoth within the Optic Nerve stand fiery glowing
And the number of his Sons is eight millions & eight.
They give delights to the man unknown; artificial riches
They give to scorn, & their posessors to trouble & sorrow & care,
Shutting the sun, & moon, & stars, & trees, & clouds, & waters,
And hills, out from the Optic Nerve & hardening it into a bone
Opake, and like the black pebble on the enraged beach.
While the poor indigent is like the diamond which tho cloth'd
In rugged covering in the mine, is open all within
And in his hallowd center holds the heavens of bright eternity
Ozoth here builds walls of rocks against the surging sea
And timbers crampt with iron cramps bar in the joys of life
From fell destruction in the Spectrous cunning or rage. He Creates
The speckled Newt, the Spider & Beetle, the Rat & Mouse,
The Badger & Fox: they worship before his feet in trembling fear.

But others of the Sons of Los build Moments & Minutes & Hours
And Days & Months & Years & Ages & Periods; wondrous buildings
And every Moment has a Couch of gold for soft repose.
(A Moment equals a pulsation of the artery)
And between every two Moments stands a Daughter of Beulah
To feed the Sleepers on their Couches with maternal care.
And every Minute has an azure Tent with silken Veils.
And every Hour has a bright golden Gate carved with skill.
And every Day & Night has Walls of brass & Gates of adamant.
Shining like precious stones & ornamented with appropriate signs:
And every Month, a silver paved Terrace builded high:
And every Year, invulnerable Barriers with high Towers.
And every Age is Moated deep with Bridges of silver & gold.
And every Seven Ages is Incircled with a Flaming Fire.
Now Seven Ages is amounting to Two Hundred Years
Each has its Guard, each Moment Minute Hour Day Month & Year.
All are the work of Fairy hands of the Four Elements
The Guard are Angels of Providence on duty evermore
Every Time less than a pulsation of the artery
Is equal in its period & value to Six Thousand Years. For

Milton 30A [K28]

Milton 30A [K28] (ABC27, D30). In the top right margin a bird (of genius) suggests giving to *airy* nothing "a habitation Delightful" (3–4). For the process of painting "with golden pen" (i.e. paintbrush) we are shown two "little weeping Spectres" (five birds represent their tears) "unform'd & wretched" but touched with goldC—one a rag-doll sort of flying horse, pinkAB or purpleD, the other a green bunch of tatters with raven beak flying toward the artist's "hands" and "clay." The fifth bird marks the hands' drawing "the indelible line" to give them immortal form (9–14). A leafing line of beauty illustrates the "integument . . . for . . . delight" (20).

A spider indicates the "Net of kindness" (25), and further down we see the second spectre beginning to resemble a purple horse; then the first turning into a bird (at line 36) and finally completed as a rosyAB or blueD bird of paradise (at line 54), an incorporation, perhaps, of both spectres, with the Pegasus idea still there.

The great tangled coil of twenty-eight or more various loops ("like a watch-spring," Keynes), with its right end raveling up to the word "Creates," introduces a paragraph on the building of "Moments . . . & Periods." The excellence of life in these is emblemed by a dragon fly and five flying birds above the Pegasus bird—under which we see, under "gold," a dark distant image of itself: for here the bird is illustrating the phoenix role of the Imagination, "every Seven Ages . . . incircled with a Flaming Fire" (57). Five more birds, below, repeat the pattern of near and distant life. (Spots of yellow lightD focus on these five and on the first tangle in the watch-spring of creative line, above.)

Milton 31^{A} [K29] (ABC28, D31). The four naked human dancers are clearly "free from . . . the four pillars of tyranny" (48–49) and able to give human illumination to the "Poets Work" (1) of description and definition (to use tyrannous words for it). The words "End of the First Book" appear at the bottom of the page in a wide valley between black (or green^{C} or copper-colored^{D}) hills—the bottom of the chasm identified in the text as the "Vale of Surrey" (57) or "Felphams Vale" (passim), also "Rephaims Vale" (21:40) where the Philistines gathered before being destroyed by David. It is also the etched or engraved furrow in the copper plate, and identified with Or-Ulro or Albion's stomach (38:14–17). We have reached the end of the systole of the poem's movement.

In the penultimate plate (49) of Book Two we shall see this valley filled with ripening grain. Here we see that Book One has been an emptying of the land, a scraping bare of the plate, a preparation.

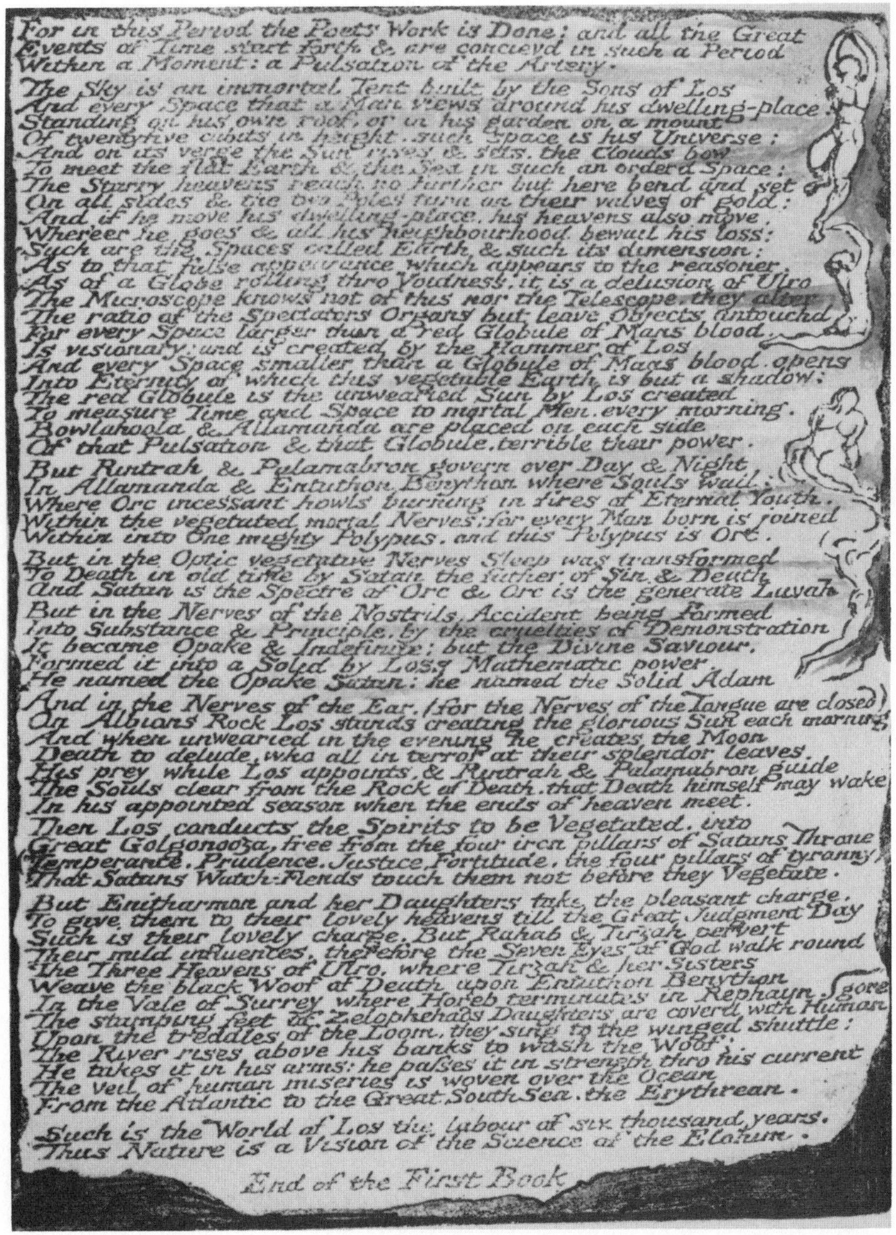

For in this Period the Poets Work is Done: and all the Great
Events of Time start forth & are concievd in such a Period
Within a Moment: a Pulsation of the Artery.

The Sky is an immortal Tent built by the Sons of Los
And every Space that a Man views around his dwelling-place:
Standing on his own roof, or in his garden on a mount
Of twentyfive cubits in height, such space is his Universe;
And on its verge the Sun rises & sets. the Clouds bow
To meet the flat Earth & the Sea in such an orderd Space:
The Starry heavens reach no further but here bend and set
On all sides & the two Poles turn on their valves of gold:
And if he move his dwelling-place, his heavens also move.
Whereer he goes & all his neighbourhood bewail his loss:
Such are the Spaces called Earth & such its dimension:
As to that false appearance which appears to the reasoner,
As of a Globe rolling thro Voidness, it is a delusion of Ulro
The Microscope knows not of this nor the Telescope. they alter
The ratio of the Spectators Organs but leave Objects untouchd
For every Space larger than a red Globule of Mans blood.
Is visionary: and is created by the Hammer of Los
And every Space smaller than a Globule of Mans blood. opens
Into Eternity of which this vegetable Earth is but a shadow:
The red Globule is the unwearied Sun by Los created
To measure Time and Space to mortal Men. every morning.
Bowlahoola & Allamanda are placed on each side
Of that Pulsation & that Globule, terrible their power.

But Rintrah & Palamabron govern over Day & Night
In Allamanda & Entuthon Benython where Souls wail:
Where Orc incessant howls burning in fires of Eternal Youth,
Within the vegetated mortal Nerves; for every Man born is joined
Within into One mighty Polypus, and this Polypus is Orc.

But in the Optic vegetative Nerves Sleep was transformed
To Death in old time by Satan the father of Sin & Death
And Satan is the Spectre of Orc & Orc is the generate Luvah

But in the Nerves of the Nostrils, Accident being formed
Into Substance & Principle, by the cruelties of Demonstration
It became Opake & Indefinite; but the Divine Saviour,
Formed it into a Solid by Los's Mathematic power.
He named the Opake Satan: he named the Solid Adam

And in the Nerves of the Ear, (for the Nerves of the Tongue are closed)
On Albions Rock Los stands creating the glorious Sun each morning
And when unwearied in the evening he creates the Moon
Death to delude, who all in terror at their splendor leaves
His prey while Los appoints, & Rintrah & Palamabron guide
The Souls clear from the Rock of Death, that Death himself may wake
In his appointed season when the ends of heaven meet.

Then Los conducts the Spirits to be Vegetated, into
Great Golgonooza, free from the four iron pillars of Satans Throne
(Temperance, Prudence, Justice, Fortitude, the four pillars of tyranny)
That Satans Watch-Fiends touch them not before they Vegetate.

But Enitharmon and her Daughters take the pleasant charge.
To give them to their lovely heavens till the Great Judgment Day
Such is their lovely charge. But Rahab & Tirzah pervert
Their mild influences, therefore the Seven Eyes of God walk round
The Three Heavens of Ulro, where Tirzah & her Sisters
Weave the black Woof of Death upon Entuthon Benython
In the Vale of Surrey where Horeb terminates in Rephaim
The stamping feet of Zelophehads Daughters are coverd with Human gore
Upon the treddles of the Loom, they sing to the winged shuttle:
The River rises above his banks to wash the Woof:
He takes it in his arms: he passes it in strength thro his current
The veil of human miseries is woven over the Ocean
From the Atlantic to the Great South Sea, the Erythrean.

Such is the World of Los the labour of six thousand years.
Thus Nature is a Vision of the Science of the Elohim.

End of the First Book

Milton 31^{A} [K29]

Milton 32A

Milton 32A (ABC29, D32). In this revised vision of William Blake's reception of Milton's "falling star" (the star first shown in Plate 2, the reception in Plate 17) the sacrificial altar of skulls and stones is replaced by three steps of hewn stone, works of art, now put behind the poet, who stands on green turfABC or on a stone pavement over black earthD. (A mirror view of the star's reception by Robert, Blake's brother and psychic double who dwells in eternity, is shown in Plate 37.) The "black cloud," held open by William's right hand, seems to rise from behind the stones and from an unseen area of pavement behind the top step rather than actually "from my left foot" (17:49–50). The Selfhood, Satan, seen in flames on his pavement in Plate 10, has now gone up in smoke; the present picture reveals the immediate consequence of the moment of bardic fusion, whereas Plate 17 shows the situation immediately preceding it.

In copy A the figure seems nude, with a black penis erect against his body (compare Plate 42); in other copies underclothes are added, green in D. The star is painted gold in C, red and gold in D.

Spiritually interpreted the star entering Blake is like the lightning striking the son of Job while plowing (in *Job* 20). Knowing it to be impossible to receive the full inspiration of Milton by the mind alone, Blake has to go and catch a falling star. The torch of bardic prophecy is transmitted in consuming fire, burning the selfhood from foot to head, with black smoke rolling over Europe. The divine imagination's entering Blake's tarsus and his falling upon the garden path (49:25) configure the conversion of Saul of Tarsus to Paul, a seizure totally annihilating the self/body, between pulsations of an artery. The splitting of the physical word "Selfhood" in Plate 18 by the tarsus of Milton's right foot is paralleled by the splitting of the altar stones into two pair of stairs (in Plates 32 and 37) visibly separated by the seized forward foot of William/Robert. (See note on Plate 37.)

In its pivotal position between Books First and Second, this reorganized picture reorganizes the first Book itself, as a stairway of thirty-one plates now behind us, a descent to this earth's surface as a place of rendezvous and illumination and redirection. William's turning away from the altar and toward his brother, each with tarsus forward, is as if the two true brothers in Plate 10, Palamabron and Rintrah, turned from the false, illusory brother Satan, falsely elevated, to confront and touch one another.

(If we look for parallels in *Jerusalem,* we may compare the three stones to the three in *Jerusalem* 69 which seem to stand for three religions.)

Milton 33ᴬ (Book the Second) [K30] (ABC30, D33). The falling star of Plate 32 (and 2 and 17) is pictured here as lightning, which does not strike the name "Milton" (as had seemed necessary from Milton's point of view, in Plate 1) but divides around it in merciful embrace. (Compare the saving interaction of wrath and mercy in *Songs* 18.) The left fork of the lightning strikes the ground; the right stays in the sky to inscribe (or point to) the subtitle. In the opened space human figures rehearse a Judgment scene. Two naked men whose falling gracefully brackets the subtitle seem to parallel the two flashes of lightning. The one at left extends his arms toward the earth, like the Satan of *Marriage* 5; the one at right leads with his elbows as though expecting, while covering his eyes and ears, to stay in the air. A naked woman beside him is already directing flight upward, for all of us. (These two are like a falling Adam and a rising Eve, who reaches up to touch the heavens: see *Ghost of Abel* 2.) Also emphasizing that this is Book *the Second* is the female toe-toucher whose hands point up and onward. In the story she stands for Ololon, the emanation of Milton, who adjoins her, right foot to right foot, as the bread the wine in Plate 2, but directly, not through vegetation. Their apparent striding in opposite directions yet continued union by touch illustrates the distinction between Contraries and Negations: though Milton turns his attention to the falling Satan, whom he points to, he does not make the error of Palamabron in Plate 10. Even while engaged in the descent and self-annihilation of Book One, he remains one with Ololon, his emanation and contrary whose attention is upon the positive face of the moment, the rising into sunlight (a yellow disk is suggested above Eve's handᴰ). The subtitles, read when "printed" in our mirrors, remind us that "Contraries are Positives," that Simplicity is not Insipidity (so much for the critics that find the tarsal pun "unfortunate")—that falling can reverse to rising, that lightning buried in ground (left side) can rise as flames of life (beside Eve's arm, strongly colored except in A): i.e. that "Nature is a vision of" Imagination (31:65). This valley among hills was shown in the preceding empty moment, when

30

How wide the Gulf & Unpassable! between Simplicity & Insipidity

Milton

Contraries are Positives

A Negation is not a Contrary

Book the Second.

There is a place where Contrarieties are equally True
This place is called Beulah, It is a pleasant lovely Shadow
Where no dispute can come. Because of those who Sleep.
Into this place the Sons & Daughters of Ololon descended
With solemn mourning into Beulahs moony shades & hills
Weeping for Milton: mute wonder held the Daughters of Beulah
Enrapturd with affection sweet and mild benevolence

Beulah is evermore Created around Eternity; appearing
To the Inhabitants of Eden. around them on all sides.
But Beulah to its Inhabitants appears within each district
As the beloved infant in his mothers bosom round incircled
With arms of love & pity & sweet compassion. But to
The Sons of Eden the moony habitations of Beulah,
Are from Great Eternity a mild & pleasant Rest.

And it is thus Created. Lo the Eternal Great Humanity
To whom be Glory & Dominion Evermore Amen
Walks among all his awful Family seen in every face
As the breath of the Almighty. such are the words of man to man
In the great Wars of Eternity, in fury of Poetic Inspiration
To build the Universe stupendous; Mental forms Creating

But the Emanations trembled exceedingly, nor could they
Live, because the life of Man was too exceeding unbounded
His joy became terrible to them they trembled & wept
Crying with one voice. Give us a habitation & a place
In which we may be hidden under the shadow of wings
For if we who are but for a time, & who pass away in winter
Behold these wonders of Eternity we shall consume
But you O our Fathers & Brothers, remain in Eternity
But grant us a Temporal Habitation. do you speak
To us; we will obey your words as you obey Jesus
The Eternal who is blessed for ever & ever. Amen

So spake the lovely Emanations; & there appeard a pleasant
Mild Shadow above: beneath: & on all sides round,

Into

Milton 33ᴬ [K30]

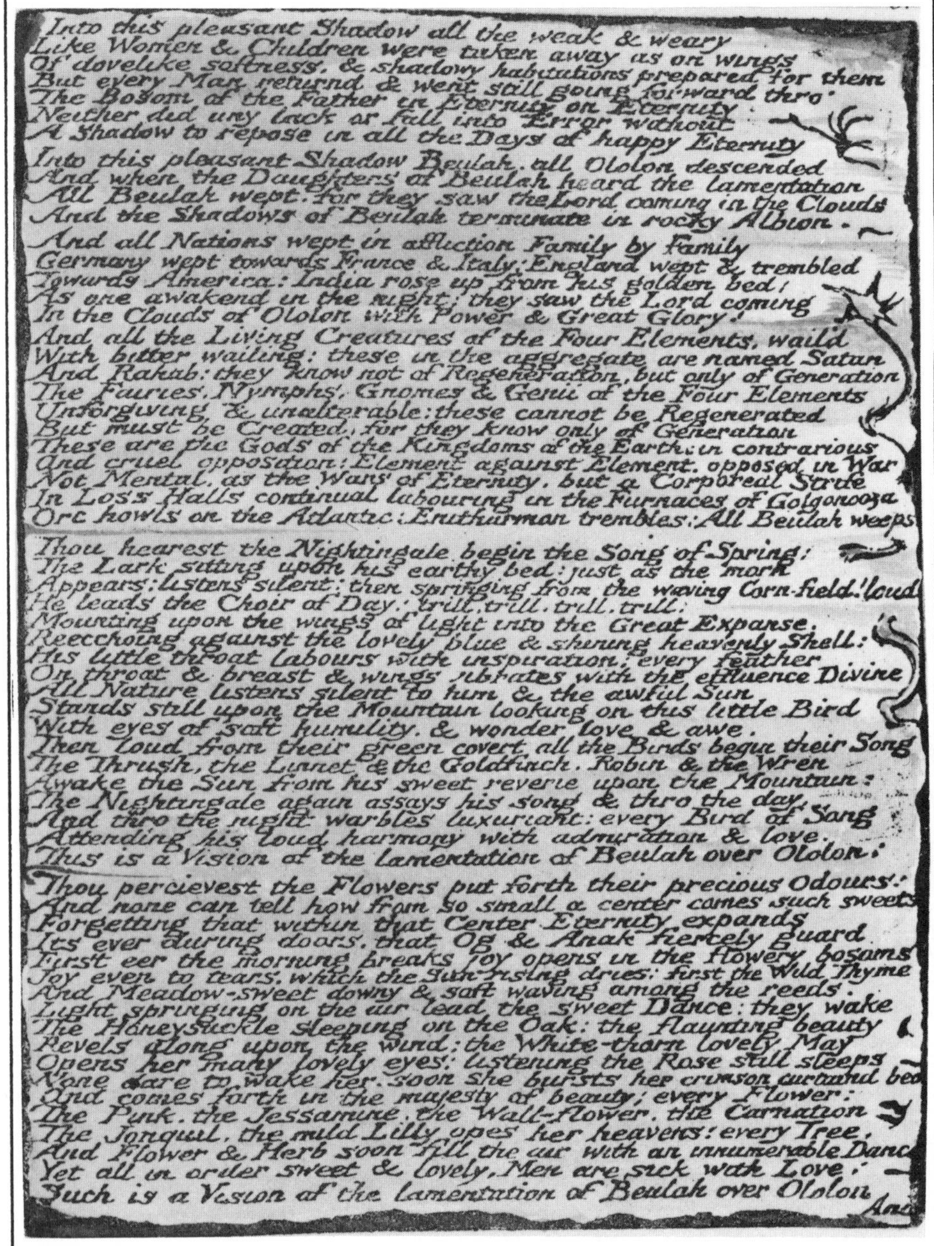

Into this pleasant Shadow all the weak & weary
Like Women & Children were taken away as on wings
Of dovelike softness, & shadowy habitations prepared for them
But every Man returnd & went still going forward thro'
The Bosom of the Father in Eternity on Eternity
Neither did any lack or fall into Error without
A Shadow to repose in all the Days of happy Eternity

Into this pleasant Shadow Beulah, all Ololon descended
And when the Daughters of Beulah heard the lamentation
All Beulah wept, for they saw the Lord coming in the Clouds
And the Shadows of Beulah terminate in rocky Albion.

And all Nations wept in affliction Family by Family
Germany wept towards France & Italy: England wept & trembled
Towards America: India rose up from his golden bed:
As one awakend in the night: they saw the Lord coming
In the Clouds of Ololon with Power & Great Glory!

And all the Living Creatures of the Four Elements, waild
With bitter wailing: these in the aggregate are named Satan
And Rahab: they know not of Regeneration, but only of Generation
The Fairies, Nymphs, Gnomes & Genii of the Four Elements
Unforgiving & unalterable: these cannot be Regenerated
But must be Created, for they know only of Generation
These are the Gods of the Kingdoms of the Earth: in contrarious
And cruel opposition: Element against Element, opposed in War
Not Mental, as the Wars of Eternity, but a Corporeal Strife
In Los's Halls continual labouring in the Furnaces of Golgonooza
Orc howls on the Atlantic: Enitharmon trembles: All Beulah weeps

Thou hearest the Nightingale begin the Song of Spring;
The Lark sitting upon his earthy bed: just as the morn
Appears; listens silent; then springing from the waving Corn-field! loud
He leads the Choir of Day! trill, trill, trill, trill,
Mounting upon the wings of light into the Great Expanse:
Reecchoing against the lovely blue & shining heavenly Shell:
His little throat labours with inspiration; every feather
On throat & breast & wings vibrates with the effluence Divine
All Nature listens silent to him & the awful Sun
Stands still upon the Mountain looking on this little Bird
With eyes of soft humility, & wonder love & awe.
Then loud from their green covert all the Birds begin their Song
The Thrush, the Linnet & the Goldfinch, Robin & the Wren
Awake the Sun from his sweet reverie upon the Mountain:
The Nightingale again assays his song, & thro the day,
And thro the night warbles luxuriant; every Bird of Song
Attending his loud harmony with admiration & love.
This is a Vision of the lamentation of Beulah over Ololon!

Thou percievest the Flowers put forth their precious Odours!
And none can tell how from so small a center comes such sweets
Forgetting that within that Center Eternity expands
Its ever during doors, that Og & Anak fiercely guard
First eer the morning breaks joy opens in the flowery bosoms
Joy even to tears, which the Sun rising dries; first the Wild Thyme
And Meadow-sweet downy & soft waving among the reeds.
Light springing on the air lead the sweet Dance: they wake
The Honeysuckle sleeping on the Oak: the flaunting beauty
Revels along upon the wind; the White-thorn lovely May
Opens her many lovely eyes: listening the Rose still sleeps
None dare to wake her. soon she bursts her crimson curtaind bed
And comes forth in the majesty of beauty; every Flower:
The Pink, the Jessamine, the Wall-flower, the Carnation
The Jonquil, the mild Lilly opes her heavens! every Tree,
And Flower & Herb soon fill the air with an innumerable Dance
Yet all in order sweet & lovely, Men are sick with Love!
Such is a Vision of the lamentation of Beulah over Ololon
And

Milton 34A [K31]

it seemed a gulf, in Plate 31. Now life springs; etching and printing (see *Marriage* 6–7) have begun.

In copy A an outer border surrounds this page and marks the scene as a Day of Judgment, with two angels near the top corners blowing contrary trumpets toward the center—instantly, as it were, reversing the gestured separation of Milton and Ololon while their feet are still together, also reversing the division of the forks of lightning. Ten spirits ascend on the left side; eleven or twelve ascend, also, on the right, the two near the top apparently children. Along the bottom are three reclining figures, somewhat slower in their awakening. Those near each corner begin to raise their heads. The one in the center, sleeping on a scroll couch, is too slightly sketched to identify—the marginal yet crucial member of Blake's audience, we may suppose (i.e. ourselves).

Milton 34A [K31] (ABC31, D34). In the upper right margin the little "unform'd" spectre of Plate 30 takes the shape of a flower flying—or swimming: a sea anemone? The yellow star-flower, with red-orangeB or whiteD center, that brackets the paragraph about those who "Know only of Generation" (22) is followed by a sort of tassel (attached to the stem only in D) or flying form that marks "the Song of Spring" (31). A gentle irony is represented by the hooded worm (changed to a stem with caterpillar on it, in D) alongside the song that thrills the lark "with the effluence Divine": even worms are listening ("All Nature listens silent": 36).

Milton 35ᴰ [K32] (C32*, D35, not in AB). (Plate added in C after the next plate, moved to this position in D. Note the cursive lettering, comparable to that in some of the added plates of *Jerusalem.*)

Thin vines with tendrils and green grape leaves carry the burden of decoration and illumination on this discursive page, which is also embellished with a Hebrew inscription. Spiral tendrils of communication grow under "Presence" (2) and "converse" (9), and above "Lineaments" (30).

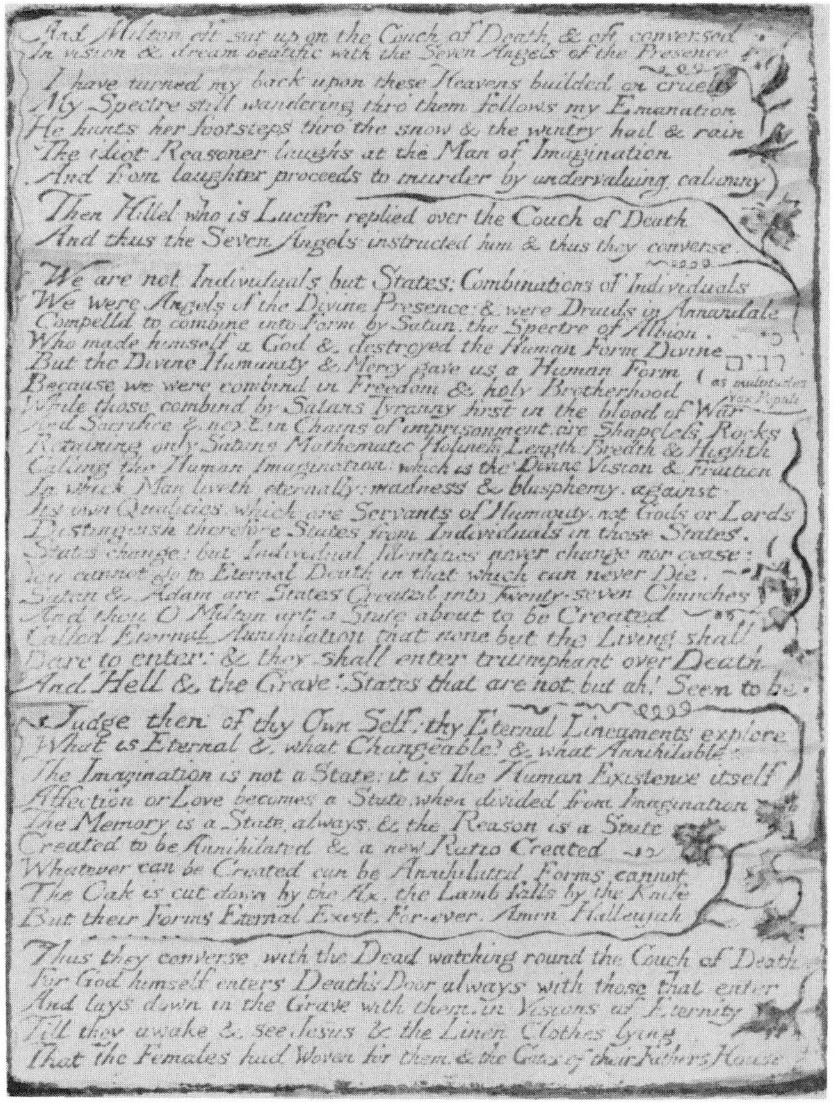

And Milton oft sat up on the Couch of Death & oft conversed
In vision & dream beatific with the Seven Angels of the Presence

I have turned my back upon these Heavens builded on cruelty
My Spectre still wandering thro' them follows my Emanation
He hunts her footsteps thro' the snow & the wintry hail & rain
The idiot Reasoner laughs at the Man of Imagination
And from laughter proceeds to murder by undervaluing calumny

Then Hillel who is Lucifer replied over the Couch of Death
And thus the Seven Angels instructed him & thus they converse

We are not Individuals but States: Combinations of Individuals
We were Angels of the Divine Presence: & were Druids in Annandale
Compelld to combine into Form by Satan, the Spectre of Albion.
Who made himself a God & destroyed the Human Form Divine
But the Divine Humanity & Mercy gave us a Human Form
Because we were combind in Freedom & holy Brotherhood
While those combind by Satans Tyranny first in the blood of War
And Sacrifice & next in Chains of imprisonment: are Shapeless Rocks
Retaining only Satans Mathematic Holiness, Length: Bredth & Highth
Calling the Human Imagination: which is the Divine Vision & Fruition
In which Man liveth eternally: madness & blasphemy, against
Its own Qualities, which are Servants of Humanity, not Gods or Lords
Distinguish therefore States from Individuals in those States.
States change: but Individual Identities never change nor cease:
You cannot go to Eternal Death in that which can never Die.
Satan & Adam are States Created into Twenty-seven Churches
And thou O Milton art a State about to be Created
Called Eternal Annihilation that none but the Living shall
Dare to enter: & they shall enter triumphant over Death
And Hell & the Grave! States that are not, but ah! Seem to be.

רבים (as multitudes Vox Populi

Judge then of thy Own Self: thy Eternal Lineaments explore
What is Eternal & what Changeable? & what Annihilable!
The Imagination is not a State: it is the Human Existence itself
Affection or Love becomes a State, when divided from Imagination
The Memory is a State always, & the Reason is a State
Created to be Annihilated & a new Ratio Created
Whatever can be Created can be Annihilated Forms cannot
The Oak is cut down by the Ax, the Lamb falls by the Knife
But their Forms Eternal Exist, For-ever. Amen Halle[l]ujah

Thus they converse with the Dead watching round the Couch of Death
For God himself enters Deaths Door always with those that enter
And lays down in the Grave with them, in Visions of Eternity
Till they awake & see Jesus & the Linen Clothes lying
That the Females had Woven for them, & the Gates of their Fathers House

Milton 35ᴰ [K32]

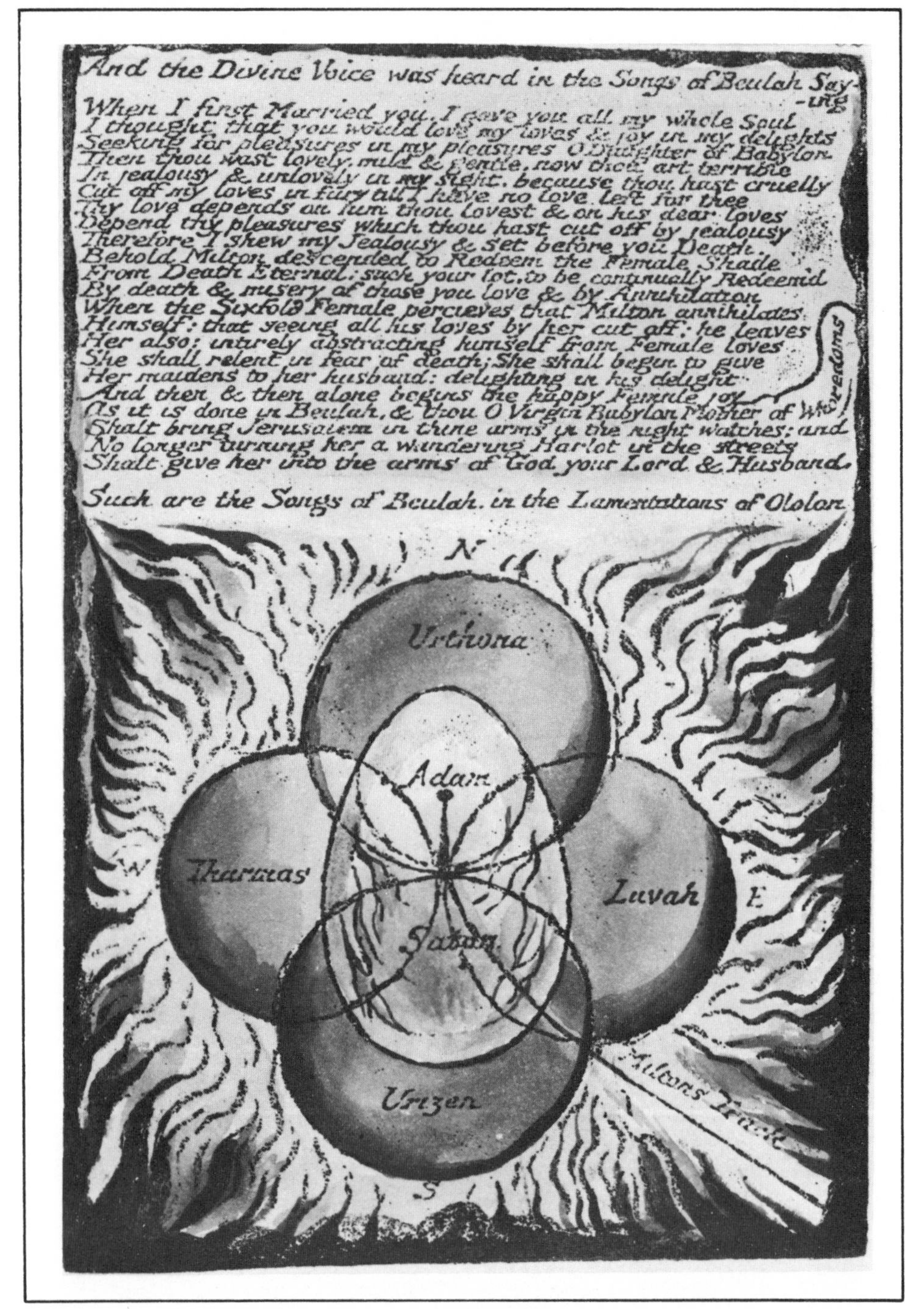

Milton 36ᴬ [K33]

❧

Milton 36ᴬ [K33] (ABC32, D36). The thread or track running from line 19 ("then alone begins . . . joy") seems to run into the margin and could be thought of as attaching text to diagram. (The "Mundane Shell" is described in 19:21–25, the relation between the "Mundane Egg" and the "Four Universes" of the "Four Zoa's" in 21:15–24.) Milton's Track enters the universes at the intersection of the eastern globe of Luvah and the southern globe of Urizen and carries him into the Egg, close to the center of Satan's realm of fire and into the earth circle—the drawing of this circle is obscured by paint in D—that fits the smaller end of the egg, with its center marked "Adam." Note that the earth, often overlooked in discussions of this diagram, is wholly within the realm of Urthona (Los), wholly outside the realm of Urizen, and only fractionally within those of Tharmas and Luvah. (But though Urthona is earth-owner, his realm is not confined to earth. In D, where the spheres are differentiated, his contains most of the blue sky.)

In A the outer flames are pale yellow, the four universes greyish, the egg sky blue with rosy flames inside; the entering track cuts a white swath. In B and C the coloring is similar. In D the inside of the mundane egg is considerably less attractive: or rather, its pale yellow fires are seen only between opaque patches of the outer shell in dull blue-black, with the space or surface above "Adam" pure white; the outer flames are variously red brown, blue grey, pink, and black and the universes mostly red brown (Urthona's bluish); the dramatic color, almost sulfur yellow, is given to the wide swath around Milton's Track (edged with gold), subdued to paler yellow inside the shell, then oddly emerging in a strong yellow swath at the opposite quadrant: did the bards leave again?

Does the ovoid space represent pity, the surrounding fires wrath? Note the question to Ololon: "Are you the Fiery Circle . . . and can you . . . pity & forgive?" (38:3–7).

❧

Milton 37[C] (ABC33, D37). Except for mention in verses in a letter (22 Nov 1802) Blake's brother Robert (d 1787) does not appear nominally or cryptically in his poetry. If he is the deeper, spiritual component of Blake's psyche and a dweller in Eternity (the stone steps behind him are four, not three except in the first copy[A]), yet he is one with William, on the ground when Milton's star falls, identically keeping his forward foot firm to receive it and flinging his body back in self-annihilation.

The star is smaller here and seems to cause less turbulence, but these effects may be simply necessary optical accommodations to the use of a dark night background; not to appear much larger than in the daytime "William" picture, the star must be smaller (though brighter). In C and D the sky outside the turbulence is deep blue-black, while the cone of turbulence consists of bright streaks, some of gold[C] fire, backed but not engulfed by black billowing smoke, not separate from the star's path like the black cloud in the "William" picture. (Pace Keynes, *no* "black cloud envelops the whole design.") In the three earlier copies the ground is green, the steps brownish. Yet they are shaped like the first steps of Jacob's "ladder" in Blake's watercolor (*Bible* 25). In D the steps, the strip of ground underfoot, the star, and the name-plate are light, i.e. the color of the paper, but the green is transferred to Robert's trunks, first outlined in B after the near nudity of A.

The separation of the two mirror-identical plates, 32 and 37, prevents us from seeing them only as opposites. That is, we are able to read them singly yet imagine them (a) as a facing pair, a perspective that emphasizes the theme of brothers standing tarsus to tarsus in positive contrast to the murdered and murdering brothers of Plate 15 (Abel who slew for sacrifice and Cain who slew the slayer) and to the brothers Rintrah and Palamabron of Plate 10, who cannot receive the light as long as they simply watch Satan burn. And we can imagine them (b) as contrary images of one person, such as Milton and his emanation Ololon, who must become one. In this perspective Robert is the Eternal form, as the fourfold stairs suggest, but William on earth is the generative form in which Robert (or Milton) must appear for the moment of light that turns eternal night to day. The pictures also present (c) a sequence of progressive contraction and expansion, of descent and ascent (simple core of the bard's prophecy): steps downward from the past, behind William, whose hands unite past and present; fourfold steps upward, behind Robert and touched[BCD] by Robert's outstretched hand, the

Milton 37[C]

And all the Songs of Beulah sounded comfortable notes
To comfort Ololons lamentation, for they said
Are you the Fiery Circle that late drove in fury & fire
The Eight Immortal Starry-Ones down into Ulro dark
Rending the Heavens of Beulah with your thunders & lightnings
And can you thus lament & can you pity & forgive?
Is terror changd to pity O wonder of Eternity!

And the Four States of Humanity in its Repose,
Were shewed them. First of Beulah a most pleasant Sleep
On Couches soft, with mild music, tended by Flowers of Beulah
Sweet Female forms, winged or floating in the air spontaneous
The Second State is Alla & the third State Al-Ulro;
But the Fourth State is dreadful; it is named Or-Ulro:
The First State is in the Head, the Second is in the Heart:
The Third in the Loins & Seminal Vessels & the Fourth
In the Stomach & Intestines terrible, deadly, unutterable
And he whose Gates are opend in those Regions of his Body
Can from those Gates view all these wondrous Imaginations

But Ololon sought the Or-Ulro & its fiery Gates
And the Couches of the Martyrs: & many Daughters of Beulah
Accompany them down to the Ulro with soft melodious tears
A long journey & dark thro Chaos in the track of Miltons course
To where the Contraries of Beulah War beneath Negations Banner

Then view'd from Miltons Track they see the Ulro: a vast Polypus
Of living fibres down into the Sea of Time & Space growing
A self-devouring monstrous Human Death Twenty-seven fold
Within it sit Five Females & the nameless Shadowy Mother
Spinning it from their bowels with songs of amorous delight
And melting cadences that lure the Sleepers of Beulah down
The River Storge (which is Arnon) into the Dead Sea:
Around this Polypus Los continual builds the Mundane Shell

Four Universes round the Universe of Los remain Chaotic
Four intersecting Globes, & the Egg formd World of Los
In midst; stretching from Zenith to Nadir, in midst of Chaos
One of these Ruind Universes is to the North named Urthona
One to the South this was the glorious World of Urizen
One to the East, of Luvah: One to the West; of Tharmas.
But when Luvah assumed the World of Urizen in the South
All fell towards the Center sinking downward in dire Ruin

Here in these Chaoses the Sons of Ololon took their abode
In Chasms of the Mundane Shell which open on all sides round
Southward & by the East within the Breach of Miltons descent
To watch the time, pitying & gentle to awaken Urizen
They stood in a dark land of death of fiery corroding waters
Where lie in evil death the Four Immortals pale and cold
And the Eternal Man even Albion upon the Rock of Ages
Seeing Miltons Shadow, some Daughters of Beulah trembling
Returnd, but Ololon remaind before the Gates of the Dead

And Ololon looked down into the Heavens of Ulro in fear
They said. How are the Wars of Man which in Great Eternity
Appear around, in the External Spheres of Visionary Life
Here renderd Deadly within the Life & Interior Vision
How are the Beasts & Birds & Fishes, & Plants & Minerals
Here fixd into a frozen bulk subject to decay & death
Those Visions of Human Life & Shadows of Wisdom & Knowledge

Milton 38ᴬ [K34]

hand and the steps both directing us forward. We see that the stones of Satan's paved terraces that had grown opaque have in an instant recovered their original glory as a luminous hewn-stone ladder of returning and going forth.

Another essential movement in the pictures is the simultaneous downward fall of the star and upward look of the human face. This translates, in the watercolor *Conversion of Saul* (*Bible* 154), into a downward look from Christ and an upward look from Saul. (The *Milton* plates correspond more literally to the Bible text, where Saul hears Christ but cannot see him.)

Here and in Plate 10 the contrary positives are male; in Plates 2 and 33 (and 42) they are male and female. In Plate 19 the grouped contraries are female at the top, male at the bottom. Thus the themes are interwoven in the visual sequence. Ultimately (see note, Plate 50) one human form will contain them all.

Milton 38ᴬ [K34] (ABC34, D38). Does the marginal squiggle after line 7 imply that the line of text is the important thing in this page? Blue washes make this an eel rather than a worm. In the early copies the washes on the page are light yellows and pinks; in D there are simply marginal patches of dark greyish blue.

Milton 39A [K35] (ABC35, D39). A bird at line 17 and the eel-worm again at 26, and a squiggle lower down, are holding the space open, which is more or less blue—as are "the clouds of Ololon" (41) except in D, where they are red brown. In B bright yellow and pink washes burst from the lower right corner in rays that imply a great sun below and to the right of the page.

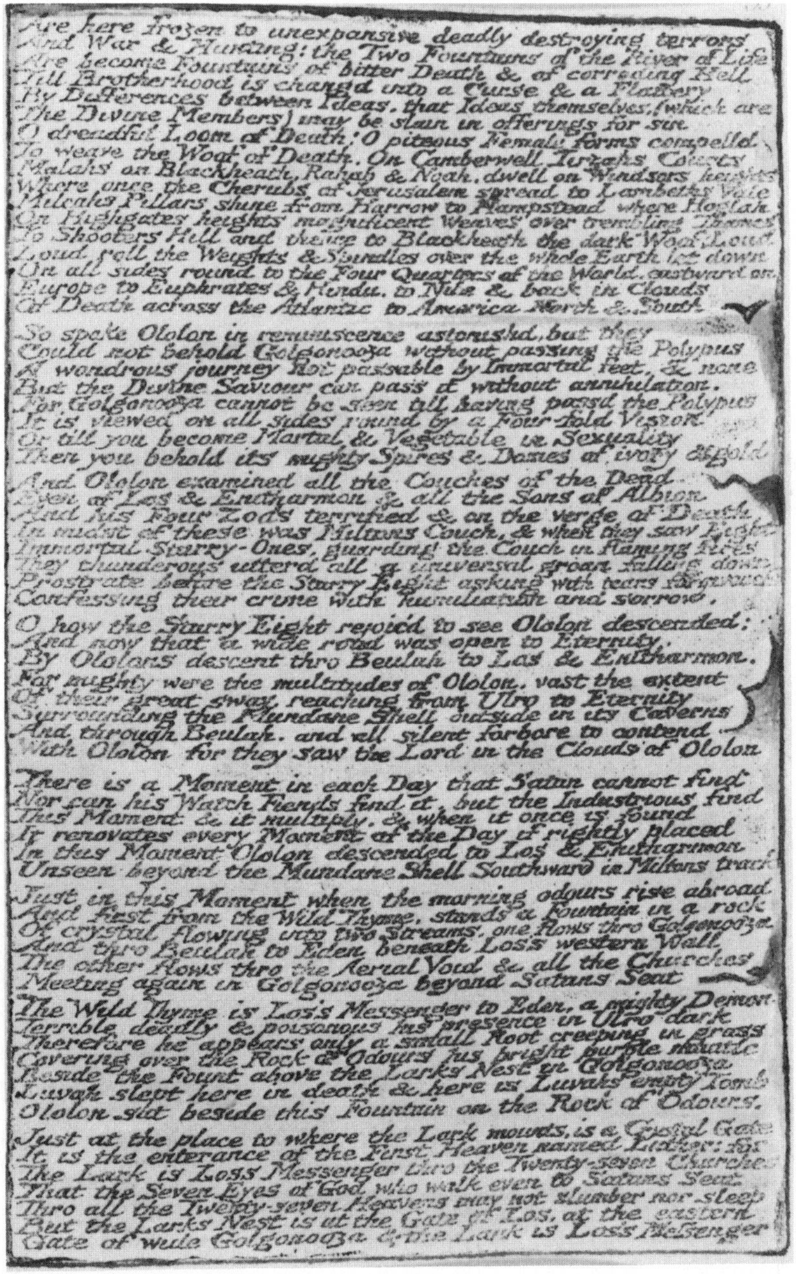

Are here frozen to unexpansive deadly destroying terrors
And War & Hunting: the Two Fountains of the River of Life
Are become Fountains of bitter Death & of corroding Hell
Till Brotherhood is changd into a Curse & a Flattery
By Differences between Ideas, that Ideas themselves, (which are
The Divine Members) may be slain in offerings for sin
O dreadful Loom of Death! O piteous Female forms compelld
To weave the Woof of Death, On Camberwell Tirzahs Courts
Malahs on Blackheath, Rahab & Noah. dwell on Windsors heights
Where once the Cherubs of Jerusalem spread to Lambeths Vale
Milcahs Pillars shine from Harrow to Hampstead where Hoglah
On Highgates heights magnificent Weaves over trembling Thames
To Shooters Hill and thence to Blackheath the dark Woof! Loud
Loud roll the Weights & Spindles over the whole Earth let down
On all sides round to the Four Quarters of the World, eastward on
Europe to Euphrates & Hindu. to Nile & back in Clouds
Of Death across the Atlantic to America North & South

So spake Ololon in reminiscence astonishd, but they
Could not behold Golgonooza without passing the Polypus
A wondrous journey not passable by Immortal feet, & none
But the Divine Saviour can pass it without annihilation.
For Golgonooza cannot be seen till having passd the Polypus
It is viewed on all sides round by a Four-fold Vision
Or till you become Mortal & Vegetable in Sexuality
Then you behold its mighty Spires & Domes of ivory & gold

And Ololon examined all the Couches of the Dead.
Even of Los & Enitharmon & all the Sons of Albion
And his Four Zoas terrified & on the verge of Death
In midst of these was Miltons Couch, & when they saw Eight
Immortal Starry-Ones, guarding the Couch in flaming fires
They thunderous utterd all a universal groan falling down
Prostrate before the Starry Eight asking with tears forgiveness
Confessing their crime with humiliation and sorrow.

O how the Starry Eight rejoic'd to see Ololon descended!
And now that a wide road was open to Eternity,
By Ololons descent thro Beulah to Los & Enitharmon.
For mighty were the multitudes of Ololon, vast the extent
Of their great sway, reaching from Ulro to Eternity
Surrounding the Mundane Shell outside in its Caverns
And through Beulah. and all silent forbore to contend
With Ololon for they saw the Lord in the Clouds of Ololon

There is a Moment in each Day that Satan cannot find
Nor can his Watch Fiends find it, but the Industrious find
This Moment & it multiply. & when it once is found
It renovates every Moment of the Day if rightly placed
In this Moment Ololon descended to Los & Enitharmon
Unseen beyond the Mundane Shell Southward in Miltons track

Just in this Moment when the morning odours rise abroad
And first from the Wild Thyme, stands a Fountain in a rock
Of crystal flowing into two Streams, one flows thro Golgonooza
And thro Beulah to Eden beneath Los's western Wall
The other flows thro the Aerial Void & all the Churches
Meeting again in Golgonooza beyond Satans Seat

The Wild Thyme is Los's Messenger to Eden, a mighty Demon
Terrible deadly & poisonous his presence in Ulro dark
Therefore he appears only a small Root creeping in grass
Covering over the Rock of Odours his bright purple mantle
Beside the Fount above the Larks Nest in Golgonooza
Luvah slept here in death & here is Luvahs empty Tomb
Ololon sat beside this Fountain on the Rock of Odours.

Just at the place to where the Lark mounts, is a Crystal Gate
It is the enterance of the First Heaven named Luther: for
The Lark is Loss Messenger thro the Twenty-seven Churches
That the Seven Eyes of God who walk even to Satans Seat
Thro all the Twenty-seven Heavens may not slumber nor sleep
But the Larks Nest is at the Gate of Los, at the eastern
Gate of wide Golgonooza & the Lark is Loss Messenger

Milton 39A [K35]

When on the highest lift of his light pinions he arrives
At that bright Gate, another Lark meets him & back to back
They touch their pinions tip tip: and each descend
To their respective Earths & there all night consult with Angels
Of Providence & with the Eyes of God all night in slumbers
Inspired: & at the dawn of day send out another Lark
Into another Heaven to carry news upon his wings
Thus are the Messengers dispatchd till they reach the Earth again
In the East Gate of Golgonooza, & the Twenty-eighth bright
Lark. met the Female Ololon descending into my Garden
Thus it appears to Mortal eyes & those of the Ulro Heavens
But not thus to Immortals. the Lark is a mighty Angel.

For Ololon step'd into the Polypus within the Mundane Shell
They could not step into Vegetable Worlds without becoming
The enemies of Humanity except in a Female Form
And as One Female, Ololon and all its mighty Hosts
Appear'd: a Virgin of twelve years nor time nor space was
To the perception of the Virgin Ololon but as the
Flash of lightning but more quick the Virgin in my Garden
Before my Cottage stood for the Satanic Space is delusion

For when Los join'd with me he took me in his firy whirlwind
My Vegetated portion was hurried from Lambeths shades
He set me down in Felphams Vale & prepard a beautiful
Cottage for me that in three years I might write all these
Visions
To display Natures cruel holiness: the deceits of Natural
Religion
Walking in my Cottage Garden, sudden I beheld
The Virgin Ololon & address'd her as a Daughter of Beulah

Virgin of Providence fear not to enter into my Cottage
What is thy message to thy friend: What am I now to do
Is it again to plunge into deeper affliction? behold me
Ready to obey, but pity thou my Shadow of Delight
Enter my Cottage, comfort her, for she is sick with fatigue

Milton 40A [K36]

Milton 40A [K36] (ABC36, D40). Beside "Blakes Cottage at Felpham," Blake, clothed (in grey or grey blueC or powder blueD) but hatless, receives the virgin Ololon, winged, descending into his garden with flying draperies. She seems to slide down an invisible trapeze wire; a tree seems to open to make way for her (effect of the spirit's entering the vegetable world), and she is just passing above the Blakes' water-pump. Her flight is mimicked by two birds in the right margin of the text.

The five birds circling Blake's chimney were inevitable, and two more are coming, under "comfort her." The humility and simplicity of the small self-portraits in Plates 14, 24, etc recur in this emblem of Blake at home; yet a certain amount of domestic pride led to some embellishments. In copy B the poet made window frames downstairs in the main house; in D he put flowers on the shrubs sketched under the double window and added shrubbery on the other side of the doorway.

This simplification of the illumination to a quiet domestic scene, in which the author and artist of the marginal self-caricatures identifies himself, with his feet on his own pathway, enables the poet to open his text (on the next plate) to sublime and terrible visions of apocalyptic immensity "reaching from heaven to earth" and through vast reaches of human and divine history. The picture also makes Blake's point (of Plate 31) that the poet's work is done in his own "neighbourhood" or not at all.

Milton 41^A [K37] (ABC37, D41). The marginal sketch curving down from "Nile" (27) looks in A vaguely like a headless figure, brown, under a grey tree. It is black and ill-defined in B and C, seems like shapeless splashing water, grey-blue, in D.

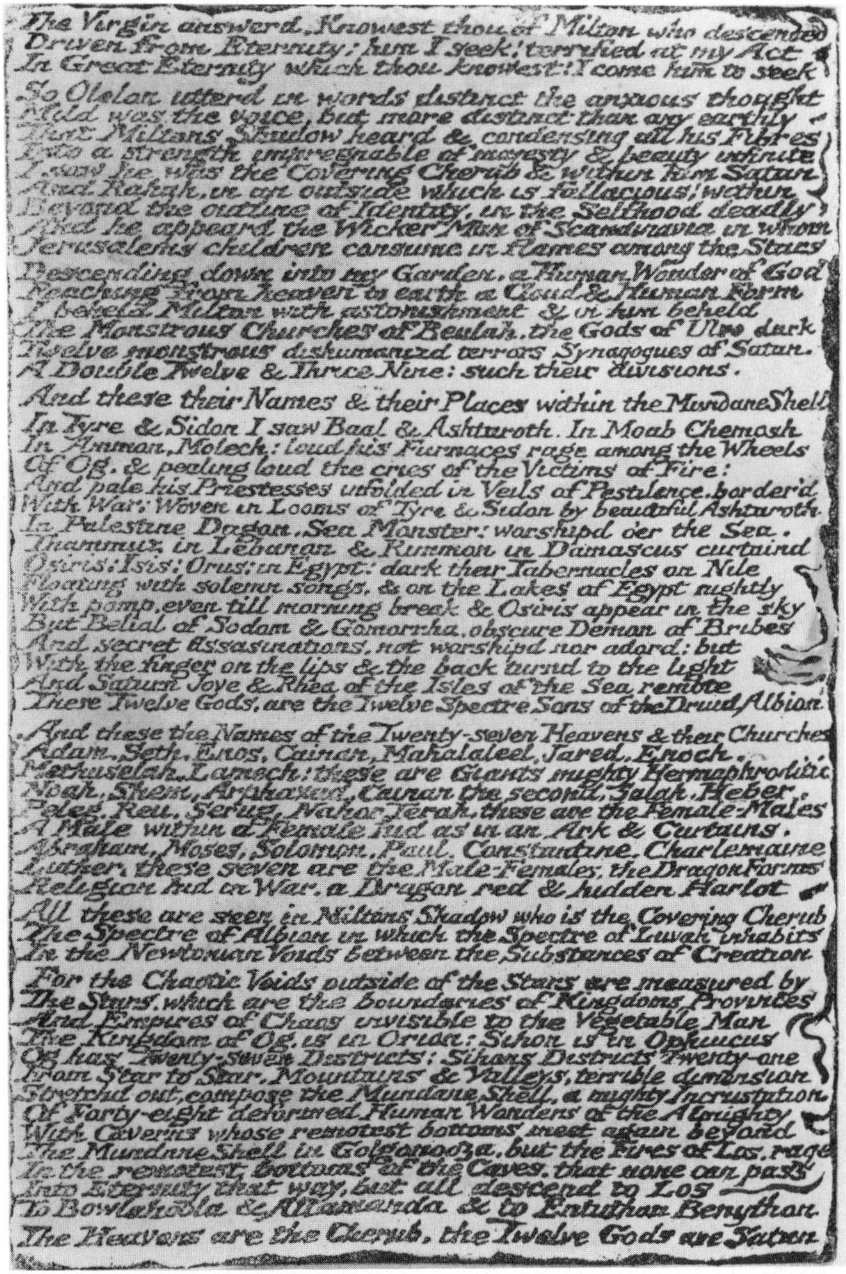

The Virgin answerd. Knowest thou of Milton who descended
Driven from Eternity; him I seek! terrified at my Act
In Great Eternity which thou knowest! I come him to seek

So Ololon utterd in words distinct the anxious thought
Mild was the voice, but more distinct than any earthly
That Miltons Shadow heard & condensing all his Fibres
Into a strength impregnable of majesty & beauty infinite
I saw he was the Covering Cherub & within him Satan
And Rahab, in an outside which is fallacious! within
Beyond the outline of Identity, in the Selfhood deadly
And he appeard the Wicker Man of Scandinavia in whom
Jerusalems children consume in flames among the Stars

Descending down into my Garden, a Human Wonder of God
Reaching from heaven to earth a Cloud & Human Form
I beheld Milton with astonishment & in him beheld
The Monstrous Churches of Beulah, the Gods of Ulro dark
Twelve monstrous dishumanizd terrors Synagogues of Satan.
A Double Twelve & Thrice Nine: such their divisions.

And these their Names & their Places within the Mundane Shell
In Tyre & Sidon I saw Baal & Ashtaroth. In Moab Chemosh
In Ammon, Molech: loud his Furnaces rage among the Wheels
Of Og. & pealing loud the cries of the Victims of Fire:
And pale his Priestesses infolded in Veils of Pestilence, border'd
With War: Woven in Looms of Tyre & Sidon by beautiful Ashtaroth.
In Palestine Dagon, Sea Monster: worshipd o'er the Sea.
Thammuz in Lebanon & Rimmon in Damascus curtaind
Osiris: Isis: Orus: in Egypt: dark their Tabernacles on Nile
Floating with solemn songs, & on the Lakes of Egypt nightly
With pomp, even till morning break & Osiris appear in the sky
But Belial of Sodom & Gomorrha, obscure Demon of Bribes
And secret Assasinations, not worshipd nor adord: but
With the finger on the lips & the back turnd to the light
And Saturn Jove & Rhea of the Isles of the Sea remote
These Twelve Gods, are the Twelve Spectre Sons of the Druid Albion.

And these the Names of the Twenty-seven Heavens & their Churches
Adam, Seth, Enos, Cainan, Mahalaleel, Jared, Enoch,
Methuselah, Lamech: these are Giants mighty Hermaphroditic
Noah, Shem, Arphaxad, Cainan the second, Salah, Heber,
Peleg, Reu, Serug, Nahor, Terah, these are the Female-Males
A Male within a Female hid as in an Ark & Curtains.
Abraham, Moses, Solomon, Paul, Constantine, Charlemaine
Luther, these seven are the Male-Females, the Dragon Forms
Religion hid in War, a Dragon red & hidden Harlot

All these are seen in Miltons Shadow who is the Covering Cherub
The Spectre of Albion in which the Spectre of Luvah inhabits
In the Newtonian Voids between the Substances of Creation

For the Chaotic Voids outside of the Stars are measured by
The Stars, which are the boundaries of Kingdoms, Provinces
And Empires of Chaos invisible to the Vegetable Man
The Kingdom of Og, is in Orion: Sihon is in Ophiucus
Og has Twenty-seven Districts: Sihons Districts Twenty-one
From Star to Star, Mountains & Valleys, terrible dimension
Stretchd out, compose the Mundane Shell, a mighty Incrustation
Of Forty-eight deformed Human Wonders of the Almighty
With Caverns whose remotest bottoms meet again beyond
The Mundane Shell in Golgonooza, but the Fires of Los, rage
In the remotest bottoms of the Caves, that none can pass
Into Eternity that way, but all descend to Los
To Bowlahoola & Allamanda & to Entuthon Benython.

The Heavens are the Cherub, the Twelve Gods are Satan

Milton 41^A [K37]

Milton 42A

Milton 42A (ABC38, D42). Here on the water's edge, where the earth-rock meets what is called in this poem "the Sea of Time & Space" (e.g. 38:25), the moment of the fall of Milton's star, the descent of Ololon, the trumpeting in the border of Plate 33, the lark's trilling, and especially the "trumpets innumerable" that wake Albion in 44:7–32, occurs as an eagle's scream waking naked lovers. Its beak and talonsD show the wrathful aspect of illuminating descent, its wings the swiftness; the silence that ensues (see below) will show the mercy. The man looks up without the enthusiasm in the upward looks of William and Robert (and Saul), and his arms remain slack. His large penis (obscuredBC, almost invisibleD) indicates that the lovers have been interrupted in—or before falling asleep after—copulation, and the sadness or concern in their faces (eyes shutB) seems post coital. It may also imply a reluctance to respond to the Last Trumpet's call to leave mortal things, rise from the "Couch Of dread repose" (44:32–33), and "go forth to the Great Harvest & Vintage" (50:1) in which nations and sexes, the bread and the wine, are consumed to arise as One in Jesus (49:10–21). Blake himself, despite his vision, returns to his "Vegetable Body" and his "sweet Shadow of Delight," though his bones tremble and she trembles "by my side" (49:27–28).

The reluctant sleepers are, archetypally, Albion and his bride Jerusalem (2:15) or, in this geographic location, "England who is Brittannia" (*Jerusalem* 95:22). In the text we hear once in a while of "the Couch of Albion" on which his "sleeping Humanity" begins to turn, when it feels "the electric flame of Miltons . . . descent," yet remains "Unwakend!" though the trumpet "hath twice sounded" (9:50; 22:25–26; 25:4–10). England is not mentioned as a woman beside him, because the terms are geographical: his rocky couch is the whole extent of the land, potentially green and pleasant, and when the giant Albion finally wakes (as shown here in miniature) he struggles to rise by moving his right foot from the "Dover cliffs" to "Cornwall" and his left foot from "near London" to "the rocks of Bognor." When he bends his head "over London" (see also 49:35) he sees his spectre trembling (at Albion's mounting anger?) and he "views Jerusalem & Babylon" and weeps (in pity for both—see Plate 10). But his strength fails when he attempts "to rise to walk into the Deep" (i.e. to cast his selfhood into the lake: compare *Jerusalem* 37), and he sinks "upon his Couch In moony Beulah" (44:32–52). Evidently his anger and pity are not enough or not properly directed. When the scene is reenacted and brought to a more successful conclusion, in *Jerusalem* 94–95, the eagle's scream and wolf's howl and ocean's "black thundering" reach a pause of "deathlike silence" and "Time was Finished!" England awakes but faints seven times on his body before her outcries against herself for his murder wake Albion. He then rises in wrath and she enters his bosom "adoring his wrathful rebuke," the union of pity and wrath achieving mutual forgiveness.

The end may seem near in this *Milton* plate; both seem awake, England turns toward her lover, not away as Eve does in *Adam and Eve Sleeping* (in the Boston *Paradise Lost* series). Albion's mouth is open[D] to breathe his wrath. Yet the ocean is only mildly turbulent nearby and calm in the distance. England keeps her arms around Albion and ignores the eagle; the fingers of his right hand dally in the sand or almost in the water[C]. (Re-engraving for copy D half succeeded in turning her body so that both legs are visible, with his thumb between them—a reversion to Blake's early sketch of the scene.)

As a prophetic center of the work, standing somewhat outside it, this plate has a function akin to that of the picture of Titania and Oberon in *Song of Los* 6. But whereas the fairy queen and king are observers, Albion and England are the observed; they represent the Lord's People whom the poem must move, or Milton and Blake will have been moved in vain. This picture also affords a glimpse of the larger epic, *Jerusalem,* which the moment of *Milton* adumbrates. The eagle, pictured here, described in *Jerusalem,* is the traditional symbol of St John and hence the living trumpet of prophecy.

~

Milton 43[A] [K38] (ABC39, D43). The marginal squiggles almost make a human form, beside the third paragraph, but this is not picked up in Blake's coloring of copies. In B a sunburst effect, in yellow and rose, radiates from the upper left corner.

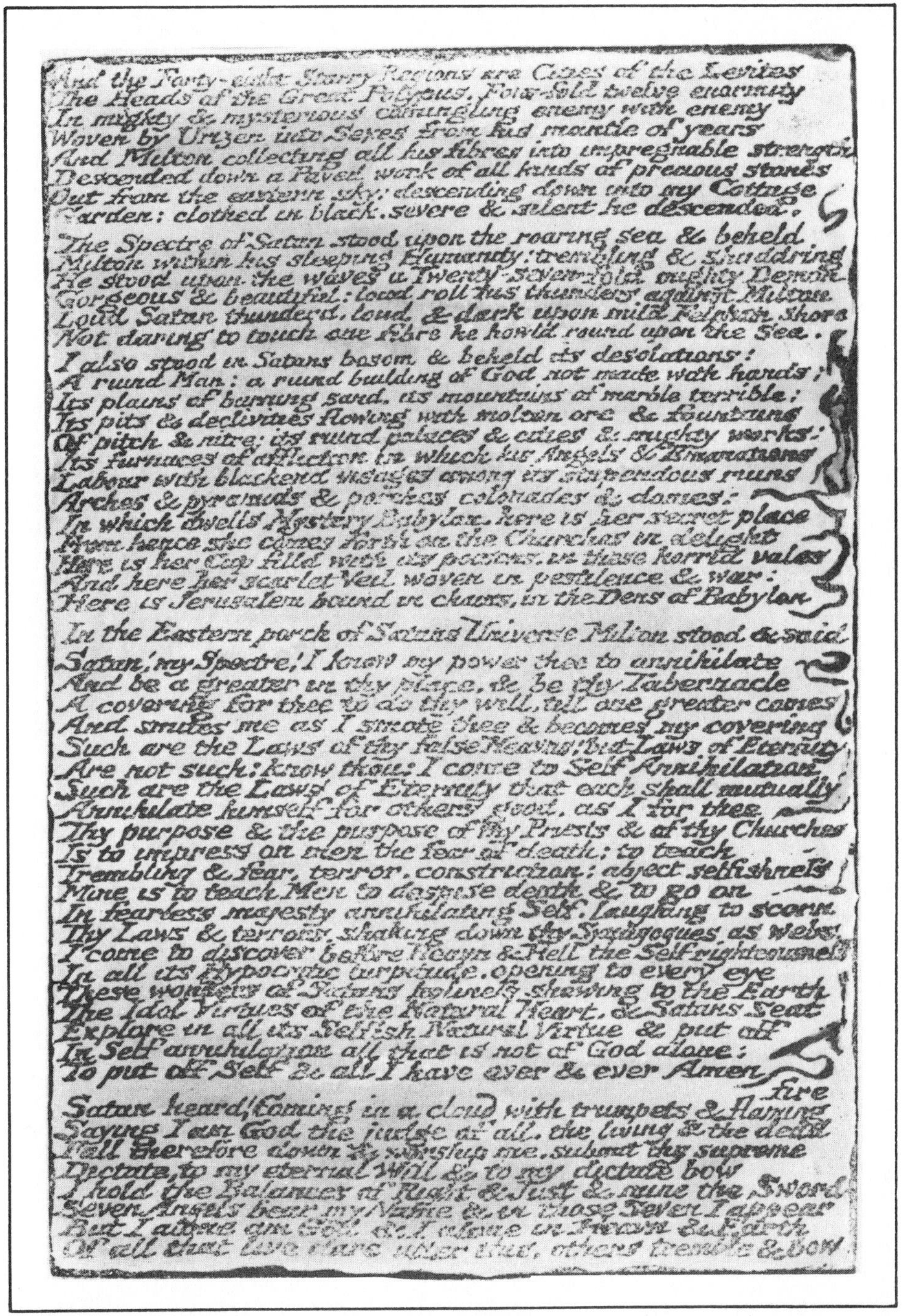

And the Forty-eight Starry Regions are Cities of the Levites
The Heads of the Great Polypus, Four-fold twelve enormity
In mighty & mysterious comingling enemy with enemy
Woven by Urizen into Sexes from his mantle of years
And Milton collecting all his fibres into impregnable strength
Descended down a Paved work of all kinds of precious stones
Out from the eastern sky; descending down into my Cottage
Garden: clothed in black. severe & silent he descended.

The Spectre of Satan stood upon the roaring sea & beheld
Milton within his sleeping Humanity: trembling & shuddring
He stood upon the waves a Twenty-seven-fold mighty Demon
Gorgeous & beautiful: loud roll his thunders against Milton
Loud Satan thunderd. loud & dark upon mild Felpham shore
Not daring to touch one fibre he howld round upon the Sea.

I also stood in Satans bosom & beheld its desolations:
A ruind Man: a ruind building of God not made with hands;
Its plains of burning sand. its mountains of marble terrible:
Its pits & declivities flowing with molten ore & fountains
Of pitch & nitre: its ruind palaces & cities & mighty works:
Its furnaces of affliction in which his Angels & Emanations
Labour with blackend visages among its stupendous ruins
Arches & pyramids & porches colonades & domes:
In which dwells Mystery Babylon. here is her secret place
From hence she comes forth on the Churches in delight
Here is her Cup filld with its poisons. in these horrid vales
And here her scarlet Veil woven in pestilence & war:
Here is Jerusalem bound in chains. in the Dens of Babylon

In the Eastern porch of Satans Universe Milton stood & said
Satan! my Spectre! I know my power thee to annihilate
And be a greater in thy place, & be thy Tabernacle
A covering for thee to do thy will. till one greater comes
And smites me as I smote thee & becomes my covering.
Such are the Laws of thy false Heavns! but Laws of Eternity
Are not such: know thou: I come to Self Annihilation
Such are the Laws of Eternity that each shall mutually
Annihilate himself for others good. as I for thee
Thy purpose & the purpose of thy Priests & of thy Churches
Is to impress on men the fear of death; to teach
Trembling & fear. terror. constriction; abject selfishness
Mine is to teach Men to despise death & to go on
In fearless majesty annihilating Self. laughing to scorn
Thy Laws & terrors, shaking down thy Synagogues as webs
I come to discover before Heavn & Hell the Self righteousness
In all its Hypocritic turpitude. opening to every eye
These wonders of Satans holiness shewing to the Earth
The Idol Virtues of the Natural Heart. & Satans Seat
Explore in all its Selfish Natural Virtue & put off
In Self annihilation all that is not of God alone:
To put off Self & all I have ever & ever Amen

Satan heard! Coming in a cloud with trumpets & flaming fire
Saying I am God the judge of all. the living & the dead
Fall therefore down & worship me. submit thy supreme
Dictate, to my eternal Will & to my dictate bow
I hold the Balances of Right & Just & mine the Sword
Seven Angels bear my Name & in those Seven I appear
But I alone am God & I alone in Heavn & Earth
Of all that live dare utter this. others tremble & bow

Milton 43[A] [K38]

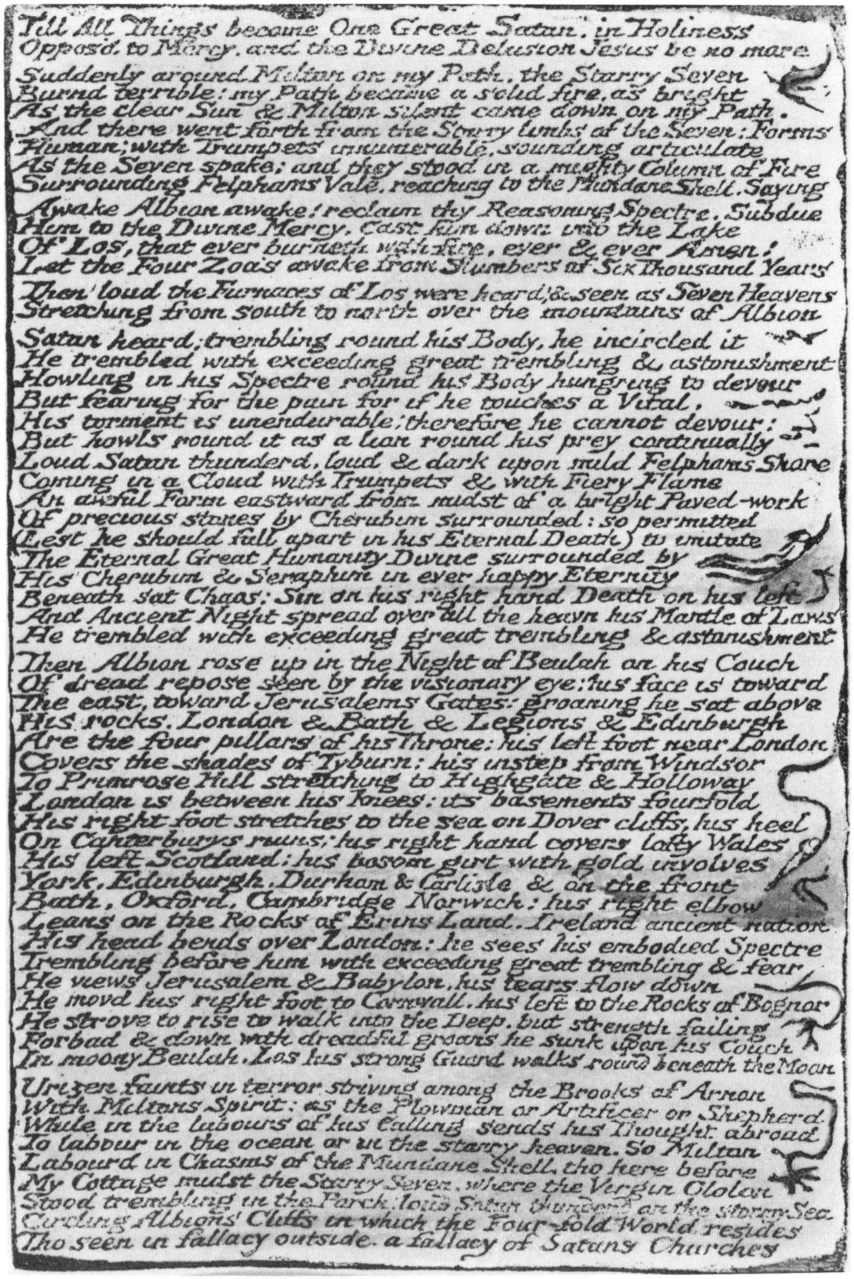

Till All Things become One Great Satan, in Holiness
Oppos'd to Mercy, and the Divine Delusion Jesus be no more

Suddenly around Milton on my Path, the Starry Seven
Burnd terrible! my Path became a solid fire, as bright
As the clear Sun & Milton silent came down on my Path.
And there went forth from the Starry limbs of the Seven: Forms
Human; with Trumpets innumerable, sounding articulate
As the Seven spake; and they stood in a mighty Column of Fire
Surrounding Felphams Vale, reaching to the Mundane Shell, Saying

Awake Albion awake! reclaim thy Reasoning Spectre. Subdue
Him to the Divine Mercy, Cast him down into the Lake
Of Los, that ever burneth with fire, ever & ever Amen!
Let the Four Zoa's awake from Slumbers of Six Thousand Years

Then loud the Furnaces of Los were heard! & seen as Seven Heavens
Stretching from south to north over the mountains of Albion

Satan heard; trembling round his Body, he incircled it
He trembled with exceeding great trembling & astonishment
Howling in his Spectre round his Body hungring to devour
But fearing for the pain for if he touches a Vital,
His torment is unendurable: therefore he cannot devour:
But howls round it as a lion round his prey continually
Loud Satan thunderd, loud & dark upon mild Felphams Shore
Coming in a Cloud with Trumpets & with Fiery Flame
An awful Form eastward from midst of a bright Paved-work
Of precious stones by Cherubim surrounded: so permitted
(Lest he should fall apart in his Eternal Death) to imitate
The Eternal Great Humanity Divine surrounded by
His Cherubim & Seraphim in ever happy Eternity
Beneath sat Chaos: Sin on his right hand Death on his left
And Ancient Night spread over all the heavn his Mantle of Laws
He trembled with exceeding great trembling & astonishment

Then Albion rose up in the Night of Beulah on his Couch
Of dread repose seen by the visionary eye; his face is toward
The east, toward Jerusalems Gates: groaning he sat above
His rocks. London & Bath & Legions & Edinburgh
Are the four pillars of his Throne; his left foot near London
Covers the shades of Tyburn: his instep from Windsor
To Primrose Hill stretching to Highgate & Holloway
London is between his knees: its basements fourfold
His right foot stretches to the sea on Dover cliffs, his heel
On Canterburys ruins; his right hand covers lofty Wales
His left Scotland; his bosom girt with gold involves
York, Edinburgh, Durham & Carlisle & on the front
Bath, Oxford, Cambridge Norwich; his right elbow
Leans on the Rocks of Erins Land, Ireland ancient nation
His head bends over London: he sees his embodied Spectre
Trembling before him with exceeding great trembling & fear
He views Jerusalem & Babylon, his tears flow down
He movd his right foot to Cornwall, his left to the Rocks of Bognor
He strove to rise to walk into the Deep, but strength failing
Forbad & down with dreadful groans he sunk upon his Couch
In moony Beulah. Los his strong Guard walks round beneath the Moon

Urizen faints in terror striving among the Brooks of Arnon
With Miltons Spirit: as the Plowman or Artificer or Shepherd
While in the labours of his Calling sends his Thought abroad
To labour in the ocean or in the starry heaven. So Milton
Labourd in Chasms of the Mundane Shell, tho here before
My Cottage midst the Starry Seven, where the Virgin Ololon
Stood trembling in the Porch: loud Satan thunderd on the stormy Sea
Circling Albions Cliffs in which the Four-fold World resides
Tho seen in fallacy outside: a fallacy of Satans Churches

Milton 44ᴬ [K39]

Milton 44ᴬ [K39] (ABC40, D44). Truer forms emerge here. Is the figure at top right a "starry" human form with a trumpet (compare 6–7) which we cannot see? Can the pointing woman leaning on a branch in mid margin and the dark bent cross below her be echoes of the Sin and Death in the adjacent text (29)? In the curve after lines 41–43 there is a cocoon, or a small watcher[D]. From the lowest vine there grows a flat dark hand with spread fingers.

❧

Milton 45ᴬ (ABC41, D45). The wrestling on the Arnon is now over, Albion having waked (temporarily) at the trumpets' sound and Urizen having fainted "in terror" in the midst of the "striving" (44:7, 32, 53); so Milton stepping out of or across the river (we never see his feet in it) affords compassionate support to the collapsed body of his "dread And awful" opponent, now "oercoverd with the mantle of years" (46:4–5). (Contrast Cain's abandonment of the collapsed body of Abel in Plate 15.) Urizen's hair is white, his garment blue or grey[D]; as in Plates 1 and 16, Milton's hair is made wavier in D and his body less lean, and in that copy the river is extended to the area behind Urizen and even put under Milton's left foot though leaving his toes dry. The making clear that both Milton's left foot and Urizen's left hand are at the surface of the water indicates the symbolic importance: Urizen's energy has gone into Milton, who simultaneously casts off his garment of selfhood and saves Urizen's human form—but his eyes look beyond, for where is Ololon? (See the text in the next plate.)

The dual sources of light, of Plate 16, are now one, though the radiation from Milton's head is enlarged to a broad band of color behind his act. Urizen seems to be kneeling on a flat stone in A (like Satan's platform in Plate 10) made grass-green in B; the hill is green in C, the whole lower area in D. The destruction/redemption of Urizen/Satan grows grass on the earth-rock. (Note that the position of Urizen's head is like that of Blake's in Plate 47.)

Milton 45ᴬ

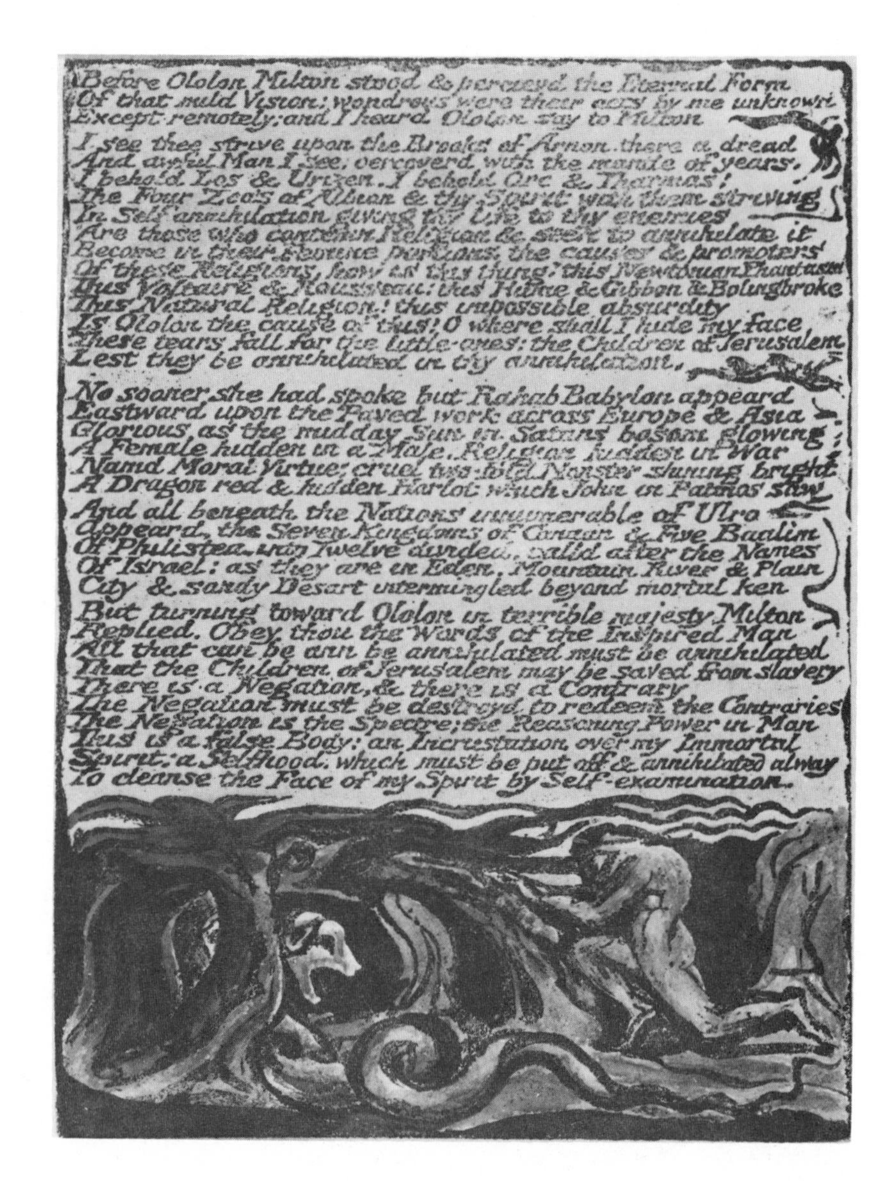
Before Ololon Milton stood & percievd the Eternal Form
Of that mild Vision; wondrous were their acts by me unknown
Except remotely; and I heard Ololon say to Milton

I see thee strive upon the Brooks of Arnon. there a dread
And awful Man I see, oercoverd with the mantle of years.
I behold Los & Urizen. I behold Orc & Tharmas;
The Four Zoa's of Albion & thy Spirit with them striving
In Self annihilation giving thy life to thy enemies
Are those who contemn Religion & seek to annihilate it
Become in their Femine portions the causes & promoters
Of these Religions, how is this thing? this Newtonian Phantasm
This Voltaire & Rousseau: this Hume & Gibbon & Bolingbroke
This Natural Religion! this impossible absurdity
Is Ololon the cause of this? O where shall I hide my face
These tears fall for the little-ones: the Children of Jerusalem
Lest they be annihilated in thy annihilation.

No sooner she had spoke but Rahab Babylon appeard
Eastward upon the Paved work across Europe & Asia
Glorious as the midday Sun in Satans bosom glowing:
A Female hidden in a Male, Religion hidden in War
Namd Moral Virtue; cruel two-fold Monster shining bright
A Dragon red & hidden Harlot which John in Patmos saw

And all beneath the Nations innumerable of Ulro
Appeard, the Seven Kingdoms of Canaan & Five Baalim
Of Philistea. into Twelve divided, calld after the Names
Of Israel: as they are in Eden. Mountain River & Plain
City & sandy Desart intermingled beyond mortal ken

But turning toward Ololon in terrible majesty Milton
Replied. Obey thou the Words of the Inspired Man
All that can be annihilated must be annihilated
That the Children of Jerusalem may be saved from slavery
There is a Negation, & there is a Contrary
The Negation must be destroyd to redeem the Contraries
The Negation is the Spectre; the Reasoning Power in Man
This is a false Body: an Incrustation over my Immortal
Spirit; a Selfhood. which must be put off & annihilated alway
To cleanse the Face of my Spirit by Self-examination.

Milton 46A [K40]

Milton 46A [K40] (ABC42, D46). The tattered fibres in the margin at the ends of the first and second paragraphs can be thought of as worn remnants of the garment of Selfhood, to "be put off & annihilated" (36). Below, the picture of Milton pushing his naked way among monstrous tree trunks (the foremost of which almost humanly mocks his stance, with a human torso and the suggestion of an eye under "cleanse") and confronting Urizen in the appearance of a mottledD serpent with two foolish heads, one a rooster/serpent with forked tongue, the other a human/dog (acting the part of Cerberus), translates Ololon's vision of the false body Milton is striving with as an "impossible absurdity" (13): a "cruel two-fold Monster shining bright A Dragon red & hidden Harlot which John in Patmos saw" (21–22). The picture, a variant of Plate 19 above, reduces dragon and harlot to domestic nuisances, a barking dog and a squawking yard fowl. (But their outcry can be as apocalyptic as the eagle's scream; in *Jerusalem* 94:16, cited above at Plate 42, a wolf's howl accompanies it.)

❧

Milton 47ᴬ (AB21, C43, D47). This plate, moved from its original location (in AB) following textual description of the scene (24:4–11) to the position (in CD) of the last full-page illumination in the poem, exalts William Blake to a position comparable to that of Urizen in the *Europe* title page, and identifies Blake/Los as "the Inspired Man" whose words Milton instructs Ololon to obey (46:29). Squatting on the green earth-rock—geographically in "the Vale of Lambeth"—Blake has bound on his sandals and is about to become "One Man" with Los. The Lambeth reference makes us realize that the "moment" of the poem reaches from the Blakes' departure from their home in London in 1800 to the end of their three years (40:21–24) in Felpham, the prophetic climax being a vision of their imminent return to London (49:31–33: though in Plate 4ᶜᴰ the reference is extended to include their residence in London again, at South Molton street). To "walk forward thro' Eternity" (24:5) Blake has bound on his sandals, with straps like bandages round his tarsus as though to bind in the energy that has now entered there (and to make a symbolic connection for us), and in the same instant Los also has "stoop'd down And bound my sandals on"—the reference being only apparently ambiguous, for Los and Blake become One with that act, presumably sharing one body. The picture, analytically, splits the moment, showing the right sandal on Blake's foot (the right foot of Los is cleverly hidden so that we cannot see whether the right sandal is there too) and Los's left foot placed bare on the green stool of earth, for the other sandal. Now we can't quite see whether Blake is wearing it. (In the Bard's song, Los "took off his left sandal placing it on his head, Signal of solemn mourning" at the "confusion" spread by Satan [8:11–12]; now it belongs on our foot as a signal of rejoicing and walking forward. But see Plate 50.) The action of Los, a divine parallel to Milton's, may be defined as "God descending according to the weakness of man" (Annotations to Lavater, *P&P* 589) or "God becomes as we are that we may be as he is" (*Religion* b12). Note that Blake's stance is the mirror opposite of Urizen's, as human compasses, in *Europe* 1, his left foot fixed, his right free to turn. But in his turning to Los, his head reaches to Los's loins—as Urizen's head touches Milton's loins in the preceding large plate (Plate 45 above). "And Los behind me stood; a terrible flaming Sun: Just close Behind my back; I turned round in terror, and behold. Los stood in that fierce glowing fire. . . ."

In Plate 45 we see the dying external husk of Urizen sup-

Milton 47ᴬ

To bathe in the Waters of Life: to wash off the Not Human
I come in Self-annihilation & the grandeur of Inspiration
To cast off Rational Demonstration by Faith in the Saviour
To cast off the rotten rags of Memory by Inspiration
To cast off Bacon, Locke & Newton from Albions covering
To take off his filthy garments, & clothe him with Imagination
To cast aside from Poetry, all that is not Inspiration
That it no longer shall dare to mock with the aspersion of Madness
Cast on the Inspired, by the tame high finisher of paltry Blots,
Indefinite, or paltry Rhymes; or paltry Harmonies.
Who creeps into State Government like a caterpiller to destroy
To cast off the idiot Questioner who is always questioning,
But never capable of answering; who sits with a sly grin
Silent plotting when to question, like a thief in a cave;
Who publishes doubt & calls it knowledge; whose Science is Despair
Whose pretence to knowledge is Envy, whose whole Science is
To destroy the wisdom of ages to gratify ravenous Envy;
That rages round him like a Wolf day & night without rest
He smiles with condescension; he talks of Benevolence & Virtue
And those who act with Benevolence & Virtue, they murder time on time
These are the destroyers of Jerusalem, these are the murderers
Of Jesus, who deny the Faith & mock at Eternal Life:
Who pretend to Poetry that they may destroy Imagination;
By imitation of Natures Images drawn from Remembrance
These are the Sexual Garments, the Abomination of Desolation
Hiding the Human Lineaments as with an Ark & Curtains
Which Jesus rent: & now shall wholly purge away with Fire
Till Generation is swallowd up in Regeneration.

Then trembled the Virgin Ololon & replyd in clouds of despair
Is this our Feminine Portion the Six-fold Miltonic Female
Terribly this Portion trembles before thee O awful Man
Altho' our Human Power can sustain the severe contentions
Of Friendship, our Sexual cannot: but flies into the Ulro.
Hence arose all our terrors in Eternity! & now remembrance
Returns upon us! are we Contraries O Milton, Thou & I
O Immortal! how were we led to War the Wars of Death
Is this the Void Outside of Existence, which if enterd into

Milton 48ᴬ [K41]

ported by the bard Milton who looks beyond that; here the naked William as Urizen reborn is not held but received by the bard Los, who looks at him hopefully (raised right hand) and thoughtfully (left hand against cheek), shortly to embrace him ("he kissed me, and wishd me health. And I became One Man with him arising in my strength"—a humanized version of the inclusion in Urthona's universe of Adam's world, diagrammed in Plate 36).

(In A, Blake's genitals are hidden with black ink, not necessarily by Blake, but in subsequent copies both figures are given underclothing.)

Milton 48ᴬ [K41] (AB43, C44, D48). "Is this our Feminine Portion the six-Fold Miltonic Female" (30)? Yes, but though "the Virgin Ololon . . . in clouds of despair" (29) may see the femininity of her friendship with Milton trembling and flying "into the Ulro" (33)—we remember the shadow figures in Plate i—we are shown those three wives (the figures more fully coloredᴰ third, fourth, and fifth from the left) and three daughters (whiter and whitely clothed)ᴰ joining hand in hand "To bathe in the Waters of Life: to wash off the Not Human" (1), the waters appearing as flames variously colored. The daughter at the right is ready only to touch fingers, but one of the two daughters at the left is touching *left* feet with one of the wives, and the same daughter is helping the wife who has her back to us to hold a crown or wreath (compare perhaps *Jerusalem* 89) over the head of the wife who looks directly toward us. This elaborate interrelating may remind us of the simpler chain game of the children in *Songs* 24. The contrast to the separate groups and individuals of Plate 19 is delightful. And the motif of tarsal touching, repeated but reversed from the First and Second book titles (the touching was of right feet in Plates 2 and 33, of mixed left and right in the emblem of errors, Plate 10), enlarges the petals-of-a-single-blossom effect into a candalabrum or broad composite flower head.

The "idiot Questioner" mentioned in line 12 scarcely begins to assume human shape, in the margin.

Milton 49A [K42] (AB44, C45, D49). The top and next marginal figures are difficult to make out: a figure huddling under a broad-brimmed hat, a large feathered wing; these in some way may relate to the Virgin's dividing and diving "into the depths Of Miltons Shadow as a Dove" (3–6). She may be the third figure, leaping with arms for wings, toward the undulations of a ribbon on "Cities of Albion" (16). Can the clothed figure sitting with arms held close, hands out in amazement, be Blake after he "fell outstretched" and his "Soul returned into its mortal state" (25–26)? I can't make out the shape of the small curve or figure beside "anger" (35).

The large naked woman hovering on a white (or purplishA) cloud must be "soft Oothoon" who "Pants in the Vales of Lambeth weeping oer her Human Harvest" (32–33). The field will be watered with tears of her joy that what she was denied will be part of the harvest. Blessings pour from her right hand as from an urn; her tears blend with the bluish rain that liquifies from the cloud under her left arm (compare the fibres pouring from the moon in *Jerusalem* 100, a transposed "harvest" emblem). The standing grain is rather green in ABC, very golden in D.

Ololon's descent as "a Moony Ark" over Felpham (7) was in Blake's immortal vision; Oothoon's ark-like hovering over Lambeth, over the Human Harvest of city-dwellers, is an emblem of Blake's former and future life in the city, to which he returns in prophetic hope: "Los & Enitharmon rose . . . Their clouds over London" (31). This is the personal content of the "old Prophecy . . . That Milton . . . Should up ascend forward from Felphams Vale" (23:35–37).

In the structuring of this poem, the penultimate plate of Book One (31) displayed the clearing away of deceit and false forgiveness, the plowing under of Druid history, comparable to the clearing of the Urizenic graffiti from the face of the sun in *The Song of Los*. But notice the transformation of this symbolism in *Milton*. *The Song of Los* ends with the surface cleared. *Milton* ends with its filling with a new and human harvest, ready to be gathered in.

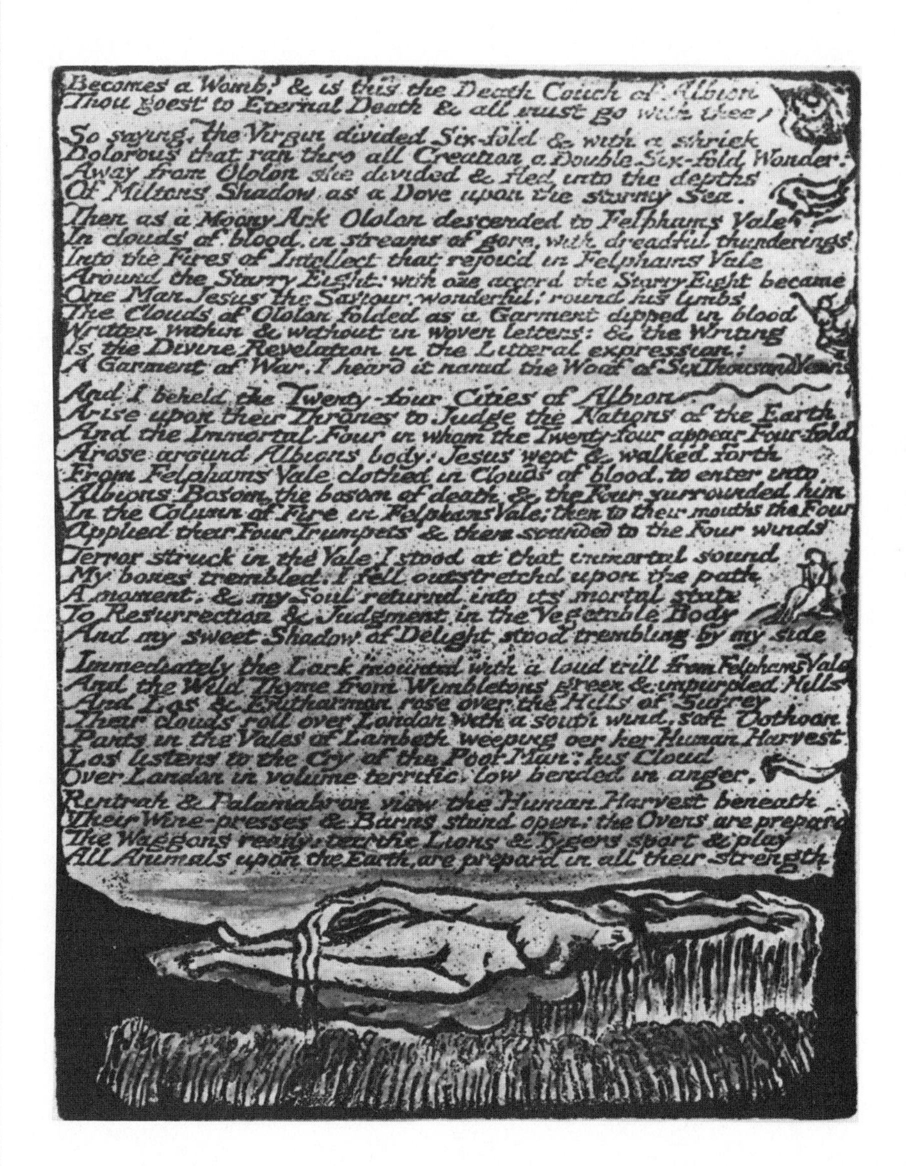

Becomes a Womb? & is this the Death Couch of Albion
Thou goest to Eternal Death & all must go with thee!

So saying, the Virgin divided Six-fold & with a shriek
Dolorous that ran thro all Creation a Double Six-fold Wonder!
Away from Ololon she divided & fled into the depths
Of Miltons Shadow as a Dove upon the stormy Sea.
Then as a Moony Ark Ololon descended to Felphams Vale
In clouds of blood, in streams of gore, with dreadful thunderings
Into the Fires of Intellect that rejoic'd in Felphams Vale
Around the Starry Eight: with one accord the Starry Eight became
One Man Jesus the Saviour. wonderful! round his limbs
The Clouds of Ololon folded as a Garment dipped in blood
Written within & without in woven letters: & the Writing
Is the Divine Revelation in the Litteral expression:
A Garment of War, I heard it namd the Woof of Six Thousand Years

And I beheld the Twenty-four Cities of Albion
Arise upon their Thrones to Judge the Nations of the Earth
And the Immortal Four in whom the Twenty-four appear Four-fold
Arose around Albions body: Jesus wept & walked forth
From Felphams Vale clothed in Clouds of blood, to enter into
Albions Bosom, the bosom of death & the Four surrounded him
In the Column of Fire in Felphams Vale; then to their mouths the Four
Applied their Four Trumpets & them sounded to the Four winds

Terror struck in the Vale I stood at that immortal sound
My bones trembled. I fell outstretchd upon the path
A moment, & my Soul returnd into its mortal state
To Resurrection & Judgment in the Vegetable Body
And my sweet Shadow of Delight stood trembling by my side

Immediately the Lark mounted with a loud trill from Felphams Vale
And the Wild Thyme from Wimbletons green & impurpled Hills
And Los & Enitharmon rose over the Hills of Surrey
Their clouds roll over London with a south wind, soft Oothoon
Pants in the Vales of Lambeth weeping oer her Human Harvest
Los listens to the Cry of the Poor Man: his Cloud
Over London in volume terrific, low bended in anger.

Rintrah & Palamabron view the Human Harvest beneath
Their Wine-presses & Barns stand open; the Ovens are prepard
The Waggons ready: terrific Lions & Tygers sport & play
All Animals upon the Earth, are prepard in all their strength

Milton 49A [K42]

Milton 50[A] [K43]

Milton 50[A] [K43] (AB45, C46, D50). The male and female human forms of the two deep rows of wheat remind us, symbolically, of the male and female harvest figures of bread and wine in Plate 2, but their shoulders look like folded wings. Alternatively, since the bread figure in Plate 2 is male, the two human rows of grain here may both be male (both W. J. T. Mitchell and Mary Lynn Johnson favor this reading). We may think of them as two brothers (of the virgin Ololon; compare the brothers of the virgin heroine in *Comus*), hence as a final vegetable appearance of the brothers of Plate 10 and of the brothers William and Robert—their readiness for the consummation of harvest being a variant of their readiness for the falling star. Yet we should expect the harvest to consume both genders of sexual garments; see below.

The crown of hair of the central figure, streaming outward symmetrically, concentrates the star and solar radiation we have seen; the grey-green* or blue[D] garment of Selfhood, held in outstretched hands, forms a trunk-like cross of self-annihilation. (Compare *Jerusalem* 76.) The vale below is English green.

In the early copies[ABC] the coloring is pale, the central figure greenish below, as though to emphasize the crucifixion, not the harvest. In A the background sky is pink rising to yellow, in B dull grey, in C with bands of gold suggesting a sun rising behind the tree-like base of the veil. In copy D the crown of hair is golden, the sky pink and blue; the further stalks, dark, are bursting into red and gold flame. The "Great Harvest & Vintage" (1) has begun or is about to begin; poet and reader are ready for the corroding fires to make a poem of the bread and wine of life, i.e. to have their human form revealed.

In D the central figure is wearing strapless sandals. Her stare, hitherto upward, is forward. Her hands, held out like those of *Christ the Mediator* (*Bible* 171), have let go of the blue veil. She is more clearly ready to go forth.

But who *is* the central figure? Is this the female Human Form Divine, a combination of Oothoon and Ololon? The faces of the male and female rows of vegetation are distinctly not those of any of the dramatis personae. Where is Milton? In Blake. Where is Blake? One Man with Los—in Jesus. The text would seem to prepare us to see in the central figure the human form divine that presides at the harvest as One Man, Jesus, in whom all the figures, male and female, have consolidated. And are not the sandals those of Los-Blake? Their lacking straps now can be symbolic of the final consummation. Yet the textual presentation is backward. In Plate 23 (58–60) we are told that when "the Family Divine as One Man even Jesus" unites "in One with Ololon" the resulting figure has "the appearance of One Man Jesus . . . coming in the Clouds of Ololon." Seventeen plates later we hear that "Ololon and all its [sic] mighty Hosts" appear "as One Female" (40:16–17). The apocalyptic vision described in Plate 49 is of "Jesus the Saviour" as "One Man" with the "Clouds of Ololon folded as a Garment dipped in blood" around his limbs and walking forth "to enter into Albions Bosom, the bosom of death" (11–21). But the word "Finis" on Plate 50 marks the end of this poem, not of Time. Albion has failed to stand up; Blake has returned to his "mortal state." And I believe that for our vision of the state of spousal *preparation* at the end of the poem—the "Wine-presses & Barns stand open: the Ovens are prepared The Waggons ready"—we must hold the volume open to its first and last plates to see Milton striding forward in self-annihilating wrath (the wrath is in the flames, not his face) and Ololon in pity removing her garment and stepping forth to the embrace of "Resurrection & Judgment" (49:26, 5–6, 37–38, 27). Seeing these giant forms step forth should free us from the need (see Mitchell and Johnson) to see both rows of the multitudinous chorus in men's clothing for want of a bridegroom. (The picture of Milton that more precisely matches this picture of his bride is on Plate 16, where he too is shedding robes. Milton is completely naked on Plate 1 because that picture has, on initial impact, to represent the entire action of the poem.)

Gates ai and Gates aii

Gates bi and *Gates* bii

THE GATES OF PARADISE

BLAKE ISSUED *The Gates of Paradise,* "a small book" (*P&P* 671) of seventeen line engravings with a title page directing them "For Children," in May 1793. Perhaps twenty-five years later, he issued them under the title "For the Sexes," with two pages of "Keys of the Gates" (here cited as *Keys*) and an Epilogue. Here copy E of "For Children" is given in the top row, copy G of "For the Sexes" in the bottom row. (Not reduced.) These are cited respectively as *a* and *b*.

For the series of emblem sketches from which these were selected for engraving, and for a study of Blake's labor in the selecting, see my edition of the *Notebook* (1973).

Gates i (Frontispiece). A caterpillar eating his way downward on the dark side of an oak leaf is contrasted with a chrysalis lying in state on the sunny side of another, human face upward. For children Blake made his caption (*a*) enigmatic, trusting them to see both views of "What is Man!"—a mortal worm and a sleeping butterfly. The ornamental initial twist on "What" implies: turn this either way. For adults solemnly wearing sexual garments, he supplied (*b*) more guidance: a message of sun's light will be unfolded in these pictures if you behold them with your spiritual eye. In *Night Thoughts* 13 (*Forms* plate 81) Blake puts the infant chrysalis and butterfly (see *Gates* 6) into the same picture.

Gates ii (title page). In *a,* a simple gowned spirit points to "Children" and directs them forward. In *b,* given a male companion, she issues the same directive; three children rising up under each spirit remind us of the eyes we still need for reading. Angels greet the sun that rises between "Gates" and "Paradise."

Gates 1. With two apple-headed infants in her apron (already shorn of their long vegetable hair) a gowned mother uproots a third mandrake child under a willow, potentially a tree of paradise. The eye that sees children as "found" vegetables will see them return to the earth and to their "mother" worm in Plate 16. Note that the child first plucked is already nearly faceless within the "Veil" (see *Keys;* see also *Jerusalem* 24). The "mother" who finds children in a garden, but doesn't let them grow up there, plainly knows only their mortal part—or insists on confining them to it. (For a happy ending, see *Song* 36.) Donne's "The Progresse of the Soule," used as a motto for one of Blake's rejected emblems for *Gates* (*N* 85), defines "a living buried man" as a "quiet mandrake" (stanza 16). See *Gates* 16.

Gates a1

Gates a2

Gates 2. Gone are the tree's leaves, and the mother; grey hairs are on man's head, his legs crossed in the immobility of "Doubt" (*Keys*). What he sees in the water must be his own image: in *a* his face shows more infatuation, in *b* his face and hands more conflict. That it must be blurred by his own "Tears" (not shown) is signified by the rain that falls on his naked body and by the surface of illusion's mirror. In first draft (*N* 95) a caption pointed to "Self slaughter," alas prohibited by "the Everlasting"; the *Keys* cite "Self Jealous Watry folly." Sit like this regarding life as a vale of tears, and your form of suicide will be stasis.

Gates b1

Gates b2

Gates a3

Gates a4

Gates b3

Gates b4

Gates 3. This titan cramped in a cave or grave of "Earth" is struggling to become the butterfly hinted at in the Frontispiece; yet he uses his arms partly to clutch his own anxious head. For a similar inward look of agony, see Blake's *Laocoön* (*P&P* pl 3). The doubter of Plate 2 was surrounding himself with matter, here solidified into "Earths Melancholy" (*Keys*), but a traveller through these emblems may think this an improvement over getting plucked for mother's apron—and will immediately, in the great leap to the next emblem, grasp the essential dynamics of the series.

Gates 4. In the air, sitting in the clouds indeed and among the stars (fourteen stars in almost recognizable constellations), naked man is freer of matter; he can see something outside himself and can do some thinking. But pressing his forehead with clenched hands and peering at futurity with his body more closed "in Shame" than the Water and Earth figures, he develops "Reasoning Cares" (i.e. "Shame and Fear": *Keys*) and "Cloudy Doubts," in other words a tendency to mistrust prophetic vision. In *a* his face shows simple worry, in *b* more rational concern.

Blake's first caption (in *Notebook* 94): "Thou hast set thy heart as the heart of God—Ezekiel," may be read straight, as an application of the prophet's warning to the King of Tyre or "covering cherub" against pride in riches and reason, but also constructively: the heart of a fully risen human must know as much as his eye sees.

Gates 5. In fire the human body opens wide—note the progressive alternations of closed and opened limbs in these four elemental emblems (Plates 2–5)—but to clutch shield and spear is to cling to the negations of earthbound vision. In *a* the sense of a climax, of a naked human rising high above "Water," balances the downward thrust of the spear. In the preliminary drawing (*Notebook* 91) he was identified with Satan when "Forthwith upright" he reared "from off the pool" (though "Forthwith upright" was then deleted). In the spirit of the Proverbs of Hell this might signify "Enough or Too Much"—although true liberation is shown not with clutched weapons but with broken chains, in for example *America* 3. In naming these four pictures by the four elements, Blake stressed their earthbound perspective; the human coming *through* the fire would be opening a book: see the conversing prophets in *Marriage* 24.

In *b* scales are forming on the warrior and on the flames (to suggest their transformation into serpent's coils); rising has turned to falling, the eyes are shut "Blind" (*Keys*). For either version these four plates have summarized and dismissed the mortal perspective as a wheel of fortune and sent the mental traveller on, unsatisfied.

Gates 6. These errors dismissed, the metamorphosis promised in the sunlit leaf of the Frontispiece is ripe: wings on the infant human, the cocoon-shell breaking. This hatching prefigures the universal jail delivery, the rending of "the Veil where the Dead dwell" (*Keys*) and the consummation of the five senses by the imagination. Here is the infant human phoenix suggested by the birds of paradise (passim); but a Cupid too, not simply winged for flight but looking in the right direction (up and onward) and leaving his weapons behind with "Fire"—or are they held behind his back? The play is not over.

Among the Notebook emblems Blake dropped from this series before its engraving are two conventional birdcage emblems, the first with a boy inside and a bird outside the cage, the second with the door open and the

Gates a5 and *Gates* a6

Gates b5 and *Gates* b6

Gates a7 and *Gates* a8

Gates b7 and *Gates* b8

boy flying out, without aid of wings. Traditionally these would signify the soul èncased in the body and then freed. The present cupid shows that one can free oneself from the mundane "shell" by breaking it open. Taking the sequence of Plates 5 to 6, we see that "Fire" was inside the shell; becoming a little child, he could break out instead of spearing himself.

Gates 7. A boy who combines the forward movement of the hatching cupid and the open body and weapon wielding of the youth in Fire tries to use his hat as the Eve mother in Plate 1 used her apron, to trap female spirits within the veil wherein the dead in spirit dwell. There is something to hope for, however, in his "Alas!" (and more wisdom in his face in *b* perhaps than in *a*). We at least can see that the forward and upward flight promised by the wings and look of cupid is possible (the top figure, a naked version of the guiding spirit of the title page, directs attention upward), although collapse into earth is possible also, as the lower female demonstrates.

Gates 8. Youth with no shield (become shameless?) but with fierce barbs on his spear can turn back from forward flight if "hatcht & nurst" in "Vain-glory" (*Keys*). King David cries out at the mutual destruction offered by his son Absalom (see 2 Samuel 18:33). His sword is a scepter too heavy for mortal wielding (see *French Revolution* 4). The throne of stony power for which they contend is death's mausoleum with no door. Its back suggests a windowless apse or synagogue wall. Thematically related is the back of Urizen's throne in *Europe* 10, which suggests a cathedral doorway blocked by his bulk and book. The tree overhead is flourishing; compare *Songs* 29.

Gates 9. A young man with hat properly on his head is going up steeply toward a waxing ("Climbing") moon. As he mounts the sky ladder he looks toward an embracing couple, the woman not too busy to wave or direct him upward. The seven stars seem well organized. This seems an auspicious rising into Air.

Gates 10. Water again. But the cry "Help! Help!" cannot go unheeded; we have moved toward energetic desire, from the Narcissism (or solipsism) of Plate 2 toward a world in which one knows there are others and hopes that they are friends. (Compare Tharmas in *FZ* 44.)

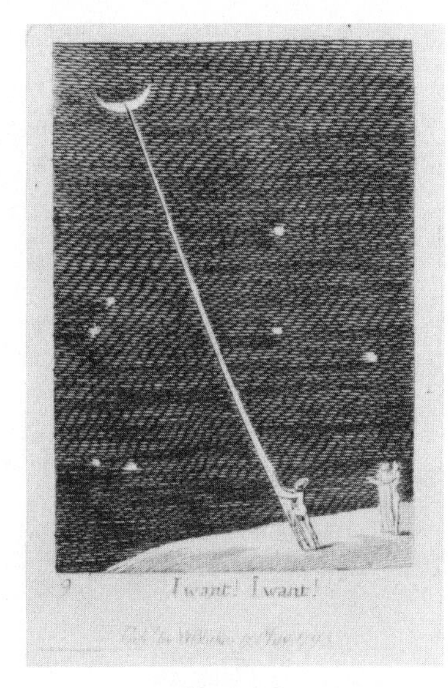

Gates a9

Gates a10

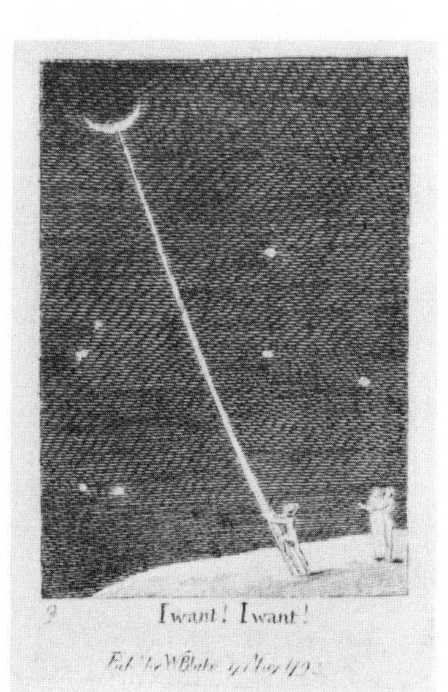

Gates b9

Gates b10

Gates a11

Gates a12

Gates b11

Gates b12

Gates 11. Youth going very much in the right direction now, right hand hailing the sunlight which he perceives, may seem threatened by Aged Ignorance—but what this King David cannot perceive is how little human flight depends on outward plumage. The only things subject to this "Holy and cold" Atropos are "Sublunary Things" such as wings not in use.

In *b* the forest behind Age is cavernous, making him seem a male variant of the sibyl in Plate 16, and the adolescent cupid is given procreative organs.

Gates 12. Inside a stone cell, sitting on a stone ledge and on rush matting, the sublunary Ugolino family are seen as one crazed father (the caption identifies him as Dante's Ugolino, jailed by priestly "vengeance") and four dying children. In Dante these are sons and grandsons, but Blake's figures rather suggest daughters (beside him) and sons (in opposite corners). The father's hair shows wild centrifugal terror; his stare is not at us but at the fancied total power of the priest. We are jailed who lack wings to fly above the nets of religion. The two "Closed" children, with legs crossed, hold their bodies pyramided into the armless stasis of their father. Those in their separate corners press their hands to the floor, but one seems rigid and hopelessly downcast, the other still flexing arms, legs, and torso and looking and calling upward. If the father is being solipsistic for the family, contemplating its suicide (like the Narcissist of Plate 2), one of the children is wakefully watching his face (like the women hoping against hope in the battlefield in *America* i and ii), and the one crying Help! seems bent on getting up. Yet the flickering spirits and wasting bodies and *almost* windowless wall here, by comparison with the variant of this scene in *Marriage* 16 where the full flesh of the pictured family of "giants" emphasizes the reversibility of a moment of incarceration which a moment of vision can transform, imply confinement endured to the moment of unendurability.

Blake himself, of course, knew that the children were boys. He had this to say to critics who mistook their sex in Fuseli's painting of Ugolino: "whether boy or girl signifies not, (but the critic must be a fool who has not read Dante, and who does not know a boy from a girl)" (*P&P* 705).

Gates 13. Coming with the swiftness of Mercy this contrary family scene has a caption that we may take for both this and the preceding death-cell pictures: "Fear & Hope are—Vision." This emblem and its message are overlooked by interpreters of Blake who argue that "To Tirzah" (*Songs* 52) with its caption, "It is Raised a Spiritual Body," represents a great change in Blake's view of the sublunary body occurring a decade or so after 1793. The Ugolino family, letting their bodies and eyes close, are closed in, and returning to, the earth. The family here, done with weeping over the dead body, look up in hope become vision. (The Notebook drawing is captioned "What we hope we see.")

The spiritual body, beginning a flight upward without need of wings, lingers to instruct the startled eldest son (whose fingers are spread but whose toes are flexed for springing), the cheered daughter—or wife, as the more aged face in *b* suggests—and the amazed but attentive younger girl and boy. In *a* these two whisper to each other with rather noncommittal faces. In *b* they recognize that something momentous is going on; the girl takes in every gesture, the boy watches us to see whether we understand too. Further iconic emphasis is given by the strong bright halo and gleam around the more humanly impressive visionary elder, the "Immortal Man that cannot die" (*Keys*). A contrary vision in the title page of Experience (*Songs* 29) shows son and daughter seeing only their parents' mortal bodies.

Gates 14. The traveller strides swiftly toward the sunlight (his legs serving as a sort of sundial) and keeps clear of the forest. Equipped with a broad-brimmed hat (like Christian's in illustrations of *The Pilgrim's Progress* made by Stothard and by Blake) and staff and tail coat, he has no visible wallet or book—needing only the sun's light which he beholds. His action reshapes the series of preceding emblems, giving them purposive direction, making actual the potential journeying implied by the cocoon's face, the struggler in Earth, the flexed legs of the hatching cupid, the halted stride of the chasing boy, the flexed hands of sons. Has the theme of potential upward flight, enacted in Plate 7, indicated by pointing hands in Plates 10 and 13 and by upraised eyes in 6 and 13, and symbolized

Gates a13

Gates a14

Gates b13

Gates b14

Gates a15

Gates a16

Gates b15

Gates b16

by the cocoon, the ladder, and the wings (of cupid and of the travelling youth), now been clipped? Or must one, as caption and *Keys* now insist, go into mortal night to reach eternal day, down to rise up; must one close one's worldly labors to get "away"? The traveller hastens through "evening shades" toward the light of the sun.

Gates 15. Did the traveller have this dark night as his destination? Did he hasten because he knew he could never reach the sun before it set, that the evening shades would darken to death? Is this old man our traveller forty years later, his staff a crutch, hat gone, fashionable coat a nightgown? Somehow his spry bare foot and forward thrust of body, not so much driven by the wind as making canny use of its current as he makes a decisive high stride over the threshold of Death's Door, seem to continue the purpose and even glad haste of the younger traveller. Note that the doorway is of hewn stone, the door of hewn oak (as the grain indicates), nature shaped by art.

In an earlier version (*Notebook* 16 and 17) the younger traveller, "glad when [he] can find the grave," gestures bravely with his fingers out (as the fingers of the son in Plate 13) in the face of a skull-headed, scythe-bearing Death inside the door, for he is going to meet his family. On the merely natural level (we learn from the *Keys*), just as the mother "found" man in the garden, so the natural man "found" the door of death open, and found "the Worm Weaving in the Ground." In a late version of this "What next?" emblem, revised for Blair's *Grave,* a woven pallet is shown within the door: this is only a resting place on the journey of vision.

Gates 16. What Job in his despair "said to the Worm" is a good definition of visions of fear. The mortal bodies found beneath a tree (Plate 1) melt back into the ground, gradually losing individuality. Of the three human heads beside the worm, only the first has distinct profile, and beard. The worm coming out of the earth spirals loosely, like a vine around a tree, about the sitting figure, a human vision of the traditional skeletal, cowled Death: the human form of natural death. We may imagine a cavity or tomb of some kind beneath the trees or roots behind this sibyl, but there is no natural way to Paradise. The traveller whom we seek is risen, has left his staff and garments. The worm and the grave clothes are all our natural eyes can see until the artist shows us this enigmatic human, to let the mental traveller see himself, his hopes and fears. In short, if we expect Life as the natural sequel to mortality, we go back to the button-molder. The imagination's way, made so explicit in Plate 13, is indicated for us this final time only by the straight staff's pointing and the poised silence of the instructress whose eyes are mirrors for our thoughts. Children or sexes having read this far must *see* for themselves.

For extensive discussion of the function of this emblem, and the original forms and interrelations of the whole series, see my edition of the *Notebook*.

Gates 17. (Greatly enlarged.) The edition "For Children" was complete with emblem 16. These two plates of Keys and the following Epilogue were added in the edition "For the Sexes." Faintly engraved figures invite the sexes, an embracing woman and man leaning against the first letter, to accept the "marriage" of soul and body, Life and Death, all Contraries into One Humanity. And perhaps what the garment-trailing or scroll-garmented figure rising beside "Keys" is holding up is a small pyramid of fire, a proper spiritual Key if we know *Job* 18; indeed this may be a miniature version of that plate—a pyramid on top of a cube (earth) modified to a pyramid atop a ring. This and the following plate have been enlarged, for the visibility of the small details.

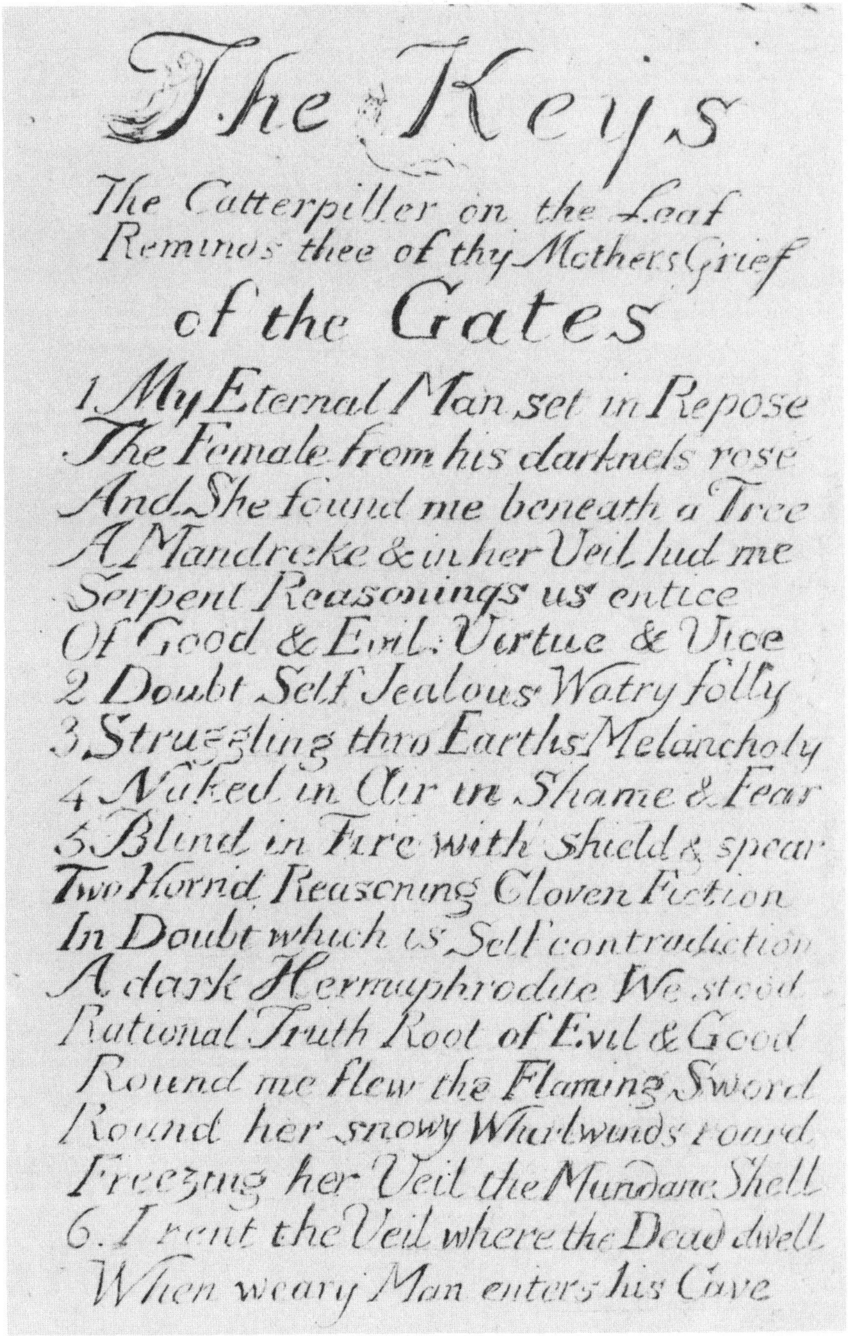

The Keys
The Catterpiller on the Leaf
Reminds thee of thy Mothers Grief
of the Gates
1 My Eternal Man set in Repose
The Female from his darkness rose
And She found me beneath a Tree
A Mandrake & in her Veil hid me
Serpent Reasonings us entice
Of Good & Evil: Virtue & Vice
2 Doubt Self Jealous Watry folly
3 Struggling thro Earths Melancholy
4 Naked in Air in Shame & Fear
5 Blind in Fire with shield & spear
Two Horrid Reasoning Cloven Fiction
In Doubt which is Self contradiction
A dark Hermaphrodite We stood
Rational Truth Root of Evil & Good
Round me flew the Flaming Sword
Round her snowy Whirlwinds roard
Freezing her Veil the Mundane Shell
6 I rent the Veil where the Dead dwell
When weary Man enters his Cave

Gates 17 (actual size $2\frac{1}{2} \times 3\frac{1}{2}$ in.)

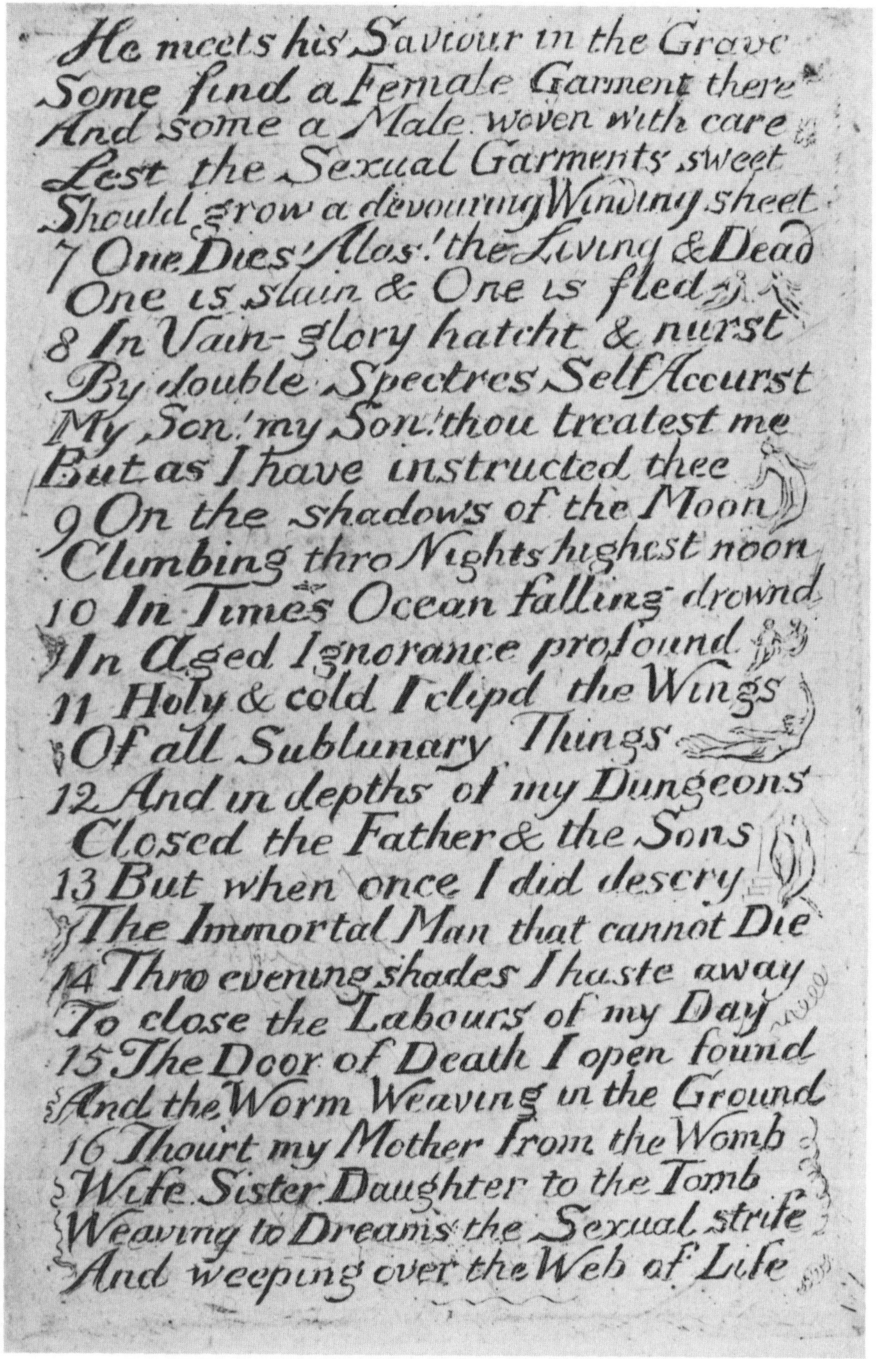

He meets his Saviour in the Grave
Some find a Female Garment there
And some a Male woven with care
Lest the Sexual Garments sweet
Should grow a devouring Winding sheet
7 One Dies! Alas! the Living & Dead
One is slain & One is fled
8 In Vain-glory hatcht & nurst
By double Spectres Self Accurst
My Son! my Son! thou treatest me
But as I have instructed thee
9 On the shadows of the Moon
Climbing thro Nights highest noon
10 In Times Ocean falling drownd
In Aged Ignorance profound
11 Holy & cold I clipd the Wings
Of all Sublunary Things
12 And in depths of my Dungeons
Closed the Father & the Sons
13 But when once I did descry
The Immortal Man that cannot Die
14 Thro evening shades I haste away
To close the Labours of my Day
15 The Door of Death I open found
And the Worm Weaving in the Ground
16 Thourt my Mother from the Womb
Wife Sister Daughter to the Tomb
Weaving to Dreams the Sexual strife
And weeping over the Web of Life

Gates 18 (actal size 2½×3½ in.)

Gates 18. (Greatly enlarged.) Tiny blossoms (or winged dresses like doll clothes) at the edges of lines 2 and 4 stand for the female and male garments. Male and female figures, naked, fly toward each other after verse 7 (to show the reunion of "Living & Dead"). An upward climbing figure with arms out in wonder faces up beside verse 9 to translate the ladder-climbing of Plate 9 into resurrection. The hands are like the infant Christ's in *The Assumption of the Virgin*. The body is bent somewhat like that of "William" receiving the star in *Milton* 32, more like that of Abel "surrounded by innocents" in *A Vision of the Last Judgment* (*Dict* figure 61) but seen from behind. In verse 10 the apostrophe on "Time's" is a flying bird; an angel flexes a broad unclipped wing in front of Aged Ignorance, and a human flies without wings beyond him (trailing a scrolled garment?). In 11, to laugh at "Sublunary Things," a dancing child with right hand high marks the left margin; a soaring cloaked figure in the left margin points over to the words and up to infinity in a variant of the gestures in Plate 13. After "descry" in verse 13 an embracing couple (compare *Jerusalem* 96) are at the steps of a Gothic door like the picture of the grave as "Heaven's golden Gate" in *To the Queen* (Blake's *Blair* i). A rejoicing boy precedes the next line. And once this 13th Key is descried, the rest is empty fabric. The only adornment of the remaining verses, which concern weaving and weeping over "the Web of life," consists of twisted threads in the left and right and bottom margins. If we have understood the "Vision" emblem, we scarcely need reminding how foolish it is to question corporeal doors and worm and tomb "concerning a Sight" (*P&P* 555).

Gates 19 (Epilogue). A thirteen-coiled serpent (ten coils actually numbered) swims in an invisible element under "This World" (see *Jerusalem* 93). A sleeping traveller, naked, his hand on his staff though a spider has spun a web at its top, lies under a hill beyond which dawn is bursting on all sides. The deity that has resided in his sleeping breast, a black bat nightmare vision of Satan pretending to power over sun, moon, and stars, must vanish like a raven of dawn since shown up as mere Dunce—yet a Lucifer (feckless but better help than no dreams at all) for temporarily lost travellers.

(An instructive analogy is the watercolor illustration for *Paradise Regained* IV 426–31, in which Christ is the sleeping traveller, just awakened by Morning, a female pilgrim with staff, who chases off phantoms, one bat-winged.)

To The Accuser who is
The God of This World

Truly My Satan thou art but a Dunce
And dost not know the Garment from the Man
Every Harlot was a Virgin once
Nor canst thou ever change Kate into Nan

Tho thou art Worshipd by the Names Divine
Of Jesus & Jehovah thou art still
The Son of Morn in weary Nights decline
The lost Travellers Dream under the Hill

Gates 19

Jerusalem 1^E^

JERUSALEM
THE EMANATION OF THE GIANT ALBION

(Reduced from about 9 by 6¼ inches)

FEW VARIANTS OCCUR among the five complete copies of *Jerusalem,* only one of which, copy E, is in color. Copies ACDF are printed from the same state of the plates, in black—with some retouching in copy C with sepia and chinese white (and green tinting of Plate 16), some retouching in copy D with india ink and slight washing in brown, and some grey washes and india ink in copy F. Copy B, consisting of chapter 1 only, is fully colored but quite differently from copy E. Copies EFB are now available in Blake Trust facsimile editions. When salient color differences occur in the first chapter (between E and B) they are noted; all subsequent color references are of course to copy E. Several proof pages exist and are cited when picture details are notably different. For a discussion of plate details see my article, "The Suppressed and Altered Passages in Blake's *Jerusalem,*" *Studies in Bibliography* XVII (1964) 1–54.

References to the commentary of Joseph Wicksteed published with the Blake Trust facsimiles of copies CE are here designated (W). For other abbreviations see Introduction. The arrangement of plates in chapter 2 follows that in copies ACF, with the pagination of copies DE given in brackets. Copy E is used for Plates 1, 99, and 100, where important details are left to the imagination in uncolored copies. Copy D is used for all the rest.

Jerusalem 1^E^ (frontispiece). An earlier state of this plate (reproduced in the Blake Trust facsimile volume of copy C) contains inscriptions on the wall and archway, in the etching and reinforced by pen and ink. These were subsequently deleted or walled up by the cutting of further lines of engraving for the shapes of bricks and stones. Plates 1 and 2 are unique in copy E in having ornamental borders outside the framing lines.

Los steps down across the threshold of a presumably oaken door (a gothic postern: W) in a stone or brick wall with arched doorway. It resembles the "wicket gate" in Blake's tenth and eleventh designs for *Pilgrim's Progress,* in the first of which Christian knocks at the gate and in the second is embraced by a bearded, haloed man as in Plate 99. Los's hat and garment and his stride suggest the traveller of *Gates* 14, while the wind from the opening that blows his hair and garment back contrasts with the wind from an opposite direction in *Gates* 15 which hastens an aged traveller into Death's Door, unarched. Los sees where he is going, carrying a sun for light instead of a staff for support. His left hand may have pushed the door open (compare Urizen in *Urizen* 23 and 27 with a similar Diogenes lantern but with hand more simply pushing); it is now in a gesture of surprise and recognition—insofar as it is like the raised hand in *Notebook* 16g of a traveller approaching wife and children in death's doorway, changing to the same hand's gesture in *Notebook* 17c where it serves to greet the family while pushing aside a skeletal image of Death. Perhaps the greeting here is for Jerusalem and her daughters, whom we first see together in Plate 46[32]. A different analogue is the Blair illustration of *The Soul Exploring the Recesses of the Grave.*

We may suppose that Los in his London human form as William Blake is entering a dark place with his illumination, as Jesus enters Hell with his key (the border[E] shows thorns below his feet, Satanic bat wings in the corners, empty manacles dangling in the side margins); that he is leading us toward a scene of action; that his arresting hand invites our attention; that he is preparing to give himself, as Milton on the title page of *Milton* (though note their mirror-opposite positions). In the words of the erased graffiti on the wall, he is entering the "Void, outside of Existence," which, when entered, we shall see become "a Womb . . . Albions Couch . . . Albions lovely Land." According to 45:3–5, Los with "his globe of fire" is searching "the interiors of Albions Bosom," searching "the tempters out." Compare and contrast Plates 97 and 100. (There are analogies also in *America* 1, the chained hero in the breached wall.)

Jerusalem 2 (title page). (From copy D, as are all plates not otherwise designated.) In the absence of "The Giant Albion" his emanation Jerusalem sleeps, her human form woven in threefold wings of potential butterfly flight into human form divine. (Los in Plates

Jerusalem 2[D]

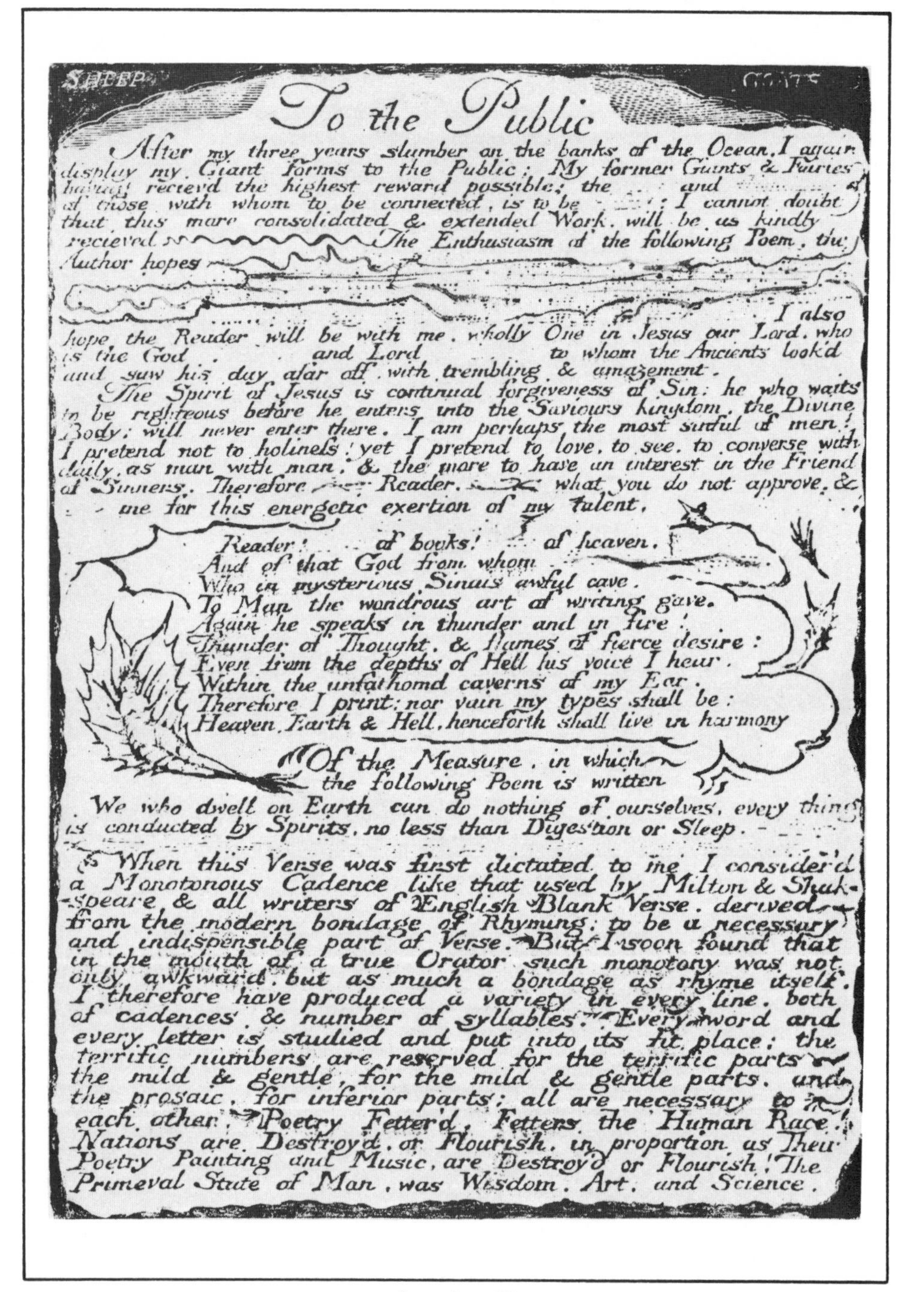

SHEEP GOATS

To the Public

After my three years slumber on the banks of the Ocean, I again display my Giant forms to the Public: My former Giants & Fairies having reciev'd the highest reward possible: the ... and ... of those with whom to be connected, is to be ...: I cannot doubt that this more consolidated & extended Work, will be as kindly recieved ... The Enthusiasm of the following Poem, the Author hopes ...

... I also hope the Reader will be with me, wholly One in Jesus our Lord, who is the God ... and Lord ... to whom the Ancients look'd and saw his day afar off, with trembling & amazement.

The Spirit of Jesus is continual forgiveness of Sin: he who waits to be righteous before he enters into the Saviours kingdom, the Divine Body; will never enter there. I am perhaps the most sinful of men! I pretend not to holiness: yet I pretend to love, to see, to converse with daily, as man with man, & the more to have an interest in the Friend of Sinners. Therefore ... Reader, ... what you do not approve, & ... me for this energetic exertion of my talent.

Reader! ... of books! ... of heaven,
And of that God from whom ...
Who in mysterious Sinais awful cave
To Man the wondrous art of writing gave,
Again he speaks in thunder and in fire!
Thunder of Thought, & flames of fierce desire:
Even from the depths of Hell his voice I hear,
Within the unfathomd caverns of my Ear.
Therefore I print; nor vain my types shall be:
Heaven, Earth & Hell, henceforth shall live in harmony

Of the Measure, in which the following Poem is written

We who dwell on Earth can do nothing of ourselves, every thing is conducted by Spirits, no less than Digestion or Sleep. ...

When this Verse was first dictated to me I consider'd a Monotonous Cadence like that used by Milton & Shakspeare & all writers of English Blank Verse, derived from the modern bondage of Rhyming; to be a necessary and indispensible part of Verse. But I soon found that in the mouth of a true Orator such monotony was not only awkward, but as much a bondage as rhyme itself. I therefore have produced a variety in every line, both of cadences & number of syllables. Every word and every letter is studied and put into its fit place: the terrific numbers are reserved for the terrific parts—the mild & gentle, for the mild & gentle parts, and the prosaic, for inferior parts: all are necessary to each other. Poetry Fetter'd, Fetters the Human Race! Nations are Destroy'd, or Flourish, in proportion as Their Poetry Painting and Music, are Destroy'd or Flourish! The Primeval State of Man, was Wisdom, Art, and Science.

Jerusalem 3D

85–86 describes her as depicted here.) Emblematically she lies in the position of the infant cocoon of *Gates* i. But head and arm fall in a parodistic easing or normalization of the grotesque *Nightmare* painting of Henry Fuseli. There the blushing dreams of the maiden include an evil gnome squatting on her breast to corrupt them; here a squatting butterfly-bat-like woman above Jerusalem echoes the concerned look and gesture of Los in Plate 1—or mocks them. A less ambiguous mourner on the right has eagle or angel wings, but her mourning hides her face. We see that Jerusalem's three sets of wings have contraries within—bat-like terminals on some—and that her future can follow the waxing moon on her right or the waning on her left. The sun and earth on her "canopy" wings (86:9) are rather dark: her threefold body is the starry night sky. (A third orb—a moon?—is split into two hemispheres, or horns, by her extended hair.) The true sun is only (but gloriously) promised in the coloring of the page (a universal rainbow spectrumE: forty-nine colors, the rainbow's seven seen sevenfold). The bracelet on her right arm signifies bondage to this world. And in copy B, as Keynes points out, the top wing membranes are shaped as the pincers of an earwig. Her daughters, also winged human forms, of Beulah, begin the poem assuming she is dead (for Albion is fallen: compare the mourning women in *America*). The bat-winged will emerge as Vala; the bird-winged, with waxing moon and bright stars, perhaps as Erin; the two green figures flying at the top (butterfly-like with antennae, bee-like with crescent tiara) are fairies urging us to start reading at the letter "J." The large grey bird flying diagonally up toward "Jerusalem" will reappear on Plates 54 and 61 as a dove of peace, though its shape may remind us of earlier eagles, its angle of flight of the birds of *Songs* 1 and *America* 13. (In B the antennae of the butterfly beside the "J" are painted as cat's ears, and the human part of the figure is given a whiskered face like that of the cat in Blake's illustrations for Gray's cat Ode.)

Smaller figures cheering our way along the title are a gold fly, a red and gold human rising without wings, and a gold moth above and in the "E," a tiptoe male dancer who points to the second "The" (Albion as "a Regency beau": W), three different small insects on "Giant," mere suggestions of forms inside "a" and "n" but a man in the curve of a scroll between these letters (perhaps a piper with back to us), another grey bird flying toward "Albion," and sketchy forms within the word.

Of the flanking mourners (whose flower caps are like the cap on "Earth" in Fuseli's frontispiece to Darwin's *Loves of the Plants*) the Vala figure at left has thin crescents (not in BE) within her wings; her right hand has the gesture of the rich mother with dead infant in *Notebook* 83a; her left cherishes herself (her squatting is not on Jerusalem but on the curve of "A"). The figure weeping into her hands is closing her face like the sad mother in *Europe* 5; near the crescent in her wing are two large stars (the lower one removed in B, the upper in E). Ingenuity can discern a progression of moon phases culminating in the tiara of the bee-winged fairy at top with a dawn moon. In E, clouds (in a pale grey border) surround the whole plate, only to be dispelled when the true sun rises.

Jerusalem 3. The words "Sheep" and "Goats" at top, on an earth curve, suggest a Judgment scene in which the judging-forgiving Christ would be sitting just above the page (his name appears in top center, Plate 4). Viewed as winged spirits, the figures on either side of the central poem might seem saved souls rising; viewed, rather more bleakly, as leaves, they are all falling. The one on the left and the lower of the two on the right are close enough to be seen as humans—simpler versions of the winged humans of the title page. The largest is like the human cocoon on a leaf in *Gates* i, but with roots suggesting a mandrake. Her root-feet are near the discussion of spirits' conducting what is done "on Earth," but she is uprooted and rose-tinted; so we may suppose that her open eyes and up-pointing wings mark a waking and arising stage beyond the sleeping of the Jerusalem leaf-butterfly on the title page.

At the top edge of cloud after the poem's first line is a bird in a nest (fairly clear in B).

Jerusalem 4 (chapter 1). At top left a benevolent naked female (a reader's guide into the poem) continues the suggested upward movement from the sleeping Jerusalem (Plate 2) to the waking cocoon (Plate 3) to wingless soaring; there are wing-like cloud edges behind her that suggest the continuity. She points to a Blakean Greek motto (Jesus only) in a slender waxing moon among stars (the large star above "S" lacking in B) and assists a

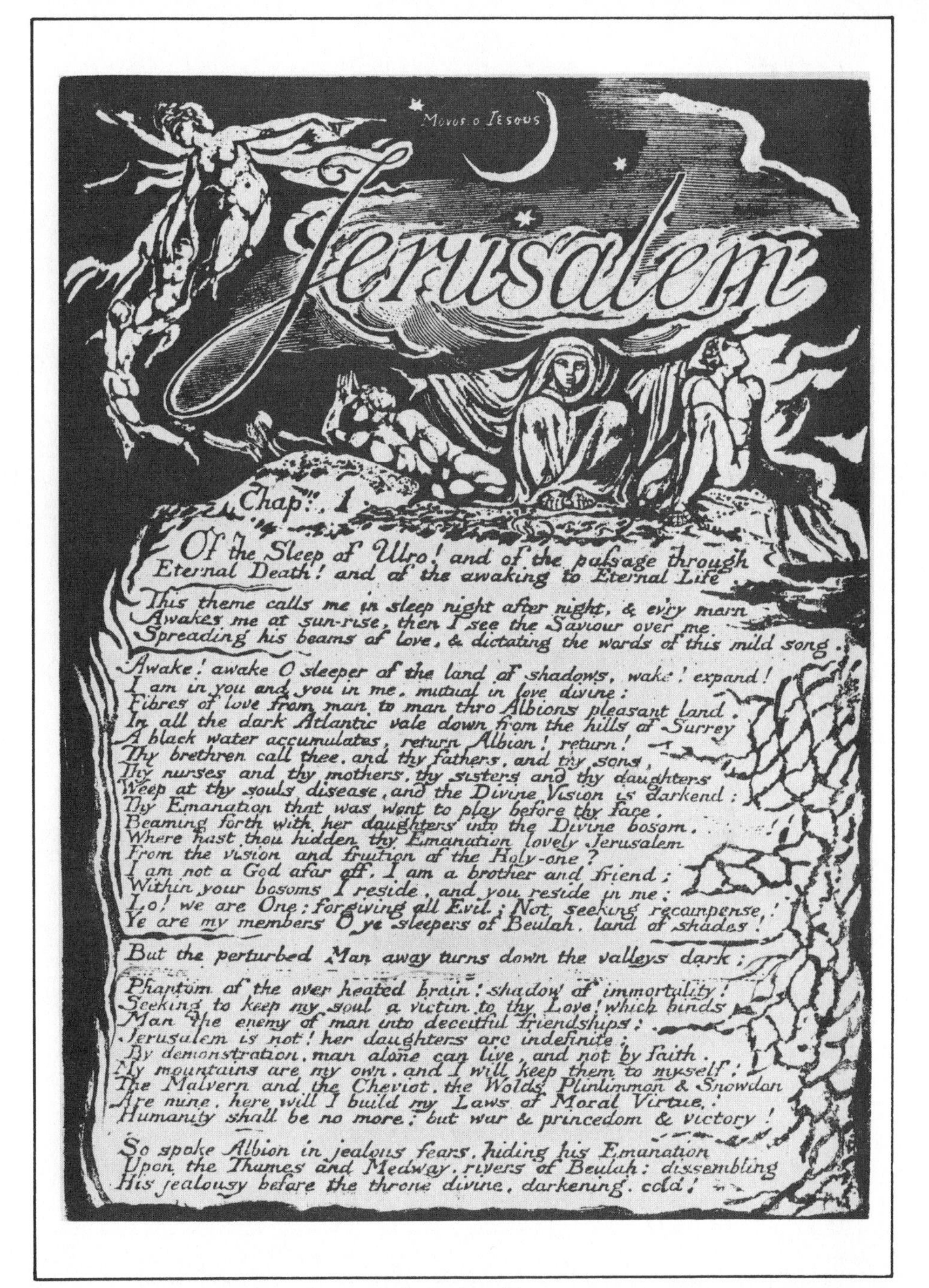

Μονος ο Ιεσους

Jerusalem

Chap: 1

Of the Sleep of Ulro! and of the passage through
Eternal Death! and of the awaking to Eternal Life.

This theme calls me in sleep night after night, & ev'ry morn
Awakes me at sun-rise, then I see the Saviour over me
Spreading his beams of love, & dictating the words of this mild song.

Awake! awake O sleeper of the land of shadows, wake! expand!
I am in you and you in me, mutual in love divine:
Fibres of love from man to man thro Albions pleasant land.
In all the dark Atlantic vale down from the hills of Surrey
A black water accumulates, return Albion! return!
Thy brethren call thee, and thy fathers, and thy sons,
Thy nurses and thy mothers, thy sisters and thy daughters
Weep at thy souls disease, and the Divine Vision is darkend:
Thy Emanation that was wont to play before thy face,
Beaming forth with her daughters into the Divine bosom.
Where hast thou hidden thy Emanation lovely Jerusalem
From the vision and fruition of the Holy-one?
I am not a God afar off, I am a brother and friend;
Within your bosoms I reside, and you reside in me:
Lo! we are One; forgiving all Evil; Not seeking recompense!
Ye are my members O ye sleepers of Beulah, land of shades!

But the perturbed Man away turns down the valleys dark;

Phantom of the over heated brain! shadow of immortality!
Seeking to keep my soul a victim to thy Love! which binds
Man the enemy of man into deceitful friendships:
Jerusalem is not! her daughters are indefinite:
By demonstration, man alone can live, and not by faith.
My mountains are my own, and I will keep them to myself!
The Malvern and the Cheviot, the Wolds Plinlimmon & Snowdon
Are mine, here will I build my Laws of Moral Virtue!
Humanity shall be no more: but war & princedom & victory!

So spoke Albion in jealous fears, hiding his Emanation
Upon the Thames and Medway, rivers of Beulah: dissembling
His jealousy before the throne divine, darkening, cold!

Jerusalem 4[D]

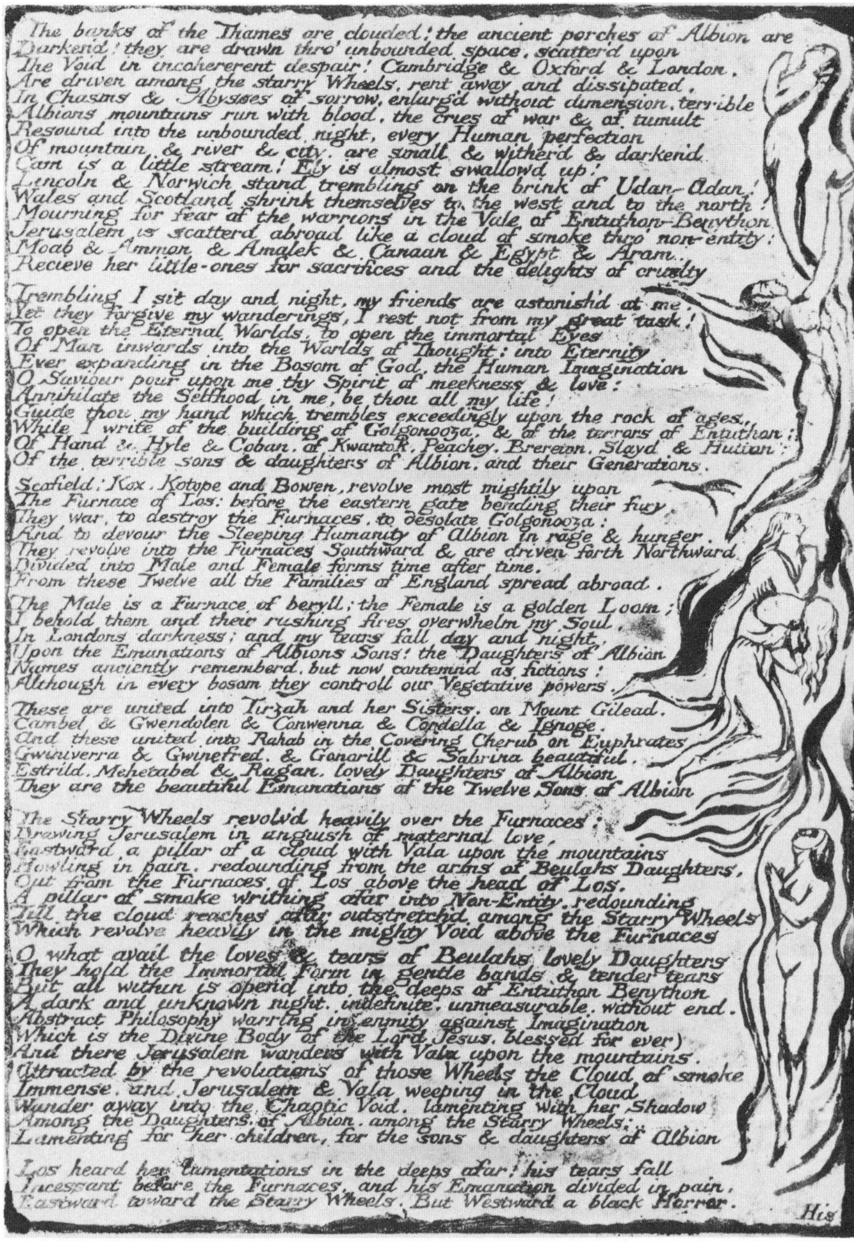

The banks of the Thames are clouded! the ancient porches of Albion are
Darkend! they are drawn thro' unbounded space, scatterd upon
The Void in incoherent despair! Cambridge & Oxford & London,
Are driven among the starry Wheels, rent away and dissipated,
In Chasms & Abysses of sorrow, enlarg'd without dimension, terrible
Albions mountains run with blood, the cries of war & of tumult
Resound into the unbounded night, every Human perfection
Of mountain & river & city, are small & witherd & darkend
Cam is a little stream! Ely is almost swallowd up!
Lincoln & Norwich stand trembling on the brink of Udan-Adan!
Wales and Scotland shrink themselves to the west and to the north!
Mourning for fear of the warriors in the Vale of Entuthon-Benython
Jerusalem is scatterd abroad like a cloud of smoke thro' non-entity:
Moab & Ammon & Amalek & Canaan & Egypt & Aram
Recieve her little-ones for sacrifices and the delights of cruelty

Trembling I sit day and night, my friends are astonish'd at me.
Yet they forgive my wanderings, I rest not from my great task!
To open the Eternal Worlds, to open the immortal Eyes
Of Man inwards into the Worlds of Thought: into Eternity
Ever expanding in the Bosom of God, the Human Imagination
O Saviour pour upon me thy Spirit of meekness & love:
Annihilate the Selfhood in me, be thou all my life!
Guide thou my hand which trembles exceedingly upon the rock of ages,
While I write of the building of Golgonooza, & of the terrors of Entuthon:
Of Hand & Hyle & Coban, of Kwantok, Peachey, Brereton, Slayd & Hutton:
Of the terrible sons & daughters of Albion, and their Generations.

Scofield! Kox, Kotope and Bowen, revolve most mightily upon
The Furnace of Los: before the eastern gate bending their fury.
They war, to destroy the Furnaces, to desolate Golgonooza:
And to devour the Sleeping Humanity of Albion in rage & hunger.
They revolve into the Furnaces Southward & are driven forth Northward
Divided into Male and Female forms time after time.
From these Twelve all the Families of England spread abroad.

The Male is a Furnace of beryll; the Female is a golden Loom;
I behold them and their rushing fires overwhelm my Soul,
In Londons darkness; and my tears fall day and night,
Upon the Emanations of Albions Sons! the Daughters of Albion
Names anciently remembred, but now contemn'd as fictions!
Although in every bosom they controll our Vegetative powers.

These are united into Tirzah and her Sisters, on Mount Gilead,
Cambel & Gwendolen & Conwenna & Cordella & Ignoge.
And these united into Rahab in the Covering Cherub on Euphrates
Gwiniverra & Gwinefred, & Gonorill & Sabrina beautiful,
Estrild, Mehetabel & Ragan, lovely Daughters of Albion
They are the beautiful Emanations of the Twelve Sons of Albion

The Starry Wheels revolv'd heavily over the Furnaces;
Drawing Jerusalem in anguish of maternal love,
Eastward a pillar of a cloud with Vala upon the mountains
Howling in pain, redounding from the arms of Beulahs Daughters,
Out from the Furnaces of Los above the head of Los.
A pillar of smoke writhing afar into Non-Entity, redounding
Till the cloud reaches afar outstretchd among the Starry Wheels
Which revolve heavily in the mighty Void above the Furnaces

O what avail the loves & tears of Beulahs lovely Daughters
They hold the Immortal Form in gentle bands & tender tears
But all within is opend into the deeps of Entuthon Benython
A dark and unknown night, indefinite, unmeasurable, without end.
Abstract Philosophy warring in enmity against Imagination
(Which is the Divine Body of the Lord Jesus, blessed for ever)
And there Jerusalem wanders with Vala upon the mountains,
Attracted by the revolutions of those Wheels the Cloud of smoke
Immense, and Jerusalem & Vala weeping in the Cloud
Wander away into the Chaotic Void, lamenting with her Shadow
Among the Daughters of Albion, among the Starry Wheels;
Lamenting for her children, for the sons & daughters of Albion

Los heard her lamentations in the deeps afar! his tears fall
Incessant before the Furnaces, and his Emanation divided in pain,
Eastward toward the Starry Wheels. But Westward a black Horror,

His

Jerusalem 5D

swirl of three rising naked children. These women are, in effect, Jerusalem and her daughters (see Plate 46).

Below the cloud-borne title is a *mis*judgment scene, presided over not by Jesus but by a cowled sibyl sitting on green land (compare the sibyl of *Gates* 16). With gestures like Enitharmon's in *Urizen* 13, she divides two images of naked Albion—at right a giant sitting on the cliffs of Dover, at left a willing follower of the emanations soaring toward Jesus. The sibyl's grip on the Albion she is misguiding "spans" his head. (In E his right hand grips a stone or bone, his left a fold of black cloth.) The full picture adumbrates the full plot of the poem, while illustrating the opening lines: Albion, accepting the isolation of sitting on his cliffs and mountains, will "build my Laws of Moral Virtue" (30)—which are drawn down the right margin as a Web of Religion (compare Urizen's woven darkness over the sun in *Song of Los* 1). Implied is the birth of Adam into the material world (*Forms* 191), with a regrouping of the sequence of the *America* Preludium (*Forms* 101).

The Albion figure turning toward Jerusalem at the left has his palms together like the youth worshipfully accepting the sibyl's instructions in *America* 14; in this contrary scene the gesture signifies active prayer, accompanied by diving up and out, away from Vala.

Jerusalem 5. In the marginal drawings here and on Plate 7 are shown samples of the plight of the "sons & daughters of Albion, and their Generations" (26) "Divided into Male and Female forms" (32). Here five females represent "Jerusalem . . . scattered abroad like a cloud of smoke" (13). At bottom "Jerusalem in anguish of maternal love" in a green and pink pillar of flame (image of anguish) (47–51) from Los's furnaces (see Plate 6); above her, two daughters, one bent over like Oothoon in *Visions* i but in a gown, disarranged, the other pleading in "loves & tears" unavailing (54). Able to soar upward, but not in harmony, are a naked (but cinctured*) open-armed daughter and a snowy white daughter in prayerful attitude. The open arms foreshadow Plate 99; the crossed ankles of Jerusalem in the flame foreshadow Plate 96.

The open-armed daughter might be mistaken for a man, in the unpainted copies.

Jerusalem 6. Los, the prophetic blacksmith, heroic form of the poet and artist himself, seems with his anvil and hammer the base of a solid pillar (compare the stone steps behind William and Robert in *Milton* 32 and 37). But what emerges above is mostly billowing smoke, for the spectre interposes his canopy of bat wings and distracts Los with arguments of despair—while covering his own ears from the noise of the furnace and from hearing what Los answers (6:7; 7:1–7). Los's mouth is now shut; his tongs and hammer are idle (the hammer and its handle genitally positioned, a positive symbol but in this context ironic); the spectre ought to stop his howling and get to work pumping the bellows. (The top chain of the bellows seems attached or attachable to the spectre's left wing. In copy B the tongs are omitted.)

We may note how spacial relation replaces temporal cause and effect. Because Los faints at the anvil he is haunted by his spectral self-shadows; *or* because they are in his mind, he faints at the forge (see *Forms* 92).

Jerusalem 6D

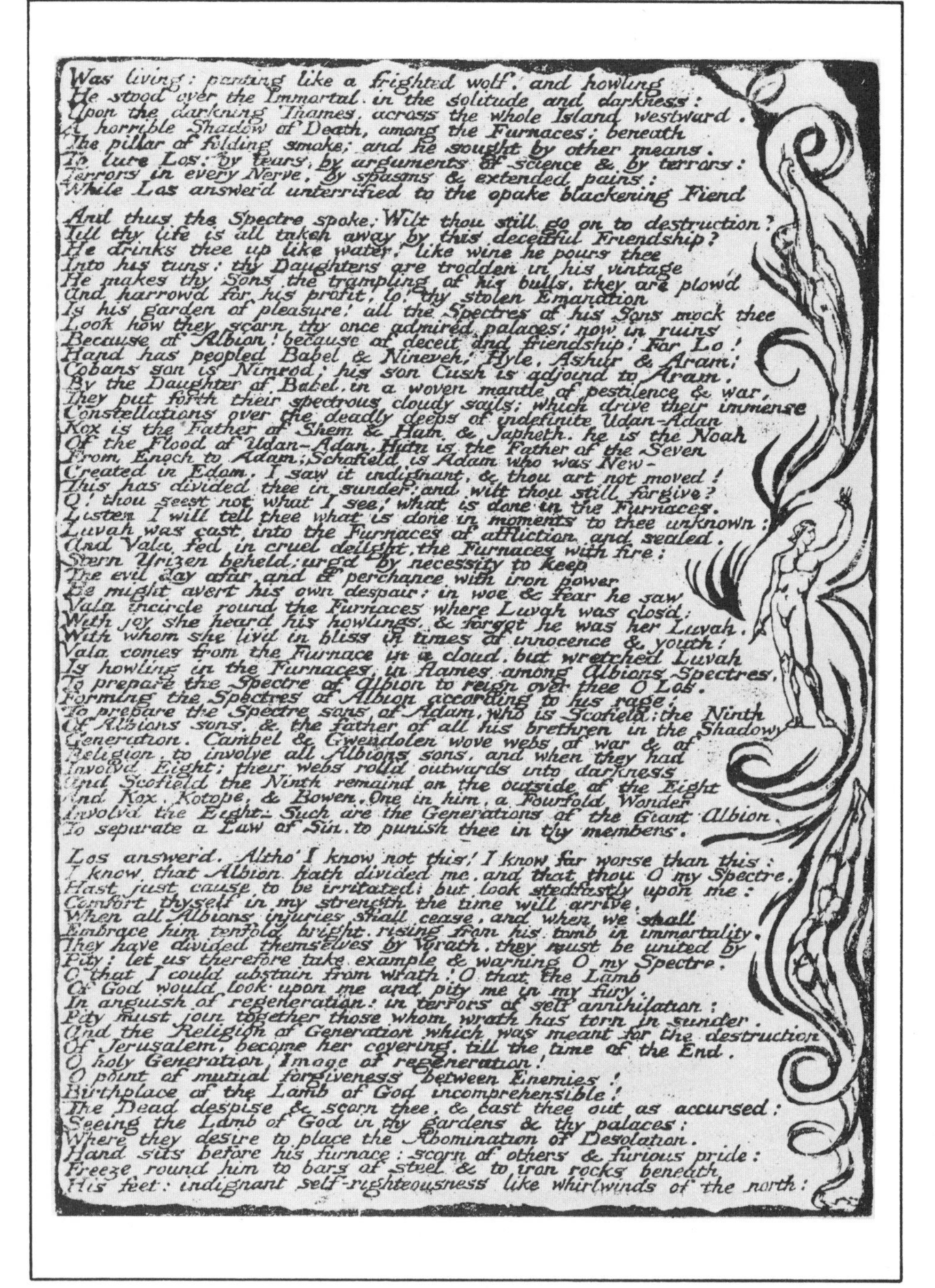

Was living: panting like a frighted wolf, and howling
He stood over the Immortal, in the solitude and darkness:
Upon the darkning Thames, across the whole Island westward.
A horrible Shadow of Death, among the Furnaces: beneath
The pillar of folding smoke; and he sought by other means.
To lure Los: by tears, by arguments of science & by terrors:
Terrors in every Nerve, by spasms & extended pains:
While Los answer'd unterrified to the opake blackening Fiend

And thus the Spectre spoke: Wilt thou still go on to destruction?
Till thy life is all taken away by this deceitful Friendship?
He drinks thee up like water! like wine he pours thee
Into his tuns: thy Daughters are trodden in his vintage
He makes thy Sons the trampling of his bulls, they are plowd
And harrowd for his profit, lo! thy stolen Emanation
Is his garden of pleasure! all the Spectres of his Sons mock thee
Look how they scorn thy once admired palaces! now in ruins
Because of Albion! because of deceit and friendship! For Lo!
Hand has peopled Babel & Nineveh: Hyle, Ashur & Aram:
Cobans son is Nimrod: his son Cush is adjoind to Aram,
By the Daughter of Babel, in a woven mantle of pestilence & war,
They put forth their spectrous cloudy sails; which drive their immense
Constellations over the deadly deeps of indefinite Udan-Adan
Kox is the Father of Shem & Ham & Japheth. he is the Noah
Of the Flood of Udan-Adan. Hutn is the Father of the Seven
From Enoch to Adam; Schofield is Adam who was New-
Created in Edom. I saw it indignant, & thou art not moved!
This has divided thee in sunder: and wilt thou still forgive?
O! thou seest not what I see! what is done in the Furnaces.
Listen I will tell thee what is done in moments to thee unknown:
Luvah was cast into the Furnaces of affliction and sealed,
And Vala fed in cruel delight, the Furnaces with fire:
Stern Urizen beheld; urgd by necessity to keep
The evil day afar, and if perchance with iron power
He might avert his own despair: in woe & fear he saw
Vala incircle round the Furnaces where Luvah was closd:
With joy she heard his howlings, & forgot he was her Luvah,
With whom she livd in bliss in times of innocence & youth!
Vala comes from the Furnace in a cloud, but wretched Luvah
Is howling in the Furnaces, in flames among Albions Spectres,
To prepare the Spectre of Albion to reign over thee O Los.
Forming the Spectres of Albion according to his rage:
To prepare the Spectre sons of Adam, who is Scofield: the Ninth
Of Albions sons, & the father of all his brethren in the Shadowy
Generation. Cambel & Gwendolen wove webs of war & of
Religion, to involve all Albions sons, and when they had
Involvd Eight; their webs rolld outwards into darkness
And Scofield the Ninth remaind on the outside of the Eight
And Kox, Kotope, & Bowen, One in him, a Fourfold Wonder
Involvd the Eight- Such are the Generations of the Giant Albion,
To separate a Law of Sin, to punish thee in thy members.

Los answerd. Altho' I know not this! I know far worse than this:
I know that Albion hath divided me, and that thou O my Spectre,
Hast just cause to be irritated: but look stedfastly upon me:
Comfort thyself in my strength the time will arrive,
When all Albions injuries shall cease, and when we shall
Embrace him tenfold bright, rising from his tomb in immortality.
They have divided themselves by Wrath, they must be united by
Pity: let us therefore take example & warning O my Spectre,
O that I could abstain from wrath! O that the Lamb
Of God would look upon me and pity me in my fury.
In anguish of regeneration: in terrors of self annihilation:
Pity must join together those whom wrath has torn in sunder,
And the Religion of Generation which was meant for the destruction
Of Jerusalem, become her covering, till the time of the End.
O holy Generation! Image of regeneration!
O point of mutual forgiveness between Enemies!
Birthplace of the Lamb of God incomprehensible!
The Dead despise & scorn thee, & cast thee out as accursed:
Seeing the Lamb of God in thy gardens & thy palaces:
Where they desire to place the Abomination of Desolation.
Hand sits before his furnace: scorn of others & furious pride:
Freeze round him to bars of steel & to iron rocks beneath
His feet: indignant self-righteousness like whirlwinds of the north:

Jerusalem 7D

Jerusalem 7. The best prophetic illumination that Los (the central figure here) can attain under these circumstances is a "pillar of folding smoke" writhing out from his furnaces (7:5; 5:50–51). He cannot turn the smoke to flame, but does make a green path of it (the swirls being colored green, shading to blue). Here, in a vertical variant of Plate 4, we see a daughter curling off in one fold, a son in the opposite direction in another, Los standing between trying to communicate with both (a motif magnified from Plate 1). "They must be united by Pity," he tells the Spectre (57–58). The son chooses a downward course, hands out for diving; the daughter is going and pointing upward. Compare the courses chosen by Albion and his Emanation in Plate 3.

To Los compare Adam in the Genesis title page (Damon *Dict* pl 2), also Jesus in *Night Thoughts* 42. Compare the smoke curling in opposite directions to the divided hair of Los in *Urizen* 16 and of Urizen in *Urizen* 12.

Jerusalem 8. The new moon of Plate 4 (accompanied by its three stars[E]) has somehow, through her resignation, become harnessed to an enslaved daughter, laboring in the smoke-cloud to keep her menstrual chariot on its course. (The spirit in which "the Fairies lead the Moon along the valley of Cherubim [children] Bleeding in torrents" in 63:12–13 is that of Druid sacrifice of others.) A new moon with the old moon in her arms is a portent of destruction (see Coleridge's *Dejection* and Shelley's *Alastor*). In Blake's symbolism it is the natural moon, of Vala, weighed down by the earthshine which, as Leonardo da Vinci pointed out, is the actual source of that "old moon" effect; to be harnessed to it is thus to be tied to the mundane (and eclipsed) moon rather than to the sun (to which Los is attaching Reuben in Plate 32). The spiritual moon of Ulro is built by Los and is also an ark (see Plates 20, 24, 39). John Grant observes that the moon and sun of Los are visions of the eventual merging of sun (illumination/perception) and moon (earth/matter) at the apocalypse.

The misallied daughter is looking grimly off stage, presumably toward her cruel masters Bacon, Newton, and Locke, whose "terrors hang like iron scourges over Albion" as long as the terrestrial and celestial wheels cannot "revolve in harmony & peace" (15:11–12, 20).

(In copy B there are an angel and a flying bird in the margin after "astonishment": 18.)

Rose up against me thundering from the Brook of Albions River
From Ranelagh & Strumbolo, from Cromwells gardens & Chelsea
The place of wounded Soldiers. but when he saw my Mace
Whirld round from heaven to earth, trembling he sat: his cold
Poisons rose up: & his sweet deceits coverd them all over
With a tender cloud. As thou art now; such was he O Spectre
I know thy deceit & thy revenges, and unless thou desist
I will certainly create an eternal Hell for thee. Listen:
Be attentive: be obedient: Lo the Furnaces are ready to recieve thee.
I will break thee into shivers: & melt thee in the furnaces of death;
I will cast thee into forms of abhorrence & torment if thou
Desist not from thine own will, & obey not my stern command:
I am closd up from my children: my Emanation is dividing
And thou my Spectre art divided against me. But mark
I will compell thee to assist me in my terrible labours. To beat
These hypocritic Selfhoods on the Anvils of bitter Death
I am inspired: I act not for myself: for Albions sake
I now am what I am: a horror and an astonishment
Shuddring the heavens to look upon me: Behold what cruelties
Are practised in Babel & Shinar, & have approachd to Zions Hill

While Los spoke, the terrible Spectre fell shuddring before him
Watching his time with glowing eyes to leap upon his prey
Los opend the Furnaces in fear. the Spectre saw to Babel & Shinar
Across all Europe & Asia. he saw the tortures of the Victims.
He saw now from the ouside what he before saw & felt from within
He saw that Los was the sole, uncontrolld Lord of the Furnaces
Groaning he kneeld before Los's iron-shod feet on London Stone,
Hungring & thirsting for Los's life yet pretending obedience.
While Los pursud his speech in threatnings loud & fierce.

Thou art my Pride & Self-righteousness: I have found thee out:
Thou art reveald before me in all thy magnitude & power
Thy Uncircumcised pretences to Chastity must be cut in sunder:
Thy holy wrath & deep deceit cannot avail against me
Nor shalt thou ever assume the triple-form of Albions Spectre
For I am one of the living: dare not to mock my inspired fury
If thou wast cast forth from my life! if I was dead upon the mountains
Thou mightest be pitied & lovd: but now I am living; unless
Thou abstain ravening I will create an eternal Hell for thee.
Take thou this Hammer & in patience heave the thundering Bellows
Take thou these Tongs: strike thou alternate with me: labour obedient
Hand & Hyle & Koban: Skofeld, Kox & Kotope. labour mightily
In the Wars of Babel & Shinar, all their Emanations were
Condensd. Hand has absorbd all his Brethren in his might
All the infant Loves & Graces were lost. for the mighty Hand
Con-

Jerusalem 8[D]

Condensd his Emanations into hard opake substances;
And his infant thoughts & desires, into cold, dark, cliffs of death.
His hammer of gold he siezd; and his anvil of adamant.
He siezd the bars of condensd thoughts, to forge them:
Into the sword of war: into the bow and arrow:
Into the thundering cannon and into the murdering gun
I saw the limbs formd for exercise, contemnd: & the beauty of
Eternity, lookd upon as deformity & loveliness as a dry tree:
I saw disease forming a Body of Death around the Lamb
Of God, to destroy Jerusalem, & to devour the body of Albion
By war and stratagem to win the labour of the husbandman:

Awkwardness armd in steel: folly in a helmet of gold:
Weakness with horns & talons; ignorance with a ravning beak:
Every Emanative joy forbidden as a Crime:
And the Emanations buried alive in the earth with pomp of religion:
Inspiration denyd; Genius forbidden by laws of punishment:
I saw terrified; I took the sighs & tears & bitter groans:
I lifted them into my Furnaces; to form the spiritual sword,
That lays open the hidden heart: I drew forth the pang
Of sorrow red hot: I workd it on my resolute anvil:
I heated it in the flames of Hand, & Hyle, & Coban
Nine times; Gwendolen & Cambel & Gwineverra

Are melted into the gold, the silver, the liquid ruby,
The crysolite, the topaz, the jacinth, & every precious stone.
Loud roar my Furnaces and loud my hammer is heard:
I labour day and night, I behold the soft affections
Condense beneath my hammer into forms of cruelty
But still I labour in hope, tho' still my tears flow down,
That he who will not defend Truth, may be compelld to defend
A Lie: that he may be snared and caught and snared and taken
That Enthusiasm and Life may not cease: arise Spectre arise!

Thus they contended among the Furnaces with groans & tears;
Groaning the Spectre heavd the bellows, obeying Los's frowns;
Till the Spaces of Erin were perfected in the furnaces
Of affliction, and Los drew them forth, compelling the harsh Spectre.

To

Jerusalem 9D

Jerusalem 9. A body of death is being formed "around the Lamb of God . . . by war and stratagem to win the labour of the husbandman" (9–11). At top a shepherd piping, with a feather in his hat and his legs crossed in ease, watches a peaceful scene of husbandry (compare the piper attending "Innocence" in *Songs* 3)—the flock with a lamb at center feeding from a ewe, a lion lying beside them, a woman about to pour milk from a pitcher (clear in F) in her left hand for a large cat (with a tail exactly like the cat's in Blake's design for Gray's cat Ode, also somewhat like the "tiger's" i.e. panther's in *Notebook* 2—but that beast has differently shaped and larger head and thorax), and a sheepdog already fed (and munching or resting) at the left. But the vine that should grow around the piper's tree has been (by stratagem) seduced to grow downward, becoming a wily serpent fed in secret by a Delilah whose man is sleeping or drugged (at center left, lacking in B). The contrasts are symmetrical: fed dog (drugged man); shepherd's wife feeding cat (begowned woman feeding serpent); lion and lamb and several sheep (serpent with several undulations). There is also a sort of reversal of the Genesis story: here Eve tempts the serpent instead of attending to her Adam. Rocky terrain is the marginal comment on Los's tale of precious stones (23 ff).

At bottom the sky is falling, and naked Albion lies fallen (from having taken the wrong direction in Plate 7); in symbolic parody of Blake's *The Morning After the Battle,* where sorrowing wives and mothers regard and embrace the slain. (The foreshortened body suggests Mantegna's *Dead Christ,* Janet Warner notes.) The central woman here abjectly worships instead of embracing the fallen warrior; the mother and children at left mourn rather than minister to him; the woman at right buries her head like Job's wife in *Job* 12. But Albion is not dead, just being grotesquely perverse, with open eyes (compare Plate 14). The stars plummeting (from Plate 4?) may parody Blake's earlier image of stars throwing down spears in surrender. This is the war related to the stratagem mentioned above; but Albion sees everything upside down.

Jerusalem 10. This page may be a late insertion, with Blake having too much to say in words to leave any room for pictures. In the colored copies the margins are given a sort of vegetal texture with suggestions of interweaving forms; this and similar borders[E] in Plates 5, 7, 9, 11, etc may imply a world inside the vegetable veil of Vala.

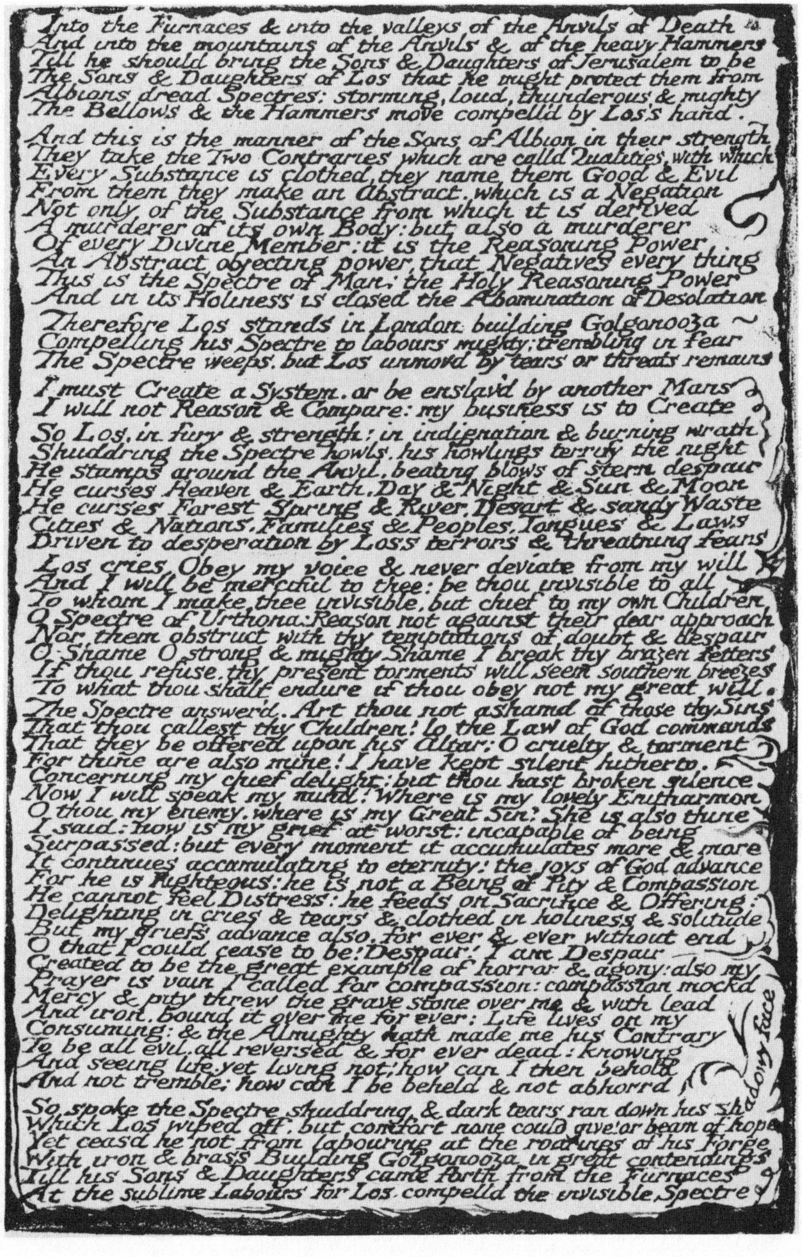

Into the Furnaces & into the valleys of the Anvils of Death
And into the mountains of the Anvils & of the heavy Hammers
Till he should bring the Sons & Daughters of Jerusalem to be
The Sons & Daughters of Los that he might protect them from
Albions dread Spectres; storming, loud, thunderous & mighty
The Bellows & the Hammers move compell'd by Los's hand.

And this is the manner of the Sons of Albion in their strength
They take the Two Contraries which are calld Qualities, with which
Every Substance is clothed, they name them Good & Evil
From them they make an Abstract, which is a Negation
Not only of the Substance from which it is derived
A murderer of its own Body: but also a murderer
Of every Divine Member: it is the Reasoning Power
An Abstract objecting power, that Negatives every thing
This is the Spectre of Man: the Holy Reasoning Power
And in its Holiness is closed the Abomination of Desolation

Therefore Los stands in London building Golgonooza
Compelling his Spectre to labours mighty; trembling in fear
The Spectre weeps, but Los unmovd by tears or threats remains

I must Create a System, or be enslav'd by another Mans
I will not Reason & Compare: my business is to Create

So Los, in fury & strength: in indignation & burning wrath
Shuddring the Spectre howls, his howlings terrify the night
He stamps around the Anvil, beating blows of stern despair
He curses Heaven & Earth, Day & Night & Sun & Moon
He curses Forest Spring & River, Desart & sandy Waste
Cities & Nations, Families & Peoples, Tongues & Laws
Driven to desperation by Los's terrors & threatning fears

Los cries, Obey my voice & never deviate from my will
And I will be merciful to thee: be thou invisible to all
To whom I make thee invisible, but chief to my own Children
O Spectre of Urthona: Reason not against their dear approach
Nor them obstruct with thy temptations of doubt & despair
O Shame O strong & mighty Shame I break thy brazen fetters
If thou refuse, thy present torments will seem southern breezes
To what thou shalt endure if thou obey not my great will.

The Spectre answer'd. Art thou not asham'd of those thy Sins
That thou callest thy Children! lo the Law of God commands
That they be offered upon his Altar: O cruelty & torment
For thine are also mine! I have kept silent hitherto.
Concerning my chief delight: but thou hast broken silence
Now I will speak my mind! Where is my lovely Enitharmon
O thou my enemy, where is my Great Sin? She is also thine
I said: now is my grief at worst: incapable of being
Surpassed: but every moment it accumulates more & more
It continues accumulating to eternity! the joys of God advance
For he is Righteous: he is not a Being of Pity & Compassion
He cannot feel Distress: he feeds on Sacrifice & Offering:
Delighting in cries & tears, & clothed in holiness & solitude
But my griefs advance also, for ever & ever without end
O that I could cease to be! Despair! I am Despair
Created to be the great example of horror & agony: also my
Prayer is vain I called for compassion: compassion mockd
Mercy & pity threw the grave stone over me & with lead
And iron, bound it over me for ever: Life lives on my
Consuming: & the Almighty hath made me his Contrary
To be all evil, all reversed & for ever dead: knowing
And seeing life, yet living not; how can I then behold
And not tremble; how can I be beheld & not abhorrd

So spoke the Spectre shuddring, & dark tears ran down his shadowy face
Which Los wiped off, but comfort none could give! or beam of hope
Yet ceas'd he not from labouring at the roarings of his Forge
With iron & brass Building Golgonooza in great contendings
Till his Sons & Daughters came forth from the Furnaces
At the sublime Labours for Los. compelld the invisible Spectre

Jerusalem 10[D]

Jerusalem 11D

Jerusalem 11. Horace, in Ode 20 (Book 2) prophesying his poetic immortality, feels himself turning into a snowy swan who will not be confined by the waters of the Styx. Blake, in his design for *Poems by Mr. Gray* depicting "The Pindaric Genius recieving his Lyre," pictures a stout naked youth accepting a lyre from the sky while giving loose rein to his mount, a swan with open (singing) mouth. Here, in a page that expresses "exceeding joy" at the success of the "art" whereby Los is creating these illuminated pages (building Golgonooza "for Jerusalems Sake": 10:63 – 11:12) yet lamentation at dangers still threatening the "foundations" (13–21)—in the top corners are suggestions of a willow for woe and an oak for ambition—the focus becomes intensely personal. We know that the poet is William Blake of South Molton Street; he has told us so inside the poem. We must think of his own work when we read here of Los's success in keeping his craftsmanship ("the invisible Spectre") subservient to "sublime Labours" (10:65) and in making the spectre wince at any divergence from creating "for Jerusalems Sake." He is unhappy that he must part from the successfully completed poems and illuminations ("Sons and Daughters") that have come forth "in perfection lovely" and (going into other people's collections) may "never more . . . see their Father" (11–14). He is in tears that there is still so much "to do for lovely Jerusalem" (17): the children who are the pages completed thus far may never reach their Father in Plate 99.

Here he paints himself—or the androgynous form of himself as poet-painter: it is an instance of his serious ("enthusiastic") clowning—as more than half turned into a snowy swan like Horace and like King Cygnus in illustrations of Ovid's *Metamorphoses* (one of which this closely resembles). His mouth is open but at the surface, improbably singing while etching; how feeble the bubbles compared to the foam of Leviathan's churning the surface and bursting up from it, in *Marriage* 20! Yet the emblem does denote the union of winged spectre and human smith there celebrated, adapting the emblem of collaboration of eagle and serpent in the printing house (*Marriage* 15). There a simple duality signified the collaboration of text and illumination or of temporal line (whether of words or outlines) and opening space (whether of shape and color or of vision). Here, "pulsations of time & extensions of space" (2) are indicated both in the etching of the copper surface (the upper picture) and in the printing and coloring of the paper (the lower), the reversal of direction representing the reversal from copper to paper.

Relief etching is employed as usual for the text, but the pictures above and below it are cut by intaglio etching (as in only ten other *Jerusalem* plates) or what Blake called woodcutting on copper (see *P&P* 672): "instead of Etching the blacks Etch the whites & bite it in"—exactly what the swan's beak is doing. The metaphor given in the text—of molten ore poured into prepared ground (3–4)—would apply literally to etching the blacks to hold the liquid ink but is pictorially transposed into a water-of-life (or death) metaphor, the continuity between upper and lower surfaces being established by five fish—one beside the swan, the others down the margin—and two eels (given viper-mouths open in opposite directions in E). (These may be thought of as single pages, or small works.)

But if the swan-human laboring within the upper surface is the artist preparing "the clay ground" (the mortal, finite surface) "with art" (4), who can the swimming-flying human moving just above the lower surface be, with arms and wings outstretched, but a human form of the eagle of Hell who, "with wings and feathers of air," produces infinite illumination? Like the serpent of Hell, the serpent-necked swan projects lineation. Like the eagle, the feather-finned skimmer adorns the surface with living colors (needing the spectral fins while the colors are wet, the feathers for rising from illustration to Illumination). What seem random bubbles in the upper surface appear as jewels adorning wrists and neck of the human form. Flying westward, this is "Erin" coming "forth from the Furnaces" (8), the contemporary form of Oothoon as the soul of freedom, with vestiges of American Indian in her appearance but wearing the pearls that adorn "Europe" in the Stedman emblem (*Prophet* plate 3).

Since, according to the text, the art is proceeding well, the unity of bird and serpent, of spectre and emanation, is implied in each of these forms. Perhaps the swan is more serpent than bird (folded wings signifying only a potential), more spectre than emanation. Yet Erin is not simply the obverse, for her human form is more nearly divine, i.e. more completely and sufficiently human. Her feathers, while suggesting the wings both of Spectre and Emanation (see them flying together in Plate 44) are becoming vestigial: free humans need none. In their present appearance both figures are adrogynous, possibly nearer Eternity than Beulah, possibly nearer Ulro. By their remaining on the oozy surface, by their heading in opposite directions, and by pearls that suggest an aquatic version of Vala/Babylon (see *Four Zoas* 128) we are reminded that the work is far from finished. This is only Plate 11. (In some

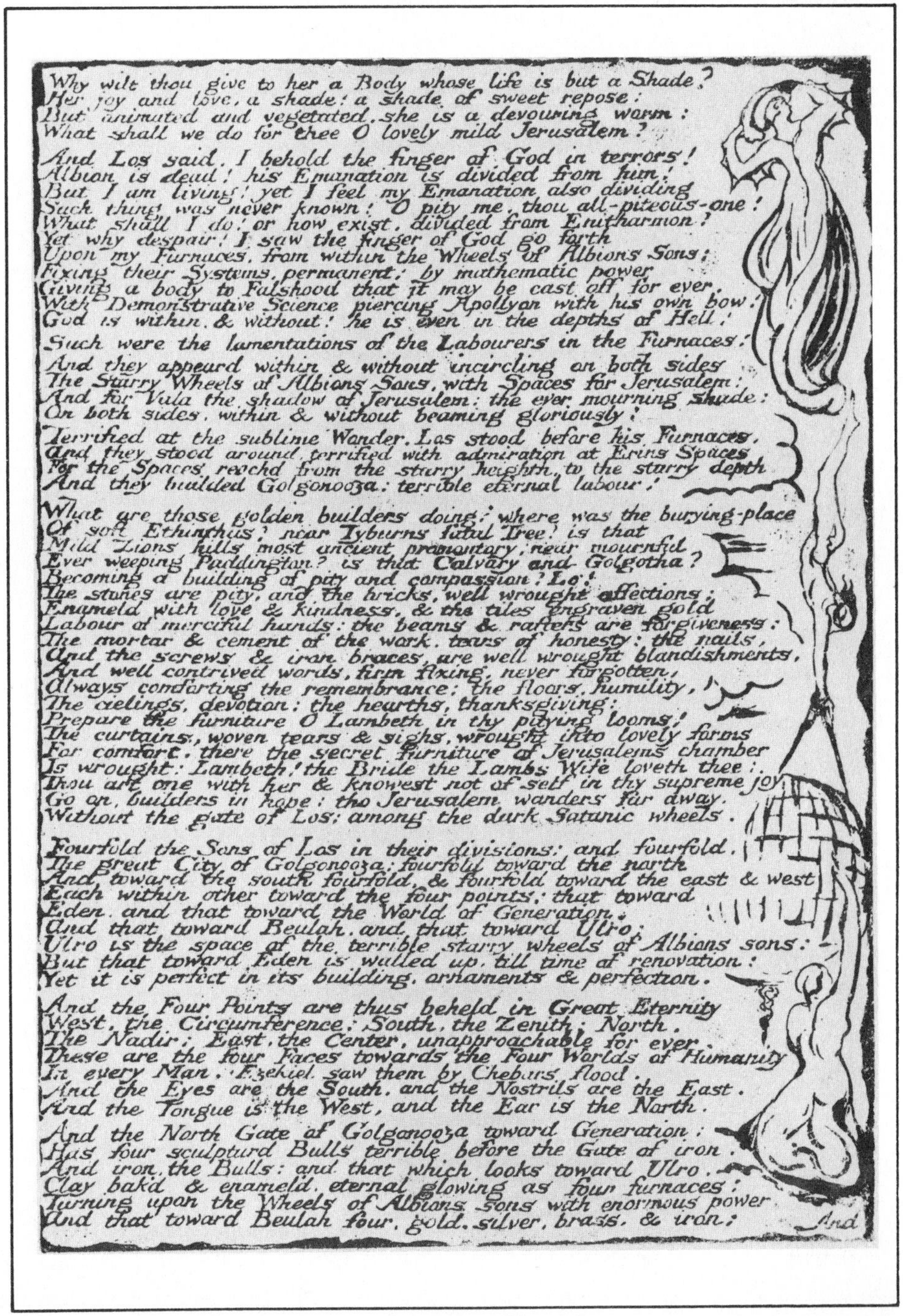

Why wilt thou give to her a Body whose life is but a Shade?
Her joy and love, a shade: a shade of sweet repose:
But animated and vegetated, she is a devouring worm:
What shall we do for thee O lovely mild Jerusalem?

And Los said. I behold the finger of God in terrors!
Albion is dead! his Emanation is divided from him!
But I am living! yet I feel my Emanation also dividing
Such thing was never known! O pity me, thou all-piteous-one!
What shall I do! or how exist, divided from Enitharmon?
Yet why despair! I saw the finger of God go forth
Upon my Furnaces, from within the Wheels of Albions Sons:
Fixing their Systems, permanent: by mathematic power
Giving a body to Falshood that it may be cast off for ever.
With Demonstrative Science piercing Apollyon with his own bow!
God is within, & without! he is even in the depths of Hell!

Such were the lamentations of the Labourers in the Furnaces!

And they appeard within & without incircling on both sides
The Starry Wheels of Albions Sons, with Spaces for Jerusalem:
And for Vala the shadow of Jerusalem: the ever mourning shade:
On both sides, within & without beaming gloriously!

Terrified at the sublime Wonder, Los stood before his Furnaces.
And they stood around, terrified with admiration at Erins Spaces
For the Spaces reachd from the starry heighth, to the starry depth.
And they builded Golgonooza: terrible eternal labour!

What are those golden builders doing? where was the burying-place
Of soft Ethinthus? near Tyburns fatal Tree? is that
Mild Zions hills most ancient promontory; near mournful
Ever weeping Paddington? is that Calvary and Golgotha?
Becoming a building of pity and compassion? Lo!
The stones are pity, and the bricks, well wrought affections:
Enameld with love & kindness, & the tiles engraven gold
Labour of merciful hands: the beams & rafters are forgiveness:
The mortar & cement of the work, tears of honesty: the nails,
And the screws & iron braces, are well wrought blandishments,
And well contrived words, firm fixing, never forgotten,
Always comforting the remembrance: the floors, humility,
The cielings, devotion: the hearths, thanksgiving:
Prepare the furniture O Lambeth in thy pitying looms!
The curtains, woven tears & sighs, wrought into lovely forms
For comfort. there the secret furniture of Jerusalems chamber
Is wrought: Lambeth! the Bride the Lambs Wife loveth thee:
Thou art one with her & knowest not of self in thy supreme joy.
Go on, builders in hope: tho Jerusalem wanders far away,
Without the gate of Los: among the dark Satanic wheels.

Fourfold the Sons of Los in their divisions: and fourfold,
The great City of Golgonooza: fourfold toward the north
And toward the south fourfold, & fourfold toward the east & west
Each within other toward the four points: that toward
Eden, and that toward the World of Generation,
And that toward Beulah, and that toward Ulro:
Ulro is the space of the terrible starry wheels of Albions sons:
But that toward Eden is walled up, till time of renovation:
Yet it is perfect in its building, ornaments & perfection.

And the Four Points are thus beheld in Great Eternity
West, the Circumference: South, the Zenith: North,
The Nadir: East, the Center, unapproachable for ever.
These are the four Faces towards the Four Worlds of Humanity
In every Man. Ezekiel saw them by Chebars flood.
And the Eyes are the South, and the Nostrils are the East.
And the Tongue is the West, and the Ear is the North.

And the North Gate of Golgonooza toward Generation;
Has four sculpturd Bulls terrible before the Gate of iron.
And iron, the Bulls: and that which looks toward Ulro,
Clay bakd & enameld, eternal glowing as four furnaces:
Turning upon the Wheels of Albions Sons with enormous power.
And that toward Beulah four, gold, silver, brass, & iron:
And

Jerusalem 12D

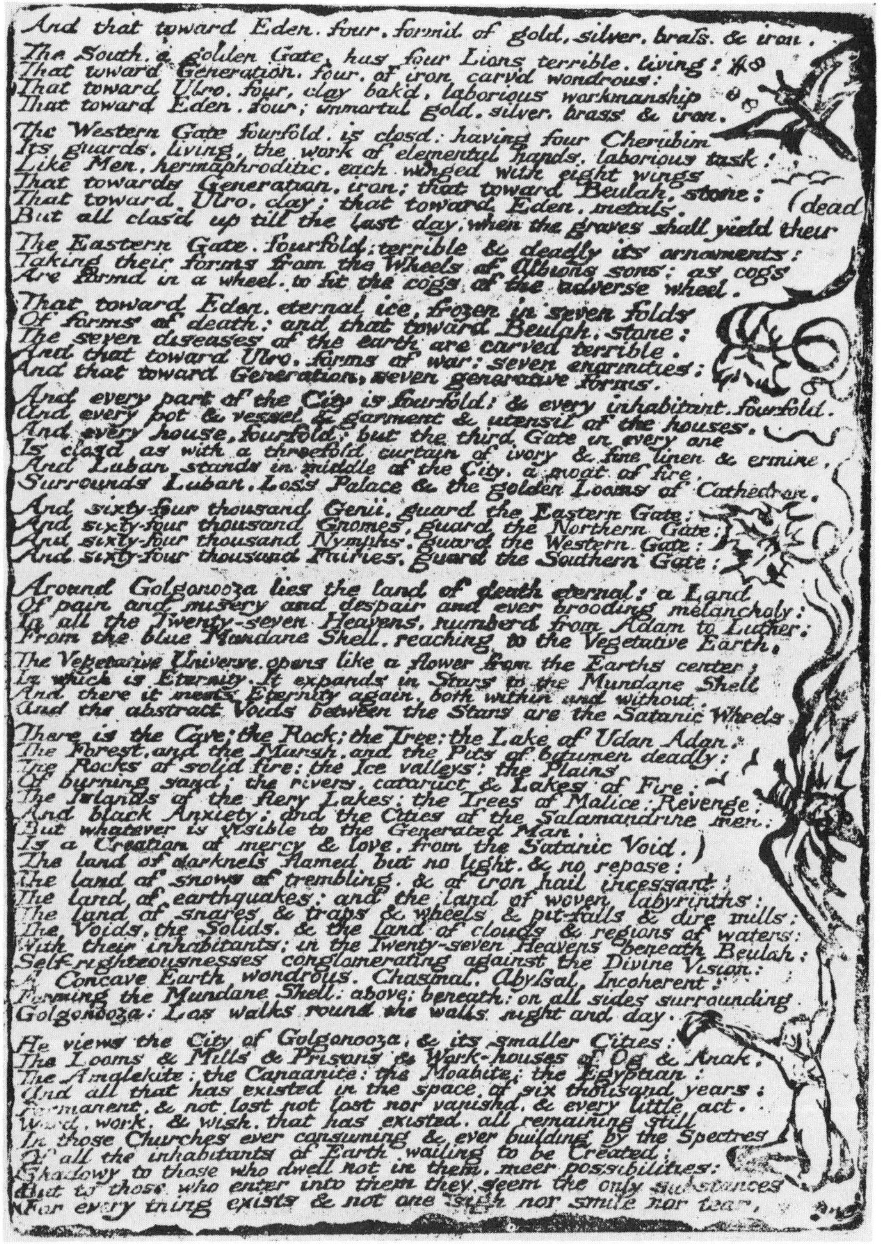

And that toward Eden. four. formd of gold. silver. brass. & iron.
The South. a golden Gate. has four Lions terrible. living!
That toward Generation. four. of iron carvd wondrous:
That toward Ulro. four, clay bakd. laborious workmanship
That toward Eden. four; immortal gold. silver. brass & iron.

The Western Gate fourfold. is closd: having four Cherubim
Its guards. living, the work of elemental hands. laborious task:
Like Men. hermaphroditic. each winged with eight wings
That towards Generation. iron; that toward Beulah. stone;
That toward Ulro. clay: that toward Eden. metals.
But all clos'd up till the last day. when the graves shall yield their (dead

The Eastern Gate. fourfold: terrible & deadly its ornaments:
Taking their forms from the Wheels of Albions sons; as cogs
Are formd in a wheel. to fit the cogs of the adverse wheel.

That toward Eden. eternal ice, frozen in seven folds
Of forms of death: and that toward Beulah. stone:
The seven diseases of the earth are carved terrible.
And that toward Ulro. forms of war: seven enormities:
And that toward Generation, seven generative forms.

And every part of the City is fourfold; & every inhabitant. fourfold.
And every pot & vessel & garment & utensil of the houses.
And every house. fourfold; but the third Gate in every one
Is clos'd as with a threefold curtain of ivory & fine linen & ermine.
And Luban stands in middle of the City. a moat of fire.
Surrounds Luban. Los's Palace & the golden Looms of Cathedron.

And sixty-four thousand Genii. guard the Eastern Gate:
And sixty-four thousand Gnomes. guard the Northern Gate:
And sixty-four thousand Nymphs. guard the Western Gate:
And sixty-four thousand Fairies. guard the Southern Gate:

Around Golgonooza lies the land of death eternal; a Land
Of pain and misery and despair and ever brooding melancholy:
In all the Twenty-seven Heavens. numberd from Adam to Luther;
From the blue Mundane Shell. reaching to the Vegetative Earth.

The Vegetative Universe. opens like a flower from the Earths center;
In which is Eternity. It expands in Stars to the Mundane Shell
And there it meets Eternity again. both within and without.
And the abstract Voids between the Stars are the Satanic Wheels

There is the Cave; the Rock; the Tree; the Lake of Udan Adan;
The Forest. and the Marsh. and the Pits of bitumen deadly:
The Rocks of solid fire: the Ice valleys: the Plains
Of burning sand: the rivers, cataract & Lakes of Fire:
The Islands of the fiery Lakes: the Trees of Malice: Revenge:
And black Anxiety; and the Cities of the Salamandrine men:
(But whatever is visible to the Generated Man.
Is a Creation of mercy & love. from the Satanic Void.)
The land of darkness flamed but no light. & no repose:
The land of snows of trembling. & of iron hail incessant:
The land of earthquakes: and the land of woven labyrinths:
The land of snares & traps & wheels & pit-falls & dire mills:
The Voids. the Solids. & the land of clouds & regions of waters:
With their inhabitants: in the Twenty-seven Heavens beneath Beulah:
Self-righteousnesses conglomerating against the Divine Vision:
A Concave Earth wondrous. Chasmal. Abyssal, Incoherent:
Forming the Mundane Shell: above; beneath: on all sides surrounding
Golgonooza: Los walks round the walls night and day.

He views the City of Golgonooza. & its smaller Cities:
The Looms & Mills & Prisons & Work-houses of Og & Anak:
The Amalekite: the Canaanite: the Moabite: the Egyptian:
And all that has existed in the space of six thousand years:
Permanent. & not lost not lost nor vanishd. & every little act.
Word, work. & wish. that has existed. all remaining still
In those Churches ever consuming & ever building by the Spectres
Of all the inhabitants of Earth wailing to be Created:
Shadowy to those who dwell not in them. meer possibilities:
But to those who enter into them they seem the only substances
For every thing exists & not one sigh nor smile nor tear,

Jerusalem 13D

respects both may be considered phases of the transmuting dragon woman, Vala, in *Four Zoas* 26.)

Jerusalem 12. The finny female at the top continues the fishy mockery of Plate 11 though with more bat-like, spectral indications. She is, of course, Vala, and "she is a devouring worm" (3), whatever her elegance of hat and gown, and vain—with the appearance of trying a plumed hat in a mirror. That she and the bejewelled woman of Plate 11 have fins (compare the human fishes in the Gray designs) means that in the course of the acid bath which is this poem the whorish garments of Babylon will be removed to reveal the naked Jerusalem.

In lines 54–60 we learn of the compass points of the human city; in the satiric cartoon in the margin Newton is giving a lesson in "Demonstrative Science" (14) with compasses and globe (scored, as in Jerusalem's right wing in Plate 2) to a gowned kneeling woman. His wooden and her human figure point to "joy" at the north pole—the nadir from the perspective of eternity (56). The south pole extends a sort of corkscrew root, perhaps a vortex.

Jerusalem 13. As the kneeling woman in pink dress sought "joy" through geometry on Plate 12, a kneeling man in green suit and cap seems to be seeking to catch or pluck something red and blue hanging from a green-leaved grape vine. We see that it is no cluster of grapes but a grotesque bat-moth, probably translucent (the blue sky shines through) like the dragon-fly through whom we can see grey cloud, above. The false actions on these plates may be, respectively, the misguided search for certain knowledge of joy and the illusory effort to gratify desire by possession. Both grape leaves, though green enough, have neither roots nor fruits.

On the other hand, perhaps the green man has just released the painted fly and is cheering it in its flight—like an artist illuminating with strong colors which have not yet reached the top fly's wings but may do so. Compare Los hammering the sun clear in *Song of Los* 8. In other words, the pictures on these two plates may signify efforts at inscribing lines and fixing colors on the pages of this illuminated book: compare Plate 36 and the gestures of the man and woman there.

Two small (or distant) birds flying near the bat-moth's feelers and four tiny or distant insects flying near the dragon-fly's draw attention to the innocent and eternal joys with which the text, narrating the building of Golgonooza, is ultimately concerned.

❧

Jerusalem 14. The "Universe within . . . Starry & glorious" (17–19) is pictured as outside Albion, miserable in his tomb beside a foaming ocean. Outside his vision are the sun, the planets—Saturn, Venus, Mercury—the earth with crescent moon, and two flat stars. A vision is offered to him of his "mild Emanation Jerusalem" (31) in her threefold butterfly form, within the arc of a rainbow in clouds. Her wings, spread as a mandorla, bear six eyes that suggest her face as the seventh; within the arc are six stars and a moon, suggesting her round apparition as a prophetic image of the true sun or seventh star.

But Albion regards her uncertainly (or with blank eyes[BE]). He cannot see that the rainbow is doubling[E] behind his head. His guardian angels at head and feet are turned from him; they and he are as stone cold as an effigy on a gothic tomb.

The scene of Albion's death-in-life is an ironic reversal of depictions of going through death to life, such as the *Angels hovering over the Body of Jesus in the Sepulchre* or *The Death of the Virgin.*

(This plate once concluded chapter 1, as a deleted colophon shows.)

One hair nor particle of dust. not one can pass away.
He views the Cherub at the Tree of Life. also the Serpent.
Orc the first born coild in the south: the Dragon Urizen:
Tharmas the Vegetated Tongue even the Devouring Tongue:
A threefold region. a false brain: a false heart:
And false bowels: altogether composing the False Tongue,
Beneath Beulah: as a watry flame revolving every way
And as dark roots and stems: a Forest of affliction: growing
In seas of sorrow. Los also views the Four Females:
Ahania, and Enion, and Vala, and Enitharmon lovely.
And from them all the lovely beaming Daughters of Albion.
Ahania & Enion & Vala. are three evanescent shades:
Enitharmon is a vegetated mortal Wife of Los:
His Emanation, yet his Wife till the sleep of death is past.
Such are the Buildings of Los: & such are the Woofs of Enitharmon:

And Los beheld his Sons, and he beheld his Daughters:
Every one a translucent Wonder: a Universe within,
Increasing inwards, into length and breadth, and heighth:
Starry & glorious: and they every one in their bright loins:
Have a beautiful golden gate which opens into the vegetative world:
And every one a gate of rubies & all sorts of precious stones
In their translucent hearts, which opens into the vegetative world:
And every one a gate of iron dreadful and wonderful.
In their translucent heads, which opens into the vegetative world
And every one has the three regions Childhood: Manhood: & Age.
But the gate of the tongue: the western gate in them is clos'd,
Having a wall builded against it: and thereby the gates
Eastward & Southward & Northward, are incircled with flaming fires.
And the North is Breadth, the South is Heighth & Depth:
The East is Inwards: & the West is Outwards every way.

And Los beheld the mild Emanation Jerusalem eastward bending
Her revolutions toward the Starry Wheels in maternal anguish
Like a pale cloud arising from the arms of Beulahs Daughters:
In Entuthon Benythons deep Vales beneath Golgonooza.

Jerusalem 14[D]

And Hand & Hyle rooted into Jerusalem by a fibre
Of strong revenge & Skofeld Vegetated by Reubens Gate
In every Nation of the Earth till the Twelve Sons of Albion
Enrooted into every Nation: a mighty Polypus growing
From Albion over the whole Earth: such is my awful Vision.

I see the Four-fold Man. The Humanity in deadly sleep
And its fallen Emanation. The Spectre & its cruel Shadow.
I see the Past, Present & Future, existing all at once
Before me; O Divine Spirit sustain me on thy wings!
That I may awake Albion from his long & cold repose.
For Bacon & Newton sheathd in dismal steel, their terrors hang
Like iron scourges over Albion, Reasonings like vast Serpents
Infold around my limbs, bruising my minute articulations

I turn my eyes to the Schools & Universities of Europe
And there behold the Loom of Locke whose Woof rages dire
Washd by the Water-wheels of Newton. black the cloth
In heavy wreathes folds over every Nation; cruel Works
Of many Wheels I view, wheel without wheel, with cogs tyrannic
Moving by compulsion each other: not as those in Eden: which
Wheel within Wheel in freedom revolve in harmony & peace.

I see in deadly fear in London Los raging round his Anvil
Of death: forming an Ax of gold: the Four Sons of Los
Stand round him cutting the Fibres from Albions hills
That Albions Sons may roll apart over the Nations
While Reuben enroots his brethren in the narrow Canaanite
From the Limit Noah to the Limit Abram in whose Loins
Reuben in his Twelve-fold majesty & beauty shall take refuge
As Abraham flees from Chaldea shaking his goary locks
But first Albion must sleep, divided from the Nations

I see Albion sitting upon his Rock in the first Winter
And thence I see the Chaos of Satan & the World of Adam
When the Divine Hand went forth on Albion in the mid Winter
And at the place of Death when Albion sat in Eternal Death
Among the Furnaces of Los in the Valley of the Son of Hin-
-nom

Jerusalem 15D

Jerusalem 15. The steepled buildings in the background (in flamesB) are "the Schools & Universities" (14), the "minatory pinnacles of Chaldea" (W), the Chaldea of sacrifice of the first born to "cruel Works" that involve folding heavy wreathes of black cloth "over every Nation" (15–17). From it Abraham, running and coming to a stand still, "flees . . . shaking his goary locks" (28) and crying out, but getting nowhere because caught up against enrooted "Hand & Hyle . . . & Skofeld" (1–2) though his arms outstretched presage Christ. (Compare *Milton* 11 and, less directly, 19 and 46.) The prone figure whose arms are turning to branches—a metamorphosis which implies of the biblical story that the sacrificial ram caught in the brambles as substitute for Isaac is only another form of blood sacrifice—and the other branches beside him may simultaneously illustrate lines 23 and 25: the cutting of fibres (i.e. oaks to make ships) from Albion's hills, to send his sons as imperial sailors "over the Nations" (compare Plate 40), and the action of one of the sons which "enroots his brethren in the narrow Canaanite," i.e. reduces man to vegetation—to produce simultaneously and chaotically (as pictured) the stripping of trees and the enrooting of humans.

Blake's fourth design for *Pilgrim's Progress* shows Christian in the same posture and anxiety as Abraham here: "he looked this way, and that way, as if he would run; yet he stood still, because . . . he could not tell which way to go." (That must be the text Blake had in mind, though he puts in the neighbors Obstinate and Pliable pursuing the pilgrim at a later moment when he is leaving the City of Destruction and knows his way.)

Jerusalem 16. A heavy page. In what little space there is, beside the second stanza, Blake puts a small figure who repeats the gestures of the top figure in Plate 4 in the up and down directions of Los in Plate 7 but with more encouragement because facing us more directly. There is a small viper after the penultimate stanza.

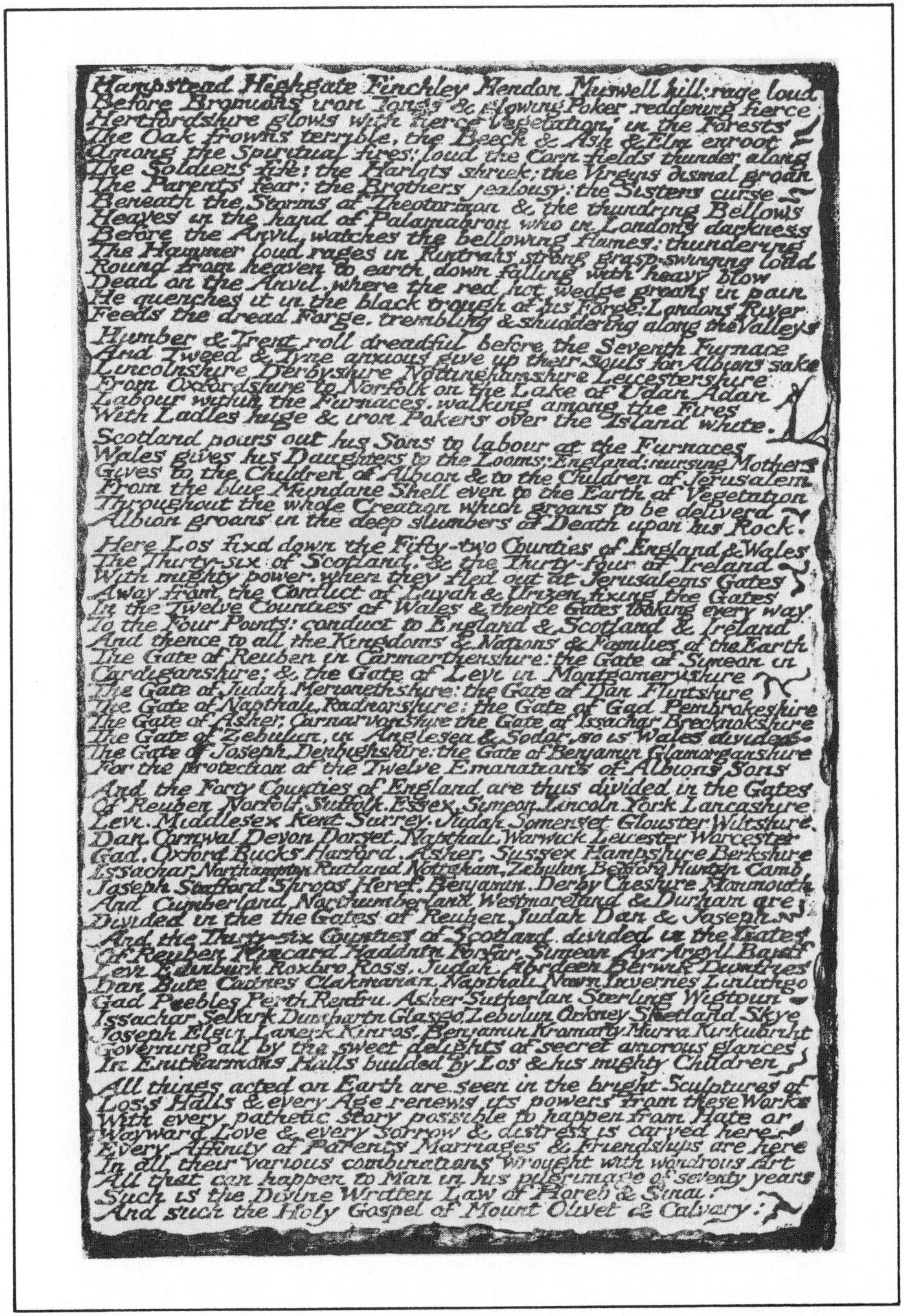

Hampstead Highgate Finchley Hendon Muswell hill: rage loud
Before Bromions iron Tongs & glowing Poker reddening fierce
Hertfordshire glows with fierce Vegetation! in the Forests
The Oak frowns terrible, the Beech & Ash & Elm enroot
Among the Spiritual fires; loud the Corn-fields thunder along
The Soldiers fife; the Harlots shriek; the Virgins dismal groan
The Parents fear: the Brothers jealousy: the Sisters curse
Beneath the Storms of Theotormon & the thundring Bellows
Heaves in the hand of Palamabron who in Londons darkness
Before the Anvil, watches the bellowing flames: thundering
The Hammer loud rages in Rintrahs strong grasp swinging loud
Round from heaven to earth down falling with heavy blow
Dead on the Anvil, where the red hot wedge groans in pain
He quenches it in the black trough of his Forge; Londons River
Feeds the dread Forge, trembling & shuddering along the Valleys

Humber & Trent roll dreadful before the Seventh Furnace
And Tweed & Tyne anxious give up their Souls for Albions sake
Lincolnshire Derbyshire Nottinghamshire Leicestershire
From Oxfordshire to Norfolk on the Lake of Udan Adan
Labour within the Furnaces, walking among the Fires
With Ladles huge & iron Pokers over the Island white.

Scotland pours out his Sons to labour at the Furnaces
Wales gives his Daughters to the Looms; England: nursing Mothers
Gives to the Children of Albion & to the Children of Jerusalem
From the blue Mundane Shell even to the Earth of Vegetation
Throughout the whole Creation which groans to be deliverd
Albion groans in the deep slumbers of Death upon his Rock.

Here Los fixd down the Fifty-two Counties of England & Wales
The Thirty-six of Scotland, & the Thirty-four of Ireland
With mighty power, when they fled out at Jerusalems Gates
Away from the Conflict of Luvah & Urizen, fixing the Gates
In the Twelve Counties of Wales & thence Gates looking every way
To the Four Points: conduct to England & Scotland & Ireland
And thence to all the Kingdoms & Nations & Families of the Earth
The Gate of Reuben in Carmarthenshire: the Gate of Simeon in
Cardiganshire: & the Gate of Levi in Montgomeryshire
The Gate of Judah Merionethshire: the Gate of Dan Flintshire
The Gate of Napthali, Radnorshire: the Gate of Gad Pembrokeshire
The Gate of Asher, Carnarvonshire the Gate of Issachar Brecknokshire
The Gate of Zebulun, in Anglesea & Sodor, so is Wales divided.
The Gate of Joseph, Denbighshire: the Gate of Benjamin Glamorganshire
For the protection of the Twelve Emanations of Albions Sons

And the Forty Counties of England are thus divided in the Gates
Of Reuben Norfolk, Suffolk, Essex, Simeon Lincoln, York Lancashire
Levi. Middlesex Kent Surrey. Judah Somerset Glouster Wiltshire.
Dan. Cornwal Devon Dorset, Napthali, Warwick Leicester Worcester
Gad. Oxford Bucks Harford. Asher, Sussex Hampshire Berkshire
Issachar, Northampton Rutland Nottgham, Zebulun Bedford Huntgn Camb
Joseph Stafford Shrops Heref. Benjamin. Derby Cheshire Monmouth
And Cumberland Northumberland Westmoreland & Durham are
Divided in the Gates of Reuben, Judah Dan & Joseph

And the Thirty-six Counties of Scotland, divided in the Gates
Of Reuben Kincard Haddntn Forfar, Simeon Ayr Argyll Banff
Levi Edinburh Roxbro Ross. Judah Abrdeen Berwik Dumfries
Dan Bute Caitnes Clakmanan. Napthali Nairn Invernes Linlithgo
Gad Peebles Perth Renfru. Asher Sutherlan Sterling Wigtoun
Issachar Selkirk Dumbartn Glasgo, Zebulun Orkney Shetland Skye
Joseph Elgin Lanerk Kinros, Benjamin Kromarty Murra Kirkubriht
Governing all by the sweet delights of secret amorous glances
In Enitharmons Halls builded by Los & his mighty Children

All things acted on Earth are seen in the bright Sculptures of
Loss Halls & every Age renews its powers from these Works
With every pathetic story possible to happen from Hate or
Wayward Love & every sorrow & distress is carved here
Every Affinity of Parents Marriages & Friendships are here
In all their various combinations wrought with wondrous Art
All that can happen to Man in his pilgrimage of seventy years
Such is the Divine Written Law of Horeb & Sinai:
And such the Holy Gospel of Mount Olivet & Calvary:

Jerusalem 16D

His Spectre divides & Los in fury compells it to divide:
To labour in the fire, in the water, in the earth, in the air,
To follow the Daughters of Albion as the hound follows the scent
Of the wild inhabitant of the forest, to drive them from his own:
To make a way for the Children of Los to come from the Furnaces
But Los himself against Albions Sons his fury bends, for he
Dare not approach the Daughters openly lest he be consumed
In the fires of their beauty & perfection & be Vegetated beneath
Their Looms, in a Generation of death & resurrection to forgetfulness
They wooe Los continually to subdue his strength: he continually
Shews them his Spectre: sending him abroad over the four points of heaven
In the fierce desires of beauty & in the tortures of repulse! He is
The Spectre of the Living pursuing the Emanations of the Dead.
Shuddring they flee: they hide in the Druid Temples in cold chastity:
Subdued by the Spectre of the Living & terrified by undisguisd desire.

For Los said: Tho my Spectre is divided: as I am a Living Man
I must compell him to obey me wholly: that Enitharmon may not
Be lost: & lest he should devour Enitharmon: Ah me!
Piteous image of my soft desires & loves: O Enitharmon!
I will compell my Spectre to obey: I will restore to thee thy Children.
No one bruises or starves himself to make himself fit for labour!

Tormented with sweet desire for these beauties of Albion
They would never love my power if they did not seek to destroy
Enitharmon: Vala would never have sought & loved Albion
If she had not sought to destroy Jerusalem; such is that false
And Generating Love: a pretence of love to destroy love:
Cruel hipocrisy unlike the lovely delusions of Beulah:
And cruel forms, unlike the merciful forms of Beulahs Night

They know not why they love nor wherefore they sicken & die
Calling that Holy Love: which is Envy Revenge & Cruelty Man.
Which separated the stars from the mountains: the mountains from
And left Man, a little grovelling Root, outside of Himself.
Negations are not Contraries: Contraries mutually Exist:
But Negations Exist Not: Exceptions & Objections & Unbeliefs
Exist not: nor shall they ever be Organized for ever & ever:
If thou separate from me, thou art a Negation: a meer
Reasoning & Derogation from me, an Objecting & cruel Spite
And Malice & Envy: but my Emanation, Alas! will become
My Contrary: O thou Negation, I will continually compell
Thee to be invisible to any but whom I please, & when
And where & how I please, and never! never! shalt thou be Organized
But as a distorted & reversed Reflexion in the Darkness
And in the Non Entity: nor shall that which is above
Ever descend into thee: but thou shalt be a Non Entity for ever
And if any enter into thee, thou shalt be an Unquenchable Fire
And he shall be a never dying Worm, mutually tormented by
Those that thou tormentest, a Hell & Despair for ever & ever.

So Los in secret with himself communed & Enitharmon heard
In her darkness & was comforted: yet still she divided away
In gnawing pain from Los's bosom in the deadly Night;
First as a red Globe of blood trembling beneath his bosom
Suspended over her he hung: he infolded her in his garments
Of wool: he hid her from the Spectre, in shame & confusion of
Face; in terrors & pains of Hell & Eternal Death, the
Trembling Globe shot forth Self-living & Los howld over it:
Feeding it with his groans & tears day & night without ceasing:
And the Spectrous Darkness from his back divided in temptations,
And in grinding agonies in threats! stiflings! & direful strugglings.

Go thou to Skofield: ask him if he is Bath or if he is Canterbury
Tell him to be no more dubious: demand explicit words
Tell him: I will dash him into shivers, where & at what time
I please: tell Hand & Skofield they are my ministers of evil
To those I hate; for I can hate also as well as they!

Jerusalem 17[D]

Jerusalem 17. Grapevines, with leaves and tendrils but no fruit, fill the margin; the leaves are left uncolored. In the text Los fears to be "Vegetated beneath" the daughters' looms (8–10).

Jerusalem 18. In a complicated emblem of division and union, the parenthetical line, "For Vala produc'd the Bodies, Jerusalem gave the Souls" (7), is illustrated paradoxically. Young body and soul are embracing swiftly (the Orc-like boy at the right presumably the body; yet recollection of the embracing female devil and perhaps male angel in *Marriage* 1 will shake our certainty), but the two giving them away look neither at them nor at each other, though they touch right toes (compare *Milton* 2, 33, and 48) and are dressed for the occasion with elegant wings and wreaths of flowers in their hair. Is it Jerusalem at the left, wearing lilies, and Vala at the right wearing red[B] roses? (Neither flower is named anywhere in *Jerusalem.*) Grant, in *Forms* 362–64, argues somewhat persuasively that the lilied figure is a stand-in for Vala, Shiloh her masculine emanation, leaving the roses to Jerusalem, the indubitable woman at the right. Elaine Kauvar notes that in Boehme a conflict between two flowers signifies regeneration. The two moon-arks suggest that our eyes are out of focus, but they are waning and waxing crescents, equipped with sails, scudding to collide or unite. (The waning crescent is made a complete sphere in B, with a shadow sail inside; compare Plate 8.)

Down the cloudy rocks of the page tumble three cast-out daughters, or rather, in illustration of the cry of Hand and Hyle to cast forth Jerusalem as "our Harlot-Sister" (30), three stages of Jerusalem's fall, ending on her head like Albion in Plate 9. (For another soaring-together of figures see Plate 20.)

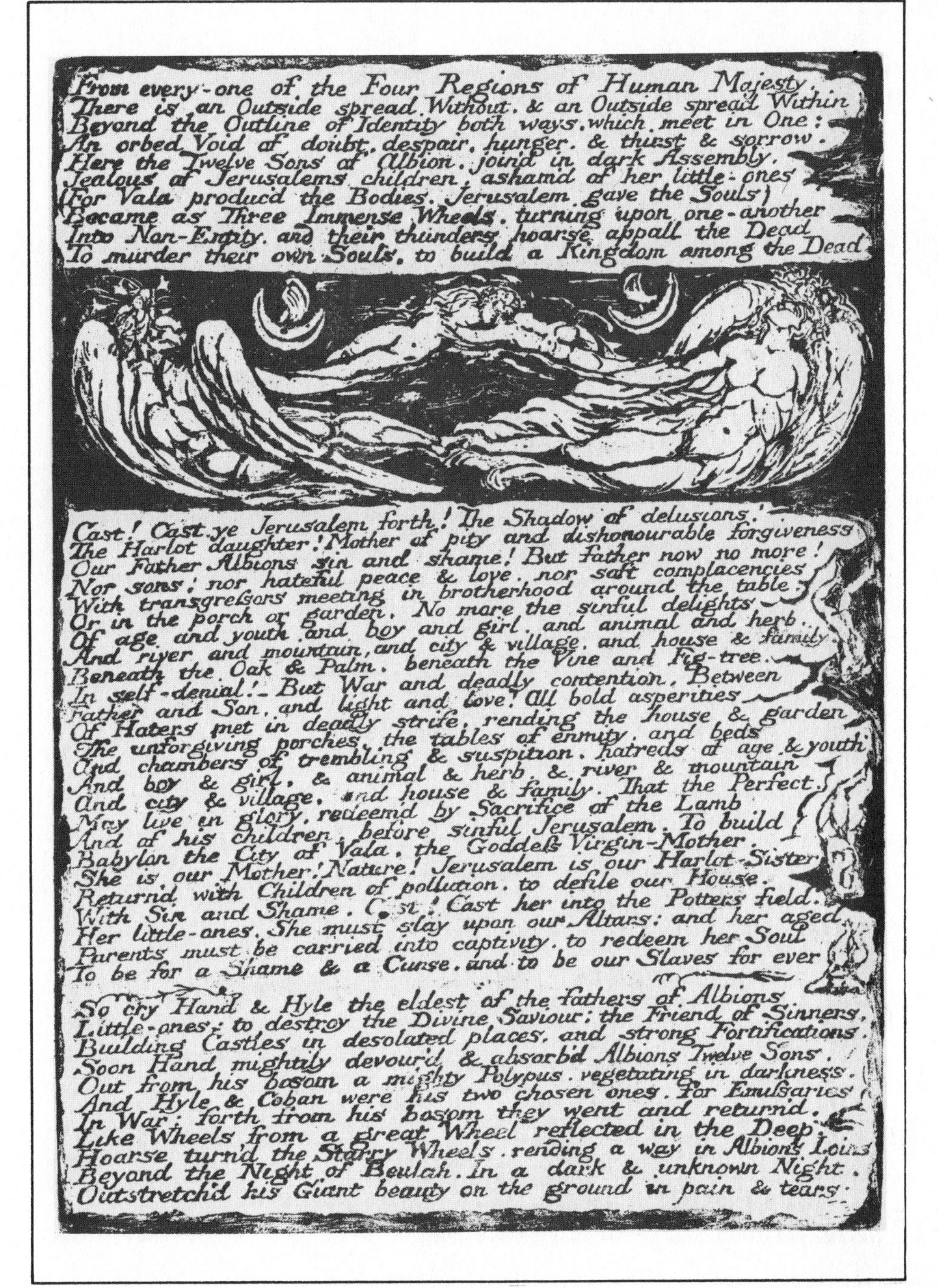

From every-one of the Four Regions of Human Majesty,
There is an Outside spread Without, & an Outside spread Within
Beyond the Outline of Identity both ways, which meet in One:
An orbed Void of doubt, despair, hunger, & thirst & sorrow.
Here the Twelve Sons of Albion, joind in dark Assembly,
Jealous of Jerusalems children, ashamd of her little-ones
(For Vala producd the Bodies, Jerusalem gave the Souls)
Became as Three Immense Wheels, turning upon one-another
Into Non-Entity, and their thunders hoarse appall the Dead
To murder their own Souls, to build a Kingdom among the Dead

Cast! Cast ye Jerusalem forth! The Shadow of delusions!
The Harlot daughter! Mother of pity and dishonourable forgiveness
Our Father Albions sin and shame! But father now no more!
Nor sons! nor hateful peace & love, nor soft complacencies
With transgressors meeting in brotherhood around the table,
Or in the porch or garden. No more the sinful delights
Of age and youth and boy and girl and animal and herb,
And river and mountain, and city & village, and house & family.
Beneath the Oak & Palm, beneath the Vine and Fig-tree.
In self-denial!—But War and deadly contention, Between
Father and Son, and light and love! All bold asperities
Of Haters met in deadly strife, rending the house & garden
The unforgiving porches, the tables of enmity, and beds
And chambers of trembling & suspition, hatreds of age & youth
And boy & girl, & animal & herb, & river & mountain
And city & village, and house & family. That the Perfect,
May live in glory, redeemd by Sacrifice of the Lamb
And of his children, before sinful Jerusalem. To build
Babylon the City of Vala, the Goddess Virgin-Mother.
She is our Mother! Nature! Jerusalem is our Harlot-Sister
Returnd with Children of pollution, to defile our House,
With Sin and Shame. Cast! Cast her into the Potters field.
Her little-ones, She must slay upon our Altars: and her aged
Parents must be carried into captivity, to redeem her Soul
To be for a Shame & a Curse, and to be our Slaves for ever

So cry Hand & Hyle the eldest of the fathers of Albions
Little-ones; to destroy the Divine Saviour; the Friend of Sinners,
Building Castles in desolated places, and strong Fortifications.
Soon Hand mightily devourd & absorbd Albions Twelve Sons.
Out from his bosom a mighty Polypus, vegetating in darkness,
And Hyle & Coban were his two chosen ones, for Emissaries
In War: forth from his bosom they went and returnd.
Like Wheels from a great Wheel reflected in the Deep.
Hoarse turnd the Starry Wheels, rending a way in Albions Loins
Beyond the Night of Beulah. In a dark & unknown Night,
Outstretchd his Giant beauty on the ground in pain & tears;

Jerusalem 18[D]

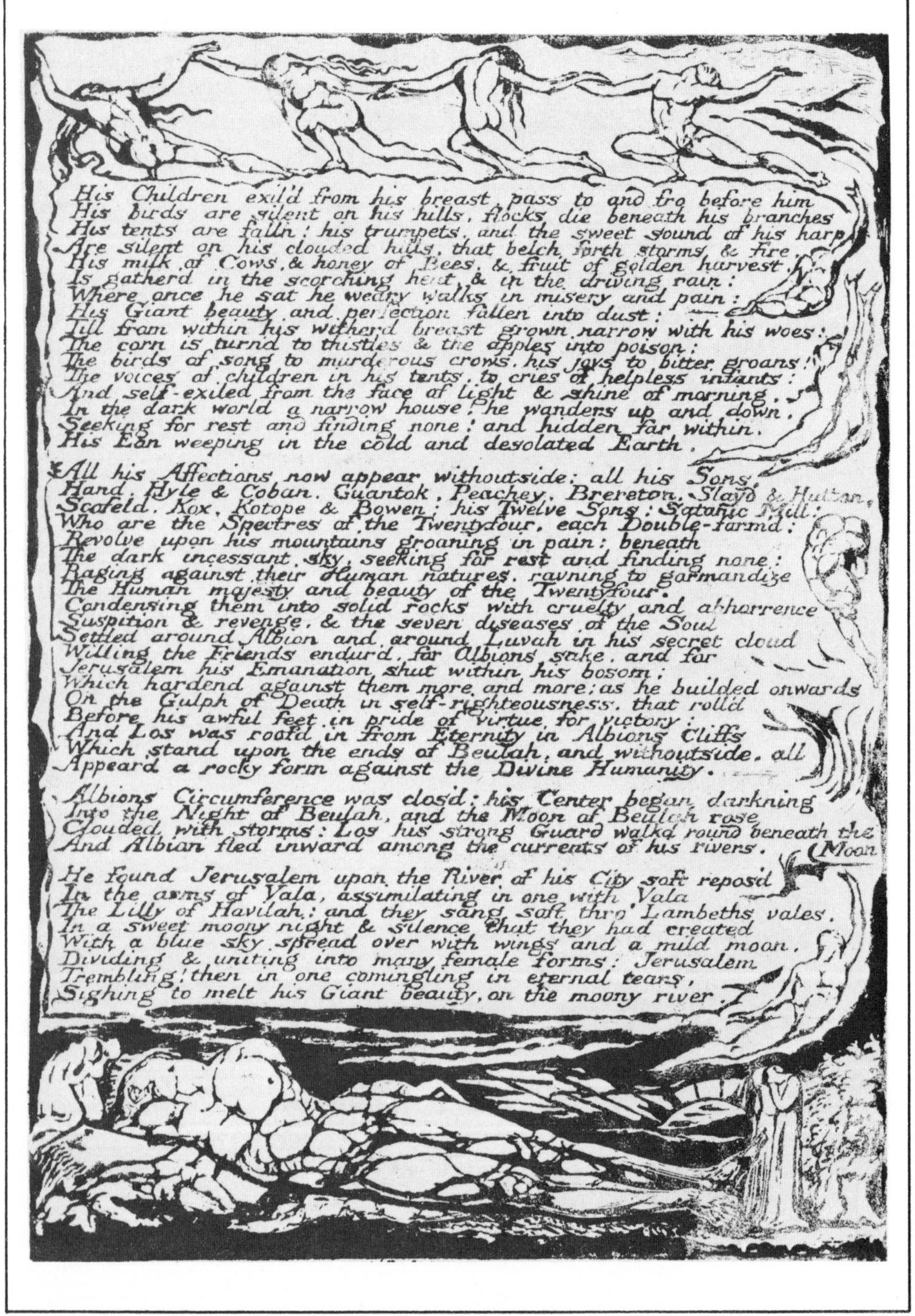

His Children exil'd from his breast pass to and fro before him
His birds are silent on his hills, flocks die beneath his branches
His tents are falln: his trumpets, and the sweet sound of his harp
Are silent on his clouded hills, that belch forth storms & fire.
His milk of Cows, & honey of Bees, & fruit of golden harvest,
Is gatherd in the scorching heat, & in the driving rain:
Where once he sat he weary walks in misery and pain:
His Giant beauty and perfection fallen into dust:
Till from within his witherd breast grown narrow with his woes:
The corn is turnd to thistles & the apples into poison:
The birds of song to murderous crows, his joys to bitter groans!
The voices of children in his tents, to cries of helpless infants:
And self-exiled from the face of light & shine of morning,
In the dark world a narrow house! he wanders up and down,
Seeking for rest and finding none! and hidden far within,
His Eon weeping in the cold and desolated Earth.

All his Affections now appear withoutside: all his Sons,
Hand, Hyle & Coban, Guantok, Peachey, Brereton, Slayd & Hutton,
Scofeld, Kox, Kotope & Bowen; his Twelve Sons: Satanic Mill!
Who are the Spectres of the Twentyfour, each Double-formd:
Revolve upon his mountains groaning in pain: beneath
The dark incessant sky, seeking for rest and finding none:
Raging against their Human natures, ravning to gormandize
The Human majesty and beauty of the Twentyfour.
Condensing them into solid rocks with cruelty and abhorrence
Suspition & revenge, & the seven diseases of the Soul
Settled around Albion and around Luvah in his secret cloud
Willing the Friends endurd, for Albions sake, and for
Jerusalem his Emanation shut within his bosom;
Which hardend against them more and more; as he builded onwards
On the Gulph of Death in self-righteousness, that rolld
Before his awful feet, in pride of virtue for victory:
And Los was roofd in from Eternity in Albions Cliffs
Which stand upon the ends of Beulah, and withoutside, all
Appeard a rocky form against the Divine Humanity.

Albions Circumference was clos'd: his Center began darkning
Into the Night of Beulah, and the Moon of Beulah rose
Clouded with storms: Los his strong Guard walkd round beneath the Moon
And Albion fled inward among the currents of his rivers.

He found Jerusalem upon the River of his City soft reposd
In the arms of Vala, assimilating in one with Vala
The Lilly of Havilah: and they sang soft thro' Lambeths vales,
In a sweet moony night & silence that they had created
With a blue sky spread over with wings and a mild moon,
Dividing & uniting into many female forms: Jerusalem
Trembling! then in one comingling in eternal tears,
Sighing to melt his Giant beauty, on the moony river.

Jerusalem 19[D]

Jerusalem 19. Across the top, "raging against their Human natures" (23), three warrior daughters and a (castrated?) son stagger with bloody knives (Druid), and blood seems running from the leading daughter's long hair. Beside the first paragraph, a description of battle, collapses a Samson-like victim, a preview of falling Albion, with just stength left to point to his murderers, the bloody daughters. His upward gesture is mimicked by two females below him who may be two daughters to match the "Double-form'd" sons (20).

Below, Albion lies "on the ground in pain & tears" (18:46), his head battered or wrenched sideways, his arms gone from sight. He seems bloody, not the marble effigy of Plate 14; yet the mourners at his head and feet, though less bent over now and facing him, still hide their faces and seem pale marble. Albion is here a defeated army (see 19:3–4), a giant among Lilliputians. A mandrake-like daughter, enrooting, lies crushed under his chest. Another daughter or son lies lifeless at his right thigh (a figure lacking in B); upon his left lies another (apparently headless[E]). An oak grove is behind the standing mourners; on the horizon is a bloody sun with spiky rays. Albion is less able to respond than he was to the rainbow of Plate 14, where he was only sulking. (His fall was rehearsed in Plate 9; the crushed female's in the head-falling of Plate 18.) Indeed the collapse of his face and the disappearance of his arm suggest that he too is melting into the earth.

Above the (setting?) sun a naked man soaring in the shape of a waxing moon (Los, with the gestures of Plate 7?) is blocked by the word "Moon." Then come "Albions Cliffs" and, above them, a climbing, struggling figure, the spectre perhaps, his back to us.

❧

Jerusalem 20. At top Vala (or Shiloh?) and Jerusalem, wreaths gone, reverse the opposition of Plate 18 but without embracing, and utter the dialogue on this page. The "web of despair" (4) puts banners on words in the next line that look like chimney smoke. "When winter" (12) is introduced by a row of indistinct lines, then two stars, then three waxing moons sinking from light into darkness, the second moon-ark having mast and sails (compare Plate 18), and finally a blazing comet (golden, with long streamers in copy B; pink with short streamers separated from the star head in E). Plainly the moon-boats are tossed on a tempestuous night sea. Further signs of storm and celestial terrestrial confusion are the scenes in the next two larger breaks, of men plowing with stars or comets, a row of flames between. Hunger and snow hide "the paths of man and beast" (12–13), but plowing and planting must go on. In the first row two figures tug at a rope or trace strung through the axis of a pinwheel of flame (an inward-rolling vortex: W) which is pushed from behind by two bearded men (one[BE]). Behind them another man (not in B) is tugging a star by its points (it is propelled by a comet tail in B). If this is the plowing (see Plate 29), the woman who follows is sowing star seeds, strewn before and behind her. Or all the people can be thought of as wanderers and captives stringing remembered moments "as on a thread of sorrow" (14–18). We see what not to do with constellations or vortices: reduce them to wheels.

In the lower row a soaring female (something like the sea goddess in the Arlington Court picture) follows the star-plows like a harvest spirit (Jerusalem, or Vala?) and four old men pull the harrow-like row of four turning stars (but it is hard to think these represent "the fourfold Man" drawing the "*out*-flaming Souls of human individuality": W). At the lower right corner are two tumbling stars, like those of Plate 9, that seem pieces fallen out of the universe. They are used by the man in the next plate for a new purpose.

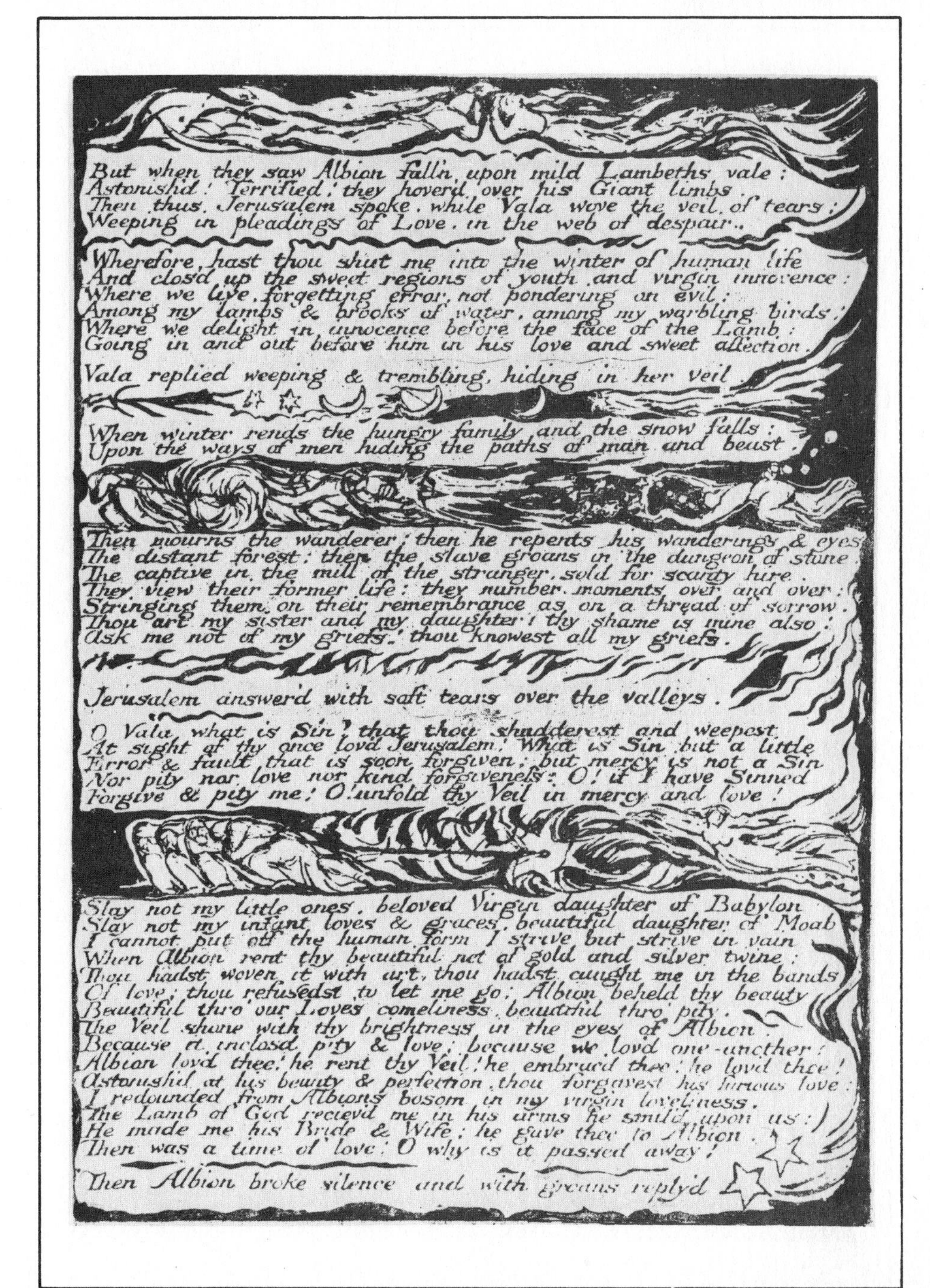

Jerusalem 20[D]

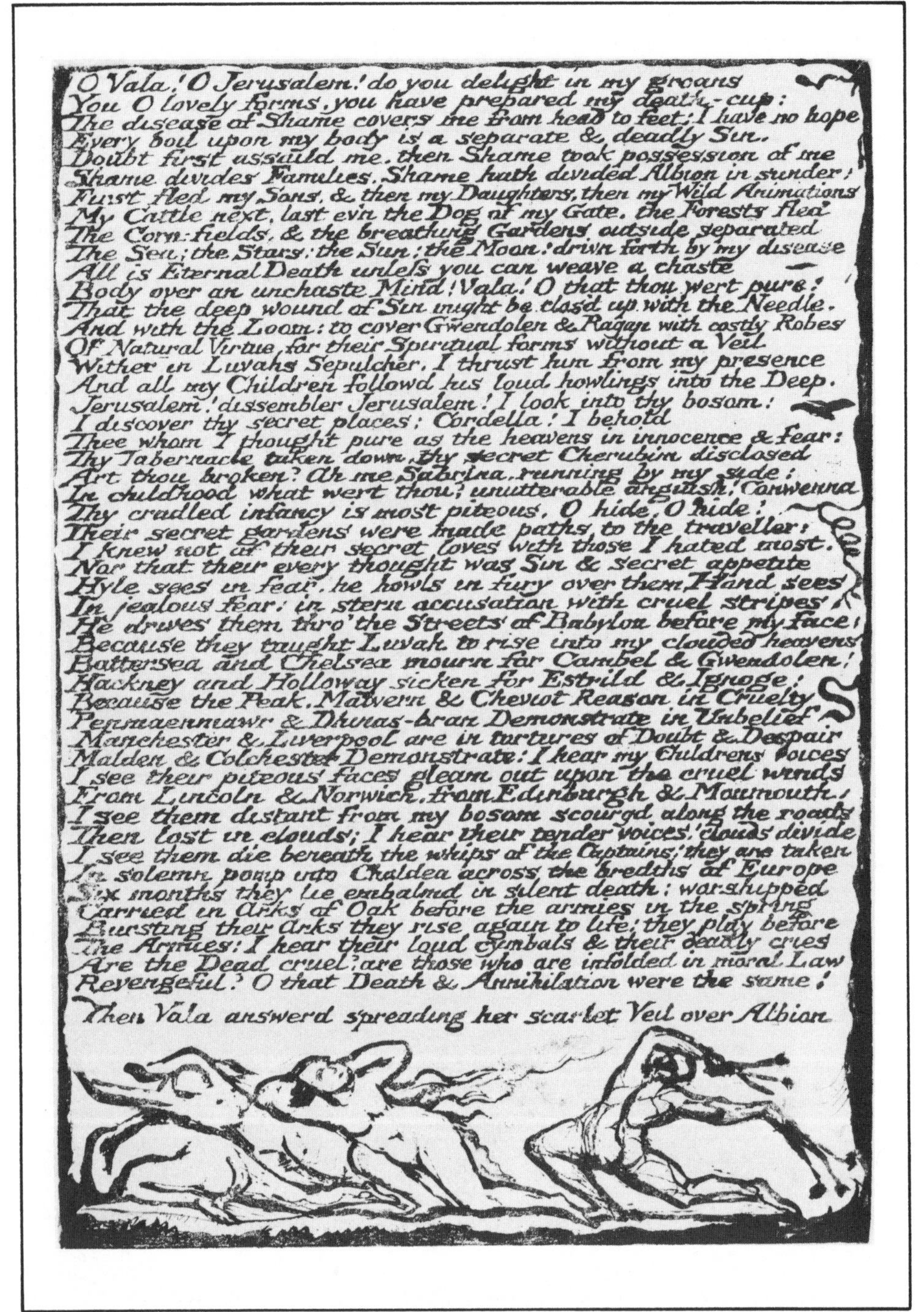
O Vala! O Jerusalem! do you delight in my groans
You O lovely forms, you have prepared my death-cup:
The disease of Shame covers me from head to feet: I have no hope
Every boil upon my body is a separate & deadly Sin.
Doubt first assaild me, then Shame took possession of me
Shame divides Families. Shame hath divided Albion in sunder!
First fled my Sons, & then my Daughters, then my Wild Animations
My Cattle next, last ev'n the Dog of my Gate. the Forests fled
The Corn-fields, & the breathing Gardens outside separated
The Sea; the Stars: the Sun: the Moon: drivn forth by my disease
All is Eternal Death unless you can weave a chaste
Body over an unchaste Mind! Vala! O that thou wert pure!
That the deep wound of Sin might be closd up with the Needle,
And with the Loom: to cover Gwendolen & Ragan with costly Robes
Of Natural Virtue, for their Spiritual forms without a Veil
Wither in Luvahs Sepulcher. I thrust him from my presence
And all my Children followd his loud howlings into the Deep.
Jerusalem! dissembler Jerusalem! I look into thy bosom:
I discover thy secret places: Cordella! I behold
Thee whom I thought pure as the heavens in innocence & fear:
Thy Tabernacle taken down, thy secret Cherubim disclosed
Art thou broken? Ah me Sabrina, running by my side:
In childhood what wert thou? unutterable anguish! Conwenna
Thy cradled infancy is most piteous. O hide, O hide!
Their secret gardens were made paths to the traveller:
I knew not of their secret loves with those I hated most.
Nor that their every thought was Sin & secret appetite
Hyle sees in fear, he howls in fury over them, Hand sees
In jealous fear: in stern accusation with cruel stripes
He drives them thro' the Streets of Babylon before my face:
Because they taught Luvah to rise into my clouded heavens
Battersea and Chelsea mourn for Cambel & Gwendolen!
Hackney and Holloway sicken for Estrild & Ignoge!
Because the Peak, Malvern & Cheviot Reason in Cruelty
Penmaenmawr & Dhinas-bran Demonstrate in Unbelief
Manchester & Liverpool are in tortures of Doubt & Despair
Malden & Colchester Demonstrate: I hear my Childrens voices
I see their piteous faces gleam out upon the cruel winds
From Lincoln & Norwich, from Edinburgh & Monmouth;
I see them distant from my bosom scourgd along the roads
Then lost in clouds; I hear their tender voices! clouds divide
I see them die beneath the whips of the Captains; they are taken
In solemn pomp into Chaldea across the bredths of Europe
Six months they lie embalmd in silent death: worshipped
Carried in Arks of Oak before the armies in the spring
Bursting their Arks they rise again to life: they play before
The Armies: I hear their loud cymbals & their deadly cries
Are the Dead cruel? are those who are infolded in moral Law
Revengeful? O that Death & Annihilation were the same!

Then Vala answerd spreading her scarlet Veil over Albion

Jerusalem 21^{D}

Jerusalem 21. Here six stars (five-pointed* as on Plate 20) appear on the cat-o'-nine-tails wielded by Hand as he pursues Albion's daughters, Cordella, Sabrina, and Conwenna, and "drives them thro' the Streets of Babylon" (28–30) for trafficking with Luvah (the Zoa associated with France and Jesus and love). Compare the man whipping women in "Milton and the Spirit of Plato," *Il Penseroso* 9. Three spirals of flame-like hair behind the most seductive daughter may not be meant as strands of her own hair but may represent the inflammatory seductiveness of the three women, just as similar spirals of red flame in *Milton* 19^{D} represent the three dancing daughters as seen by the three wives.

Above the words "cruel stripes" (29) and "Cruelty" and "Unbelief" (34–35) are a marginal looped tendril growing downward and a twisted strap. The bird above "innocence & fear" (20) hardly dares take shape.

Jerusalem 22. At top Vala is "spreading her scarlet Veil" (21:50) over someone whose identity it almost hides, Albion according to the text, though we have not seen him with wings before. Three birds fly in the margin beside Albion's lament, near mentions of Love and Jerusalem. At bottom four winged Cherubim form a human chain above three black cogwheels, in illustration of Jerusalem's question (34–35). The wheels are described in 18:8–10: "Three Immense Wheels turning upon one-another Into Non-Entity . . . To murder their own Souls." They churn in water which foams[B] at the intersections of the cogs; behind them and the Cherubim are pink[B] or sulfur[E] flames.

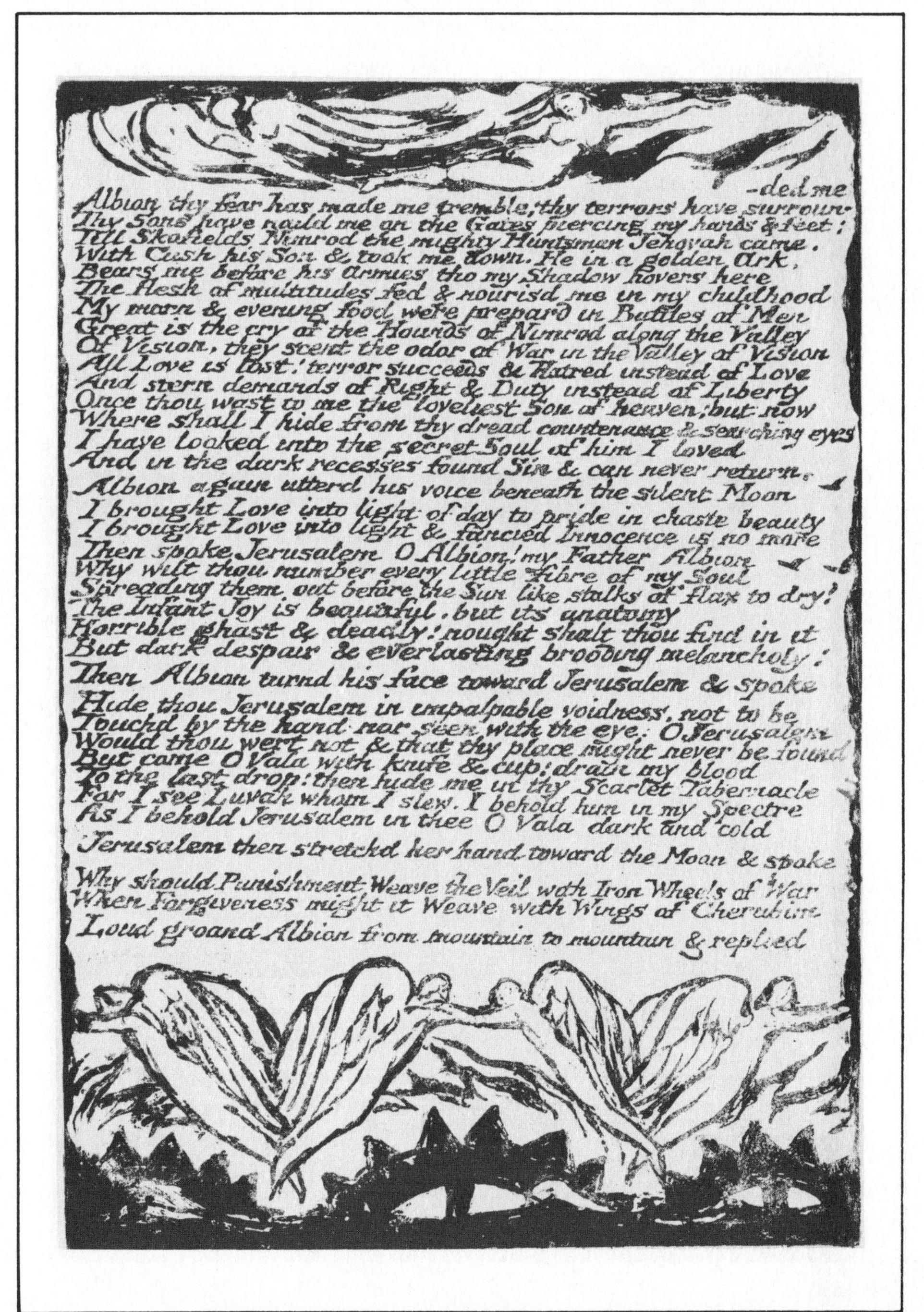

Jerusalem 22[D]

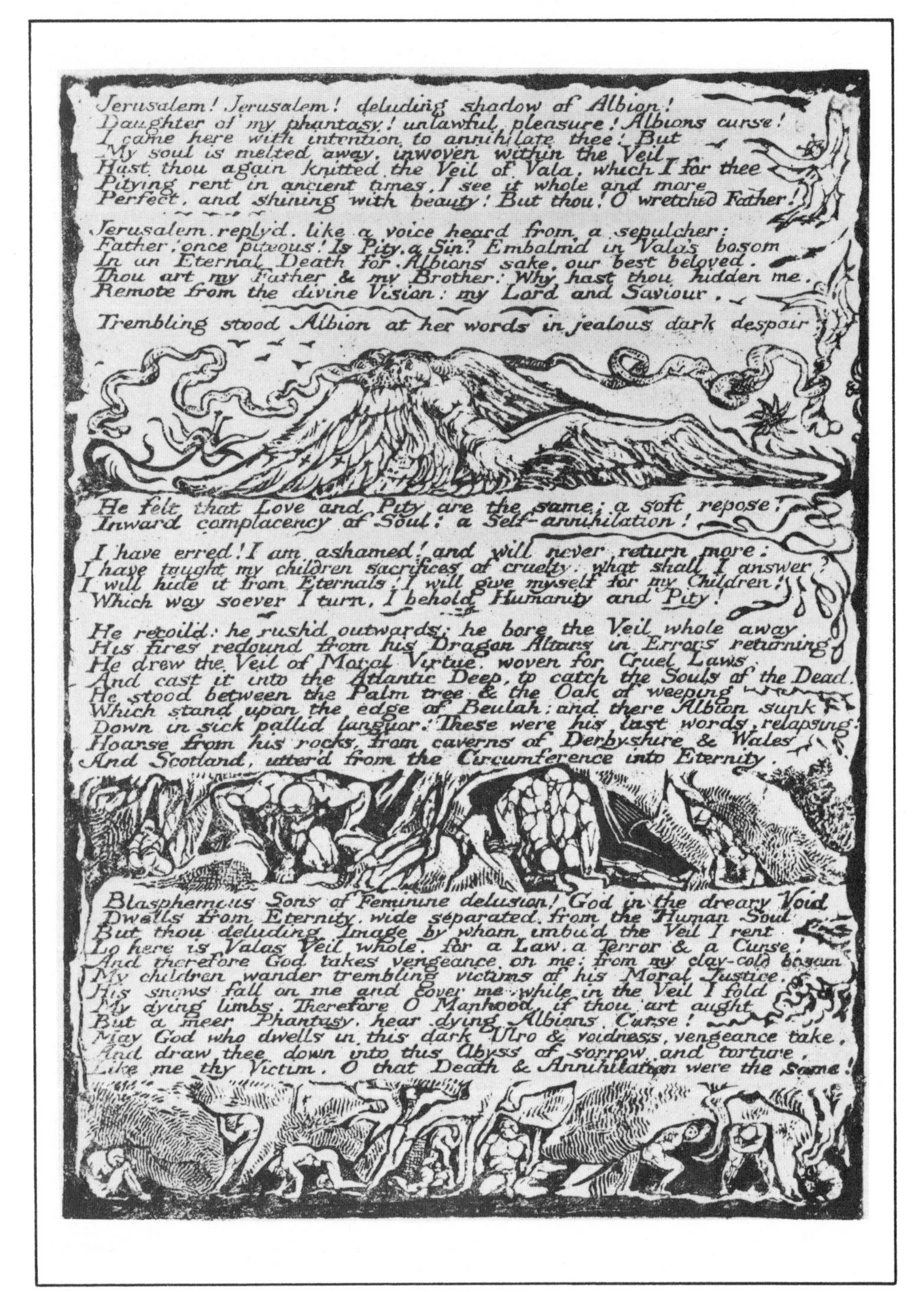

Jerusalem! Jerusalem! deluding shadow of Albion!
Daughter of my phantasy! unlawful pleasure! Albions curse!
I came here with intention to annihilate thee! But
My soul is melted away, inwoven within the Veil
Hast thou again knitted the Veil of Vala, which I for thee
Pitying rent in ancient times. I see it whole and more
Perfect, and shining with beauty! But thou! O wretched Father!

Jerusalem reply'd, like a voice heard from a sepulcher:
Father! once piteous! Is Pity a Sin? Embalmd in Vala's bosom
In an Eternal Death for Albions sake, our best beloved.
Thou art my Father & my Brother: Why hast thou hidden me,
Remote from the divine Vision: my Lord and Saviour.

Trembling stood Albion at her words in jealous dark despair:

He felt that Love and Pity are the same; a soft repose!
Inward complacency of Soul: a Self-annihilation!

I have erred! I am ashamed! and will never return more:
I have taught my children sacrifices of cruelty: what shall I answer?
I will hide it from Eternals! I will give myself for my Children!
Which way soever I turn, I behold Humanity and Pity!

He recoild: he rushd outwards; he bore the Veil whole away
His fires redound from his Dragon Altars in Errors returning
He drew the Veil of Moral Virtue, woven for Cruel Laws,
And cast it into the Atlantic Deep, to catch the Souls of the Dead.
He stood between the Palm tree & the Oak of weeping
Which stand upon the edge of Beulah; and there Albion sunk
Down in sick pallid languor! These were his last words, relapsing!
Hoarse from his rocks, from caverns of Derbyshire & Wales
And Scotland, utter'd from the Circumference into Eternity.

Blasphemous Sons of Feminine delusion! God in the dreary Void
Dwells from Eternity, wide separated from the Human Soul
But thou deluding Image by whom imbu'd the Veil I rent
Lo here is Valas Veil whole, for a Law, a Terror & a Curse!
And therefore God takes vengeance on me: from my clay-cold bosom
My children wander trembling victims of his Moral Justice.
His snows fall on me and cover me, while in the Veil I fold
My dying limbs. Therefore O Manhood, if thou art aught
But a meer Phantasy, hear dying Albions Curse!
May God who dwells in this dark Ulro & voidness, vengeance take,
And draw thee down into this Abyss of sorrow and torture,
Like me thy Victim. O that Death & Annihilation were the same!

Jerusalem 23D

Jerusalem 23. Jerusalem with eagle wings, only half recumbent and able to speak to Albion (compare his body outstretched in Plate 19), yet speaks as "from a sepulcher" (8), is partly enrooted, and is caught in a twisted visceral scarf (the "Veil of Vala" which Albion imagines "whole and more Perfect, and shining with beauty!": 6–7). Above this veil at right fly two human butterflies (whom we will recognize in Plate 44 as the witnesses, the Spectre and Emanation of Los). They are not joining hands as the Cherubim of Plate 22, but they fly toward each other; and the scattered birds above Jerusalem—one near each of the butterflies, four and four in the paragraph breaks—are arranged as a flight of five above the head of Jerusalem. (In F looping tendrils are added in the left margin of lines 10–12 and a floral piece below "Trembling.") Another hopeful though vegetative sign is the replacement of stony or stone mourners at Jerusalem's head and feet by blossoming, polenating lily (of Calvary: W) and star-flower (of Bethlehem: W), flowers of Beulah.

Below her, however, we see the interior of a mountain of which her still stony figure forms the peak, the "caverns of Derbyshire" (27–28) (one called "the Devil's Arse": *Dict*) where Albion's imprisoned multitudes are closed not only from light of day but from seeing or touching one another. Only one small bird adorns this zone of text. From the "will" of Albion's decision that he "will never return" (16) a banner loops off, splits, and turns back on itself or runs down into fishy tears in the right margin. The "victims" in the coal mines repeat the incarceration of the Ugolino family (see *Gates* 12 and *Marriage* 16; but also *Gates* 3 and *Urizen* 4, 9, 10) but multiplied and isolated (even so, like seeds in the earth). The man on all fours, at bottom, third from left, is like Nebuchadnezzar, especially as he crops the grass in *Night Thoughts* 299. Wicksteed notes that on the wing feathers of Jerusalem are a series of Golgotha crosses.

❧

Jerusalem 24. Rain in web form reveals the deluge to be an illusion which the dove brooding in the moon-ark (given a human face in BE) can signal the escape from. The water foams* around the boat. This illumination marks Albion's momentary recovery of the truth about Jerusalem and Babylon and the Divine Body of the Human Imagination (17–25 etc). But his falling back into doubt (54 ff), his assumption that accepting the mercy of the Savior is to die in his arms (59–60), gives the Veil continued existence. Its rushing "from his hand, Vegetating Knot by Knot" (61–62) is illustrated by the sequence of human forms dwindling into visceral lumps, across and down the page. The O-mouthed faces at the start of the sequence may seem to show a potentially hopeful outcry, but even the second of these falls back into the line of silent, pyramid-building slaves; the open mouths (of consumers or devourers) are but the start of the intestinal tract. At the bend in the tract-veil, Vala squats with an alluring glance (we have seen her in the same position in *Milton* 26).

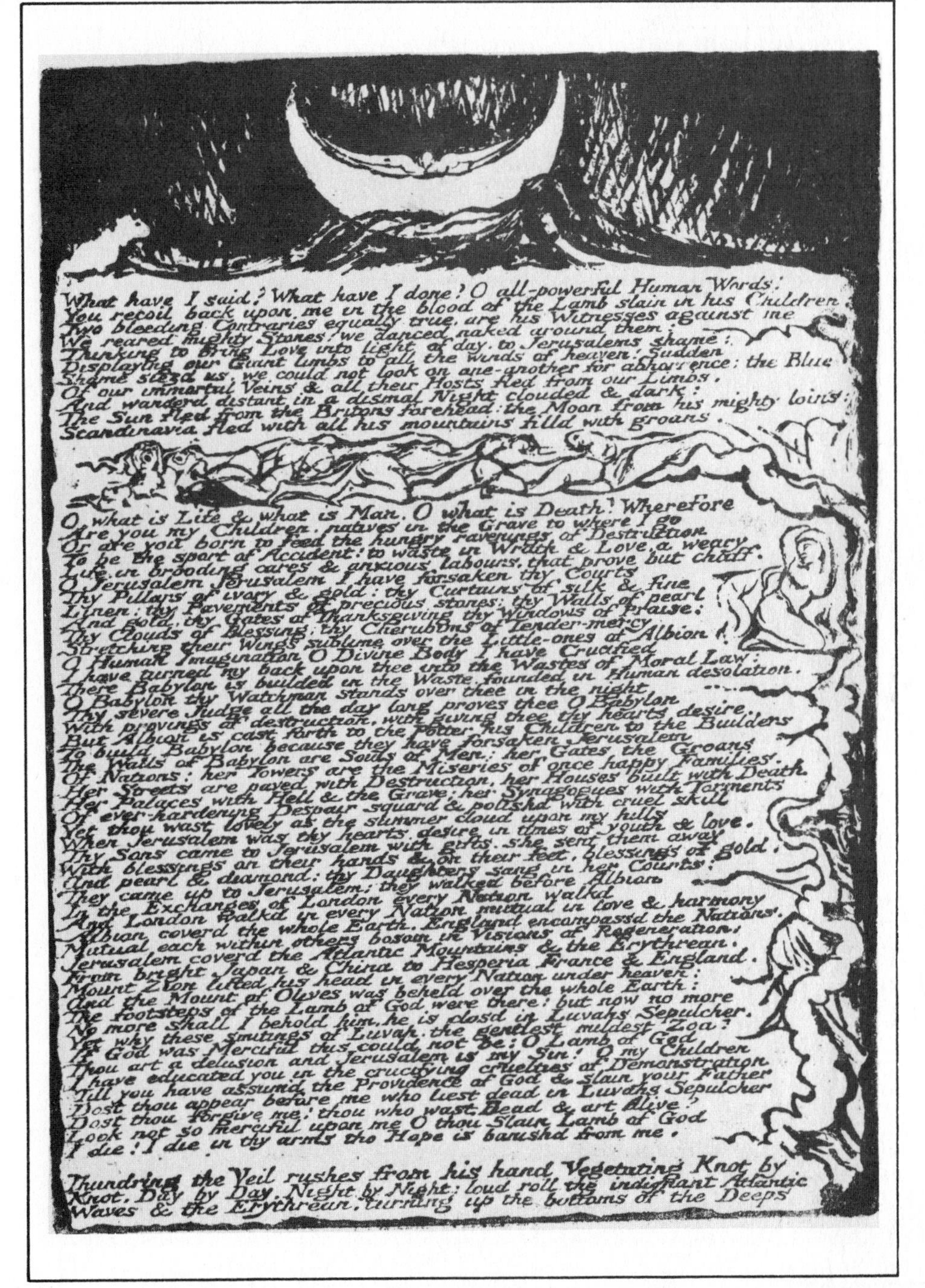

Jerusalem 24D

Jerusalem 25[D]

Jerusalem 25. Albion's plight at the chapter's end is that of a victim of Druid sacrifice, of the sparagmos of his human divinity, as three wilful maidens play the three fates with his thread of life. This emblem culminates the series, Plates 9, 14, 19, 22 (top), 24, depicting Albion's fall and entrapment.

Not yet "fled from the mighty limbs" (27:16) are the "Starry Heavens," represented by two bright stars (Jupiter or Mars and Venus), Orion's belt, and the seven Pleiades, and a crescent moon (given eyes in E) and an angry (or surprised[B]) sun (which rightly belongs in his forehead: 24:10). But under the veil which Vala holds up as an operating tent, he is now the victim rather than the form and former of the universe; he is now inside the intestine-veil, though its fibres are potentially grain (see *Milton* 49) or benign atmosphere (see Plate 100) or "fibres of life" (67:1–14). Rahab, with left leg crossed over right, fixes his attention mesmerically (her right hand behind her back: compare Gwendolen with her falsehood in Plate 81), while Tirzah, (weeping tears[E]) and seated on a stepped stone, draws from his body and winds into a ball (see *Forms* plate 6) a cord that may be seen as, symbolically, his umbilical cord to "Nature" which had never been cut, his own intestines (see Plate 24, also Poussin's *Martyrdom of St. Erasmus: Blake Newsletter* 19, plate 6 and, for a graphic source, plate 7, *Le Tre Parche*), or his spinal cord, the central line Blake draws as the body's axis even when depicting a front view. The tight covering of his genitals is symbolic, if also perhaps a concession to Blake's contemporaries.

This torture is how Albion imagines Luvah-Christ's sacrifice to have been. With a reversal of his attitude, the situation could be as depicted in the design for "To Tirzah" (*Songs* 52). Contrast the golden string of Plate 77.

Jerusalem 26. This chapter divider is in solid color as are Plates 1, 51, 76, and 100. Naked, in red, black, and yellow flames, Hand (whom we saw as flagellator on Plate 21) is a marching crucifix, with nails in hands and (perhaps) feet (none shown in E). The flames form a halo around his head and a (brazen) serpent around his arms. He is walking (like Los in Plate 1) into the wind, perhaps leading Jerusalem *into* Hades (as Orpheus was leading Euridyce *out*). She is reacting with pity and repulsion. Does his looking back at her—or the horror he is leading her toward—stop her in her tracks? In Plate 4 she had held out a hand to lead humans upward. (From this point on, all color references are to copy E as the only colored copy.)

Jerusalem 26D (exact size)

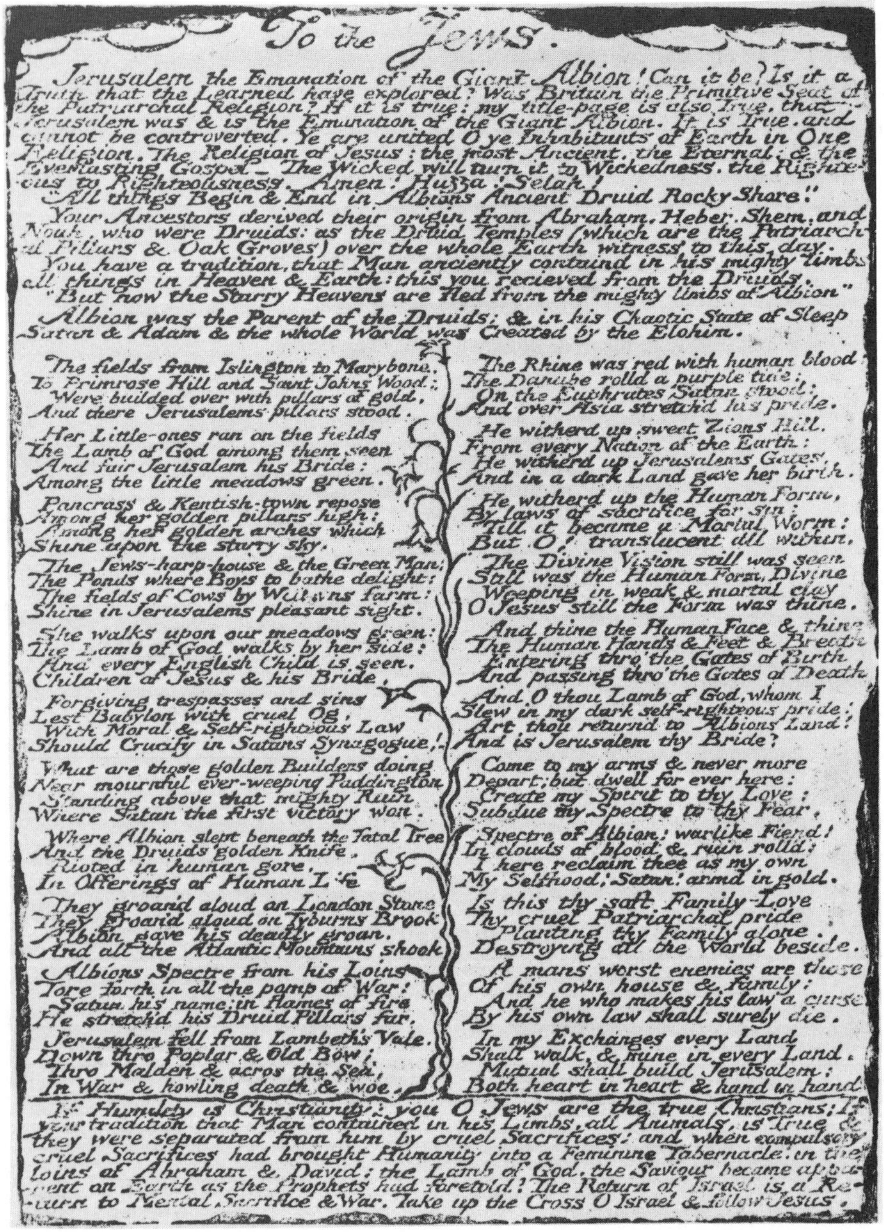

To the Jews.

Jerusalem the Emanation of the Giant Albion! Can it be? Is it a Truth that the Learned have explored? Was Britain the Primitive Seat of the Patriarchal Religion? If it is true: my title-page is also True, that Jerusalem was & is the Emanation of the Giant Albion. It is True, and cannot be controverted. Ye are united O ye Inhabitants of Earth in One Religion. The Religion of Jesus: the most Ancient, the Eternal: & the Everlasting Gospel— The Wicked will turn it to Wickedness, the Righteous to Righteousness. Amen! Huzza! Selah!

"All things Begin & End in Albions Ancient Druid Rocky Shore."

Your Ancestors derived their origin from Abraham, Heber, Shem, and Noah, who were Druids: as the Druid Temples (which are the Patriarchal Pillars & Oak Groves) over the whole Earth witness to this day.

You have a tradition, that Man anciently containd in his mighty limbs all things in Heaven & Earth: this you recieved from the Druids.

"But now the Starry Heavens are fled from the mighty limbs of Albion"

Albion was the Parent of the Druids; & in his Chaotic State of Sleep Satan & Adam & the whole World was Created by the Elohim.

The fields from Islington to Marybone,
To Primrose Hill and Saint Johns Wood:
Were builded over with pillars of gold,
And there Jerusalems pillars stood.

Her Little-ones ran on the fields
The Lamb of God among them seen
And fair Jerusalem his Bride:
Among the little meadows green.

Pancrass & Kentish-town repose
Among her golden pillars high:
Among her golden arches which
Shine upon the starry sky.

The Jews-harp-house & the Green Man;
The Ponds where Boys to bathe delight:
The fields of Cows by Willans farm:
Shine in Jerusalems pleasant sight.

She walks upon our meadows green:
The Lamb of God walks by her side:
And every English Child is seen,
Children of Jesus & his Bride,

Forgiving trespasses and sins
Lest Babylon with cruel Og,
With Moral & Self-righteous Law
Should Crucify in Satans Synagogue!

What are those golden Builders doing
Near mournful ever-weeping Paddington
Standing above that mighty Ruin
Where Satan the first victory won.

Where Albion slept beneath the Fatal Tree
And the Druids golden Knife,
Rioted in human gore,
In Offerings of Human Life

They groand aloud on London Stone
They groand aloud on Tyburns Brook
Albion gave his deadly groan,
And all the Atlantic Mountains shook

Albions Spectre from his Loins
Tore forth in all the pomp of War!
Satan his name: in flames of fire
He stretchd his Druid Pillars far.

Jerusalem fell from Lambeths Vale,
Down thro Poplar & Old Bow;
Thro Malden & acros the Sea,
In War & howling death & woe.

The Rhine was red with human blood:
The Danube rolld a purple tide:
On the Euphrates Satan stood:
And over Asia stretchd his pride.

He witherd up sweet Zions Hill,
From every Nation of the Earth:
He witherd up Jerusalems Gates,
And in a dark Land gave her birth.

He witherd up the Human Form,
By laws of sacrifice for sin:
Till it became a Mortal Worm:
But O! translucent all within.

The Divine Vision still was seen
Still was the Human Form, Divine
Weeping in weak & mortal clay
O Jesus still the Form was thine.

And thine the Human Face & thine
The Human Hands & Feet & Breath
Entering thro' the Gates of Birth
And passing thro' the Gates of Death

And O thou Lamb of God, whom I
Slew in my dark self-righteous pride:
Art thou returnd to Albions Land!
And is Jerusalem thy Bride?

Come to my arms & never more
Depart; but dwell for ever here:
Create my Spirit to thy Love:
Subdue my Spectre to thy Fear.

Spectre of Albion! warlike Fiend!
In clouds of blood & ruin rolld:
I here reclaim thee as my own
My Selfhood; Satan! armd in gold.

Is this thy soft Family-Love
Thy cruel Patriarchal pride
Planting thy Family alone,
Destroying all the World beside.

A mans worst enemies are those
Of his own house & family;
And he who makes his law a curse,
By his own law shall surely die.

In my Exchanges every Land
Shall walk, & mine in every Land,
Mutual shall build Jerusalem:
Both heart in heart & hand in hand.

If Humility is Christianity; you O Jews are the true Christians: If your tradition that Man contained in his Limbs, all Animals, is True & they were separated from him by cruel Sacrifices: and when compulsory cruel Sacrifices had brought Humanity into a Feminine Tabernacle, in the loins of Abraham & David: the Lamb of God, the Saviour became apparent on Earth as the Prophets had foretold? The Return of Israel is a Return to Mental Sacrifice & War. Take up the Cross O Israel & follow Jesus.

Jerusalem 27D

Jerusalem 27. The central dividing stems support five lily blossoms —only on the left side, for that's where the spaces occur; in the text, Jesus and his Bride are hailed in both columns. The right column is given a light blue wash, and the top corners of sky above the cloud of text are colored blue, pink, and purple, suggesting dawn or a rainbow.

Jerusalem 28. This vision of what Albion calls "unnatural consanguinities" (7) was revised from its proof state (see Appendix) by removal of a phallic caterpillar (still partly visible) from the lower leaf of the lotos lily and by a reshaping of thighs and spine from a position of copulation to a sort of side-saddle sitting (and in E a removal of the front figure's right hand). At first the embracing pair were male (at left) and female; they now seem to fit the references to Jerusalem, on the Thames, reposing "in the arms of Vala, assimilating in one with Vala The Lilly of Havilah" (19:40–42; compare 29:44). Vala would be the one facing us, half inflorescence, half woman. The great lily on the Thames can represent, in Blake's art, the bright illumination of a deep text. Albion sees in the embrace "darkness immingled with light" (29:32) on his "furrowd field" (often a metaphor for lines engraved in copper). But Vala imposes on Albion when she scoffs at her once loving union with Jerusalem, "embracing in the Vision of Jesus," concluding that love "never yet Immingled God & Man" (29:44–46).

Grant (*Essays* 354–62) makes an excellent case for reading the unrevised plate as an emblem of Albion's prelapsarian "furious love" for Vala when he rent her "beautiful net of gold and silver twine" (not then a smoky veil) and embraced her in "a time of love" (20:30–41). It can symbolize the Fall, not because happy copulation or rending the veil was wrong (Christ's rending of the veil to the Temple is exemplary for Blake in 44:40 and 69:38–40), but because Albion "made the mistake of repudiating his positive action and, as the text [here] declares, fell, to become 'the punisher and judge' of 'every labour of love In all the Garden of Eden'" (compare 1–4). As revised, the picture can still bear these meanings, whether read as an act of his own that Albion now blindly condemns or as a hobgoblin of his accusing jealousy. Albion curses, just as Dante swoons at the sight of the embracing of Paolo and Francesca in this same chaste but passionate manner; yet we can see (as could Dante, in Blake's depiction, *in* his swoon) that such "embracing in the Vision of Jesus" renders Vala's net harmless, transformed to fertility—a stylized stamen that matches the golden sky and makes no stain on the lily bright.

In the text Albion, not simply perverse as pictured in Plate 14 but a righteous judge of the underworld, in effect still accepts the Plate 25 version of love as unnatural. And in the marginal illumination the water imagery of Plate 11 recurs, with four fish in

Jerusalem 28[D]

Turning his back to the Divine Vision, his Spectrous
Chaos before his face appeard: an Unformed Memory.
Then spoke the Spectrous Chaos to Albion darkning cold
From the back & loins where dwell the Spectrous Dead
I am your Rational Power O Albion & that Human Form
You call Divine, is but a Worm seventy inches long
That creeps forth in a night & is dried in the morning sun
In fortuitous concourse of memorys accumulated & lost
It plows the Earth in its own conceit. it overwhelms the Hills
Beneath its winding labyrinths, till a stone of the brook
Stops it in midst of its pride among its hills & rivers
Battersea & Chelsea mourn. London & Canterbury tremble
Their place shall not be found as the wind passes over
The ancient Cities of the Earth remove as a traveller
And shall Albions Cities remain when I pass over them
With my deluge of forgotten remembrances over the tablet

So spoke the Spectre to Albion. he is the Great Selfhood
Satan: Worshipd as God by the Mighty Ones of the Earth
Having a white Dot calld a Center from which branches out
A Circle in continual gyrations. this became a Heart
From which sprang numerous branches varying their motions
Producing many Heads three or seven or ten, & hands & feet
Innumerable at will of the unfortunate contemplator
Who becomes his food such is the way of the Devouring Power
And this is the cause of the appearance in the frowning Chaos
Albions Emanation which he had hidden in Jealousy
Appeard now in the frowning Chaos prolific upon the Chaos
Reflecting back to Albion in Sexual Reasoning Hermaphroditic
Albion spoke. Who art thou that appearest in gloomy pomp
Involving the Divine Vision in colours of autumn ripeness
I never saw thee till this time, nor beheld life abstracted
Nor darkness immingled with light on my furrowd field
Whence camest thou! who art thou O loveliest? the Divine Vision
Is as nothing before thee. faded is all life and joy
Vala replied in clouds of tears Albions garment embracing
I was a City & a Temple built by Albions Children.
I was a Garden planted with beauty I allured on hill & valley
The River of Life to flow against my walls & among my trees
Vala was Albions Bride & Wife in great Eternity
The loveliest of the daughters of Eternity when in day-break
I emanated from Luvah over the Towers of Jerusalem
And in her Courts among her little Children offering up
The Sacrifice of fanatic love! why loved I Jerusalem!
Why was I one with her embracing in the Vision of Jesus
Wherefore did I loving create love, which never yet
Immingled God & Man, when thou & I, hid the Divine Vision
In cloud of secret gloom which behold involve me round about
Know me now Albion: look upon me I alone am Beauty
The Imaginative Human Form is but a breathing of Vala
I breathe him forth into the Heaven from my secret Cave
Born of the Woman to obey the Woman O Albion the mighty
For the Divine appearance is Brotherhood, but I am Love

Jerusalem 29[33]D

the last two stanza breaks and other sea creatures in the right margin. He sees every ornament of perfection and labor of love as criminal: "I therefore condense them into solid rocks" (10). This is to condemn all art except sculpture, and what it does to the creatures of Los-Blake's illuminating fluids (the medium indicated here as in Plate 11) is to show them as freaks: a sort of shrimp-dog at lower right, an oyster near the top. But in revenge, just where Albion is declaring, "here I plant my seat!" (12), the artist depicts a man putting his head into a snail shell (which makes a dunce cap) and holding a falling star-of-Bethlehem lily (see Plate 23) which turns into a star-fish.

Jerusalem 29[33]. The spectre's account of the human form (not divine) is illustrated literally: "It plows the Earth in its own conceit" (9). Plowing (on the ground level, engraving or etching) seems to the spectre or journeyman a mad business for philosophers. His vision of three wise men of Gotham pulling and guiding the plow shows his contempt for the abstract theorists (which Blake would share) but lumped together with contempt for the prophetic Imagination (which he would not). The efforts of the prophet pushing rather than guiding the plow are as futile as the superciliousness of the conceited lion-bodied theorists in front. It is the spectre who belongs in the traces, with Los in control. In context, the upward glances of the lion men and the furrow-watching of the plowman are parodistic.

(Compare the usurpation of the celestial plows in Plate 20 and the uniquely energy-and-wisdom charged but motionless contraption of Plate 41.)

❧

Jerusalem 30[34]. After the words of Los's cry, "O Albion why wilt thou Create a Female Will?" (31) a naked woman leaps forth. Her feet and hands are only sketched, perhaps to show that she is no more than a smoky figment of Albion's brain. The hieroglyph is comparable to figures in the *Marriage* who represent "Soul"; the concept of the Female Will has evolved from the idea that to think of soul and body as separate entities is an error.

This plate and the one preceding are apparently quite early pages; Plate 29 was evidently a first explanation of the term "Spectre"; the style of lettering and incidental illustration seem to represent an early format.

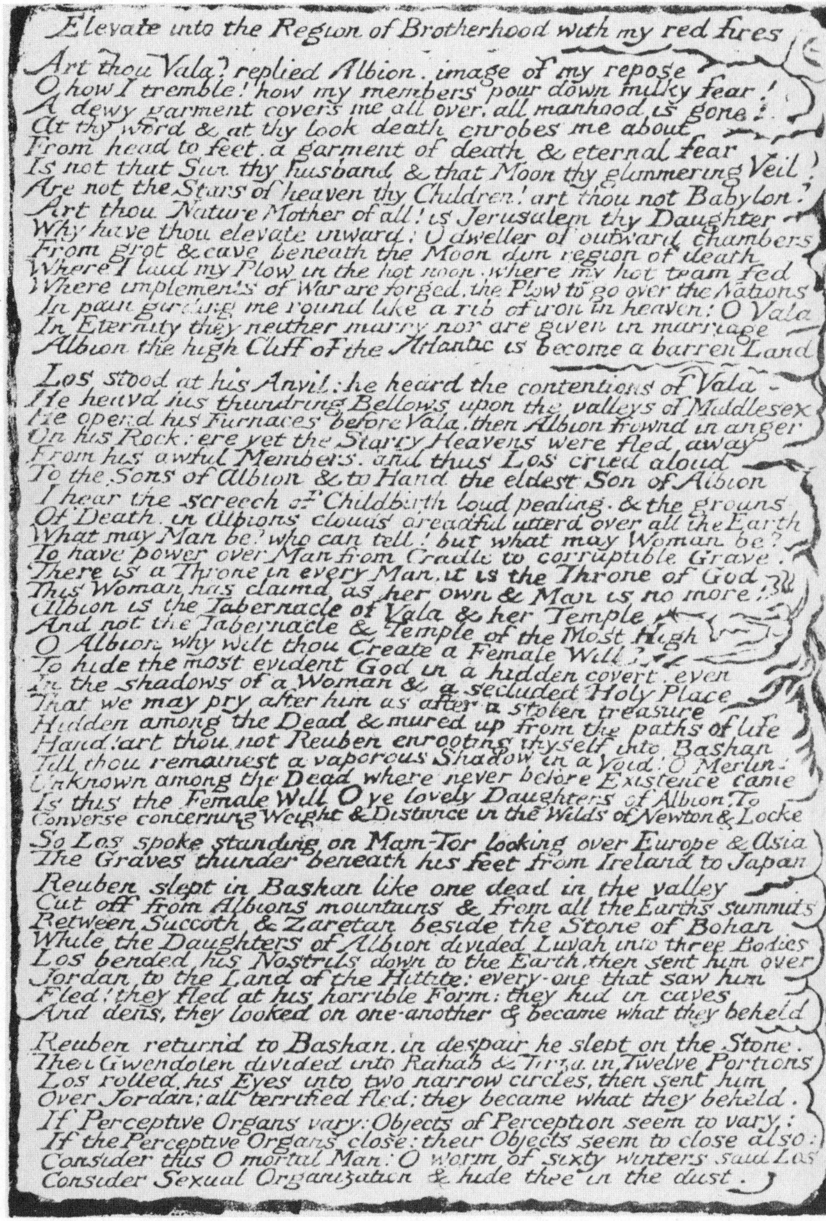

Elevate into the Region of Brotherhood with my red fires
Art thou Vala? replied Albion. image of my repose
O how I tremble! how my members pour down milky fear!
A dewy garment covers me all over. all manhood is gone!
At thy word & at thy look death enrobes me about
From head to feet. a garment of death & eternal fear
Is not that Sun thy husband & that Moon thy glimmering Veil?
Are not the Stars of heaven thy Children! art thou not Babylon?
Art thou Nature Mother of all! is Jerusalem thy Daughter
Why have thou elevate inward: O dweller of outward chambers
From grot & cave beneath the Moon dim region of death
Where I laid my Plow in the hot noon. where my hot team fed
Where implements of War are forged. the Plow to go over the Nations
In pain girding me round like a rib of iron in heaven: O Vala
In Eternity they neither marry nor are given in marriage
Albion the high Cliff of the Atlantic is become a barren Land

Los stood at his Anvil: he heard the contentions of Vala
He heavd his thundring Bellows upon the valleys of Middlesex
He opend his Furnaces before Vala. then Albion frownd in anger
On his Rock: ere yet the Starry Heavens were fled away
From his awful Members. and thus Los cried aloud
To the Sons of Albion & to Hand the eldest Son of Albion
I hear the screech of Childbirth loud pealing. & the groans
Of Death. in Albions clouds dreadful utterd over all the Earth
What may Man be? who can tell! but what may Woman be?
To have power over Man from Cradle to corruptible Grave.
There is a Throne in every Man, it is the Throne of God
This Woman has claimd as her own & Man is no more!
Albion is the Tabernacle of Vala & her Temple
And not the Tabernacle & Temple of the Most High
O Albion why wilt thou Create a Female Will?
To hide the most evident God in a hidden covert. even
In the shadows of a Woman & a secluded Holy Place
That we may pry after him as after a stolen treasure
Hidden among the Dead & mured up from the paths of life
Hand! art thou not Reuben enrooting thyself into Bashan
Till thou remainest a vaporous Shadow in a Void! O Merlin!
Unknown among the Dead where never before Existence came
Is this the Female Will O ye lovely Daughters of Albion. To
Converse concerning Weight & Distance in the Wilds of Newton & Locke

So Los spoke standing on Mam-Tor looking over Europe & Asia
The Graves thunder beneath his feet from Ireland to Japan

Reuben slept in Bashan like one dead in the valley
Cut off from Albions mountains & from all the Earths summits
Between Succoth & Zaretan beside the Stone of Bohan
While the Daughters of Albion divided Luvah into three Bodies
Los bended his Nostrils down to the Earth. then sent him over
Jordan to the Land of the Hittite: every-one that saw him
Fled! they fled at his horrible Form: they hid in caves
And dens, they looked on one-another & became what they beheld

Reuben returnd to Bashan. in despair he slept on the Stone.
Then Gwendolen divided into Rahab & Tirza in Twelve Portions
Los rolled his Eyes into two narrow circles, then sent him
Over Jordan; all terrified fled: they became what they beheld.
If Perceptive Organs vary: Objects of Perception seem to vary:
If the Perceptive Organs close: their Objects seem to close also:
Consider this O mortal Man: O worm of sixty winters said Los
Consider Sexual Organization & hide thee in the dust.

Jerusalem 30[34]D

Jerusalem 31[35]D

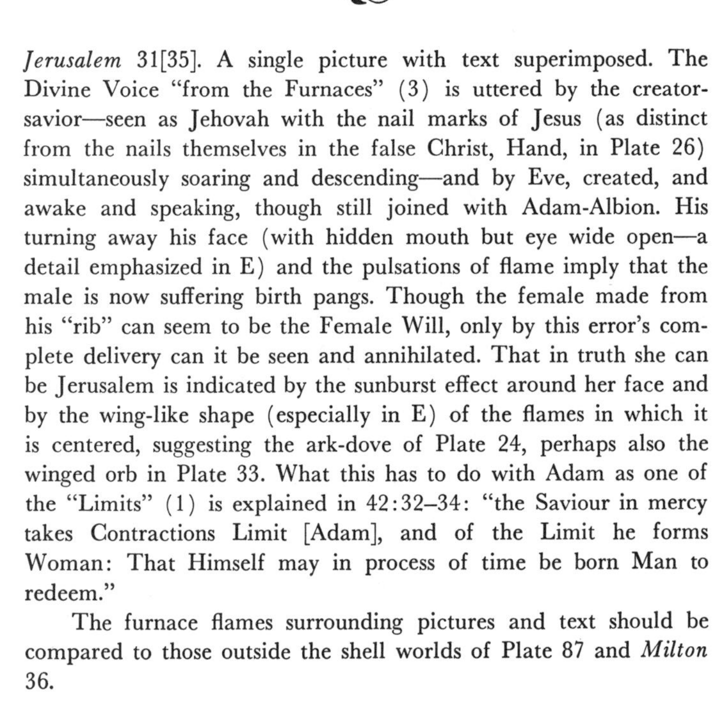

Jerusalem 31[35]. A single picture with text superimposed. The Divine Voice "from the Furnaces" (3) is uttered by the creator-savior—seen as Jehovah with the nail marks of Jesus (as distinct from the nails themselves in the false Christ, Hand, in Plate 26) simultaneously soaring and descending—and by Eve, created, and awake and speaking, though still joined with Adam-Albion. His turning away his face (with hidden mouth but eye wide open—a detail emphasized in E) and the pulsations of flame imply that the male is now suffering birth pangs. Though the female made from his "rib" can seem to be the Female Will, only by this error's complete delivery can it be seen and annihilated. That in truth she can be Jerusalem is indicated by the sunburst effect around her face and by the wing-like shape (especially in E) of the flames in which it is centered, suggesting the ark-dove of Plate 24, perhaps also the winged orb in Plate 33. What this has to do with Adam as one of the "Limits" (1) is explained in 42:32–34: "the Saviour in mercy takes Contractions Limit [Adam], and of the Limit he forms Woman: That Himself may in process of time be born Man to redeem."

The furnace flames surrounding pictures and text should be compared to those outside the shell worlds of Plate 87 and *Milton* 36.

Jerusalem 32[36]. At top, Los's "Building the Moon of Ulro plank by plank" (i.e. building the moon-ark of Plates 18 and 24) and "rib by rib" (i.e. the average man, here called Reuben) is pictured in terms of smithery. Each time Los swings his hammer, Reuben is sent for another trial run. Umbilical fibres attach him to the solar source (which is rising off the anvil: see Plate 93 note on the emergence of bright yellow coloring here). The implications of building a moon out of sunlight may be compared to the implications of the creation of Eve (a Vala shadow of Jerusalem) in Plate 31.

In the right margin Blake lets the word "returned" bend upward (9), the word "Judgment" (42) downward, into flames (red and yellow, matching the sun above). The odd leaf that grows up from the name "Merlin" (41) may be meant to remind us that Merlin (here Reuben's "Immortal Imagination": 24) was trapped in a tree, analogue of crucifixion.

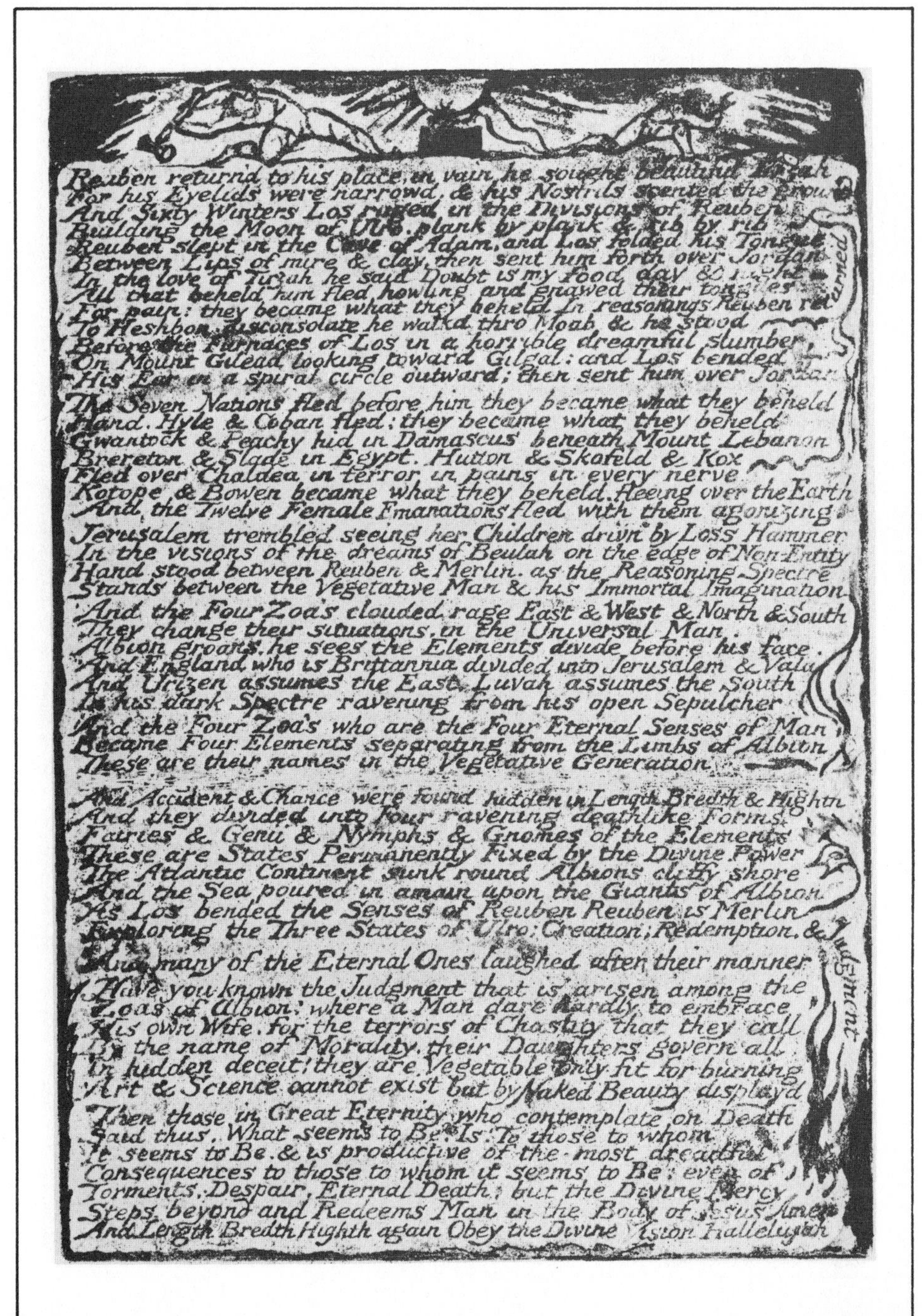
Reuben returnd to his place, in vain he sought beautiful Tirzah
For his Eyelids were narrowd, & his Nostrils scented the ground
And Sixty Winters Los raged in the Divisions of Reuben
Building the Moon of Ulro, plank by plank & rib by rib
Reuben slept in the Cave of Adam, and Los folded his Tongue
Between Lips of mire & clay, then sent him forth over Jordan
In the love of Tirzah he said Doubt is my food day & night
All that beheld him fled howling and gnawed their tongues
For pain: they became what they beheld In reasonings Reuben returned
To Heshbon, disconsolate he walkd thro Moab & he stood
Before the Furnaces of Los in a horrible dreamful slumber,
On Mount Gilead looking toward Gilgal: and Los bended
His Ear in a spiral circle outward; then sent him over Jordan

The Seven Nations fled before him they became what they beheld
Hand. Hyle & Coban fled: they became what they beheld
Gwantock & Peachy hid in Damascus beneath Mount Lebanon
Brereton & Slade in Egypt. Hutton & Skofeld & Kox
Fled over Chaldea in terror in pains in every nerve
Kotope & Bowen became what they beheld. fleeing over the Earth
And the Twelve Female Emanations fled with them agonizing.

Jerusalem trembled seeing her Children drivn by Loss Hammer
In the visions of the dreams of Beulah on the edge of Non-Entity
Hand stood between Reuben & Merlin. as the Reasoning Spectre
Stands between the Vegetative Man & his Immortal Imagination

And the Four Zoa's clouded rage East & West & North & South
They change their situations, in the Universal Man.
Albion groans. he sees the Elements divide before his face.
And England who is Brittannia divided into Jerusalem & Vala
And Urizen assumes the East, Luvah assumes the South
In his dark Spectre ravening from his open Sepulcher

And the Four Zoa's who are the Four Eternal Senses of Man
Became Four Elements separating from the Limbs of Albion
These are their names in the Vegetative Generation.

And Accident & Chance were found hidden in Length Bredth & Highth
And they divided into Four ravening deathlike Forms.
Fairies & Genii & Nymphs & Gnomes of the Elements.
These are States Permanently Fixed by the Divine Power
The Atlantic Continent sunk round Albions cliffy shore
And the Sea poured in amain upon the Giants of Albion
As Los bended the Senses of Reuben Reuben is Merlin
Exploring the Three States of Ulro; Creation; Redemption. & Judgment

And many of the Eternal Ones laughed after their manner
Have you known the Judgment that is arisen among the
Zoas of Albion; where a Man dare hardly to embrace
His own Wife. for the terrors of Chastity that they call
By the name of Morality. their Daughters govern all
In hidden deceit! they are Vegetable only fit for burning
Art & Science cannot exist but by Naked Beauty displayd

Then those in Great Eternity who contemplate on Death
Said thus. What seems to Be: Is: To those to whom
It seems to Be. & is productive of the most dreadful
Consequences to those to whom it seems to Be: even of
Torments. Despair. Eternal Death; but the Divine Mercy
Steps beyond and Redeems Man in the Body of Jesus Amen
And Length Bredth Highth again Obey the Divine Vision Hallelujah

Jerusalem 32[36][D]

Jerusalem 33[37]D

Jerusalem 33[37]. The top picture recalls 23:24–26: Albion "stood between the Palm tree & the Oak of weeping Which stand upon the edge of Beulah; and there Albion sunk Down in sick pallid languor!" His foot on the winged moon, the ark which Noah-Los has been building, is on the edge of moony Beulah, in a starry night sky clouded by text. But the picture adds a next stage (from Plate 24), his sensation of dying in the arms of the "Slain Lamb of God," a ghost he cannot accept as savior but whom we see as Los-Jesus radiating sunshine. If in alchemical symbolism a winged sun represents primeval chaos, this winged moon built by the imagination (Los) is a limit or raft on its surface ("visions . . . on the edge of Non-Entity" 32:22). (The continents drawn on it are of the moon, not earth.)

Jerusalem sees all this (her "visions . . . on the edge"), even though the red-winged spectre still darkens communication (as he does Los's in Plate 6); indeed vision can transpose his bat wings and ravenous head into the dove wings and red globe supporting Albion's right foot. (Compare the mirror contraries of the outstretched arms of Hand, Plate 26, and Jesus, Plate 76—anticipated in Plate 31—or of Urizen and Orc in *America* 8 and 10. For Albion in a similar but opposite dependency, see Plate 25.) That the spectre's bat-winged displacement of Jerusalem's butterfly wings is powerful, however, is indicated by the lower moon's turning, impossibly, its wrong side to the lower sun. If we want to think of cause and effect, we must see this both ways: because Albion faints, the spectre is in the ascendant; or, because the spectre hides Jerusalem, Albion faints. Yet the sun can shine through, its human form divine being shown in the savior's head above and shedding light past the oak of Druid sacrifice (with one acorn*) as well as onto the fruit-laden palm (six coconuts*) of suffering. The palm of pilgrimage through error—its fecundity signifying preservation of the spirit—points to the Palm Sunday of triumphal entry, as the sacrifice oak implies the crucifixion (see Plate 76). The bright stars in the middle distance number twenty-one (the bottom eight grouped differently in E)—perhaps to be read, from left to right and downward, as solitary Venus, the great dipper (in the autumn sky, pouring its milk), corona borealis, and (perhaps) Hercules (if three constellations, in autumnal evening positions, may be inferred).

Jerusalem 34[38]. Vegetation that defies anybody to see a human form in it (rather than a chain) fills the left margin; compare the vegetal networks in *Songs* 27 and 53 with climbers in them. The right margin (a variant of Plate 7 without Los) encourages us to believe that "Rivers & Mountains Are . . . Men; every thing is Human" (47–48). Is the naked form at bottom, swimming or diving downward, a river or branch? Is the clothed form above an eddy in a river or a tree trunk? In color Blake picks out these two forms as distinctly human—but in vegetable yellow-green. Conversely, vegetation can communicate prophetically: at line 19 the marginal verdure puts forth a human hand, which is also a flower, to point to "One Man," the object of all our beholding.

Below line 28, "I see them in the Vision of God," five birds fly. Other birds—three, then one, and then five again—fly in the lower open spaces. One flies above "Jerusalem" (25).

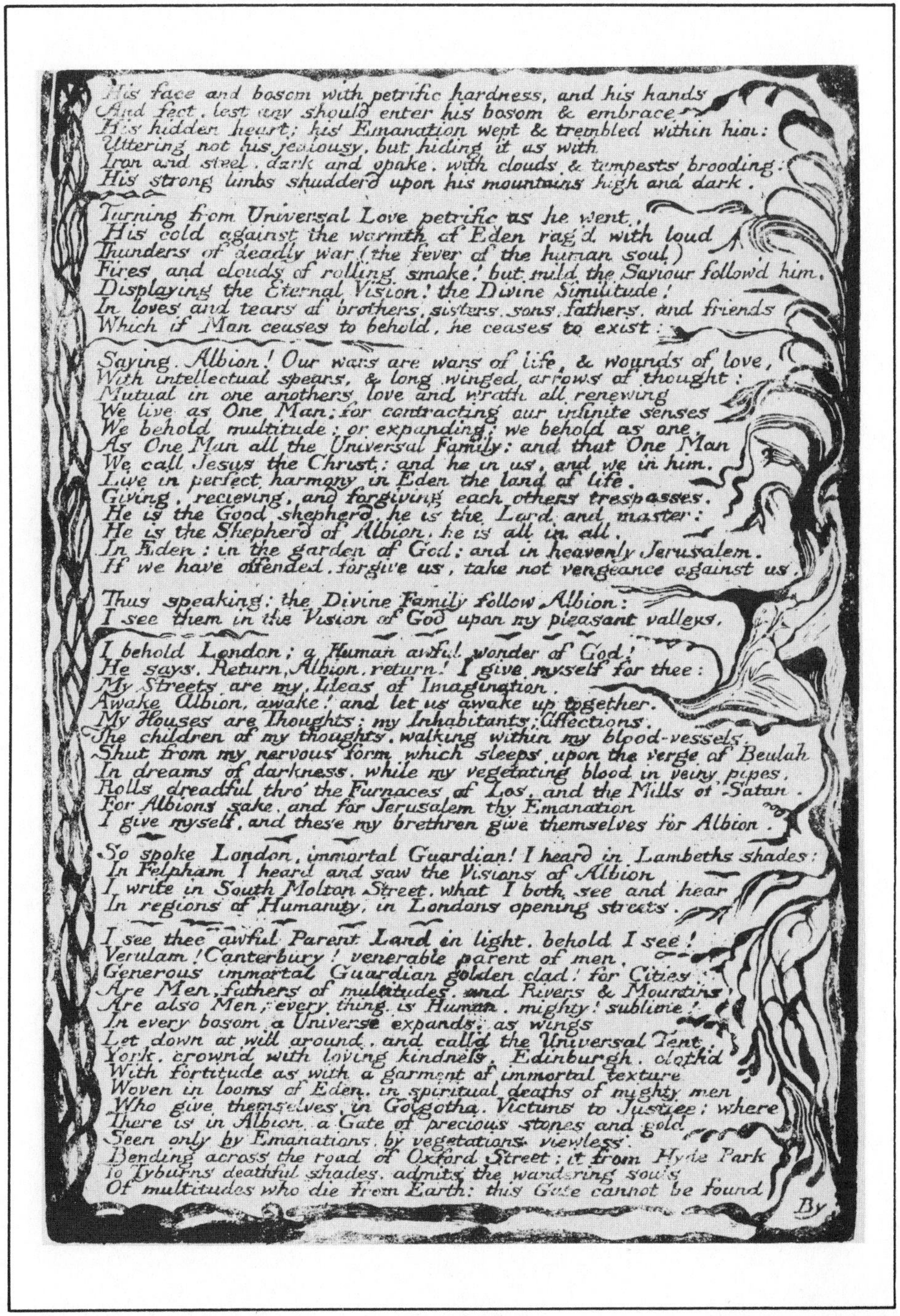

His face and bosom with petrific hardness, and his hands
And feet, lest any should enter his bosom & embrace
His hidden heart; his Emanation wept & trembled within him:
Uttering not his jealousy, but hiding it as with
Iron and steel, dark and opake, with clouds & tempests brooding:
His strong limbs shudderd upon his mountains high and dark.

Turning from Universal Love petrific as he went,
His cold against the warmth of Eden rag'd with loud
Thunders of deadly war (the fever of the human soul)
Fires and clouds of rolling smoke! but mild the Saviour followd him,
Displaying the Eternal Vision! the Divine Similitude!
In loves and tears of brothers, sisters, sons, fathers, and friends
Which if Man ceases to behold, he ceases to exist:

Saying, Albion! Our wars are wars of life, & wounds of love,
With intellectual spears, & long winged arrows of thought:
Mutual in one anothers love and wrath all renewing
We live as One Man; for contracting our infinite senses
We behold multitude; or expanding: we behold as one,
As One Man all the Universal Family: and that One Man
We call Jesus the Christ: and he in us, and we in him,
Live in perfect harmony in Eden the land of life,
Giving, recieving, and forgiving each others trespasses.
He is the Good shepherd, he is the Lord and master:
He is the Shepherd of Albion, he is all in all,
In Eden: in the garden of God: and in heavenly Jerusalem.
If we have offended, forgive us, take not vengeance against us.

Thus speaking; the Divine Family follow Albion:
I see them in the Vision of God upon my pleasant valleys.

I behold London; a Human awful wonder of God!
He says: Return, Albion, return! I give myself for thee:
My Streets are my, Ideas of Imagination.
Awake Albion, awake! and let us awake up together.
My Houses are Thoughts: my Inhabitants; Affections.
The children of my thoughts, walking within my blood-vessels,
Shut from my nervous form which sleeps upon the verge of Beulah
In dreams of darkness, while my vegetating blood in veiny pipes,
Rolls dreadful thro' the Furnaces of Los, and the Mills of Satan.
For Albions sake, and for Jerusalem thy Emanation
I give myself, and these my brethren give themselves for Albion.

So spoke London, immortal Guardian! I heard in Lambeths shades:
In Felpham I heard and saw the Visions of Albion
I write in South Molton Street, what I both see and hear
In regions of Humanity, in Londons opening streets.

I see thee awful Parent Land in light, behold I see!
Verulam! Canterbury! venerable parent of men,
Generous immortal Guardian golden clad! for Cities
Are Men, fathers of multitudes, and Rivers & Mountins
Are also Men; every thing is Human, mighty! sublime!
In every bosom a Universe expands, as wings
Let down at will around, and call'd the Universal Tent.
York, crownd with loving kindness, Edinburgh, cloth'd
With fortitude as with a garment of immortal texture
Woven in looms of Eden, in spiritual deaths of mighty men
Who give themselves, in Golgotha, Victims to Justice; where
There is in Albion a Gate of precious stones and gold
Seen only by Emanations, by vegetations viewless,
Bending across the road of Oxford Street; it from Hyde Park
To Tyburns deathful shades, admits the wandering souls
Of multitudes who die from Earth: this Gate cannot be found
By

Jerusalem 34[38][D]

Jerusalem 35[39]D

Jerusalem 35[39]. Above Blake's anxious assurance that "Satans Watch-fiends" can never find "the Gate of Los," rides a multi-bowed archer, the Urizenic spectre (Apollyon whose bow is "Demonstrative Science" 12:14) as three horsemen in one, bat-winged and demonstrating (see 36:32–37) what "mighy arms" the spectre would brandish should Albion fall and "Let loose the enormous Spectre on the darkness." The sun below, setting behind low hills, radiates spikes that make it seem like one of the cogwheels of Plate 22. Even so, some light reaches the clouds at top left. The picture adumbrates the vision in later plates of "the Covering Cherub coming on in darkness" (96:17; see 89:9, 44). Spatially one may imagine "a rank of archers mounted on flying horses" (Stevenson); temporally a pulsation of shots, as the Satanic time-clock shoots shaft after shaft of anguish and fear: between every two pulsations there is a spiritual interval (W).

~

Jerusalem 36[40]. The left border deviates from the motif of Plate 34 into twining branches with tentative human and leaf[E] forms. The right continues interrelated human and plant forms—but with a startling difference: a panache of color and line that quite defy the despair of the upper text. The two humans here are naked and seem less a part of the vegetation than creators of its form and color: the woman (flesh pink against yellow) reaching a large cluster of purple grapes (shaped with india ink in F) as if placing it on the vine or adding the purple; the man (pink against blue) flinging his right arm joyously back as he looks upward into the mundane shell (W), from his left armpit extruding three leaf and vine stems, the longest dividing threefold into tendrils and leaves. (Compare the more sinister sevenfold dividing of Hand in Plate 50.) Is the cape-like swirl behind his shoulders a growth of wings?

These two are Los and Enitharmon working in line and color, but in their mundane vehicles (not their elemental forms as in Plate 85, q.v.), i.e. William and Catherine Blake. We have seen them busy illuminating in *Milton* 22; him, with similar exuberance, in 24; in the next plate below he depicts himself writing his own text, with a sadder sequel in Plate 49. Here he is walking in the line (like the runner in *Marriage* 7), which his right foot sends spiraling down to Catherine's arms and feet. This leaves the poet's writing arm free while his sixfold painting arm can fill the sky with grape leaves in three color varieties and spin a tight wiry coil of communication to break past its limit—and even send up a tendril banner to put a scythe blade arching above "Eternal Death" (3)! Not to mention the reds and blues that drop from his lowered paintbrush arm and two splashes of red that seem to boomerang from the blue and green leaf arm behind his head. Thus Blake illuminates his own parenthesis here: "Los built the stubborn structure of the Language, acting against Albions melancholy, who must else have been a Dumb despair" (59–60). Catherine's influence turns the vine to green ribbons; a spare paintbrush with five red-dipped fingers and a flower brush curls at her other side.

Rainbow colors suffuse the page.

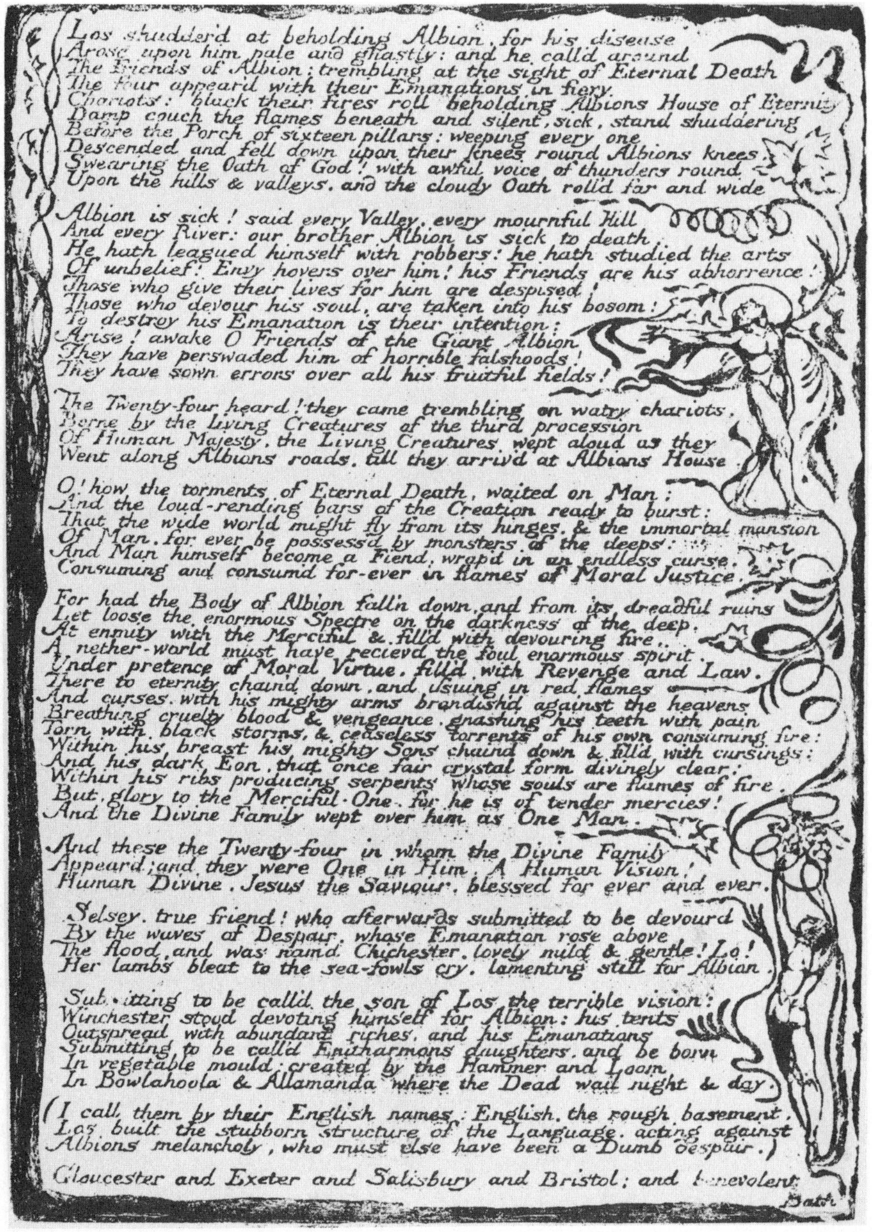

Los shudderd at beholding Albion, for his disease
Arose upon him pale and ghastly: and he calld around
The Friends of Albion: trembling at the sight of Eternal Death
The four appeard with their Emanations in fiery
Chariots: black their fires roll beholding Albions House of Eternity
Damp couch the flames beneath and silent, sick, stand shuddering
Before the Porch of sixteen pillars: weeping every one
Descended and fell down upon their knees round Albions knees,
Swearing the Oath of God! with awful voice of thunders round
Upon the hills & valleys, and the cloudy Oath rolld far and wide

Albion is sick! said every Valley, every mournful Hill
And every River: our brother Albion is sick to death.
He hath leagued himself with robbers: he hath studied the arts
Of unbelief! Envy hovers over him! his Friends are his abhorrence!
Those who give their lives for him are despised!
Those who devour his soul, are taken into his bosom!
To destroy his Emanation is their intention:
Arise! awake O Friends of the Giant Albion
They have perswaded him of horrible falshoods!
They have sown errors over all his fruitful fields!

The Twenty-four heard! they came trembling on watry chariots,
Borne by the Living Creatures of the third procession
Of Human Majesty, the Living Creatures wept aloud as they
Went along Albions roads, till they arriv'd at Albions House.

O! how the torments of Eternal Death, waited on Man:
And the loud-rending bars of the Creation ready to burst:
That the wide world might fly from its hinges, & the immortal mansion
Of Man, for ever be possessd by monsters of the deeps:
And Man himself become a Fiend, wrapd in an endless curse,
Consuming and consumd for-ever in flames of Moral Justice.

For had the Body of Albion falln down, and from its dreadful ruins
Let loose the enormous Spectre on the darkness of the deep,
At enmity with the Merciful & filld with devouring fire,
A nether-world must have recievd the foul enormous spirit,
Under pretence of Moral Virtue, filld with Revenge and Law.
There to eternity chaind down, and issuing in red flames
And curses, with his mighty arms brandishd against the heavens
Breathing cruelty blood & vengeance, gnashing his teeth with pain
Torn with black storms, & ceaseless torrents of his own consuming fire:
Within his breast his mighty Sons chaind down & filld with cursings:
And his dark Eon, that once fair crystal form divinely clear:
Within his ribs producing serpents whose souls are flames of fire.
But, glory to the Merciful-One, for he is of tender mercies!
And the Divine Family wept over him as One Man.

And these the Twenty-four in whom the Divine Family
Appeard; and they were One in Him. A Human Vision!
Human Divine, Jesus the Saviour, blessed for ever and ever.

Selsey, true friend! who afterwards submitted to be devourd
By the waves of Despair, whose Emanation rose above
The flood, and was namd Chichester, lovely mild & gentle! Lo!
Her lambs bleat to the sea-fowls cry, lamenting still for Albion.

Sub-itting to be calld the son of Los the terrible vision:
Winchester stood devoting himself for Albion: his tents
Outspread with abundant riches, and his Emanations
Submitting to be calld Enitharmons daughters, and be born
In vegetable mould: created by the Hammer and Loom
In Bowlahoola & Allamanda where the Dead wail night & day.

(I call them by their English names: English, the rough basement,
Los built the stubborn structure of the Language, acting against
Albions melancholy, who must else have been a Dumb despair.)

Gloucester and Exeter and Salisbury and Bristol; and benevolent
Bath

Jerusalem 36[40][D]

Jerusalem 37[41]D

Jerusalem 37[41]. It is not for want of reading matter that Albion sits in dumb despair (see above). On either knee is half of a limp-bound book, onto which his head has collapsed, and we may suppose he has been forced to buy one of those books that Urizen so busily duplicates and displays in *Urizen* 1 and 5. Graphically and iconically this picture is related to the picture of the scroll of proverbial wisdom in the devil's lap in *Marriage* 10 and to *Night Thoughts* 7 (*Forms* plate 75), where the writer has fallen asleep like this (not Blake but Young) and his scroll is being delivered to Urizen, and *Night Thoughts* 5 (*Forms* plate 73), where the poet (Young, not Blake) has his pen ready on his scroll but despairs from failing light. Here a scroll like the devil's either lies across Albion's lap or is being sat upon. And the poet, Blake himself, sits upon the fresh end with pen ready. But he shows no signs of despair or of failing light. The writing is inside out, but he is a professional at reading his "type" before printing. And when that giant Albion, all the people for whom English is "the rough basement" (36:58) and beside whom Blake feels himself about the size of a fairy, finally wakes up he will find a mirror to read in—the watery shore which Blake has painted right up to the chalk edge of the green carpet which Albion's toes delimit. Albion is in the position of the despairing suicide in *Gates* 2 named "Water." The merry proverb Blake has just written for him, however, will simply tell him for goodness' sake to jump:

> Each Man is in his Spectre's power
> Until the arrival of that hour,
> When his Humanity awake
> And cast his Spectre into the Lake.

The visceral pillar of cloud behind him will then go up in smoke.

In *Song of Los* 1 we saw Urizen in a similar collapse over his book.

Jerusalem 38[43]. The kneeling, praying (or anguished) figure at bottom right, against grey blue cloud, is probably one of those who have "caught the infection of Sin & stern Repentance" (75). He or she seems identical to the vegetable person in about the same location on Plate 34[38], with hair gone and flourishing vegetation replaced by heavy clouds. Where the other figure was there is only a leafless coil. This was not the inevitable way to go. (Compare the central figures in Plate 5.)

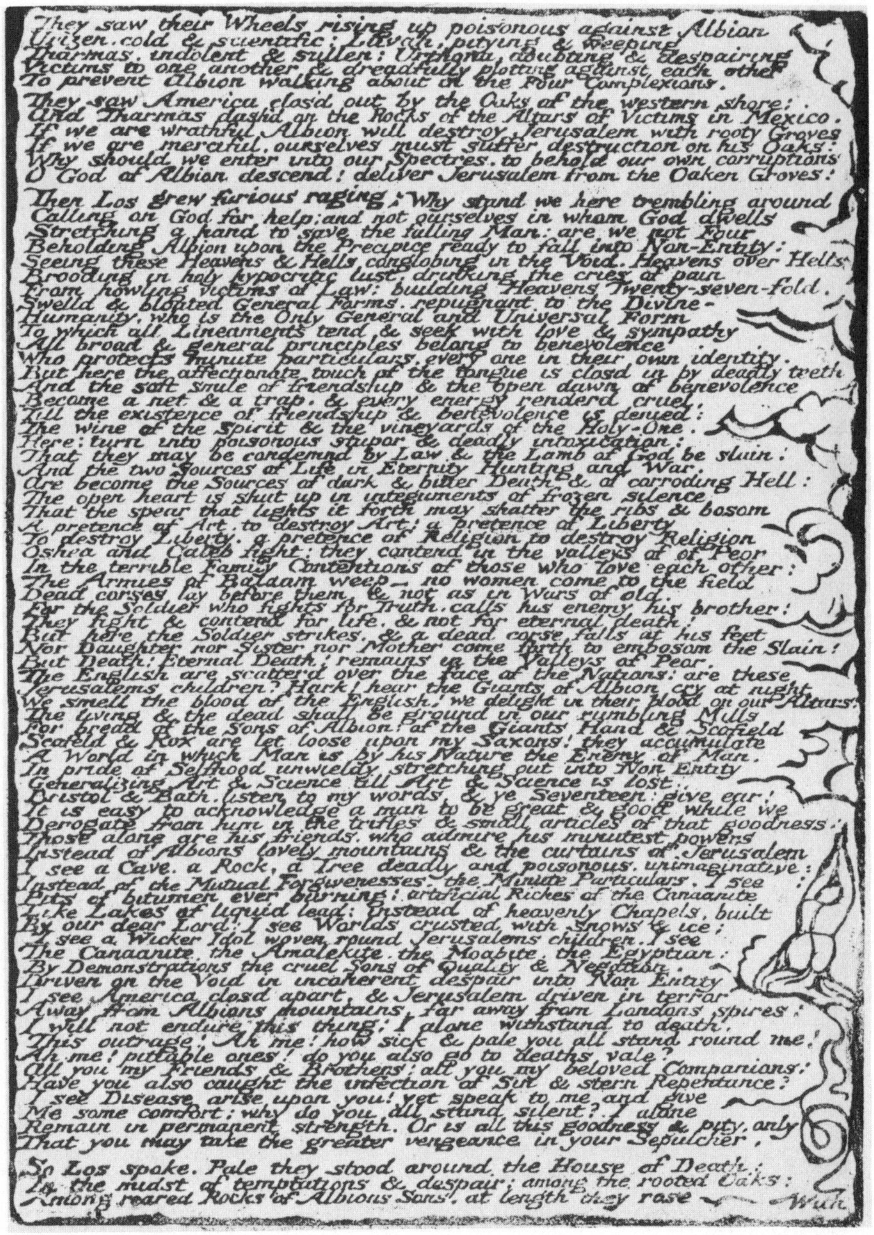

They saw their Wheels rising up poisonous against Albion
Urizen, cold & scientific: Luvah, pitying & weeping
Tharmas, indolent & sullen: Urthona, doubting & despairing
Victims to one another & dreadfully plotting against each other
To prevent Albion walking about in the Four Complexions.

They saw America closd out by the Oaks of the western shore;
And Tharmas dashd on the Rocks of the Altars of Victims in Mexico.
If we are wrathful Albion will destroy Jerusalem with rooty Groves
If we are merciful, ourselves must suffer destruction on his Oaks:
Why should we enter into our Spectres, to behold our own corruptions
O God of Albion descend! deliver Jerusalem from the Oaken Groves!

Then Los grew furious raging: Why stand we here trembling around
Calling on God for help; and not ourselves in whom God dwells
Stretching a hand to save the falling Man: are we not Four
Beholding Albion upon the Precipice ready to fall into Non-Entity:
Seeing these Heavens & Hells conglobing in the Void. Heavens over Hells
Brooding in holy hypocritic lust, drinking the cries of pain
From howling victims of Law: building Heavens Twenty-seven-fold.
Swelld & bloated General Forms, repugnant to the Divine-
Humanity, who is the Only General and Universal Form
To which all Lineaments tend & seek with love & sympathy
All broad & general principles belong to benevolence
Who protects minute particulars, every one in their own identity.
But here the affectionate touch of the tongue is closd in by deadly teeth
And the soft smile of friendship & the open dawn of benevolence
Become a net & a trap, & every energy renderd cruel,
Till the existence of friendship & benevolence is denied:
The wine of the Spirit & the vineyards of the Holy-One.
Here: turn into poisonous stupor & deadly intoxication:
That they may be condemnd by Law & the Lamb of God be slain:
And the two Sources of Life in Eternity Hunting and War,
Are become the Sources of dark & bitter Death & of corroding Hell:
The open heart is shut up in integuments of frozen silence
That the spear that lights it forth may shatter the ribs & bosom
A pretence of Art, to destroy Art: a pretence of Liberty
To destroy Liberty. a pretence of Religion to destroy Religion
Oshea and Caleb fight: they contend in the valleys of of Peor
In the terrible Family Contentions of those who love each other:
The Armies of Balaam weep — no women come to the field
Dead corses lay before them, & not as in Wars of old.
For the Soldier who fights for Truth, calls his enemy his brother:
They fight & contend for life, & not for eternal death!
But here the Soldier strikes, & a dead corse falls at his feet
Nor Daughter nor Sister nor Mother come forth to embosom the Slain!
But Death! Eternal Death! remains in the Valleys of Peor.
The English are scatterd over the face of the Nations: are these
Jerusalems children? Hark! hear the Giants of Albion cry at night
We smell the blood of the English! we delight in their blood on our Altars:
The living & the dead shall be ground in our rumbling Mills
For bread of the Sons of Albion: of the Giants Hand & Scofield
Scofeld & Kox are let loose upon my Saxons! they accumulate
A World in which Man is by his Nature the Enemy of Man.
In pride of Selfhood unwieldy stretching out into Non Entity
Generalizing Art & Science till Art & Science is lost.
Bristol & Bath, listen to my words, & ye Seventeen: give ear!
It is easy to acknowledge a man to be great & good while we
Derogate from him in the trifles & small articles of that goodness:
Those alone are his friends, who admire his minutest powers
Instead of Albions lovely mountains & the curtains of Jerusalem
I see a Cave, a Rock, a Tree deadly and poisonous, unimaginative:
Instead of the Mutual Forgivenesses, the Minute Particulars, I see
Pits of bitumen ever burning: artificial Riches of the Canaanite
Like Lakes of liquid lead: instead of heavenly Chapels, built
By our dear Lord: I see Worlds crusted with snows & ice;
I see a Wicker Idol woven round Jerusalems children. I see
The Canaanite, the Amalekite, the Moabite, the Egyptian:
By Demonstrations the cruel Sons of Quality & Negation.
Driven on the Void in incoherent despair into Non Entity
I see America closd apart, & Jerusalem driven in terror
Away from Albions mountains, far away from Londons spires:
I will not endure this thing! I alone withstand to death,
This outrage! Ah me! how sick & pale you all stand round me!
Ah me! pitiable ones! do you also go to deaths vale?
All you my Friends & Brothers! all you my beloved Companions!
Have you also caught the infection of Sin & stern Repentance?
I see Disease arise upon you! yet speak to me and give
Me some comfort: why do you all stand silent? I alone
Remain in permanent strength. Or is all this goodness & pity, only
That you may take the greater vengeance in your Sepulcher,

So Los spoke. Pale they stood around the House of Death:
In the midst of temptations & despair; among the rooted Oaks:
Among reared Rocks of Albions Sons, at length they rose — With

Jerusalem 38[43]D

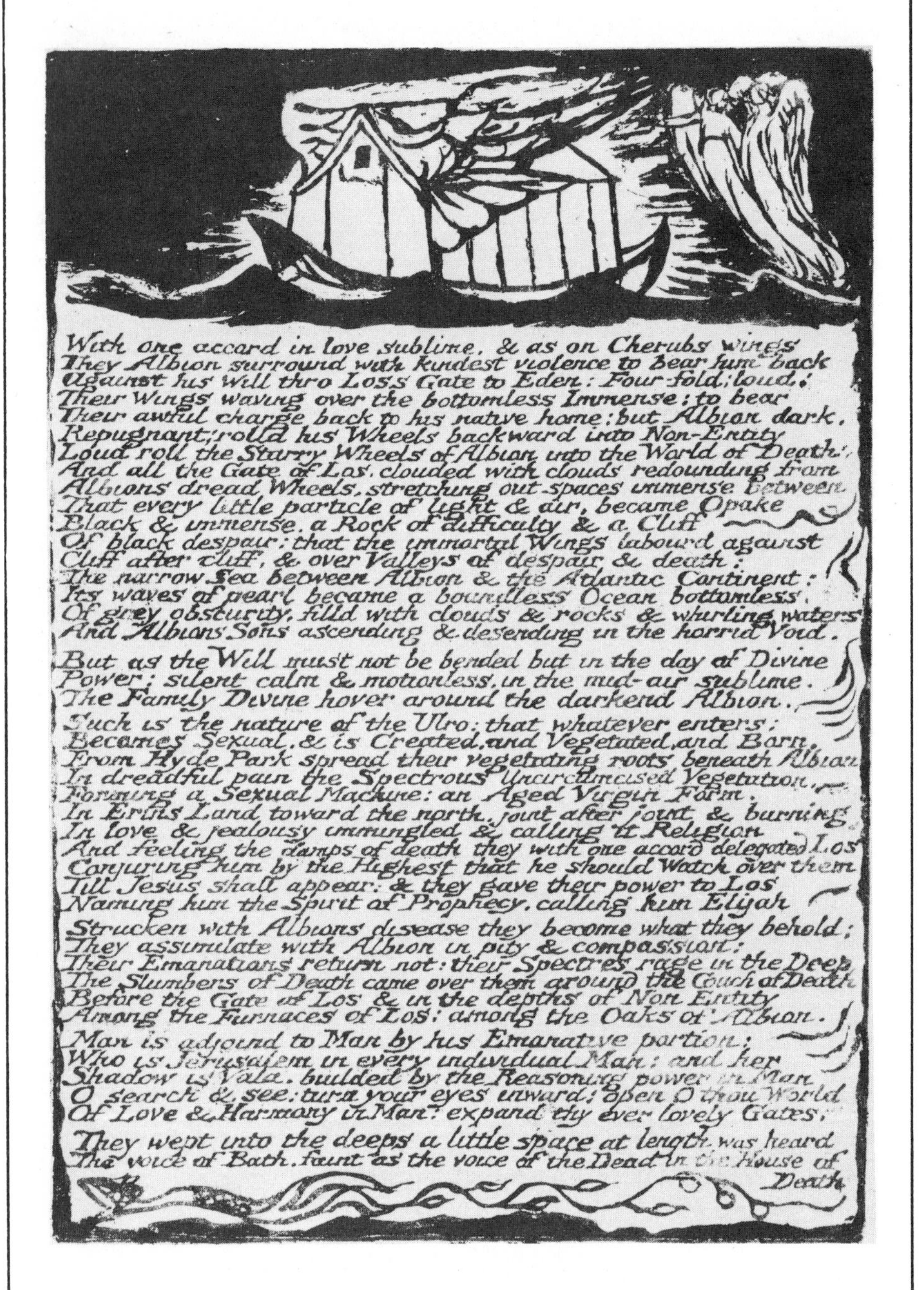

Jerusalem 39[44]D

Jerusalem 39[44]. Two "Friends & Brothers" of Los (38:74), responding to his exhortation, try "Four-fold! loud! Their Wings waving over the bottomless Immense" (39:3–4) to bear Albion back to Eden against his will—"thro Los's Gate," that is by making him read the Bible (if we understand Plate 37). For their purpose the ark of Plate 24 is shaped into a house-boat like Noah's with "loud" dove's wings. The Friends, a sort of supervising committee, must be "silent calm & motionless, in the mid-air" (18–20) until Albion's imagination effects a change in his volition. The symbols of hope are of course meant to remind him quietly of the sunlight, reflected by the moon, the garden of Paradise, witnessed by the dove, and the bow of promise, bestowed as heaven's reward for Noah's trusting his home to the flood waters.

The open-mouthed serpent rolling, at the bottom, in the ark's direction offers an analogue of transmutation, from spine to flame to vine to fruit—painted rainbow colors so that the serpent head and body are red, orange, yellow, the leaves green, the fruit blue and violet. (The tongue, lacking but supplied in the colored copy, does not appear to dart poison but to become again a vine for the left margin.) Followers of Blake's vipers as emblems of his text will see an exemplar of the unity of line and color, or rather the marriage of them.

Jerusalem 40 [45]. Here puns in text and pictures aid symbolic multiplicity. Against a section of Vala's cloud (pouring rain as in *Visions* ii) with her red net Vala is catching that poor fish Albion, still hiding his head. He lies exhausted (like the black African in *Visions* 2) and snagged on a barren tree in England's green land: caught in the machinery of enslavement to a modern Helen—cutting oaks for the navy (see Plate 15) and exporting textiles (her "scarlet Veil over Albion": 21:50). Vala the exporter needs his body for Nimrod's imperialism; he still imagines her borne "in a golden Ark . . . before [the] Armies" (22:2–5—the picture repeats at closer view the top scene of Plate 22 and the cloud behind her is painted golden). (On the text of Plate 40 as a sermon against aggressive war see *Prophet* 475–81.)

Thus nurturing Selfhood (eyes shut) and caught in war, Albion's maritime existence threatens to become his death. His "machines are woven [pun on textile economy] with his life" (25); England cannot cease being maritime and textile but must return to international exchanges "mutual in love & harmony" (24:42–43). Destroying Africa's chains and dark machines (the slave trade conflated with pyramid building) was simpler; it freed Africa, and "the Man" lived to repent (19–22). The appropriate mediator is "Bath"; below his name a big fish swallowing smaller ones (contrast the groups of large and small birds) illustrates maritime Selfhood. In contrast the water serpent and three different fish in the margin above seaweed exemplify variety and freedom. The serpent, open mouthed at "fruitful are our fields" (12), links sea and land, as did the snake on Plate 39.

In this plate Blake does not emphasize the symbolism of liquid as media (compare Plates 11, 28, 37, 39) but it must be part of a full reading.

Bath, healing City! whose wisdom in midst of Poetic
Fervor: mild spoke thro' the Western Porch in soft gentle tears

O Albion mildest Son of Eden! clos'd is thy Western Gate
Brothers of Eternity: this Man whose great example
We all admir'd & lov'd, whose all benevolent countenance, seen
In Eden, in lovely Jerusalem, drew even from envy
The tear: and the confession of honesty, open & undisguis'd
From mistrust and suspition. The Man is himself become
A piteous example of oblivion. To teach the Sons
Of Eden, that however great and glorious; however loving
And merciful the Individuality; however high
Our palaces and cities, and however fruitful are our fields
In Selfhood, we are nothing: but fade away in mornings breath.
Our mildness is nothing: the greatest mildness we can use
Is incapable and nothing: none but the Lamb of God can heal
This dread disease: none but Jesus: O Lord descend and save!
Albions Western Gate is clos'd: his death is coming apace:
Jesus alone can save him; for alas we none can know
How soon his lot may be our own. When Africa in sleep
Rose in the night of Beulah, and bound down the Sun & Moon
His friends cut his strong chains, & overwhelm'd his dark
Machines in fury & destruction, and the Man reviving repented
He wept before his wrathful brethren, thankful & considerate
For their well timed wrath. But Albions sleep is not
Like Africa's: and his machines are woven with his life
Nothing but mercy can save him! nothing but mercy interposing
Lest he should slay Jerusalem in his fearful jealousy
O God descend! gather our brethren, deliver Jerusalem
But that we may omit no office of the friendly spirit
Oxford take thou these leaves of the Tree of Life: with eloquence
That thy immortal tongue inspires; present them to Albion:
Perhaps he may recieve them, offer'd from thy loved hands.

So spoke, unheard by Albion, the merciful Son of Heaven
To those whose Western Gates were open, as they stood weeping
Around Albion: but Albion heard him not; obdurate; hard:
He frown'd on all his Friends, counting them enemies in his sorrow

And the Seventeen conjoining with Bath, the Seventh:
In whom the other Ten shone manifest, a Divine Vision!
Assimilated and embrac'd Eternal Death for Albions sake.

And these the names of the Eighteen combining with those Ten.

Jerusalem 40[45]D

Bath, mild Physician of Eternity, mysterious power
Whose springs are unsearchable & knowledg infinite.
Hereford, ancient Guardian of Wales, whose hands
Builded the mountain palaces of Eden, stupendous works!
Lincoln, Durham & Carlisle, Councellors of Los.
And Ely, Scribe of Los, whose pen no other hand
Dare touch: Oxford, immortal Bard! with eloquence
Divine, he wept over Albion: speaking the words of God
In mild perswasion: bringing leaves of the Tree of Life.

Thou art in Error Albion, the Land of Ulro:
One Error not removd, will destroy a human Soul
Repose in Beulahs night, till the Error is removd
Reason not on both sides. Repose upon our bosoms
Till the Plow of Jehovah, and the Harrow of Shaddai
Have passed over the Dead, to awake the Dead to Judgment.
But Albion turnd away refusing comfort.

Oxford trembled while he spoke, then fainted in the arms
Of Norwich, Peterboro, Rochester, Chester awful, Worcester,
Litchfield, Saint Davids, Landaff, Asaph, Bangor, Sodor,
Bowing their heads devoted: and the Furnaces of Los
Began to rage, thundering loud the storms began to roar
Upon the Furnaces, and loud the Furnaces rebellow beneath

And these the Four in whom the twenty-four appeard four-fold:
Verulam, London, York, Edinburgh, mourning one towards another
Alas!—The time will come, when a mans worst enemies
Shall be those of his own house and family: in a Religion
Of Generation, to destroy by Sin and Atonement, happy Jerusalem,
The Bride and Wife of the Lamb. O God thou art Not an Avenger!

Jerusalem 41[46][D]

Jerusalem 41[46]. To awake us all is the purpose of this curious vision of "the Plow of Jehovah and the Harrow of Shaddai" (13–15), as complicated a contrivance as the plow of Plate 29 was simple. It reflects both the parlous apathy of Albion as charioteer and the desperation of the prophetic artist to construct a vehicle of life to replace the "scythed chariots of Britain" (47:11). We see two ox-hooved, lion-maned, man-headed unicorns crowned with fillets of bay-colored leaves, standing in traces formed by stretched bodies of serpents. (Blake has taken up God's ironic challenge to Job: "Canst thou bind the unicorn . . . in the furrow?"—Job 39.9.) From the three interwoven serpents' necks, we infer two unseen serpent bodies coming up between and on the far side of the unicorns. The human face of the farther quadruped looks solemnly forward, and a hand on the top of his spiral ram-like horn points forward. The other's face has a furrowed brow and an inward look suiting the backward direction of his spiral horn, from which a hand reaches for a quill held forth by one of two eagle-men, harpy-like but not woman-faced, who ride with wings high. (Compare the "Eagle like men" in the printing house of *Marriage* 15.) The serpents' tongues dart in the direction pointed by the hand; their tails form impossible spiral wheels above which sit, on a wagon seat amid flames (extended up the page in E) from the "Furnaces of Los" (20), a small, veiled, even nun-like woman and a bearded ancient man looking like Jehovah hitched up to his own untrusted unicorns. (In Plate 96 we shall see them awake, embracing, the woman England or Brittannia, the man Albion as Jehovah.) For Jehovah in a similar but fiery-horse drawn chariot, see the famous color print of *God Judging Adam*.

In the immediate narrative context, the failure of Bath and the Bard of Oxford to reach warring Albion with words of peace and life (Plates 40–41), this is an emblem of continuing effort and hope amid futility. As a comment on Blake's whole labor of art, it is an emblem of his self-conscious determination to use every means to intensify the "thundering" and rebellowing of volcanic fires "beneath" the fainting cities of England (17–22). It is his yoking of the arts to produce *Jerusalem* to rescue Jerusalem. The serpents are plowing with their tongues, i.e. cutting the airy way with messages (compare the lightning and the serpent of *Marriage* 11 and 15), and they are harrowing with their spiral tails (compare the starry pinwheel harrows of Plate 20, also pulled by human draft animals. The brain-based horns take the spiral shape of serpent-trumpets yet are but ink-horns, requiring quills. The lion-ox grafting seems a Urizenically desperate attempt to find a law of voluntary collaboration of lion and patient ox. The serpent traces and the eagle-winged riders are an offer of serpent power and eagle spirit (etching and coloring) to tempt Los and Urizen to come under one yoke—and be crowned with bays. Compared to the exuberant collaboration of eagle and snake depicted in *Marriage* 15, this intricate teaming is highly sophisticated and resourceful—and static. If Los points forward and Urizen thinks back, will it get us anywhere? Can the serpents see the pointing hand? Does it all finally await Albion's tugging on the reins now limp in his hand? Of course. Blake knows that the whole contraption would look ridiculous beside a fiery Pegasus. But he is deadly serious about the need to get off dead center—and serious if mysterious about the many forces and their intricate interplay that constitute this illuminated work.

Jerusalem 42. A coiling line down the left margin brackets the lines (45–61) illustrated in the right: "Man lives by deaths of Men" (Albion thinks: 49). Spectres of these dead, e.g. Oxford groaning "in his iron furnace Winchester in his den & cavern" (58–59), imagine happiness as joining to build up Babylon, for "Rahab is ours . . . in pomp and glory of victory" (63–64). At top, in a huge "pomp" of purple grapes (such as the spies brought from the promised land, at Eschol—the living tree that will be crushed upon the wine-press of the cross), we see Vala and Rahab and Tirzah balanced on a pyramid of four men, the top one blinded by fat Tirzah's foot on his face. Rahab in turn stands on her eyes and breast. Vala, drawing the grapes to her mouth, stands tiptoe on the lips of Rahab.

Tirzah and the two men below her are flesh-tinted; Vala and Rahab are the white of the page, as are the two bottom men. The stony color may remind us of the stony figures at head and foot of Albion's effigy (Plates 14, 19). Here Albion would seem to be the totally exploited lowest man. Is that Los above him, like a caryatid, facing forward, unblinded, and keeping one ear free? This may be an improvement on the lifeless structures in the left margins of Plates 34 and 36, but there are better ways of forming human chains

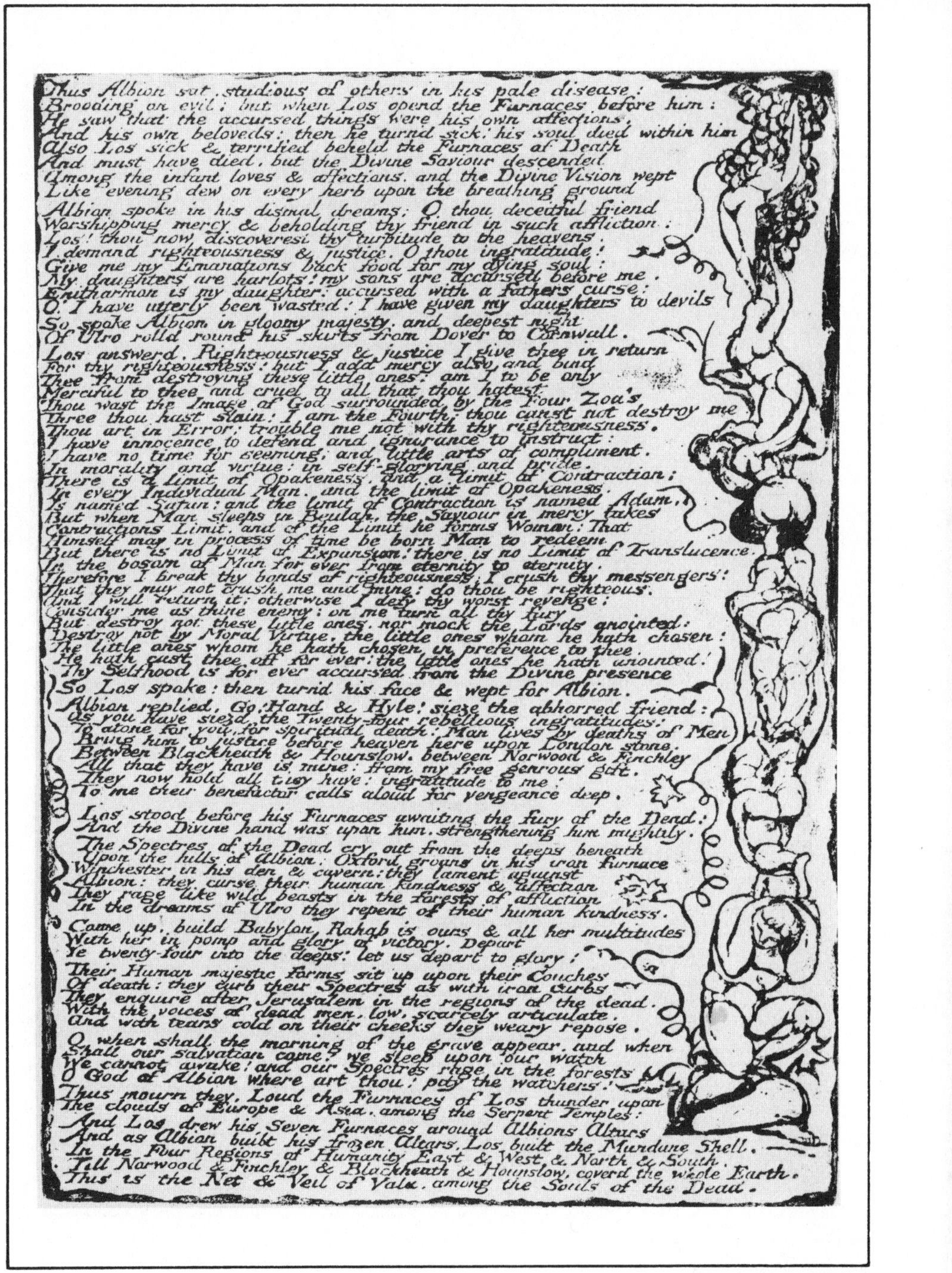

Thus Albion sat, studious of others in his pale disease:
Brooding on evil: but when Los opend the Furnaces before him:
He saw that the accursed things were his own affections,
And his own beloveds: then he turnd sick: his soul died within him
Also Los sick & terrified beheld the Furnaces of Death
And must have died, but the Divine Saviour descended
Among the infant loves & affections, and the Divine Vision wept
Like evening dew on every herb upon the breathing ground

Albion spoke in his dismal dreams: O thou deceitful friend
Worshipping mercy & beholding thy friend in such affliction:
Los! thou now discoverest thy turpitude to the heavens.
I demand righteousness & justice. O thou ingratitude!
Give me my Emanations back food for my dying soul:
My daughters are harlots: my sons are accursed before me.
Enitharmon is my daughter: accursed with a fathers curse:
O! I have utterly been wasted: I have given my daughters to devils
So spoke Albion in gloomy majesty, and deepest night
Of Ulro rolld round his skirts from Dover to Cornwall.

Los answerd. Righteousness & justice I give thee in return
For thy righteousness: but I add mercy also, and bind
Thee from destroying these little ones: am I to be only
Merciful to thee and cruel to all that thou hatest?
Thou wast the Image of God surrounded by the Four Zoa's
Three thou hast slain: I am the Fourth: thou canst not destroy me
Thou art in Error; trouble me not with thy righteousness.
I have innocence to defend and ignorance to instruct:
I have no time for seeming; and little arts of compliment,
In morality and virtue: in self-glorying and pride.
There is a limit of Opakeness, and a limit of Contraction;
In every Individual Man, and the limit of Opakeness,
Is named Satan: and the limit of Contraction is named Adam.
But when Man sleeps in Beulah, the Saviour in mercy takes
Contractions Limit, and of the Limit he forms Woman: That
Himself may in process of time be born Man to redeem
But there is no Limit of Expansion! there is no Limit of Translucence.
In the bosom of Man for ever from eternity to eternity.
Therefore I break thy bonds of righteousness; I crush thy messengers!
That they may not crush me and mine: do thou be righteous,
And I will return it; otherwise I defy thy worst revenge:
Consider me as thine enemy: on me turn all thy fury
But destroy not these little ones, nor mock the Lords anointed:
Destroy not by Moral Virtue, the little ones whom he hath chosen:
The little ones whom he hath chosen in preference to thee.
He hath cast thee off for ever: the little ones he hath anointed!
Thy Selfhood is for ever accursed from the Divine presence
So Los spoke: then turnd his face & wept for Albion.

Albion replied. Go! Hand & Hyle! sieze the abhorred friend:
As you have siezd the Twenty-four rebellious ingratitudes:
To atone for you, for spiritual death! Man lives by deaths of Men
Bring him to justice before heaven here upon London stone,
Between Blackheath & Hounslow, between Norwood & Finchley
All that they have is mine: from my free genrous gift,
They now hold all they have: ingratitude to me:
To me their benefactor calls aloud for vengeance deep.

Los stood before his Furnaces awaiting the fury of the Dead:
And the Divine hand was upon him, strengthening him mightily.
The Spectres of the Dead cry out from the deeps beneath
Upon the hills of Albion: Oxford groans in his iron furnace
Winchester in his den & cavern: they lament against
Albion: they curse their human kindness & affection
They rage like wild beasts in the forests of affliction
In the dreams of Ulro they repent of their human kindness.

Come up, build Babylon, Rahab is ours & all her multitudes
With her in pomp and glory of victory. Depart
Ye twenty-four into the deeps! let us depart to glory!

Their Human majestic forms sit up upon their Couches
Of death: they curb their Spectres as with iron curbs
They enquire after Jerusalem in the regions of the dead.
With the voices of dead men, low, scarcely articulate,
And with tears cold on their cheeks they weary repose.

O when shall the morning of the grave appear, and when
Shall our salvation come? we sleep upon our watch
We cannot awake! and our Spectres rage in the forests
O God of Albion where art thou! pity the watchers!

Thus mourn they. Loud the Furnaces of Los thunder upon
The clouds of Europe & Asia, among the Serpent Temples!

And Los drew his Seven Furnaces around Albions Altars
And as Albion built his frozen Altars, Los built the Mundane Shell,
In the Four Regions of Humanity East & West & North & South,
Till Norwood & Finchley & Blackheath & Hounslow, coverd the whole Earth.
This is the Net & Veil of Vala, among the Souls of the Dead.

Jerusalem 42D

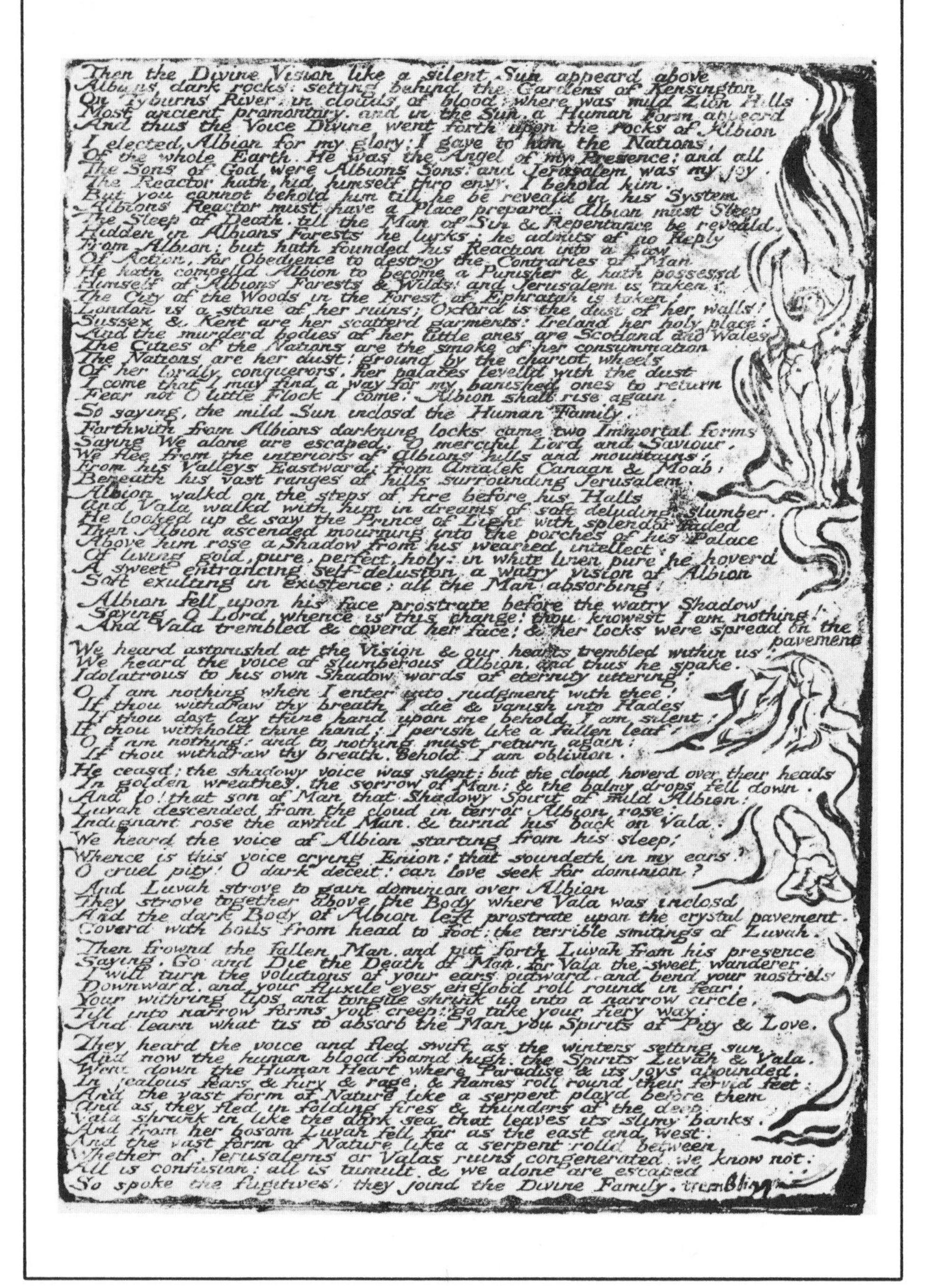

Then the Divine Vision like a silent Sun appeard above
Albions dark rocks: setting behind the Gardens of Kensington
On Tyburns River, in clouds of blood: where was mild Zion Hills
Most ancient promontory, and in the Sun, a Human Form appeard
And thus the Voice Divine went forth upon the rocks of Albion

I elected Albion for my glory; I gave to him the Nations,
Of the whole Earth. He was the Angel of my Presence: and all
The Sons of God were Albions Sons: and Jerusalem was my joy.
The Reactor hath hid himself thro envy. I behold him.
But you cannot behold him till he be reveald in his System
Albions Reactor must have a Place prepard: Albion must Sleep
The Sleep of Death, till the Man of Sin & Repentance be reveald.
Hidden in Albions Forests he lurks: he admits of no Reply
From Albion: but hath founded his Reaction into a Law
Of Action, for Obedience to destroy the Contraries of Man
He hath compelld Albion to become a Punisher & hath possessd
Himself of Albions Forests & Wilds: and Jerusalem is taken:
The City of the Woods in the Forest of Ephratah is taken!
London is a stone of her ruins; Oxford is the dust of her walls!
Sussex & Kent are her scatterd garments: Ireland her holy place:
And the murderd bodies of her little ones are Scotland and Wales
The Cities of the Nations are the smoke of her consummation
The Nations are her dust! ground by the chariot wheels
Of her lordly conquerors, her palaces levelld with the dust
I come that I may find a way for my banished ones to return
Fear not O little Flock I come: Albion shall rise again.

So saying, the mild Sun inclosd the Human Family.

Forthwith from Albions darkning locks came two Immortal forms
Saying We alone are escaped. O merciful Lord and Saviour,
We flee from the interiors of Albions hills and mountains!
From his Valleys Eastward: from Amalek Canaan & Moab;
Beneath his vast ranges of hills surrounding Jerusalem.

Albion walkd on the steps of fire before his Halls
And Vala walkd with him in dreams of soft deluding slumber.
He looked up & saw the Prince of Light with splendor faded
Then Albion ascended mourning into the porches of his Palace
Above him rose a Shadow from his wearied intellect:
Of living gold, pure, perfect, holy: in white linen pure he hoverd
A sweet entrancing self-delusion a watry vision of Albion
Soft exulting in existence; all the Man absorbing!

Albion fell upon his face prostrate before the watry Shadow
Saying O Lord whence is this change! thou knowest I am nothing!
And Vala trembled & coverd her face; & her locks were spread on the pavement

We heard astonishd at the Vision & our hearts trembled within us:
We heard the voice of slumberous Albion, and thus he spake.
Idolatrous to his own Shadow words of eternity uttering:

O I am nothing when I enter into judgment with thee!
If thou withdraw thy breath I die & vanish into Hades
If thou dost lay thine hand upon me behold I am silent:
If thou withhold thine hand; I perish like a fallen leaf:
O I am nothing: and to nothing must return again:
If thou withdraw thy breath. Behold I am oblivion.

He ceasd: the shadowy voice was silent: but the cloud hoverd over their heads
In golden wreathes, the sorrow of Man; & the balmy drops fell down.
And lo! that son of Man that Shadowy Spirit of mild Albion:
Luvah descended from the cloud in terror Albion rose:
Indignant rose the awful Man. & turnd his back on Vala.

We heard the voice of Albion starting from his sleep;

Whence is this voice crying Enion! that soundeth in my ears?
O cruel pity! O dark deceit: can love seek for dominion?

And Luvah strove to gain dominion over Albion
They strove together above the Body where Vala was inclosd
And the dark Body of Albion left prostrate upon the crystal pavement.
Coverd with boils from head to foot: the terrible smitings of Luvah.

Then frownd the fallen Man. and put forth Luvah from his presence
Saying. Go and Die the Death of Man. for Vala the sweet wanderer.
I will turn the volutions of your ears outward: and bend your nostrils
Downward, and your fluxile eyes englobd roll round in fear;
Your withring lips and tongue shrink up into a narrow circle,
Till into narrow forms you creep: go take your fiery way:
And learn what tis to absorb the Man you Spirits of Pity & Love.

They heard the voice and fled swift as the winters setting sun.
And now the human blood foamd high. the Spirits Luvah & Vala.
Went down the Human Heart where Paradise & its joys abounded.
In jealous fears & fury & rage, & flames roll round their fervid feet:
And the vast form of Nature like a serpent playd before them
And as they fled in folding fires & thunders of the deep:
Vala shrunk in like the dark sea that leaves its slimy banks.
And from her bosom Luvah fell far as the east and west:
And the vast form of Nature like a serpent rolld between,
Whether of Jerusalems or Valas ruins congenerated we know not:
All is confusion: all is tumult. & we alone are escaped
So spoke the fugitives: they joind the Divine Family. trembling

Jerusalem 43[29]D

(see 22 and 75). Until people learn to sacrifice themselves (which doesn't just mean accepting exploitation) instead of stepping on each other's faces, it will be Babylon, not Jerusalem. Ultimately (Plate 91) Los will bring down these "pyramids of pride."

Jerusalem 43[29]. The flames at top (yellow, pink, rising to blue) may signify the "steps of fire" (33) which reflect the Human Sun that Albion cannot see (1–4) and where "Vala walkd with him in dreams" (34). The naked female stepping forward with upraised arms is Vala, then, and the duplication of the lines of her body (in the flames at her left side, obscured in E), up to her breasts but not farther, suggests Albion's shadowy relation to her—while as a consequence *he* sees the Savior (Luvah) as a mere "Shadow from his wearied intellect" (37). (Departing from the text with prophetic irony, we can see the living Jerusalem stepping through purgatorial flames and shedding the illusory Vala: generation, image of regeneration.)

The voice of Jesus (Luvah), even as shadow, throws Vala into confusion; she is shown, mid-page, with "her locks . . . spread on the pavement" (43)—her spiritual body the shadow now (pink, as above, at the left) and her dark illusory one resuming visibility—and Albion, below, repeats his fall of Plate 9. (This is another version of what we see happening to him in Plates 22 and 40.) Both are shown as, literally, fallen, heads downward. But perhaps these two figures are to illustrate the passage below them: Vala "shrunk in like the dark sea" and Luvah fallen "from her bosom . . . far" (78–79). (The narrative pairings overlap; so the pictures will do for both.)

❧

Jerusalem 44[30]. Los puts forth his hands to take into his bosom his bat-winged spectre and butterfly-winged emanation (1–2, 16–17), witnesses and fugitives from the preceding "confusion" (43:82). We have seen them, at a distance, in Plate 23; the finny web on the spectre's *leg* suggests kinship with the human fish of Plate 11. The spectre is painted fiery red but with black and blue on wing edges and light blue on his fin; the emanation's wings are sky blue. After all that catatonic machinery of the vehicle in Plate 41, this simple reunion is like a return to the diabolic collaboration of serpent (with the spectre's function of working in fire and biting fluid) and eagle (with the emanation's function of working with "wings and feathers of [blue] air": *Marriage* 15). That the reunion benefits Los's bardic power is emphasized by the four strings drawn between his thigh and chest (and bound round his apron[DF]) that make him look like a harp. (In E a line extended below his thigh permits us to make the more rational perception of a fluted column behind him—compare *Europe* 15.)

The vine at the bottom of the page in full (green) leaf but not yet fruitful accompanies the textual assertion that Los continues life while following Albion among clouds of death. It may also be taken to signify the line of Los's engraving spectre, its putting forth leaves but not fruit implying his keeping the vision even in time of trouble (15).

Jerusalem 44[30][D]

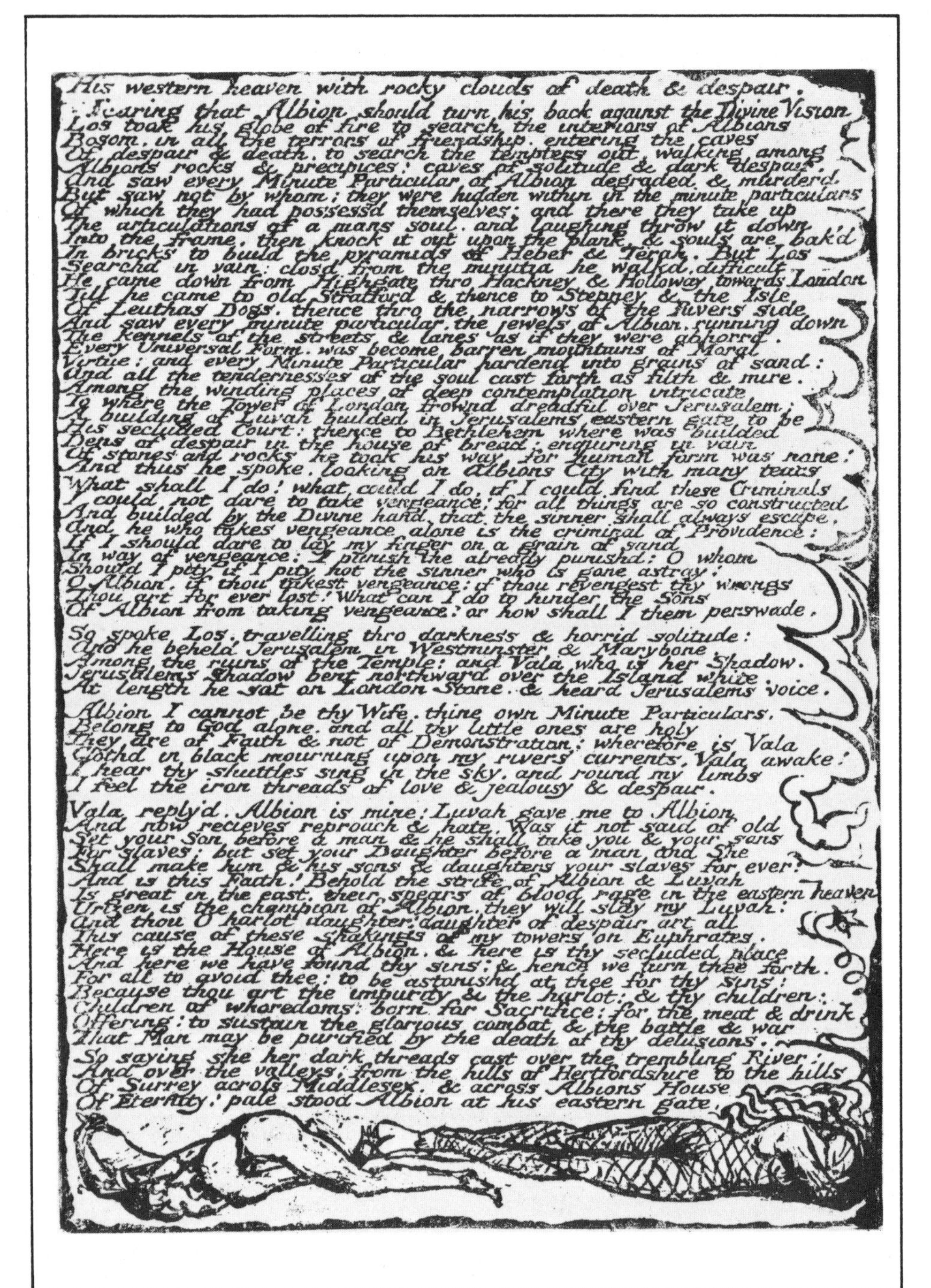

His western heaven with rocky clouds of death & despair.
Fearing that Albion should turn his back against the Divine Vision
Los took his globe of fire to search the interiors of Albions
Bosom, in all the terrors of friendship, entering the caves
Of despair & death, to search the tempters out, walking among
Albions rocks & precipices: caves of solitude & dark despair,
And saw every Minute Particular of Albion degraded & murderd
But saw not by whom; they were hidden within in the minute particulars
Of which they had possessd themselves; and there they take up
The articulations of a mans soul, and laughing throw it down
Into the frame, then knock it out upon the plank, & souls are bak'd
In bricks to build the pyramids of Heber & Terah. But Los
Searchd in vain: closd from the minutia he walkd, difficult.
He came down from Highgate thro Hackney & Holloway towards London
Till he came to old Stratford & thence to Stepney & the Isle
Of Leuthas Dogs, thence thro the narrows of the Rivers side
And saw every minute particular, the jewels of Albion, running down
The kennels of the streets & lanes as if they were abhorrd.
Every Universal Form, was become barren mountains of Moral
Virtue: and every Minute Particular hardend into grains of sand:
And all the tendernesses of the soul cast forth as filth & mire.
Among the winding places of deep contemplation intricate
To where the Tower of London frownd dreadful over Jerusalem;
A building of Luvah builded in Jerusalems eastern gate to be
His secluded Court: thence to Bethlehem where was builded
Dens of despair in the house of bread: enquiring in vain
Of stones and rocks he took his way, for human form was none:
And thus he spoke, looking on Albions City with many tears

What shall I do! what could I do, if I could find these Criminals
I could not dare to take vengeance; for all things are so constructed
And builded by the Divine hand, that the sinner shall always escape,
And he who takes vengeance alone is the criminal of Providence:
If I should dare to lay my finger on a grain of sand
In way of vengeance: I punish the already punishd: O whom
Should I pity if I pity not the sinner who is gone astray;
O Albion, if thou takest vengeance: if thou revengest thy wrongs
Thou art for ever lost! What can I do to hinder the Sons
Of Albion from taking vengeance? or how shall I them perswade.

So spoke Los, travelling thro darkness & horrid solitude:
And he beheld Jerusalem in Westminster & Marybone,
Among the ruins of the Temple: and Vala who is her Shadow.
Jerusalems Shadow bent northward over the Island white.
At length he sat on London Stone, & heard Jerusalems voice.

Albion I cannot be thy Wife, thine own Minute Particulars,
Belong to God alone, and all thy little ones are holy
They are of Faith & not of Demonstration: wherefore is Vala
Clothd in black mourning upon my rivers currents, Vala awake!
I hear thy shuttles sing in the sky, and round my limbs
I feel the iron threads of love & jealousy & despair.

Vala reply'd. Albion is mine! Luvah gave me to Albion
And now recieves reproach & hate. Was it not said of old
Set your Son before a man & he shall take you & your sons
For slaves: but set your Daughter before a man and She
Shall make him & his sons & daughters your slaves for ever!
And is this Faith? Behold the strife of Albion & Luvah
Is great in the east, their spears of blood rage in the eastern heaven
Urizen is the champion of Albion, they will slay my Luvah:
And thou O harlot daughter! daughter of despair art all
This cause of these shakings of my towers on Euphrates.
Here is the House of Albion, & here is thy secluded place
And here we have found thy sins: & hence we turn thee forth,
For all to avoid thee: to be astonishd at thee for thy sins:
Because thou art the impurity & the harlot: & thy children:
Children of whoredoms: born for Sacrifice: for the meat & drink
Offering: to sustain the glorious combat & the battle & war
That Man may be purified by the death of thy delusions.

So saying she her dark threads cast over the trembling River:
And over the valleys; from the hills of Hertfordshire to the hills
Of Surrey across Middlesex, & across Albions House
Of Eternity! pale stood Albion at his eastern gate,

Jerusalem 45[31]D

❧

Jerusalem 45[31]. The account (58–70) of Vala's expulsion of Jerusalem as a "harlot daughter: daughter of despair" and of Vala's casting "her dark threads . . . over the trembling River: And over the valleys . . ." is illustrated by an acrobatic vignette, in the spirit of Plate 42. Vala grasps in her right hand (dramatically spread wide for our attention) one of the "shuttles" (48) from which she casts her threads; with her left she gropes grotesquely between her legs for a thread which binds the human Jerusalem (human form of the river and valleys and hills)—who feels "the iron threads of love & jealousy & despair" around her limbs (48–49). Vala's action in binding Jerusalem is a counterpart to her action in Plate 40 of tangling Albion in her web. As a sequel to Plate 44 with its harp strings this is a parodistic demonstration of the wrong use of string.

Jerusalem 46[32]. On green turf beside a river (Euphrates if Vala prevails, Thames if not) Jerusalem and three daughters in a yellowish green cloud that opens infinitely at the top are lured by Vala toward the Babylonian church (a cross and dome like St Paul's—the dome unmistakable in E) at the left, that she may throw her smog-blue veil over their naked beauty. The gothic church at the right, Westminster Abbey representing the cathedral cities, looks as static, except for its spires, as St Paul's, but a loop of cloud that does not obscure the spires, indicates the clarity of the visionary cloud. (This works in the black and white copies; in E Blake colors the cloud and so needs blue sky behind the spires; obscuring them with color would subvert the idea. He also puts a grey shadow across the lower part of the church, which hides its portal. Jerusalem would not be puzzled if the contrast were too clear. In the Preston copy of this plate (*Forms* plate 7) both churches are redrawn, Westminster not much changed, St Paul's shaped as a roundish stone with a simple cross—comparable to the cross-topped globe of power in Satan's right hand in *Satan in his Original Glory*.

One of the children points the true direction for imaginative building and has begun soaring, but Jerusalem, instead of leading the Jacob's ladder procession as in Plate 4, is almost mesmerized by Vala (compare the mesmerizing of Albion in Plate 25). The daughters tugging at her on either side are not easy to read. The insistent one on tiptoe looks very concerned about her mother and does have her back to Vala; the other is calling attention to the rising sister's upward pointing, which her left hand repeats, but her legs are crossed (as are Vala's) and her arm may be restraining rather than aiding the soarer. In the text, Los begins "Shouting loud for aid Divine" (9).

Jerusalem 46[32]D

Jerusalem 47D

Jerusalem 47. With Jerusalem looking the wrong way (Plate 46), Albion tries to run one way while looking the other (into the void). His turning his face equals his having uttered his "last words" (18). Jerusalem and Vala (his split Emanation) have been howling (2). Jerusalem, not having looked *up* (Plate 46), tumbles down. Vala, standing on her shoulders (compare Plate 42), is still trying her arts on Albion. We can recognize her grossly seductive gesture as that used in Plate 24 at the point where people were sucked so completely into her digestive system that their course was straight down.

The hillock on which Albion's feet and thighs are pivoting is yellow and perhaps grassy. His left arm suggests he is peering strenuously. Along the bottom of the page there is a very slight indication of hope in the growth of barren netting into thin wavy stems, even under the words "Hope is banish'd."

Jerusalem 48. This is a quiet page, after 46 and 47, but as the imagination works "in silence" (5) in a spirit of "tender mercy" (depicted by a bowing woman at top right, whom we may associate also with the weeping in line 51), it is alive with ornament: a bird over "the Graves" (13), a scroll of contrary ends (flame and intestine) after "Contrarieties are . . . true" (14); sketches of a flying bird, tiny trees of shelter, and a rising bird of paradise between lines 20 and 21 (for the "lovely shadowy Universe" of Beulah: 19). Even when the heart gates close (25), there follow looping and reaching vines, three flying insects, a tendril suggesting the flying serpent; then, after a shaggy "terrible," small versions of the spectre bat and the emanation butterfly (see Plate 44). Marigolds blossom (28) when the "Woman" named Erin (for Ireland was the new center of revolution since America had been closed off) begins to open a "Moment of Time" (31). Instead of the rainbow mentioned we are shown, in the margin, birds, moths, butterflies (beside 30–36), then several small birds and an eagle (at 48). At Erin's name (53) vegetation springs, even a palm tree on "Dead." Then much tendril work and, at bottom, a large butterfly or moth.

Wicksteed sees the influence of "the merciful Saviour" (1) as causing the whole page "to breathe with a love and sorrow touched with tender hope," the "Cloud" (4) in which the Lord ensconces himself to burst "into fertile leafage as it stretches out to meet and envelop the Redeemer," the initial letters to "blossom into exuberant life," even the palm tree of suffering, on "Dead," being "of that vicarious suffering which liberates the happy stream of birds and flitting insects that rise up . . . to reach the Cloud in which the Saviour hides himself to build in silence." Nevertheless in coloring this page[E] Blake applied no rainbow brightness to the wings and bodies of birds and moths, indeed no colors at all but a dull grey wash over most of the surface fading to a mere suggestion of tan in the lower right corner. All the life delineated remains potential rather than actual, and we are left to walk with the daughters of Beulah "among the ornaments solemn mourning" (42).

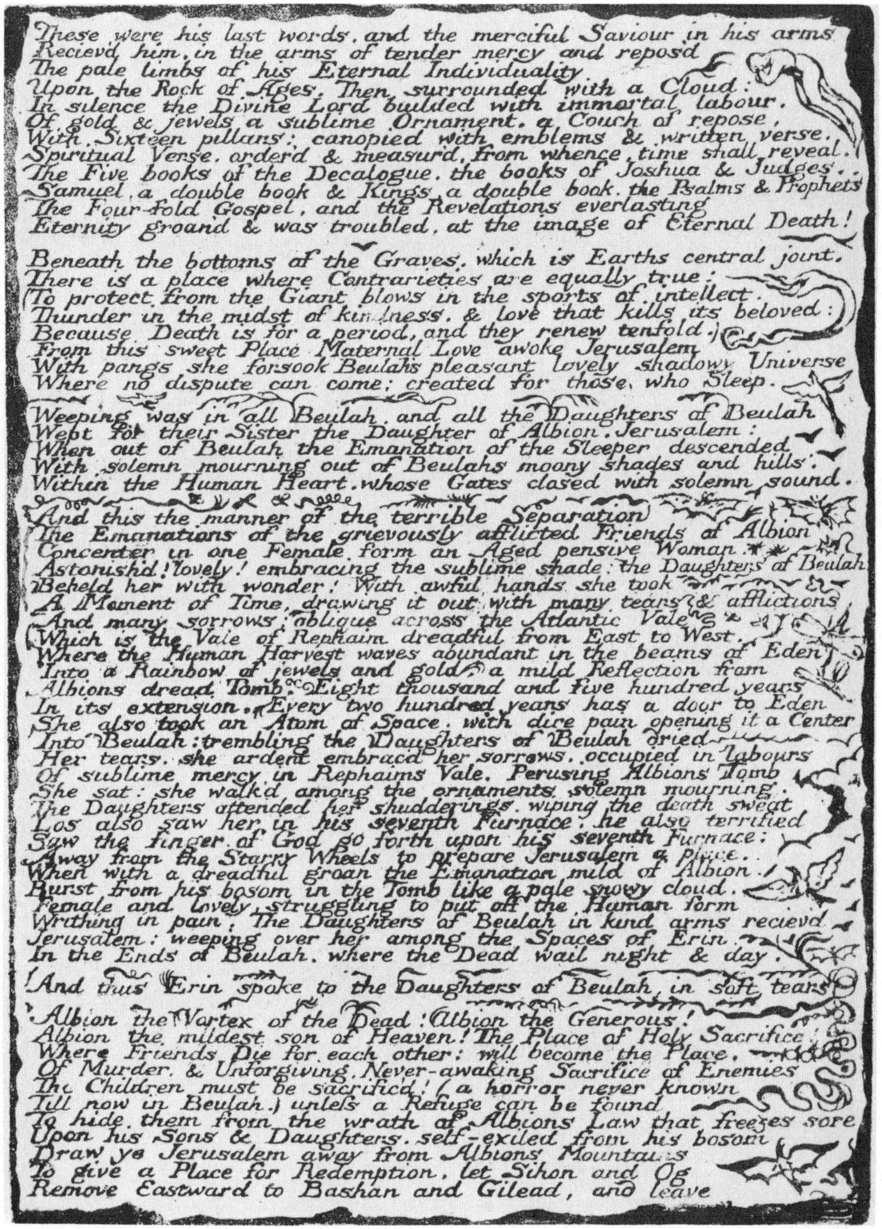

These were his last words, and the merciful Saviour in his arms
Recievd him, in the arms of tender mercy and reposd
The pale limbs of his Eternal Individuality
Upon the Rock of Ages. Then, surrounded with a Cloud:
In silence the Divine Lord builded with immortal labour,
Of gold & jewels a sublime Ornament, a Couch of repose,
With Sixteen pillars: canopied with emblems & written verse.
Spiritual Verse, orderd & measurd, from whence, time shall reveal.
The Five books of the Decalogue, the books of Joshua & Judges,
Samuel, a double book & Kings, a double book, the Psalms & Prophets
The Four-fold Gospel, and the Revelations everlasting
Eternity groand & was troubled, at the image of Eternal Death!

Beneath the bottoms of the Graves, which is Earths central joint,
There is a place where Contrarieties are equally true:
(To protect from the Giant blows in the sports of intellect,
Thunder in the midst of kindness, & love that kills its beloved:
Because Death is for a period, and they renew tenfold.)
From this sweet Place Maternal Love awoke Jerusalem
With pangs she forsook Beulahs pleasant lovely shadowy Universe
Where no dispute can come; created for those who Sleep.

Weeping was in all Beulah, and all the Daughters of Beulah
Wept for their Sister the Daughter of Albion, Jerusalem:
When out of Beulah the Emanation of the Sleeper descended
With solemn mourning out of Beulahs moony shades and hills:
Within the Human Heart, whose Gates closed with solemn sound.

And this the manner of the terrible Separation
The Emanations of the grievously afflicted Friends of Albion
Concenter in one Female form an Aged pensive Woman.
Astonishd! lovely! embracing the sublime shade: the Daughters of Beulah
Beheld her with wonder! With awful hands she took
A Moment of Time, drawing it out with many tears & afflictions
And many sorrows: oblique across the Atlantic Vale
Which is the Vale of Rephaim dreadful from East to West,
Where the Human Harvest waves abundant in the beams of Eden
Into a Rainbow of jewels and gold, a mild Reflection from
Albions dread Tomb. Eight thousand and five hundred years
In its extension. Every two hundred years has a door to Eden
She also took an Atom of Space, with dire pain opening it a Center
Into Beulah: trembling the Daughters of Beulah dried
Her tears. she ardent embracd her sorrows. occupied in labours
Of sublime mercy in Rephaims Vale. Perusing Albions Tomb
She sat: she walk'd among the ornaments solemn mourning.
The Daughters attended her shudderings, wiping the death sweat
Los also saw her in his seventh Furnace, he also terrified
Saw the finger of God go forth upon his seventh Furnace:
Away from the Starry Wheels to prepare Jerusalem a place.
When with a dreadful groan the Emanation mild of Albion.
Burst from his bosom in the Tomb like a pale snowy cloud,
Female and lovely, struggling to put off the Human form
Writhing in pain. The Daughters of Beulah in kind arms recievd
Jerusalem: weeping over her among the Spaces of Erin,
In the Ends of Beulah, where the Dead wail night & day.

And thus Erin spoke to the Daughters of Beulah, in soft tears

Albion the Vortex of the Dead! Albion the Generous!
Albion the mildest son of Heaven! The Place of Holy Sacrifice!
Where Friends Die for each other: will become the Place,
Of Murder, & Unforgiving, Never-awaking Sacrifice of Enemies
The Children must be sacrificd! (a horror never known
Till now in Beulah.) unless a Refuge can be found
To hide them from the wrath of Albions Law that freezes sore
Upon his Sons & Daughters, self-exiled from his bosom
Draw ye Jerusalem away from Albions Mountains
To give a Place for Redemption, let Sihon and Og
Remove Eastward to Bashan and Gilead, and leave

Jerusalem 48[D]

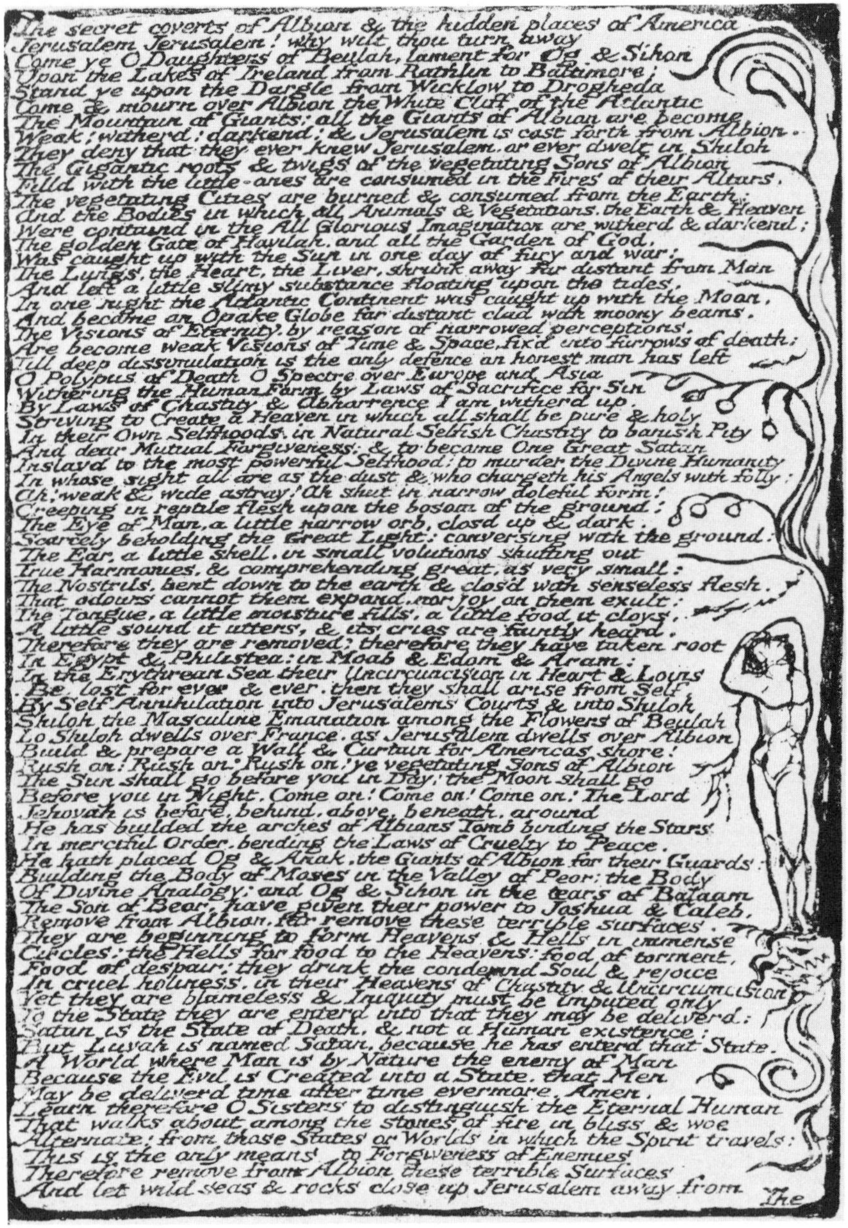

The secret coverts of Albion & the hidden places of America
Jerusalem Jerusalem! why wilt thou turn away
Come ye O Daughters of Beulah, lament for Og & Sihon
Upon the Lakes of Ireland from Rathlin to Baltimore;
Stand ye upon the Dargle from Wicklow to Drogheda
Come & mourn over Albion the White Cliff of the Atlantic
The Mountain of Giants: all the Giants of Albion are become
Weak; witherd; darkend; & Jerusalem is cast forth from Albion.
They deny that they ever knew Jerusalem, or ever dwelt in Shiloh
The Gigantic roots & twigs of the vegetating Sons of Albion
Filld with the little-ones are consumed in the Fires of their Altars.
The vegetating Cities are burned & consumed from the Earth;
And the Bodies in which all Animals & Vegetations, the Earth & Heaven
Were containd in the All Glorious Imagination are witherd & darkend;
The golden Gate of Havilah, and all the Garden of God,
Was caught up with the Sun in one day of fury and war;
The Lungs, the Heart, the Liver, shrunk away far distant from Man
And left a little slimy substance floating upon the tides.
In one night the Atlantic Continent was caught up with the Moon,
And became an Opake Globe far distant clad with moony beams.
The Visions of Eternity, by reason of narrowed perceptions,
Are become weak Visions of Time & Space, fixd into furrows of death;
Till deep dissimulation is the only defence an honest man has left
O Polypus of Death O Spectre over Europe and Asia
Withering the Human Form by Laws of Sacrifice for Sin
By Laws of Chastity & Abhorrence I am witherd up.
Striving to Create a Heaven in which all shall be pure & holy
In their Own Selfhoods, in Natural Selfish Chastity to banish Pity
And dear Mutual Forgiveness; & to become One Great Satan
Inslavd to the most powerful Selfhood: to murder the Divine Humanity
In whose sight all are as the dust & who chargeth his Angels with folly:
Ah! weak & wide astray! Ah shut in narrow doleful form!
Creeping in reptile flesh upon the bosom of the ground;
The Eye of Man, a little narrow orb, closd up & dark.
Scarcely beholding the Great Light; conversing with the ground:
The Ear, a little shell, in small volutions shutting out
True Harmonies, & comprehending great, as very small:
The Nostrils, bent down to the earth & closd with senseless flesh.
That odours cannot them expand, nor joy on them exult:
The Tongue, a little moisture fills, a little food it cloys,
A little sound it utters, & its cries are faintly heard.
Therefore they are removed; therefore they have taken root
In Egypt & Philistea: in Moab & Edom & Aram;
In the Erythrean Sea their Uncircumcision in Heart & Loins
Be lost for ever & ever. then they shall arise from Self,
By Self Annihilation into Jerusalems Courts & into Shiloh
Shiloh the Masculine Emanation among the Flowers of Beulah
Lo Shiloh dwells over France, as Jerusalem dwells over Albion
Build & prepare a Wall & Curtain for Americas shore!
Rush on: Rush on! Rush on! ye vegetating Sons of Albion
The Sun shall go before you in Day; the Moon shall go
Before you in Night. Come on! Come on! Come on! The Lord
Jehovah is before, behind, above, beneath, around
He has builded the arches of Albions Tomb binding the Stars
In merciful Order, bending the Laws of Cruelty to Peace.
He hath placed Og & Anak, the Giants of Albion for their Guards:
Building the Body of Moses in the Valley of Peor: the Body
Of Divine Analogy; and Og & Sihon in the tears of Balaam
The Son of Beor, have given their power to Joshua & Caleb.
Remove from Albion, far remove these terrible surfaces.
They are beginning to form Heavens & Hells in immense
Circles: the Hells for food to the Heavens: food of torment,
Food of despair; they drink the condemnd Soul & rejoice
In cruel holiness, in their Heavens of Chastity & Uncircumcision
Yet they are blameless & Iniquity must be imputed only
To the State they are enterd into that they may be deliverd:
Satan is the State of Death, & not a Human existence:
But Luvah is named Satan, because he has enterd that State.
A World where Man is by Nature the enemy of Man
Because the Evil is Created into a State. that Men
May be deliverd time after time evermore. Amen.
Learn therefore O Sisters to distinguish the Eternal Human
That walks about among the stones of fire in bliss & woe
Alternate: from those States or Worlds in which the Spirit travels:
This is the only means to Forgiveness of Enemies
Therefore remove from Albion these terrible Surfaces
And let wild seas & rocks close up Jerusalem away from
The

Jerusalem 49[D]

Jerusalem 49. Suddenly but not surprisingly, the fertile leafage and exuberant blossoming and happy stream of birds and insects of Plate 48 are gone utterly from the page; the "Gigantic roots & twigs," Erin explains, "all Animals & vegetations . . . contained in the All Glorious Imagination are witherd & darkend" (10–14). She fears that Albion is fallen into such a state that to save "the Eternal Human That walks about among . . . these terrible Surfaces" his emanation Jerusalem must be removed from Albion (60–76). Erin herself is (quite evidently) "witherd up" by his "Laws of Chastity & Abhorrence" (26).

William Blake is too, as he shows us by repeating from Plate 36 the picture of himself as standing naked and looking up, with vegetations springing from his right foot and left arm. Now his emanation and assistant colorist is removed. His left arm that was so colorfully and variously prolific is withered to a scrawny branch with five twig fingers, leafless. His right foot extrudes only some modest root structures, still out of habit taking the form of scrolls. What he sees above his head is a leafless tree bearing five apples, two either shriveled or not fully formed. Blake when coloring the page put a blue wash behind himself, as in Plate 36, some grey blue but no pink on his body, a faint grey wash over the rest of the page, and a touch of yellow green on the tree trunk but no color on the fruit or the roots.

Jerusalem 50. The picture illustrates Erin's concluding speech, mostly on this page, and the Daughters' reply. To "let the Sun go down" (at bottom right, its yellow disk almost sunken into the black sea) in a remembrance of "Sin" (27–30) is "a Woe & a Horror! A brooder of an Evil Day" (here a sevenfold but hornless —compare Plate 76—and human version of the apocalyptic Beast, sitting below the chalk cliffs of green England, legs in the surf[E]—compare the human swan in Plate 11) "and a Sun rising in blood"—shown as a smaller, blotchy sun (compare *Song of Los* 1) rising above the true (sulfur) sun, streaming black and red rays and causing an eclipse of the earth just beyond it. A clouded but full moon is at the left, beside a cormorant belching a zigzag of lightning. (Perhaps we are to think of Satan's sitting on the tree of life like a cormorant, in *Paradise Lost* IV 196.)

In a parody of Jerusalem's daughter who points in Plate 46 (and compare Plate 4), the top and most fully individuated person of the Beast is pointing with accusation of sin toward the figures of Plate 51 (itself a parody and reverse image of Plate 100), who constitute an emblem of the "State of Death" (49:67) produced by accusations. (Compare the triple and last accusers in Plate 93.)

The first three heads, two crowned, recall the engraving of three Accusers first called *Our End is Come* (*Marriage* i: Appendix). A passage in Plate 70 identifies this imperial monster as "the form of mighty Hand," with an orifice between key-bones and chest whence issue from three to nine "Sons of Albion" (70:1–16). When combined into "Three Forms" they are "Bacon & Newton & Locke." From Erin we learn (48:53) that this creature or state is, in effect, Albion as "Vortex of the Dead!" The cloud funneling up from the base of the vortex is Vala's veil again.

(See Lesnick, *Forms* 395–97).

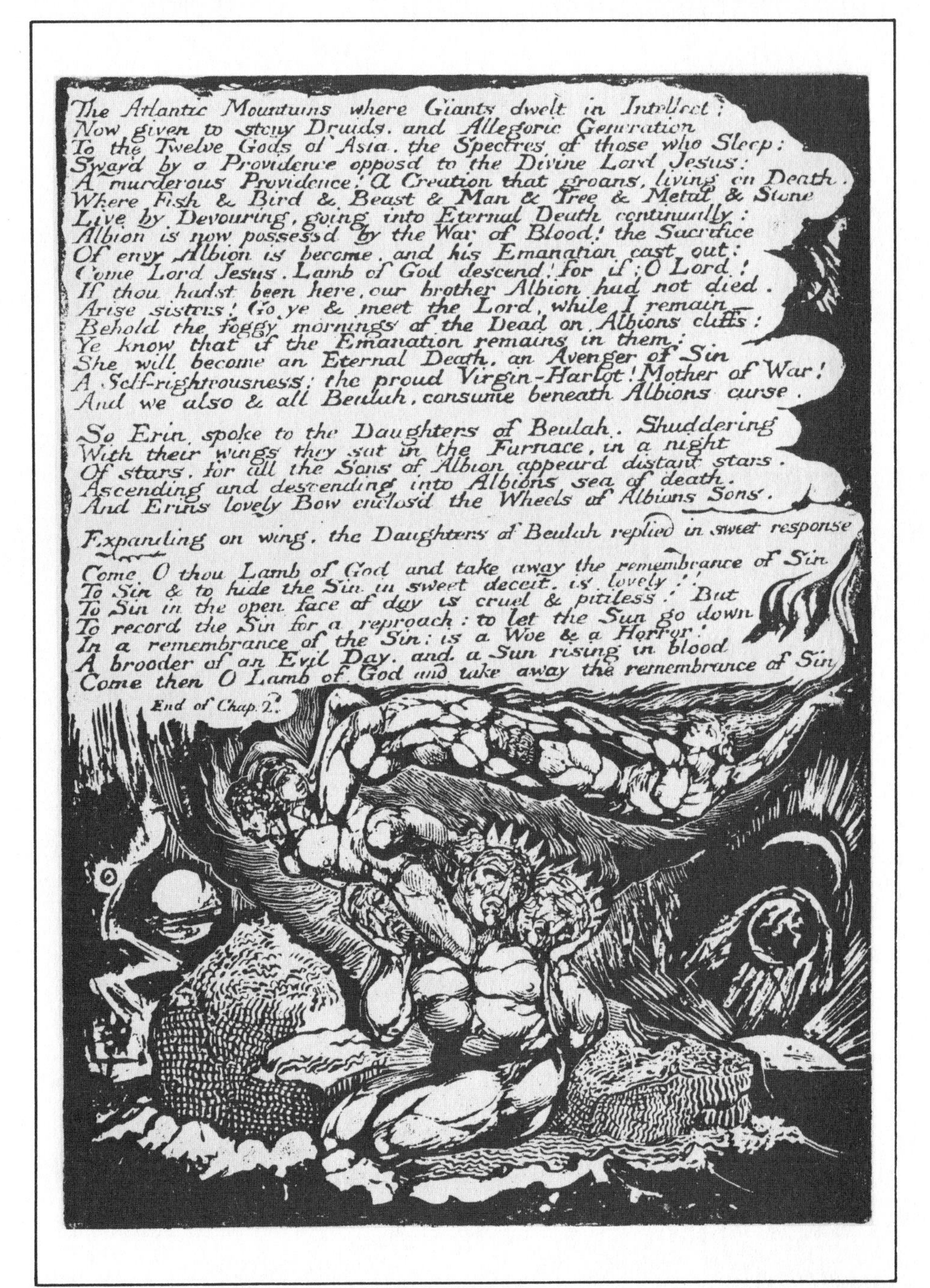

Jerusalem 50[D]

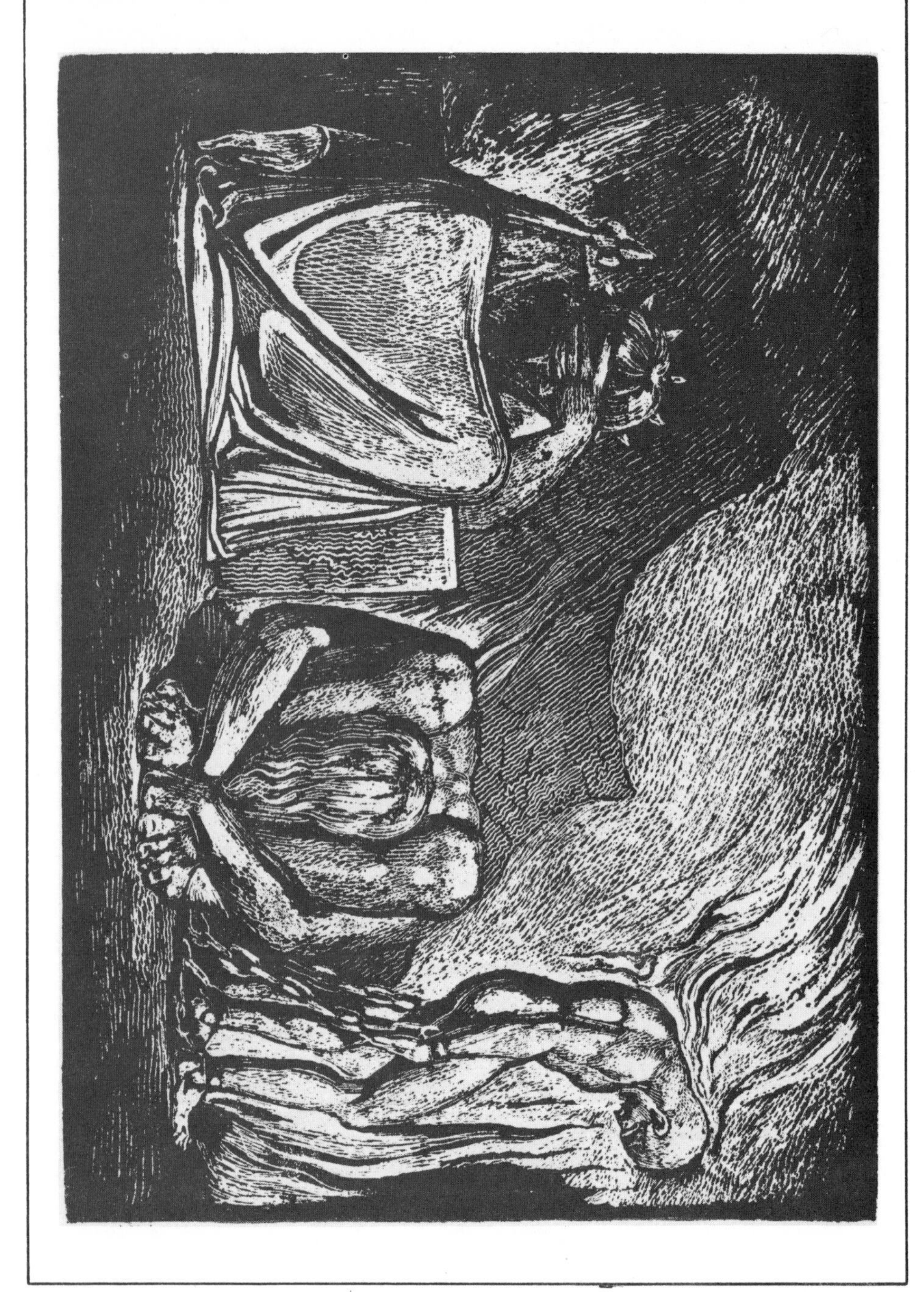

Jerusalem 51^{D} (exact size)

Jerusalem 51. This vision of the "stones of fire" and "terrible Surfaces" that must be removed (49:73–76) is the center of the poem and nadir or reverse of Plate 100. Vala, Hyle, and Skofield (so titled by Blake in separate prints of this plate) preside with heavy heads in Vala's court of despair. With scepter held like the wand of the sibyl in *Gates* 16 and a spiked crown which makes her a Whore queen to match the Beast kings of Plate 50, Vala rules from a black stone throne. Her head is held a bit higher than Albion's in Plate 37; yet the living can take comfort from her plight, which recalls that of the King of France in the first lines of Blake's *French Revolution:* "his strong hand outstretched, from his shoulder down the bone, Runs aching cold into the scepter too heavy for mortal grasp. No more To be swayed by visible hand. . . ." In the center Hyle, with head even lower than Albion's, recalls Theotormon in *Visions* 4. The Prime Minister of Vala's court, he represents the importance of mere rationalism (W). Skofield, burning in hotter flames (yellow-white near his body) than Hand in Plate 26, the soldier who indicted Blake in 1803, is chained by his own accusations (he had hoped to see Blake led off in chains, noted Gilchrist apropos this picture)—and is seen not as a menace but another "hapless soldier." (Lesnick, *Forms* 397.)

Jerusalem 52. This is the least ornamented of the prose interchapters, because the most crowded, partly. The small tree or vine between the columns of verse continues the barrenness of Plate 49, but with no fruit or human form.

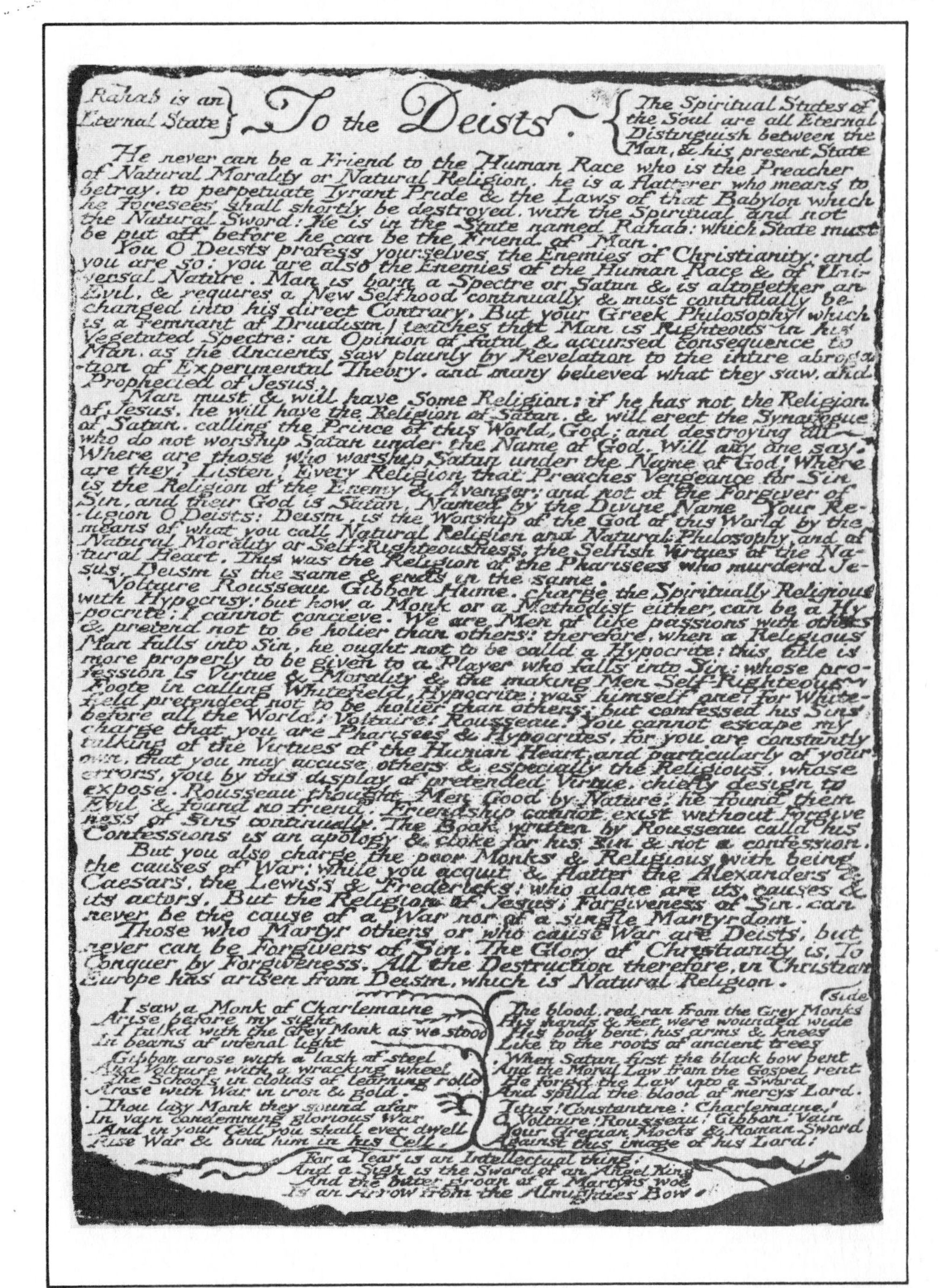

Rahab is an Eternal State

To the Deists.

The Spiritual States of the Soul are all Eternal Distinguish between the Man, & his present State

He never can be a Friend to the Human Race who is the Preacher of Natural Morality or Natural Religion. he is a flatterer who means to betray. to perpetuate Tyrant Pride & the Laws of that Babylon which he foresees shall shortly be destroyed. with the Spiritual and not the Natural Sword: He is in the State named Rahab: which State must be put off before he can be the Friend of Man.

You O Deists profess yourselves the Enemies of Christianity: and you are so: you are also the Enemies of the Human Race & of Universal Nature. Man is born a Spectre or Satan & is altogether an Evil, & requires a New Selfhood continually & must continually be changed into his direct Contrary. But your Greek Philosophy (which is a remnant of Druidism) teaches that Man is Righteous in his Vegetated Spectre: an Opinion of fatal & accursed consequence to Man. as the Ancients saw plainly by Revelation to the intire abrogation of Experimental Theory. and many believed what they saw. and Prophecied of Jesus.

Man must & will have Some Religion: if he has not the Religion of Jesus. he will have the Religion of Satan. & will erect the Synagogue of Satan. calling the Prince of this World, God; and destroying all who do not worship Satan under the Name of God. Will any one say: Where are those who worship Satan under the Name of God! Where are they? Listen! Every Religion that Preaches Vengeance for Sin is the Religion of the Enemy & Avenger; and not of the Forgiver of Sin, and their God is Satan, Named by the Divine Name. Your Religion O Deists: Deism, is the Worship of the God of this World by the means of what you call Natural Religion and Natural Philosophy, and of Natural Morality or Self-Righteousness, the Selfish Virtues of the Natural Heart. This was the Religion of the Pharisees who murderd Jesus. Deism is the same & ends in the same.

Voltaire Rousseau Gibbon Hume. charge the Spiritually Religious with Hypocrisy! but how a Monk or a Methodist either, can be a Hypocrite! I cannot concieve. We are Men of like passions with others & pretend not to be holier than others: therefore, when a Religious Man falls into Sin, he ought not to be calld a Hypocrite: this title is more properly to be given to a Player who falls into Sin; whose profession is Virtue & Morality & the making Men Self-Righteous. Foote in calling Whitefield, Hypocrite; was himself one: for Whitefield pretended not to be holier than others; but confessed his Sins before all the World; Voltaire! Rousseau! You cannot escape my charge that you are Pharisees & Hypocrites, for you are constantly talking of the Virtues of the Human Heart, and particularly of your own, that you may accuse others & especially the Religious, whose errors, you by this display of pretended Virtue, chiefly design to expose. Rousseau thought Men Good by Nature; he found them Evil & found no friend. Friendship cannot exist without Forgiveness of Sins continually. The Book written by Rousseau calld his Confessions is an apology & cloke for his Sin & not a confession.

But you also charge the poor Monks & Religious with being the causes of War: while you acquit & flatter the Alexanders & Caesars, the Lewis's & Fredericks: who alone are its causes & its actors. But the Religion of Jesus, Forgiveness of Sin, can never be the cause of a War nor of a single Martyrdom.

Those who Martyr others or who cause War are Deists, but never can be Forgivers of Sin. The Glory of Christianity is, To Conquer by Forgiveness. All the Destruction therefore, in Christian Europe has arisen from Deism, which is Natural Religion.

I saw a Monk of Charlemaine
Arise before my sight
I talkd with the Grey Monk as we stood
In beams of infernal light

Gibbon arose with a lash of steel
And Voltaire with a wracking wheel
The Schools in clouds of learning rolld
Arose with War in iron & gold.

Thou lazy Monk they sound afar
In vain condemning glorious War
And in your Cell you shall ever dwell
Rise War & bind him in his Cell.

The blood. red ran from the Grey Monks side
His hands & feet were wounded wide
His body bent. his arms & knees
Like to the roots of ancient trees

When Satan first the black bow bent
And the Moral Law from the Gospel rent
He forgd the Law into a Sword
And spilld the blood of mercys Lord.

Titus! Constantine! Charlemaine!
O Voltaire! Rousseau! Gibbon! Vain
Your Grecian Mocks & Roman Sword
Against this image of his Lord!

For a Tear is an Intellectual thing;
And a Sigh is the Sword of an Angel King
And the bitter groan of a Martyrs woe
Is an Arrow from the Almighties Bow!

Jerusalem 52D

Jerusalem 53D

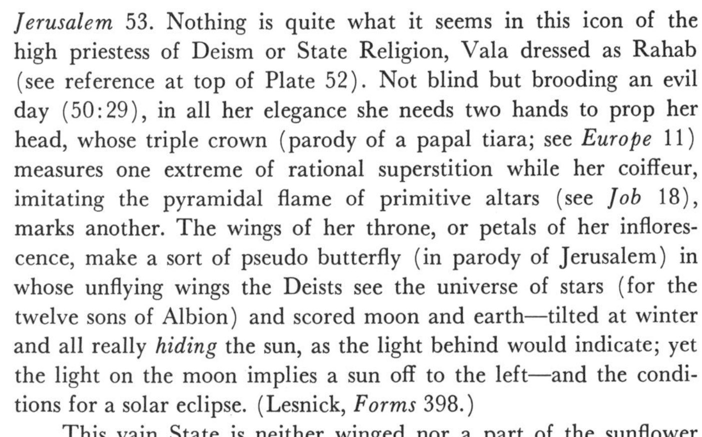

Jerusalem 53. Nothing is quite what it seems in this icon of the high priestess of Deism or State Religion, Vala dressed as Rahab (see reference at top of Plate 52). Not blind but brooding an evil day (50:29), in all her elegance she needs two hands to prop her head, whose triple crown (parody of a papal tiara; see *Europe* 11) measures one extreme of rational superstition while her coiffeur, imitating the pyramidal flame of primitive altars (see *Job* 18), marks another. The wings of her throne, or petals of her inflorescence, make a sort of pseudo butterfly (in parody of Jerusalem) in whose unflying wings the Deists see the universe of stars (for the twelve sons of Albion) and scored moon and earth—tilted at winter and all really *hiding* the sun, as the light behind would indicate; yet the light on the moon implies a sun off to the left—and the conditions for a solar eclipse. (Lesnick, *Forms* 398.)

This vain State is neither winged nor a part of the sunflower she sits on—which is rising in water (a striking contrast to the waterlily of Plate 28) and so probably the business end of a sea-anemone (a form of polypus) from a watery perspective—and her throne and wings but illusory extensions of her self. Erasmus Darwin may be quoted on the helianthus as a "barren" and "unprolific" flower. Brahma floats on a lotos.

The figures in the right margin are puzzling. A long-legged boy lies back with head and shoulders in a woman's lap—a Pieta of Natural Religion, the mother who treasures the dead body of her child (W). Below, Wicksteed sees "the Angel of the Resurrection calling the Soul" (as in Blake's title page for Blair's *Grave*)—but the lower figure, a naked female in a natural grave, acts like body, not soul, and clutches the line that would have been the Angel's trumpet if she had permitted Blake to complete the drawing. Vala, no doubt.

Jerusalem 54. In this diagrammatic page Blake both illustrates and disputes Albion's fallen vision of his own falling. Albion's view is that he "fell down a Rocky fragment from Eternity" (6); Blake adds: "hurld By his own . . . Reasoning Power . . . Into his own Chaos" (6–8) but obliges with a diagram of a round lumpy earth stone labeled "This World" with the four Eternals in every man reduced to four cardinal areas labeled "Reason" (really Urizen), "Desire" (Luvah), "Pity" (Los as Palamabron), "Wrath" (Tharmas as Rintrah). Then Blake proceeds to give this stone vision the laugh by adding human forms, four, clothed, on the right, five or six naked on the left, who at first glance appear to be in This World's orbit yet are not rolled round by it. Indeed they are all dancing the upward dance shown, on the left side only, in Plate 4, in a vortex rising toward the unfallen zone at top. That upper area, illustrating the first stanza's definition of the life and liberty of "every particular form" in Great Eternity (1), is filled with living particulars flying free: twenty-seven birds in the space below Albion's nonsense about Chaos, sixteen more (including an eagle perhaps) up the right margin. (In *Milton* it takes twenty-eight larks to soar free of the twenty-seven heavens: *P&P* 135.)

Albion's spectre named Arthur, now in charge, declares flatly against the credibility of "an unknown Eternal Life"; you can't turn "stones to bread"; the artist is a "Vain foolish Man!" (remember the angel in *Marriage* 17 who called Blake "pitiable foolish young man" for challenging his vision of his own Abyss) for trying to "build a World of Phantasy upon my Great Abyss!" (20–23). These human forms are mere "Shapes in craving lust & devouring appetite" (24). Very well, Blake obliges by drawing segments of Vala's intestinal veil at the curved sides of this stomach area, enclosing the human forms—but then, slyly, in the colored copy he changes them to spiralling flames and adds a young lad (Orc?) at the right to push the veil aside.

Next Arthur demonstrates that he can constrict himself into four "Druid Rocks round Canaan Agag & Aram & Pharoh" (26). Blake obliges only to the extent of drawing four rock-like heads on one body sunk into the ground—Arthur the spectre as four rocky fragments: not really dead but open eyed, looking up and outward, blessed with five five-pointed stars (a motif carried from the pairs of falling stars in Plates 9 and 20), for even fallen senses may have their own light of perception (see 2–3). In Plate 92 we shall see these four heads grown older.

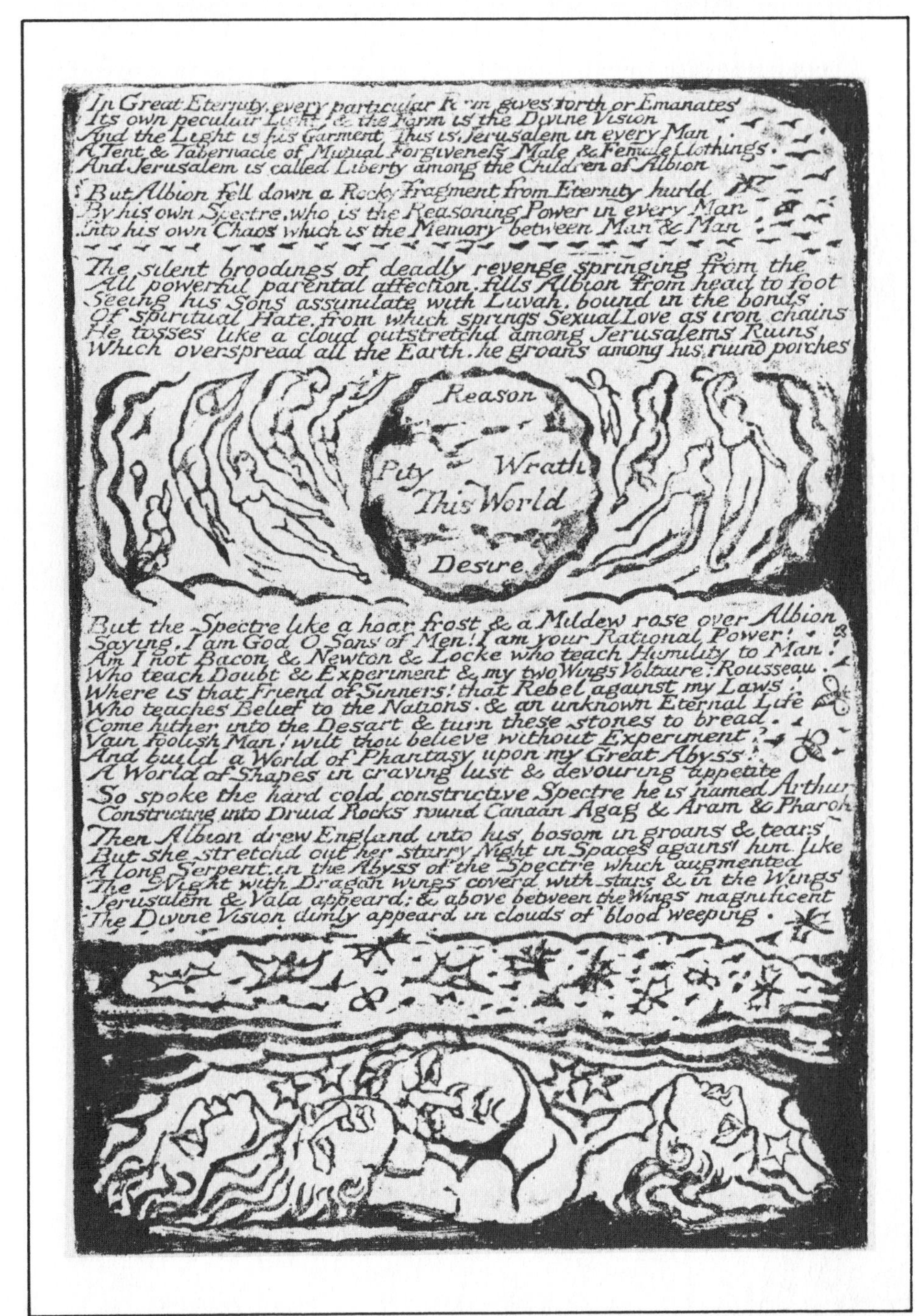
In Great Eternity, every particular Form gives forth or Emanates
Its own peculiar Light, & the Form is the Divine Vision
And the Light is his Garment This is Jerusalem in every Man
A Tent & Tabernacle of Mutual Forgiveness Male & Female Clothings.
And Jerusalem is called Liberty among the Children of Albion

But Albion fell down a Rocky Fragment from Eternity hurld
By his own Spectre, who is the Reasoning Power in every Man
Into his own Chaos which is the Memory between Man & Man

The silent broodings of deadly revenge springing from the
All powerful parental affection, fills Albion from head to foot
Seeing his Sons assimilate with Luvah, bound in the bonds
Of spiritual Hate, from which springs Sexual Love as iron chains
He tosses like a cloud outstretchd among Jerusalems Ruins
Which overspread all the Earth, he groans among his ruind porches

But the Spectre like a hoar frost & a Mildew rose over Albion
Saying, I am God O Sons of Men! I am your Rational Power!
Am I not Bacon & Newton & Locke who teach Humility to Man!
Who teach Doubt & Experiment & my two Wings Voltaire: Rousseau.
Where is that Friend of Sinners! that Rebel against my Laws!
Who teaches Belief to the Nations. & an unknown Eternal Life
Come hither into the Desart & turn these stones to bread.
Vain foolish Man! wilt thou believe without Experiment?
And build a World of Phantasy upon my Great Abyss!
A World of Shapes in craving lust & devouring appetite

So spoke the hard cold constructive Spectre he is named Arthur
Constricting into Druid Rocks round Canaan Agag & Aram & Pharoh

Then Albion drew England into his bosom in groans & tears
But she stretchd out her starry Night in Spaces against him. like
A long Serpent, in the Abyss of the Spectre which augmented
The Night with Dragon wings coverd with stars & in the Wings
Jerusalem & Vala appeard; & above between the Wings magnificent
The Divine Vision dimly appeard in clouds of blood weeping.

Jerusalem 54D

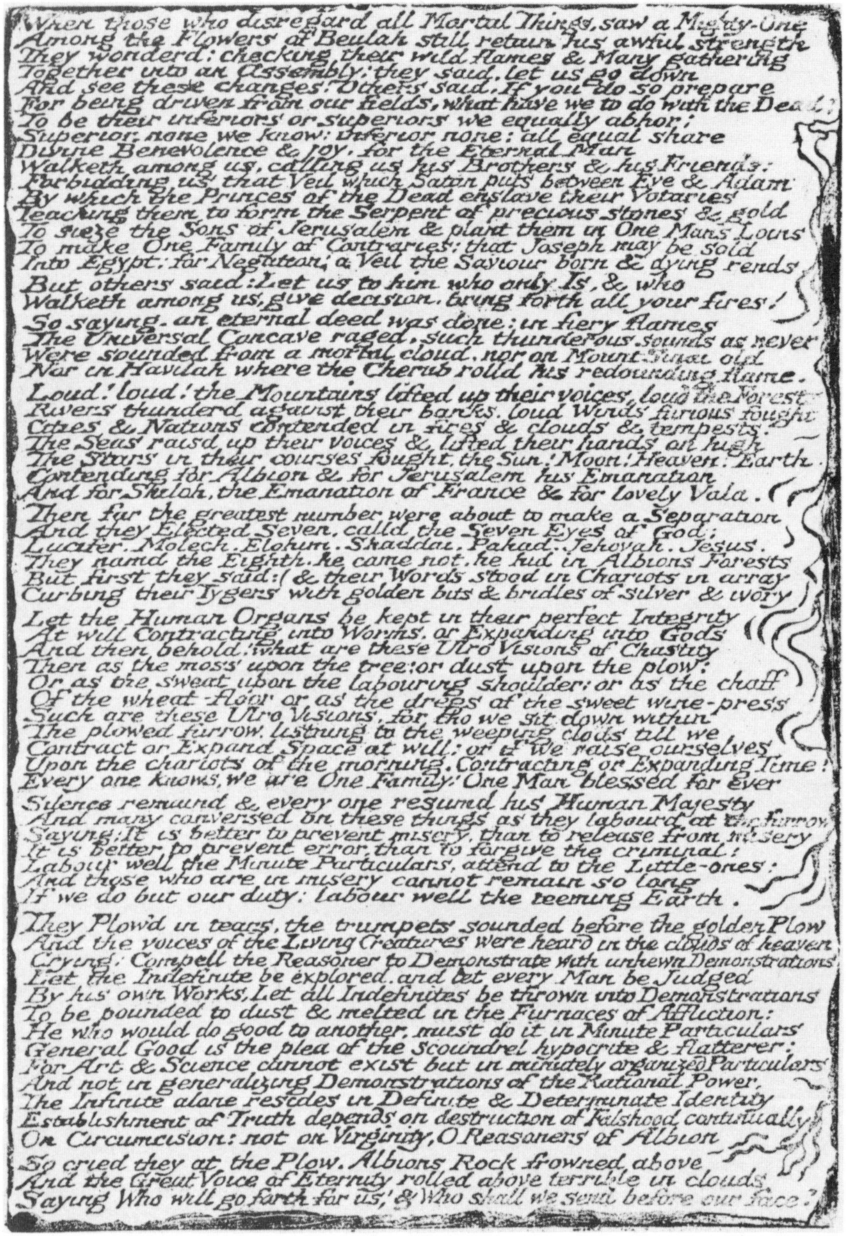

When those who disregard all Mortal Things, saw a Mighty-One
Among the Flowers of Beulah still retain his awful strength
They wonder'd; checking their wild flames & Many gathering
Together into an Assembly; they said, let us go down
And see these changes! Others said, If you do so prepare
For being driven from our fields, what have we to do with the Dead?
To be their inferiors or superiors we equally abhor;
Superior, none we know: inferior none: all equal share
Divine Benevolence & joy, for the Eternal Man
Walketh among us, calling us his Brothers & his Friends:
Forbidding us that Veil which Satan puts between Eve & Adam
By which the Princes of the Dead enslave their Votaries
Teaching them to form the Serpent of precious stones & gold
To seize the Sons of Jerusalem & plant them in One Mans Loins
To make One Family of Contraries: that Joseph may be sold
Into Egypt: for Negation; a Veil the Saviour born & dying rends.

But others said: Let us to him who only Is, & who
Walketh among us, give decision. bring forth all your fires!

So saying, an eternal deed was done: in fiery flames
The Universal Concave raged, such thunderous sounds as never
Were sounded from a mortal cloud, nor on Mount Sinai old
Nor in Havilah where the Cherub rolld his redounding flame.

Loud! loud! the Mountains lifted up their voices, loud the Forests
Rivers thunderd against their banks, loud Winds furious fought
Cities & Nations contended in fires & clouds & tempests.
The Seas raisd up their voices & lifted their hands on high
The Stars in their courses fought. the Sun! Moon! Heaven! Earth.
Contending for Albion & for Jerusalem his Emanation
And for Shiloh, the Emanation of France & for lovely Vala.

Then far the greatest number were about to make a Separation
And they Elected Seven, calld the Seven Eyes of God;
Lucifer. Molech. Elohim. Shaddai. Pahad. Jehovah. Jesus.
They namd the Eighth. he came not, he hid in Albions Forests
But first they said: (& their Words stood in Chariots in array
Curbing their Tygers with golden bits & bridles of silver & ivory)

Let the Human Organs be kept in their perfect Integrity
At will Contracting into Worms, or Expanding into Gods
And then behold! what are these Ulro Visions of Chastity
Then as the moss upon the tree: or dust upon the plow:
Or as the sweat upon the labouring shoulder: or as the chaff
Of the wheat-floor or as the dregs of the sweet wine-press
Such are these Ulro Visions. for tho we sit down within
The plowed furrow. listning to the weeping clods till we
Contract or Expand Space at will: or if we raise ourselves
Upon the chariots of the morning. Contracting or Expanding Time!
Every one knows, we are One Family: One Man blessed for ever

Silence remaind & every one resumd his Human Majesty
And many conversed on these things as they labourd at the furrow
Saying: It is better to prevent misery, than to release from misery
It is better to prevent error, than to forgive the criminal:
Labour well the Minute Particulars, attend to the Little-ones:
And those who are in misery cannot remain so long
If we do but our duty: labour well the teeming Earth.

They Plowd in tears, the trumpets sounded before the golden Plow
And the voices of the Living Creatures were heard in the clouds of heaven
Crying: Compell the Reasoner to Demonstrate with unhewn Demonstrations
Let the Indefinite be explored. and let every Man be Judged
By his own Works, Let all Indefinites be thrown into Demonstrations
To be pounded to dust & melted in the Furnaces of Affliction:
He who would do good to another, must do it in Minute Particulars
General Good is the plea of the scoundrel hypocrite & flatterer:
For Art & Science cannot exist but in minutely organized Particulars
And not in generalizing Demonstrations of the Rational Power.
The Infinite alone resides in Definite & Determinate Identity
Establishment of Truth depends on destruction of Falshood continually
On Circumcision: not on Virginity, O Reasoners of Albion

So cried they at the Plow. Albions Rock frowned above
And the Great Voice of Eternity rolled above terrible in clouds
Saying Who will go forth for us! & Who shall we send before our face?

Jerusalem 55D

Finally, parted from his Reasoning Power, Albion tries "groans & tears" to entice "England into his bosom" (27)—but instead she chooses to emanate *her* peculiar light, which is to stretch out a banner of "her starry Night . . . like A long Serpent," to replace the spectre's chaos with a microform version of the title page: "Dragon wings coverd with stars & in the Wings Jerusalem & Vala . . ." pictured as a lower sky filled with flying creatures, mostly butterflies and distant birds, but one fine grey dove under the second word of "Divine Vision," as harbinger for the Holy Spirit. So much for Albion's very own Chaos!

From the artist's perspective this world rock is the "rock of ages" on which he writes and etches with trembling hand, the human brain being opened to "the Human Imagination" (5:20–23). It is also the stony island occupied by sevenfold Hand in Plate 50.

Jerusalem 55. "Silence remaind" (47) is sufficient comment on the treatment of the margins, darkened gently with purple and blue in E.

Jerusalem 56. The webs in the margin (compare Plate 4) illustrate the simplest form of the "weaving" dwelt upon in the text; a very complex form appears on Plate 57.

The style of poetry and of lettering on this page is curiously different, though Plates 61 and 88 are somewhat similar; no plausible explanation has been proposed. (See my "Suppressed and Altered Passages in Blake's *Jerusalem*," *Studies in Bibliography*, 1964.)

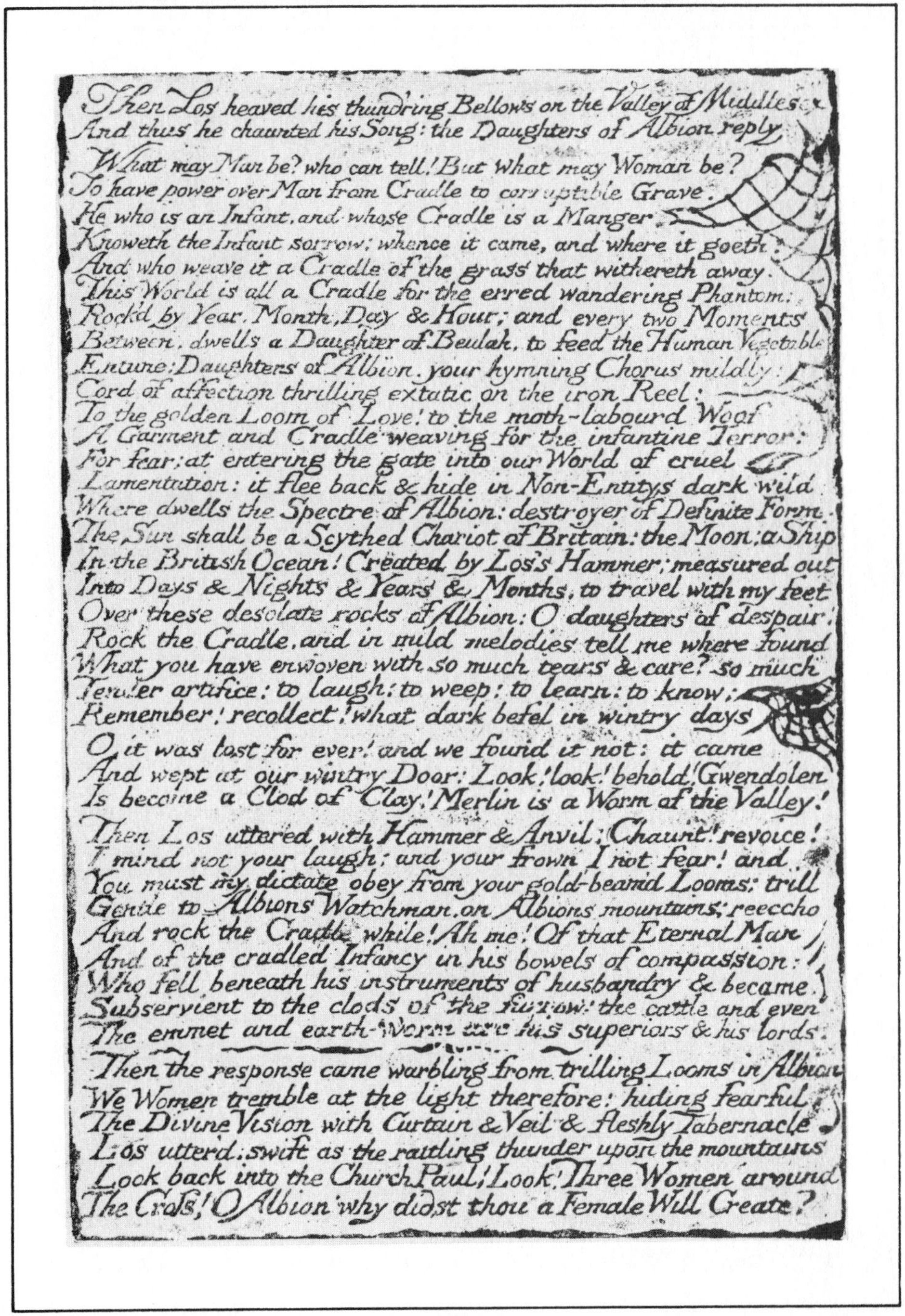

Then Los heaved his thundring Bellows on the Valley of Middlesex
And thus he chaunted his Song: the Daughters of Albion reply.

What may Man be? who can tell! But what may Woman be?
To have power over Man from Cradle to corruptible Grave.
He who is an Infant. and whose Cradle is a Manger
Knoweth the Infant sorrow: whence it came, and where it goeth:
And who weave it a Cradle of the grass that withereth away.
This World is all a Cradle for the erred wandering Phantom:
Rock'd by Year. Month. Day & Hour; and every two Moments
Between. dwells a Daughter of Beulah. to feed the Human Vegetable
Entune: Daughters of Albion. your hymning Chorus mildly!
Cord of affection thrilling extatic on the iron Reel:
To the golden Loom of Love! to the moth-labourd Woof
A Garment and Cradle weaving for the infantine Terror:
For fear; at entering the gate into our World of cruel
Lamentation: it flee back & hide in Non-Entitys dark wild
Where dwells the Spectre of Albion: destroyer of Definite Form.
The Sun shall be a Scythed Chariot of Britain: the Moon; a Ship
In the British Ocean! Created by Los's Hammer; measured out
Into Days & Nights & Years & Months. to travel with my feet
Over these desolate rocks of Albion: O daughters of despair!
Rock the Cradle. and in mild melodies tell me where found
What you have enwoven with so much tears & care? so much
Tender artifice: to laugh: to weep: to learn: to know;
Remember! recollect! what dark befel in wintry days

O it was lost for ever! and we found it not: it came
And wept at our wintry Door: Look! look! behold! Gwendolen
Is become a Clod of Clay! Merlin is a Worm of the Valley!

Then Los uttered with Hammer & Anvil: Chaunt! revoice!
I mind not your laugh: and your frown I not fear! and
You must my dictate obey from your gold-beam'd Looms; trill
Gentle to Albions Watchman. on Albions mountains; reeccho
And rock the Cradle while! Ah me! Of that Eternal Man
And of the cradled Infancy in his bowels of compassion:
Who fell beneath his instruments of husbandry & became
Subservient to the clods of the furrow! the cattle and even
The emmet and earth-Worm are his superiors & his lords.

Then the response came warbling from trilling Looms in Albion
We Women tremble at the light therefore: hiding fearful
The Divine Vision with Curtain & Veil & fleshly Tabernacle
Los utterd: swift as the rattling thunder upon the mountains
Look back into the Church Paul! Look! Three Women around
The Cross! O Albion why didst thou a Female Will Create?

Jerusalem 56[D]

Jerusalem 57D

Jerusalem 57. This transforming vision of Albion's abstract nightmare of Plate 54 shows us "A World of Generation continually Creating out of The . . . World of Rocky destiny" (58:50–51), though Los's own response is ambiguous: "Look back into the Church Paul! [i.e. St Paul's, shown at the top of the globe] Three Women around The Cross!" (56:42–43). Very well, though the cross on St Paul's is almost invisible, not ready for the illumination of Plate 84 (q.v.). But his next outcry, "O Albion why didst thou a Female Will Create?" implies suspicion. Yet these three lovely naked women with gentle faces, though they may "tremble at the light" from the "trilling Looms" they work in (56:39, 38) as they crouch, kneel, and lie around a globe that is not rough stone but soft green earth with cities and churches, are a generative contrast to the cruel Parcae of Plate 25. The churches of "London" (subsuming "York") and "Jerusalem" are not posed as rival images. The women are weaving a stained-glass window for "bright Cathedrons golden Hall" (59:25), the vine-like tracery or leading of which forms no intestinal veil but is filled with bright stars (against deep blue sky), four and seven stars at the top, three with Jerusalem. The vine is woven or rather extruded from their hands the way fibres are from Vala's hands in Plate 25 but also the way life springs from the artist's in Plate 36, always potentially "fibres of life." (See Plate 85.) If these are spiders of Female Will and Generation, then their message of Regeneration is very loud.

The golden arch of the gothic window, with faint outlines of carved angels on its surface, cuts across the top corners of the page, with dark shadows (shading into the blue sky in E). Jerusalem's right foot against the earth seems to be assisting its clockwise movement (W); that position for her leg was an afterthought, contrived after the space had been etched with vines. The hair of Jerusalem (not of the others) seems to be a source of fibres.

❧

Jerusalem 58. In the grotesque pictures at the top and bottom of the page the female-male, soul-body, emanation-spectre opposition has become an opposition of pudenda (bat-winged but butterfly-colored—and note the similarity to the hair of Vala in Plate 25) to greenish dry skeleton, in red flames. The gateway of birth is alluded to in the words "porticoes," "portico," and "porch" (27, 33). The skeleton lying in a bed of flames that suggests the "cave" etched in the copper plate (*Marriage* 15) indicates what it means to the artist to labor in "A World of Generation continually Creating; out of The Hermaphroditic Satanic World of rocky destiny" (50–51, and see Plate 57 note). Grant (*Forms* 109) has called attention to the symbolic relation of this pair of images to the pair in *America* 13 as emblems of the effect on women (top scene) and men (lower scene) of the physical and psychological horrors of war.

In beauty the Daughters of Albion divide & unite at will
Naked & drunk with blood Gwendolen dancing to the timbrel
Of War: reeling up the Street of London she divides in twain
Among the Inhabitants of Albion. the People fall around
The Daughters of Albion. divide & unite in jealousy & cruelty
The Inhabitants of Albion at the Harvest & the Vintage
Feel their Brain cut round beneath the temples shrieking
Bonifying into a Scull, the Marrow exuding in dismal path
They flee over the rocks bonifying: Horses: Oxen: feel the knife.
And while the Sons of Albion by severe War & Judgment, bonify
The Hermaphroditic Condensations are divided by the Knife
The obdurate Forms are cut asunder by Jealousy & Pity.

Rational Philosophy and Mathematic Demonstration
Is divided in the intoxications of pleasure & affection
Two Contraries War against each other in fury & blood,
And Los fixes them on his Anvil, incessant his blows:
He fixes them with strong blows, placing the stones & timbers
To Create a World of Generation from the World of Death:
Dividing the Masculine & Feminine: for the comingling
Of Albions & Luvahs Spectres was Hermaphroditic

Urizen wrathful strode above directing the awful Building:
As a Mighty Temple; delivering Form out of confusion
Jordan sprang beneath its threshold bubbling from beneath
Its pillars: Euphrates ran under its arches: white sails
And silver oars reflect on its pillars. & sound on its ecchoing
Pavements: where walk the Sons of Jerusalem who remain Ungenerate
But the revolving Sun and Moon pass thro its porticoes.
Day & night, in sublime majesty & silence they revolve
And shine glorious within: Hand & Koban archd over the Sun
In the hot noon. as he traveld thro his journey: Hyle & Skofield
Archd over the Moon at midnight & Los Fixd them there,
With his thunderous Hammer; terrified the Spectres rage & flee
Canaan is his portico; Jordan is a fountain in his porch;
A fountain of milk & wine to relieve the traveller:
Egypt is the eight steps within. Ethiopia supports his pillars;
Lybia & the Lands unknown. are the ascent without;
Within is Asia & Greece. ornamented with exquisite art:
Persia & Media are his halls: his inmost hall is Great Tartary.
China & India & Siberia are his temples for entertainment
Poland & Russia & Sweden. his soft retired chambers
France & Spain & Italy & Denmark & Holland & Germany
Are the temples among his pillars. Britain is Loss Forge:
America North & South are his baths of living waters.

Such is the Ancient World of Urizen in the Satanic Void
Created from the Valley of Middlesex by Londons River
From Stone-henge & from London Stone, from Cornwall to Cathnes
The Four Zoa's rush around on all sides in dire ruin
Furious in pride of Selfhood the terrible Spectres of Albion
Rear their dark Rocks among the Stars of God: stupendous
Works! A World of Generation continually Creating; out of
The Hermaphroditic Satanic World of rocky destiny.

Jerusalem 58[D]

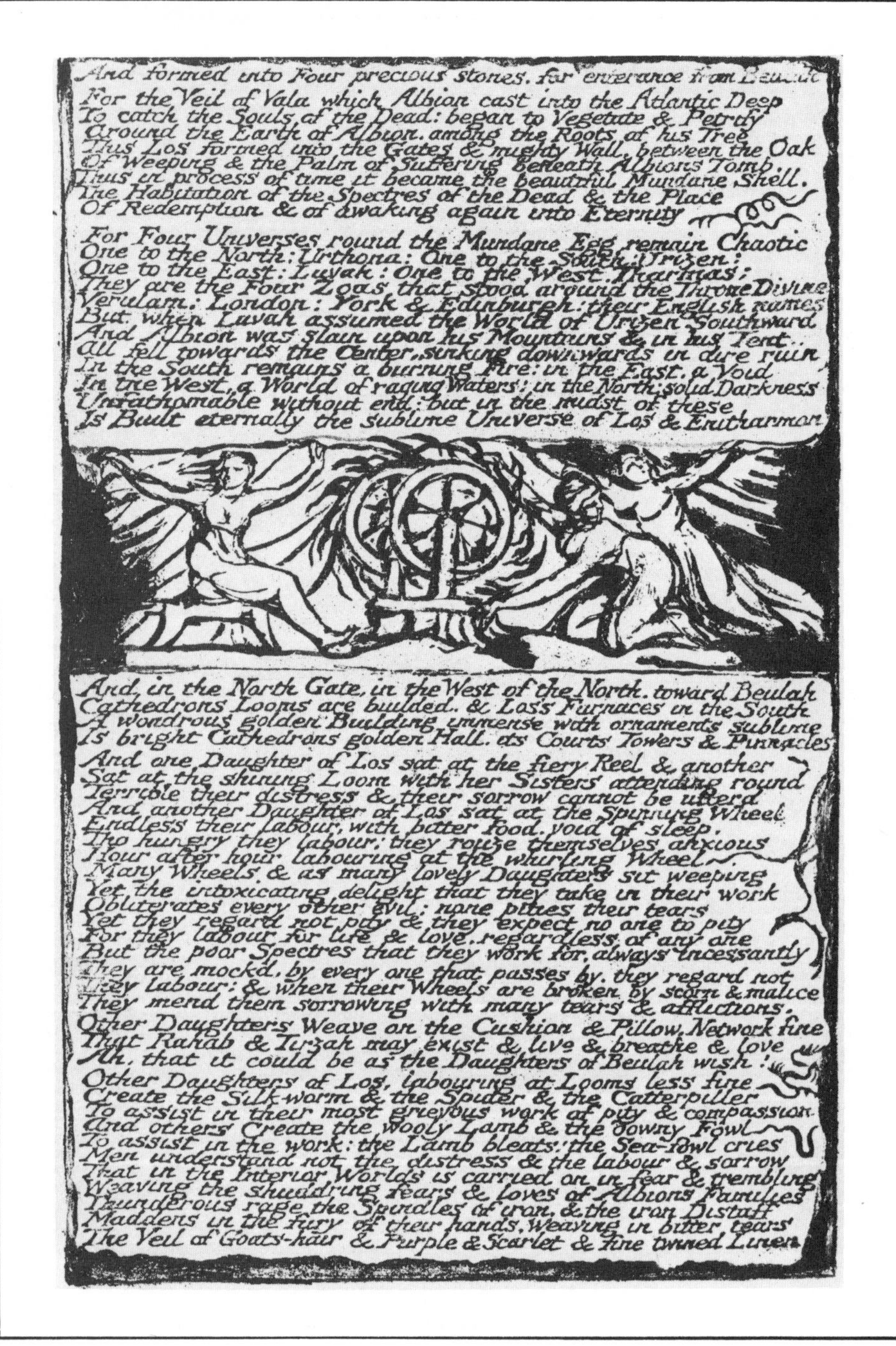

And formed into Four precious stones. for enterance from Beulah
For the Veil of Vala which Albion cast into the Atlantic Deep
To catch the Souls of the Dead: began to Vegetate & Petrify
Around the Earth of Albion. among the Roots of his Tree
This Los formed into the Gates & mighty Wall, between the Oak
Of Weeping & the Palm of Suffering beneath Albions Tomb.
Thus in process of time it became the beautiful Mundane Shell.
The Habitation of the Spectres of the Dead & the Place
Of Redemption & of awaking again into Eternity

For Four Universes round the Mundane Egg remain Chaotic
One to the North: Urthona: One to the South: Urizen:
One to the East: Luvah: One to the West. Tharmas;
They are the Four Zoas that stood around the Throne Divine
Verulam: London: York & Edinburgh: their English names
But when Luvah assumed the World of Urizen Southward
And Albion was slain upon his Mountains & in his Tent.
All fell towards the Center, sinking downwards in dire ruin
In the South remains a burning Fire: in the East. a Void
In the West, a World of raging Waters; in the North; solid Darkness
Unfathomable without end: but in the midst of these
Is Built eternally the sublime Universe of Los & Enitharmon

And in the North Gate, in the West of the North. toward Beulah
Cathedrons Looms are builded. & Los's Furnaces in the South
A wondrous golden Building immense with ornaments sublime
Is bright Cathedrons golden Hall. its Courts Towers & Pinnacles

And one Daughter of Los sat at the fiery Reel & another
Sat at the shining Loom with her Sisters attending round
Terrible their distress & their sorrow cannot be utterd
And another Daughter of Los sat at the Spinning Wheel
Endless their labour, with bitter food. void of sleep.
Tho hungry they labour: they rouze themselves anxious
Hour after hour labouring at the whirling Wheel
Many Wheels & as many lovely Daughters sit weeping
Yet the intoxicating delight that they take in their work
Obliterates every other evil; none pities their tears
Yet they regard not pity & they expect no one to pity
For they labour for life & love. regardless of any one
But the poor Spectres that they work for, always incessantly
They are mockd. by every one that passes by. they regard not
They labour; & when their Wheels are broken by scorn & malice
They mend them sorrowing with many tears & afflictions.
Other Daughters Weave on the Cushion & Pillow, Network fine
That Rahab & Tirzah may exist & live & breathe & love
Ah, that it could be as the Daughters of Beulah wish!
Other Daughters of Los, labouring at Looms less fine
Create the Silk-worm & the Spider & the Catterpiller
To assist in their most grievous work of pity & compassion
And others Create the wooly Lamb & the downy Fowl
To assist in the work: the Lamb bleats: the Sea-fowl cries
Men understand not the distress & the labour & sorrow
That in the Interior Worlds is carried on in fear & trembling
Weaving the shuddring fears & loves of Albions Families
Thunderous rage the Spindles of iron. & the iron Distaff
Maddens in the fury of their hands. Weaving in bitter tears
The Veil of Goats-hair & Purple & Scarlet & fine twined Linen

Jerusalem 59D

Jerusalem 59. The word "Chaotic" (10) is flagged by three varieties of tendrils on one stem, going three ways. The three Daughters below (sisters of the three Fates) repeat this motif. One "Daughter of Los," at left, sits "at the shining Loom" (not shown); for the other two, "sitting" is a euphemism: one is tending "the fiery Reel . . . another . . . the spinning Wheel" (26–29). Nor does Blake quite mean that their delight in their work "Obliterates every other evil" (34–35), for they are looking offstage with considerable anxiety.

The central area behind the wheels is yellow, sprinkled with gold, in copy E, suggesting a central light source; the lines are muted that indicated tongues of flame spun outward from the wheels in the uncolored copies.

Wicksteed suggests that the wheels, revolving clockwise, represent the rolling on of time, also the processes of digestion and reproduction (signified by the flames) and lastly the labors of Los and Enitharmon, Blake and his wife.

Jerusalem 60. The Divine Vision is speaking to Jerusalem (10–15) but she doesn't think she can hear or see him (54–61). Working "at the Mills" like the Daughters on Plate 59, under the tyranny of the incessant "Wheel of Hand," she pleads to him (51 ff) as pictured in the right margin, kneeling in prayer as the children in *Songs* 18 imploring "Mercy Pity Peace and Love," her "feet naked Cut with the flints, her tears run[ning] down," etc (41–42). She appears naked; in E she is given a deep flame-pink gown.

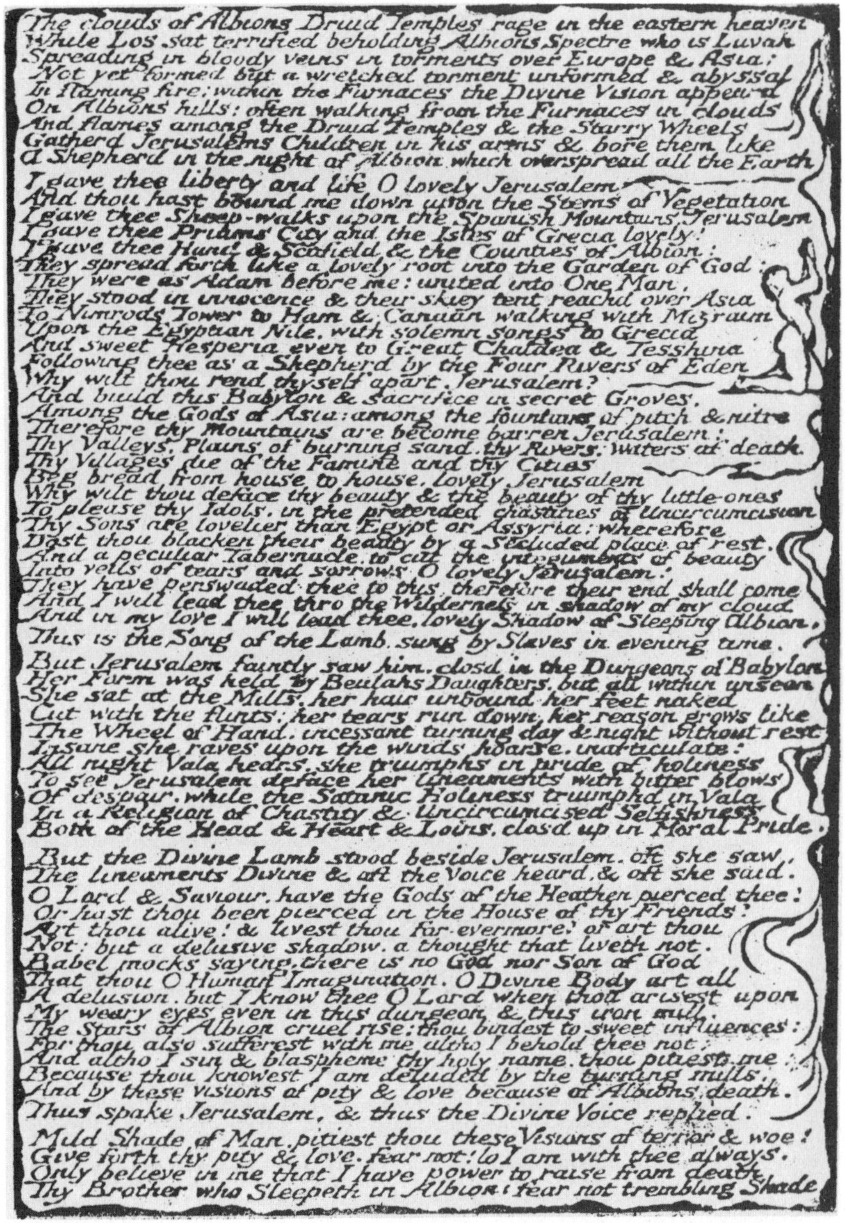

The clouds of Albions Druid Temples rage in the eastern heaven
While Los sat terrified beholding Albions Spectre who is Luvah
Spreading in bloody veins in torments over Europe & Asia;
Not yet formed but a wretched torment unformed & abyssal
In flaming fire; within the Furnaces the Divine Vision appeard
On Albions hills: often walking from the Furnaces in clouds
And flames among the Druid Temples & the Starry Wheels
Gatherd Jerusalems Children in his arms & bore them like
A Shepherd in the night of Albion which overspread all the Earth

I gave thee liberty and life O lovely Jerusalem
And thou hast bound me down upon the Stems of Vegetation
I gave thee Sheep-walks upon the Spanish Mountains Jerusalem
I gave thee Priams City and the Isles of Grecia lovely!
I gave thee Hand & Scofield & the Counties of Albion:
They spread forth like a lovely root into the Garden of God:
They were as Adam before me: united into One Man,
They stood in innocence & their skiey tent reachd over Asia
To Nimrods Tower to Ham & Canaan walking with Mizraim
Upon the Egyptian Nile, with solemn songs to Grecia
And sweet Hesperia even to Great Chaldea & Tesshina
Following thee as a Shepherd by the Four Rivers of Eden
Why wilt thou rend thyself apart, Jerusalem?
And build this Babylon & sacrifice in secret Groves,
Among the Gods of Asia: among the fountains of pitch & nitre
Therefore thy Mountains are become barren Jerusalem!
Thy Valleys, Plains of burning sand. thy Rivers: waters of death
Thy Villages die of the Famine and thy Cities
Beg bread from house to house, lovely Jerusalem
Why wilt thou deface thy beauty & the beauty of thy little-ones
To please thy Idols, in the pretended chastities of Uncircumcision
Thy Sons are lovelier than Egypt or Assyria; wherefore
Dost thou blacken their beauty by a Secluded place of rest.
And a peculiar Tabernacle, to cut the integuments of beauty
Into veils of tears and sorrows O lovely Jerusalem!
They have perswaded thee to this, therefore their end shall come
And I will lead thee thro the Wilderness in shadow of my cloud
And in my love I will lead thee, lovely Shadow of Sleeping Albion.

This is the Song of the Lamb, sung by Slaves in evening time.

But Jerusalem faintly saw him, closd in the Dungeons of Babylon
Her Form was held by Beulahs Daughters. but all within unseen
She sat at the Mills, her hair unbound her feet naked
Cut with the flints: her tears run down, her reason grows like
The Wheel of Hand. incessant turning day & night without rest
Insane she raves upon the winds hoarse, inarticulate:
All night Vala hears, she triumphs in pride of holiness
To see Jerusalem deface her lineaments with bitter blows
Of despair. while the Satanic Holiness triumphd in Vala
In a Religion of Chastity & Uncircumcised Selfishness
Both of the Head & Heart & Loins, closd up in Moral Pride.

But the Divine Lamb stood beside Jerusalem. oft she saw
The lineaments Divine & oft the Voice heard, & oft she said:
O Lord & Saviour, have the Gods of the Heathen pierced thee:
Or hast thou been pierced in the House of thy Friends?
Art thou alive! & livest thou for-evermore? or art thou
Not: but a delusive shadow, a thought that liveth not.
Babel mocks saying, there is no God nor Son of God
That thou O Human Imagination, O Divine Body art all
A delusion. but I know thee O Lord when thou arisest upon
My weary eyes even in this dungeon & this iron mill.
The Stars of Albion cruel rise; thou bindest to sweet influences:
For thou also sufferest with me altho I behold thee not;
And altho I sin & blaspheme thy holy name, thou pitiest me;
Because thou knowest I am deluded by the turning mills.
And by these visions of pity & love because of Albions death.
Thus spake Jerusalem, & thus the Divine Voice replied.

Mild Shade of Man, pitiest thou these Visions of terror & woe!
Give forth thy pity & love. fear not! lo I am with thee always.
Only believe in me that I have power to raise from death
Thy Brother who Sleepeth in Albion: fear not trembling Shade

Jerusalem 60[D]

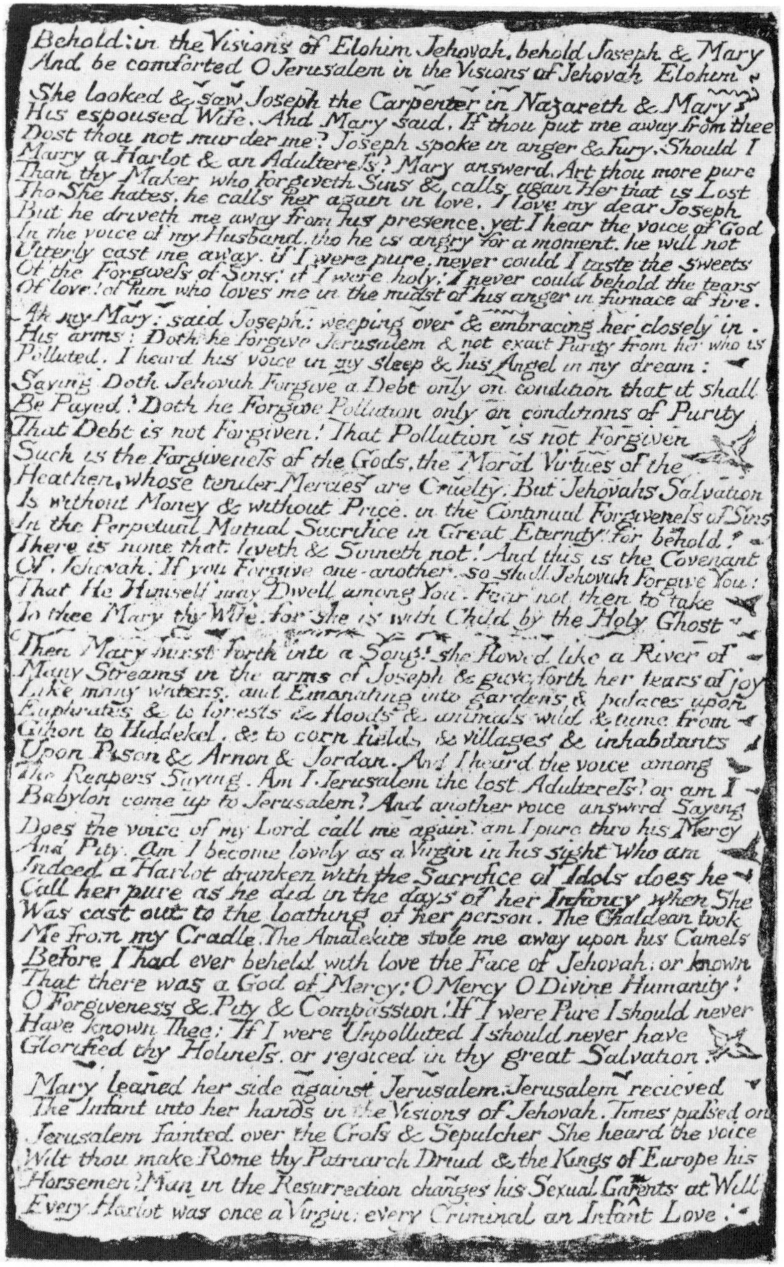

Behold: in the Visions of Elohim Jehovah, behold Joseph & Mary
And be comforted O Jerusalem in the Visions of Jehovah Elohim
She looked & saw Joseph the Carpenter in Nazareth & Mary
His espoused Wife. And Mary said, If thou put me away from thee
Dost thou not murder me? Joseph spoke in anger & fury. Should I
Marry a Harlot & an Adulteress? Mary answerd, Art thou more pure
Than thy Maker who forgiveth Sins & calls again Her that is Lost
Tho She hates. he calls her again in love. I love my dear Joseph
But he driveth me away from his presence. yet I hear the voice of God
In the voice of my Husband. tho he is angry for a moment, he will not
Utterly cast me away. if I were pure, never could I taste the sweets
Of the Forgivefs of Sins: if I were holy: I never could behold the tears
Of love! of him who loves me in the midst of his anger in furnace of fire.

Ah my Mary: said Joseph: weeping over & embracing her closely in
His arms: Doth he forgive Jerusalem & not exact Purity from her who is
Polluted. I heard his voice in my sleep & his Angel in my dream:
Saying Doth Jehovah Forgive a Debt only on condition that it shall
Be Payed? Doth he Forgive Pollution only on conditions of Purity
That Debt is not Forgiven! That Pollution is not Forgiven
Such is the Forgivenefs of the Gods, the Moral Virtues of the
Heathen, whose tender Mercies are Cruelty. But Jehovahs Salvation
Is without Money & without Price, in the Continual Forgivenefs of Sins
In the Perpetual Mutual Sacrifice in Great Eternity! for behold!
There is none that liveth & Sinneth not! And this is the Covenant
Of Jehovah: If you Forgive one-another, so shall Jehovah Forgive You:
That He Himself may Dwell among You. Fear not then to take
To thee Mary thy Wife, for she is with Child by the Holy Ghost

Then Mary burst forth into a Song! she flowed like a River of
Many Streams in the arms of Joseph & gave forth her tears of joy
Like many waters, and Emanating into gardens & palaces upon
Euphrates & to forests & floods & animals wild & tame from
Gihon to Hiddekel, & to corn fields & villages & inhabitants
Upon Pison & Arnon & Jordan. And I heard the voice among
The Reapers Saying, Am I Jerusalem the lost Adulterefs? or am I
Babylon come up to Jerusalem? And another voice answerd Saying
Does the voice of my Lord call me again? am I pure thro his Mercy
And Pity. Am I become lovely as a Virgin in his sight who am
Indeed a Harlot drunken with the Sacrifice of Idols does he
Call her pure as he did in the days of her Infancy when She
Was cast out to the loathing of her person. The Chaldean took
Me from my Cradle. The Amalekite stole me away upon his Camels
Before I had ever beheld with love the Face of Jehovah; or known
That there was a God of Mercy: O Mercy O Divine Humanity!
O Forgiveness & Pity & Compassion! If I were Pure I should never
Have known Thee; If I were Unpolluted I should never have
Glorified thy Holinefs, or rejoiced in thy great Salvation.

Mary leaned her side against Jerusalem, Jerusalem recieved
The Infant into her hands in the Visions of Jehovah. Times passed on
Jerusalem fainted over the Crofs & Sepulcher She heard the voice
Wilt thou make Rome thy Patriarch Druid & the Kings of Europe his
Horsemen? Man in the Resurrection changes his Sexual Garments at Will
Every Harlot was once a Virgin: every Criminal an Infant Love!

Jerusalem 61D

Jerusalem 61. The dialogue of Joseph and Mary, seen and heard by Jerusalem, is ornamented with five flying birds at the top, then two or three, then a scattering down the right margin—including a dove above "Salvation" (21) and anther beside the same word again (46), followed by a row of five small birds. Small banners appear on some of the letters. It is very earthy across the bottom in E.

The animation of the interlinear and marginal spaces recalls Plate 48.

Jerusalem 62. Here the text is written on a stone or a wall held by, or resting on, an anguished giant. Pictures of the giant Enceladus flattened by Mount Etna, in illustrations of Ovid, are like this. The text suggests "Victims" on Druid altars, howling (33–34); the open mouth has a round red tongue. Désirée Hirst (*Hidden Riches* 54) sees here a free transposition of the Vitruvian figure in the title page of Robert Fludd's *Utriusque Cosmi*.

Though "the Sun set in Tyburns Brook," Los "beheld the Divine Vision among the flames" (34–35). But the small figure who sees only the flaming feet (an allusion to Revelation 10.1?) is probably Blake rather than his giant Los (compare Plate 37). The gigantic victim is Luvah, a fallen savior whose cloud, when "the Lamb of God" speaks, reddens above and bursts forth "in streams of blood upon the heavens" (30–31). A brazen (not a living) serpent is bound on his head like an instrument of torture, perhaps a symbolic crown of thorns: long, pointed spikes backed by peacock feathers protrude from the circlet, though an optical switch can make them simply spaces between the feathers.

Politically, Luvah is the revolution in France, of fire and promise; Jesus (18–20) as "the Resurrection & the Life" announces that "Luvah must be Created, And Vala. . . ." The feathery radiation, somewhat rainbow colored, suggests a phoenix burning. It also suggests the potentially infinite *vision* of giant man renovated and "Eyed as the Peacock" (*J* 98:14—see Thomas R. Frosch, *The Awakening of Albion* 143).

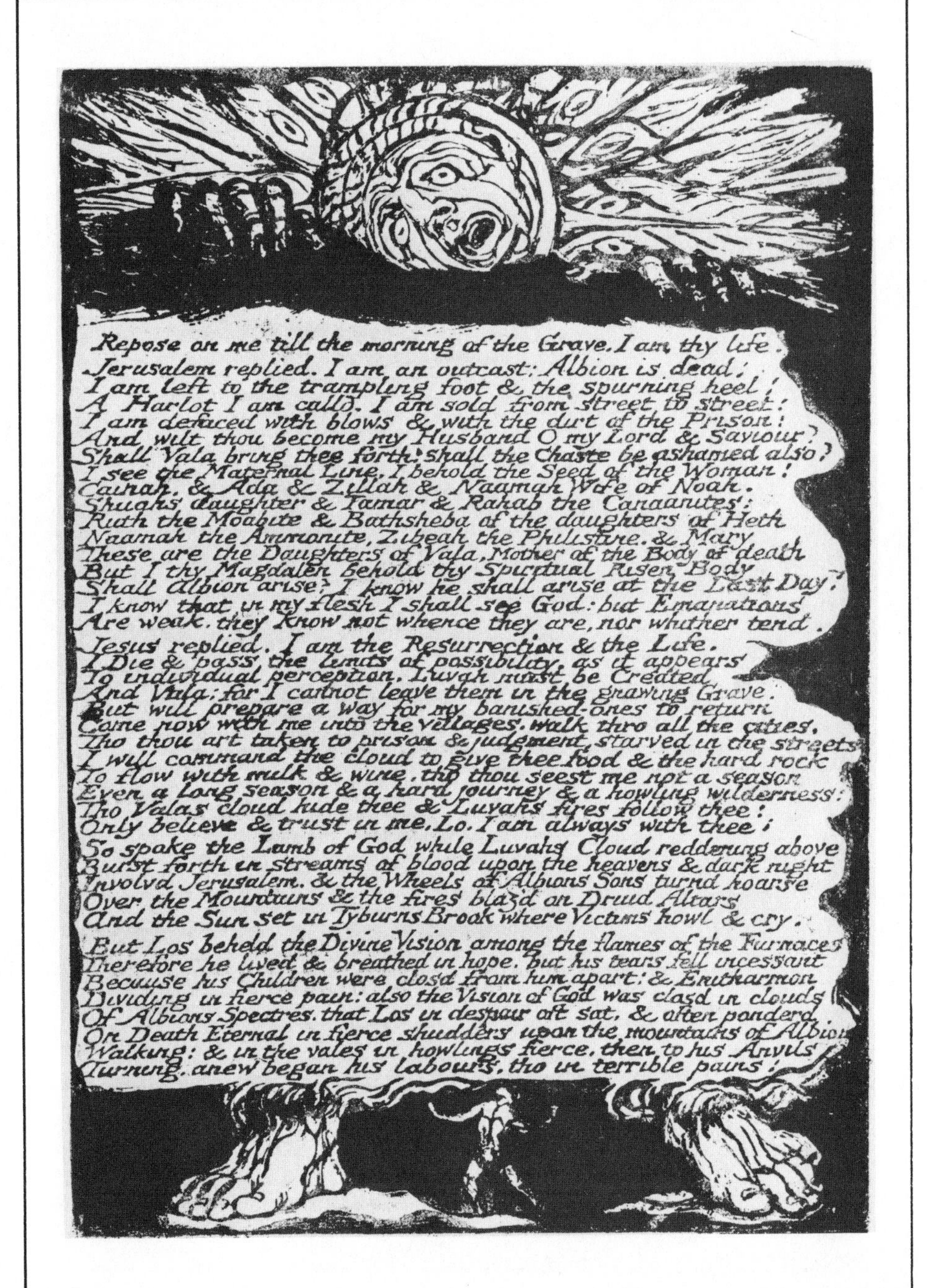

Repose on me till the morning of the Grave. I am thy life.
Jerusalem replied. I am an outcast: Albion is dead;
I am left to the trampling foot & the spurning heel!
A Harlot I am calld. I am sold from street to street!
I am defaced with blows & with the dirt of the Prison:
And wilt thou become my Husband O my Lord & Saviour?
Shall Vala bring thee forth! shall the Chaste be ashamed also?
I see the Maternal Line, I behold the Seed of the Woman!
Cainah, & Ada & Zillah & Naamah Wife of Noah.
Shuahs daughter & Tamar & Rahab the Canaanites:
Ruth the Moabite & Bathsheba of the daughters of Heth
Naamah the Ammonite, Zibeah the Philistine. & Mary
These are the Daughters of Vala, Mother of the Body of death
But I thy Magdalen behold thy Spiritual Risen Body
Shall Albion arise? I know he shall arise at the Last Day!
I know that in my flesh I shall see God: but Emanations
Are weak. they know not whence they are, nor whither tend.

Jesus replied. I am the Resurrection & the Life.
I Die & pass the limits of possibility, as it appears
To individual perception. Luvah must be Created
And Vala; for I cannot leave them in the gnawing Grave.
But will prepare a way for my banished-ones to return
Come now with me into the villages. walk thro all the cities.
Tho thou art taken to prison & judgment, starved in the streets
I will command the cloud to give thee food & the hard rock
To flow with milk & wine, tho thou seest me not a season
Even a long season & a hard journey & a howling wilderness:
Tho Valas cloud hide thee & Luvahs fires follow thee:
Only believe & trust in me, Lo. I am always with thee:

So spake the Lamb of God while Luvahs Cloud reddening above
Burst forth in streams of blood upon the heavens & dark night
Involvd Jerusalem. & the Wheels of Albions Sons turnd hoarse
Over the Mountains & the fires blazd on Druid Altars
And the Sun set in Tyburns Brook where Victims howl & cry.

But Los beheld the Divine Vision among the flames of the Furnaces
Therefore he lived & breathed in hope. but his tears fell incessant
Because his Children were closd from him apart: & Enitharmon
Dividing in fierce pain: also the Vision of God was closd in clouds
Of Albions Spectres. that Los in despair oft sat, & often ponderd
On Death Eternal in fierce shudders upon the mountains of Albion
Walking: & in the vales in howlings fierce. then to his Anvils
Turning. anew began his labours. tho in terrible pains!

Jerusalem 62[D]

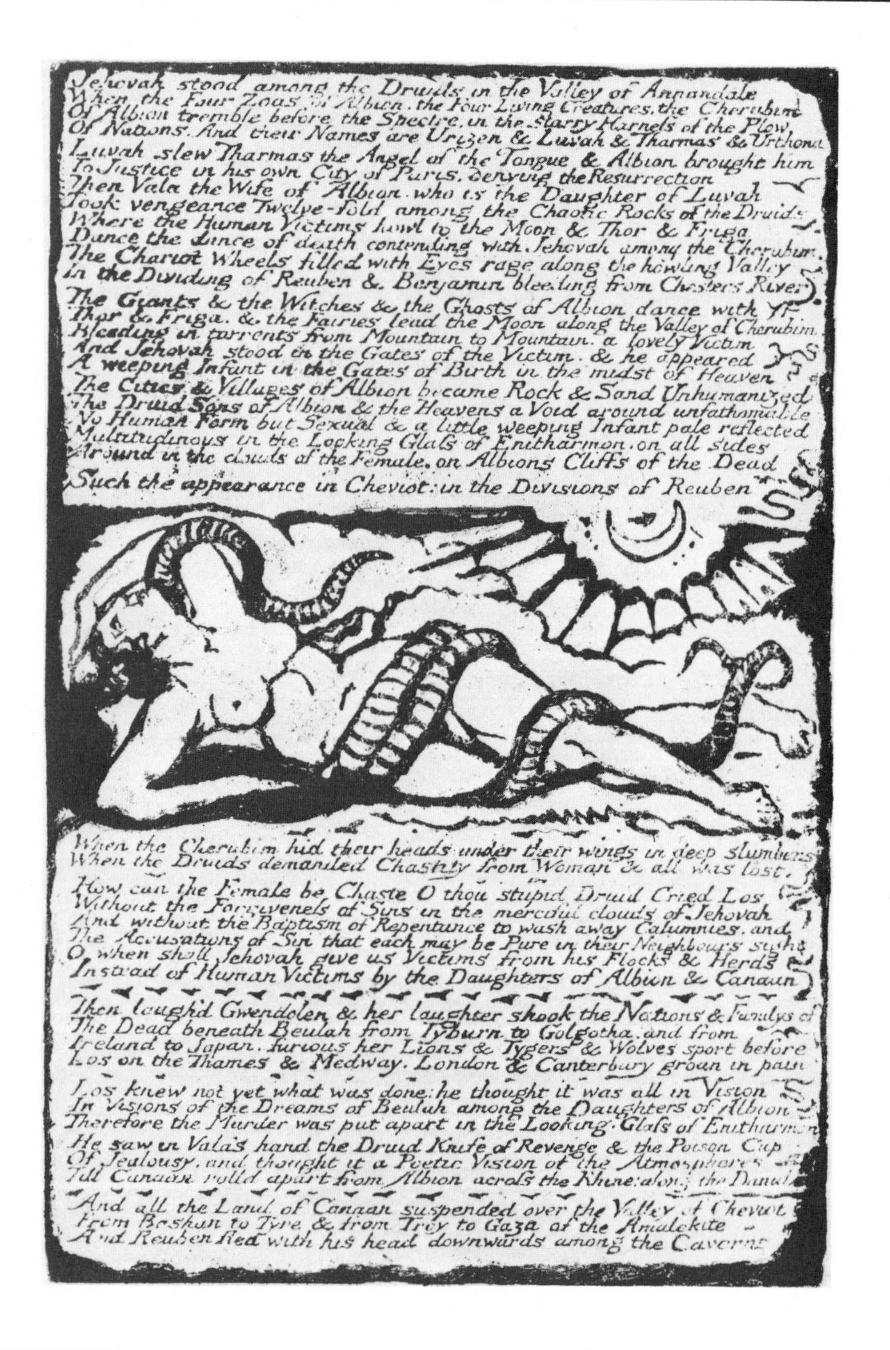
Jehovah stood among the Druids in the Valley of Annandale
When the Four Zoas of Albion, the Four Living Creatures, the Cherubim
Of Albion tremble before the Spectre, in the starry Harness of the Plow,
Of Nations. And their Names are Urizen & Luvah & Tharmas & Urthona
Luvah slew Tharmas the Angel of the Tongue & Albion brought him
To Justice in his own City of Paris, denying the Resurrection
Then Vala the Wife of Albion, who is the Daughter of Luvah
Took vengeance Twelve-fold among the Chaotic Rocks of the Druids
Where the Human Victims howl to the Moon & Thor & Friga
Dance the dance of death contending with Jehovah among the Cherubim.
The Chariot Wheels filled with Eyes rage along the howling Valley
In the Dividing of Reuben & Benjamin bleeding from Chesters River
The Giants & the Witches & the Ghosts of Albion dance with
Thor & Friga, & the Fairies lead the Moon along the Valley of Cherubim
Bleeding in torrents from Mountain to Mountain, a lovely Victim
And Jehovah stood in the Gates of the Victim, & he appeared
A weeping Infant in the Gates of Birth in the midst of Heaven
The Cities & Villages of Albion became Rock & Sand Unhumanized
The Druid Sons of Albion & the Heavens a Void around unfathomable
No Human Form but Sexual & a little weeping Infant pale reflected
Multitudinous in the Looking Glass of Enitharmon, on all sides
Around in the clouds of the Female, on Albions Cliffs of the Dead
Such the appearance in Cheviot: in the Divisions of Reuben

When the Cherubim hid their heads under their wings in deep slumbers
When the Druids demanded Chastity from Woman & all was lost.
How can the Female be Chaste O thou stupid Druid Cried Los
Without the Forgiveness of Sins in the merciful clouds of Jehovah
And without the Baptism of Repentance to wash away Calumnies. and
The Accusations of Sin that each may be Pure in their Neighbours sight
O when shall Jehovah give us Victims from his Flocks & Herds
Instead of Human Victims by the Daughters of Albion & Canaan
Then laughd Gwendolen & her laughter shook the Nations & Familys of
The Dead beneath Beulah from Tyburn to Golgotha, and from
Ireland to Japan. furious her Lions & Tygers & Wolves sport before
Los on the Thames & Medway. London & Canterbury groan in pain
Los knew not yet what was done: he thought it was all in Vision
In Visions of the Dreams of Beulah among the Daughters of Albion
Therefore the Murder was put apart in the Looking-Glass of Enitharmon
He saw in Valas hand the Druid Knife of Revenge & the Poison Cup
Of Jealousy, and thought it a Poetic Vision of the Atmospheres
Till Canaan rolld apart from Albion across the Rhine: along the Danube
And all the Land of Canaan suspended over the Valley of Cheviot
From Bashan to Tyre & from Troy to Gaza of the Amalekite
And Reuben fled with his head downwards among the Caverns

Jerusalem 63D

Jerusalem 63. In his *Apotheosis of Nelson* Blake shows a naked female "Nation" clutching her head shorn of long locks by the folds of a scaly Leviathan, to signify France shorn of sea power by Nelson at the battle of Trafalgar. On this plate the text (5–6) describes Albion as bringing Luvah "To Justice in his own City of Paris, denying the resurrection," i.e. the Revolution, denied by Luvah in the deeds of Napoleon and denied by Albion in his accusations of Sin. The naked woman clutching her shorn hair (note the strand or strands beside her left hip, parallel to the worm, comparable to the locks that emerge between loops of the Leviathan) must be the nation of France, shorn of land power when the allied armies entered Paris. The shaking of "the Nations" (32) is alluded to here, the battles on Plate 65. But to fit her into the Blakean mythology involves accommodation to the exception Blake made when, out of respect for the entrenched convention that personifies Albion as masculine and France as feminine, he gave France a "Masculine Emanation" (49:47), named Shiloh, the only male "among the Flowers of Beulah" but a needed allegorical peer to Jerusalem: "Lo Shiloh dwells over France, as Jerusalem dwells over Albion." (This is little more than a matter of protocol; when Blake wants to describe the triumph of revolution in France he forgets Shiloh and gives Jerusalem the line, "France was wholy mine": 79:39.) France, then, will have to serve also as Vala, here—Luvah's emanation, it is true, but reserved in *Jerusalem* for other purposes than representing nations. Her ostentatiously crossed legs may mean that she is falsely doubling in the role. In the Vala-Albion contest of visions, Albion's appearing as a worm seems to confirm her outcry: "The Human is but a Worm . . . The Human Divine is Womans Shadow" (64:12–14). In this vein she is the proper Whore to preside over the "Court of Justice" in Paris, and over the whole war. Her feet are "two Armies in Battle," her precious hair is what the nations fight over: "Storms & Pestilence in her Locks . . . & the Ruin of Cities & Nations" (64:9–11). Her false role as well as her false vision cause the partial eclipse of the bloody sun we are shown—for the blood-red rays piercing a yellow cloud are much too strong for moonlight.

It is an angrily beautiful sun nevertheless, and flakes of gold are added at its edge and among its beams, and to the green grass. In the upper text area there are two very thin birds (and added leaves in F), but below the picture there are two or three more, one or two in the next break, and then nineteen in the next, mere dots in the next, but a dozen birds in the lowest row.

❧

Jerusalem 64. At top the green "Web Of Ages & Generations" folds and unfolds "like a Veil of Cherubim" (2–3), unfurled by two Daughters into a wing-like shape (compare the green bee-winged fairy in Plate 2). At bottom this scroll of Natural Religion (see 66:8) reaches "the Rational Power" (5), the "Indefinite Spectre" Urizen, with fingers on book, checking with his index finger the message of the blots and blurs on the veil—in a reminiscence of *Urizen* 1, where he scans similar blots and blurs with his big toe; his posture resembles that in *Song of Los* 2; but Blake is most specifically borrowing from his *Night Thoughts* 7 (see *Forms* plate 75), where a poet sleeps on his scroll at the top and Urizen makes a copy at the bottom. (Compare the angel as learner in *Marriage* 10; Urizen as learner in *Urizen* 1.)

The figure blindly writing the scroll, sleeping on it, yet with a sunburst (yellow against pink) of potential halo around her head, is evidently Vala—in Los's eyes equivalent to all the Daughters of Albion in One! (6). She will need only to sit up and pay attention (like the transcribing angel in *Marriage* 10) to become wise and beautiful and transform the veil of nature into the garments of the Bride.

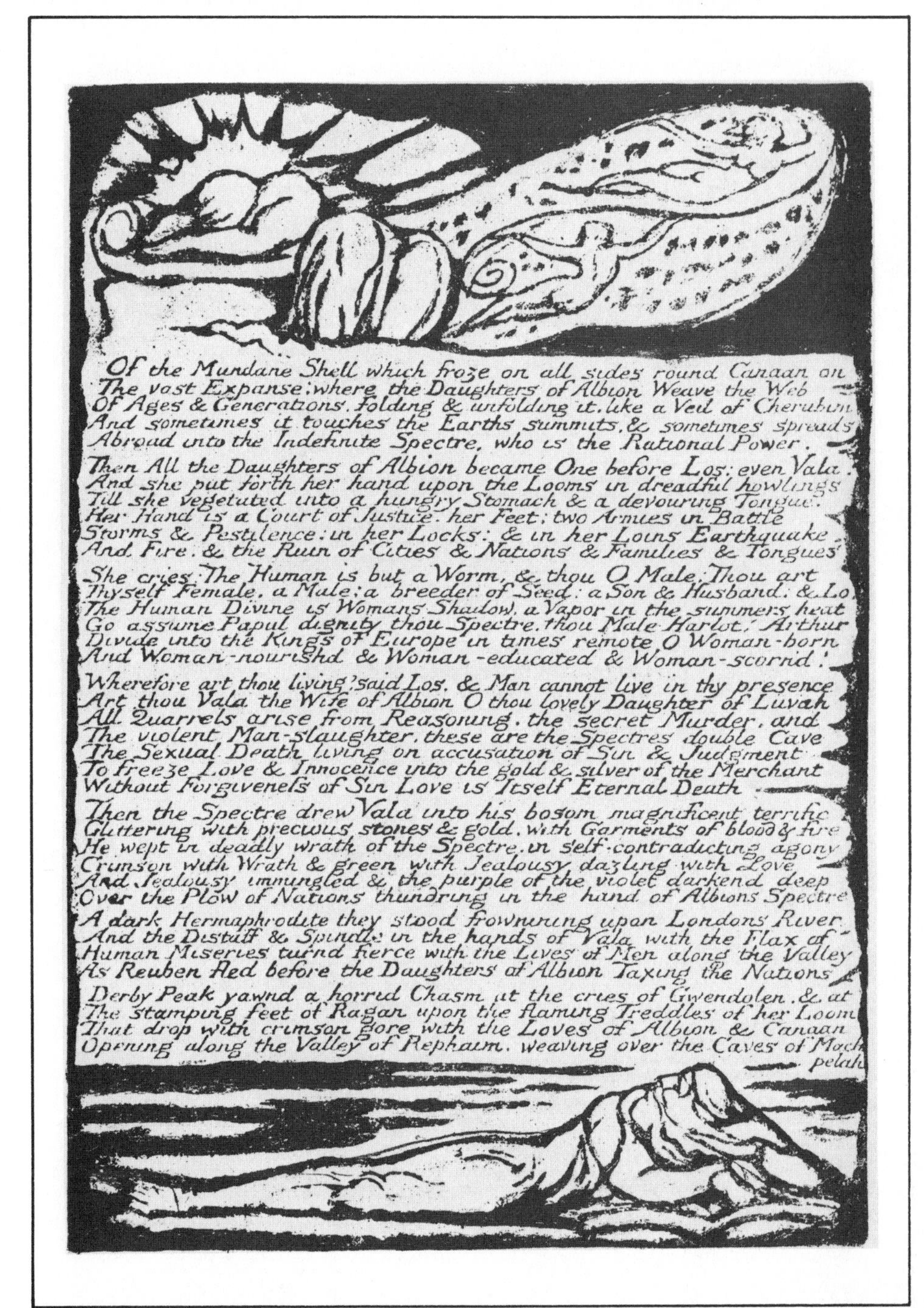

Of the Mundane Shell which froze on all sides round Canaan on
The vast Expanse: where the Daughters of Albion Weave the Web
Of Ages & Generations. Folding & unfolding it. like a Veil of Cherubim
And sometimes it touches the Earths summits. & sometimes spreads
Abroad into the Indefinite Spectre. who is the Rational Power.

Then All the Daughters of Albion became One before Los: even Vala.
And she put forth her hand upon the Looms in dreadful howlings
Till she vegetated into a hungry Stomach & a devouring Tongue.
Her Hand is a Court of Justice. her Feet: two Armies in Battle
Storms & Pestilence: in her Locks: & in her Loins Earthquake.
And Fire. & the Ruin of Cities & Nations & Families & Tongues

She cries: The Human is but a Worm, & thou O Male: Thou art
Thyself Female. a Male: a breeder of Seed: a Son & Husband: & Lo
The Human Divine is Womans Shadow, a Vapor in the summers heat
Go assume Papal dignity thou Spectre. thou Male Harlot! Arthur
Divide into the Kings of Europe in times remote O Woman-born
And Woman-nourishd & Woman-educated & Woman-scornd!

Wherefore art thou living? said Los. & Man cannot live in thy presence
Art thou Vala the Wife of Albion O thou lovely Daughter of Luvah
All Quarrels arise from Reasoning. the secret Murder. and
The violent Man-slaughter. these are the Spectres double Cave
The Sexual Death living on accusation of Sin & Judgment
To freeze Love & Innocence into the gold & silver of the Merchant
Without Forgiveness of Sin Love is Itself Eternal Death

Then the Spectre drew Vala into his bosom magnificent terrific
Glittering with precious stones & gold. with Garments of blood & fire
He wept in deadly wrath of the Spectre. in self-contradicting agony
Crimson with Wrath & green with Jealousy, dazling with Love
And Jealousy immingled & the purple of the violet darkend deep
Over the Plow of Nations thundring in the hand of Albions Spectre

A dark Hermaphrodite they stood frowning upon Londons River
And the Distaff & Spindle in the hands of Vala with the Flax of
Human Miseries turnd fierce with the Lives of Men along the Valley
As Reuben fled before the Daughters of Albion Taxing the Nations

Derby Peak yawnd a horrid Chasm at the cries of Gwendolen. & at
The stamping feet of Ragan upon the flaming Treddles of her Loom
That drop with crimson gore with the Loves of Albion & Canaan
Opening along the Valley of Rephaim. weaving over the Caves of Mach
pelah

Jerusalem 64[D]

To decide Two Worlds with a great decision: a World of Mercy, and
A World of Justice: the World of Mercy for Salvation
To cast Luvah into the Wrath, and Albion into the Pity
In the Two Contraries of Humanity & in the Four Regions.

For in the depths of Albions bosom in the eastern heaven,
They sound the clarions strong! they chain the howling Captives:
They cast the lots into the helmet: they give the oath of blood in Lambeth
They vote the death of Luvah, & they naild him to Albions Tree in Bath:
They staind him with poisonous blue, they inwove him in cruel roots
To die a death of Six thousand years bound round with vegetation
The sun was black & the moon rolld a useless globe thro Britain!

Then left the Sons of Urizen the plow & harrow, the loom
The hammer & the chisel, & the rule & compasses; from London fleeing
They forgd the sword on Cheviot, the chariot of war & the battle-ax,
The trumpet fitted to mortal battle, & the flute of summer in Annandale
And all the Arts of Life, they changd into the Arts of Death in Albion.
The hour-glass contemnd because its simple workmanship.
Was like the workmanship of the plowman, & the water wheel,
That raises water into cisterns: broken & burnd with fire:
Because its workmanship. was like the workmanship of the shepherd.
And in their stead, intricate wheels invented, wheel without wheel:
To perplex youth in their outgoings, & to bind to labours in Albion
Of day & night the myriads of eternity that they may grind
And polish brass & iron hour after hour laborious task:
Kept ignorant of its use, that they might spend the days of wisdom
In sorrowful drudgery, to obtain a scanty pittance of bread:
In ignorance to view a small portion & think that All,
And call it Demonstration: blind to all the simple rules of life.

Now: now the battle rages round thy tender limbs O Vala
Now smile among thy bitter tears: now put on all thy beauty
Is not the wound of the sword sweet! & the broken bone delightful?
Wilt thou now smile among the scythes when the wounded groan in the field
We were carried away in thousands from London; & in tens
Of thousands from Westminster & Marybone in ships closd up:
Chaind hand & foot, compelld to fight under the iron whips
Of our captains; fearing our officers more than the enemy.
Lift up thy blue eyes Vala & put on thy sapphire shoes:
O melancholy Magdalen behold the morning over Malden break;
Gird on thy flaming zone, descend into the sepulcher of Canterbury.
Scatter the blood from thy golden brow, the tears from thy silver locks:
Shake off the waters from thy wings! & the dust from thy white garments
Remember all thy feigned terrors on the secret couch of Lambeths Vale
When the sun rose in glowing morn, with arms of mighty hosts
Marching to battle who was wont to rise with Urizens harps
Girt as a sower with his seed to scatter life abroad over Albion:
Arise O Vala! bring the bow of Urizen: bring the swift arrows of light.
How ragd the golden horses of Urizen, compelld to the chariot of love!
Compelld to leave the plow to the ox, to snuff up the winds of desolation
To trample the corn fields in boastful neighings: this is no gentle harp
This is no warbling brook, nor shadow of a mirtle tree:
But blood and wounds and dismal cries, and shadows of the oak:
And hearts laid open to the light, by the broad grizly sword:
And bowels hid in hammerd steel rip'd quivering on the ground.
Call forth thy smiles of soft deceit: call forth thy cloudy tears:
We hear thy sighs in trumpets shrill when morn shall blood renew.

So sang the Spectre Sons of Albion round Luvahs Stone of Trial:
Mocking and deriding at the writhings of their Victim on Salisbury:
Drinking his Emanation in intoxicating bliss rejoicing in Giant dance;
For a Spectre has no Emanation but what he imbibes from deceiving
A Victim! Then he becomes her Priest & she his Tabernacle.
And his Oak Grove, till the Victim rend the woven Veil.
In the end of his sleep when Jesus calls him from him his grave

Howling the Victims on the Druid Altars yield their souls
To the stern Warriors: lovely sport the Daughters round their Victims;
Drinking their lives in sweet intoxication. hence arose from Bath
Soft deluding odours, in spiral volutions intricately winding
Over Albions mountains, a feminine indefinite cruel delusion.
Astonishd: terrified & in pain & torment. Sudden they behold
Their own Parent the Emanation of their murderd Enemy
Become their Emanation and their Temple and Tabernacle
They knew not. this Vala was their beloved Mother Vala Albions Wife.
Terrified at the sight of the Victim: at his distorted sinews!
The tremblings of Vala vibrate thro' the limbs of Albions Sons:
While they rejoice over Luvah in mockery & bitter scorn:
Sudden they become like what they behold in howlings & deadly pain.
Spasms smite their features, sinews & limbs: pale they look on one another.
They turn, contorted: their iron necks bend unwilling towards
Luvah: their lips tremble: their muscular fibres are crampd & smitten
They become like what they behold! Yet immense in strength & power,

Jerusalem 65[D]

Jerusalem 65. Instead of web or veil or garment, suggested on Plate 64, we see nothing but a heavy chain (line 6: "they chain the howling Captives"). There are further chains in 66:2 and 5 and in the images and picture of Plate 67. Thus evolves a chain of being (66:5; compare Plate 67) from the Chain of Jealousy: see *Urizen* 21. In Plate 65 it has no "anti-personnel" implications; by Plate 67 a human life is riveted into the chain. The youth of England compelled to "grind And polish brass & iron hour after hour . . . Kept ignorant of its use" (23–25) discover it as they find themselves "Marching to battle" and "quivering on the ground" (44–53).

Jerusalem 66. Under the "Knife of flint In the hands of Albions Daughters, among the Druid Temples" (83–84) the Divine Vision has become a bloody flame on the altar of sacrifice, "a column of fire" (41–42)—shown in the right margin. Within this replacement of Vala's intestinal column "the Victim" struggles under the knife held, in her left hand, by a daughter who has laid aside her garments (19) and clamps the victim's head between her thighs to perform the tortures itemized in the text alongside. For his further adventures in this same position on the page, see Plates 74, 80, and 83. A simple variant of the Beast and Whore motif; compare Plate 75.

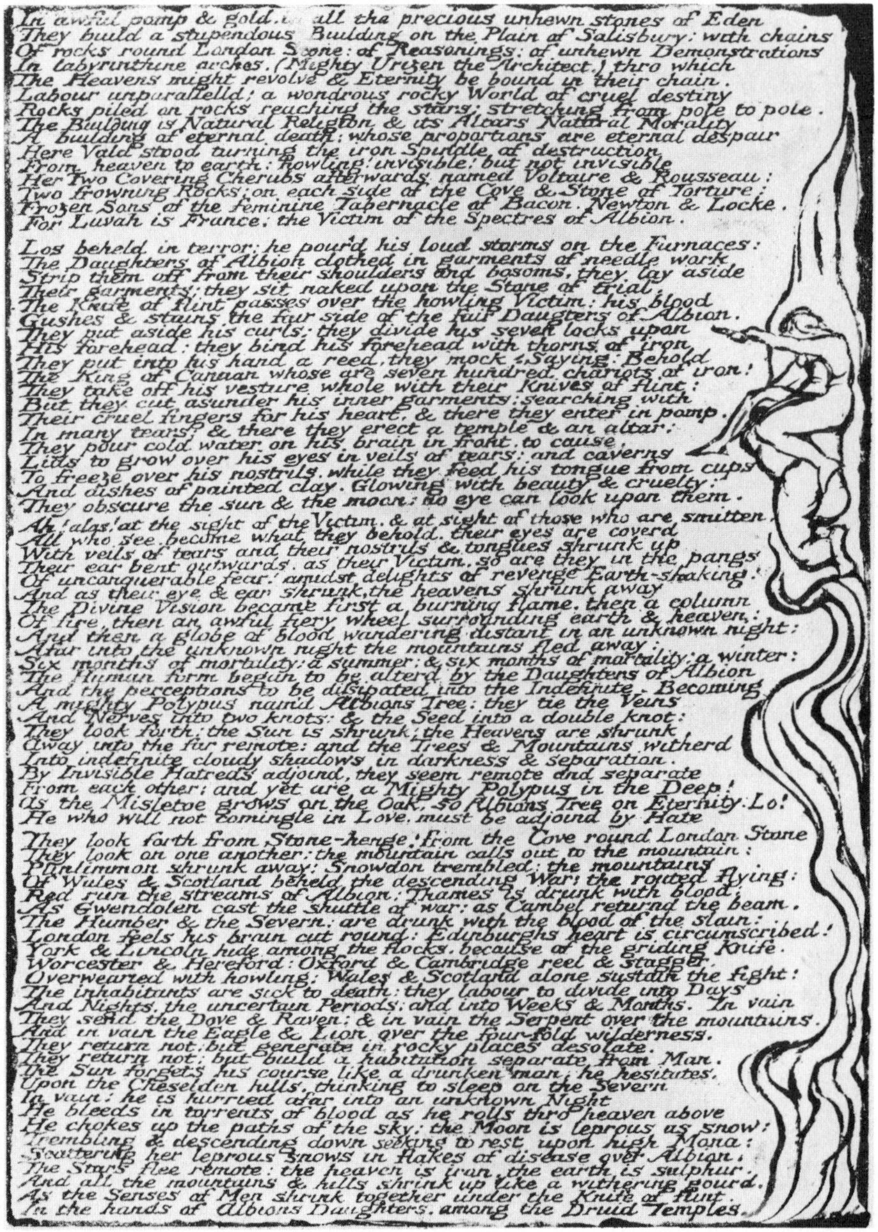

In awful pomp & gold, in all the precious unhewn stones of Eden
They build a stupendous Building on the Plain of Salisbury; with chains
Of rocks round London Stone: of Reasonings: of unhewn Demonstrations
In labyrinthine arches. (Mighty Urizen the Architect.) thro which
The Heavens might revolve & Eternity be bound in their chain.
Labour unparallelld! a wondrous rocky World of cruel destiny
Rocks piled on rocks reaching the stars: stretching from pole to pole.
The Building is Natural Religion & its Altars Natural Morality
A building of eternal death: whose proportions are eternal despair
Here Vala stood turning the iron Spindle of destruction
From heaven to earth: howling! invisible! but not invisible
Her Two Covering Cherubs afterwards named Voltaire & Rousseau:
Two frowning Rocks: on each side of the Cove & Stone of Torture:
Frozen Sons of the feminine Tabernacle of Bacon. Newton & Locke.
For Luvah is France: the Victim of the Spectres of Albion.

Los beheld in terror: he pour'd his loud storms on the Furnaces:
The Daughters of Albion clothed in garments of needle work
Strip them off from their shoulders and bosoms, they lay aside
Their garments; they sit naked upon the Stone of trial.
The Knife of flint passes over the howling Victim: his blood
Gushes & stains the fair side of the fair Daughters of Albion.
They put aside his curls; they divide his seven locks upon
His forehead: they bind his forehead with thorns of iron
They put into his hand a reed, they mock: Saying: Behold
The King of Canaan whose are seven hundred chariots of iron!
They take off his vesture whole with their Knives of flint:
But they cut asunder his inner garments: searching with
Their cruel fingers for his heart, & there they enter in pomp,
In many tears; & there they erect a temple & an altar:
They pour cold water on his brain in front, to cause.
Lids to grow over his eyes in veils of tears: and caverns
To freeze over his nostrils. while they feed his tongue from cups
And dishes of painted clay. Glowing with beauty & cruelty:
They obscure the sun & the moon: no eye can look upon them.

Ah! alas! at the sight of the Victim, & at sight of those who are smitten,
All who see. become what they behold. their eyes are coverd
With veils of tears and their nostrils & tongues shrunk up
Their ear bent outwards. as their Victim, so are they in the pangs
Of unconquerable fear! amidst delights of revenge Earth-shaking!
And as their eye & ear shrunk, the heavens shrunk away
The Divine Vision became first a burning flame, then a column
Of fire, then an awful fiery wheel surrounding earth & heaven:
And then a globe of blood wandering distant in an unknown night:
Afar into the unknown night the mountains fled away:
Six months of mortality; a summer: & six months of mortality; a winter:
The Human form began to be alterd by the Daughters of Albion
And the perceptions to be dissipated into the Indefinite. Becoming
A mighty Polypus nam'd Albions Tree: they tie the Veins
And Nerves into two knots: & the Seed into a double knot:
They look forth: the Sun is shrunk: the Heavens are shrunk
Away into the far remote: and the Trees & Mountains witherd
Into indefinite cloudy shadows in darkness & separation.
By Invisible Hatreds adjoind, they seem remote and separate
From each other; and yet are a Mighty Polypus in the Deep!
As the Misletoe grows on the Oak, so Albions Tree on Eternity: Lo!
He who will not comingle in Love, must be adjoind by Hate

They look forth from Stone-henge! from the Cove round London Stone
They look on one another: the mountain calls out to the mountain:
Plinlimmon shrunk away: Snowdon trembled: the mountains
Of Wales & Scotland beheld the descending War: the routed flying:
Red run the streams of Albion: Thames is drunk with blood:
As Gwendolen cast the shuttle of war: as Cambel returnd the beam.
The Humber & the Severn: are drunk with the blood of the slain:
London feels his brain cut round: Edinburghs heart is circumscribed!
York & Lincoln hide among the flocks. because of the griding Knife.
Worcester & Hereford: Oxford & Cambridge reel & stagger.
Overwearied with howling: Wales & Scotland alone sustain the fight:
The inhabitants are sick to death: they labour to divide into Days
And Nights. the uncertain Periods: and into Weeks & Months. In vain
They send the Dove & Raven: & in vain the Serpent over the mountains.
And in vain the Eagle & Lion over the four-fold wilderness.
They return not: but generate in rocky places desolate.
They return not; but build a habitation separate from Man.
The Sun forgets his course like a drunken man; he hesitates,
Upon the Cheselden hills, thinking to sleep on the Severn
In vain: he is hurried afar into an unknown Night
He bleeds in torrents of blood as he rolls thro heaven above
He chokes up the paths of the sky; the Moon is leprous as snow:
Trembling & descending down seeking to rest upon high Mona:
Scattering her leprous snows in flakes of disease over Albion.
The Stars flee remote: the heaven is iron, the earth is sulphur.
And all the mountains & hills shrink up like a withering gourd.
As the Senses of Men shrink together under the Knife of flint.
In the hands of Albions Daughters. among the Druid Temples.

Jerusalem 66D

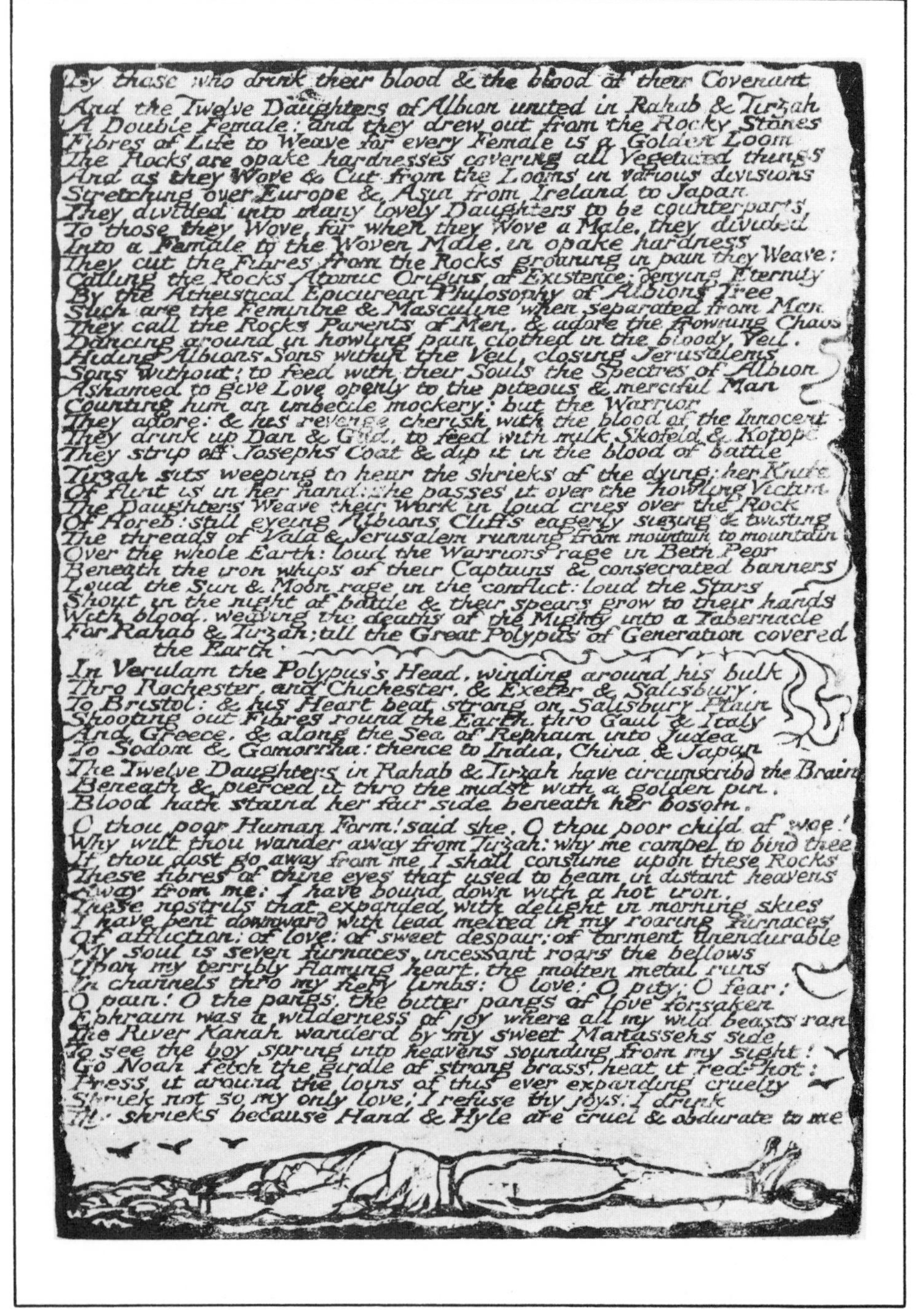

By those who drink their blood & the blood of their Covenant
And the Twelve Daughters of Albion united in Rahab & Tirzah
A Double Female: and they drew out from the Rocky Stones
Fibres of Life to Weave for every Female is a Golden Loom
The Rocks are opake hardnesses covering all Vegetated things
And as they Wove & Cut from the Looms in various divisions
Stretching over Europe & Asia from Ireland to Japan
They divided into many lovely Daughters to be counterparts
To those they Wove, for when they Wove a Male, they divided
Into a Female to the Woven Male. in opake hardness
They cut the Fibres from the Rocks groaning in pain they Weave;
Calling the Rocks Atomic Origins of Existence; denying Eternity
By the Atheistical Epicurean Philosophy of Albions Tree
Such are the Feminine & Masculine when separated from Man
They call the Rocks Parents of Men, & adore the frowning Chaos
Dancing around in howling pain clothed in the bloody Veil.
Hiding Albions Sons within the Veil, closing Jerusalems
Sons without; to feed with their Souls the Spectres of Albion
Ashamed to give Love openly to the piteous & merciful Man
Counting him an imbecile mockery: but the Warrior
They adore: & his revenge cherish with the blood of the Innocent
They drink up Dan & Gad, to feed with milk Skofeld & Kotope
They strip off Josephs Coat & dip it in the blood of battle

Tirzah sits weeping to hear the shrieks of the dying: her Knife
Of flint is in her hand: she passes it over the howling Victim
The Daughters Weave their Work in loud cries over the Rock
Of Horeb: still eyeing Albions Cliffs eagerly siezing & twisting
The threads of Vala & Jerusalem running from mountain to mountain
Over the whole Earth: loud the Warriors rage in Beth Peor
Beneath the iron whips of their Captains & consecrated banners
Loud the Sun & Moon rage in the conflict: loud the Stars
Shout in the night of battle & their spears grow to their hands
With blood, weaving the deaths of the Mighty into a Tabernacle
For Rahab & Tirzah; till the Great Polypus of Generation covered
the Earth

In Verulam the Polypus's Head, winding around his bulk
Thro Rochester, and Chichester, & Exeter & Salisbury,
To Bristol: & his Heart beat strong on Salisbury Plain
Shooting out Fibres round the Earth, thro Gaul & Italy
And Greece, & along the Sea of Rephaim into Judea
To Sodom & Gomorrha: thence to India, China & Japan

The Twelve Daughters in Rahab & Tirzah have circumscribd the Brain
Beneath & pierced it thro the midst with a golden pin.
Blood hath staind her fair side beneath her bosom.

O thou poor Human Form! said she. O thou poor child of woe!
Why wilt thou wander away from Tirzah: why me compel to bind thee
If thou dost go away from me I shall consume upon these Rocks
These fibres of thine eyes that used to beam in distant heavens
Away from me: I have bound down with a hot iron.
These nostrils that expanded with delight in morning skies
I have bent downward with lead melted in my roaring furnaces
Of affliction; of love; of sweet despair; of torment unendurable
My soul is seven furnaces, incessant roars the bellows
Upon my terribly flaming heart, the molten metal runs
In channels thro my fiery limbs: O love: O pity: O fear:
O pain! O the pangs, the bitter pangs of love forsaken
Ephraim was a wilderness of joy where all my wild beasts ran
The River Kanah wanderd by my sweet Manassehs side
To see the boy spring into heavens sounding from my sight!
Go Noah fetch the girdle of strong brass, heat it red-hot:
Press it around the loins of this ever expanding cruelty
Shriek not so my only love; I refuse thy joys: I drink
Thy shrieks because Hand & Hyle are cruel & obdurate to me

Jerusalem 67^D

Jerusalem 67. A thin line of vegetation is drawn below mention of "the Great Polypus of Generation" covering the earth (34). At page bottom we see the iron form of the Polypus, a chain attached to the victim's wrists and ankles, while the text suggests other kinds of torture. "The Victim" is, universally, the "poor Human Form" (44) or "Man" (19); in the previous context he is Luvah, in the central plot Albion.

The division and shrinking of "the Senses of Men" (66:83) is signified here by the usual five birds' being separated: three at the victim's head (like three vultures), two above his feet. (Man chained into the Time process, yet birds of Innocence over him: W.) The significance of his tight belt escapes me. (Its buckle is removed in E.)

If we compare Plates 14 and 19 we see that the guardian angels and mourners at head and feet have turned to steel.

The color washes upon the text blush red on this page, yellow on the page before (as on the torture scene of Plate 21).

Jerusalem 68. The first five birds, larger than others on the page, alert us to references to the five senses, and such we find: hearing in lines 6 ("ear") and 10 ("Songs"), beside each of which two birds hover; taste in line 12 ("drunk with blood"), with one bird; sight in 16 ("the eyes of the Kings"), with one; sound again, for the bird at line 20 ("howlings & deadly War"); touch for the bird and worm near line 25 ("tender Nerves"). For smell we must look back to the preceding page ("nostrils" in line 49, but with no bird), and we will see two birds there, beside "sight!" (67:58) and "hot" (59, in a passage continuing "Press it around the loins . . .").

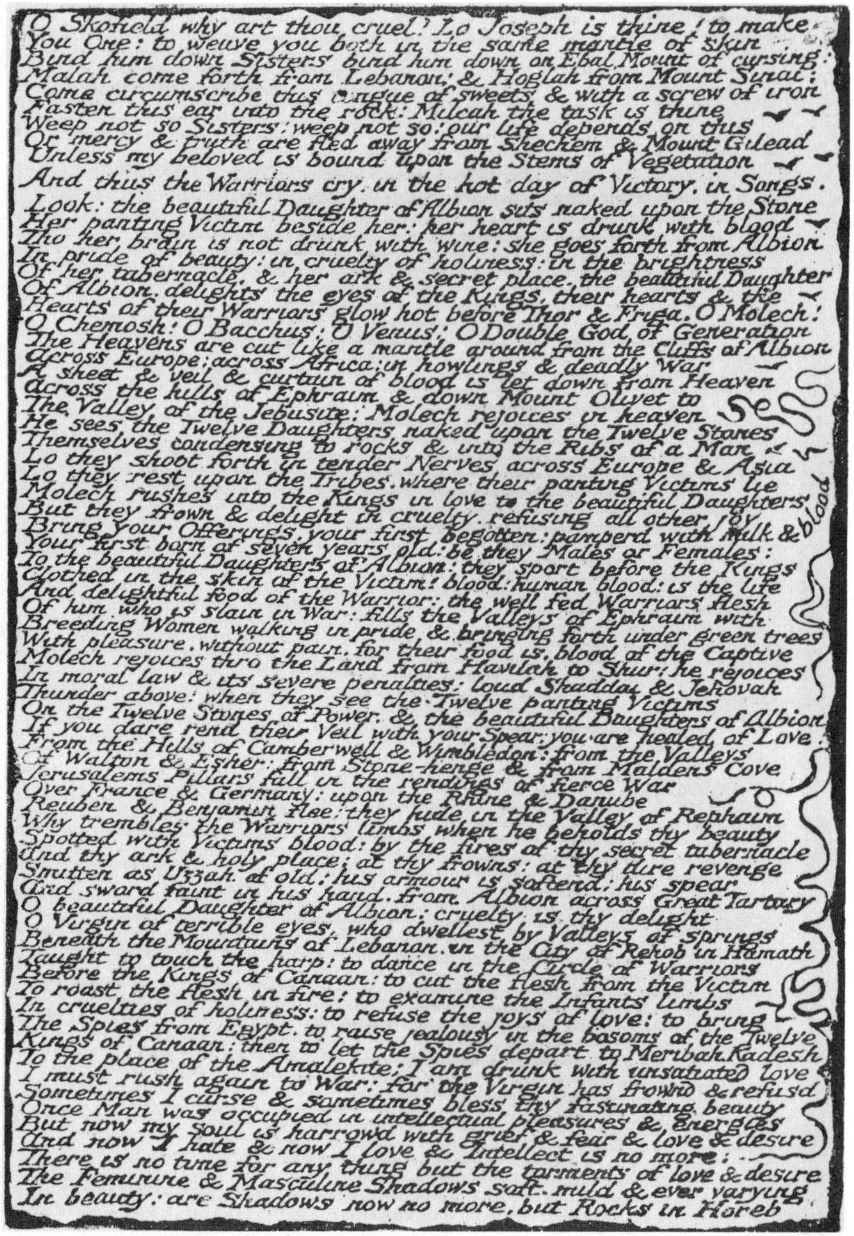

O Skofeld why art thou cruel? Lo Joseph is thine! to make
You One: to weave you both in the same mantle of skin
Bind him down Sisters bind him down on Ebal, Mount of cursing:
Malah come forth from Lebanon: & Hoglah from Mount Sinai:
Come circumscribe this tongue of sweets & with a screw of iron
Fasten this ear into the rock: Milcah the task is thine
Weep not so Sisters: weep not so: our life depends on this
Or mercy & truth are fled away from Shechem & Mount Gilead
Unless my beloved is bound upon the Stems of Vegetation
And thus the Warriors cry. in the hot day of Victory. in Songs.
Look: the beautiful Daughter of Albion sits naked upon the Stone
Her panting Victim beside her: her heart is drunk with blood
Tho her brain is not drunk with wine: she goes forth from Albion
In pride of beauty: in cruelty of holiness: in the brightness
Of her tabernacle, & her ark & secret place. the beautiful Daughter
Of Albion. delights the eyes of the Kings. their hearts & the
Hearts of their Warriors glow hot before Thor & Friga. O Molech!
O Chemosh! O Bacchus! O Venus! O Double God of Generation
The Heavens are cut like a mantle around from the Cliffs of Albion
Across Europe; across Africa; in howlings & deadly War
A sheet & veil & curtain of blood is let down from Heaven
Across the hills of Ephraim & down Mount Olivet to
The Valley of the Jebusite: Molech rejoices in heaven
He sees the Twelve Daughters naked upon the Twelve Stones
Themselves condensing to rocks & into the Ribs of a Man
Lo they shoot forth in tender Nerves across Europe & Asia
Lo they rest upon the Tribes. where their panting Victims lie
Molech rushes into the Kings in love to the beautiful Daughters
But they frown & delight in cruelty. refusing all other joy
Bring your Offerings. your first begotten: pamperd with milk & blood
Your first born of seven years old: be they Males or Females:
To the beautiful Daughters of Albion: they sport before the Kings
Clothed in the skin of the Victim! blood: human blood: is the life
And delightful food of the Warrior: the well fed Warriors flesh
Of him who is slain in War: fills the Valleys of Ephraim with
Breeding Women walking in pride & bringing forth under green trees
With pleasure. without pain. for their food is. blood of the Captive
Molech rejoices thro the Land from Havilah to Shur: he rejoices
In moral law & its severe penalties: loud Shaddai & Jehovah
Thunder above: when they see the Twelve panting Victims
On the Twelve Stones of Power. & the beautiful Daughters of Albion
If you dare rend their Veil with your Spear; you are healed of Love!
From the Hills of Camberwell & Wimbledon: from the Valleys
Of Walton & Esher: from Stone-henge & from Maldens Cove
Jerusalems Pillars fall in the rendings of fierce War
Over France & Germany: upon the Rhine & Danube
Reuben & Benjamin flee: they hide in the Valley of Rephaim
Why trembles the Warriors limbs when he beholds thy beauty
Spotted with Victims blood: by the fires of thy secret tabernacle
And thy ark & holy place: at thy frowns: at thy dire revenge
Smitten as Uzzah of old: his armour is softend: his spear
And sword faint in his hand. from Albion across Great Tartary
O beautiful Daughter of Albion: cruelty is thy delight
O Virgin of terrible eyes, who dwellest by Valleys of springs
Beneath the Mountains of Lebanon. in the City of Rehob in Hamath
Taught to touch the harp: to dance in the Circle of Warriors
Before the Kings of Canaan: to cut the flesh from the Victim
To roast the flesh in fire: to examine the Infants limbs
In cruelties of holiness: to refuse the joys of love: to bring
The Spies from Egypt. to raise jealousy in the bosoms of the Twelve
Kings of Canaan: then to let the Spies depart to Meribah Kadesh
To the place of the Amalekite; I am drunk with unsatiated love
I must rush again to War: for the Virgin has frownd & refusd
Sometimes I curse & sometimes bless thy fascinating beauty
Once Man was occupied in intellectual pleasures & energies
But now my soul is harrowd with grief & fear & love & desire
And now I hate & now I love & Intellect is no more:
There is no time for any thing but the torments of love & desire
The Feminine & Masculine Shadows soft. mild & ever varying
In beauty: are Shadows now no more, but Rocks in Horeb

Jerusalem 68[D]

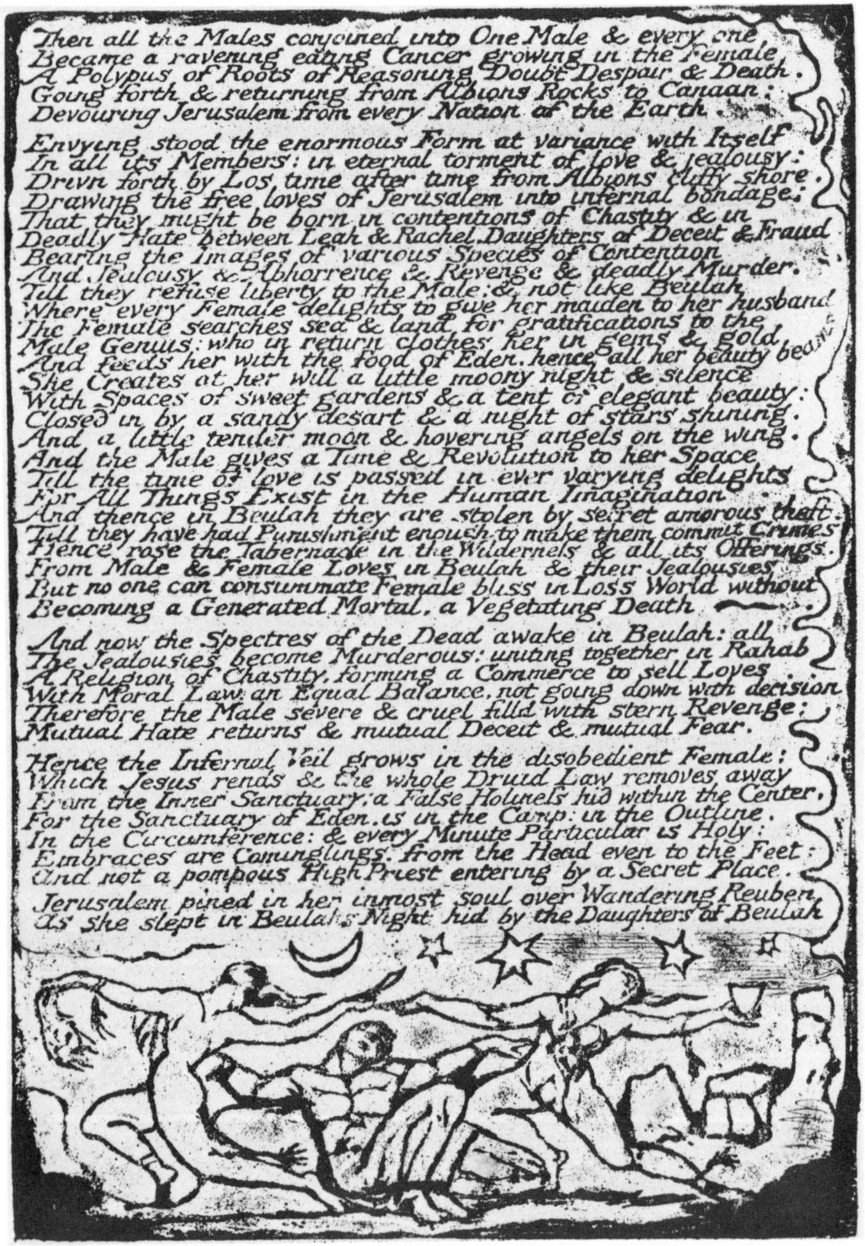

Then all the Males conjoined into One Male & every one
Became a ravening eating Cancer growing in the Female
A Polypus of Roots of Reasoning Doubt Despair & Death.
Going forth & returning from Albions Rocks to Canaan:
Devouring Jerusalem from every Nation of the Earth.

Envying stood the enormous Form at variance with Itself
In all its Members: in eternal torment of love & jealousy:
Drivn forth by Los time after time from Albions cliffy shore.
Drawing the free loves of Jerusalem into infernal bondage;
That they might be born in contentions of Chastity & in
Deadly Hate between Leah & Rachel Daughters of Deceit & Fraud
Bearing the Images of various Species of Contention
And Jealousy & Abhorrence & Revenge & deadly Murder.
Till they refuse liberty to the Male; & not like Beulah
Where every Female delights to give her maiden to her husband
The Female searches sea & land for gratifications to the
Male Genius: who in return clothes her in gems & gold
And feeds her with the food of Eden. hence all her beauty beams
She Creates at her will a little moony night & silence
With Spaces of sweet gardens & a tent of elegant beauty:
Closed in by a sandy desart & a night of stars shining.
And a little tender moon & hovering angels on the wing.
And the Male gives a Time & Revolution to her Space
Till the time of love is passed in ever varying delights
For All Things Exist in the Human Imagination
And thence in Beulah they are stolen by secret amorous theft.
Till they have had Punishment enough to make them commit Crimes
Hence rose the Tabernacle in the Wildernes & all its Offerings.
From Male & Female Loves in Beulah & their Jealousies
But no one can consummate Female bliss in Los's World without
Becoming a Generated Mortal, a Vegetating Death

And now the Spectres of the Dead awake in Beulah: all
The Jealousies become Murderous: uniting together in Rahab
A Religion of Chastity, forming a Commerce to sell Loves
With Moral Law an Equal Balance, not going down with decision
Therefore the Male severe & cruel filld with stern Revenge:
Mutual Hate returns & mutual Deceit & mutual Fear.

Hence the Infernal Veil grows in the disobedient Female:
Which Jesus rends & the whole Druid Law removes away
From the Inner Sanctuary: a False Holines hid within the Center,
For the Sanctuary of Eden. is in the Camp: in the Outline.
In the Circumference: & every Minute Particular is Holy:
Embraces are Cominglings: from the Head even to the Feet:
And not a pompous High Priest entering by a Secret Place.

Jerusalem pined in her inmost soul over Wandering Reuben
As she slept in Beulahs Night hid by the Daughters of Beulah

Jerusalem 69[D]

Jerusalem 69. In this and the two preceding plates the marginal ornamental lines suggest whips rather than vines. The climactic torture orgy fills the bottom of this page. Under a thin moon and four (fallen) stars of very unequal sizes (compare Plates 9 and 54), two drunken daughters brandish knives above a stunned victim whose wrists and ankles are manacled (the ankles not so in E). The otherwise naked priestesses wear scalps of other victims dangling from their left wrists and flayed hands from their left ankles (not retained in E). One holds "the grim image of a flayed face" (W) in her left hand; both have sketchily indicated bloody horrors (other parts of male bodies?) dangling over their breasts. One daughter holds out a large cup toward a phallic stone pillar (inked over in C) beside a Druid trilithon and a Christian gravestone, at the right. This gives a sinister import indeed to the statement that "they feed his tongue from cups And dishes of painted clay" while closing his senses (66:32–33). The victim's arms lie in the position of crucifixion; the bands on his wrists and ankles recall Orc chained to the rock in *America* 1. The grass is green.

In a more charitable view, the woman with the cup may be trying to catch a falling star; it is a tiny one.

Can the three symbolic stones be meant to refer, from right to left, to the three chapters in this work addressed respectively to Jews, Deists, and Christians? (Was the phallic stone suggested by descriptions of Hindu temples?)

Jerusalem 70. The revised catchword ("His" changed to "And" in copy C) and textual continuity suggest that this plate once preceded Plate 19, again associating the trilithon with human sacrifice. (See also *Milton* 4 and 7.) The association imposed by Plate 69, where it is drawn as stony companion to the stone phallus, is of the Female Will, here looming vast over human forms and framing an occulted sun. The pillars of smoke, presumably drifting up from sacrificial altars, that assist in the occulting are also, of course, Vala's intestinal veil presented as a vortex not yet passed. The traveller on the right of the three on a road under the Stonehenge "clock" is holding what may be a Druid harp (removed in E). (The eclipse of the sun is also modified in E to mere smoggy pallor.) Two trees against the hill behind the travellers and a cluster of trees at the base of the other pillar indicate "the Oak Groves of Albion which overspread all the Earth" (16). (The two trees and some shadows are painted out in E, as are indications of houses or barns along the distant road.) The grass and hills are shades of green. (The similarity of the three standing figures, with harp, to the three standing angels, with lyre, in *Songs* 21 is curious.)

And this the form of mighty Hand sitting on Albions cliffs
Before the face of Albion, a mighty threatning Form.
His bosom wide & shoulders huge overspreading wondrous
Bear Three strong sinewy Necks & Three awful & terrible Heads
Three Brains in contradictory council brooding incessantly.
Neither daring to put in act its councils, fearing each-other.
Therefore rejecting Ideas as nothing & holding all Wisdom
To consist. in the agreements & disagreents of Ideas.
Plotting to devour Albions Body of Humanity & Love.

Such Form the aggregate of the Twelve Sons of Albion took; & such
Their appearance when combind: but often by birth-pangs & loud groans
They divide to Twelve: the key-bones & the chest dividing in pain
Disclose a hideous orifice; thence issuing the Giant-brood
Arise as the smoke of the furnace, shaking the rocks from sea to sea.
And there they combine into Three Forms, named Bacon & Newton & Locke.
In the Oak Groves of Albion which overspread all the Earth.

Imputing Sin & Righteousness to Individuals; Rahab
Sat deep within him hid: his Feminine Power unreveald
Brooding Abstract Philosophy. to destroy Imagination, the Divine-
-Humanity A Three-fold Wonder: feminine: most beautiful: Three-fold
Each within other. On her white marble & even Neck, her Heart
Inorb'd and bonified: with locks of shadowing modesty, shining
Over her beautiful Female features. soft flourishing in beauty
Beams mild, all love and all perfection, that when the lips
Recieve a kiss from Gods or Men, a threefold kiss returns
From the pressd loveliness: so her whole immortal form three-fold
Three-fold embrace returns: consuming lives of Gods & Men
In fires of beauty melting them as gold & silver in the furnace
Her Brain enlabyrinths the whole heaven of her bosom & loins
To put in act what her Heart wills: O who can withstand her power
Her name is Vala in Eternity: in Time her name is Rahab

The Starry Heavens all were fled from the mighty limbs of Albion His

Jerusalem 70[D]

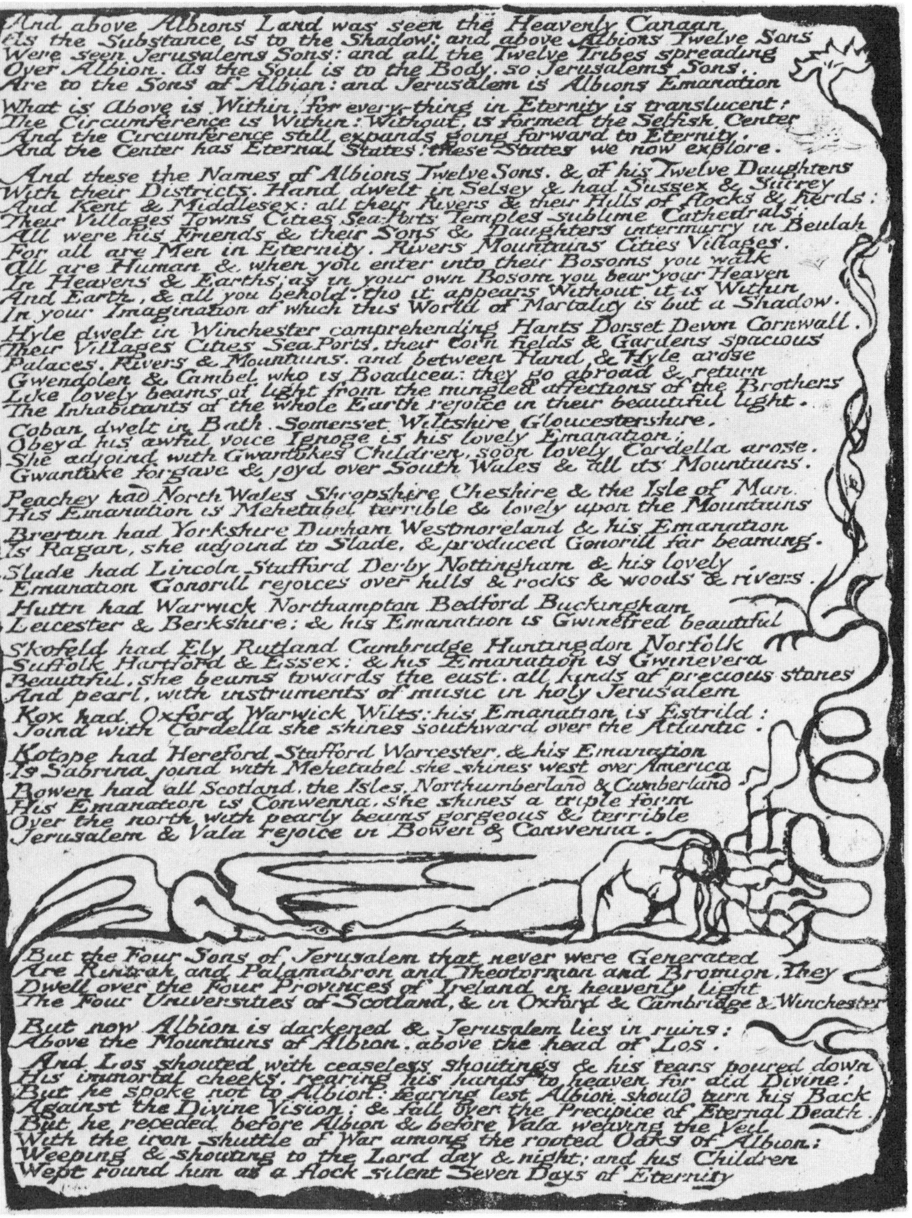

And above Albions Land was seen the Heavenly Canaan
As the Substance is to the Shadow: and above Albions Twelve Sons
Were seen Jerusalems Sons: and all the Twelve Tribes spreading
Over Albion. As the Soul is to the Body, so Jerusalems Sons,
Are to the Sons of Albion: and Jerusalem is Albions Emanation
What is Above is Within, for every-thing in Eternity is translucent:
The Circumference is Within: Without, is formed the Selfish Center
And the Circumference still expands going forward to Eternity.
And the Center has Eternal States! these States we now explore.
And these the Names of Albions Twelve Sons. & of his Twelve Daughters
With their Districts. Hand dwelt in Selsey & had Sussex & Surrey
And Kent & Middlesex: all their Rivers & their Hills of flocks & herds:
Their Villages Towns Cities Sea-Ports Temples sublime Cathedrals;
All were his Friends & their Sons & Daughters intermarry in Beulah
For all are Men in Eternity. Rivers Mountains Cities Villages.
All are Human & when you enter into their Bosoms you walk
In Heavens & Earths; as in your own Bosom you bear your Heaven
And Earth, & all you behold, tho it appears Without it is Within
In your Imagination of which this World of Mortality is but a Shadow.
Hyle dwelt in Winchester comprehending Hants Dorset Devon Cornwall.
Their Villages Cities SeaPorts. their Corn fields & Gardens spacious
Palaces, Rivers & Mountains. and between Hand & Hyle arose
Gwendolen & Cambel who is Boadicea: they go abroad & return
Like lovely beams of light from the mingled affections of the Brothers
The Inhabitants of the whole Earth rejoice in their beautiful light.
Coban dwelt in Bath. Somerset Wiltshire Gloucestershire.
Obeyd his awful voice Ignoge is his lovely Emanation;
She adjoind with Gwantokes Children, soon lovely Cordella arose.
Gwantoke forgave & joyd over South Wales & all its Mountains.
Peachey had North Wales Shropshire Cheshire & the Isle of Man.
His Emanation is Mehetabel terrible & lovely upon the Mountains
Brertun had Yorkshire Durham Westmoreland & his Emanation
Is Ragan, she adjoind to Slade, & produced Gonorill far beaming.
Slade had Lincoln Stafford Derby Nottingham & his lovely
Emanation Gonorill rejoices over hills & rocks & woods & rivers.
Huttn had Warwick Northampton Bedford Buckingham
Leicester & Berkshire: & his Emanation is Gwinefred beautiful
Skofeld had Ely Rutland Cambridge Huntingdon Norfolk
Suffolk Hartford & Essex: & his Emanation is Gwinevera
Beautiful, she beams towards the east, all kinds of precious stones
And pearl, with instruments of music in holy Jerusalem
Kox had Oxford Warwick Wilts: his Emanation is Estrild:
Joind with Cordella she shines southward over the Atlantic.
Kotope had Hereford Stafford Worcester, & his Emanation
Is Sabrina joind with Mehetabel she shines west over America
Bowen had all Scotland, the Isles, Northumberland & Cumberland
His Emanation is Conwenna, she shines a triple form
Over the north with pearly beams gorgeous & terrible
Jerusalem & Vala rejoice in Bowen & Conwenna.

But the Four Sons of Jerusalem that never were Generated
Are Rintrah and Palamabron and Theotormon and Bromion. They
Dwell over the Four Provinces of Ireland in heavenly light
The Four Universities of Scotland, & in Oxford & Cambridge & Winchester
But now Albion is darkened & Jerusalem lies in ruins:
Above the Mountains of Albion. above the head of Los.
And Los shouted with ceaseless shoutings & his tears poured down
His immortal cheeks, rearing his hands to heaven for aid Divine!
But he spoke not to Albion: fearing lest Albion should turn his Back
Against the Divine Vision: & fall over the Precipice of Eternal Death.
But he receded before Albion & before Vala weaving the Veil
With the iron shuttle of War among the rooted Oaks of Albion:
Weeping & shouting to the Lord day & night; and his Children
Wept round him as a flock silent Seven Days of Eternity

Jerusalem 71[D]

Jerusalem 71. This is an emblem of the mythic origins of murder and war, with allusions to Cain and Abel and to Zeus and Leda, the role of Zeus as swan being played by Albion's spectre, the role of Leda by Vala or one of her daughters. Wicksteed's comment is suggestive, though it runs too quickly to Blake's reminder that life can spring eternal: "The figure represents Sex in Female form but as a spiritual vehicle between the bat- or dragon-winged Swan—an alchemist phallic symbol—and the tendrils rising from the rationalizing process spun out of her head, with the precious flower of Human fertility at the crest of the chain of ascending tendrils, a process which stretches from Hell through Earth to Heaven".

Although the network that seems to grow from Vala's head, dividing upward and downward, whip-like at first, does eventuate in tendrils, foliage, and a flower-like leaf, given no color, the structure that it forms on ground level, given a grey wash (with which Vala is also shaded, greenish grey) resembles too closely for accident the stone altar beside which Cain slays Abel in *Milton* 15; even the rounded beginnings of two stone faces are here. As for Vala's seduction of Albion's spectre, as etched she looks down, as the "maiden Queen" in the Notebook drawing for *Songs* 41 or the jealous Rosetree in *Songs* 43, but in E she is redrawn with her face smiling back like Vala's in Plate 24 (or Eve's in *Songs* 1). Her waist is flabby and her hair slovenly, but the spectre in swan disguise (compare his limp worm-like neck to the firm arching neck of Blake's swan in Plate 11) is modified by passion, violet on the lighted wing and body surfaces, and fatuously kissing or nibbling at the toes of this daughter of man named Leda, from whose union with the spectre of Zeus came Helen and all the Greek and Trojan woe.

Jerusalem 72. Two guardian angels, more like the friends who follow the ark on Plate 39 than those we have seen at Albion's head and feet in Plates 14 and 19, brood over a diagram of the universal States defined in these plates: Circumference-Center, Love-Jealousy, Building-Decaying, Within-Without. And this globe, somewhat less lumpy than "This World" of Plate 54, yet an interruption in the chain of loving angels (Plate 22 and, coming, Plate 75), is the metal in Los's furnace: note the flames here, and see it placed on his anvil in Plate 73. The lump, the flames, and the text area below are washed sulfur yellow, the dominant color in the anvil scene of Plate 73.

At page bottom the serpent's secret for our mirror is: "Women the Comforters of Men become the Tormenters & Punishers."

And the Thirty-two Counties of the Four Provinces of Ireland
Are thus divided: The Four Counties are in the Four Camps
Munster South in Reubens Gate. Connaut West in Josephs Gate
Ulster North in Dans Gate. Leinster East in Judahs Gate

For Albion in Eternity has Sixteen Gates among his Pillars
But the Four towards the West were Walled up & the Twelve
That front the Four other Points were turned Four Square
By Los for Jerusalems sake & called the Gates of Jerusalem
Because Twelve Sons of Jerusalem fled successive thro the Gates
But the Four Sons of Jerusalem who fled not but remaind
Are Rintrah & Palamabron & Theotormon & Bromion
The Four that remain with Los to guard the Western Wall
And these Four remain to guard the Four Walls of Jerusalem
Whose foundations remain in the Thirty-two Counties of Ireland
And in Twelve Counties of Wales. & in the Forty Counties
Of England & in the Thirty-six Counties of Scotland

And the names of the Thirty-two Counties of Ireland are these
Under Judah & Issachar & Zebulun are Lowth Longford
Eastmeath Westmeath Dublin Kildare Kings County
Queens County Wicklow Catherloh Wexford Kilkenny
And those under Reuben & Simeon & Levi are these
Waterford Tipperary Cork Limerick Kerry Clare
And those under Ephraim Manasseh & Benjamin are these
Galway Roscommon Mayo Sligo Leitrim
And those under Dan Asher & Napthali are these
Donnegal Antrim Tyrone Fermanagh Armagh Londonderry
Down Managhan Cavan. These are the Land of Erin

All these Center in London & in Golgonooza. from whence
They are Created continually East & West & North & South
And from them are Created all the Nations of the Earth
Europe & Asia & Africa & America, in fury Fourfold!

Continually Building. Continually Decaying because of Love & Jealousy

And Thirty-two the Nations: to dwell in Jerusalems Gates
O Come ye Nations Come ye People Come up to Jerusalem
Return Jerusalem, & dwell together as of old: Return
Return: O Albion let Jerusalem overspread all Nations
As in the times of old: O Albion awake! Reuben wanders
The Nations wait for Jerusalem. they look up for the Bride

France Spain Italy Germany Poland Russia Sweden Turkey
Arabia Palestine Persia Hindostan China Tartary Siberia
Egypt Lybia Ethiopia Guinea Caffraria Negroland Morocco
Congo Zaara Canada Greenland Carolina Mexico
Peru Patagonia Amazonia Brazil. Thirty-two Nations
And under these Thirty-two Classes of Islands in the Ocean
All the Nations Peoples & Tongues throughout all the Earth

And the Four Gates of Los surround the Universe Within and
Without; & whatever is visible in the Vegetable Earth. the same
Is visible in the Mundane Shell; reversd in mountain & vale
And a Son of Eden was set over each Daughter of Beulah to guard
In Albions Tomb the wondrous Creation: & the Four-fold Gate
Towards Beulah is to the South Fenelon, Guion, Teresa,
Whitefield & Hervey, guard that Gate; with all the gentle Souls
Who guide the great Wine-press of Love; Four precious Stones that
Gate:

Women the Comforters of Men become the Tormenters & Punishers

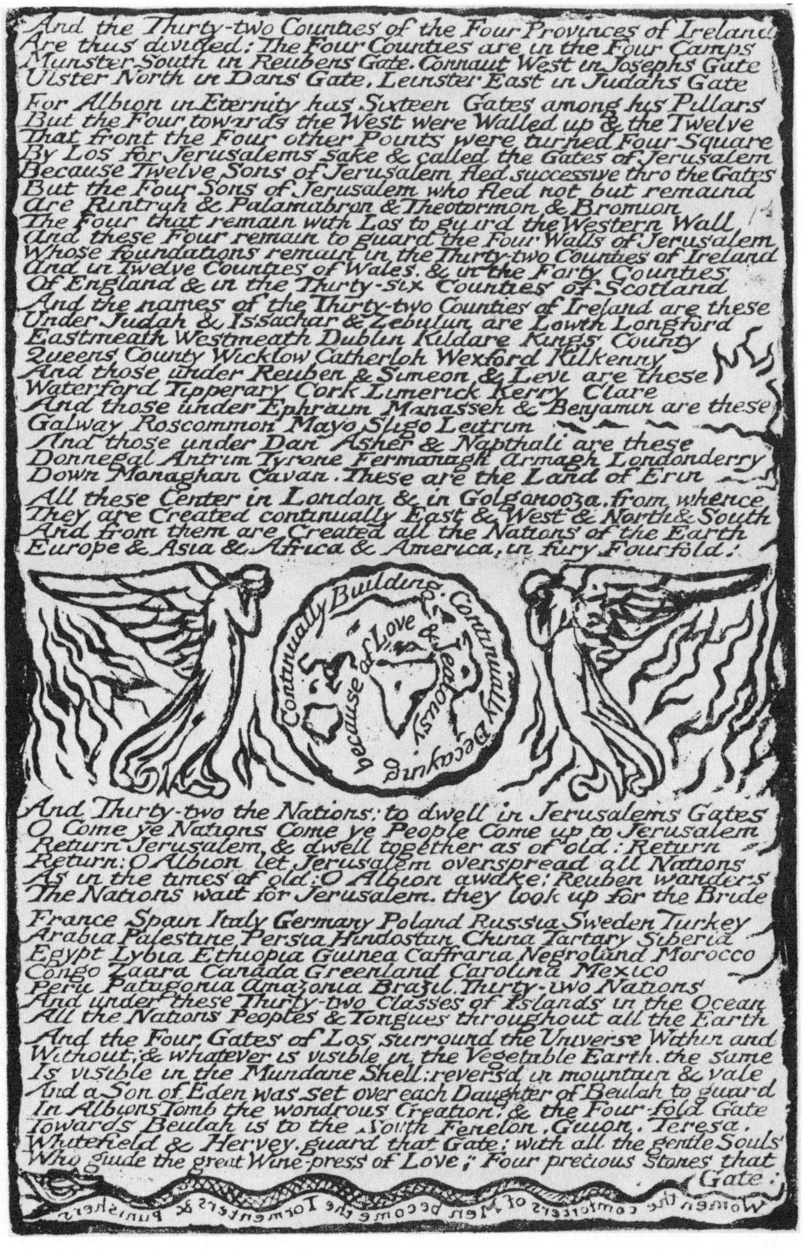

Jerusalem 72[D]

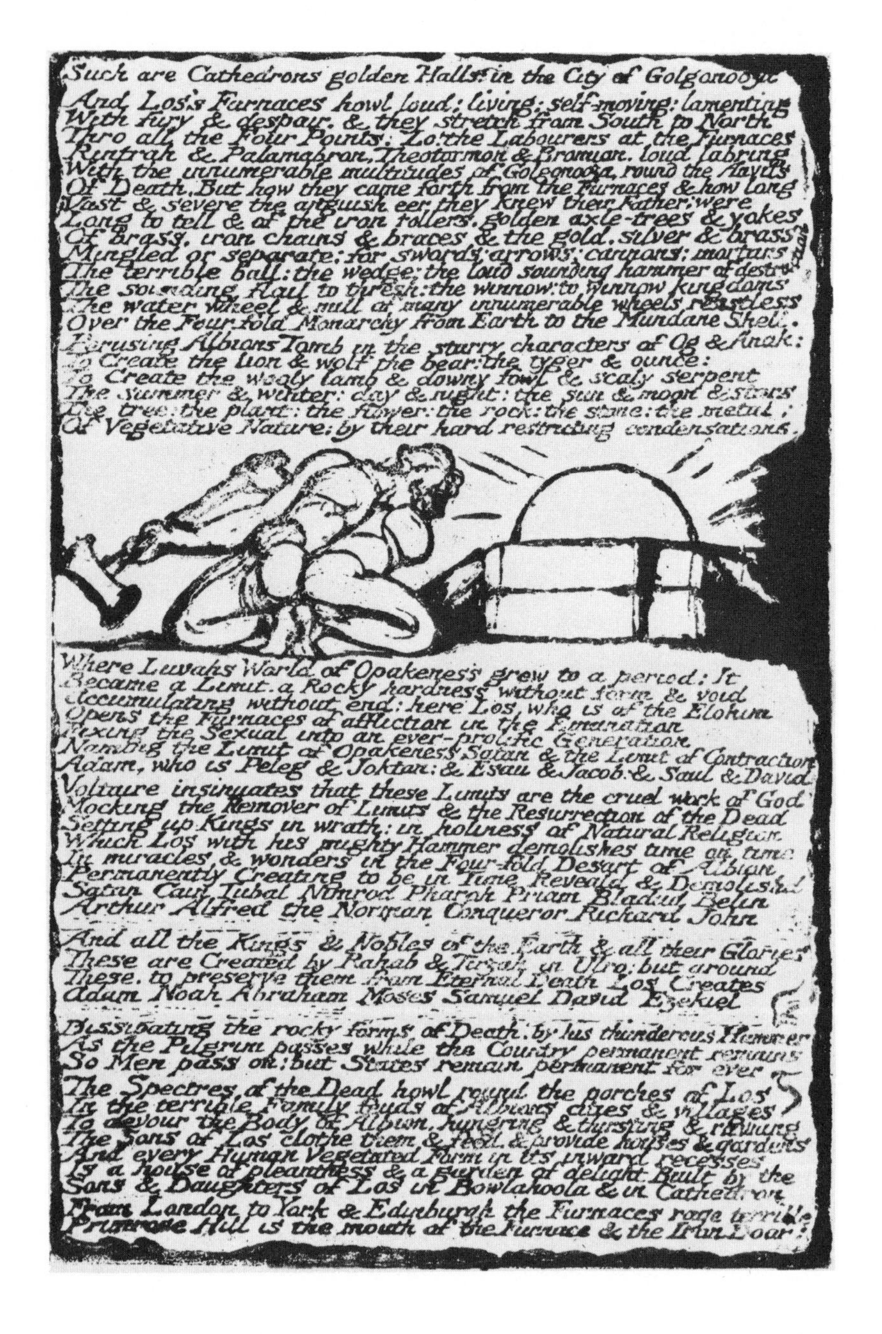

Such are Cathedrons golden Halls: in the City of Golgonooza
And Los's Furnaces howl loud; living: self-moving: lamenting
With fury & despair, & they stretch from South to North
Thro all the Four Points: Lo! the Labourers at the Furnaces
Rintrah & Palamabron, Theotormon & Bromion, loud labring
With the innumerable multitudes of Golgonooza, round the Anvils
Of Death. But how they came forth from the Furnaces & how long
Vast & severe the anguish eer they knew their Father; were
Long to tell & of the iron rollers, golden axle-trees & yokes
Of brass, iron chains & braces & the gold, silver & brass
Mingled or separate: for swords; arrows; cannons; mortars
The terrible ball: the wedge: the loud sounding hammer of destruction
The sounding flail to thresh: the winnow: to winnow kingdoms
The water wheel & mill of many innumerable wheels resistless
Over the Four-fold Monarchy from Earth to the Mundane Shell.
Perusing Albions Tomb in the starry characters of Og & Anak:
To Create the lion & wolf the bear: the tyger & ounce:
To Create the wooly lamb & downy fowl & scaly serpent
The summer & winter: day & night: the sun & moon & stars
The tree: the plant: the flower: the rock: the stone: the metal:
Of Vegetative Nature: by their hard restricting condensations.

Where Luvahs World of Opakeness grew to a period: It
Became a Limit, a Rocky hardness without form & void
Accumulating without end: here Los, who is of the Elohim
Opens the Furnaces of affliction in the Emanation
Fixing the Sexual into an ever-prolific Generation
Naming the Limit of Opakeness Satan & the Limit of Contraction
Adam, who is Peleg & Joktan: & Esau & Jacob: & Saul & David
Voltaire insinuates that these Limits are the cruel work of God
Mocking the Remover of Limits & the Resurrection of the Dead
Setting up Kings in wrath: in holiness of Natural Religion
Which Los with his mighty Hammer demolishes time on time
In miracles & wonders in the Four-fold Desart of Albion
Permanently Creating to be in Time Reveald & Demolishd
Satan Cain Tubal Nimrod Pharah Priam Bladud Belin
Arthur Alfred the Norman Conqueror Richard John

And all the Kings & Nobles of the Earth & all their Glories
These are Created by Rahab & Tirzah in Ulro: but around
These, to preserve them from Eternal Death Los Creates
Adam Noah Abraham Moses Samuel David Ezekiel

Dissipating the rocky forms of Death, by his thunderous Hammer
As the Pilgrim passes while the Country permanent remains
So Men pass on: but States remain permanent for ever
The Spectres of the Dead howl round the porches of Los
In the terrible Family feuds of Albions cities & villages
To devour the Body of Albion, hungring & thirsting & ravning
The Sons of Los clothe them & feed & provide houses & gardens
And every Human Vegetated Form in its inward recesses
Is a house of pleasantness & a garden of delight Built by the
Sons & Daughters of Los in Bowlahoola & in Cathedron
From London to York & Edinburgh the Furnaces rage terrible
Primrose Hill is the mouth of the Furnace & the Iron Door;

Jerusalem 73D

Jerusalem 73. The orange and yellow sun suffuses yellow light up into the text, arched at the left into a rainbow of soft yellow to mild indigo. If the task of Los—an industrial Orpheus bringing sunrise—is to transform the round globe into living forms, compelling the natural sun "into an ever-prolific Generation" (26) and "dissipating the rocky forms of Death" (43)—visually he is refining that lump of Albion's fall on Plates 54 and 72—then by comparison to Plate 32 we may guess his work to be half done. (In Plate 6 it is scarce begun.) Compare *Song of Los* 8.

In lines 37 and 42 had been etched the names of monarchs "to be in Time Reveald & Demolishd"—Edward, Henry, Elizabeth, James, Charles, William, George—and of liberators from Eternal Death—Pythagoras, Socrates, Euripedes, Virgil, Dante, Milton. But Blake gouged the lines from the copper plate, from some impulse of secrecy perhaps, fainting at his task as Los, but an action not inconsistent with his message for Albion against "Vengeance."

Jerusalem 74. In the right margin, the figures we saw in the altar flames on Plate 66, priestess with knife and victim whose head is vised between her thighs, are now apart—his head gone but replaced by a coiling worm. She soars upward with knife held in triumph, but the points of the text-cloud beside her suggest bat wings (clearly painted in E as ruddy wings, and the knife drawn in sharp black). The adjacent text (6–12) defines the separation as the Zoas' all entering "into the Reasoning Power" (the priestess with that knife) and "forsaking Imagination," to abandon the human body to Beulah and "destroy . . . the Divine Body by Martyrdoms & Wars." The replacing of the victim's head by a worm-serpent shows what immediately happens in a paradise without imagination.

At bottom a male or hermaphroditic body enrooting (moving toward the process above), by the growth of vegetation from hair and fingers and loins, interprets the enrooting of Reuben, Simeon, Levi, Judah mentioned in lines 42–49. The roots seem to sprout from the neck as well, where wings would be the right thing (see Plate 75). The nearest analogue is the growth from Vala's head on Plate 71; an obviously intended contrast is to the body of Jerusalem in Plate 57 building a cathedral window with tracery growing from her head and hands but not neck or loins. See also Plate 85.

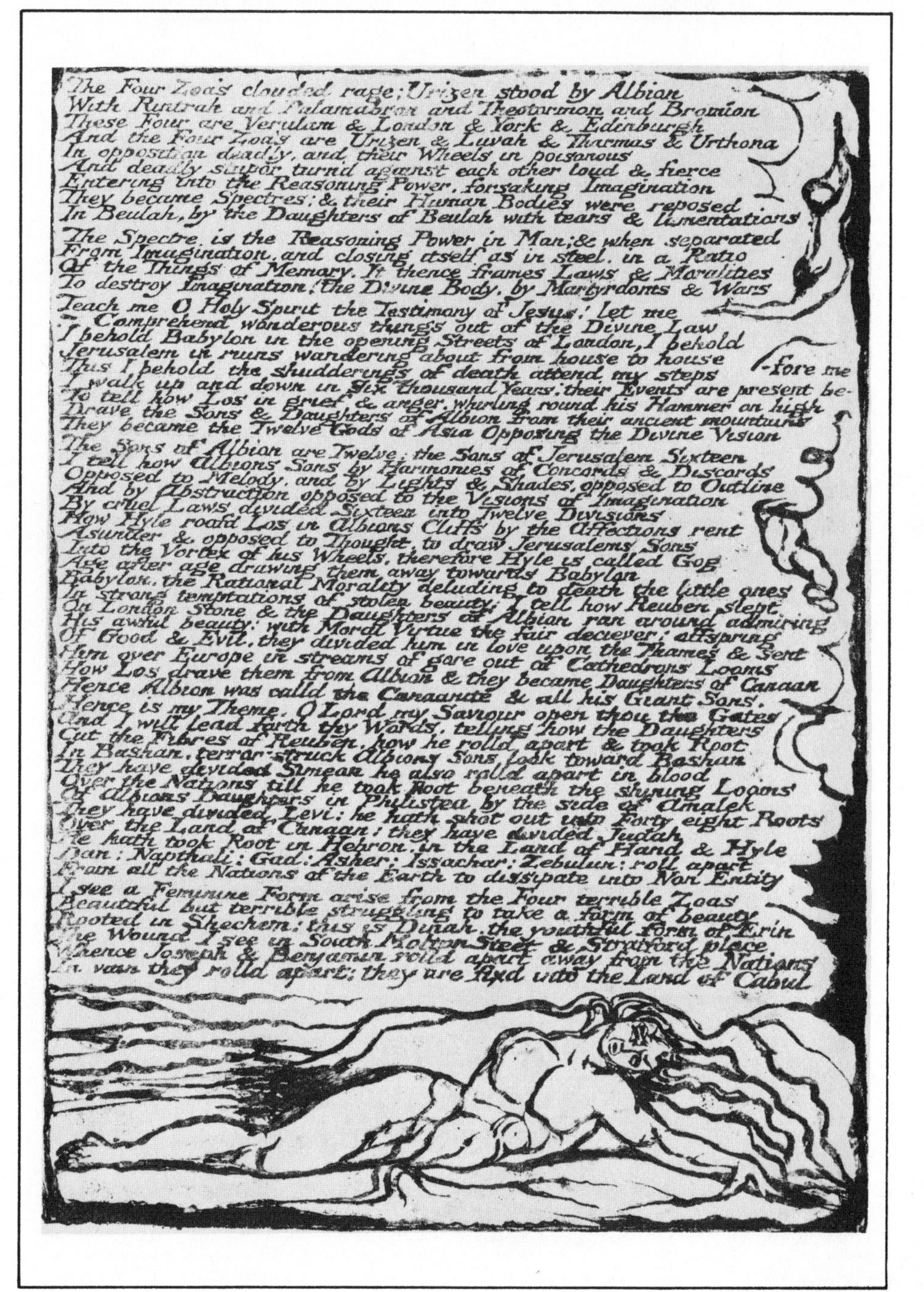
The Four Zoas clouded rage; Urizen stood by Albian
With Rintrah and Palamabron and Theotormon and Bromion
These Four are Verulam & London & York & Edinburgh
And the Four Zoas are Urizen & Luvah & Tharmas & Urthona
In opposition deadly, and their Wheels in poisonous
And deadly stupor turnd against each other loud & fierce
Entering into the Reasoning Power, forsaking Imagination
They became Spectres; & their Human Bodies were reposed
In Beulah, by the Daughters of Beulah with tears & lamentations

The Spectre is the Reasoning Power in Man; & when separated
From Imagination, and closing itself as in steel, in a Ratio
Of the Things of Memory. It thence frames Laws & Moralities
To destroy Imagination! the Divine Body, by Martyrdoms & Wars

Teach me O Holy Spirit the Testimony of Jesus! let me
Comprehend wonderous things out of the Divine Law
I behold Babylon in the opening Streets of London, I behold
Jerusalem in ruins wandering about from house to house
This I behold the shudderings of death attend my steps
I walk up and down in Six thousand Years: their Events are present be-fore me
To tell how Los in grief & anger, whirling round his Hammer on high
Drave the Sons & Daughters of Albion from their ancient mountains
They became the Twelve Gods of Asia Opposing the Divine Vision

The Sons of Albion are Twelve: the Sons of Jerusalem Sixteen
I tell how Albions Sons by Harmonies of Concords & Discords
Opposed to Melody, and by Lights & Shades, opposed to Outline
And by Abstraction opposed to the Visions of Imagination
By cruel Laws divided Sixteen into Twelve Divisions
How Hyle roofd Los in Albions Cliffs by the Affections rent
Asunder & opposed to Thought, to draw Jerusalems Sons
Into the Vortex of his Wheels, therefore Hyle is called Gog
Age after age drawing them away towards Babylon
Babylon, the Rational Morality deluding to death the little ones
In strong temptations of stolen beauty; I tell how Reuben slept
On London Stone & the Daughters of Albion ran around admiring
His awful beauty: with Moral Virtue the fair deciever; offspring
Of Good & Evil, they divided him in love upon the Thames & sent
Him over Europe in streams of gore out of Cathedrons Looms
How Los drave them from Albion & they became Daughters of Canaan
Hence Albion was calld the Canaanite & all his Giant Sons.
Hence is my Theme. O Lord my Saviour open thou the Gates
And I will lead forth thy Words, telling how the Daughters
Cut the Fibres of Reuben, how he rolld apart & took Root
In Bashan, terror-struck Albions Sons look toward Bashan
They have divided Simeon he also rolld apart in blood
Over the Nations till he took Root beneath the shining Looms
Of Albions Daughters in Philistea by the side of Amalek
They have divided Levi: he hath shot out into Forty eight Roots
Over the Land of Canaan: they have divided Judah
He hath took Root in Hebron, in the Land of Hand & Hyle
Dan: Napthali: Gad: Asher: Issachar: Zebulun: roll apart
From all the Nations of the Earth to dissipate into Non Entity

I see a Feminine Form arise from the Four terrible Zoas
Beautiful but terrible struggling to take a form of beauty
Rooted in Shechem: this is Dinah, the youthful form of Erin
The Wound I see in South Molton Street & Stratford place
Whence Joseph & Benjamin rolld apart away from the Nations
In vain they rolld apart; they are fixd into the Land of Cabul

Jerusalem 74D

And Rahab Babylon the Great hath destroyed Jerusalem
Bath stood upon the Severn with Merlin & Bladud & Arthur
The Cup of Rahab in his hand: her Poisons Twenty-seven-fold
And all her Twenty-seven Heavens now hid & now reveal'd
Appear in strong delusive light of Time & Space drawn out
In shadowy pomp by the Eternal Prophet created evermore
For Los in Six Thousand Years walks up & down continually
That not one Moment of Time be lost & every revolution
Of Space he makes permanent in Bowlahoola & Cathedron.

And these the names of the Twenty-seven Heavens & their Churches
Adam. Seth. Enos. Cainan. Mahalaleel, Jared, Enoch.
Methuselah, Lamech: these are the Giants mighty, Hermaphroditic
Noah, Shem, Arphaxad, Cainan the Second, Salah, Heber,
Peleg, Reu, Serug, Nahor, Terah: these are the Female Males:
A Male within a Female hid as in an Ark & Curtains.
Abraham, Moses, Solomon, Paul, Constantine, Charlemaine
Luther. these Seven are the Male Females: the Dragon Forms
The Female hid within a Male: thus Rahab is reveald
Mystery Babylon the Great: the Abomination of Desolation
Religion hid in War: a Dragon red, & hidden Harlot
But Jesus breaking thro' the Central Zones of Death & Hell
Opens Eternity in Time & Space; triumphant in Mercy
Thus are the Heavens form'd by Los within the Mundane Shell
And where Luther ends Adam begins again in Eternal Circle
To awake the Prisoners of Death; to bring Albion again
With Luvah into light eternal, in his eternal day.
But now the Starry Heavens are fled from the mighty limbs of Albion

Jerusalem 75[D]

Jerusalem 75. An endless band (i.e. nine and two halves) of angelic wheels within wheels illustrates how Imagination makes "every revolution . . . permanent" (8–9); compare Plate 22. At bottom we see the same interlinking circles, minus angels, in about fourteen loops drawn in place of scales on the coils of the serpent body (at right) of the revealed seven-headed (and moon-horned) dragon (17–20), some of whose heads are embraced by two semi-human forms of the "hidden Harlot" (20), crowned with wreaths, probably Tirzah at the left, ending in fish tail, probably Rahab at the right, all woman as far as we can see (yet scaly), embracing and being embraced and effectually shutting the mouth of the favored head (a Circean or Titania-Bottom variant of the embrace of priestess and victim of Plate 66). The other heads are active, their darting and cloven tongues prominent. The head at lower right is like a dolphin's.

The duplication of the angelic wheels on the dragon's coils, like the happy exhibition of the serpentine temple of Druid trilithons in Plate 100, illustrates how the Imagination can "open Eternity" and be "triumphant in Mercy" (22) toward this erroneous yet revealed form of creation.

This closing picture of chapter 3 forms instructive contrasts to the picture of the beast at the end of chapter 2. (One of Blake's sources is his earlier mélange of dragon and human forms in *Urizen* 25.)

Jerusalem 76. On an ancient oak, with golden[E] (or white[F]) acorns suggesting apples (five in A, nine or ten in EF, obscured in CD), Christ with crown of thorns and nails in hands and feet takes on himself "the Satanic Body of Holiness" (90:38). The Druids practicing sacrifice of others would "seek studiously for an oak-tree, large and handsome, growing up with two principal arms in form of a cross, beside the main stem upright," according to Stuckeley (*Stonehenge* 269), and consecrate it by cutting in the bark "the word Hesus" (compare the "Monos ho Iesus" of Plate 4). Affixed to vegetation, to generation, Jesus becomes the Satanic Selfhood, the bodily Victim (see Plates 66–69, 75, and crucially 25)—an enigma that requires Albion, in stretching out his arms becoming what he beholds, properly looking up, to see the object of his rising upon his feet (for the first time in seventy-six plates) to be not only the worshipped God of This World and himself as the passive victim of Plate 25, but by this Act the resurrected Humanity. There are still two suns (behind Jesus' head and on the leftward horizon) in this picture; Albion is at an acme of Satanic worship of a vegetated Christ; but he has now made the crucial identification, and the clues in this rehearsal of the true awakening instruct him that the natural sun could be setting, the sun of imagination bursting forth in noonday glory. The living Jesus will not display wooden hands but embrace his brother Albion.

The names "Albion" and "Jesus" are incised beneath the figures, but deleted[DE], or "Albion" is left showing but "Jesus" deleted[CF]. Readers are not to mistake this for the true Jesus. Mitchell notes that the posture of Albion is in effect a quotation of pictures of St Francis receiving the stigmata.

Jerusalem 76[D]

To the Christians.

Devils are
False Religions
"Saul Saul"
Why persecutest thou me.

I give you the end of a golden string,
Only wind it into a ball:
It will lead you in at Heavens gate,
Built in Jerusalems wall.

We are told to abstain from fleshly desires that we may lose no time from the
Work of the Lord. Every moment lost, is a moment that cannot be redeemed
every pleasure that intermingles with the duty of our station is a folly unre-
-deemable & is planted like the seed of a wild flower among our wheat. All
the tortures of repentance. are tortures of self-reproach on account of our lea-
-ving the Divine Harvest to the Enemy, the struggles of intanglement with incoherent roots. I know of no other Christianity and of no other Gospel than
the liberty both of body & mind to exercise the Divine Arts of Imagination.
Imagination the real & eternal World of which this Vegetable Universe is
but a faint shadow & in which we shall live in our Eternal or Imaginative
Bodies, when these Vegetable Mortal Bodies are no more. The Apostles knew
of no other Gospel. What were all their spiritual gifts? What is the Divine
Spirit? is the Holy Ghost any other than an Intellectual Fountain? What is
the Harvest of the Gospel & its Labours? What is that Talent which it is a
curse to hide? What are the Treasures of Heaven which we are to lay up for
ourselves, are they any other than Mental Studies & Performances? What
are all the Gifts of the Gospel, are they not all Mental Gifts? Is God a
Spirit who must be worshipped in Spirit & in Truth and are not the Gifts
of the Spirit Every-thing to Man? O ye Religious discountenance every
one among you who shall pretend to despise Art & Science! I call upon
you in the Name of Jesus! What is the Life of Man but Art & Science?
is it Meat & Drink? is not the Body more than Raiment? What is Mortality
but the things relating to the Body, which Dies? What is Immortality but the
things relating to the Spirit, which Lives Eternally! What is the Joy of Hea-
-ven but Improvement in the things of the Spirit? What are the Pains of Hell
but Ignorance, Bodily Lust, Idleness & devastation of the things of the Spirit
Answer this to yourselves, & expel from among you those who pretend to des-
-pise the labours of Art & Science, which alone are the labours of the Gos-
-pel: Is not this plain & manifest to the thought? Can you think at all, &
not pronounce heartily! That to Labour in Knowledge. is to Build up Jerusa-
-lem: and to Despise Knowledge, is to Despise Jerusalem & her Builders.
And remember: He who despises & mocks a Mental Gift in another; calling
it pride & selfishness & sin; mocks Jesus the giver of every Mental Gift.
which always appear to the ignorance-loving Hypocrite, as Sins. but that
which is a Sin in the sight of cruel Man, is not so in the sight of our kind God.
Let every Christian as much as in him lies engage himself openly & publicly
before all the World in some Mental pursuit for the Building up of Jerusalem

I stood among my valleys of the south
And saw a flame of fire, even as a Wheel
Of fire surrounding all the heavens: it went
From west to east against the current of
Creation, and devourd all things in its loud
Fury & thundering course round heaven & earth
By it the Sun was rolld into an orb:
By it the Moon faded into a globe.
Travelling thro the night; for from its dire
And restless fury, Man himself shrunk up
Into a little root a fathom long.
And I asked a Watcher & a Holy-One
Its Name? he answerd. It is the Wheel of Religion
I wept & said. Is this the law of Jesus
This terrible devouring sword turning every way
He answerd; Jesus died because he strove
Against the current of this Wheel: its Name
Is Caiaphas, the dark Preacher of Death

Of sin, of sorrow, & of punishment:
Opposing Nature! It is Natural Religion
But Jesus is the bright Preacher of Life
Creating Nature from this fiery Law.
By self-denial & forgiveness of Sin:
Go therefore, cast out devils in Christs name
Heal thou the sick of spiritual disease
Pity the evil. for thou art not sent
To smite with terror & with punishments
Those that are sick. like to the Pharisees
Crucifying & encompasing sea & land
For proselytes to tyranny & wrath.
But to the Publicans & Harlots go;
Teach them True Happiness. but let no curse
Go forth out of thy mouth to blight their peace
For Hell is opend to Heaven; thine eyes beheld
The dungeons burst & the Prisoners set free.

England! awake! awake! awake!
Jerusalem thy Sister calls!
Why wilt thou sleep the sleep of death?
And close her from thy ancient walls.

Thy hills & valleys felt her feet.
Gently upon their bosoms move:
Thy gates beheld sweet Zions ways;
Then was a time of joy and love.

And now the time returns again:
Our souls exult & Londons towers.
Recieve the Lamb of God to dwell
In Englands green & pleasant bowers.

Jerusalem 77D

Jerusalem 77. The properly instructed reader (a child, as we must become to enter) of Blake's scroll (clue thread of text) has an active grip on the golden line inside the illuminated cave of text (see *Marriage* 15). She begins beside the cliffs of Dover, Jerusalem's wall, which we have seen from different perspectives in Plates 4, 33, 50. (The analogue of *Night Thoughts* 362 suggests that Blake may have intended a forest originally—note the four trunk-like columns sketched behind the child—but in coloring copy E he confirmed the chalk cliff effect of the uncolored copies; there are similar but more closely spaced cliff lines in Plate 78.) The way in (up) can be seen to involve climbing, beside a mountain stream (of living waters?) (or along the edge of a green hill). But in this homely picture map and in the bare vines bordering the poem below, the absence of any celebration is noteworthy.

(In the rocky corners of the plate bottom, Blake originally inscribed some words of advice about where to recognize "The Real Selfhood" but did not ink them for legibility.)

Jerusalem 78. The final chapter opens with a clue that the night of death "is far spent, the day is at hand" (to quote Romans 13.12). (Yet in E the whole chapter heading is blacked out, as though Blake did not want anybody to be sure.) The sons of Albion are now condensed (from their seven-headed condition of Plate 50) into Hand, with "ravening" beak (see 8:43–9:13; 19:23–24; 78:2–3) and a cock's comb—a signal of the morning (93:26) "eloquent of the Christian symbol upon Church steeples recalling Peter's denial of his Lord and the bitter repentance that was to make him the 'Rock' upon which the church itself was founded" (W). On the rocky cliff of Albion he sits, like St John on the Isle of Patmos awaiting the apocalypse (Mitchell), disconsolate but eying us closely, across the water from a large, brown-rayed sun, plainly the setting material sun—a signal for the rising of a more bright sun. Duality is gently indicated also by the tendril which, growing out of the *g* in "viewing Jerusalem" (10), splits westward into the text (extended almost all across in E) and eastward and down the margin for adornment (but as seaweed, a vegetable polypus suggestion).

Only two birds fly (in the second paragraph break), for Jerusalem's giants are, almost everywhere, in chains.

In the painting of E a sort of webbing between Hand and the rock (or an ugly growth on his right hip) has been removed.

Jerusalem 78^D^

My tents are fall'n! my pillars are in ruins! my children dashd
Upon Egypts iron floors, & the marble pavements of Assyria;
I melt my soul in reasonings among the towers of Heshbon;
Mount Zion is become a cruel rock & no more dew
Nor rain: no more the spring of the rock appears: but cold
Hard & obdurate are the furrows of the mountain of wine & oil:
The mountain of blessing is itself a curse & an astonishment:
The hills of Judea are fallen with me into the deepest hell
Away from the Nations of the Earth, & from the Cities of the Nations;
I walk to Ephraim. I seek for Shiloh: I walk like a lost sheep
Among precipices of despair: in Goshen I seek for light
In vain: and in Gilead for a physician and a comforter.
Goshen hath follow'd Philistea: Gilead hath join'd with Og!
They are become narrow places in a little and dark land:
How distant far from Albion: his hills & his valleys no more
Recieve the feet of Jerusalem: they have cast me quite away:
And Albion is himself shrunk to a narrow rock in the midst of the sea!
The plains of Sussex & Surrey. their hills of flocks & herds
No more seek to Jerusalem nor to the sound of my Holy-ones.
The Fifty-two Counties of England are hardend against me
As if I was not their Mother, they despise me & cast me out
London coverd the whole Earth. England encompassd the Nations:
And all the Nations of the Earth were seen in the Cities of Albion:
My pillars reachd from sea to sea: London beheld me come
From my east & from my west: he blessed me and gave
His children to my breasts. his sons & daughters to my knees
His aged parents sought me out in every city & village:
They discernd my countenance with joy: they shewd me to their sons
Saying Lo Jerusalem is here! she sitteth in our secret chambers
Levi and Judah & Issachar: Ephram. Manasseh. Gad and Dan.
Are seen in our hills & valleys: they keep our flocks & herds:
They watch them in the night: and the Lamb of God appears among us
The river Severn stayd his course at my command:
Thames poured his waters into my basons and baths:
Medway mingled with Kishon: Thames recievd the heavenly Jordan
Albion gave me to the whole Earth to walk up & down; to pour
Joy upon every mountain; to teach songs to the shepherd & plowman
I taught the ships of the sea to sing the songs of Zion.
Italy saw me, in sublime astonishment: France was wholly mine:
As my garden & as my secret bath; Spain was my heavenly couch:
I slept in his golden hills: the Lamb of God met me there.
There we walked as in our secret chamber among our little ones
They looked upon our loves with joy: they beheld our secret joys:
With holy raptures of adoration rapd sublime in the Visions of God.
Germany. Poland & the North wooed my footsteps they found
My gates in all their mountains & my curtains in all their vales
The furniture of their houses was the furniture of my chamber
Turkey & Grecia saw my instrments of music. they arose
They seizd the harp: the flute: the mellow horn of Jerusalems joy
They sounded thanksgivings in my courts: Egypt & Lybia heard
The swarthy sons of Ethiopia stood round the Lamb of God
Enquiring for Jerusalem: he led them up my steps to my altar:
And thou America! I once beheld thee but now behold no more
Thy golden mountains where my Cherubim & Seraphim rejoicd
Together among my little-ones. But now, my Altars run with blood:
My fires are corrupt, my incense is a cloudy pestilence
Of seven diseases! Once a continual cloud of salvation. rose
From all my myriads; once the Four-fold World rejoicd among
The pillars of Jerusalem, between my winged Cherubim:
But now I am closd out from them in the narrow passages
Of the valleys of destruction. into a dark land of pitch & bitumen.
From Albions Tomb afar and from the four-fold wonders of God
Shrunk to a narrow doleful form in the dark land of Cabul;
There is Reuben & Gad & Joseph & Judah & Levi, closd up
In narrow vales: I walk & count the bones of my beloveds
Along the Valley of Destruction, among these Druid Temples
Which overspread all the Earth in patriarchal pomp & cruel pride
Tell me O Vala thy purposes; tell me wherefore thy shuttles
Drop with the gore of the slain; why Euphrates is red with blood
Wherefore in dreadful majesty & beauty outside appears
Thy Masculine from thy Feminine hardening against the heavens
To devour the Human! Why dost thou weep upon the wind among
These cruel Druid Temples: O Vala! Humanity is far above
Sexual organization; & the Visions of the Night of Beulah
Where Sexes wander in dreams of bliss among the Emanations
Where the Masculine & Feminine are nursd into Youth & Maiden
By the tears & smiles of Beulahs Daughters till the time of Sleep is past.
Wherefore then do you realize these nets of beauty & delusion
In open day to draw the souls of the Dead into the light.
Till Albion is shut out from every Nation under Heaven.

Jerusalem 79D

Jerusalem 79. Jerusalem's lament is piteous but recalls Edenic joys. The marginal foliage, lacking supporting vines, yet manages some fine full grape leaves, one growing on "Druid Temples" (66), another on a reference to America unbeheld (53), and at length, between two dark green leaves, a reddish cluster of ripe grapes, above which soars a pale green bird of paradise, the shape of the birds in *Songs* 1 and 5 but singing, as the two doves in Plate 61. Near the top a distant hawk is sketched. (This plate matches 48 and 61 in adornment but not in script.)

Jerusalem 80. In the right margin Cambel and Gwendolen, daughters who replace Vala henceforth, are repeating their mother's visceral activities but with a hopeful difference. Whereas Vala, on Plate 24, lured human forms into her vermiform veil, Cambel (at page bottom) after much labor "In the Furnaces of Los & in the Wine-press [of Luvah] treading day & night Naked among the human clusters" (82:64–65)—which earns her the bright green grape leaf dangling from her knee (one of the unattached leaves of Plate 79)—is striving to generate a human form. She holds up a small worm-like object in her left hand, wrapped in swaddling cloth. It is a poor start on the humanizing of her lover, Hand, but enough to convert her sister Gwendolen, who "saw the Infant in her sisters arms" (82:72) and joined the group who "give their souls away in the Furnaces of affliction" (82:79) under Los's discipline. She too has her grape-leaf badge, not very firmly attached; her lover, Hyle, already a large long worm, is beginning to develop a head outside the veil and a back that gives us a new recognition of the almost human backs on two of the dragon forms in Plate 75. Seeing this beginning of a change of the worm "into a form of love by tears & pain," other sisters join—to Los's great comfort (82:76–80).

Cambel kneels near "Skiddaws snow" (74); Gwendolen steps off from the "Plain of Salisbury" (49).

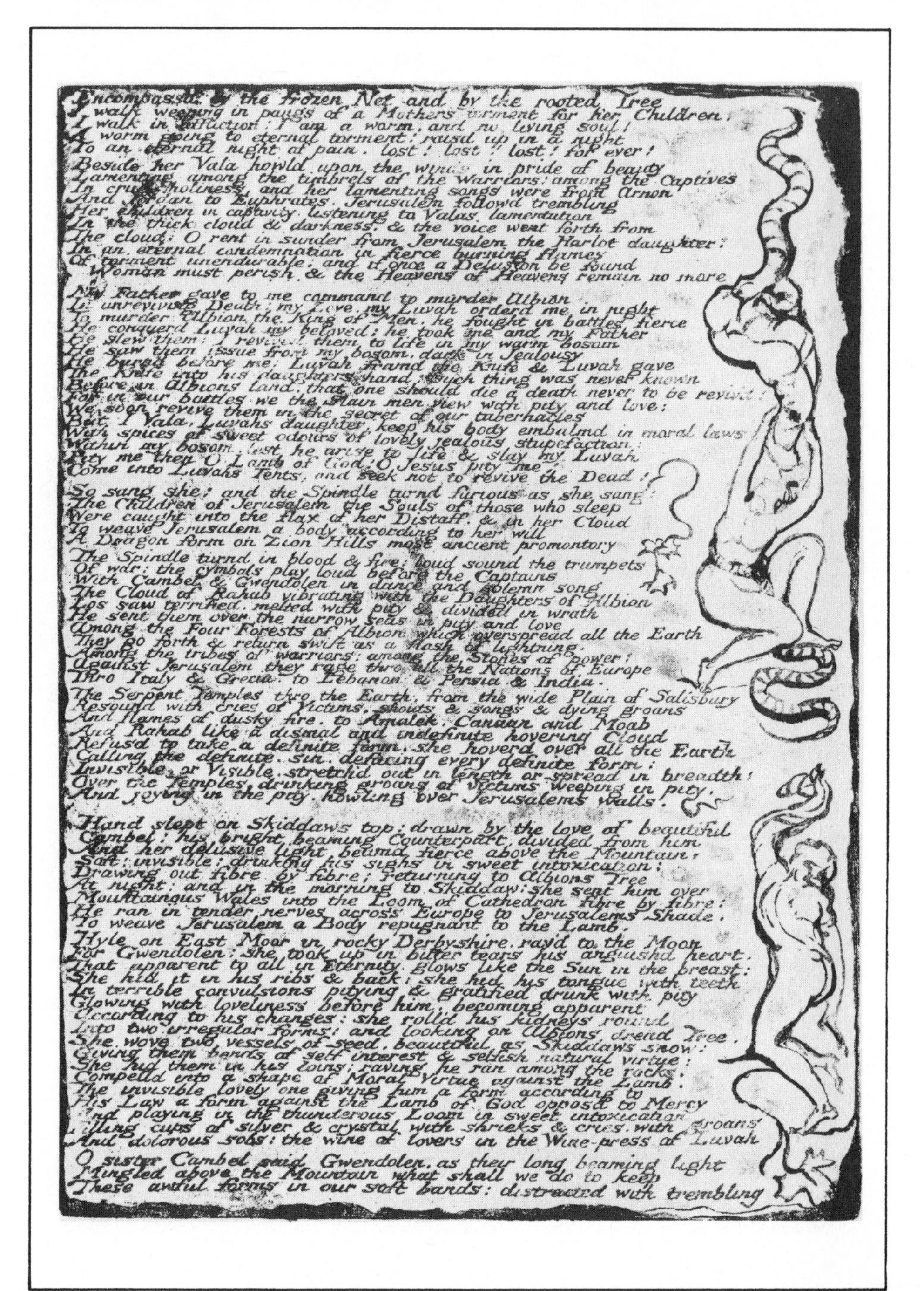

Encompassd by the frozen Net and by the rooted Tree
I walk weeping in pangs of a Mothers torment for her Children:
I walk in affliction: I am a worm, and no living soul!
A worm going to eternal torment! raisd up in a night
To an eternal night of pain. lost! lost! lost! for ever!
Beside her Vala howld upon the winds in pride of beauty
Lamenting among the timbrels of the Warriors: among the Captives
In cruel holiness, and her lamenting songs were from Arnon
And Jordan to Euphrates. Jerusalem followd trembling
Her children in captivity. listening to Valas lamentation
In the thick cloud & darkness. & the voice went forth from
The cloud. O rent in sunder from Jerusalem the Harlot daughter!
In an eternal condemnation in fierce burning flames
Of torment unendurable: and if once a Delusion be found
Woman must perish & the Heavens of Heavens remain no more

My Father gave to me command to murder Albion
In unreviving Death; my Love, my Luvah orderd me in night
To murder Albion the King of Men. he fought in battles fierce
He conquerd Luvah my beloved: he took me and my Father
He slew them: I revived them to life in my warm bosom
He saw them issue from my bosom, dark in Jealousy
He burnd before me: Luvah framd the Knife & Luvah gave
The Knife into his daughters hand! such thing was never known
Before in Albions land. that one should die a death never to be reviv'd!
For in our battles we the Slain men view with pity and love:
We soon revive them in the secret of our tabernacles
But I Vala, Luvahs daughter, keep his body embalmd in moral laws
With spices of sweet odours of lovely jealous stupefaction:
Within my bosom. lest he arise to life & slay my Luvah
Pity me then O Lamb of God! O Jesus pity me!
Come into Luvahs Tents, and seek not to revive the Dead!

So sang she: and the Spindle turnd furious as she sang:
The Children of Jerusalem the Souls of those who sleep
Were caught into the flax of her Distaff. & in her Cloud
To weave Jerusalem a body according to her will
A Dragon form on Zion Hills most ancient promontory
The Spindle turnd in blood & fire: loud sound the trumpets
Of war: the cymbals play loud before the Captains
With Cambel & Gwendolen in dance and solemn song
The Cloud of Rahab vibrating with the Daughters of Albion
Los saw terrified. melted with pity & divided in wrath
He sent them over the narrow seas in pity and love
Among the Four Forests of Albion which overspread all the Earth
They go forth & return swift as a flash of lightning.
Among the tribes of warriors: among the Stones of power;
Against Jerusalem they rage thro all the Nations of Europe
Thro Italy & Grecia: to Lebanon & Persia & India.
The Serpent Temples thro the Earth, from the wide Plain of Salisbury
Resound with cries of Victims, shouts & songs & dying groans
And flames of dusky fire. to Amalek, Canaan and Moab
And Rahab like a dismal and indefinite hovering Cloud
Refusd to take a definite form. she hoverd over all the Earth
Calling the definite, sin. defacing every definite form:
Invisible, or Visible. stretchd out in length or spread in breadth:
Over the Temples drinking groans of victims weeping in pity,
And joying in the pity. howling over Jerusalems walls.

Hand slept on Skiddaws top: drawn by the love of beautiful
Cambel: his bright beaming Counterpart, divided from him
And her delusive light beamd fierce above the Mountain,
Soft: invisible: drinking his sighs in sweet intoxication:
Drawing out fibre by fibre: returning to Albions Tree
At night: and in the morning to Skiddaw: she sent him over
Mountainous Wales into the Loom of Cathedron fibre by fibre:
He ran in tender nerves across Europe to Jerusalems Shade:
To weave Jerusalem a Body repugnant to the Lamb.
Hyle on East Moor in rocky Derbyshire, ravd to the Moon
For Gwendolen: she took up in bitter tears his anguishd heart.
That apparent to all in Eternity. glows like the Sun in the breast:
She hid it in his ribs & back: she hid his tongue with teeth
In terrible convulsions pitying & gratified drunk with pity
Glowing with loveliness before him, becoming apparent
According to his changes: she rolld his kidneys round
Into two irregular forms: and looking on Albions dread Tree.
She wove two vessels of seed, beautiful as Skiddaws snow:
Giving them bends of self interest & selfish natural virtue:
She hid them in his loins; raving he ran among the rocks.
Compelld into a shape of Moral Virtue against the Lamb.
The invisible lovely one giving him a form according to
His Law a form against the Lamb of God opposd to Mercy
And playing in the thunderous Loom in sweet intoxication
Filling cups of silver & crystal with shrieks & cries. with groans
And dolorous sobs: the wine of lovers in the Wine-press of Luvah

O sister Cambel said Gwendolen, as their long beaming light
Mingled above the Mountain what shall we do to keep
These awful forms in our soft bands: distracted with trembling

Jerusalem 80D

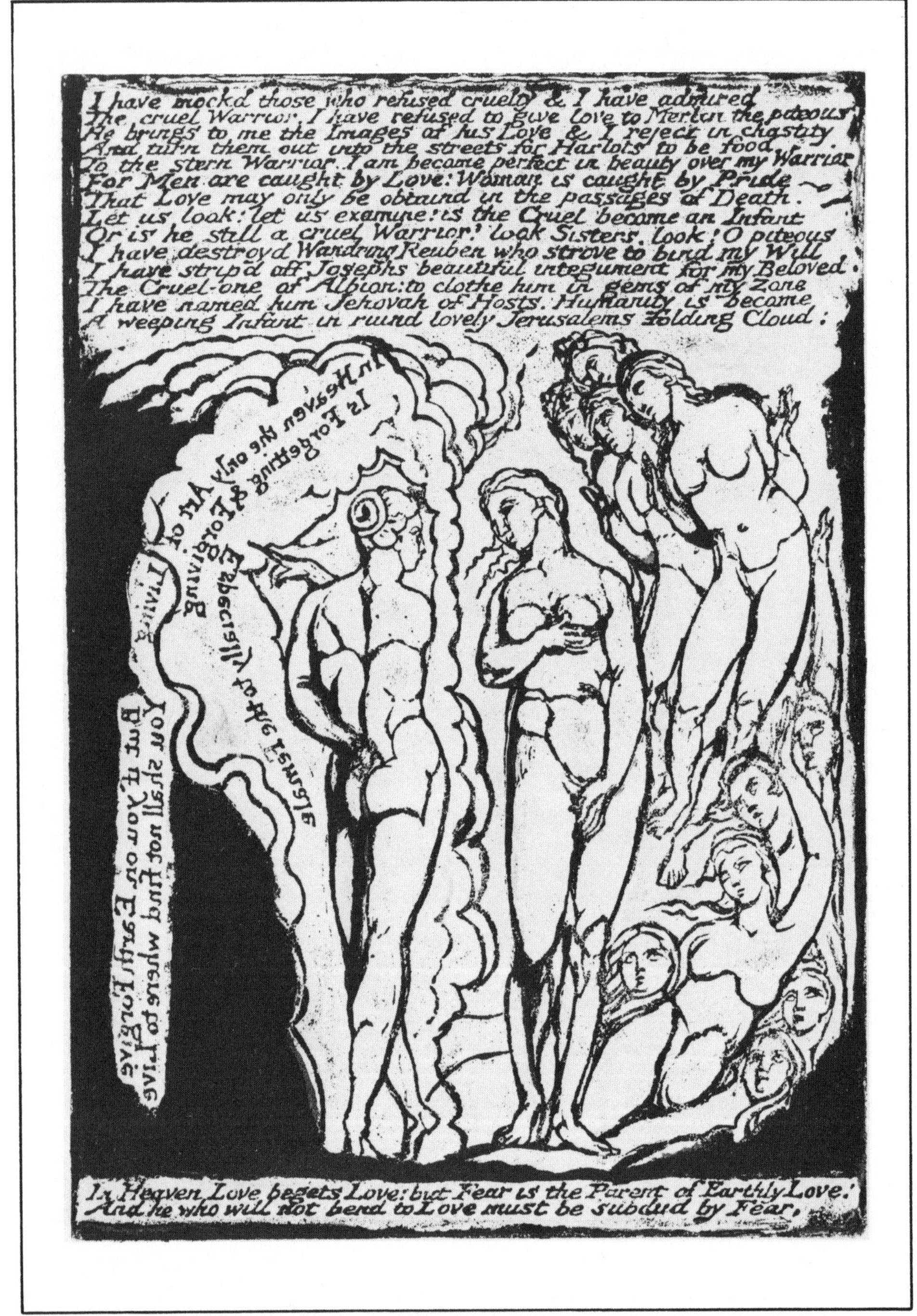

Jerusalem 81D

Jerusalem 81. Gwendolen, Cambel, and the other ten daughters of Albion are shown in an argument-temptation scene (described in 82:10–21) that descends from the confrontation in Plate 46 of Vala and Jerusalem and her three children. This scene precedes the conversion to unselfish action in Los's furnaces and Luvah's wine-press described later in Plate 82 but pictured in Plate 80. (Before we seek deep meanings in this arrangement, we may notice that the text on Plate 82 does not leave the width of margin needed for the pictures on Plate 80.)

Gwendolen, her hair drawn up in a Psyche knot and her legs crossed, holds a "falshood" in her left hand, out of her sisters' sight, and gives Sibylline advice (in mirror writing) to Cambel amounting to cruel accusations of Sin. The cloud column in which she stands, a vortex with its own internal patches of sky, is both visceral and vermicular. Cambel, fallen into shame as Jerusalem was not, stands in the attitude of Venus in Blake's *Judgment of Paris.* (Her locks are loose, as are Venus' there, while Juno has short hair and her hand behind her, holding a helmet: one might otherwise conjecture that the falsehood held by Gwendolen is that apple of contention.)

The four sisters who stand in the air, like the upward-pointing daughter of Jerusalem in Plate 46, appear credulous (throwing up their hands) and falling. The six other sisters seem already fallen, and since two have arms raised as that daughter of Jerusalem and all lie in a vortex of flame that begins under the feet of Cambel, we must come to realize of them that "they saw the Furnaces opend" (82:78) from afar off and did not wait to be called. The point of course is that the falsehood, as we come to expect of worldly wisdom, is only the truth turned inside out. It consists of the second half of Gwendolen's quatrain in mirror writing, "But if you on Earth Forgive, You shall not find where to Live." The true message? If you want to live in heaven, then start "Forgetting & Forgiving," which "In Heaven [is] the only Art of Living"—the first half of the quatrain. (The second half is almost completely painted out in E: Blake hiding the falsehood so that we are safe with the remainder read ironically or straight.) Her line of comment, "Especially to the Female," marks her false feminism.

Jerusalem 82. Human form is now none: a seven-curved worm (counting each double curve including the small ones at the bottom: these would be the loops or coils if it curled up) tells the story of mortal futility. This is what Gwendolen's lover Hyle looks like before her conversion. Its discovery involves her drawing aside "her Veil from Mam-Tor to Dovedale" (45), "clearly symbols of her feminine parts" (W). This is another nadir and turning-point image; shortly both sisters get drawn into the efforts pictured on Plate 80, to form, with Los's help, "the Worm into a form of love by tears & pain" (76).

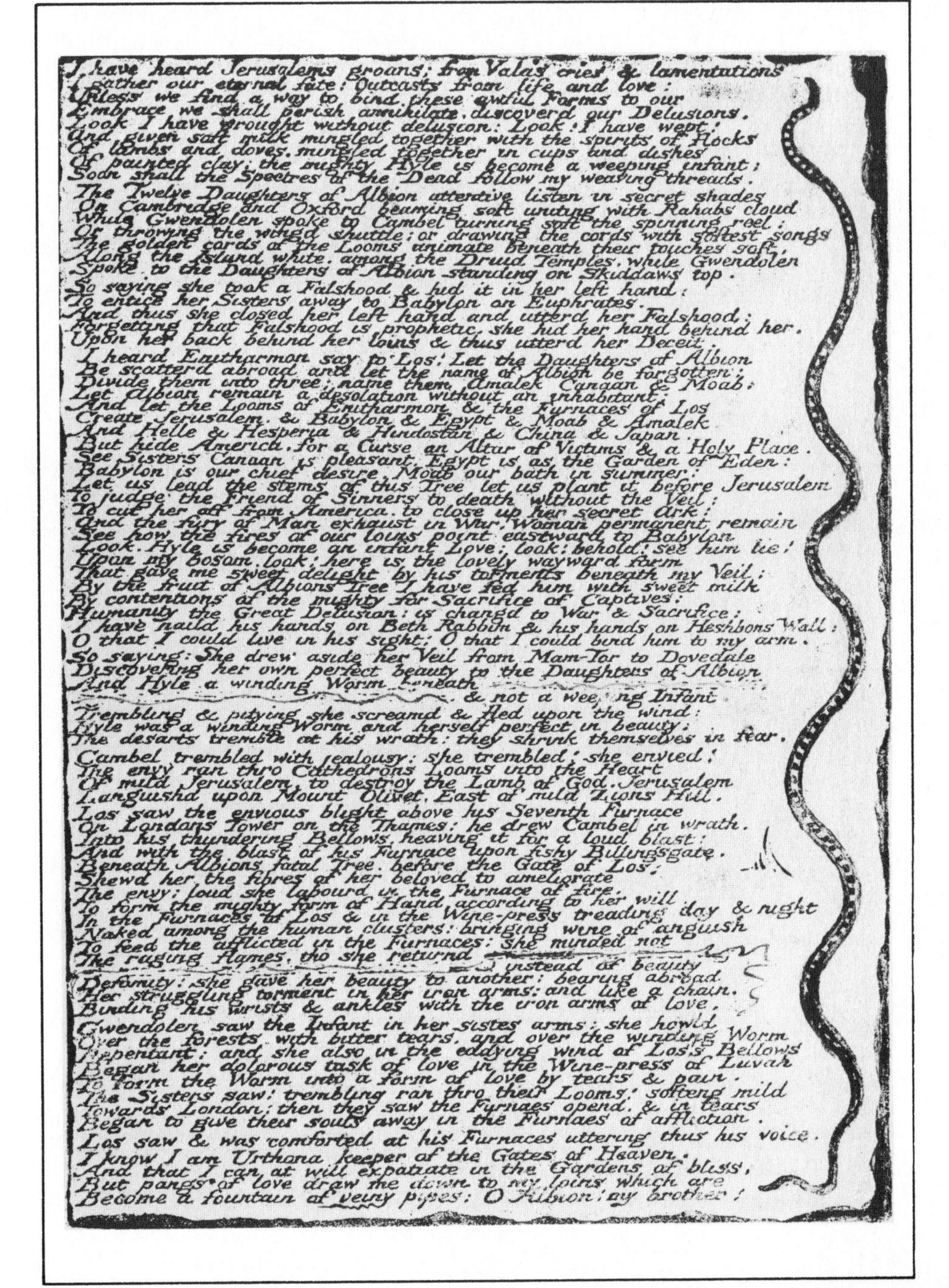
I have heard Jerusalems groans; from Valas cries & lamentations
I gather our eternal fate: Outcasts from life and love:
Unless we find a way to bind these awful Forms to our
Embrace we shall perish annihilate, discoverd our Delusions.
Look I have wrought without delusion: Look! I have wept!
And given soft milk mingled together with the spirits of flocks
Of lambs and doves, mingled together in cups and dishes
Of painted clay; the mighty Hyle is become a weeping infant;
Soon shall the Spectres of the Dead follow my weaving threads.
The Twelve Daughters of Albion attentive listen in secret shades
On Cambridge and Oxford beaming soft uniting with Rahabs cloud
While Gwendolen spoke to Cambel turning soft the spinning reel;
Or throwing the wingd shuttle; or drawing the cords with softest songs
The golden cords of the Looms animate beneath their touches soft,
Along the Island white, among the Druid Temples, while Gwendolen
Spoke to the Daughters of Albion standing on Skiddaws top.
So saying she took a Falshood & hid it in her left hand:
To entice her Sisters away to Babylon on Euphrates.
And thus she closed her left hand and utterd her Falshood;
Forgetting that Falshood is prophetic, she hid her hand behind her.
Upon her back behind her loins & thus utterd her Deceit.
I heard Enitharmon say to Los: Let the Daughters of Albion
Be scatterd abroad and let the name of Albion be forgotten:
Divide them into three; name them Amalek Canaan & Moab:
Let Albion remain a desolation without an inhabitant:
And let the Looms of Enitharmon & the Furnaces of Los
Create Jerusalem, & Babylon & Egypt & Moab & Amalek
And Helle & Hesperia & Hindostan & China & Japan.
But hide America, for a Curse an Altar of Victims & a Holy Place.
See Sisters Canaan is pleasant, Egypt is as the Garden of Eden:
Babylon is our chief desire, Moab our bath in summer:
Let us lead the stems of this Tree let us plant it before Jerusalem
To judge the Friend of Sinners to death without the Veil:
To cut her off from America, to close up her secret Ark:
And the fury of Man exhaust in War; Woman permanent remain
See how the fires of our loins point eastward to Babylon
Look. Hyle is become an infant Love; look! behold! see him lie!
Upon my bosom. look! here is the lovely wayward form
That gave me sweet delight by his torments beneath my Veil;
By the fruit of Albions Tree I have fed him with sweet milk
By contentions of the mighty for Sacrifice of Captives:
Humanity the Great Delusion: is changd to War & Sacrifice;
I have naild his hands on Beth Rabbim & his hands on Heshbons Wall:
O that I could live in his sight: O that I could bind him to my arm.
So saying: She drew aside her Veil from Mam-Tor to Dovedale
Discovering her own perfect beauty to the Daughters of Albion
And Hyle a winding Worm beneath
& not a wee[illegible]ng Infant
Trembling & pitying she screamd & fled upon the wind:
Hyle was a winding Worm and herself perfect in beauty:
The desarts tremble at his wrath: they shrink themselves in fear.
Cambel trembled with jealousy: she trembled! she envied!
The envy ran thro Cathedrons Looms into the Heart
Of mild Jerusalem, to destroy the Lamb of God. Jerusalem
Languishd upon Mount Olivet, East of mild Zions Hill.
Los saw the envious blight above his Seventh Furnace
On Londons Tower on the Thames: he drew Cambel in wrath.
Into his thundering Bellows, heaving it for a loud blast:
And with the blast of his Furnace upon fishy Billingsgate.
Beneath Albions fatal Tree. before the Gate of Los:
Shewd her the fibres of her beloved to ameliorate
The envy: loud she labourd in the Furnace of fire.
To form the mighty form of Hand according to her will
In the Furnaces of Los & in the Wine-press treading day & night
Naked among the human clusters: bringing wine of anguish
To feed the afflicted in the Furnaces: she minded not
The raging flames, tho she returnd
instead of beauty
Deformity: she gave her beauty to another: bearing abroad
Her struggling torment in her iron arms: and like a chain.
Binding his wrists & ankles with the iron arms of love.
Gwendolen saw the Infant in her sisters arms; she howld
Over the forests with bitter tears, and over the winding Worm
Repentant: and she also in the eddying wind of Los's Bellows
Began her dolorous task of love in the Wine-press of Luvah
To form the Worm into a form of love by tears & pain.
The Sisters saw: trembling ran thro their Looms; softening mild
Towards London: then they saw the Furnaes opend, & in tears
Began to give their souls away in the Furnaes of affliction.
Los saw & was comforted at his Furnaces uttering thus his voice.
I know I am Urthona keeper of the Gates of Heaven,
And that I can at will expatiate in the Gardens of bliss,
But pangs of love draw me down to my loins which are
Become a fountain of veiny pipes: O Albion! my brother!

Jerusalem 82[D]

Corruptibility appears upon thy limbs, and never more
Can I arise and leave thy side, but labour here incessant
Till thy awaking! yet alas I shall forget Eternity!
Against the Patriarchal pomp and cruelty, labouring incessant
I shall become an Infant horror: Enion! Tharmas! friends
Absorb me not in such dire grief: O Albion, my brother!
Jerusalem hungers in the desart! affection to her children!
The scorn'd and contemnd youthful girl, where shall she fly?
Sussex shuts up her Villages. Hants, Devon & Wilts
Surrounded with masses of stone in orderd forms, determine then
A form for Vala and a form for Luvah, here on the Thames
Where the Victim nightly howls beneath the Druids knife:
A Form of Vegetation, nail them down on the stems of Mystery:
O when shall the Saxon return with the English his redeemed brother!
O when shall the Lamb of God descend among the Reprobate!
I woo to Amalek to protect my fugitives Amalek trembles:
I call to Canaan & Moab in my night watches, they mourn:
They listen not to my cry, they rejoice among their warriors
Woden and Thor and Friga wholly consume my Saxons:
On their enormous Altars built in the terrible north:
From Irelands rocks to Scandinavia Persia and Tartary:
From the Atlantic Sea to the universal Erythrean.
Found ye London! enormous City! weeps thy River?
Upon his parent bosom lay thy little ones O Land
Forsaken. Surrey and Sussex are Enitharmons Chamber.
Where I will build her a Couch of repose & my pillars
Shall surround her in beautiful labyrinths: Oothoon!
Where hides my child? in Oxford hidest thou with Antamon?
In graceful hidings of error: in merciful deceit
Lest Hand the terrible destroy his Affection, thou hidest her:
In chaste appearances for sweet deceits of love & modesty
Immingled, interwoven, glistening to the sickening sight.
Let Cambel and her Sisters sit within the Mundane Shell:
Forming the fluctuating Globe according to their will.
According as they weave the little embryon nerves & veins
The Eye, the little Nostrils, & the delicate Tongue & Ears
Of labyrinthine intricacy: so shall they fold the World
That whatever is seen upon the Mundane Shell, the same
Be seen upon the Fluctuating Earth woven by the Sisters.
And sometimes the Earth shall roll in the Abyss & sometimes
Stand in the Center & sometimes stretch flat in the Expanse,
According to the will of the lovely Daughters of Albion.
Sometimes it shall assimilate with mighty Golgonooza:
Touching its summits: & sometimes divided roll apart.
As a beautiful Veil so these Females shall fold & unfold
According to their will the outside surface of the Earth
An outside shadowy Surface superadded to the real Surface;
Which is unchangeable for ever & ever Amen: so be it!
Separate Albions Sons gently from their Emanations,
Weaving bowers of delight on the current of infant Thames
Where the old Parent still retains his youth as I alas!
Retain my youth eight thousand and five hundred years.
The labourer of ages in the Valleys of Despair!
The land is markd for desolation & unless we plant
The seeds of Cities & of Villages in the Human bosom
Albion must be a rock of blood: mark ye the points
Where Cities shall remain & where Villages for the rest:
It must lie in confusion till Albions time of awaking.
Place the Tribes of Llewellyn in America for a hiding place!
Till sweet Jerusalem emanates again into Eternity
The night falls thick: I go upon my watch: be attentive:
The Sons of Albion go forth; I follow from my Furnaces:
That they return no more: that a place be prepard on Euphrates
Listen to your Watchmans voice: sleep not before the Furnaces
Eternal Death stands at the door. O God pity our labours.

So Los spoke to the Daughters of Beulah while his Emanation
Like a faint rainbow waved before him in the awful gloom
Of London City on the Thames from Surrey Hills to Highgate:
Swift turn the silver spindles, & the golden weights play soft
And lulling harmonies beneath the Looms, from Caithness in the north
To Lizard-point & Dover in the south: his Emanation
Joy'd in the many weaving threads in bright Cathedrons Dome
Weaving the Web of life for Jerusalem. the Web of life
Down flowing into Entuthons Vales glistens with soft affections.

While Los arose upon his Watch, and down from Golgonooza
Putting on his golden sandals to walk from mountain to mountain,
He takes his way, girding himself with gold & in his hand
Holding his iron mace: The Spectre remains attentive
Alternate they watch in night: alternate labour in day
Before the Furnaces labouring. while Los all night watches
The stars rising & setting, & the meteors & terrors of night.
With him went down the Dogs of Leutha. at his feet
They lap the water of the trembling Thames then follow swift
And thus he heard the voice of Albions daughters on Euphrates.

Our Father Albions land: O it was a lovely land! & the Daughters of Be
Walked up and down in its green mountains: but Hand is fled
Away: & mighty Hyle: & after them Jerusalem is gone: Awake

Jerusalem 83[D]

Jerusalem 83. The visceral clouds in the right margin remind us we are still in Vala's world. The small figure beside the word "alas!" (51) sits stiff-legged and seems blindfolded, with hands tied behind his back (redrawn in E; see below). The larger, naked figure above, with head missing or buried in the cloud, recalls the headless (but worm-headed) body in the same position in Plate 74 and the victim in Plate 66. The body forming in the worm-form of Hyle on Plate 80 is in the same position on the page, and if we take Plate 83 as the constructive side of the bare worm of Plate 82 we may join Los in taking some comfort (82:80) even though Hyle has now lost his head again. A sign that we are meant to do so may be the redrawing[E] of the smaller figure, with his hands moved to his lap and his legs relaxed against the curve of the cloud. This is hardly Los, but perhaps another of the small figures that seem to be plain William Blake; for the tremendous significance of his hands, see Plates 36 and 49.

In copy D the vine-like ironwork at the bottom, not repeated in other copies, is somewhat like the briar-binding on freshly buried coffins, as in *Songs* 44. Can it have been prompted by some personal loss, the death of William Hayley (incorporated into Blake's myth as Hyle) in 1820?

❧

Jerusalem 84. "I see London, blind & age-bent begging thro the Streets Of Babylon, led by a child," say the lamenting daughters of Albion uniting with Rahab; "his tears run down his beard" (11–12). We do not see tears; we see several very hopeful things: a little child who shall lead London, on crutches, past the Roman-Babylonian church (of which the portal is hidden by the child's body) toward the door of the Gothic church. (Compare the door in Plate 1 and the domed and spired churches on the opposite sides of Plate 46.) Looking again at the similar picture in "London" (*Songs* 46) we see that they have passed Death's Door and are turning a corner. (If that is a remnant of a Druid trilithon behind the boy's guiding arm, it exerts no pull.)

Yet now the two churches side by side, with "the curtains of night . . . drawn back" (W) to illuminate the cross on St Paul's, suggest an amalgamation. Entrance must be through the Gothic door, but the cross marks the whole edifice—and in copy E a sun of gold is rising above a hill behind the three[E] leftward spires that sends its beams to a cloud-edge exactly above the cross: the prophetic message is the same as that of Plate 76, the transformation of crucifixion into resurrection, the Druid and Christian churches becoming one.

Four lines are erased from the plate after line 16; in D the space is filled by seven double curves of intertwining vines; in E by a sort of willow branch.

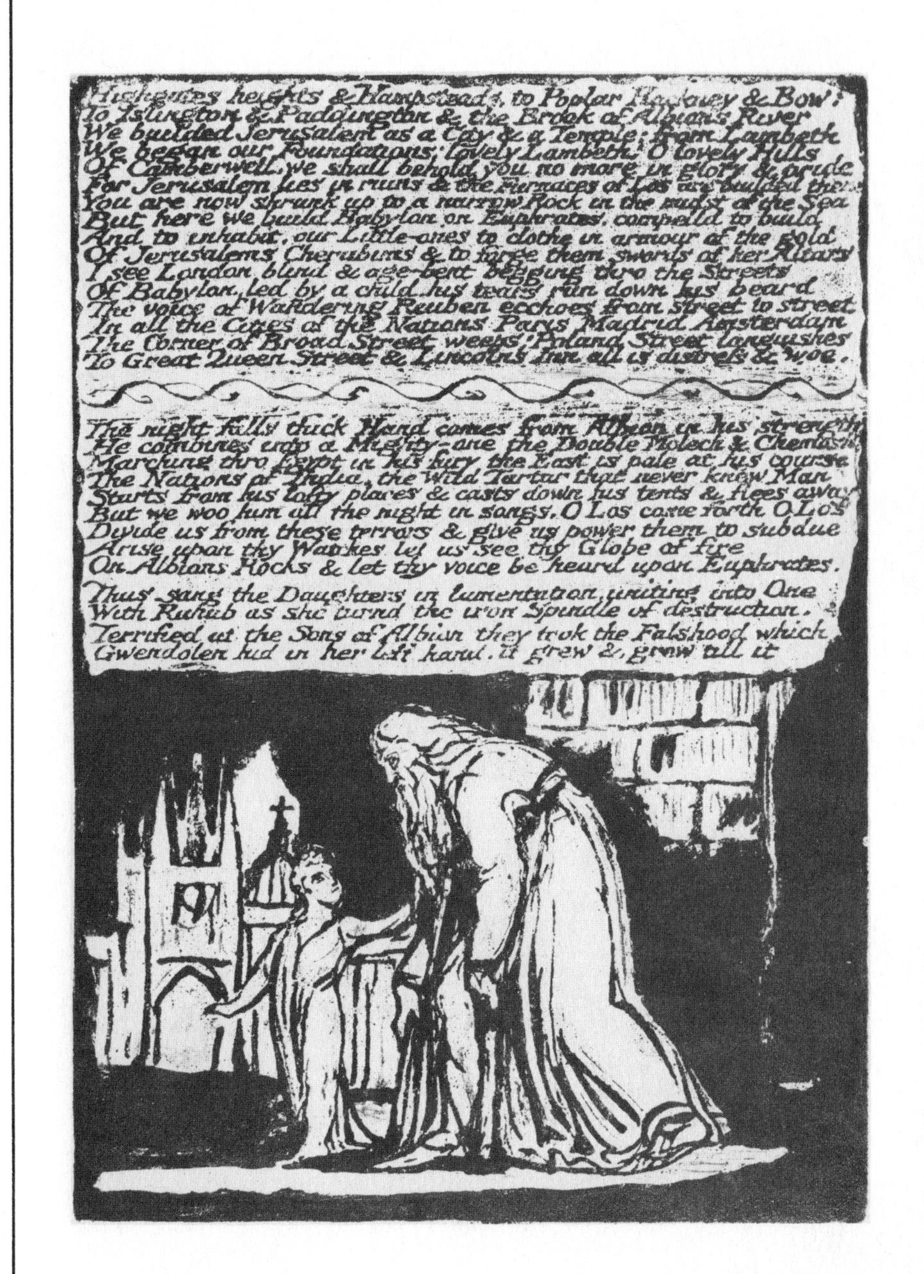
Highgates heights & Hampsteads, to Poplar Hackney & Bow:
To Islington & Paddington & the Brook of Albions River
We builded Jerusalem as a City & a Temple; from Lambeth
We began our Foundations; lovely Lambeth! O lovely Hills
Of Camberwell, we shall behold you no more in glory & pride
For Jerusalem lies in ruins & the Furnaces of Los are builded there
You are now shrunk up to a narrow Rock in the midst of the Sea
But here we build Babylon on Euphrates, compelld to build
And to inhabit. our Little-ones to clothe in armour of the gold
Of Jerusalems Cherubims & to forge them swords of her Altars
I see London blind & age-bent begging thro the Streets
Of Babylon, led by a child. his tears run down his beard
The voice of Wandering Reuben ecchoes from street to street
In all the Cities of the Nations Paris Madrid Amsterdam
The Corner of Broad Street weeps; Poland Street languishes
To Great Queen Street & Lincolns Inn all is distress & woe.

The night falls thick Hand comes from Albion in his strength
He combines into a Mighty-one the Double Molech & Chemosh
Marching thro Egypt in his fury the East is pale at his course
The Nations of India, the Wild Tartar that never knew Man
Starts from his lofty places & casts down his tents & flees away
But we woo him all the night in songs. O Los come forth O Los
Divide us from these terrors & give us power them to subdue
Arise upon thy Watches let us see thy Globe of fire
On Albions Rocks & let thy voice be heard upon Euphrates.

Thus sang the Daughters in lamentation, uniting into One
With Rahab as she turnd the iron Spindle of destruction.
Terrified at the Sons of Albion they took the Falshood which
Gwendolen hid in her left hand. it grew & grew till it

Jerusalem 84[D]

Became a Space & an Allegory around the Winding Worm
They namd it Canaan & built for it a tender Moon
Los smild with joy thinking on Enitharmon & he brought
Reuben from his twelvefold wandrings & led him into it
Planting the Seeds of the Twelve Tribes & Moses & David
And gave a Time & Revolution to the Space Six Thousand Years
He calld it Divine Analogy, for in Beulah the Feminine
Emanations Create Space. the Masculine Create Time, & plant
The Seeds of beauty in the Space: listning to their lamentation
Los walks upon his ancient Mountains in the deadly darkness
Among his Furnaces directing his laborious Myriads watchful
Looking to the East: & his voice is heard over the whole Earth
As he watches the Furnaces by night, & directs the labourers

And thus Los replies upon his Watch: the Valleys listen silent:
The Stars stand still to hear: Jerusalem & Vala cease to mourn:
His voice is heard from Albion: the Alps & Appenines
Listen: Hermon & Lebanon bow their crowned heads
Babel & Shinar look toward the Western Gate, they sit down
Silent at his voice: they view the red Globe of fire in Los's hand
As he walks from Furnace to Furnace directing the Labourers
And this is the Song of Los: the Song that he sings on his Watch

O lovely mild Jerusalem! O Shiloh of Mount Ephraim!
I see thy Gates of precious stones: thy Walls of gold & silver
Thou art the soft reflected Image of the Sleeping Man
Who stretchd on Albions rocks reposes amidst his Twenty-eight
Cities: where Beulah lovely terminates, in the hills & valleys of Albion
Cities not yet embodied in Time and Space: plant ye
The Seeds O Sisters in the bosom of Time & Spaces womb
To spring up for Jerusalem: lovely Shadow of Sleeping Albion
Why wilt thou rend thyself apart & build an Earthly Kingdom
To reign in pride & to opress & to mix the Cup of Delusion
O thou that dwellest with Babylon! Come forth O lovely-one

Jerusalem 85[D]

Jerusalem 85. "Plant ye the Seeds" (27–28), Los now urges the daughters. There follow several pages of discussion with Enitharmon about the collaboration necessary for true converse—argument rather than quarrel, for they have reached the modus vivendi shown here. He insists upon her accepting his "Fibres of dominion" (88:13); she has her own plans, which amount to jealousy of Jerusalem: Enitharmon resists becoming the Jerusalem named Liberty who will rejoice in his free "Human Four-fold" expression "in thunders of Intellect" (88:7). Presumably she wishes to plant flowers (in E the vines running down from her breasts—out of sight because her back is turned—reach the ground and send rooty fibres along under both bodies) rather than ripen the harvest grapes for *Jerusalem*.

Los pleads that his love and admiration for Enitharmon so warm his blood that unless she seizes his "wild fibres" (which shoot from his heart and loins, conveying his blood and glandous wine: see *Song of Los* 7:38) they will rapidly enroot and hide him from sight (compare the enrooting figures in Plates 15, 50, 71, 74). To have vines to weave she must seize his fibres with her hands and infuse them with "milky Love" from her breasts (87:3–11; 88:24–29). (These intermingling creators are symbolically more elemental than the figures of William and Catherine Blake in Plate 38, who work with their hands in the illuminated-printing house.)

The page must be seen in color[E] for the full picture of the symmetries of their collaboration and disharmony and for its rainbow promise of the "reunification not only of the masculine and the feminine and the sublime and the pathetic, but also of day and night and line and color," which Edward Rose finds in Plate 100 (Edward J. Rose in *Criticism* xiii [1971] 65). On the vine that marks Los's song, in mid page, only the leaves on the left side are colored; those on Enitharmon's side are left blank. The sulfur sun is on her side, and though it is still web-bound (W) its color flows up into Los's song and pours downward a rainbow of orange and yellow through pink and violet to green (coloring the whole strip of grass) and blue (in the sky on his side, in the foreground suggesting water on hers). His grapes are greenish, some not colored at all; her potential lilies are perhaps only leaves, green or orange brown, but a hyacinth-like flower cluster opens on the fourth from the bottom of the five stems. The star beside Los reminds us of the fallen stars beside fallen Albion (Plates 9 and 54) but the colonic cloud of Vala beside it is melting; it is tinted with violet and the new moon cradle with pink as though in the dawn light that surrounds Enitharmon. The star or comet shooting across from night to day means life if the two become one, chaos if they divide. (In *Night Thoughts* 443, a similar starlike image illustrates the words "Comets good Omens are when duly scann'd.") Consider the weaving of a star window in Plate 57.

Jerusalem 86. There is no illumination on this plate, and there cannot be, for in it Los is describing in detail his vision of Jerusalem which Blake supplies in elaborate color in the title page (Plate 2). The effect of this full reference to it, fourteen plates from the work's end, is to clinch the argument just illustrated and to put in strong contrast the dark images of the next page.

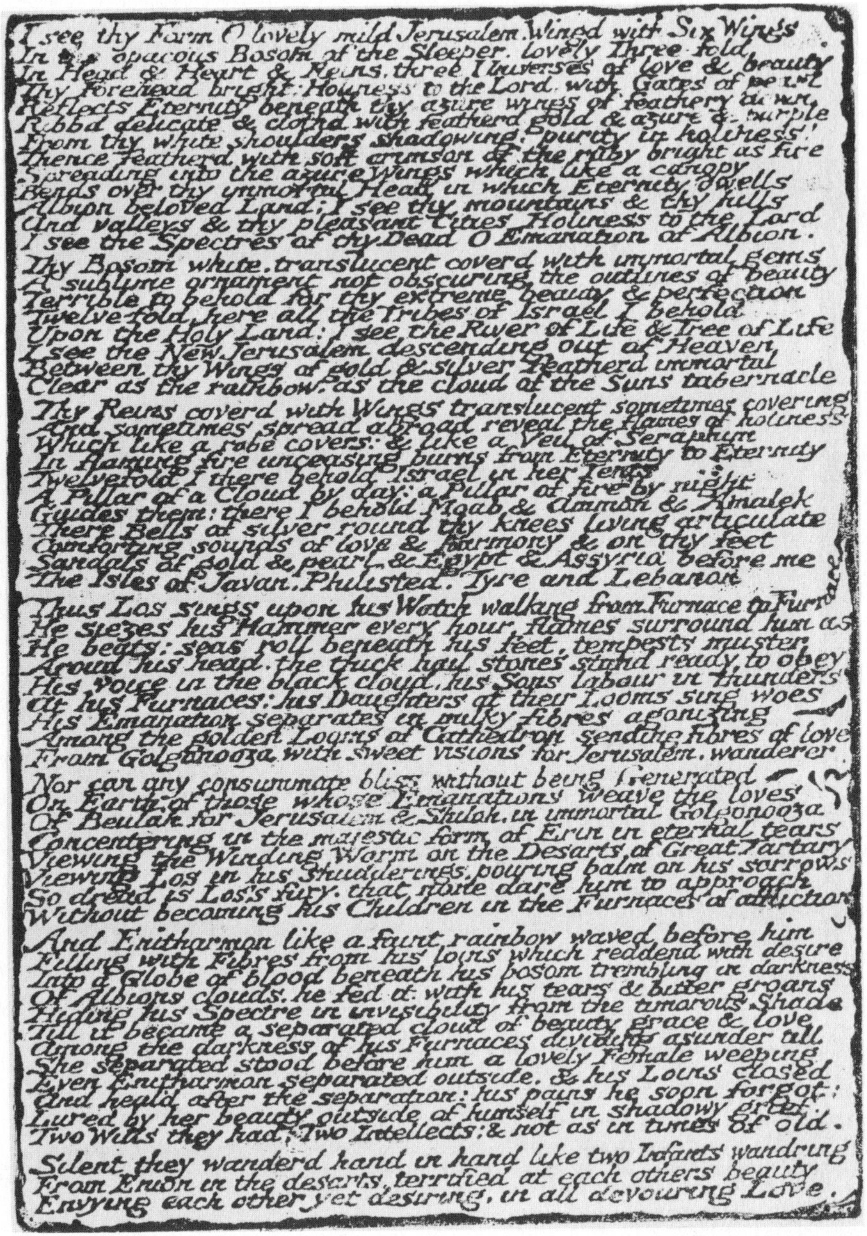

I see thy Form O lovely mild Jerusalem, Wingd with Six Wings
In the opacous Bosom of the Sleeper, lovely Three-fold
In Head & Heart & Reins, three Universes of love & beauty
Thy forehead bright: Holiness to the Lord, with Gates of pearl
Reflects Eternity beneath thy azure wings of feathery down
Ribbd delicate & clothd with featherd gold & azure & purple
From thy white shoulders shadowing, purity in holiness!
Thence featherd with soft crimson of the ruby bright as fire
Spreading into the azure Wings which like a canopy
Bends over thy immortal Head in which Eternity dwells
Albion beloved Land; I see thy mountains & thy hills
And valleys & thy pleasant Cities Holiness to the Lord
I see the Spectres of thy Dead O Emanation of Albion.

Thy Bosom white, translucent coverd with immortal gems
A sublime ornament not obscuring the outlines of beauty
Terrible to behold for thy extreme beauty & perfection
Twelve-fold here all the Tribes of Israel I behold
Upon the Holy Land: I see the River of Life & Tree of Life
I see the New Jerusalem descending out of Heaven
Between thy Wings of gold & silver featherd immortal
Clear as the rainbow, as the cloud of the Suns tabernacle

Thy Reins coverd with Wings translucent sometimes covering
And sometimes spread abroad reveal the flames of holiness
Which like a robe covers: & like a Veil of Seraphim
In flaming fire unceasing burns from Eternity to Eternity
Twelvefold I there behold Israel in her Tents
A Pillar of a Cloud by day: a Pillar of fire by night
Guides them: there I behold Moab & Ammon & Amalek
There Bells of silver round thy knees living articulate
Comforting sounds of love & harmony & on thy feet
Sandals of gold & pearl, & Egypt & Assyria before me
The Isles of Javan, Philistea, Tyre and Lebanon

Thus Los sings upon his Watch walking from Furnace to Furnace.
He siezes his Hammer every hour, flames surround him as
He beats: seas roll beneath his feet, tempests muster
Around his head. the thick hail stones stand ready to obey
His voice in the black cloud, his Sons labour in thunders
At his Furnaces; his Daughters at their Looms sing woes
His Emanation separates in milky fibres agonizing
Among the golden Looms of Cathedron sending fibres of love
From Golgonooza with sweet visions for Jerusalem, wanderer.

Nor can any consummate bliss without being Generated
On Earth, of those whose Emanations weave the loves
Of Beulah for Jerusalem & Shiloh, in immortal Golgonooza
Concentering in the majestic form of Erin in eternal tears
Viewing the Winding Worm on the Desarts of Great Tartary
Viewing Los in his shudderings, pouring balm on his sorrows
So dread is Los's fury, that none dare him to approach
Without becoming his Children in the Furnaces of affliction

And Enitharmon like a faint rainbow waved before him
Filling with Fibres from his loins which reddend with desire
Into a Globe of blood beneath his bosom trembling in darkness
Of Albions clouds. he fed it, with his tears & bitter groans
Hiding his Spectre in invisibility from the timorous Shade
Till it became a separated cloud of beauty grace & love
Among the darkness of his Furnaces dividing asunder till
She separated stood before him a lovely Female weeping
Even Enitharmon separated outside, & his Loins closed
And heald after the separation: his pains he soon forgot;
Lured by her beauty outside of himself in shadowy grief.
Two Wills they had; Two Intellects: & not as in times of old.

Silent they wanderd hand in hand like two Infants wandring
From Enion in the desarts, terrified at each others beauty
Envying each other yet desiring, in all devouring Love.

Jerusalem 86[D]

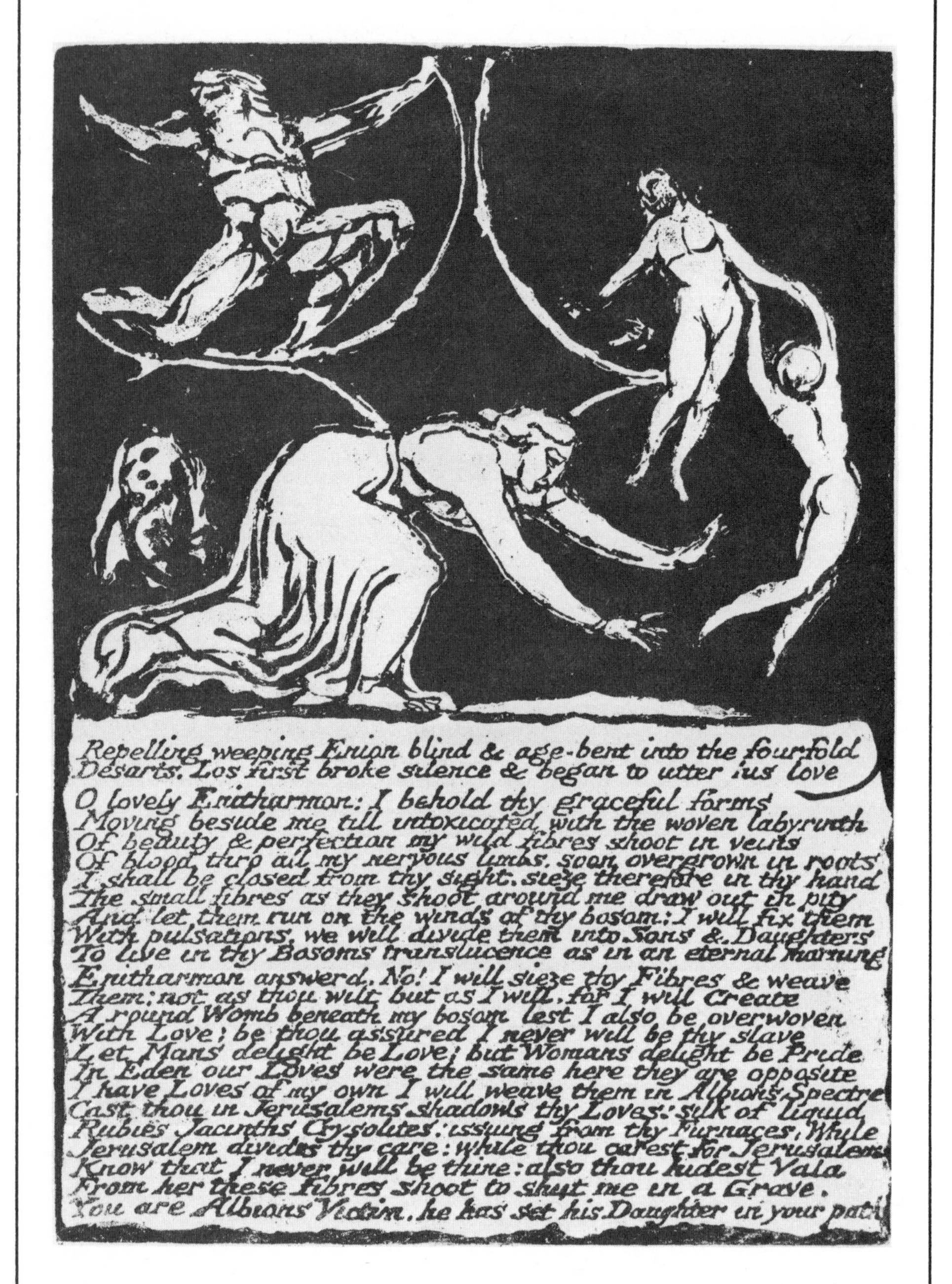

Jerusalem 87D

Jerusalem 87. In the "fourfold Desarts" (1–2) Los and Enitharmon, the upper and lower figures in and crossing between the two right "folds" (in an earlier stage of their argument illustrated on Plate 85 and quoted on Plate 88), wander, terrified at each other's beauty, envying, yet desiring; they repell "weeping Enion blind & age-bent" (1), the anonymity ("Enion" as anyone) of the visionless body. See *Four Zoas* p 9. Enitharmon's repelling takes the form of her stepping out of Enion's reach, while enticing Los; his of viewing Enion with pity or concern (compare his backward look toward Vala's cloud in Plate 85). In the top left fold the spectre takes the form of Urizen (or Tharmas?: W), also age-bent, stretching out his arms in the illusion of divine power ("Knowing himself the author of their divisions": 88:34–35) but confined in a globe—this is a capsule recollection of *Urizen*. FlamesE fill the space outside the spheres, forming a fiery pyramid above Enion.

The sad face in the fourth fold (bottom left) is, in the immediate context, Erin "in eternal tears, Viewing the Winding Worm on the Desarts," in whom is now concentered all hope of regeneration (86:42–46). We have seen the worm, Hyle concentering all lost Humanity, on Plate 82. (A similar sad face is addedF in the sphere behind Los.) Compare the diagram in *Milton* 36.

Jerusalem 88. Ornamenting the margins of this page Blake allowed some wormy wriggles of emphasis at the end of Enitharmon's speech of "dominion" and "jealousy" (41–42) but filled the other spaces with birds flying—appropriately near the "Bellows of his Furnaces" (1), the "force" of his Hammer (50), his "love on the wind" even though "scatterd" (51): seven birds under the bellows, five near "who loves Jesus" (if we select the most apt words nearby), two at "alternate torments," four after "milky Love"; then a reclining human (or angelic?) figure between lines 33 and 34 (why?) and further birds in clusters of three, five, four, and perhaps two.

The basic fact is that Los is hard at work; the birds indicate that his sparks are flying.

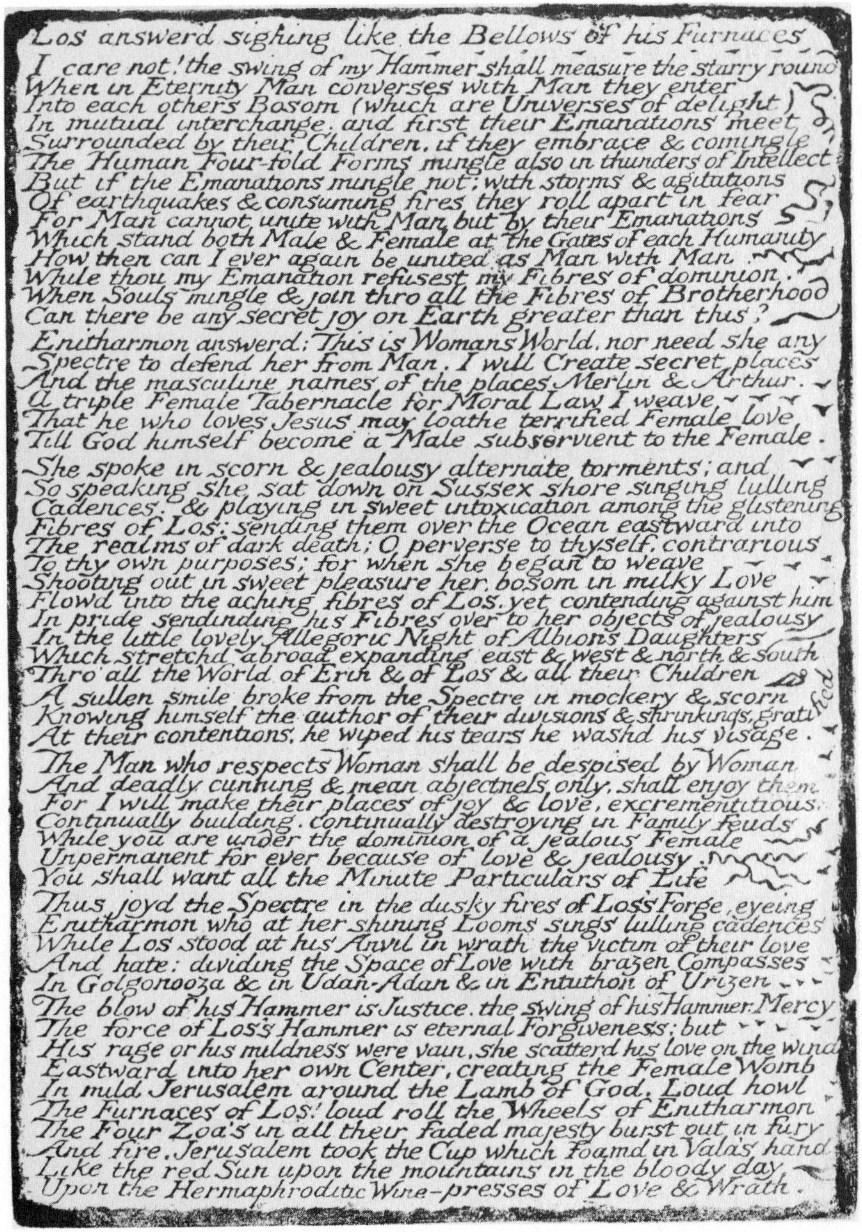

Los answerd sighing like the Bellows of his Furnaces
I care not! the swing of my Hammer shall measure the starry round
When in Eternity Man converses with Man they enter
Into each others Bosom (which are Universes of delight)
In mutual interchange. and first their Emanations meet
Surrounded by their Children. if they embrace & comingle
The Human Four-fold Forms mingle also in thunders of Intellect
But if the Emanations mingle not; with storms & agitations
Of earthquakes & consuming fires they roll apart in fear
For Man cannot unite with Man but by their Emanations
Which stand both Male & Female at the Gates of each Humanity
How then can I ever again be united as Man with Man
While thou my Emanation refusest my Fibres of dominion.
When Souls mingle & join thro all the Fibres of Brotherhood
Can there be any secret joy on Earth greater than this?
Enitharmon answerd: This is Womans World. nor need she any
Spectre to defend her from Man. I will Create secret places
And the masculine names of the places Merlin & Arthur.
A triple Female Tabernacle for Moral Law I weave
That he who loves Jesus may loathe terrified Female love
Till God himself become a Male subservient to the Female.
She spoke in scorn & jealousy alternate torments; and
So speaking she sat down on Sussex shore singing lulling
Cadences. & playing in sweet intoxication among the glistening
Fibres of Los: sending them over the Ocean eastward into
The realms of dark death; O perverse to thyself, contrarious
To thy own purposes; for when she began to weave
Shooting out in sweet pleasure her bosom in milky Love
Flowd into the aching fibres of Los. yet contending against him
In pride sendinding his Fibres over to her objects of jealousy
In the little lovely Allegoric Night of Albions Daughters
Which stretchd abroad expanding east & west & north & south
Thro all the World of Erin & of Los & all their Children
A sullen smile broke from the Spectre in mockery & scorn
Knowing himself the author of their divisions & shrinkings, gratified
At their contentions, he wiped his tears he washd his visage.
The Man who respects Woman shall be despised by Woman
And deadly cunning & mean abjectness only, shall enjoy them
For I will make their places of joy & love, excrementitious.
Continually building. continually destroying in Family feuds
While you are under the dominion of a jealous Female
Unpermanent for ever because of love & jealousy.
You shall want all the Minute Particulars of Life
Thus joyd the Spectre in the dusky fires of Los's Forge, eyeing
Enitharmon who at her shining Looms sings lulling cadences
While Los stood at his Anvil in wrath the victim of their love
And hate: dividing the Space of Love with brazen Compasses
In Golgonooza & in Udan-Adan & in Entuthon of Urizen
The blow of his Hammer is Justice. the swing of his Hammer: Mercy
The force of Los's Hammer is eternal Forgiveness; but
His rage or his mildness were vain, she scatterd his love on the wind
Eastward into her own Center, creating the Female Womb
In mild Jerusalem around the Lamb of God. Loud howl
The Furnaces of Los! loud roll the Wheels of Enitharmon
The Four Zoa's in all their faded majesty burst out in fury
And fire. Jerusalem took the Cup which foamd in Vala's hand
Like the red Sun upon the mountains in the bloody day
Upon the Hermaphroditic Wine-presses of Love & Wrath.

Jerusalem 88ᴰ

Tho divided by the Cross & Nails & Thorns & Spear
In cruelties of Rahab & Tirzah permanent endure
A terrible indefinite Hermaphroditic form
A Wine-press of Love & Wrath double Hermaphroditic
Twelvefold in Allegoric pomp in selfish holiness
The Pharisaion. the Grammateis. the Presbuterion.
The Archiereus, the Iereus, the Saddusaion, double
Each withoutside of the other, covering eastern heaven

Thus was the Covering Cherub reveald majestic image
Of Selfhood. Body put off. the Antichrist accursed
Coverd with precious stones. a Human Dragon terrible
And bright. stretchd over Europe & Asia gorgeous
In three nights he devourd the rejected corse of death

His Head dark. deadly. in its Brain incloses a reflexion
Of Eden all perverted; Egypt on the Gihon many tongued
And many mouthd: Ethiopia. Lybia. the Sea of Rephaim
Minute Particulars in slavery I behold among the brick-kilns
Disorganizd. & there is Pharoh in his iron Court:
And the Dragon of the River & the Furnaces of iron.
Outwoven from Thames & Tweed & Severn awful streams
Twelve ridges of Stone frown over all the Earth in tyrant pride
Frown over each River stupendous Works of Albions Druid Sons
And Albions Forests of Oaks coverd the Earth from Pole to Pole

His Bosom wide reflects Moab & Ammon on the River
Pison. since calld Arnon. there is Heshbon beautiful
The Rocks of Rabbath on the Arnon & the Fish-pools of Heshbon
Whose currents flow into the Dead Sea by Sodom & Gomorra
Above his Head high arching Wings black filld with Eyes
Spring upon iron sinews from the Scapulae & Os Humeri.
There Israel in bondage to his Generalizing Gods
Molech & Chemosh. & in his left breast is Philistea
In Druid Temples over the whole Earth with Victims Sacrifice
From Gaza to Damascus Tyre & Sidon & the Gods
Of Javan thro the Isles of Grecia & all Europes Kings
Where Hiddekel pursues his course among the rocks
Two Wings spring from his ribs of brass. starry. black as night
But translucent their blackness as the dazling of gems

His Loins inclose Babylon on Euphrates beautiful
And Rome in sweet Hesperia: there Israel scatterd abroad
In martyrdoms & slavery I behold: ah vision of sorrow!
Inclosed by eyeless Wings. glowing with fire as the iron
Heated in the Smiths forge. but cold the wind of their dread fury

But in the midst of a devouring Stomach. Jerusalem
Hidden within the Covering Cherub as in a Tabernacle
Of threefold workmanship in allegoric delusion & woe
There the Seven Kings of Canaan & Five Baalim of Philistea
Sihon & Og the Anakim & Emim. Nephilim & Gibborim
From Babylon to Rome & the Wings spread from Japan
Where the Red Sea terminates the World of Generation & Death
To Irelands farthest rocks where Giants builded their Causeway
Into the Sea of Rephaim. but the Sea oerwhelmd them all.

A Double Female now appeard within the Tabernacle.
Religion hid in War. a Dragon red & hidden Harlot
Each within other. but without a Warlike Mighty-one
Of dreadful power. sitting upon Horeb pondering dire
And mighty preparations mustering multitudes innumerable
Of warlike sons among the sands of Midian & Aram
For multitudes of those who sleep in Alla descend
Lured by his warlike symphonies of tabret pipe & harp
Burst the bottoms of the Graves & Funeral Arks of Beulah
Wandering in that unknown Night beyond the silent Grave
They become One with the Antichrist & are absorbd in him

Jerusalem 89ᴰ

Jerusalem 89. While the text describes the Covering Cherub now revealed as "majestic image of Selfhood" (9–10), the margin continues flights of birds: four below and three between branches of a merciful tree-vine at bottom right, five around a reformed Druid priestess reaching up to receive a scalloped basket such as angels fill with bread for Christ after his triumph, in Blake's watercolor for *Paradise Regained* IV 581–95—from a descending spirit dressed in pale green. A variant of the handing down of grapes. Or perhaps the Druid priestess is unreformed, for this figure is very like the knife-wielding and almost bat-winged female at the top of Plate 74. The coloring and detail in E make the identification clear: in Plate 89 she still holds a knife, but now carefully sideways in her left hand; she is clothed in a sort of body-stocking in both plates, orange-pink in 74, rose in 89; in both her shape and dancing form are similar. (The upper figure has trailing hair, left partly white in E, where a beard effect is produced by the redrawing of features, but it may not be intentional. He or she is looking back up toward some directing deity.) In any event, preparations for a banquet are suggested.

Jerusalem 90. In the third paragraph Los speaks out against the cruel practices of Selfhood described in preceding and following paragraphs. From his utterance firm coils reach up to contain the upper paragraph and down to contain the lower and then on to show reversal of direction (coils reversed) when Los resumes speaking. The edge all round is shaped into brown twists and flames in E, with green and brown bay leaves across the bottom like a wreath and starting up the right edge: "These beautiful Witchcrafts . . . gratifyd by Cruelty" (68).

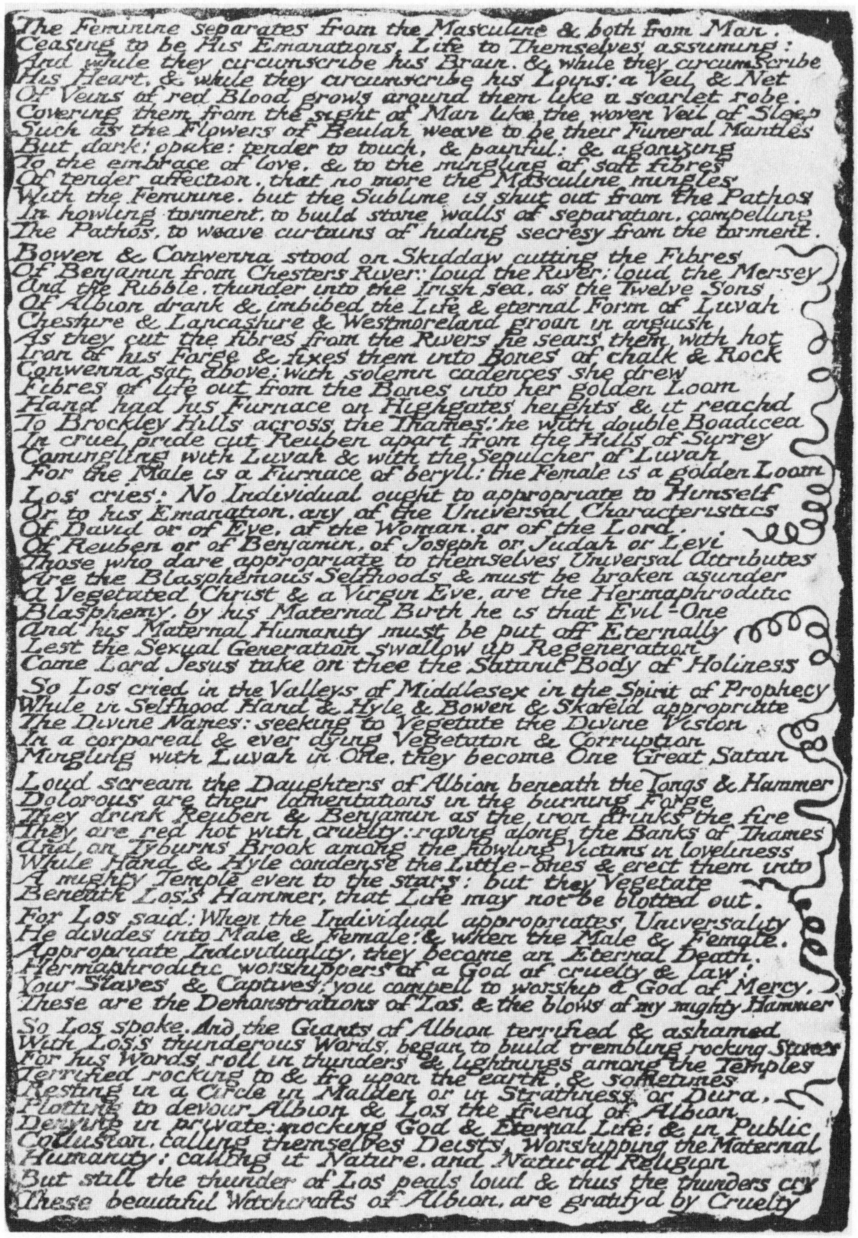

The Feminine separates from the Masculine & both from Man,
Ceasing to be His Emanations, Life to Themselves assuming:
And while they circumscribe his Brain, & while they circumscribe
His Heart, & while they circumscribe his Loins: a Veil & Net
Of Veins of red Blood grows around them like a scarlet robe.
Covering them from the sight of Man like the woven Veil of Sleep
Such as the Flowers of Beulah weave to be their Funeral Mantles
But dark: opake: tender to touch, & painful: & agonizing
To the embrace of love, & to the mingling of soft fibres
Of tender affection, that no more the Masculine mingles
With the Feminine. but the Sublime is shut out from the Pathos
In howling torment, to build stone walls of separation, compelling
The Pathos, to weave curtains of hiding secresy from the torment.

Bowen & Conwenna stood on Skiddaw cutting the Fibres
Of Benjamin from Chesters River: loud the River; loud the Mersey
And the Ribble, thunder into the Irish sea, as the Twelve Sons
Of Albion drank & imbibed the Life & eternal Form of Luvah
Cheshire & Lancashire & Westmoreland groan in anguish
As they cut the fibres from the Rivers he sears them with hot
Iron of his Forge & fixes them into Bones of chalk & Rock
Conwenna sat above: with solemn cadences she drew
Fibres of life out from the Bones into her golden Loom
Hand had his Furnace on Highgates heights & it reachd
To Brockley Hills across the Thames: he with double Boadicea
In cruel pride cut Reuben apart from the Hills of Surrey
Comingling with Luvah & with the Sepulcher of Luvah
For the Male is a Furnace of beryll: the Female is a golden Loom

Los cries: No Individual ought to appropriate to Himself
Or to his Emanation, any of the Universal Characteristics
Of David or of Eve, of the Woman, or of the Lord,
Of Reuben or of Benjamin, of Joseph or Judah or Levi
Those who dare appropriate to themselves Universal Attributes
Are the Blasphemous Selfhoods & must be broken asunder
A Vegetated Christ & a Virgin Eve, are the Hermaphroditic
Blasphemy, by his Maternal Birth he is that Evil-One
And his Maternal Humanity must be put off Eternally
Lest the Sexual Generation swallow up Regeneration
Come Lord Jesus take on thee the Satanic Body of Holiness

So Los cried in the Valleys of Middlesex in the Spirit of Prophecy
While in Selfhood Hand & Hyle & Bowen & Skofeld appropriate
The Divine Names: seeking to Vegetate the Divine Vision
In a corporeal & ever dying Vegetation & Corruption
Mingling with Luvah in One, they become One Great Satan

Loud scream the Daughters of Albion beneath the Tongs & Hammer
Dolorous are their lamentations in the burning Forge
They drink Reuben & Benjamin as the iron drinks the fire
They are red hot with cruelty: raving along the Banks of Thames
And on Tyburns Brook among the howling Victims in loveliness
While Hand & Hyle condense the Little-Ones & erect them into
A mighty Temple even to the stars: but they Vegetate
Beneath Los's Hammer, that Life may not be blotted out.
For Los said: When the Individual appropriates Universality
He divides into Male & Female: & when the Male & Female,
Appropriate Individuality, they become an Eternal Death.
Hermaphroditic worshippers of a God of cruelty & law!
Your Slaves & Captives; you compell to worship a God of Mercy.
These are the Demonstrations of Los, & the blows of my mighty Hammer

So Los spoke. And the Giants of Albion terrified & ashamed
With Los's thunderous Words, began to build trembling rocking Stones
For his Words roll in thunders & lightnings among the Temples
Terrified rocking to & fro upon the earth, & sometimes
Resting in a Circle in Malden or in Strathness or Dura,
Plotting to devour Albion & Los the friend of Albion
Denying in private: mocking God & Eternal Life: & in Public
Collusion, calling themselves Deists, Worshipping the Maternal
Humanity; calling it Nature, and Natural Religion
But still the thunder of Los peals loud & thus the thunders cry
These beautiful Witchcrafts of Albion, are gratifyd by Cruelty

Jerusalem 90[D]

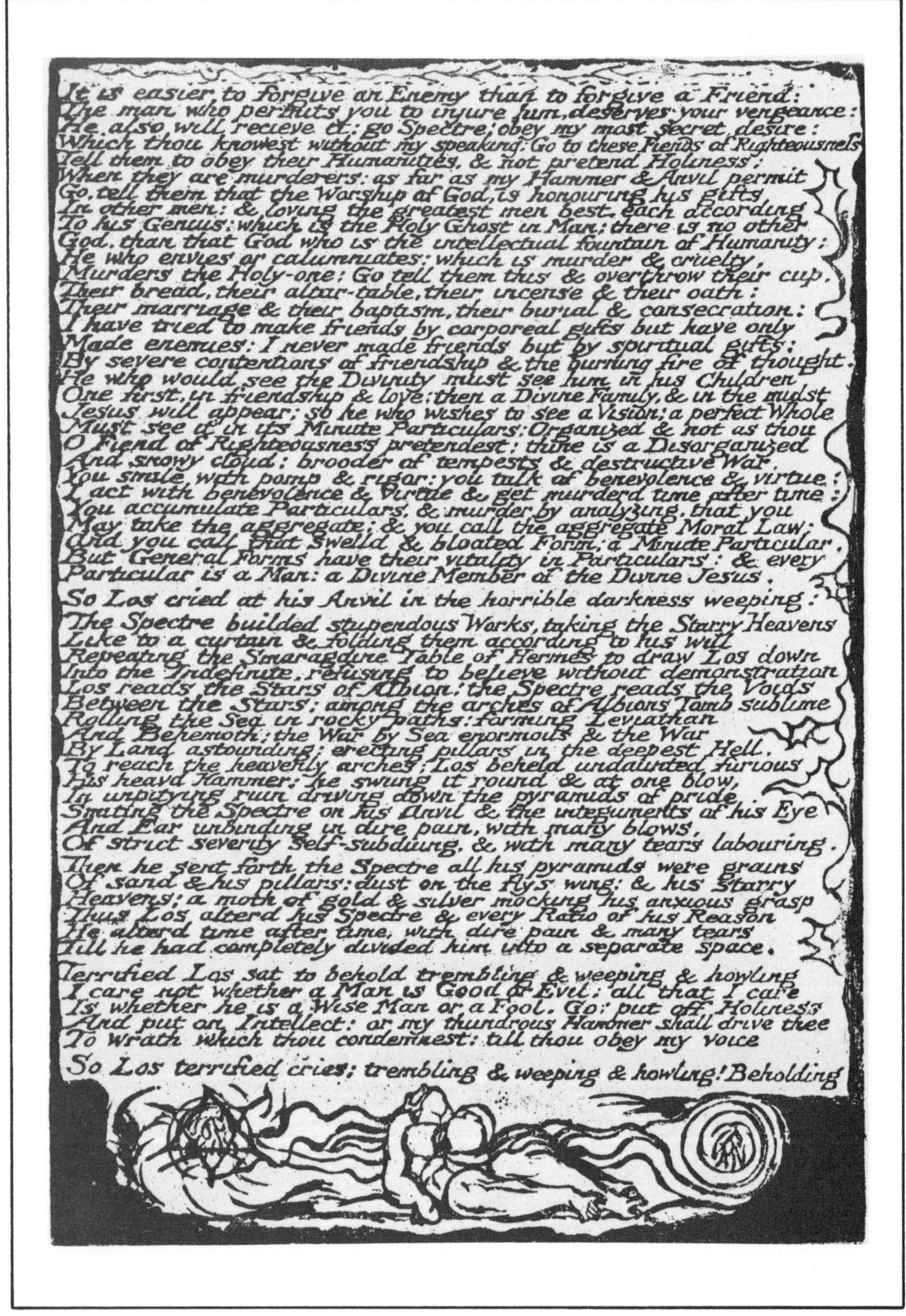

It is easier to forgive an Enemy than to forgive a Friend:
The man who permits you to injure him, deserves your vengeance:
He also will recieve it; go Spectre; obey my most secret desire:
Which thou knowest without my speaking: Go to these Fiends of Righteousness
Tell them to obey their Humanities, & not pretend Holiness;
When they are murderers: as far as my Hammer & Anvil permit
Go, tell them that the Worship of God, is honouring his gifts
In other men: & loving the greatest men best, each according
To his Genius: which is the Holy Ghost in Man; there is no other
God, than that God who is the intellectual fountain of Humanity;
He who envies or calumniates: which is murder & cruelty,
Murders the Holy-one: Go tell them this & overthrow their cup,
Their bread, their altar-table, their incense & their oath:
Their marriage & their baptism, their burial & consecration:
I have tried to make friends by corporeal gifts but have only
Made enemies: I never made friends but by spiritual gifts;
By severe contentions of friendship & the burning fire of thought.
He who would see the Divinity must see him in his Children
One first, in friendship & love; then a Divine Family, & in the midst
Jesus will appear; so he who wishes to see a Vision; a perfect Whole
Must see it in its Minute Particulars; Organized & not as thou
O Fiend of Righteousness pretendest; thine is a Disorganized
And snowy cloud: brooder of tempests & destructive War
You smile with pomp & rigor: you talk of benevolence & virtue;
I act with benevolence & Virtue & get murderd time after time:
You accumulate Particulars, & murder by analyzing, that you
May take the aggregate; & you call the aggregate Moral Law:
And you call that Swelld & bloated Form; a Minute Particular.
But General Forms have their vitality in Particulars: & every
Particular is a Man; a Divine Member of the Divine Jesus.

So Los cried at his Anvil in the horrible darkness weeping:

The Spectre builded stupendous Works, taking the Starry Heavens
Like to a curtain & folding them according to his will
Repeating the Smaragdine Table of Hermes to draw Los down
Into the Indefinite, refusing to believe without demonstration
Los reads the Stars of Albion: the Spectre reads the Voids
Between the Stars; among the arches of Albions Tomb sublime
Rolling the Sea in rocky paths: forming Leviathan
And Behemoth: the War by Sea enormous & the War
By Land astounding: erecting pillars in the deepest Hell,
To reach the heavenly arches; Los beheld undaunted furious
His heavd Hammer; he swung it round & at one blow,
In unpitying ruin driving down the pyramids of pride
Smiting the Spectre on his Anvil & the integuments of his Eye
And Ear unbinding in dire pain, with many blows,
Of strict severity self-subduing, & with many tears labouring.

Then he sent forth the Spectre all his pyramids were grains
Of sand & his pillars: dust on the flys wing: & his starry
Heavens; a moth of gold & silver mocking his anxious grasp
Thus Los alterd his Spectre & every Ratio of his Reason
He alterd time after time, with dire pain & many tears
Till he had completely divided him into a separate space.

Terrified Los sat to behold trembling & weeping & howling
I care not whether a Man is Good or Evil; all that I care
Is whether he is a Wise Man or a Fool. Go! put off Holiness
And put on Intellect: or my thundrous Hammer shall drive thee
To wrath which thou condemnest: till thou obey my voice

So Los terrified cries: trembling & weeping & howling! Beholding

Jerusalem 91D

Jerusalem 91. Holly leaves appear in the margin of Los's sermon and the account of his metamorphoses of the spectre's warlike actions into acts of peace—Christmas holly? Below, the victim (Albion—see Plates 25 and 67 and 69—and the spectre) is still caught in knowing "whether a Man is Good or Evil" (54). His fibres are being pulled from him left and right and wound (compare Plate 25 and St Erasmus again) into emblems of the Old Testament (Solomon's seal: compare the star Blake puts below the singing warbler in his third design for Gray's *Spring*) and the New (an ear of wheat)—i.e. Law and Mercy.

In this area of the page we have seen Albion torn apart by chains (Plate 67), fibres forming a stone altar (71), fibres enrooting (74), fibres beginning to bear flower and fruit (85); Albion's fibres being unwound (with his head in this position) in Plate 25. They are now pulled between belief in a god of geometry, in a burning (green) bush—and hunger for the mercy of the living bread.

❧

Jerusalem 92. "The Poets Song draws to its period" (8) in a more positive sense than Enitharmon understands. Jerusalem, sitting up in human form, not fully unclothed but in her right mind, is no longer spellbound by Vala. Her hands are raised in creative compassion; her head is bent but unbowed and is the center of a scene of dawn (compare the dawn tints in Plate 85) that embraces her written name. On bright greensward she sits among four forms of Albion's selfhood—whose sleeping heads may be taken as her four sons named in 71:50–52 but also as the Four Zoas almost ready for their resurrection in Plate 95. In Plate 54 we saw them, entombed alive, in illustration and defiance of the spectre's efforts, as Alfred, to constrict life to four "Druid Rocks" in chaos. Los now sees the reverse of the process of warfare among nations seeking sole dominion, attributed to Saxon Alfred: "I see The Briton Saxon Roman Norman amalgamating . . . into One Nation" (1–2). Like the heads of the dead in *Gates* 16, these are almost completely assimilated unto the earth to be reborn. The worms at lower right indicate what their bodies are becoming (and perhaps suggest a connection with the snake-city of Plate 100). In short the corporeal war is drawing to its period.

The inscription of the name "Jerusalem" beside her living body but also in the dawn sky above the stones of Druid England foretells the resurrection of Jerusalem as woman and city. (See Plates 99 and 100; also Blake's painting *The Fall of Man* in which the original garden wall of Eden is a row of perfect trilithons.) Here her giant form between divided and broken segments of the stone structure recalls *America* 1. She is in the breach in the wall of Druidic Babylon (as Orc was) but her face is not buried and she is not in chains; she combines the fallen male Orc and the surviving, lamenting mother and wife among the bodies of the fallen warriors —with an echo, as noted, of the sibyl of *The Gates of Paradise* (and see Plate 4). The picture illuminates the prophecy of Isaiah 3.25–26: "Thy men shall fall by the sword, and thy mighty in the war. And her [Jerusalem's] gates shall lament and mourn; and she being desolate shall sit upon the ground." For a similar look and bending of the head see *Song of Los* 8.

Jerusalem 92D

Anytus Melitus & Lycon thought Socrates a Very Pernicious Man

So Caiphas thought Jesus

Enitharmon heard. She raisd her head like the mild Moon

O Rintrah! O Palamabron! What are your dire & awful purposes
Enitharmons name is nothing before you: you forget all my Love!
The Mothers love of obedience is forgotten & you seek a Love
Of the pride of dominion. that will Divorce Ocalythron & Elynittria
Upon East Moor in Derbyshire & along the Valleys of Cheviot
Could you Love me Rintrah, if you Pride not in my Love
As Reuben found Mandrakes in the field & gave them to his Mother
Pride meets with Pride upon the Mountains in the stormy day
In that terrible Day of Rintrahs Plow & of Satans driving the Team.
Ah! then I heard my little ones weeping along the Valley:
Ah! then I saw my beloved ones fleeing from my Tent
Merlin was like thee Rintrah among the Giants of Albion
Judah was like Palamabron: O Simeon! O Levi! ye fled away
How can I hear my little ones weeping along the Valley
Or how upon the distant Hills see my beloveds Tents.

Then Los again took up his speech as Enitharmon ceast

Fear not my Sons this Waking Death. he is become One with me
Behold him here! We shall not Die! we shall be united in Jesus.
Will you suffer this Satan this Body of Doubt that Seems but Is Not
To occupy the very threshold of Eternal Life. if Bacon. Newton. Locke
Deny a Conscience in Man & the Communion of Saints & Angels
Contemning the Divine Vision & Fruition. Worshiping the Deus
Of the Heathen. The God of This World. & the Goddess Nature
Mystery Babylon the Great. The Druid Dragon & hidden Harlot
Is it not that Signal of the Morning which was told us in the Beginning
Thus they converse upon Mam-Tor. the Graves thunder under their feet

Jerusalem 93D

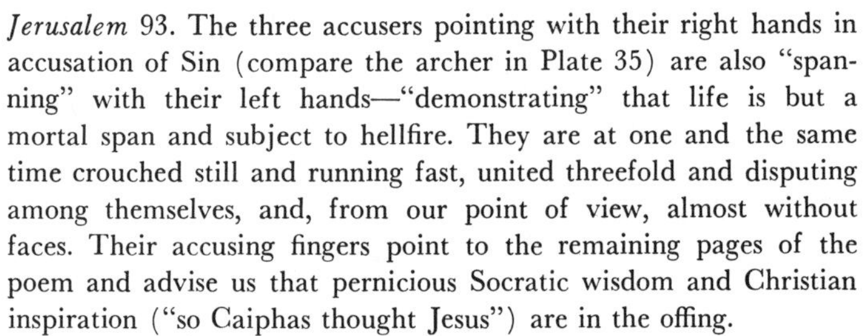

Jerusalem 93. The three accusers pointing with their right hands in accusation of Sin (compare the archer in Plate 35) are also "spanning" with their left hands—"demonstrating" that life is but a mortal span and subject to hellfire. They are at one and the same time crouched still and running fast, united threefold and disputing among themselves, and, from our point of view, almost without faces. Their accusing fingers point to the remaining pages of the poem and advise us that pernicious Socratic wisdom and Christian inspiration ("so Caiphas thought Jesus") are in the offing.

Below, a sad placid Enitharmon looking up (at the accusers?—in *Four Zoas* 138 she sits in water looking up the same way, to be reunited to Los, ready for the end) sits in a sulfur bath in the red and yellow flames of the "furnaces of affliction." They are mentioned in Plates 7 and 8, in 55 and 73; Gwendolen and other daughters of Albion began giving their souls away in the furnaces in 82:79 (which comforted Los) and became Los's children by doing so (86:49, apropos the vision of the title page). Albion will throw himself into them, for visionary transmutation, in 96:35. During the whole poem Jerusalem has been in them. Taking her place, Enitharmon now raises "her head like the mild Moon" (1) to be consumed and "vanish for ever" (92:11) as the Female Will or "Goddess Nature" (24) and be reborn as Jerusalem. Emanation and selfhood (the decaying male bodies of Plate 92) die that Man may be born a Spiritual body. Note the viper shape of the flames along the bottom.

In E the color shock of this page—sulfur yellow behind the darkened pink accusers and around the bathing female, turning to strong red in the flames at left—is the most vivid visual effect in the book. All the colors on other pages are pale in comparison. There is a touch of bright yellow above Los's bellows in Plate 6, a yellow wash in Plate 21, some bright yellow in Plate 28 behind the chapter title "Jerusalem Chap: 2." But the yellows of the title page, of the ark on Plate 24, the suns in Plates 37, 39, 50, 73, 85, are all paler, the sunflower of Plate 53 darker. Anticipations of the brighter yellow here are a bright yellow behind the red sun on the anvil in Plate 36, the yellow wash below the portal of birth in Plate 58, a yellow green around the head of the woman writing in Plate 64—and the gold leaf on the sun over the churches in Plate 84. Clearly times are ending, the alchemical transmutation is at hand, true dawn is bursting, the illuminated poem is coming to its period.

Jerusalem 94. The triple accuser tumbles from the thrust of that last accusation, heads, shoulders, segments of chest and belly collapsing into a heap of rocks at the top of the page (an effect muted in E) and trailing enrooted fibres that presumably caused the fall, then, at bottom, amalgamating into fallen Albion "cold . . . upon his Rock" (1), an aging, dying warrior on the battlefield of Plate 92 (and *America*) embraced by a mourning female. A revolutionary sunburst fills the breach—only two trilithons of the Druid city wall (one in C) remaining—in red and orange with a band of gold on the horizon. Textually this sunshine is the "Breath Divine" (18) and the human scene represents "England" awaking "from Death on Albions bosom" and fainting seven times (20–21). Visually this is the next gesture following Jerusalem's pity for the mouldering bodies on Plate 92. Blake's repeated explanation, "England who is Brittannia" (20), may mean that the true England is at present the fallen, imperial Britannia, whore or jealous wife of the tyrant Albion who "Taxed the Nations into Desolation" (98:53).

One flying bird on Plate 93 beneath the first line and two on Plate 49 after the fourth must be noted, the first flying creatures since Plate 89.

We may also note that the fall of the Accusers exhibits the collapse of the Babylonian pyramid of Plate 42 and the end of the tug-of-war last shown in Plate 81.

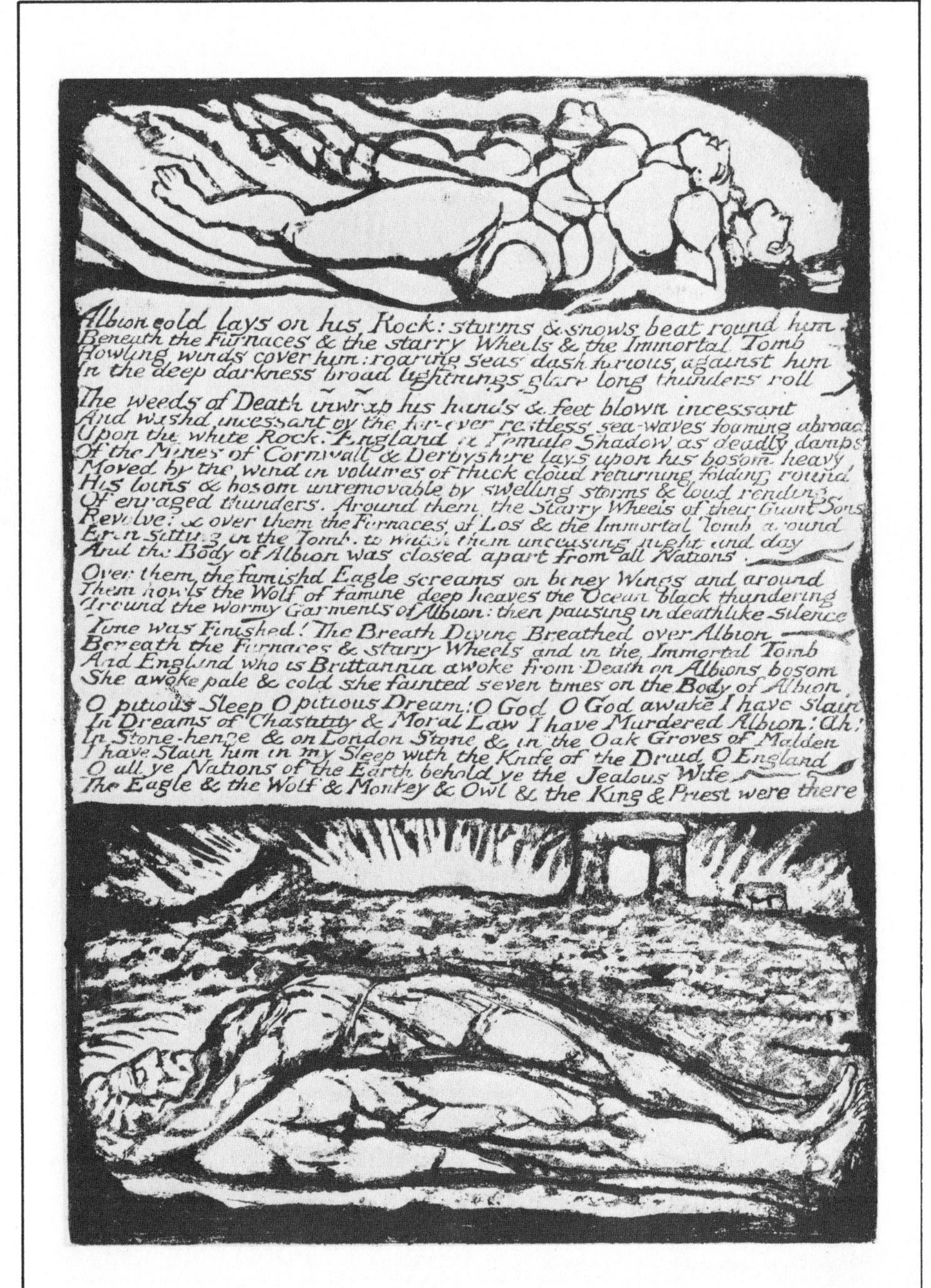

Jerusalem 94D

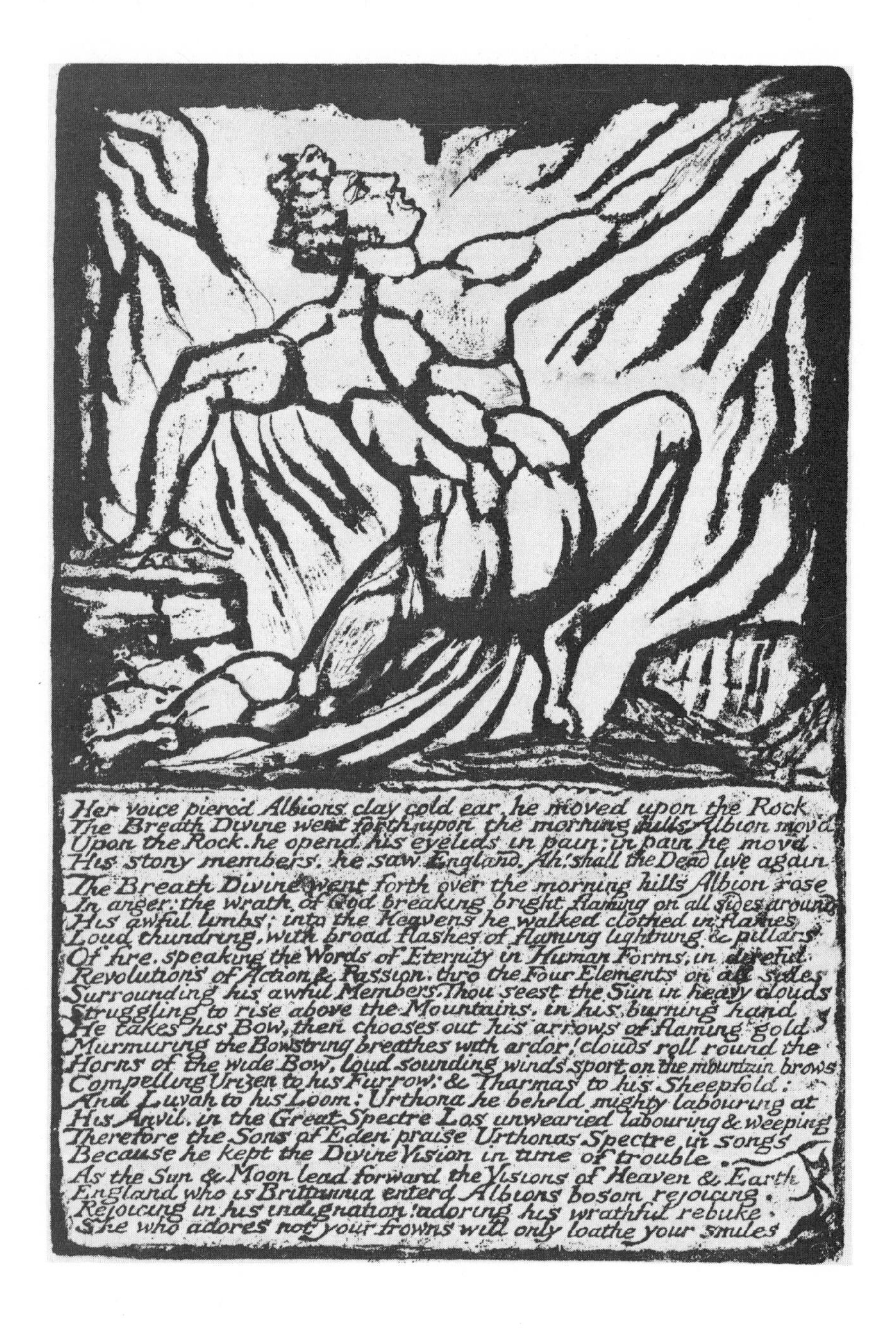
Her voice pierced Albions clay cold ear. he moved upon the Rock
The Breath Divine went forth upon the morning hills, Albion movd
Upon the Rock, he opend his eyelids in pain; in pain he movd
His stony members, he saw England. Ah! shall the Dead live again
The Breath Divine went forth over the morning hills Albion rose
In anger: the wrath of God breaking bright flaming on all sides around
His awful limbs: into the Heavens he walked clothed in flames
Loud thundring, with broad flashes of flaming lightning & pillars
Of fire, speaking the Words of Eternity in Human Forms, in direful
Revolutions of Action & Passion, thro the Four Elements on all sides
Surrounding his awful Members. Thou seest the Sun in heavy clouds
Struggling to rise above the Mountains. in his burning hand
He takes his Bow, then chooses out his arrows of flaming gold
Murmuring the Bowstring breathes with ardor! clouds roll round the
Horns of the wide Bow, loud sounding winds sport on the mountain brows
Compelling Urizen to his Furrow; & Tharmas to his Sheepfold;
And Luvah to his Loom: Urthona he beheld mighty labouring at
His Anvil, in the Great Spectre Los unwearied labouring & weeping
Therefore the Sons of Eden praise Urthonas Spectre in songs
Because he kept the Divine Vision in time of trouble.
As the Sun & Moon lead forward the Visions of Heaven & Earth
England who is Brittannia enterd Albions bosom rejoicing
Rejoicing in his indignation! adoring his wrathful rebuke.
She who adores not your frowns will only loathe your smiles

Jerusalem 95D

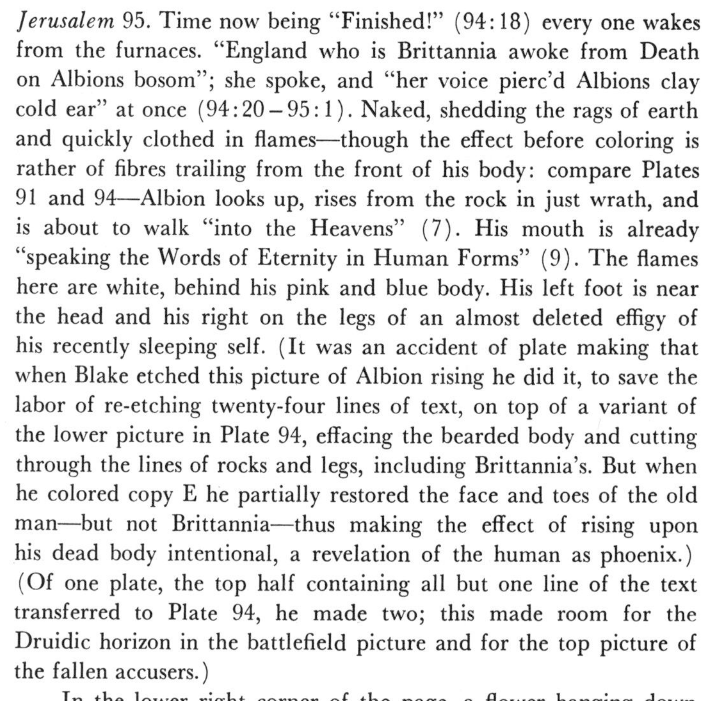

Jerusalem 95. Time now being "Finished!" (94:18) every one wakes from the furnaces. "England who is Brittannia awoke from Death on Albions bosom"; she spoke, and "her voice pierc'd Albions clay cold ear" at once (94:20–95:1). Naked, shedding the rags of earth and quickly clothed in flames—though the effect before coloring is rather of fibres trailing from the front of his body: compare Plates 91 and 94—Albion looks up, rises from the rock in just wrath, and is about to walk "into the Heavens" (7). His mouth is already "speaking the Words of Eternity in Human Forms" (9). The flames here are white, behind his pink and blue body. His left foot is near the head and his right on the legs of an almost deleted effigy of his recently sleeping self. (It was an accident of plate making that when Blake etched this picture of Albion rising he did it, to save the labor of re-etching twenty-four lines of text, on top of a variant of the lower picture in Plate 94, effacing the bearded body and cutting through the lines of rocks and legs, including Brittannia's. But when he colored copy E he partially restored the face and toes of the old man—but not Brittannia—thus making the effect of rising upon his dead body intentional, a revelation of the human as phoenix.) (Of one plate, the top half containing all but one line of the text transferred to Plate 94, he made two; this made room for the Druidic horizon in the battlefield picture and for the top picture of the fallen accusers.)

In the lower right corner of the page, a flower hanging down like the lily in *Songs* 43 is bestowed upon Los for having "kept the Divine Vision in time of trouble" (20). In E the shape of the lily is enlarged, and a worm is added along the bottom border, marked into about seventy segments.

Jerusalem 96. Before the insertion of the picture of youthful Albion rising in Plate 95, this page evidently followed the view of aged Albion embraced by England horizontally on the battlefield with this view of them rising together, still surprised that he is not dead! (Compare the mortal and spiritual images of the father in *Gates* 13.) Shortly, as the first lines of text on this page announce, "England who is Brittannia" (and with whom all the female persons of the drama are now amalgamated) will enter "Albions bosom rejoicing" (2), as we are shown on Plate 99. All the male persons now speak "in" this Jehovah-like Albion or "Universal Father," and in this "Vision of Albion" (97:5–6) we see male and female, age and youth, he in the robe of bard or hermit (compare "Milton in his Old Age sitting in his 'Mossy Cell'" in the last *Il Penseroso* design), she naked, with her legs still crossed, rising in the clouds where the Breath Divine goes "forth upon the morning hills" (95:2). Radiation pours from the cloud, or from behind it. When the embrace is completed, Plate 99, the clouds will kindle. Yet the interpolation, Plate 95, of Albion as naked youth, repeated on Plate 97 to show us youthful Albion as Los-Urthona-Jesus, prevents our settling down with the incongruity of the Universal Man as solely pater familias! In Plate 99, regardless of the apparent sexual garments, the young person will have to represent all youth, the elder all age. With time ended, all these aspects vanish and come to life in one plenitude of Universal Brotherhood and Human Form Divine. This does not erase but validates all the Illuminations in these one hundred plates, just as it preserves the Druid temple in the one hundredth.

(On the earlier use of this plate which gave the picture area its bell shape, see my article cited in the *Jerusalem* headnote, above.)

In E and F the cloak lines are redrawn.

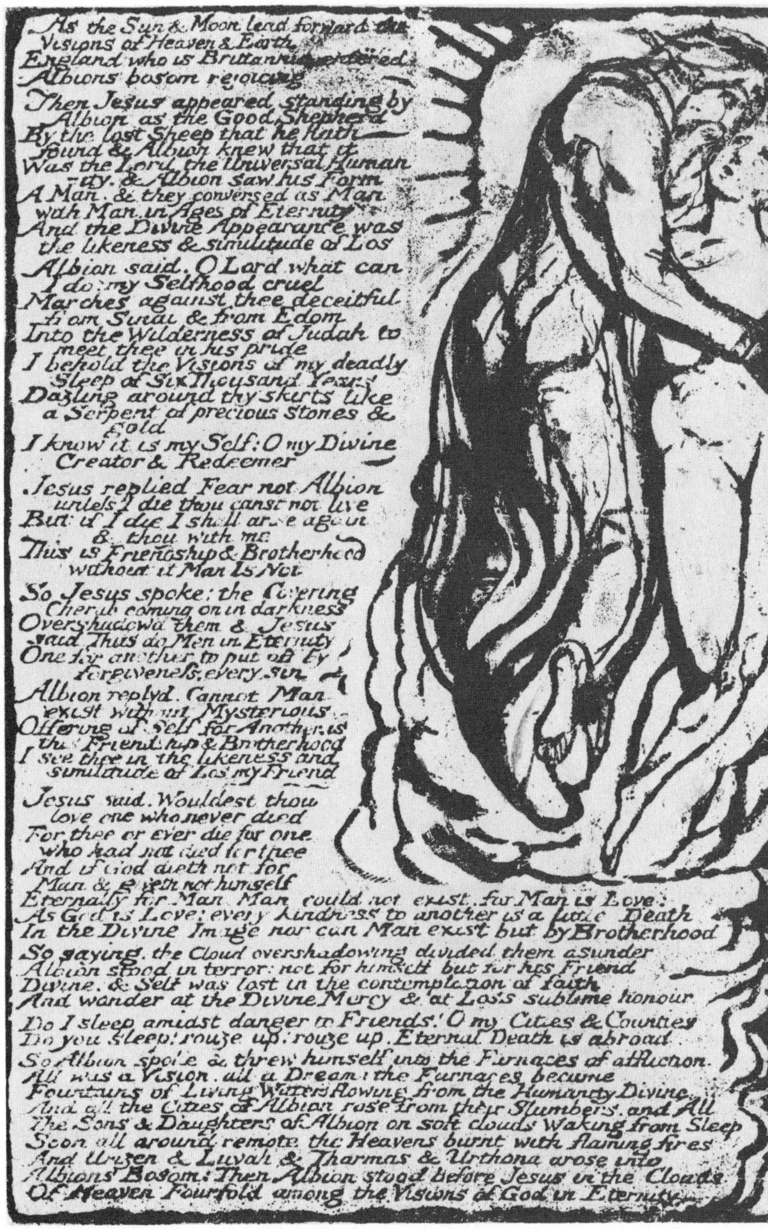

Jerusalem 96[D]

Jerusalem 97ᴰ

❧

Jerusalem 97. "Then Albion stretched his hand into Infinitude And took his Bow. Fourfold the Vision" (6–7). In the picture we see Albion as Los (naked but with a token of worker's apron) taking in his left hand the sun—what the text calls fourfold flaming Arrows of Intellect and of Love (97:12, 98:1–7). We see these as a single flaming globe, but other perspectives are offered. "Clouds roll round the horns Of the wide Bow" (98:4–5), and the wide band of light around the globe (obscured in C and F) with rays lying across it may be seen as a variant of the image in Blake's *Rout of the Rebel Angels* (Raine fig 174): six arrow shafts lie across a similar band of light between the sun, in which Jesus kneels, and the horns of his bow. (The effect, and the symbolic analogy, can hardly be accidental.) Another effect (also obscured in CF) is that all the whitish sunlight may be seen as an open left hand "stretchd . . . into Infinitude," holding the sun as a ball in its palm, the fingers spreading (and dividing, but the effect of five is kept in E) infinitely toward the waning but dawn moon and morning star, the thumb disappearing off left. (The other radiation, which would be between thumb and forefinger, is distinguished by its yellower color and more diffuse shading.)

A fourth "fold" of this vision is suggested by the wings of red light on the upper edges of the sun (on the right side only except in E); these recall the bat wings of the spectre: arisen and supplying the light of Eternity, this giant is Urthona and the sun of imagination is his spectre. (Blake made a pencil drawing of a more personal version entitled "The Journey of Life" [Keynes *Drawings* 56] in which the human figure is the same but carries a traveller's staff instead of the sun and sees higher mountains ahead on either side.)

Los-Urthona's work is but begun; the traveller who entered death's door as a Diogenes or a pilgrim with lantern in Plate 1 has found the honest Man, his own Human Form Divine; is springing from the tomb; and now journeys on the mountain top (green as the hill rising in Plate 77 from the cliffs). His right hand is held up —to shade his eyes from the sun, one thinks until noting its position (in "The Journey of Life" one assumes a sun up above somewhere) —or to concentrate his vision. He is looking forward to see the prospect, like an architect surveying his building site. On Plate 100 he has begun building, carrying the sun as a hod of mortar. (Compare also the position of his raised arm in Plate 85.)

❧

Jerusalem 98. All "the Living Creatures of the Earth" (54) are represented singly (not in pairs; this is no limiting ark of rescue) and in multitudes. The serpent at top in great variety of coiling is not confined to repetitious spirals or undulations, certainly not to his role in Plate 72: he is shedding his skin. The worm, last seen on Plate 82 (but compare *Songs* 43) is establishing the same freedom at bottom, with snail, frog (the left one in *Songs* 32), inch worm (in arc), spider (hanging by its thread from the "G" of "Golgonooza" and doing a handstand because Blake has now given him eight legs: compare *Europe* 12 and 14), and two flying butterflies or moths. The living lines now coil into infinity, not into vegetation as in Plates 9 and 44. (Is the last worm arc, at the right, another inch worm? Is there another small worm behind it?)

The birds are symbolically grouped: seven after line 15, a large one after "rejoicing in Unity" (21), a small one after the list ending "Eagle. Dove. Fly. Worm" (43), and at bottom twenty-eight small birds (the senses become fourfold seven) plus a large one for the imagination (leading into the group from the right margin). These living creatures also represent the endless circles of "Years Months Days & Hours" (99). The small birds must be the twenty-eight larks of *Milton*.

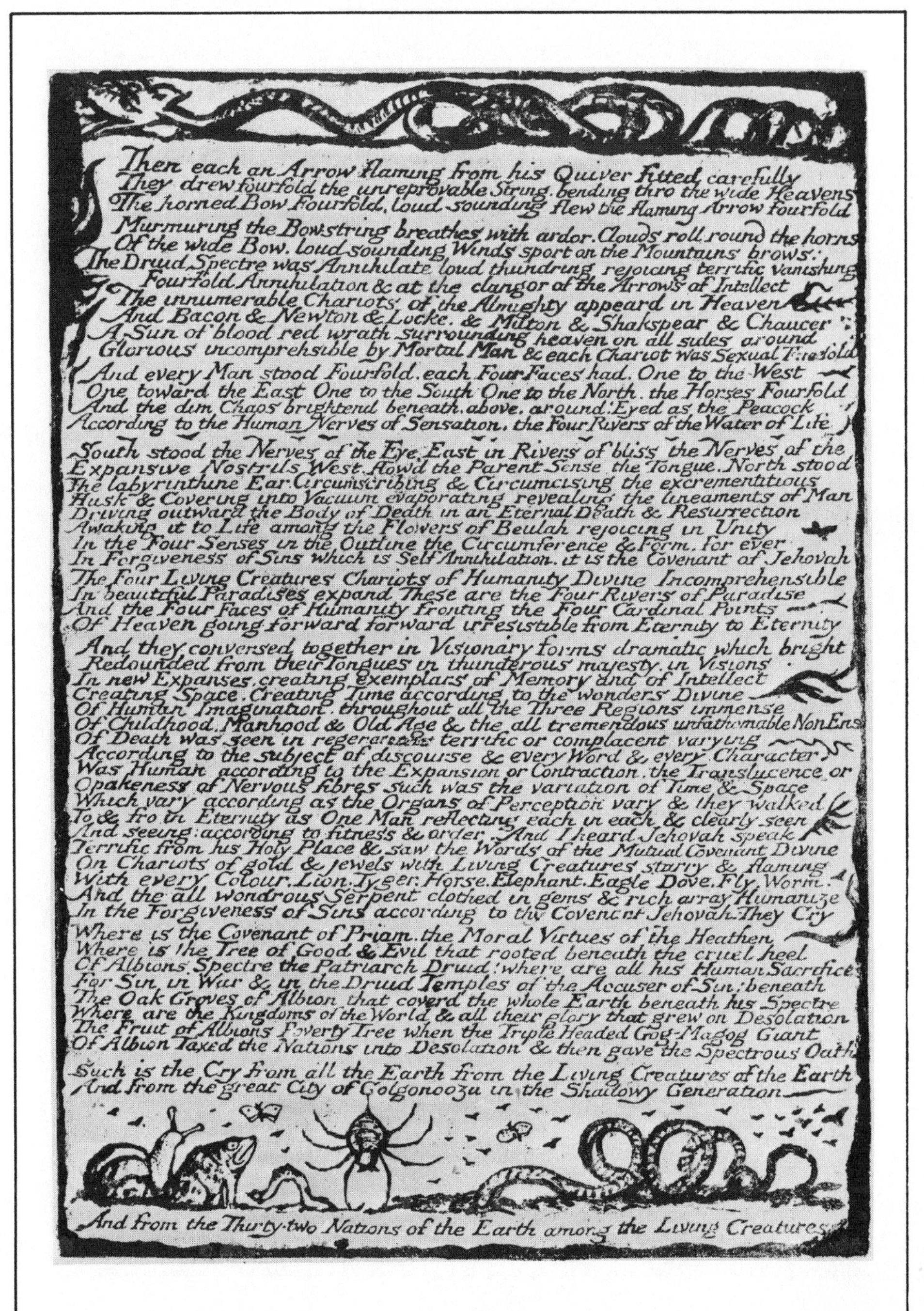
Then each an Arrow flaming from his Quiver fitted carefully
They drew fourfold the unreprovable String. bending thro the wide Heavens
The horned Bow Fourfold. loud sounding flew the flaming Arrow fourfold
Murmuring the Bowstring breathes with ardor. Clouds roll round the horns
Of the wide Bow. loud sounding Winds sport on the Mountains brows:
The Druid Spectre was Annihilate loud thundring rejoicing terrific vanishing
Fourfold Annihilation & at the clangor of the Arrows of Intellect
The innumerable Chariots of the Almighty appeard in Heaven
And Bacon & Newton & Locke. & Milton & Shakspear & Chaucer
A Sun of blood red wrath surrounding heaven on all sides around
Glorious incomprehsible by Mortal Man & each Chariot was Sexual Threefold
And every Man stood Fourfold. each Four Faces had. One to the West
One toward the East One to the South One to the North. the Horses Fourfold
And the dim Chaos brightend beneath. above. around: Eyed as the Peacock
According to the Human Nerves of Sensation. the Four Rivers of the Water of Life
South stood the Nerves of the Eye. East in Rivers of bliss the Nerves of the
Expansive Nostrils West. flowd the Parent Sense the Tongue. North stood
The labyrinthine Ear. Circumscribing & Circumcising the excrementitious
Husk & Covering into Vacuum evaporating revealing the lineaments of Man
Driving outward the Body of Death in an Eternal Death & Resurrection
Awaking it to Life among the Flowers of Beulah rejoicing in Unity
In the Four Senses in the Outline the Circumference & Form. for ever
In Forgiveness of Sins which is Self Annihilation. it is the Covenant of Jehovah
The Four Living Creatures Chariots of Humanity Divine Incomprehensible
In beautiful Paradises expand These are the Four Rivers of Paradise
And the Four Faces of Humanity fronting the Four Cardinal Points
Of Heaven going forward forward irresistible from Eternity to Eternity
And they conversed together in Visionary forms dramatic which bright
Redounded from their Tongues in thunderous majesty. in Visions
In new Expanses. creating exemplars of Memory and of Intellect
Creating Space. Creating Time according to the wonders Divine
Of Human Imagination. throughout all the Three Regions immense
Of Childhood. Manhood & Old Age & the all tremendous unfathomable Non Ens
Of Death was seen in regenerations terrific or complacent varying
According to the subject of discourse & every Word & every Character
Was Human according to the Expansion or Contraction. the Translucence or
Opakeness of Nervous fibres such was the variation of Time & Space
Which vary according as the Organs of Perception vary & they walked
To & fro in Eternity as One Man reflecting each in each & clearly seen
And seeing: according to fitness & order. And I heard Jehovah speak
Terrific from his Holy Place & saw the Words of the Mutual Covenant Divine
On Chariots of gold & jewels with Living Creatures starry & flaming
With every Colour. Lion. Tyger. Horse. Elephant. Eagle Dove. Fly. Worm.
And the all wondrous Serpent clothed in gems & rich array Humanize
In the Forgiveness of Sins according to thy Covenant Jehovah. They Cry
Where is the Covenant of Priam. the Moral Virtues of the Heathen
Where is the Tree of Good & Evil that rooted beneath the cruel heel
Of Albions Spectre the Patriarch Druid: where are all his Human Sacrifice
For Sin in War & in the Druid Temples of the Accuser of Sin: beneath
The Oak Groves of Albion that coverd the whole Earth beneath his Spectre
Where are the Kingdoms of the World & all their glory that grew on Desolation
The Fruit of Albions Poverty Tree when the Triple Headed Gog-Magog Giant
Of Albion Taxed the Nations into Desolation & then gave the Spectrous Oath
Such is the Cry from all the Earth from the Living Creatures of the Earth
And from the great City of Golgonooza in the Shadowy Generation
And from the Thirty-two Nations of the Earth among the Living Creatures

Jerusalem 98[D]

Jerusalem 99ᴱ

Jerusalem 99ᴱ. The "End of The Song" is set in flames which are become "Fountains of Living Waters" (96:36–37) within which Jerusalem and Jehovah-Albion rectify the embrace begun on Plate 96—there coming together in pity and mercy, here in joy and giving. "The Deity on Plate 96 is . . . lifting in his embrace the restored . . . England. . . . The Deity on Plate 99 is descending . . . into the Abyss [and is] received into the arms" of Jerusalem (W). Yet the embrace is intellectual; he holds his body sideways, as she did in Plate 96.

The large-brimmed traveller's hat of Jesus-Jehovah, halo-like, seems blue sky (living waters) between the light blue spears of light from his head and the encircling flames. God does not appear as beams of light to outshine the flames of Hell but as a human father welcoming a lost prodigal. (Compare Goodwill's welcome to Christian in Blake's eleventh design for Bunyan.) The gestures and function of Jerusalem are like those of the fulfilled woman rising to embrace her father at the "End of The Dream" in *Four Zoas* 139; and compare Isaiah 62:5. These two persons must now symbolize all the divided persons in the now whole Song: he all the flayed, chained, decapitated, deluded, accusing and divided men in the poem, now united in One; she all the separated and separating women, now ready for trust and love. The repainting of their faces in E, however, seems to make *both* more male than female and to strengthen a prodigal son allusion.

In Plate 97 we saw Los ready to undertake the true building of the City of Art. Here Enitharmon is ready to weave the furnishings. In E the swirling clouds are picked out here and there in red as shapes of thread-laden spindles, the most prominent just below the fingers of her right hand. Tomorrow Urizen (Jehovah) will resume reading the Everlasting Gospel—or at least that was the original idea: etched on the plate, and visible in A, C, and posthumous copies, but carefully deleted in others, is a small book in which he holds his left index finger even while embracing. Urthona will limp (he is still Hephaestus, god of fire and a blacksmith) to the temple-building, and Enitharmon will spin and weave: see Plate 100.

Jerusalem 100E. Los faces us for the curtain call (but this plate faces back into the work), resting wearied from his successful labor with hammer and compass-like tongs (see Plates 6, 32, 74) —now willing to make equal use of both, since Urizen (as explained in 97:7–8) is now transformed and united with him. Los's genitals are restored (in E). The spectre of Urthona (the radiationE around his head still rather bat-like) makes a giant leap up from the serpent temple, shouldering his golden hod. Yet light from it pours down onto the mended or perfected wall of trilithons and suffuses the illuminated page. Perhaps his building a new Jerusalem is precisely a matter of *illuminating* the serpent line, the Jerusalem we have always known. The trilithons were once Eden's wall (see note Plate 92) and monuments of Britain in "its ancient glory" (*DC* 5). The cruelties of fallen Druidism are annihilated, the serpent temple is transformed or transfigured, by the radiance of sunlight and moonlight poured on its stones as ink and color onto these hundred copper stones printed into *Jerusalem*. The poet's emanation, Enitharmon (her bluish dark skin and veil of night sky retaining associations with Vala in Plate 46), unwinds from a shuttle in her left hand the "aching fibres of Los" (88:29) which he "will fix . . . With pulsations" (87:10—see Plate 82 note) and drapes them over the moon-ark of Generation, a cup (whiteF, goldenE) filling with blood and glandous wine, Vala's cup transformed, to fall as red rain, veins of mortal life immortal (compare *America* 4:5), to be woven into "the Immortal atmospheres" (*Four Zoas* 37:8—compare Plate 63:40). The temple represents "the all wondrous Serpent . . . Humanize[d]" (98:44). There are five stars under Enitharmon's left arm, two above it, two above the moon. Los's tongs hold earth, are a creative counterpart of the compasses in *Europe* i. Perhaps the most instructive anticipation of the work of Illumination in this plate is to be found in the text of Plate 82 and in the picture of Los and Enitharmon in Plate 85. She needed a spindle and found one in the moon: was she entangling the sun, in 85? He, unable to cope with the moon, now shoulders the sun.

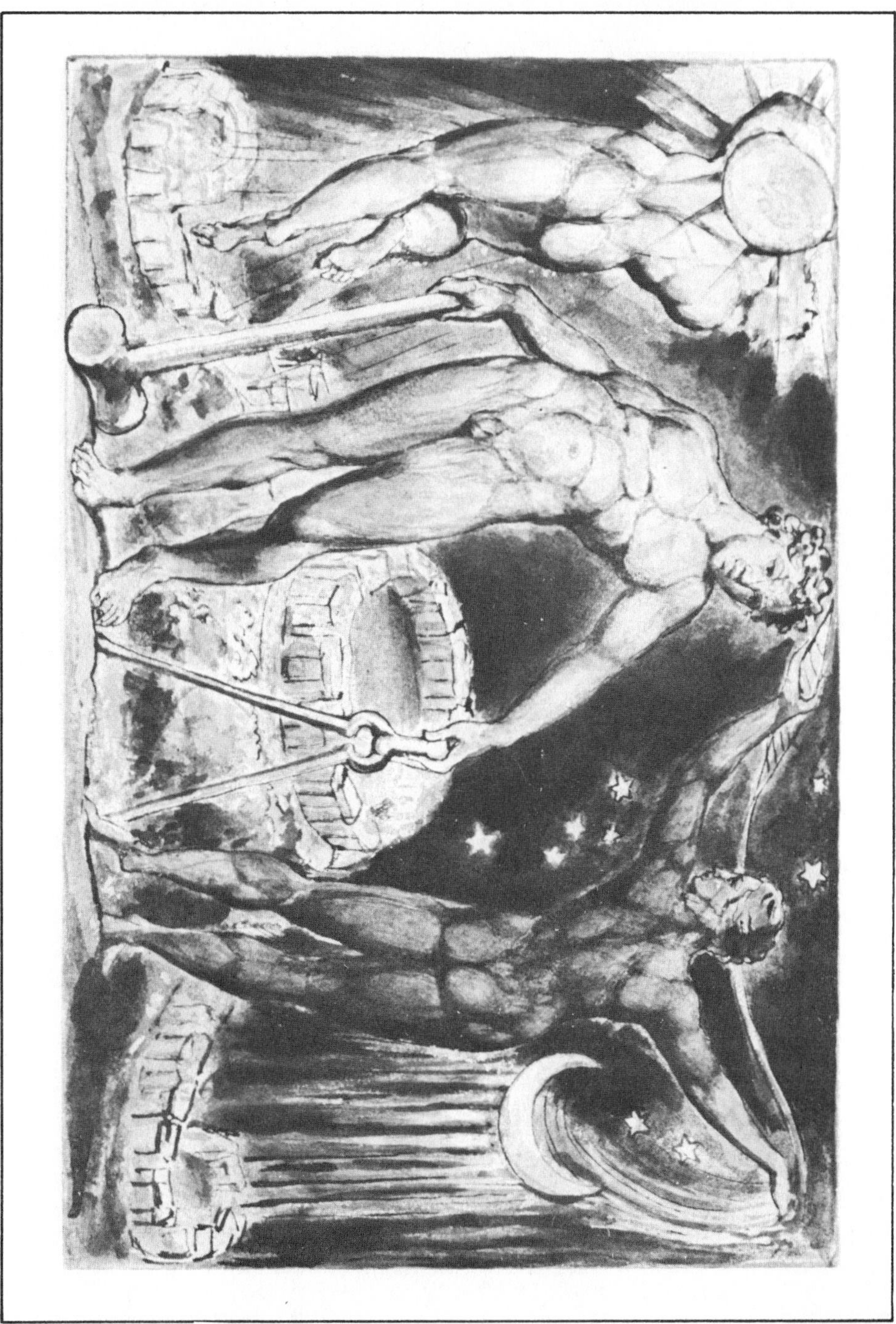

Jerusalem 100E (exact size)

On Homers Poetry

Every Poem must necessarily be a perfect Unity, but why Homers is peculiarly so, I cannot tell: he has told the story of Bellerophon & omitted the Judgment of Paris which is not only a part, but a principal part of Homers subject
But when a Work has Unity it is as much in a Part as in the Whole. the Torso is as much a Unity as the Laocoon
As Unity is the cloke of folly so Goodness is the cloke of knavery Those who will have Unity exclusively in Homer come out with a Moral like a sting in the tail: Aristotle says Characters are either Good or Bad: now Goodness or Badness has nothing to do with Character. an Apple tree a Pear tree a Horse a Lion, are Characters but a Good Apple tree or a Bad, is an Apple tree still: a Horse is not more a Lion for being a Bad Horse. that is its Character: its Goodness or Badness is another consideration.
It is the same with the Moral of a whole Poem as with the Moral Goodness of its parts Unity & Morality, are secondary considerations & belong to Philosophy & not to Poetry, to Exception & not to Rule, to Accident & not to Substance. the Ancients calld it eating of the tree of good & evil.

The Classics, it is the Classics! & not Goths nor Monks, that Desolate Europe with Wars.

On Virgil

Sacred Truth has pronounced that Greece & Rome as Babylon & Egypt: so far from being parents of Arts & Sciences as they pretend: were destroyers of all Art. Homer Virgil & Ovid confirm this opinion & make us reverence The Word of God. the only light of antiquity that remains unperverted by War. Virgil in the Eneid Book VI. line 848 says Let others study Art: Rome has somewhat better to do, namely War & Dominion

Rome & Greece swept Art into their maw & destroyd it a Warlike State never can produce Art. It will Rob & Plunder & accumulate into one place, & Translate & Copy & Buy & Sell & Criticise, but not Make. Grecian is Mathematic Form
Gothic is Living Form
Mathematic Form is Eternal in the Reasoning Memory. Living Form is Eternal Existence

On Homers Poetry[D]

ON HOMERS POETRY AND ON VIRGIL

On Homers Poetry[D]. A scroll of five twists on the left of the title and a white visceral cloud on the right recall Vala's intestinal veil in *Jerusalem* (e.g. 24, 83, 85). We are in This World, though "Homers" is lifted somewhat by a flourish from the lighter word "Poetry."

The whole first paragraph of writing constitutes the leafage of a tree whose trunk is drawn below "eating of the tree." Another trunk at the left beside a bard with harp suggests a grove, oak no doubt: Homer is a Druid bard, with standing audience (see *Songs* 54). The one listening attentively with hand held against right cheek will be Virgil receiving the Druid theme from Homer. (In his eighth design for Dante's Inferno, "Homer and the Ancient Poets," Blake removes Homer from an oak grove where a piper is playing and exposes him holding a sword with four silent but leaf-crowned companions in a thicket of beech. The ancient poet beside him stands in the posture given Virgil here.)

Out of the grass beside the central tree a serpentine coil rises under the title "On Virgil"—a bend and ten loops, becoming flame-like and matched by a flame-vine from the top of the "V," to join strong flames that rise from the illustration of "War & Dominion" below: two humans, Albion (shall we say?) lying prone on a battlefield of fire, Jerusalem fallen backward away from him, not comforting him as in *Jerusalem* 94 but taking the feet-to-feet position of *Jerusalem* 18, 40, 45; see 71.

The sketchiness of drawing at the bottom is meant to indicate the inadequacy of "Grecian . . . Mathematic Form": at left some arcs and angles of vegetation, perhaps, then a measured row of stone-like human figures. One under "Gothic" is coming to life, rising, and beckoning the others (including a dark blob above them) toward the right corner—where a prone figure, or one hunched as Eve in *Songs* 1, is opening one eye toward two human faces among the shadows. (Contrast the beckoning and movement of forms in *Jerusalem* 24.)

THE GHOST OF ABEL
A REVELATION IN THE VISIONS OF JEHOVAH

Ghost of Abel 1D. The title is in human quotation marks, a clothed pair directing us into it, a naked seductive pair of dancers at the right, among other celebrants. Life springing from Abel's death, seen in spiritual vision, is indicated by the family of happy humans using the stiff gravestone letters of "ABEL" (compare the acrobats on "THEL" in that title page): a child leans against A, an infant flies above it toward a boy standing on B; another sits on E; a tiny figure flies below; a hand reaches up from someone stooping in L to the outstretched arm of a large woman—all the rest being children, or fairies?

An ascending figure with outstretched arms rises into the top right corner; it is the ghost of Abel. Directly below, separated from this spiritual form by flames or a cloud edge, the first murder is enacted, Cain with extended knife about to slay his brother, who hides his face as they run into brambles. In a forest above "To Lord Byron" a lion is chasing a bounding stag as an emblem of Lord Byron "in the Wilderness" doubting "the Visions" of a Jehovah-Messiah (the stag having served traditionally for Christ). But the passage in *The Mental Traveller* (*P&P* 477) in which male and female wander in "the desart wild," he like "Lion Wolf & Boar," she fleeing "Like the wild Stag," suggests that the allusion may be primarily to Byron's vaunted entrapment in corporeal desires. (For pictures of a lion and stag on the same page see *Marriage* 8; for other stags see *Marriage* 26 and *America* 16, the latter in a positive visionary role.) At the left of "Scene" two small figures stand on the handle of a sort of flail.

In the first line of dialogue we see the flaming altar of sacrifice, Abel's slain body, and Cain with knife fleeing to the right. Before Jehovah speaks we are apprised that he is the Savior-Creator by the (tiny) flying bird before his name in the line above Cain, picking up the four small birds flying above "Can a Poet" (in the opening paragraph), and by the shooting star at his outcry of "Adam!" (line 1). Note that other birds accompany his name here and on most subsequent occurrences, including a large bird when he is saying "lift thine eyes" (7), perhaps a dove or eagle. Under "Adam—" (2) a gowned figure soars leftward, probably represent-

THE GHOST of ABEL
A Revelation In the Visions of Jehovah
Seen by William Blake
To LORD BYRON in the Wilderness
What doest thou here Elijah?
Can a Poet doubt the Visions of Jehovah? Nature has no Outline:
but Imagination has. Nature has no Tune: but Imagination has!
Nature has no Supernatural & dissolves: Imagination is Eternity
Scene. A rocky Country. Eve fainted over the dead body
of Abel which lays near a Grave. Adam kneels by her. Jehovah
stands above
Jehovah— Adam!
Adam— I will not hear thee more thou Spiritual Voice
Is this Death?
Jehovah— Adam!
Adam— It is in vain: I will not hear thee
Henceforth! Is this thy Promise that the Womans Seed
Should bruise the Serpents head: Is this the Serpent? Ah!
Seven times O Eve thou hast fainted over the Dead Ah! Ah!
Eve revives
Eve— Is this the Promise of Jehovah! O it is all a vain delusion
This Death & this Life & this Jehovah!
Jehovah— Woman: lift thine eyes
A Voice is heard coming on
Voice— O Earth cover not thou my Blood! cover not thou my Blood
Enter the Ghost of Abel
Eve— Thou Visionary Phantasm thou art not the real Abel.
Abel— Among the Elohim a Human Victim I wander I am their House
Prince of the Air & our dimensions compass Zenith & Nadir
Vain is thy Covenant O Jehovah I am the Accuser & Avenger
Of Blood O Earth Cover not thou the Blood of Abel
Jehovah— What Vengeance dost thou require
Abel— Life for Life! Life for Life!
Jehovah— He who shall take Cains life must also Die O Abel
And who is he: Adam wilt thou, or Eve thou do this
Adam— It is all a Vain delusion of the all creative Imagination
Eve come away & let us not believe these vain delusions
Abel is dead & Cain slew him: We shall also Die a Death
And then! what then! be as poor Abel a Thought: or as
This! O what shall I call thee Form Divine! Father of Mercies
That appearest to my Spiritual Vision: Eve seest thou also
Eve— I see him plainly with my Minds Eye. I see also Abel living:
Tho terribly afflicted as We also are. yet Jehovah sees him

Ghost of Abel 1D

ing "Spiritual Voice" the way such figures represent "Soul" in *Marriage*. Just below, clothed angels fly left with two birds when Adam recognizes this Voice, though his refusal to listen to it brings an emblem of the serpent making devious coils beside a bough with seven apples and an oak leaf. In the next emblem, of Eve and Adam amid fruit, there are eight apples on her side, only three on his. Briars from near Adam's feet precede "Eve revives," but a leafing and fruiting tendril follows. Even as the tiny birds fly in to be named by her, however, the "Voice . . . coming on" sends coils up to emphasize "vain delusion" (6) and to whip down (from A) toward "Eve." Or rather, the coils (with a good message: see their grape leaves) warn us that the Voice, not Jehovah, is "a vain delusion" and, running down to her next remark, a "Visionary Phantasm" (9). A good conjuror, a watchman type, points to the bloody waves from "the Ghost of Abel" and then to the words "not the real Abel" (9) to spare us (or Byron) from confusion. The next vignette, at left, shows the ghost soaring above Eve who lies under barren trees like Lyca in the forest in *Songs* 35.

At Abel's words (14) no clear shape emerges, except deletion signs pulling three *f*'s out of his words, making the line read: "Life for Lie! Lie or Life!" We next see Adam and Eve naked under the fruitless tree, turning away from each other, alongside his remarks which begin with mistrust of Jehovah and end with true recognition of Jehovah as the Form Divine.

Ghost of Abel 2D. At top left, circled by five or six birds, Eve, who now sees "Abel living: Tho terribly afflicted as We also are" (1:23–24), is bent over carrying his (empty) coffin. Flames with lightning edges rise from the name "Abel" (4) as he asks of true sacrifices, and Jehovah's name, repeated a step below itself, sends intertwining vine banners to herald five infinitely various birds at a line from "Spirit" (4). The next picture shows Eve seated and Abel struggling with his attempt to deny, his left hand pushing her head, his right raised to ward off contrition. Another gowned spirit (see 1:11) soars among the many birds trying to connect Abel with Jehovah; its flight leftward may mark their failure to prevail against the gospel of sacrifice, despite their flying under "the Blood" (12) and over "Human Blood . . . not" (13), for now arises "Satan Armed"—though we see him naked, arguing in the air, backwards, with the seated Adam-Jehovah, "Thou Human O Jehovah" (15). Jehovah's legs are crossed, like a conjuror's—but so are Christ's in *Paradise Regained* 9, where Satan is twisting in the air this way.

When Jehovah says "Such is My Will" (19), small hieroglyphs summarize the Gospel story: Jesus as a child, parting from parents, then receiving shafts (unseen: compare *Marriage* 22) of sacrificial arrows from an archer holding his bow (under the "cr" of "Sacrificed": 18), Jesus enacting his passion on the "Thy" of "Thyself," then risen a spiritual body and received by three women. The stage direction "Thunders" is given echoic leaves of sound at one end and zigzags of lightning at the other. Adam and Eve beside the tree now see Satan's sacrificing his serpent form (twisted round the tree's pyramidal girth with its head emerging at the top, the branches making arms of a cross, from which a branch of three, or four, apples depends) as Satan's contribution, by self annihilation, to resurrection. Eve while walking away reaches and looks up, for spiritual fruit. Four birds fly under "My Will" (19) and one under "following" (below 21).

At the bottom the vengeful face of the pointing accusing "Voice of Abels Blood," wearing a halo, shouts as he soars in a cloud-phantom form up from the blood spilled from the head of Abel's body, upon which his brother now lies, skin-clad, in almost exactly the position of Jerusalem upon slain Albion in *Jerusalem* 94; the "Brotherhood and Love" on the ground triumph over the Phantom in the air.

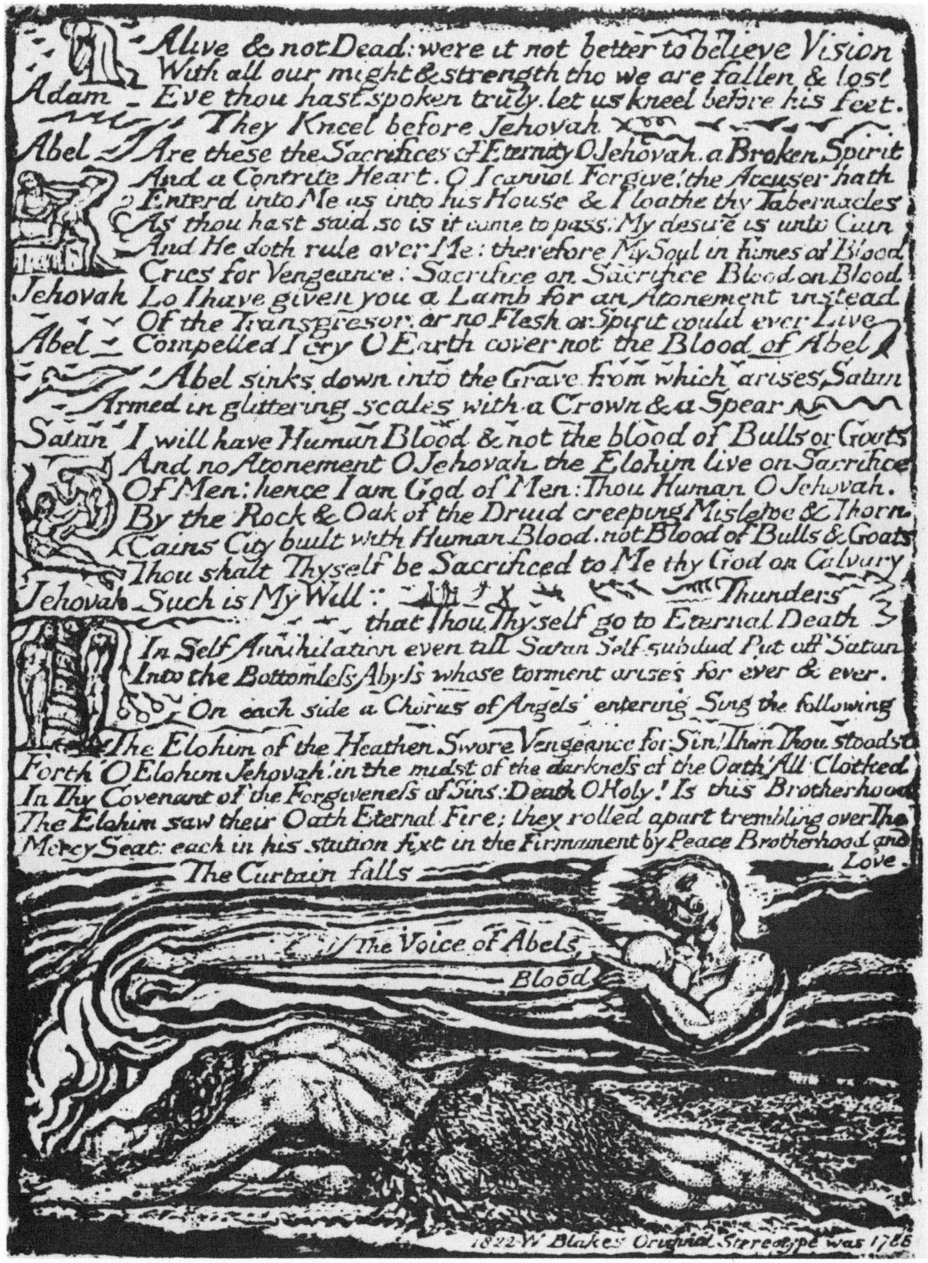

Alive & not Dead: were it not better to believe Vision
With all our might & strength tho we are fallen & lost
Adam - Eve thou hast spoken truly. let us kneel before his feet.
They Kneel before Jehovah
Abel Are these the Sacrifices of Eternity O Jehovah. a Broken Spirit
And a Contrite Heart. O I cannot Forgive! the Accuser hath
Enterd into Me as into his House & I loathe thy Tabernacles
As thou hast said so is it come to pass: My desire is unto Cain
And He doth rule over Me: therefore My Soul in fumes of Blood
Cries for Vengeance: Sacrifice on Sacrifice Blood on Blood
Jehovah Lo I have given you a Lamb for an Atonement instead
Of the Transgresor, or no Flesh or Spirit could ever Live
Abel Compelled I cry O Earth cover not the Blood of Abel
Abel sinks down into the Grave. from which arises Satan
Armed in glittering scales with a Crown & a Spear
Satan I will have Human Blood & not the blood of Bulls or Goats
And no Atonement O Jehovah the Elohim live on Sacrifice
Of Men: hence I am God of Men: Thou Human O Jehovah.
By the Rock & Oak of the Druid creeping Mistletoe & Thorn
Cains City built with Human Blood. not Blood of Bulls & Goats
Thou shalt Thyself be Sacrificed to Me thy God on Calvary
Jehovah Such is My Will: Thunders
that Thou Thyself go to Eternal Death
In Self Annihilation even till Satan Self-subdud Put off Satan
Into the Bottomless Abyss whose torment arises for ever & ever.
On each side a Chorus of Angels entering Sing the following
The Elohim of the Heathen Swore Vengeance for Sin! Then Thou stoodst
Forth O Elohim Jehovah! in the midst of the darkness of the Oath! All Clothed
In Thy Covenant of the Forgiveness of Sins: Death O Holy! Is this Brotherhood
The Elohim saw their Oath Eternal Fire; they rolled apart trembling over The
Mercy Seat: each in his station fixt in the Firmament by Peace Brotherhood and Love.
The Curtain falls
The Voice of Abels Blood
1822 W Blakes Original Stereotype was 1788

Ghost of Abel 2D

APPENDIX: PROOFS AND VARIANTS

Songs 1U

SONGS OF INNOCENCE AND OF EXPERIENCE

Songs 1U (general title page). Among the many copies I have seen, this one is unique in placing a golden apple in the mouth of the rising bird. See the discussion above.

Songs 4^{U} Introduction (Innocence). The details retraced with a fine pen in this copy seem generally closer to the original details in the etched plate than is usual for this page.

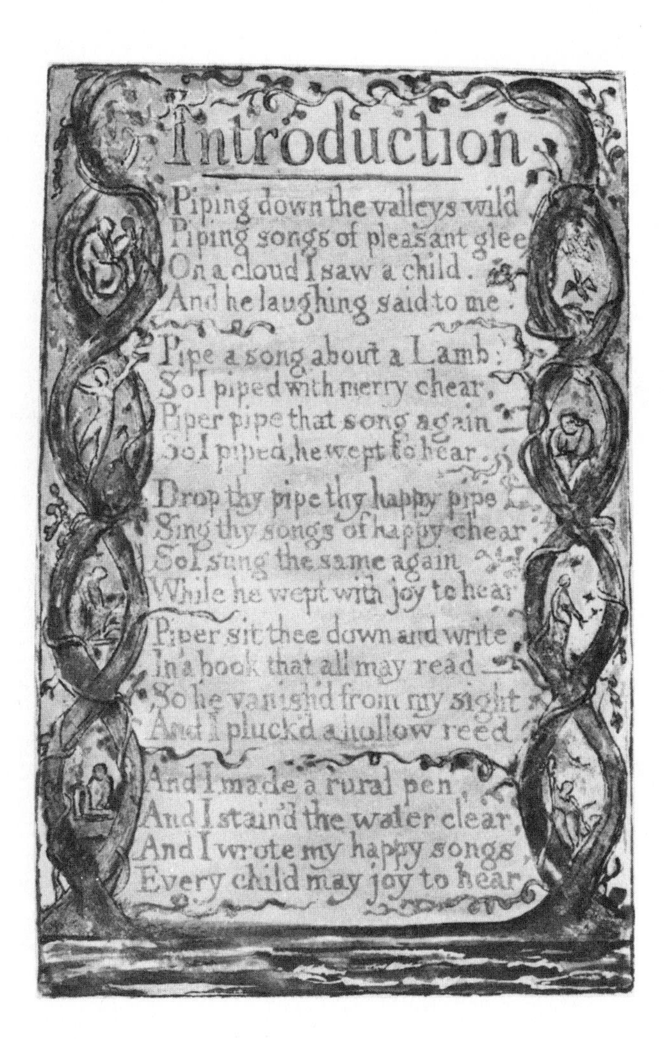

Introduction

Piping down the valleys wild
Piping songs of pleasant glee
On a cloud I saw a child.
And he laughing said to me.

Pipe a song about a Lamb:
So I piped with merry chear,
Piper pipe that song again
So I piped, he wept to hear.

Drop thy pipe thy happy pipe
Sing thy songs of happy chear
So I sung the same again
While he wept with joy to hear

Piper sit thee down and write
In a book that all may read
So he vanish'd from my sight
And I pluck'd a hollow reed

And I made a rural pen,
And I stain'd the water clear,
And I wrote my happy songs
Every child may joy to hear

Songs 4^{U}

Songs a[C]

Songs a[C] (Rejected tailpiece, used in copies BCD, then replaced by *Songs* 52, "To Tirzah"). In both copies[CD] for which we know Blake's arrangement of plates, the series of songs culminates with "The Clod and the Pebble," bringing the question of human sympathy for "another" to an impasse, right after[C] or shortly after (in D, where the page of threatened flower-loves comes between) the "Holy Thursday" that sees children reduced to misery. In the nick of time comes this appearance of God as Human Form Divine, as Father of children, our maker ever nigh. In these two copies *Songs* 27, "On Anothers Sorrow," conveying the same message fully in words and only mysteriously in illumination (see note) is placed early in the Innocence group (the fifth song in D, the tenth in C).

Keynes and Raine (I 397n) see "a majestic androgynous figure upborne by six winged cherubs," but the figure of God as Father is no more (and no less) androgynous here than in "The Little Boy Found" and "The Little Black Boy." Reference to "the traditional attitude of prayer" found in non-Blakean paintings of the Christian Virgin is less to the point than to paintings of the Ascension of Christ or Blake's own "God Blessing the Seventh Day." "On Anothers Sorrow" should remind us that the children gathering here are supporting the Savior in the sense that their belief (like the piper's in *Songs* 27) enables them and us to see his human form. When Blake replaced this picture with "To Tirzah" he was choosing another way to say "It is Raised a Spiritual Body." (See note on *Songs* 52.)

Songs b (A Divine Image). Printed posthumously; unpublished by Blake (this reproduction from a reconstitution of a "plate-perfect image" by John Wright). Originally etched for *Songs of Experience* (the style of lettering puts it earlier than the plates used, not later), this Song was replaced by "The Human Abstract" (*Songs* 47), a subtler contrary to "The Divine Image" (*Songs* 18).

At the left of the first line stands a faintly printed figure with trumpet (the effect in copy a) or raised hand initiating the movement continued in whip-like lines running out from the "C" and "l" of "Cruelty." (Above, at the left of the title, is an image that prints badly in all copies but, as developed in this reconstitution, suggests a human or angel—possibly wielding the thick line above the title like a lash.) In the stanza break, and thus between two lines about "Human Dress," a vegetable (fibrous) undulation carries a fashion show in its five valleys suggesting free and innocent human dress: a man and woman (perhaps) running or dancing, with arms flung wide, in the first two valleys; a man standing fully clothed in the next; a more stately pair in the last two, reaching toward each other. Leaves grow down from the snaky stem, for part of the length, but it becomes barren and loops about to form a divided whip above the tiny human figure that is attached to "forged" (5) while trying to fly. Another human leaps back into the right margin from "Forge" (6). A tiny bird flies at the end of "Face" (7).

As a naked young blacksmith, backed by a cloud and a waxing moon and surrounded by flecks of sweat (or sparks), applies effort and anxiety to his hammer, the beginning of a human face on the sun he is laboring at opens one eye, and three of the spikes of solar radiation are becoming fibrous and wavy like hair—though still all too much like "forged Iron."

The blacksmith, identifiable later as Los, is engaged in an effort of imagination like that of the piper in *Songs* 27. The emblem shows that his blows to unseal the furnace of the "Human Face" (7) are simultaneously bringing the sunrise. For his similar later efforts at this anvil, compare *Jerusalem* 32 and 73; also 62.

Songs b

Marriage i^B

THE MARRIAGE OF HEAVEN AND HELL

Marriage i^B (Our End is come). (Imprint line omitted by the photographer: "Publish'd June 5 1793 by WBlake Lambeth"; this is the first state of the plate, not the second, though so designated in Keynes *Catalogue of Blake's Separate Engravings,* where it is reproduced complete.) Frontispiece in copy B.

The binding of this print into the Bodleian copy of *The Marriage of Heaven and Hell* (bought by Francis Douce from George Dyer in Blake's lifetime, 1821, but lacking pagination by Blake) just may have been at Blake's direction, and the appropriateness is worth considering. The caption as an allusion to *America* 15:16 implies that a certain king (with his warrior chiefs) has stepped over the threshold of his doom; as a frontispiece to *Marriage* it implies an identification of the "jealous king" of "A Song of Liberty" who leads his hosts "thro' the waste wilderness . . . glancing his beamy eyelids over the deep in dark dismay" (verses 15–18).

As an addition to the portfolio of political caricatures in *Europe* (or an anticipation of them, chronologically) we have here the mad King George, identified by spiked crown and an insane look, not toward the external menace that the others see at the left (as Bromion in *Visions* i) but as if expressing intolerable horrors within. The sword-clutching warrior may be identified with Rintrah as Pitt in *Europe* 6; the other warrior, holding a spear behind the king, looks more like Thurlow or Dundas than Burke, though any of these identifications could be defended.

Points of comparison and contrast can be made with the frontispiece of *America,* where the human form filling a gap in a wall is winged but chained, the wall stony but broken. Here the wooden wall, threshold, and floor, oak grained, will be shown in later states of the plate as flaming (*The Accusers*) or gone up in smoke (the color print) leaving the heroes shivering on a wet lake (of brimstone?).

VISIONS
OF THE DAUGHTERS
OF ALBION

Visions 1c. Unique in this copy, I believe, is the angel with wings and arms outspread, who seems just to have descended into the lap of the woman riding the horse-like cloud above the letter i. See discussion above.

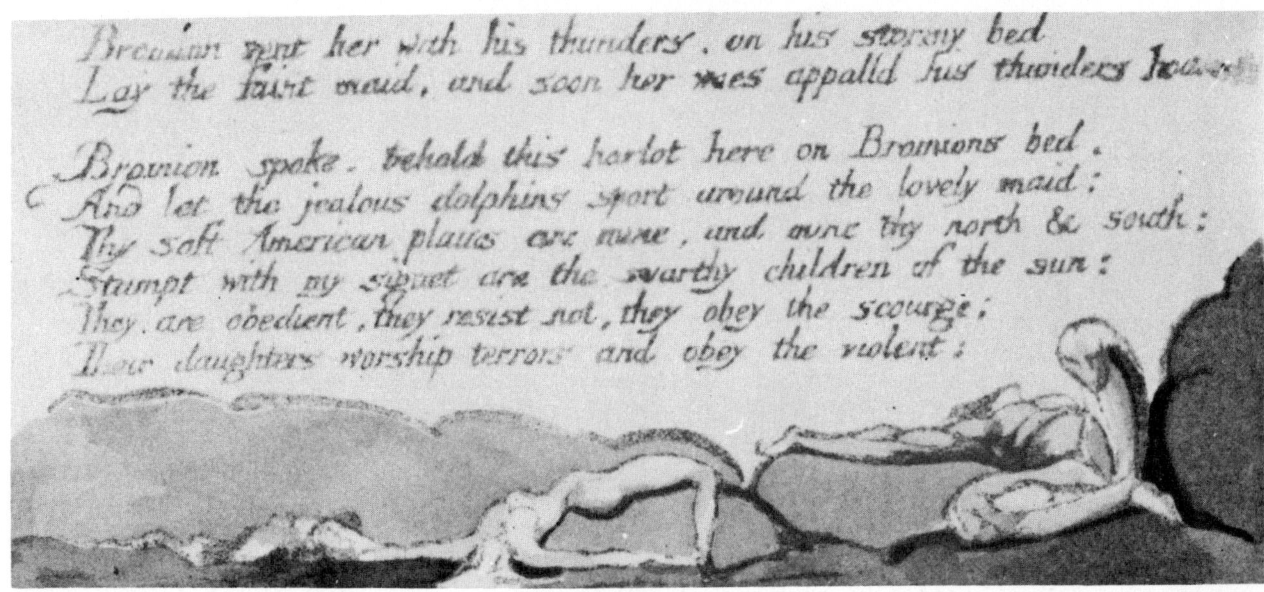

Visions 1c (detail, slightly enlarged)

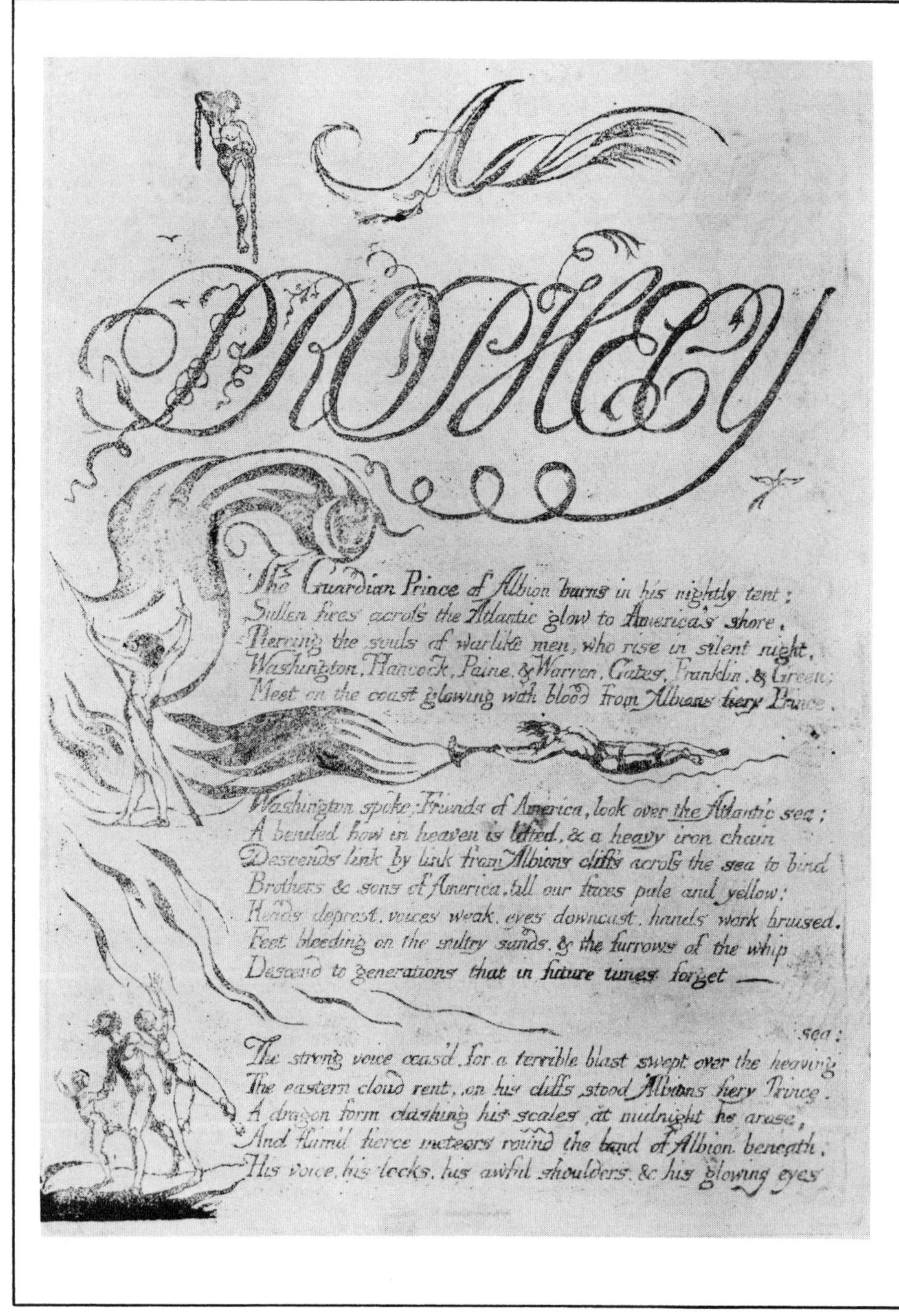

A PROPHECY

The Guardian Prince of Albion burns in his nightly tent:
Sullen fires across the Atlantic glow to America's shore,
Piercing the souls of warlike men, who rise in silent night,
Washington, Hancock, Paine, & Warren, Gates, Franklin, & Green;
Meet on the coast glowing with blood from Albions fiery Prince.

Washington spoke; Friends of America, look over the Atlantic sea;
A bended bow in heaven is lifted, & a heavy iron chain
Descends link by link from Albions cliffs across the sea to bind
Brothers & sons of America, till our faces pale and yellow;
Heads deprest, voices weak, eyes downcast, hands work bruised,
Feet bleeding on the sultry sands, & the furrows of the whip
Descend to generations that in future times forget —

The strong voice ceas'd; for a terrible blast swept over the heaving sea;
The eastern cloud rent; on his cliffs stood Albions fiery Prince,
A dragon form clashing his scales at midnight he arose,
And flam'd fierce meteors round the band of Albion beneath.
His voice, his locks, his awful shoulders, & his glowing eyes

America a

AMERICA A PROPHECY

(Reduced from about 9 by 6 inches)

America a (cancelled variant of *America* 3). Unique proof copy. The text when redrawn was slightly changed with slightly different ornamentation. The three birds became six, lily shapes were added to the title in place of vaguer terminals, and spirals were given more freedom and strength. I think the page was remade to adapt the figure of Orc soaring in chains (top left) to the Preludium when it was invented and inserted. In Plate a, Orc seems to rise from the text mass; in Plate 3 he rises at an angle identifying him with the figure crouched to spring in Plate 2. Blake also wanted, obviously, to remove the flag and flag-bearer, eliminating even the tiny flag on "The" (1), for reasons we can only guess. Note that the staff ends as a spear and that what the apparent bearer really holds, in both hands, is a small banner or wide broadside: the Declaration of Independence, we may surmise. The flag, near its end, seems to divide and form a loop (or there may be flames issuing from the loop) beyond which it tapers to a sort of proboscis that gropes toward the feeling end of the looped line below "*PROPHECY*."

America b (*America* variant of 6). When redrawn for Plate 6, with different text leaving more room for the figures, there was an amplification of King George's three forms. The dragon form became more human in body, face, and hands (these being rather frog-like here), with one fewer kink in his tail. In Plate b his human form, at bottom, is alone, and although he looks in alarm at a monster near him, we see it as a fallen birch trunk; in Plate 4 it is in the water, at left, a beached sea monster. Perhaps the mystery of the topless birch trunk in *America* 12, next to the living birch with roots like the one here, could receive some light from this coincidence.

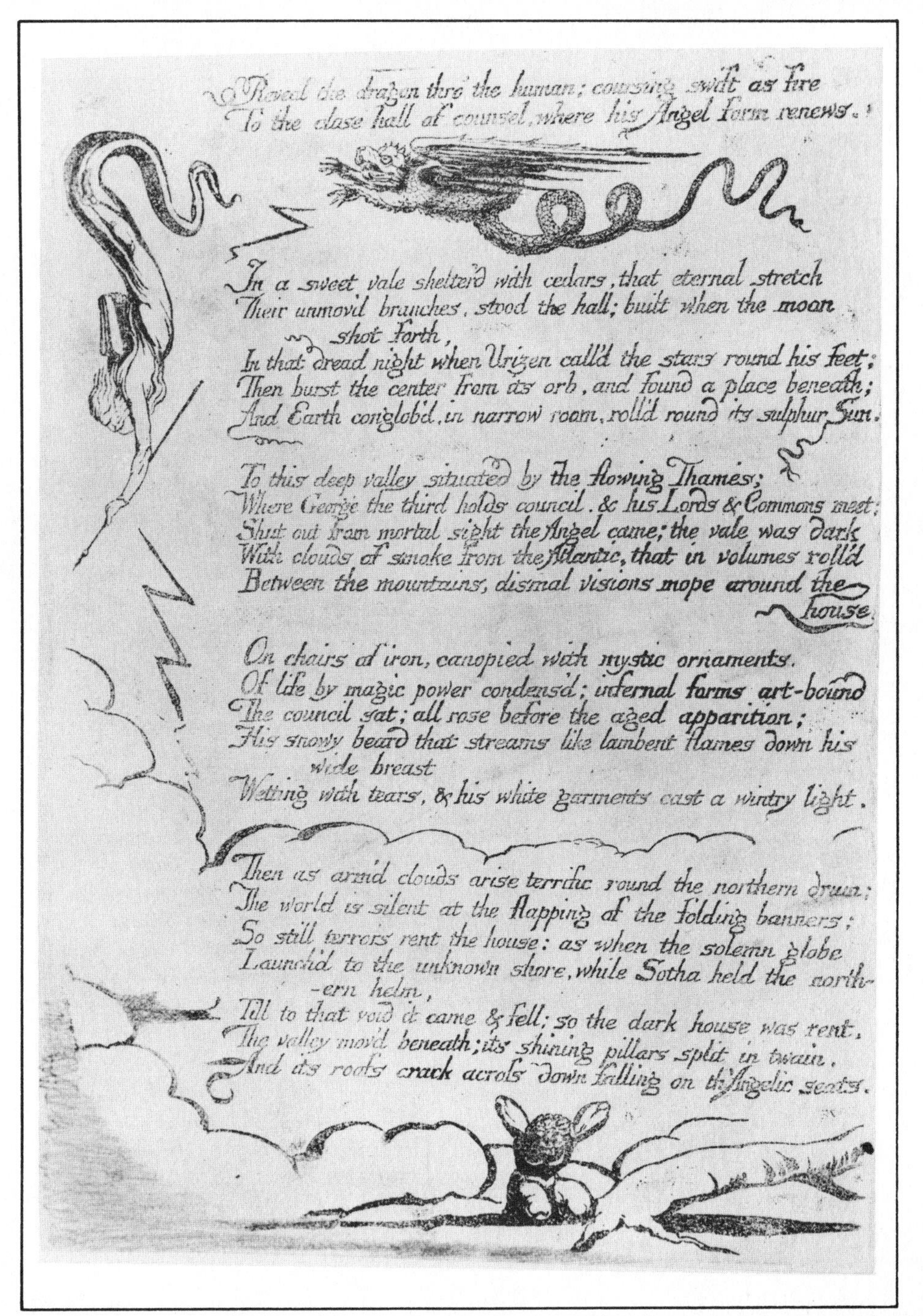
Reveal the dragon thro' the human; coursing swift as fire
To the close hall of counsel, where his Angel form renews.

In a sweet vale shelter'd with cedars, that eternal stretch
Their unmov'd branches, stood the hall; built when the moon
shot forth,
In that dread night when Urizen call'd the stars round his feet;
Then burst the center from its orb, and found a place beneath;
And Earth conglob'd, in narrow room, roll'd round its sulphur Sun.

To this deep valley situated by the flowing Thames;
Where George the third holds council. & his Lords & Commons meet;
Shut out from mortal sight the Angel came; the vale was dark
With clouds of smoke from the Atlantic, that in volumes roll'd
Between the mountains, dismal visions mope around the
house.

On chairs of iron, canopied with mystic ornaments.
Of life by magic power condens'd; infernal forms art-bound
The council sat; all rose before the aged apparition;
His snowy beard that streams like lambent flames down his
wide breast
Wetting with tears, & his white garments cast a wintry light.

Then as arm'd clouds arise terrific round the northern drum;
The world is silent at the flapping of the folding banners;
So still terrors rent the house: as when the solemn globe
Launch'd to the unknown shore, while Sotha held the north-
-ern helm,
Till to that void it came & fell; so the dark house was rent,
The valley mov'd beneath; its shining pillars split in twain,
And its roofs crack across down falling on th'Angelic seats.

America b

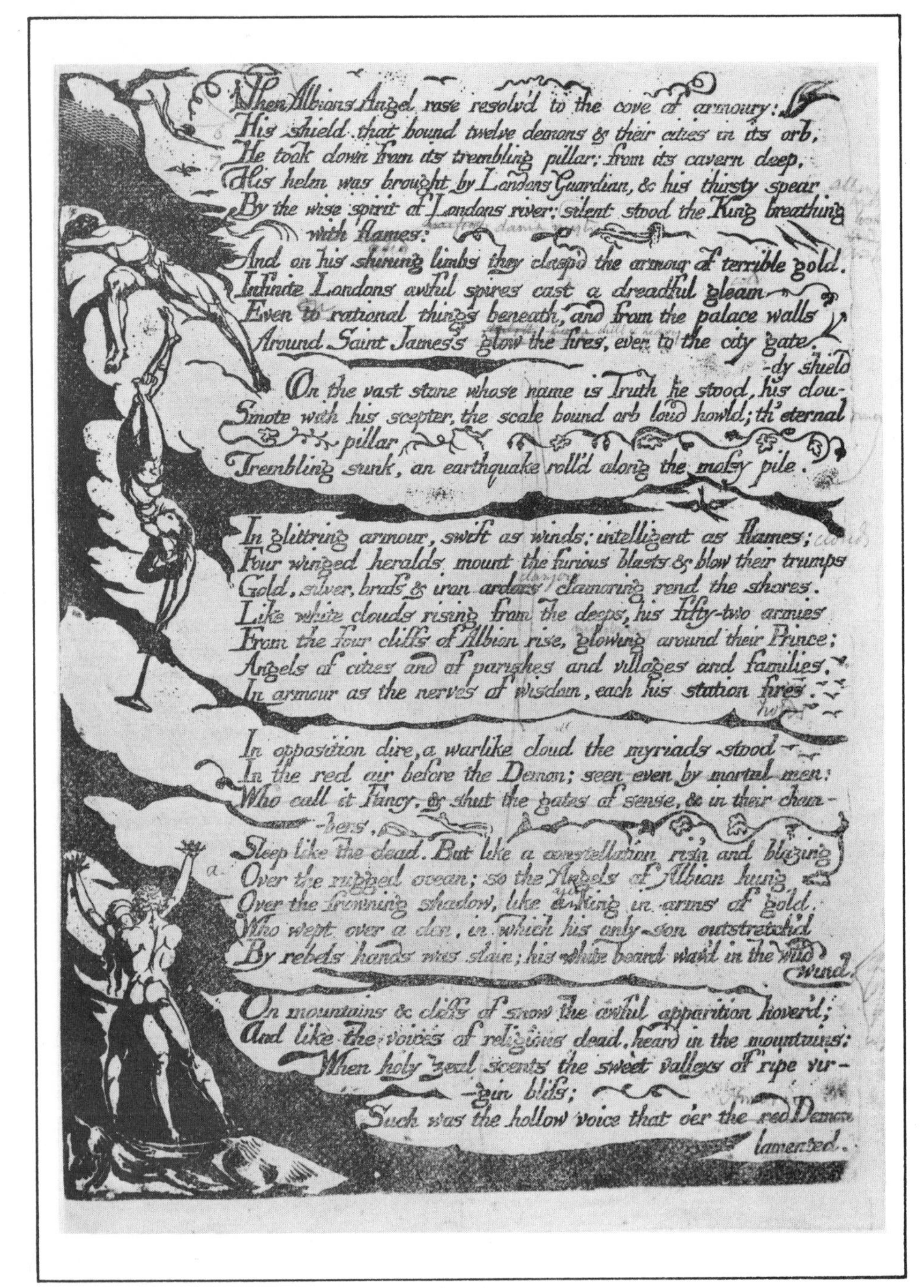
When Albions Angel rose resolv'd to the cove of armoury:
His shield that bound twelve demons & their cities in its orb,
He took down from its trembling pillar; from its cavern deep,
His helm was brought by Londons Guardian, & his thirsty spear
By the wise spirit of Londons river: silent stood the King breathing
with flames:
And on his shining limbs they clasp'd the armour of terrible gold.
Infinite Londons awful spires cast a dreadful gleam
Even to rational things beneath, and from the palace walls
Around Saint James's glow the fires, even to the city gate.

On the vast stone whose name is Truth he stood, his clou-
-dy shield
Smote with his scepter, the scale bound orb loud howl'd; th' eternal
pillar
Trembling sunk, an earthquake roll'd along the mossy pile.

In glittring armour, swift as winds; intelligent as flames;
Four winged heralds mount the furious blasts & blow their trumps
Gold, silver, brass & iron ardors clamoring rend the shores.
Like white clouds rising from the deeps, his fifty-two armies
From the four cliffs of Albion rise, glowing around their Prince;
Angels of cities and of parishes and villages and families,
In armour as the nerves of wisdom, each his station fires.

In opposition dire, a warlike cloud the myriads stood
In the red air before the Demon; seen even by mortal men:
Who call it Fancy, & shut the gates of sense, & in their cham-
-bers,
Sleep like the dead. But like a constellation ris'n and blazing
Over the rugged ocean; so the Angels of Albion hung
Over the frowning shadow, like a King in arms of gold.
Who wept over a den, in which his only son outstretch'd
By rebels hands was slain; his white beard wav'd in the wild
wind.

On mountains & cliffs of snow the awful apparition hover'd;
And like the voices of religious dead, heard in the mountains:
When holy zeal scents the sweet valleys of ripe vir-
-gin bliss;
Such was the hollow voice that o'er the red Demon
lamented.

America c

America c (cancelled plate eliminated in revision). This plate may have followed Plate b, some of its motifs being absorbed into the illuminations of Plate 5, some logically possible after Plate 8. At lower left on the Atlantic rock where Oothoon lies under the eagle on Plate 13, a naked man attacks a naked woman whose head is flung back, hands up, hair dangling (a realistic version of Oothoon's nightmare position?). Above them a long trumpet is blown by a naked spirit upside down, falling or leaping from a cloud on which a naked youth buries his head in his arms. (Orc crucified in Plate 1 may evolve from this.)

Before the first word of text a little king, with train, walks leftward, presumably "to the cove of armoury" (1). Two birds and two eccentric squiggles go in the same direction, but the birds may be flying *up*. An open hand or flower ends the line. In front of the king a looping finger points to a soaring figure being clutched by a hand out of a cloud. Below him two birds fly up, perhaps lapwing and gull. Under "silent stood the King" (5) a beard-dangling man soars right, with one arm back over his body, the other extended forward, fingers spanning (or rather like Urizen's in Plate 8). A headless bird shape and flames slant above "terrible gold" (6), but despite the "dreadful" arming in the next lines, irrepressible flowers grow, down from "gleam" and up from "gate." From "Smote" (11) a vine with one leaf and seven berries (not grapes?) grows toward "pillar" followed by a looped seven-branched root touched by a dancing human, then a vine-like branch with eight acorns and four oak leaves.

A crying bird flies up between paragraphs; nine gulls in the next break. Above "Sleep like the dead" (23) are four figures, the first, third, and fourth reclining or sitting on cloud curves, the second soaring perhaps to wake them; at right is another oak branch with perhaps two acorns and three leaves—perhaps a general symbol on this page for Albion (England).

America d "As when a dream of Thiralatha" (*P&P* p 58), text painted over and perhaps unrelated to illustration. A bowed woman naked to the waist, buries her face in defeat and is totally vaulted over by a barren tree which is rooted at right and bent to the ground at left. It is what the monster of rebellion looks like to kings (A 4). Just outside the clutches of its four branches, a naked mother and infant walk westward. Has the revolutionary storm (compare *Songs of Los* 6) defeated the bowed woman but released the naked one, who receives the infant as if from above, the new-born child of the new dawn? This fragment is not closely related to any part of the extant text of *America*.

America d

Europe ii a

EUROPE A PROPHECY

(Altered title pages;
reduced from about 9 by 7 inches)

Europe ii a (watercolor on proof; Pierpont Morgan Library). The word "EUROPE" is visible but invaded by pencil and ink sketches of three soaring human figures descending toward Urizen with outstretched right arms as if dropping plagues (compare the revolutionary threat of "spotted plague" to Albion's Guardian in *America* 15:2 or the fairy trumpeters of plague in *Europe* 9, or compare *Visions* 1). The sequel for these three (compare *Europe* 2) may be the trip to Hades shown in version c, below.

Urizen, interrupted, looks up from his task, which is to subdue—or ignore—the serpent on which his elderly bearded body makes its divan, by writing on tablets such as we see behind him in *Urizen* 1. Note that he holds his pen in the left hand, the tablets in his right. The drawing of the serpent has been reversed (though his head as printed shows traces under the largest plague-dropper) with tail at top and head—with a very large eye—down underneath Urizen in the center of numerous coils, though Blake has not done away with the original tail at lower right. In this version Urizen's determination to treat his adversary as nonexistent is both more absurd—physically he seems frail and quite dependent on the serpent's whim—and more perturbed. In the published frontispiece there is nothing in Urizen's environment that might make him look up. And although placing him here with the coils of the leviathan constituting on all sides his actual environment is symbolically like Newton's appearance of being at work on his geometry under the ocean (in the color print), Urizen is not as absorbed in his work nor as firmly settled. (For comment on this and the following variants, see Introduction.)

Europe ii b (watercolors on proof; private collection). No hills or mountains are shown. Flames around the serpent, as his natural element, have now kindled the title as they only threaten to do in the standard version of this plate; "EUROPE" is all in flames, and of "PROPHECY" only the first three letters remain. In the center, his left leg flexed, his right extended and digging into the earth and flame, a nude male whose hair appears to identify him as Los "in snaky thunders clad" (15:11) is not now calling his sons but busy (and with a fairly confident yet perhaps anxious look) pulling with his two hands the two largest coils of the serpent, as though to roll them toward himself, i.e. forward, like wheels. Is he afraid that the revolution is stalled and, if it doesn't move forward, may burn up Europe and his Prophecy as well? (Consider the shattered harp quatrain in *America* 2.) The position of his legs constitutes a sort of parody or contrast to the compass position of Urizen's legs in the frontispiece. This and the following variant seem to have been made some time after the original publication of *Europe;* the preceding variant might seem to have been made earlier, since its design appears to assume the lack of a frontispiece or at least of the present frontispiece; yet all three—it is more likely—may have been made later. A colored proof of Jerusalem 46 is on the other side of Plate ii c. Each of these alterations of the *Europe* title page seems intended not so much as a trial revision for a new printing as a caricature or criticism of the original work, a graphic comment on its failure as prophecy of an English revolution, and as such a probably rather private statement.

Europe ii b

Europe ii c

Europe ii c (watercolors on proof; trimmed at top, bottom, and right side; collection of Kerrison Preston). The serpent remains but an extra serpent head, somewhat enlarged, and six other figures have been added. The small figures are very tentatively sketched. At bottom left two naked females seem to be sporting with the rising phallic trunk of the serpent as fearlessly as Enitharmon and her children in the pictures of Plate 4 and the text of Plates 4 and 14. One presses the length of her body against the rising serpent body, reaching up to its loop above her head as though picking fruit. The other lies half underneath the serpent, pillowed half upright and clasping her hands together as though receiving his weight with pleasure. They are oblivious of the other parts and the unbound strength of "terrible Orc" (14:37).

The key to the upper scene, sketched over the erased word "PROPHECY," lies in the identity of the half-human figure who sits with legs dangling down the curve of the serpent's second coil. He is the Egyptian god Anubis, ruler of the dead, with the head and feet of a jackal or dog. (Blake's pencil sketch of him in almost the same sitting posture was recently published by Michael Tolley on the cover of *Blake Studies* magazine for Spring 1971.) This Egyptian Cerberus awaits three spirits drifting between him and the new serpent's head (compare three similarly drifting above the river Lethe in Blake's *L'Allegro* 6; *Forms* plate 1); these three obviously *have* been confronted by the terrible jaws; presumably they are fleeing their bodies and can see the tongue darting above them as the blade of the guillotine (consider the meanings of *America* 5).

JERUSALEM

Jerusalem 28 (early state). This proof, on paper with an 1802 watermark, is tipped into copy F (Pierpont Morgan Library). The caterpillar on the petal, or leaf, almost but not quite deleted in the later state of the plate, seems grotesquely phallic, especially since it lacks a clearly delineated caterpillar head and since it emerges from the shadow in such a way as to imply its attachment to one of the human bodies above it. In this state the two embracing humans appear to be male (facing left, with short hair and knotted back muscles) and female, in an embrace from head to thigh (and perhaps feet, not in sight) that implies copulation.

In the final state of the plate (slightly but not significantly modified by a few ink lines in copies D and F and, of course, colored in copy E), the sexual differences are less distinct (possibly to suit the picture to the embrace of Vala and Jerusalem), the (former) man's left leg below the knee has been removed by an upward spread of the petals he rests upon; he has been given a right thigh, and his buttocks have been (ineffectively) moved round to the left, so that he appears to sit side-saddle and is turned the other way from the other figure; his back muscles are flattened (and his spine surely broken). A left thigh has been created for the (former) woman out of what was the man's left thigh, so that she now appears to sit side-saddle on the petal. (For a more elaborate discussion, see p 18–20 of "The Suppressed and Altered Passages in Blake's *Jerusalem,*" *Studies in Bibliography* XVII, 1964.)

Jerusalem.
Chap: 2.

Every ornament of perfection. and every labour of love,
In all the Garden of Eden. & in all the golden mountains
Was become an envied horror. and a remembrance of jealousy:
And every Act a Crime. and Albion the punisher & judge.

And Albion spoke from his secret seat and said

All these ornaments are crimes. they are made by the labours
Of loves: of unnatural consanguinities and friendships
Horrid to think of when enquired deeply into; and all
These hills & valleys are accursed witnesses of Sin
I therefore condense them into solid rocks. stedfast:
A foundation and certainty and demonstrative truth:
That Man be separate from Man, & here I plant my seat.

Cold snows drifted around him: ice coverd his loins around
He sat by Tyburns brook, and underneath his heel, shot up:
A deadly Tree. he nam'd it Moral Virtue. and the Law
Of God who dwells in Chaos hidden from the human sight.

The Tree spread over him its cold shadows. (Albion groand)
They bent down. they felt the earth and again enrooting
Shot into many a Tree: an endless labyrinth of woe!

From willing sacrifice of Self. to sacrifice of (miscall'd) Enemies
For Atonement: Albion began to erect twelve Altars,
Of rough unhewn rocks. before the Potters Furnace
He nam'd them Justice, and Truth. And Albions Sons
Must have become the first Victims. being the first transgressors
But they fled to the mountains to seek ransom: building A Strong
Fortification against the Divine Humanity and Mercy.
In Shame & Jealousy to annihilate Jerusalem!

Jerusalem 28 (proof)

INDEX

An index to the pictures including variants described in the notes, but not to the other content of the notes (with one or two minor exceptions). When two or more possible identifications of an object are noted, all are included in the index. But many entries are obviously not exhaustive—e.g. "abyss" or "arms"—and dots of elision (. . .) meaning *et passim* are inserted in entries meant to be no more than representative.

Blake's works are referred to in the order in which they are traditionally arranged, by the following simple abbreviations. Numbers refer to plates of the work indicated, not to pages in this edition. Pictures in the Appendix are referred to by "App".

R a, b	*There is No Natural Religion*	*E*	*Europe a Prophecy*
Rs	*All Religions Are One* (series a and b)	*SL*	*The Song of Los*
T	*The Book of Thel*	*U*	*The Book of Urizen*
S	*Songs of Innocence and of Experience*	*Ah*	*The Book of Ahania*
MHH	*The Marriage of Heaven and Hell*	*L*	*The Book of Los*
V	*Visions of the Daughters of Albion*	*M*	*Milton a Poem*
A	*America a Prophecy*	*G*	*The Gates of Paradise*
		J	*Jerusalem*
		O	*On Homers Poetry and On Virgil*
		Gh	*The Ghost of Abel*

ACKNOWLEDGMENTS

To my students and lecture audiences, first of all, I am indebted for inspiring questions and provocative answers. To many fellow scholars, including seminar students, I am indebted for help often amounting to collaboration: preeminently to John E. Grant, Donald K. Moore, and Irene Tayler, ever helpful; to Jerry S. Blake, Tom Dargan, Marlene Deverell-Van Meter, Sally Sevcik, and Robert Waxler for much critical assistance and hard work; for suggestions, corrections, encouragement to Terry Bases, Nancy Bogen, Veronica Brucker, Irene Chayes, Stuart Curran, Morris Eaves, Martha W. England, Robert Essick, Everett C. Frost, Mary V. Jackson, Mary Lynn Johnson, Maurice Johnson, Elaine M. Kauvar, Geoffrey Keynes, Donald Lasko, Henry J. Lesnick, Anne Mellor, W. J. T. Mitchell, Morton Paley, Edward J. Rose, Donald Ross, Florence Sandler, Robert E. Simmons, John Sutherland, Michael J. Tolley, Audrey Toulmin, and Janet A. Warner.

For encouragement and favors of various kinds I am grateful to Harold Bloom, Martin Butlin, Lord Cunliffe, Arnold Fawcus, Anne Freedgood, Donald K. Fry, Marilyn S. Gaull, Virginia Goolsby, Jean Hagstrum, Thomas H. Helmstadter, John Howard, Noelle Jackson, Carolyn E. Jakeman, Lawrence J. Lipking, Paul Mellon, Genevieve Oswald, Michael J. Philips, George Quasha, Anthony Rosati, Lessing J. Rosenwald, Charles Ryskamp, Lola Szladits, Lewis Stark, Robert Stoddard, James Thorpe, Ruthven Todd, Willis Van Devanter, Bert Waggott, Reginald Williams, John Williams Wright, Majorie C. Wynn, and Rose Zimbardo.

For permission to reproduce illuminated pages in their collections I am indebted to the Auckland Public Library (plates from *America* copy N and *Europe* copy I); the Beinecke Rare Book and Manuscript Library, Yale University (plates from *America* copy K); the Henry W. and Albert A. Berg Collection, The New York Public Library, Astor, Lenox and Tilden Foundations (a plate from *Visions of the Daughters of Albion* copy K); the Trustees of the British Museum (plates from *Thel* copy D, *Song of Los* copies A and D, *Book of Los* copy A, and *Milton* copy A); the Cincinnati Art Museum and Mr and Mrs John J. Emery donors (plates from *Thel* copy N); the Fitzwilliam Museum (plates from *Thel* copy F and *Marriage of Heaven and Hell* copy I); Harvard College Library (plates from *Europe* copy H and *Jerusalem* copy D); the Huntington Library, San Marino, California (plates from *All Religions are One* and from *Song of Los* copy E); Sir Geoffrey Keynes (plates from *There is No Natural Religion* copy L and *Marriage of Heaven and Hell* copy E); Paul Mellon (plates from *America* copy M, in color for the cover, *Urizen* copy A, *Gates of Paradise,* For Children, copy E; For the Sexes, copy G, and *Jerusalem* copy E); the Pierpont Morgan Library (plates from *No Natural Religion* copy G, *Marriage of Heaven and Hell* copy C, and a variant title page for *Europe*); the Kerrison Preston Collection, Westminster Public Library (variant title page for *Europe*); the Rare Book Division, The New York Public Library, Astor, Lenox and Tilden Foundations (plates from *Milton,* copy C); the Lessing J. Rosenwald Collection, Library of Congress (plates from *No Natural Religion* copies C and F, *Thel* copy F, *Visions of the Daughters of Albion* copy J, *Urizen* copy G, *Ahania* copy A, *Milton* copy D, *Songs of Innocence and of Experience* copies C and a, *America* canceled plates); Trinity College Library, Hartford (plates from *On Homers Poetry* copy D and *Ghost of Abel* copy D); the Widener Collection, Harvard University (*Songs of Innocence and of Experience* copy I).